NERO

C000060496

This book portrays Nero, not as the murderous tyrant of tradition, but as a young man ever reluctant to fulfil his responsibilities as emperor and ever anxious to demonstrate his genuine skills as a sportsman and an artist. This reluctance caused him to allow others to rule, and rule surprisingly well, in his name. On its own terms, the Neronian Empire was in fact remarkably successful. Nero's senior ministers were many and various, but notably they included a number of powerful women, such as his mother, Agrippina II, and his second and third wives, Poppaea Sabina and Statilia Messalina. Using the most recent archaeological, epigraphic, numismatic and literary research, the book explores issues such as court politics, banter and free speech; literary, technological and scientific advances; the Fire of 64, 'the persecution of Christians' and Nero's 'Golden House'; and the huge underlying strength, both constitutional and financial, of the Julio-Claudian Empire.

JOHN F. DRINKWATER is Emeritus Professor of Roman Imperial History at the University of Nottingham. He has been joint editor of the *Derbyshire Archaeological Journal* and is now honorary lecturer in Archaeology at the University of Sheffield. He has been elected a Fellow of the Society of Antiquaries of London. His principal field of research is the Roman West, and his publications include *Roman Gaul* (1983); *The Gallic Empire* (1987); *Fifth-Century Gaul* (ed., with Hugh Elton, Cambridge 1992); and *The Alamanni and Rome* (2007).

NERO

Emperor and Court

JOHN F. DRINKWATER

University of Nottingham

CAMBRIDGE
UNIVERSITY PRESS

CAMBRIDGE
UNIVERSITY PRESS

University Printing House, Cambridge CB2 8BS, United Kingdom

One Liberty Plaza, 20th Floor, New York, NY 10006, USA

477 Williamstown Road, Port Melbourne, VIC 3207, Australia

314-321, 3rd Floor, Plot 3, Splendor Forum, Jasola District Centre, New Delhi - 110025, India

79 Anson Road, #06-04/06, Singapore 079906

Cambridge University Press is part of the University of Cambridge.

It furthers the University's mission by disseminating knowledge in the pursuit of education, learning and research at the highest international levels of excellence.

www.cambridge.org
Information on this title: www.cambridge.org/9781108460071
DOI: 10.1017/9781108472647

© J. F. Drinkwater 2019

First published 2019
First paperback edition 2021

A catalogue record for this publication is available from the British Library

Library of Congress Cataloging in Publication data
NAMES: Drinkwater, J. F., author.
TITLE: Nero : emperor and court / John F. Drinkwater, University of Nottingham.
DESCRIPTION: 1st edition. | Cambridge ; New York, NY : University Printing House, [2018]
IDENTIFIERS: LCCN 2018021308 | ISBN 9781108472647 (hardback) | ISBN 9781108460071 (pbk.)
SUBJECTS: LCSH: Nero, Emperor of Rome, 37–68. | Emperors–Rome–Biography. | Nero, Emperor of Rome, 37–68–Friends and associates. | Rome–Court and courtiers. | Rome–History–Nero, 54–68.
CLASSIFICATION: LCC DG285 .D75 2018 | DDC 937/.07092 [B] –dc23
LC record available at https://lccn.loc.gov/2018021308

ISBN 978-1-108-47264-7 Hardback
ISBN 978-1-108-46007-1 Paperback

To Vicky, Neil, Ella and Daniel

Contents

Preface

This book began as a short survey of the 'office of emperor' in the first century AD. My plan was to catalogue its main characteristics and then illustrate their operation by reference to the reigns of particular rulers. Having roughed out a list of characteristics, I looked first at Nero but quickly discovered that my list hardly fitted his principate. In addition, as a later Roman historian used to imperial decline, I was struck by how successful his period of office was despite the very negative impression of him given by the sources and began to feel that the Empire could not have been run as they describe. I decided that Nero's administration deserved its own study, which then took some years to complete. My principal theme – that Nero never acted alone – also probably derives from the Late Empire, in which there was always a plurality of political actors: multiple emperors and heirs, wives, sisters, eunuchs, generals, bishops, holy men etc.

I was able to present my first thoughts on Nero at a symposium held in St Andrews in 2008. I must thank Alisdair Gibson for inviting me to attend and for seeing my paper through to publication in 2013. I am likewise grateful to Julia Hillner, Jane Rempel and Charles West for encouraging me to talk on Nero and the Fire at a Sheffield Medieval and Ancient Research Seminar (MARS) meeting in 2010. I owe much of what I say about Nero's charioteering to a paper read by Dr Andy Fear, University of Manchester, to MARS in February 2012. Julia Hillner and members of the Sheffield Late Antiquity Reading Group also heard me on Agrippina in 2016 and offered useful comments and advice on further reading. Guidance on assessing Nero's mental and physical condition was given by Professor Anthony Barker, Department of Medical Physics, Royal Hallamshire Hospital, Sheffield; Professor David Clarke and Dr A. Sunderland, School of Psychology, University of Nottingham; and Professor Mike Gleeson, School of Sport, Exercise and Health Science, Loughborough University. In this respect, I am particularly indebted to Oliver James, author of *They F*** You Up* (2007), for his prompt and positive response to my request for help. Dr Werner Lütkenhaus, a former pupil at Nottingham, Simon Malloch, Department of Classics, University of Nottingham, and Professor Morris Silver, Department of Economics, City College of the City University of New York, kindly read and commented on elements of the text. Professor Eric Moormann, Radboud Universiteit, helped me understand aspects of Neronian architecture and supplied me with hard-to-get material. Professor Lawrence Keppie, Hunterian Museum, Glasgow, gave me useful topographical information. Welcome long-term encouragement and support came from Professor Maureen Carroll, Department of Archaeology, University of Sheffield; Professor Nick Henck, Faculty of Law, Keio University; Professor Fritz-Heiner Mutschler, Department of Classics, Universities of Dresden and Peking; and former Sheffield pupil, Adrian Pearson. I particularly appreciate the suggestions of the two anonymous readers of Cambridge University Press, most of which I have attempted to incorporate in my text. Throughout, the Press's patient and indefatigable Michael Sharp has given me indispensable encouragement and support.

No research is possible without good library facilities, and for these I owe much to the Hallward Library, University of Nottingham for its physical and its online stock. Odd gaps were filled by the University Library, Sheffield and, especially, by Sue Willetts and the impeccable postal loan service of the Joint Library of the Hellenic and Roman Societies, London. Prof. Dr Renate Bol, University of Mainz, Dr Julie Lenaghan, Aphrodisias Excavations, Oxford, Mr Simon Parkin, Roma Numismatics Ltd, London and Dr Elena Stolyarik, American Numismatic Society, went well beyond the call of duty in supplying me with photographic images.

I first came into contact with Nero through Jack Roberts, who taught me Latin at Sale Boys' Grammar School and who organised a memorable sixth form trip to Italy in 1963. I owe him a great debt, which I am delighted to have the opportunity to acknowledge here. I must, again, thank my wife, Gillian, for her unstinting patience and support. I wrote this book during a period of great family change and dedicate it to my daughter, Vicky, her husband, Neil Sampson, and their children, Ella and Daniel. The appearance of Ella and Daniel significantly increased the time it took to write this book but was of course hugely welcome and, I hope, by preventing me from rushing completion, significantly improved its quality.

Abbreviations

References to ancient authors and texts follow the conventions of the *Oxford Classical Dictionary*. The following abbreviations are used both in footnotes and in the References section.

AJPh	*American Journal of Philology*
atkinsglobal	http://www.atkinsglobal.com/en-gb/media-centre/news-releases/2010/group/2010-01-11 [11/01/2010].
Barrington Atlas	R. J. Talbert (ed.), *Barrington Atlas of the Greek and Roman World*, Princeton NJ, 2000
BMCR	*Bryn Mawr Classical Review*
CAH 9²	*Cambridge Ancient History Vol. IX* (2nd edn). *The Last Age of the Roman Republic, 146–43 BC*, J. A. Crook, A. Lintott and E. Rawson (eds), Cambridge, 1992
CAH 10²	*Cambridge Ancient History Vol. X* (2nd edn). *The Augustan Empire, 3 BC–AD 69*, A. K. Bowman, E. Champlin and A. Lintott (eds), Cambridge, 1996.
CAH 12²	*Cambridge Ancient History Vol. XII* (2nd edn). *The Crisis of Empire*, AD 193–337, A. K. Bowman, P. Garnsey and Averil Cameron (eds), Cambridge, 2005
CJ	*Classical Journal*
EEC	A. Di Bartino (ed.), *Encyclopedia of the Early Church*, New York NY, 1992
FRHist.	T. J. Cornell (ed.), *The Fragments of the Roman Historians*, Oxford, 2013
JRS	*Journal of Roman Studies*
OCD⁴	S. Hornblower, A. Spawforth and E. Eidinow (eds), *The Oxford Classical Dictionary* (4th edn), Oxford, 2012

RIC 1²	*Roman Imperial Coinage* vol. 1 (2nd edn), H. V. Sutherland and R. A. G. Carson, London 1984
RIC 2²	*Roman Imperial Coinage* vol. 2, part 1 (2nd rev. edn), I. Carradice and T. V. Buttrey, London, 2007

Figures

Tables

Introduction

This book is not a 'life and reign' of the emperor Nero. It is, rather, an attempt to understand how the Roman Empire was run from the centre in the middle years of the first century AD. The Empire could not have been directed by a single individual, however admirable his character and abilities. My aim is to present a more dynamic picture of political life by identifying those involved alongside Nero, to set these people in their contexts – metropolitan, provincial and foreign – and to make them move in the landscape. My main argument is that in the 50s and 60s the central administrative institution, the Principate, was still very plastic, allowing room for experiment and change. I propose that Nero was never fully in control of affairs and that, increasingly diverted by sport and art, he allowed others to act in his name.

I use the term 'emperor' in my title because it is expected. However, throughout my main text I avoid it. This is because 'emperor' comes with a baggage of medieval and modern associations out of keeping with the reality of the position of the leader of the Roman state in the first century AD: an autocrat who was not a king, who exercised power and influence independently (sometimes, perhaps, in spite) of the offices he held in a purportedly continuing Republic. For this reason I was tempted by 'First Man' and 'Leader',[1] but too frequent a use of these is awkward and too reminiscent of 'il Duce' and 'der Führer'. Having toyed with 'the Boss', 'the Chief' and even 'the Supreme One', I, like Rutledge and Romm,[2] opted for *princeps*. Though my focus is not Nero, it is impossible to keep him out of the picture. I experienced most difficulty in establishing his frame of mind: bluntly, was he mad? I felt obliged to consider his psychology head on and came to the conclusion that, while he was not mad, he suffered mental problems after the death of Poppaea in 65 and underwent some sort of breakdown after his return from Greece in 67.

---

[1] Cf. Osgood 2011, 19. [2] Rutledge 2001; Romm 2014.

Though I began with no intention to whitewash Nero's historical reputation, in the end, consonant with a contemporary current of research in which, for example, Winterling has presented a 'new' Gaius and Osgood and Barrett have offered a 'new' Agrippina and Claudius, I propose a 'new' Nero: more innocent but much less engaged in affairs than he of the source tradition.

Study of Nero and the Neronian age began at the dawn of modern Ancient History and is still a very lively field. It has generated a multitude of publications of which I have been able to read and consider only a tiny proportion. I apologise in advance for any oversight of important contributions and any unintended reinvention of published thinking. As a newcomer to the period, I was greatly aided by the availability of a number of key studies. My cherished copy of Bradley's *Suetonius' Life of Nero*, given to me in friendship by the author many years ago and making him a constant companion in spirit, was indispensable. Cizek's *Néron* and Griffin's *Nero* remain mines of information and stimulation, and in my assessment of Nero I was much influenced by Champlin's *Nero*.[3] In addition to these monographs I was able to draw on volumes of collected papers, beginning with Elsner and Master's *Reflections of Nero* and including more recently Buckley and Dinter's *Companion to the Neronian Age*, Gibson's *Julio-Claudian Succession*, Walde's *Neros Wirklichkeiten* and Bartsch and Schiesaro's *Cambridge Companion to Seneca*.[4] These enabled me to engage with a much wider range of topics than would otherwise have been possible. Other monographs, for example Rudich's *Political Dissidence*, Bartsch's *Actors and Audiences*, Rutledge's *Imperial Inquisitions*, Ginsburg's *Representing Agrippina*, Cottier *et al.* 's, *Customs Law*, Winterling's *Politics and Society*, Meyboom and Moormann's *Le decorazioni dipinte*, Butcher and Ponting's *Metallurgy of Roman Silver Coinage* and Kimmerle's *Lucan*, I found especially stimulating.[5] In understanding Neronian Rome I would have been lost without Tomi and Rea's detailed and magnificently illustrated *Nerone*, the companion volume to the exhibition of April to September 2011 which I was fortunate to be able to attend.[6]

---

[3] Bradley 1978a; Cizek 1982; Griffin 1984; Champlin 2003.
[4] Elsner and Masters 1994; Buckley and Dinter 2013; Gibson 2013; Walde 2013; Bartsch and Schiesaro 2015.
[5] Rudich 1993; Bartsch 1994; Rutledge 2001; Ginsburg 2006; Cottier *et al.* 2008; Meyboom and Moormann 2013; Butcher and Ponting 2014; Kimmerle 2015.
[6] Tome and Rea 2011.

Because I provide no continuous narrative, and because points and arguments made at one point are cited or corroborated in others, I have been generous with internal cross-references.

My approach is not based on any theorising but is a consciously 'old-fashioned, cautiously positivist, empirical and evidence-based enquiry'.[7] However, what struck me throughout in dealing with the age of Nero is that, if we are to go beyond the suspect tale of our literary sources, we have to accept that Ancient History is disciplined novel writing: as long as we do not go beyond the evidence and reasonable plausibility, we must dare a high degree of speculation.

Except where otherwise stated, I take translations of Greek and Latin authors from the Loeb series, occasionally amending them to make them sound more modern or bring out particular points. In the text and on maps I have not striven for consistency with place names but have used those which I felt will be most familiar to anglophones, usually, but not always, the modern forms: so Lyon not Lugdunum and Padua not Patavium; but Misenum, not Miseno, and Sinope, not Sinop etc. All dates are AD unless otherwise stated.

---

[7] Vervaet on his approach to late Roman Republican history, quoted by Lanfranchi 2015.

PART I

Background

Figure 1   The West and Greece

CHAPTER I

Nero, 'Bad' or 'Good'?

1.1 Introduction

In Chapters 1 – 7, I consider the origins, operation and character of the Neronian administration. I begin by sketching out the *princeps'* life and historiography, and explaining my approach to him and his principate

1.2 Biography

Nero was born on 15 December 37.[1] His mother was Agrippina II, daughter of Germanicus and Agrippina I, and sister of the incumbent *princeps*, Gaius. Nero was her only child. His father was Gn. Domitius Ahenobarbus, a high-ranking aristocrat. Taking his name from his father, he was first called Lucius Domitius Ahenobarbus. His father died in late 39 or early 40, and his mother remarried twice, the second time to Gaius' successor, Claudius, in 49. Having betrothed L. Domitius Ahenobarbus to his daughter, Octavia, in 49, Claudius adopted him as his son on 25 February 50 and changed his name to Nero Claudius Caesar Drusus Germanicus. Nero married Octavia in 53. He replaced Claudius as *princeps* on 13 October 54. At just under 17 years of age, he was the youngest to date but he was also to be the last Julio-Claudian. He committed suicide in June 68 following rebellions by Vindex in Gaul and Galba in Spain, and desertion by his own followers in Rome.

1.3 Demonisation

Even before his death, Nero suffered growing denigration and soon there seemed to be no monstrosity of which he was thought incapable.[2] In the early Flavian pseudo-Senecan drama *Octavia*, he is depicted as 'the

---

[1] Bradley 1978a, 48, 53; Kienast 2004, 96. [2] Hohl 1918, 350–1; Rathbone 2008, 276.

7

proverbial tyrant, robbed of any personal characteristics, a mere incarnation of the will to evil'.[3] Written when a new dynasty of *principes* encouraged disparagement of the later Julio-Claudians to justify itself as their replacement, the play helped to establish the memory of Nero as a 'monster'.[4] He joined the 'mad' Gaius in the canon of 'wickedest' *principes*.[5] Wider vilification resulted from Jewish loathing of him as the instigator of the war that destroyed Jerusalem and its Temple. Jewish resentment was adopted and developed by later Christians, who made Nero the first great persecutor of the faith.[6] Also out of Judaism, but through the New Testament book of 'Revelation', came the Christian view of Nero as either the herald of the Anti-Christ or the Anti-Christ in person, which shaped the ever more grotesque late Antique and medieval view of him. Each age needs its own 'bad' Nero.[7] Ancient and medieval demonisation determined modern conceptions of this emperor. At the academic level, for example, preconceptions of the actions and demeanour of Nero the 'tyrant' and 'theocrat' have influenced both the identification of 'tyrannical'- and 'theocratic'-looking statue heads and busts as his and the interpretation of wall-paintings.[8] At the popular level, Nero the 'monster' is widely known thanks mostly to Henrik Sienkiewicz's novel *Quo Vadis?*, first published in Polish in 1896, and to various screen-dramatisations of the work from 1901. The most striking, directed by Mervyn LeRoy and starring Peter Ustinov as Nero, was released in 1951. There can be no doubt that Ustinov's Nero – mad, bad and dangerous to know – has become the Nero of popular imagination.[9] Novels, films and television dramas continue to project the 'evil' Nero.[10] Our own society seems to be particularly obsessed by 'the villains of history'.[11] Nero has joined Jack the Ripper as a character more fictional than real – an instantly

---

[3] Griffin 1984, 100.
[4] Cf. Mart. *Spect.* 2: Nero as the *ferus rex* ('mad king'). Henderson 1905, 419; Barton 1994, 50; Rubiés 1994, 40; Champlin 2003, 104; Reitz 2006, 49; Rathbone 2008, 252; Buckley 2013a, 218; Buckley 2013b, 133–4, 140–2, 145–148, 151; Hurley 2013, 30, 34–7; Mordine 2013, 102–3.
[5] Cf. Winterling 2007, 178.   [6] Maier 2013, 386; below 244.
[7] Henderson 1905, 10, 418, 420–1; Grant 1970, 94; Cizek 1982, 16–18; Wiseman 1991, xii; Fini 1994, 9–11; Wyke 1994, 12; Champlin 2003, 13–14, 17–19; Waldherr 2005, 9; Reitz 2006, 4–9; Maier 2013, 387–91, 394, 400. Cf. Rubiés 1994 for the Tacitean 'Nero', and its use in the Renaissance.
[8] Bragantini 2011, 191–3; Cadario 2011, 177, 182, 184, 188; Kreikenbom 2013; cf. Ginsburg 2006, 55.
[9] Fini 1994, 11; Wyke 1994; Pucci 2011; cf. Miziolek 2011, 60–1.
[10] E.g. as in the BBC's *Ancient Rome: The Decline and Fall of an Empire* (2006).
[11] Barrett 1996, xii.

recognisable, disturbingly fascinating stereotype of 'inconceivable wickedness and unnatural horror'.[12]

1.4 Rationalisation

There are two ways of dealing with the denigrated, vilified and demonised Nero. The first is to assume that, though in places distorted, the ancient tradition is correct: Nero was a tyrant, so we should not be surprised if subsequent generations made him a monster. This was the view of Sir Ronald Syme, who argued that Tacitus, writing 'of times within the reach of memory or of reliable testimony', produced a broadly accurate account of his principate. Tacitus' account closely resembles those of Suetonius and Cassius Dio, our other main sources, because they, too, were reconstructing the same truth from the same historical material. All three draw a picture of the *princeps* that 'corresponds in a large measure to the facts'.[13] The second is to treat the consonance between Tacitus, Suetonius and Dio as suspect. It is, in fact, now generally agreed that all drew the bulk of their information from an earlier established anti-Neronian historiographical tradition. This tradition was available in a number of now vanished works: by Pliny I, Cluvius Rufus and Fabius Rusticus, of whom the first was particularly hostile to the *princeps*.[14] These authors themselves, however, drew on existing negative assessments of Nero manifested, as we have seen, in the *Octavia*.[15] Thus, despite Syme, it is now accepted that Tacitus, the most influential extant writer, and one certainly capable of independent research into details of Nero's principate,[16] was overall no detached reporter of the truth. Rather, he manipulated the common tradition for his own highly moralising ends, in particular to develop the *Octavia*'s theme of 'corruption under tyranny'.[17] A confection of all his 'dramatic skills', Tacitus' Nero is 'a literary figure', not 'the object of dispassionate historical scrutiny'.[18] Suetonius and Dio, likewise, had their own authorial strategies. Suetonius has been described as a 'rhetorician', taking up stock themes of invective: Nero is an ugly man behaving in an ugly and depraved fashion.[19] Dio, writing under the autocratic Severans, is the harshest judge

---

[12] Henderson 1905, 421.   [13] Syme 1958, 437.   [14] Cf. Doody 2013, 295–6.

[15] Levi 1949, 7–40; Townend 1967, 96; Griffin 1984, 37–9, 235–8; Reitz 2006, 4–8; Hurley 2013, 29–310; above 7.

[16] Below 244.   [17] Cf. Tac. *Ann.* 3.55.2–6. Rubiés 1994, 35–6 (quotation).

[18] Rubiés 1994, 40 (quotation); Reitz 2006, 7: 'Nero ist bei Tacitus also eine literarische Gestalt, nicht Gegenstand objektiver historichen Beobachtung'; cf. Bartsch 1994, 23–4.

[19] Barton 1994, 48 (quotation), 50–8.

of Nero, whom he regarded as their political ancestor.[20] As historians have
increasingly appreciated the existence of the common tradition, they have
attempted to identify and correct its distortions. It is now acknowledged
that its denigration obscured a contemporary line of thinking, discernible
even in our main sources, which proposed a 'good' or, at least, not wholly
bad Nero.[21] Its validity is confirmed by the fact that Nero's memory did
not suffer formal condemnation by the state; by the play that Otho and
Vitellius made of his name; by the continued honouring of his tomb; and
by the appearance of at least three 'false Neros'.[22] Indeed, he appears to
have enjoyed remarkable, if sometimes misguided, continuing public
affection. Dio Chrysostom, who flourished around 100, remarks in a
way that brings to mind purported sightings of Elvis Presley, 'even now
everyone wishes he were still alive. And the great majority do believe that
he is'.[23] Modern scholars have pitched this alternative Nero against Nero
the 'monster', but their efforts have had little effect on public imagination
and, even on their own terms, have often been marred by an insidious
tendency to see Roman history from an upper-class viewpoint, and so still
to condemn Nero as the scourge of the Senate: testimony to the power of
the 'senatorial tradition'.[24]

1.5   Reassessment

Rejection of the uncritical acceptance of Nero the 'tyrant' and 'monster'
can be traced back to Gerolamo Cardano (1501–1576) in his *Encomium
Neronis*.[25] However, like many before him, Cardano created his own
'Nero' for his own ends,[26] and it was more than three centuries before a
considered assessment of the *princeps* was published in English.[27] Since
then Nero has attracted significant attention. Some historians have
remained content to follow the main source tradition's depiction of a
man who became a monster, either more or less as it stands, as with Malitz

---

[20] Hurley 2013, 32.
[21] See Suet. *Ner.* 1.19.3, with Joseph. *AJ.* 20.154–6. Bradley 1978a, 66, 119; Champlin 2003, 24–5;
      Rathbone 2008, 252; Maier 2013, 386; Hurley 2013, 31–2.
[22] *Damnatio memoriae*: Champlin 2003, 29. Otho and Vitellius: Tac. *Hist.* 1.78, 2.95. Rudich 1993,
      229–30. Tomb Suet. *Ner.* 57.1. Three false Neros: Tac. *Hist.* 2.8; Cass. Dio 64.9.3b–c; Suet. *Ner.*
      57.3; Bradley 1978a, 294–5; Champlin 2003, 10–12; Grünewald 2004, 151–4; Barratt *et al.* 2016,
      280 and n. 63. Otho and Vitellius: Tac. *Hist.* 1.78, 2.95. Rudich 1993, 229–30.
[23] Dio Chrys. *Or.* 21.10. Cf. Rubiés 1994, 40; Champlin 2003, 29–34; Waldherr 2005, 268–70.
[24] So Henderson 1905, 12–13; cf. below 18.   [25] Rubiés 1994, 33; Reitz 2006, 9.
[26] Maier 2013, 396–7.
[27] Dawson 1964, 263: by G. H. Lewes in a *Cornhill Magazine* article of 1863.

and, in massive detail, Krüger, or with some mitigating explanation and justification of his actions, as with Waldherr and Shotter.[28] Others, however, have proposed a striking variety of interpretations, as can be seen from a short survey of specialist works published from 1900. Henderson's Nero is a good ruler but a bad man: an effective administrator but 'a helpless prisoner to his lower appetites'.[29] Levi's Nero is a flawed idealist.[30] His objective was the re-establishment of the Augustan Golden Age through an intensification of the Hellenisation of Roman cultural life and the extension of the monarchical powers of the *princeps*. He countered consequent upper-class hostility by turning to the people and the army, but his vices eventually destroyed his popularity and exposed him to senatorial attack. Grant's Nero is depraved and indolent, increasingly leaving the running of the Empire to others.[31] Cizek's Nero is, in contrast, an active ruler and an original thinker, set on instituting a new theocratic autocracy for a new world-state: 'Neronism'. 'Cultivated to the point of preciosity, vulgar to the point of brutality', he was destroyed by his flawed and unstable personality.[32] Griffin's Nero also actively directs imperial affairs and is also destroyed by his vicious personality. However, he is no great political reformer and fell victim to the 'unresolved contradictions' of the Augustan Principate, in which he was forced to operate and against which, urged on by unscrupulous intimates, he unsuccessfully rebelled.[33] Fini agrees with 'Nero his own man', but enthusiastically reinstates 'Nero the great reformer', albeit as a secularist, not a theocrat, with popularist and internationalist leanings well ahead of his time. He failed because he was a narcissistic dreamer, but his vices have been exaggerated and his virtues discounted.[34] Holland offers a more negative duality. From 56, Nero took the reins of power and, aspiring to be a Hellenistic monarch and with some dreams of divinity, pursued policies aimed at securing the happiness and moral elevation of his people. However, psychologically damaged by an insecure childhood, he rejected traditional morality and was easily lured into excess by strong-willed associates. Champlin's Nero is 'a bad man and a bad ruler' but he is no devil. Rather, drifting into an ever closer exploration, self-explanation and reconstruction of himself as a great figure of myth and history, expressed in sporting and artistic performance, he simply neglected his duties as *princeps*.[35] A recent striking

---

[28] Malitz 1999; Waldherr 2005; Shotter 2008; Krüger 2012.
[29] Henderson 1905 (quotation: 423).   [30] Levi 1949.   [31] Grant 1970.
[32] Cizek 1982 ('raffiné jusq'à la preciosité, plébeian jusq'à la brutalité': 48).
[33] Griffin 1984 (quotation: 187–8); Griffin 2013, 479.   [34] Fini 1994.
[35] Champlin 2003 (quotation: 52).

demonstration of Nero's endless mutability is provided by Shumate who, having sought a reasoned rebuttal of Nero the 'monster', was moved by her perception of gross irrationalities within the White House of George W. Bush to accept Tacitus' identification of these in the court of Nero.[36]

Starting from an interest in the office of Augustan *princeps* – 'the job of emperor' – and so in Nero as a ruler whose principate is sufficiently well-documented to provide a useful case study of the operation of the system, I expected to develop Griffin's reasoning: that Nero attempted but inevitably failed to run a system that was so raw that it was hardly yet a system at all – a monarchy that was not a monarchy, a 'half-baked Principate'.[37] However, consideration of political context led me closer to Grant and to Elsner and Masters' brief 're-writing' of his principate that envisages not 'an omnipotent boy-king who squanders his destiny' but 'a pawn in other people's political games' played in a powerful, self-interested and self-renewing imperial court. The notion of a Nero only 'superficially' in charge of his government has also recently been proposed by Meier and further developed by Kimmerle.[38] My Nero is a man who never controlled events.[39] He became emperor through the scheming of others. He did his best to act the difficult role of *princeps* but increasingly found the position not to his taste. He therefore disengaged from his responsibilities, threw himself into sport and art, and left the running of the Empire to others. Not wicked or depraved, indeed in some respects bourgeois in his values, Nero fell because when he chose to intervene in events his interventions were disruptive and because his refusal to accept the military duties of a *princeps* eventually broke the loyalty of his supporters.

1.6   Caveats

Before proceeding, one must ask whether any reinterpretation of the evidence can establish a more historically 'authentic' Nero. Rubiés, while arguing against 'traditional readings' of Nero the 'tyrant', notes the difficulties of separating truth from prejudice in Tacitus. Even to attempt this 'distorts the conventions and intentions of ancient historiography' which

---

[36] Shumate 2013, 349.   [37] Drinkwater 2013.

[38] Elsner and Masters 1994, 3; cf. Kraus 1994: 'the contributors suggest a scenario ... in which imperial court factions control an essentially powerless *princeps* who is allowed to follow his desires only if they further the wishes of his keepers'; Meier 2008, esp. 573–4, 588 ('überflächlich'), 602; Kimmerle 2015, 109–10, 305. Cf. Romm 2014, xvii, 95 and Osgood 2011, 25–7 on the limitations of thematic and synchronic approaches in understanding individual emperors; also below 59.

[39] Cf. below 56.

allowed the deployment of countless tendentious 'facts'.[40] How can we possibly winnow reality from rhetoric? The answer is that we cannot with any certainty, but we must still make the effort. The historical tradition, however much distorted by invective, records important occurrences, such as the revolt of Boudica, corroborative evidence for which may be found on inscriptions, coins and papyri and in archaeological excavation. To understand these events we must set them in their political context, which necessarily means coming to grips with the character and policies of Nero. This involves identifying likely distortions in the traditional picture of the *princeps*, estimating their degree and attempting to correct them. Such an approach is the basis of all modern studies of individual *principes*, seeking to establish 'what really happened' under each.[41] Correction involves imagination. Elsner and Masters observe that 'the traditional picture we have of Nero is . . . impossibly crude'. We can accept it as it stands, reject it entirely or attempt some sort of compromise, even if compromise requires the historian becoming something of an historical novelist.[42] The last is not to be despised. The difference between the historian offering reasoned speculation about the operation of the Neronian world and the skilled novelist recreating it from reading and intuition is small.[43] It is, however, significant, since the historian must never drift into fantasy. Everything in the sources has to be considered for inclusion and, if excluded, its exclusion acknowledged and explained.[44] The historian must also practise considered inconsistency, accepting one statement by an ancient author, or one interpretation of an archaeological find or feature, on the grounds of plausibility while rejecting another.[45] With regard to 'bad' *principes*, such as Nero, correction must also avoid whitewash. Contemporary obsession with youth, good looks, celebrity, spectacle, multiculturalism and 'spin' should not lead unthinkingly to 'Nero the Hero'.[46]

1.7   Initial Success

We should, however, begin by considering the positive (in Roman imperial terms) side of Nero's principate, starting with his excellent claim to

---

[40] Rubiés 1994, 36 (quotation), 41.
[41] Winterling 2007, 11: 'was denn tatsächlich unter seiner Herrschaft vorgefallen ist'.
[42] Elsner and Masters 1994, 1 (quotation), 5; cf. Rudich 1993, 41.
[43] As brilliantly expounded in Mantel 2017.   [44] Drinkwater 2014.
[45] E.g. Suetonius on Nero's physical state; the location of the operating centre of the Golden House: below 255, 303.
[46] Griffin 2013, 467–9 (quotations), 472–4.

succeed Claudius.[47] To say that his adoption was almost a formality is to
go too far,[48] but Nero was no interloper. He was not, as the *Octavia*
depicts him from the point of view of Claudius' blood heirs Britannicus
and Octavia, the usurping son of a wicked stepmother, the cuckoo in the
nest.[49] The Principate was a complex autocracy, not a sovereign monarchy.[50] A *princeps* could not in principle determine a successor: when he
died, both his principate and the Principate died with him. There was no *le
roi est mort, vive le roi!*[51] In practice, however, the supreme position was
treated from the start as a family heirloom, a policy favoured by the Roman
people, the army and provincials.[52] In the absence of a strong tradition of
primogeniture, the Roman concept of inheritance was very flexible, and
Nero's claim to the leadership of the Julio-Claudian *domus* was better than
most of his male relations: another aspect of the 'half-baked Principate'.[53]
Through Agrippina II, Claudius' niece as well as his wife, Nero was, as
Claudius' grandnephew, a near relative of the *princeps*.[54] And, as both the
great-great-grandson and great-great-grandnephew of Augustus, Nero had
a better claim to be family head than Britannicus, who was only Augustus'
great-grandnephew.[55] What really distinguished him was his maternal
grandfather, Germanicus. Nero's accession represented a second attempt
to realise the long-postponed 'dream ticket' succession of the line of
Agrippina I and Germanicus (the first had been that of his maternal uncle,
Gaius) frustrated by Germanicus' death in 19.[56] Awareness of his status
and destiny will have been instilled in him by his mother, the proud and
steely daughter of a proud and steely mother and an equally proud

---

[47] Wiedemann 1996a, 241.   [48] As Henderson 1905, 21–2.

[49] Ps.-Sen. *Oct.* l. 249: *Nero insitivus, Domitio genitus patre* – literally 'grafted on Nero', whose real
father was Domitius, not Claudius; Ps.-Sen. *Oct.* ll. 170–1: *saeva … noverca*. Cf. Tac. *Ann.*
13.14.3: Nero as *insitus et adoptivus*, unlike Britannicus, *vera et dignaque stirps*. Gowers 1994,
136; Buckley 2013b, 137.

[50] Below 8, 90.   [51] Winterling 2007, 19; cf. below 173.

[52] Winterling 2007, 20; Osgood 2013, 24–33.

[53] This caused problems in dealing with likely rivals: Tac. *Ann.* 13.1.2. Fini 1994, 17, 115, 144;
Osgood 2011, 212; below 172.

[54] The complex intertwining of Roman aristocratic pedigrees is also visible in the fact that, through
their mother and his paternal first cousin, Messalina, Nero was also related to Octavia and
Britannicus.

[55] Tac. *Ann.* 13.1.2; Smallwood no. 386. Like Britannicus, Nero was also descended from Mark
Antony, a great-great-grandfather, and also on this side of his family related to Augustus. Levi
(1949, e.g. 105, 215) places too much emphasis on Nero's Domitian descent, and his adoption into
the Julio-Claudian dynasty, which he regards as weakening his right to the principate. Nero's
maternal ancestry gave him as good a claim as any.

[56] Below 36; cf. Warmington 1969, 31–2; Barrett 1996, 152; Wiedemann 1996a, 239; Shotter 2008,
21; Osgood 2011, 23, 34, 62, 91, 215–17, 219–20; Gibson 2013, 117; Seager 2013, 42–6. Cf.
Winterling 2007, 53–6.

and hugely famous father.[57] Adoption was a long-established means of strengthening a family.[58] Once a few legal obstacles had been removed,[59] Nero was by virtue of his adoption unquestionably Claudius' son. By being betrothed to Octavia, by being adopted by her father, and by subsequently being given various privileges, responsibilities, offices and titles – the key ones of which were *Princeps Iuventutis* ('Leader of the Youth') and consul designate with proconsular authority outside Rome, both in 51 – he was elevated far above the younger Britannicus and clearly designated Claudius' successor.[60] The capstone of the whole structure was the eventual deification of Claudius. Whatever Seneca, Nero's former tutor and now senior counsellor, encouraged him to think of the event,[61] it made the new *princeps* 'the son of a god', the first since Augustus, and was as such made much of by Agrippina.[62]

Next to be noticed is Nero's adroit handling of the Roman 'political community'.[63] His coming to power consisted in addressing and being accepted by the Praetorians and the Senate. The former were ready to welcome him as a Julian and the grandson of Germanicus.[64] To cement their loyalty, Nero announced a huge donative of 15,000 *sestertii* (the coin denomination of account, abbreviated HS) per man.[65] This secured him the all-important title of *Imperator*, 'Commander-in-Chief'.[66] All that remained was for the Senate, in a process commencing unusually late, taking the rest of the working day, and not formally completed until 4 December,[67] formally to confer upon him the secular and religious powers of his predecessors.[68] He was now unquestionably sole ruler, 'Augustus'. Presumably it was the same sitting of the Senate that agreed Claudius' grand state funeral and additional honours for his widow including, unusually, in advance of an actual decree of deification, her appointment as priestess of the new cult.[69] A few days later, Nero did his filial duty by

---

[57] Cf. Barrett 1996, 22, 26–30, 41; Seager 2013, 47–8, 50–1; Vout 2013, 72.

[58] Waldherr 2005, 47–8; below 172.   [59] Romm 2014, 37–8.

[60] Henderson 1905, 38–9; Hohl 1918, 351–3; Grant 1970, 29–30; Bradley 1978a, 57–8, 61; Griffin, 1984, 29–30; Barrett 1996, 116–18; Kienast 2004, 96; Waldherr 2005, 50–1; Osgood 2011, 225–7, 239–41.

[61] Below 102.   [62] Below 44.   [63] Flaig 2011, 278.

[64] The Praetorians, and their commander, Burrus, were close to Agrippina: below 35.

[65] Below 329.   [66] Tac. *Ann.* 12.69.3.

[67] Smallwood 1967, no. 19, ll.14–15; *RIC* I² p. 133. Cizek 1982, 94; Talbert 1984, 191; Barrett 1996, 144.

[68] Tac. *Ann.* 12.69.4; Suet. *Ner.* 8. Brunt 1977, 98–9; Bradley 1978a, 64–5; Talbert 1984, 354–5 Barrett 1996, 51–2, 144; below 83.

[69] Tac. *Ann.* 13.2.6; Suet. *Ner.* 9. Furneaux 1907, 153; Krüger 2012, 35–6; below 46.

delivering Claudius' funeral eulogy, composed by Seneca.[70] In perhaps two
following speeches to the Senate (again probably the work of Seneca) he
formally requested Claudius' deification and laid out the principles of his
administration.[71] Tacitus' summary of the latter makes them sound anti-
Claudian and so suggests that Nero promised a wholly fresh start, but it is
more likely, against a background of already improving relations with the
Senate, that Nero committed himself to 'business as usual'.[72] The succession had gone as easily as could be hoped. From the strategic delay in
announcing Claudius' death – to give the new regime time to secure its
position – onwards, events were carefully choreographed.[73] Though this
must have been the work of Agrippina and her ministers,[74] the principal
part was Nero's, and he played it flawlessly. He always spoke and carried
himself well in public. He first demonstrated these skills as an adolescent
under Claudius, before his adoption.[75] Later, in the process of being
brought on as heir, he addressed the Praetorians and People, and spoke
in the Senate on various matters, both ceremonial and substantive.[76]
During an ancient festival he behaved with particular distinction as acting
senior magistrate in Rome.[77] It seems clear that Nero, helped by a
wonderful memory for faces and names,[78] thoroughly enjoyed roles that
made him the centre of attention.[79] Now, with his advisers, in particular
Seneca, feeding him exactly the right lines, he was able to act the *civilis
princeps* – not king, not autocrat, but leader of his peers – to perfection.[80]
This, together with the youth, good looks, energy and health that made
him a welcome change from Claudius,[81] and again his descent from
Germanicus, assured his popularity with the third key political element,
the People of Rome, without whose approval no *princeps* could ever rest
easy.[82] Though the idea that the poet Calpurnius Siculus announced a new

---

[70] Tac. *Ann.* 13.3.2. Barrett 1996, 144–7: 13 October, death, followed by five days of lying in state;
18 October, funeral; 19 October, speech to Senate, including the request for deification; 24
October, ashes deposited in mausoleum.

[71] Tac. *Ann.* 13.2.6, 4; Suet. *Ner.* 9, 10.1. Griffin 1984, 41.

[72] Tac. *Ann.* 13.4; Suet. *Ner.* 10.1. Below 50.

[73] Suet. *Ner.* 8.1. Hohl 1918, 355–6; Bradley 1978a, 62–3, 68; Osgood 2011, 240; Romm 2014, 60.

[74] Tac. *Ann.* 13.2.5; Suet. *Ner.* 9. Hohl 1918, 356; below 35.

[75] Suet. *Ner.* 7.1. Bradley 1978a, 53.

[76] Tac. *Ann.* 12.58; Suet. *Ner.* 7.2. Osgood 2011, 166–7, 225–6 (noting that, in contrast, Claudius
was a poor public speaker).

[77] Suet. *Ner.* 7.2: *praefectus feriarum Latinarum.* Bradley 1978a, 61.   [78] Suet. *Ner.* 10.2.

[79] Wiedemann 1996a, 246.   [80] Wallace-Hadrill 1982; Griffin 1984, 62; below 18, 50.

[81] Griffin 1984, 132; below 305.

[82] Waldherr 2005, 200–2; Osgood 2011, 32; cf. below 193 on the trouble a dissident mob
caused Nero.

Golden Age of Apollo in 54 has recently been questioned, it is in keeping with other contemporary sentiments and remains the *communis opinio*.[83] Perhaps encouraged by Agrippina, there must have been a feeling abroad, even before Nero's accession, that with him as *princeps* things could only get better.[84]

For a long time Nero satisfied the chief criterion for being regarded an *optimus princeps*: the possession of a good relationship with the Senate. His respect for this body was demonstrated in his first addresses to it in 54. Particularly significant is his early policy speech which promised to continue an established policy of co-operation with the Senate.[85] It guaranteed no abuse of power in the palace (in particular, no secret political trials of senators and no undue influence by females and freedmen), and so a clear distinction between court and state[86] and acceptance of the shared responsibility between *princeps* and Senate which went back to Augustus.[87] But shared responsibility did not mean equal power.[88] The *princeps*, commander-in-chief of the armed forces, remained supreme.[89] Tacitus probably accurately summarises Nero's rejection of openly autocratic power and deft exposition of the ideal relationship between *princeps* and Senate: 'Let the Senate retain its old prerogatives! Let Italy and the public provinces take their stand before the judgement seats of the consuls, and let the consuls grant them access to the Fathers; for the armies delegated to his charge he would himself be responsible'.[90] The Senate would administer the peaceful inner territories, while its representative, the *princeps*, governed all those frontier regions where, after Gaius had removed control of the African legion from the Senate, most major provincial troop concentrations lay.[91] This division of responsibilities signified no formal apportioning of power between Senate and *princeps*: no 'dyarchy'.[92] From the

---

[83] Calp. *Ecl.* 1.42–5; 4.5–8, 83–6; 7.79–84; *Carm. Einsid.* 1.36, 2.38; Sen. *Apocol.* 1.4; Luc. 1.60–5. Levi 1949, 76–7; Champlin 1978; Mayer 1980; Townend 1980; Griffin 1984, 37–8; Rudich 1993, 4; Bartsch 1994, 54 and n. 34, 134–5; Gowers 1994, 131–2, 144–5; Reitz 2006, 112–14; Osgood 2011, 249; Maes 2013, 288 and n. 3. *Contra* Champlin 2003, 113; Stover 2015. (Based on their transmission and language, Stover redates the *Carmina Einsidlensia* (below 267 and n. 27) and, by implication, Calpurnius Siculus, to the later fourth century. Cf. below 267, 268.)

[84] Bol 2013, 184; below 42.   [85] Above 16; below 34, 50.

[86] Tac. *Ann.* 13.4.2: *discretam domum et rem publicam.* Griffin 1976, 105, 109; cf. below 60.

[87] Griffin 1984, 51, 55, 63; cf. Champlin 2003, 139.   [88] Griffin 1976, 113.   [89] Cf. below 20.

[90] Tac. *Ann.* 13.4.3: *Teneret antiqua munia senatus, consulum tribunalibus Italia et publicae provinciae adsisterent: illi patrum aditum praeberent, se mandatis exercitibus consulturum.* Krüger 2012, 36–7.

[91] Talbert 1984, 392–3, 425–7; cf. below 85.

[92] *Contra* Henderson 1905, 54–6. (I use 'dyarchy' as the term has come to be understood in a Roman context: the sharing of real power between two partners in government. The term was coined by Mommsen but, as Winterling (2009, 123–9, 132, 134) points out, to denote constitutional, not

start, every *princeps* must take an interest in and occasionally (legitimately, as consul or proconsul of the Republic) intervene in the affairs of the whole Empire, including the senatorial provinces, Italy and Rome.[93] In addition, provincials, whether 'senatorial' or 'frontier', knowing where true power lay, were more likely to turn to the *princeps* for help than to the Senate.[94] On the other hand, Nero's manifesto accepted that no *princeps* could ignore the Senate. The essence of the Principate was that while the *princeps* might be allowed special privileges, hold senior magistracies, and expect to decide on important matters that fell outside his nominal remit,[95] the Republic should otherwise operate as it always had done. Senators remained an irreplaceable part of the administration,[96] and recourse to the Senate continued to be had by inhabitants of all provinces, both senatorial and imperial. This could not work without a close partnership between *princeps* and Senate.[97] Thus, though Nero's policy speech gave senators more respect than power, it was precisely such respect that assured the continuation of the Republic and the fulfilment of senators' expectations of traditional office and dignity: of their 'senatorial tradition'.[98]

1.8 Senatorial Tradition

The culture in which all senators and aspiring senators, including Nero, were raised remained that of the old Republic in its 'finest hour': the late third and early second centuries BC, when it faced down Carthage and laid the foundations of world empire. This 'Scipionic' Republic disappeared in the civil strife of the late second and first centuries BC but remained the standard by which all subsequent political institutions were judged.[99] It was the Scipionic Republic that Octavian/Augustus 'restored' after Actium,[100] but the manner of his restoration had two awkward consequences. The old Republic detested kingship, but had occasionally accepted one-man rule in the office of *dictator*. Dictatorship was, however, strictly an emergency measure and, as Julius Caesar found, the concept of a permanent dictatorship was wholly unacceptable. Augustus, therefore,

---

political power: a means of expressing the Senate's crucial role in validating a *princeps*, both at the beginning and end of his principate.)
[93] Talbert 1984, 400–1. Cf. Tac. *Ann.* 14.59.5 (on the fall of Sulla and Plautus): *sibi incolumitatem rei publicae magna cura haberi.*
[94] Talbert 1984, 383, 419–20; Bowman 1996a, 347.
[95] Cf. Tac. *Ann.* 14.49. 2 (trial of Antistius Sosianus).   [96] Talbert 1984, 416–20; cf. below 24.
[97] Cf. Rudich 1993, 5; Michel 2015, 249–51.   [98] Cf. Malitz 1999, 18–19; below 286.
[99] Griffin 1984, 90.   [100] Cf. Crook 1996a, 77; below 83.

sought a more traditional way of retaining power, through the Principate. The first awkward consequence was that the continuance of the Republic cast all *principes* as interlopers: not sovereign monarchs but caretakers, enjoying privileges granted by the Senate in the name of the People.[101] The underlying conceit was that the state was experiencing temporary difficulties which it was each *princeps'* job to resolve. When this was achieved, the last *princeps* would return power to a renascent Scipionic Republic. Until then, the political community might continue to honour that Republic and judge all *principes* by its moral and political criteria. Under Nero, this allowed the consular C. Cassius Longinus to exult in his descent from one of the assassins of Caesar.[102] Pragmatic senatorial politicians, probably the vast majority, will have appreciated that the restoration of the Scipionic Republic was just a dream, that the Principate was the only means of achieving peace and preserving aristocratic privilege, and that the state was destined for ever to lie under the protection and direction of a great man and his *domus*.[103] In this they will have been encouraged by the ideology that the Augustan 'restored' Republic was the end of history.[104] This view, however, produced the second awkwardness: that there remained a model Republic, albeit Augustan, not Scipionic, against which the actions of all future *principes* would be judged. Either way, successive *principes*, all with an eye to their place in history, were aware that the political community was continually assessing them in terms of Republican, not monarchical, virtues and vices, and that on their death 'virtue' would win them deification and 'vice' non-deification or, worse, *damnatio memoriae* – being rendered a 'non-person', all by decree of the Senate. This constant looking back to the Republic explains the initial 'Augustan' promises made by Gaius, Claudius and Nero,[105] and amounts to Wallace-Hadrill's 'pose of denial' and Osgood's key political weakness at the heart of the Empire, considered further below as Winterling's series of constitutional 'paradoxes'.[106] The power of the senatorial tradition was probably also responsible for the absence of any serious intellectual consideration of the *princeps'* position. By the time of Nero there had been no penetrating politico-philosophical explanation, definition or justification of the Principate, nor would there ever be. Seneca did not provide one; Pliny II's treatment of it in his panegyric of Trajan is indirect, circumspect and tendentious; and while Dio's 'Maecenas debate' is insightful, it is late

---

[101] Cf. below 84.   [102] Cf. Griffin 1984, 195; below 70; cf. 90.   [103] Below 90.
[104] Cf. Drinkwater 2007b, 69–70.   [105] Wiedemann 1996a, 222, 232; Winterling 2007, 54–7.
[106] Wallace-Hadrill 1982, 36; Osgood 2011, 8; below 98.

and anachronistic.[107] The most accurate contemporary observer we have is
the anonymous author of the *Octavia*.[108] This impeded the emergence of a
political vocabulary that enabled people to engage with the way in which
the Roman state was run. A significant exception, indicating that people
could respond to change, was the invention of *Augusta*, first as a name and
then as a title, to designate the most senior women – 'empresses' – of the
ruling dynasty.[109] However, there remained no special word for 'emperor'.
Imperator, 'Caesar', *Augustus* and *princeps* were all borrowed terms, used
very flexibly. 'Caesar', the old Julian family name, appears to have been the
one in commonest use, with the rest, rather more specialised, deployed on
specific occasions.[110] Likewise, to the end there emerged no specific term
for 'usurper'. A wide variety of words were used, with a favourite being
'tyrant'.[111]

The coexistence of the fiction of a 'restored' Republic and the reality of
developing autocracy always had the potential to produce tension, but in
October 54 any threat of this was charmed away by Nero's policy speech
which accepted the model of the Augustan Republic. The convention by
which the *princeps* was the unquestioned captain of the ship of state with
the Senate as his trusty first mate was accepted and advertised as working
better than ever.[112] Nero's words were so well received that the Senate had
them inscribed on silver and read out at the beginning of every year at the
swearing in of the new consuls. Griffin sees the decree as conventional and
tasteless, but public endorsement of the Augustan Principate, perhaps
down to Nero's fall (there is no mention of the decree's being revoked),
is significant.[113] As had happened at the accession of Gaius and Claudius,
the 'Augustan clock' had been reset, or rather, notice was given that its
resetting under Claudius and Agrippina would continue under Nero.[114]

---

[107] Seneca: below 156; Pliny: Hekster 2002, 18–19; Cass. Dio 52.1–40; Crook 1996a, 71. Cf.
Osgood 2011, 7.
[108] Below 285.   [109] Cf. Suet. *Ner.* 28. Below 36.   [110] E.g. Petron. *Sat.* 51, 60, 76.
[111] Neri 1996.   [112] Cf. Griffin 1976, 112–17; 1984, 59–60.
[113] Cass. Dio 61.3.1; 60.10.2. Griffin 1984, 51.
[114] Cf. above 17. Cass. Dio 59.6.7; 60.10.1. Griffin 1976, 104 and n. 51. Such 'clock-setting' was not
restricted to the metropolis. Cf. Osgood 2011, 71–2, on the interchange between centre and
periphery at the start of a new principate: 'At the start of the new reign . . . Claudius and Rome's
subjects, looking back on the founder Augustus and his measures, reenacted the birth of the
empire, knitting together as they exchanged favors with one another'.

1.9 Nero and the Senate (i)

Concrete examples of Nero's good relationship with the Senate early in his principate are few but important. Taking their cue from his policy speech, senators quickly acted in matters affecting Italy and the central provinces.[115] The earliest known instance, in 54, included changes in charges for legal services and the freeing of aspiring quaestors from the obligation to put on expensive gladiatorial shows. They were supposedly opposed by Agrippina because they appeared to be anti-Claudian. This is probably another Tacitean tweak, but the legislation itself will have strengthened confidence in Nero's promises.[116] For his part, in 54 Nero suppressed two accusations against aristocrats which might have led to charges of *maiestas minuta* ('diminished majesty'): the compromising, through deed, word or gesture, of the security or good name of the state or its representatives, now extended to cover the ruling family – high treason.[117] At the start of 55, upon entering into his first consulship, Nero restrained his fellow consul, L. Antistius Vetus, from making the full pledge, demanded every 1 January of senators and state officials, to recognise the validity of those administrative and judicial decisions of all *principes*, past and present, which did not have the force of statute. The provision went back to Caesar and Augustus and demonstrates the need to paper over legal cracks caused by the emergence of autocracy alongside republic.[118] Now strictly speaking unnecessary, since everything a *princeps* did to secure the state was validated by the legislation that confirmed him in office, his *lex de imperio*,[119] it was an uncomfortable reminder of the sham of the 'restored' Republic and so anything that sugared the pill would have been welcomed by conservatives. Vetus therefore swore obedience to the *acta* of Nero's predecessors but not to those of Nero: substantively meaningless, but a courteous recognition of the Republican convention of the strict equality of each consul.[120] In the same year, having pledged himself to clemency, Nero made a practical display of mercy by restoring Plautius Lateranus to full senatorial rank after his degradation by Claudius.[121] More generally, Nero

[115] Tac. *Ann.* 13.5.1: *arbitrio Senatus.* Griffin 1976, 105–13.
[116] Tac. *Ann.* 13.5.1–2. Barrett 1996, 162; above 16; below 51.
[117] Tac. *Ann.* 4.34.3; 13.10.3. Rudich 1993, xxv; Bartsch 1994, 66; Barrett 1996, 4; Rutledge 2001, 87; Shotter 2008, 185; Winterling 2007, 29; below 187.
[118] Cf. Cass. Dio 51.20.1 (29 BC). Talbert 1984, 11–2, 200–1; above 15; cf. below 217.
[119] Below 84.
[120] Tac. *Ann.* 13.10–11.1. Hohl 1918, 359; Griffin 1976, 120–1; Bradley 1978a, 279.
[121] Tac. *Ann.* 13.11.2. Following this, Seneca produced his *De clementia*: below 156; cf. 26.

acted as *civilis princeps* in showing sensitivity to senatorial feelings in respect of offices and titles.[122] The most prized office was that of consul, whether 'ordinary' (one of the first two of the year, whose names gave it its date) or 'suffect' (supernumerary, taking the place of the *ordinarii*, usually after six months). Thus, for example, though as a matter of course he almost immediately became *consul ordinarius*, he was careful to take only four such consulships (in 55, 57, 58 and 60; his fifth, in 68, was extraordinary),[123] and in 58 he refused the offer of a consulship for life.[124] This accorded with Republican tradition and gave other aristocrats more chance of gaining the top office.[125] Nero showed further regard for tradition in respect of the consulship by taking fellow *ordinarii* mainly from the old nobility.[126] In the best Augustan fashion, he also initially declined the title of *pater patriae* ('Father of his country') on the grounds of his youth, though he adopted it in late 55 or early 56 following the regime's early success against Parthia.[127] He objected to being depicted in gold and silver statues and to the reordering of the calendar to make his birth month, December, the first of the year.[128] Conservatives would probably also have approved of his honouring of his birth father, Lucius Domitius Ahenobarbus.[129] At first he did not use *Imperator* as a name; and, in a very Augustan gesture, he immediately placed the *corona civica*, the symbol of liberty, on his coins.[130] He sought to protect the status and improve the career prospects of senators by forbidding the admission of sons of freedmen into the Senate and by, for example, standardising the length of consulships to six months, a period which reflected the dignity of the office while enabling it to be shared by more aspirants.[131] That he was less generous than Claudius in respect of the rights and privileges of slaves and freedmen, and in the extension of Roman citizenship and membership of the Senate, will also have gratified conservatives.[132] His relaxing, perhaps around 62, of the enforcement of legislation coercing aristocrats to marry

---

[122] Griffin 1984, 120.   [123] Suet. *Ner.* 14; Hohl 1918, 391; Bradley 1978a, 91–2; below 144, 397.
[124] Tac. *Ann.* 13.41.5. Below 135 and n. 42; for the embarrassing antecedents of the concept see Levi 1949, 130–1.
[125] Warmington 1969, 41–2; Griffin 1976, 121–2; Bradley 1978a, 92 (contrasting the Flavians); Waldherr 2005, 180.
[126] Below 144.
[127] *RIC* I² p. 149 nos. 8–9; cf. Sen. *Clem.* 1.14.2; Suet. *Ner.* 10.2. Levi 1949, 127 and n. 1; Bradley 1978a, 79; Griffin 1984,120.
[128] Tac. *Ann.* 13.10.1–2.   [129] Tac. *Ann.* 13.10.1; Suet. *Ner.* 9. Hohl 1918, 357.
[130] *RIC* I² p. 148 nos. 1–3. Levi 1949, 17; Griffin 1976, 115; Griffin 1984, 62; Wiedemann 1996a, 242, 246; below 94.
[131] Suet. *Ner.* 15.2. Bradley 1978a, 96–8; Talbert 1984, 21.
[132] Levi 1949, 97–8, 133; Warmington 1969, 33–4, 52–3.

and have legitimate children must likewise have been welcomed by them.[133] In these early years Nero very much acted the senator, attending senatorial meetings, participating in debates and enthusiastically involving himself in judicial, political and fiscal matters.[134] In 56, for example, he initiated lasting reform of the main public treasury (*Aerarium populi Romani/Aerarium Saturni*: henceforth *Aerarium*),[135] and in 57 and 62 he subsidised it from his own resources.[136] In 58, Nero was persuaded of the impracticality of his ideas on the reform of indirect taxation by 'senators' – either in debate or in an advisory capacity.[137] Also in 58, he gave pensions to impoverished senators,[138] and in 58 and 59 acknowledged senatorial authority in the affairs of Cyrenaica and Italy.[139] In 60 he enhanced the standing of the Senate as an appellate civil court.[140] Suetonius favourably reports his further respecting senatorial sensitivities when a consul died on the last day of the year, and approves his having at least some of his addresses to the Senate read by one of the consuls not, as was usual, a *quaestor Augusti*.[141] After the displacement of Agrippina, he played a direct role in the destruction of hated figures of the Claudian regime, such as Suillius Rufus in 58.[142] One has to be careful. Ultimate power still remained with the *princeps*. The praetorians whom the Senate sent to quell civil disorder at Puteoli can have moved only on the direct orders of Nero.[143] Furthermore, we see him involved in senatorial business for reasons which are sometimes obvious (court matters, specialist knowledge, treason[144]), sometimes not (mild treatment of corrupt provincial governors[145]). However, 'captain' and 'first mate' generally worked together well.

---

[133] Suet. *Ner.* 10.1. Bradley 1978a, 74–5.
[134] Judicial: Tac. *Ann.* 13.43.4; Suet. *Ner.* 15.1. Warmington 1969, 36–7; Talbert 1984, 475–6; Wiedemann 1996a, 246. Fiscal: Tac. *Ann.* 13.50–51; below 351.
[135] Tac. *Ann.* 13.28.5–29. Below 351.   [136] Tac. *Ann.* 13.31.2; 15.18.4. Below 334.
[137] Tac. *Ann.* 13.50.2: *senatores* amended to *seniores* by Lipsius. Hohl 1918, 366 favours the Senate, as do Syme 1958, 416, Griffin 1984, 92 (cautiously) and Günther 2013, 116 and n. 13. On the other hand, Furneaux 1907, 219 favours *seniores* and the notion of a 'private cabinet', as do Crook; below 78, Millar 1977, 259 and Talbert 1984, 172. Though the *communis opinio* seems to favour *seniores*, Tac. *Ann.* 13.48 and 13.49 are about the Senate, its activities and its purview.
[138] Tac. *Ann.* 13.34. Cf. Talbert 1996, 326, for Augustan precedents.
[139] Cyrenaica: 14.18.1–2 [59]; Italy: 13.48 (Puteoli) [58]; 13.49.1 (Syracuse) [58]; 14.17.3 (Pompeii and Nuceria) [59]. Waldherr 2005, 178.
[140] Tac. *Ann.* 14.28.2. Talbert 1984, 469.
[141] Suet. *Ner.* 15.2. Bradley 1978a, 99; Griffin 1984, 62.
[142] Tac. *Ann.* 13.43.4. Rudich 1993, 28; cf. below 51.
[143] Tac. *Ann.* 13.48.3. Warmington 1969, 37; below 227.
[144] Tac. *Ann.* 14.50 [access]; 14.18.3–4 [knowledge]; 14.49.3 [treason].
[145] Tac. *Ann.* 13.33.1–2; 13.52.

Tacitus, indeed, gives the impression that, at the start of – and perhaps throughout[146] – Nero's principate, magistrates and Senate handled the bulk of routine matters within their competence, referring only the most contentious, such as the treatment of errant freedmen, to the *princeps* and his ministers.[147] The Julio-Claudian Senate met relatively frequently, in regular and supernumerary sessions, and gave full consideration to important matters, both secular and religious.[148] Such activity, involving, for example, Republican constitutional 'housekeeping', problems arising out of legislation, legislation itself and occasional participation in trials of senators for murder and corruption (since they expected to be tried by their peers[149]), was important and was a wholly appropriate employment of the education and training of all involved.[150] Routine but effective measures against the forging of wills and other reforms of legal business may well have been suggested and implemented by senatorial lawyers.[151] Because the sources focus on Nero's activities, we hear little of this other extensive field of public business, a rare exception being the existence and membership of a three-man commission of enquiry into indirect taxation, operating in 62.[152] Such business was an indispensable part of imperial administration; and though at times arduous and boring,[153] for many it must have been hugely satisfying, and a useful experience for future provincial governors.[154] Furthermore, despite the persistence of their tradition, senators were willing to take on a range of new, non-Republican

---

[146] Tacitus reports an unusually high number of senatorial cases involving provincial governors in the period 54–61: Tac. *Ann.* 13.30.1, 13.33.3–4; 14.18.1; 14.28.3, 14.46.1. This could be a real historical phenomenon – so Warmington 1969, 59: reflecting Seneca's influence on Nero – or an artefact of the evidence – Tacitus noted these for reasons unknown to us. I follow Wiedemann's (1996a, 249) implication of a real phenomenon, due at least in part to real senatorial interest (in both senses of the word) in the issue, which would have continued after the major trials.

[147] Freedmen: Tac. *Ann.* 13.26–27; 14.45.4 (cf. 13.32.1). Cf. Bradley 1978a, 94–5, on the apparently very few cases heard by Nero until the Pisonian conspiracy; and Talbert 1984, 475, on Nero's careful choice of cases in his 'interference' in the extortion trials of 58 and 59; 468, on the possibility that in 61 issues over slaves and freedmen were discussed in senatorial committee, before being passed to the full house and then to Nero.

[148] Cf. Talbert 1984, 185, on 'the current misconception that the senate met seldom and speedily despatched its business'); 213–15, 221–2, 249–51, on the likelihood that under the 'restored' Republic junior members were given more opportunity to express their views than previously; 387–91, 407, 459, 463, on legal business as the most time-consuming.

[149] Talbert 1984, 43, 466–9.

[150] Talbert 1984, 268, 285; cf. 195: 'For many senators it would have been a pleasure, not a penance, to listen to a Pliny . . . speaking for hours on end'.

[151] Suet. *Ner.* 17. Bradley 1978a, 105–10; cf. Talbert 1984, 442.

[152] Tac. *Ann.* 15.18.4. Below 352.   [153] Cf. Talbert 1984, 66–8, 192–95, 262, 413–15, 489.

[154] Experience: Talbert 1984, 459.

but important and probably highly lucrative, positions in Rome and Italy.[155] Although the likelihood of the Senate's seriously opposing a *princeps* was minimal,[156] the acceptance of employment by senators *qua* senators should not be disparaged as people using membership of a prestigious but moribund institution to promote their own interests.[157] They continued to meet in the Senate, which as a body remained a functioning organ of administration. Tacitus describes a lively dispute between a praetor and a tribune of the people over their respective powers in 56 as giving a lingering impression of the old Republic.[158]

Though some who were qualified to do so did not attempt to become senators, and some senators failed to pursue full careers,[159] competition to get into, and on in, the Senate was generally high.[160] In 60, when the number of candidates for praetorships exceeded the number of vacancies, Nero had to provide senior military posts as consolation prizes:[161] a clever use of available talent given current heavy fighting in Britain and the East.[162] Senatorial self-confidence was reflected in 58, in an attack on Thrasea Paetus for making a meal of a routine item: the Senate's business was to discuss peace and war, not minutiae.[163] And in 61, when, following the murder of Pedanius Secundus by one of his slaves, the Senate considered the fate of the rest of his household, the high aristocrat, veteran consular and distinguished jurist, C. Cassius Longinus, remarked upon changes in law and custom that had already been put to the body, no doubt including those before Nero but making the current principate part of a continuing process.[164] In 62, in the context of a senatorial trial for treason, Nero conceded that the Senate had the right to decide as it pleased, and allowed it to do so.[165] This was not a cowed and dejected body. The likelihood of relatively free speech between *princeps* and senators at Nero's court – 'banter' – is discussed further below.[166] It may have been because he feared criticism there that he reported the death of Agrippina to the Senate from the safe distance of Naples.[167] It is also

---

[155] Talbert 1984, 372–3, 383–6.   [156] Talbert 1984, 290; cf. below 100.
[157] As Rudich 1993, xx, xxiv (typically taking too much of his tone from Tacitus).
[158] Tac. *Ann.* 13.28.1: *manebat nihilo minus quaedam imago rei publicae.* Warmington 1969, 35–6; Griffin 1976, 122–3; cf. below 27, 187.
[159] Talbert 1984, 76–8, noting the absence of Seneca's brother, Annaeus Mela: cf. below 350, 363.
[160] Talbert 1984, 131–3, 342.   [161] Tac. *Ann.* 14.28.1. Cf. Talbert 1984, 19–20 and below 389.
[162] Shotter 2008, 86; Barrett *et al.* 2016, 37 and n. 47; Table 3; cf. below 145.
[163] Tac. *Ann.* 13.49.
[164] Tac. *Ann.* 14.43.1. His wife, Junia Lepida, was a great-great-granddaughter of Augustus: Wiedemann 1996a, 250.
[165] Tac. *Ann.* 14.49.4–5: *statuerent ut vellent.* Cf. below 27.   [166] Below 128.
[167] Tac. *Ann.* 14.10.5.

significant that Tacitus, always quick to criticise the Neronian Senate for servility, has two mutinous legions swearing allegiance to it and the People of Rome on 1 January 69, and has Otho praise it as 'the head of the Empire and the glory of all the provinces'.[168] The high status of senators was never in doubt.[169]

Nero did not neglect to honour the lower aristocracy, the *equites*, for example by giving the order the distinction of its own seating in the Circus.[170] He also attempted to show more co-operation with the People, towards 55 suspending the use of praetorians to police the games – places of rowdy, violent or even hostile behaviour. Though the experiment lasted only one year, it showed consideration.[171] His care for the provisioning of Rome; his giving of lavish games and entertainments; his building of grand new venues for these – part of a general programme of construction which will have given employment; and his generous scattering of gift-tokens at spectacles, will also have endeared him to the populace.[172]

In the early part of his principate Nero was, therefore, the perfect *civilis princeps*, dancing in step with a willing Senate in affirming the existence of a fully 'restored' Republic.[173] Senators demanded their rights but accepted restrictions and control, mitigated by clemency, even though this was an essentially autocratic virtue.[174] The established view is that this accord could not last, and that in the later part of the principate it collapsed utterly. Strictly speaking this is incontrovertible, since in 68 the Senate condemned Nero as a public enemy. However, this condemnation came at the end of a complex process; and the evidence suggests that – a *fil rouge* of this study – Nero never quarrelled with the Senate as an institution.[175] He never set out to break its power and impose himself on the state as despot; still less did he seek to annihilate its members.[176] The fact that most examples of Nero's good relationship with the Senate come from the

---

[168] Tac. *Hist.* 1.56; 1.84: *caput imperii et decora omnium provinciarum.* Talbert 1984, 81–2.
[169] Talbert 1984, 87–90.   [170] Tac. *Ann.* 15.32.2; Suet. *Ner.* 11.1. Bradley 1978a, 82.
[171] Tac. *Ann.* 13.24.1, 25.4. Bingham 2013, 104–5.
[172] Suet. *Ner.* 11, 12.1, 3. Grant 1970, 50–2; Griffin 1976, 123; Bradley 1978a, 81–5, 288. Below 315, 330–1.
[173] Cf. Griffin 1976, 127.
[174] Griffin 1976, 124: 'Nothing better illustrated how far the senate accepted the real monarchical powers of the *Princeps* (while insisting on the formal masking of it), than in its enthusiasm for his displays of *liberalitas, clementia* and *comitas* towards them'. Cf. above 21.
[175] Similar: Talbert 1984, 177–8.
[176] *Contra*, e.g. Henderson 1905, 87: 'Nero's courtesy turned to bitter hate'; Hohl 1918, 392: 'In stets wachsendem Maß fühlt sich Nero als Despot, als absoluter Monarch ... man darf es glauben, daß er am liebsten den Senat völlig beseitigen hätte, um die gesamte Verwaltung den Rittern und den Freigelassen anzutrauen'; Levi 1949, 144–6, 151–2; Cizek 1982, 60. Cf. below 147, 263.

earlier period suits the notion of his degeneration into monstrosity, and the belief in a *quinquennium Neronis* – an initial five-year period when all went well but after which came disaster. Though the *quinquennium* is now generally (though not wholly) discounted,[177] the conviction that Nero's 'monstrosity' led to a complete rupture between him and the Senate continues to attract support. However, the validity of this rupture is questionable. In 59, Thrasea Paetus, arch-champion of senatorial privilege, showed his disapproval of excessive celebration of Agrippina's killing by walking out of the Senate, but does not appear to have objected to the death itself.[178] He had enjoyed a successful career under Claudius and Nero,[179] and appears to have remained willing to work with Nero to at least as late as 62, when he intervened to mitigate the punishment of Antistius Sosianus, condemned on a trumped-up charge under the revived treason law.[180] He used the occasion to heap praise on 'an excellent *princeps*, and a Senate unfettered by any restriction'.[181] In the same year he gave a textbook demonstration of the *princeps*/Senate partnership at work in the senatorial trial of an arrogant provincial aristocrat. Paetus got the Senate to minute a decree defending its own honour, which Nero moderated and had put into action.[182] Many have seen 62, which also saw the death of Burrus, Nero's praetorian prefect and counsellor and great ally of Seneca, the partial retirement of Seneca, the death of Octavia and Nero's marriage with Poppaea, as the turning-point of Nero's principate, after which he went increasingly to the bad,[183] but this is to adopt the

---

[177] Tacitus (*Ann.* 14.13.3) identifies the year 59, immediately after the murder of Agrippina, as the time when Nero started to go to the bad, which makes the 'good' period the four years or so between October 54 and March 59. However, the term *quinquennium Neronis* derives from the fourth-century historian Aurelius Victor (*Caes.* 5.2). For its application to the first five years of Nero's principate see Henderson 1905, 75–6 and, more recently, Cizek 1982, 93 and Rudich 1993, 11 (detecting 'spinning' by Seneca's circle). Malitz 1999, 17–18 and Waldherr 2005, 95 see the difficulties involved, but are still inclined to accept this. Hohl 1918, 392; Griffin 1976, 423–6; and Reitz 2006, 11 are not wholly opposed to the idea, but prefer to see a major turning-point in 62, not 59; cf. below 194. Griffin 1984, 37–8, 43 is more sceptical; and Bradley 1978a, 71–2, Wiedemann 1996a 243–4, and Hurley 2013, 34 are dismissive. Fini 1994, 47 is unique in attaching it to the last five years of Nero's principate.

[178] Tac. *Ann.* 14.12.2. Cf. Rudich 1993, 38, and below 82; his protest was against excessive dissimulation.

[179] Wirszubski 1950, 140.

[180] Tac. *Ann.* 14.48–9. Cf. above 21. Despite the slant that Tacitus puts on the story, it seems likely that the original charge was the work of Nero's over-enthusiastic advisers, especially Tigellinus, and not that of the *princeps* himself. This may well reflect the power-struggles that marked 62: below 187.

[181] Tac. *Ann.* 14.48:5: *egregio sub principe et nulla necessitate obstricto senatu.*

[182] Tac. *Ann.* 15.20–22.2.　　[183] Above n. 177; also Malitz 1999, 22; Waldherr 2005, 184–5.

prejudices of the common source tradition. Though Thrasea Paetus showed disquiet at certain events of 62, he continued as a member of Nero's inner circle.[184] Only this can explain the snub he suffered early in 63 when, presumably still prepared to show himself in support of the regime, he was forbidden to accompany the rest of the Senate to Anzio (Figure 1) to celebrate the birth of Nero's daughter. This was the start of his downfall, but even then he enjoyed a reconciliation with Nero and it was only later that he began the retreat from public life which, in 66, was interpreted as treason.[185] However, as late as 66 he had to be ordered not to attend Nero's reception of Tiridates, which suggests that he was still regarded as a senior statesman.[186] Likewise, that Nero indicated that Cassius Longinus had lost his favour by forbidding his attendance at Poppaea's funeral shows that until 65 Longinus, the proud descendant of one of the men who killed Julius Caesar and no great friend of the regime, was still tolerated at court.[187]

    Above all, however, it has to be reckoned that Paetus and Longinus and their supporters comprised only a small minority of senators. To the end of May 68 most were, like the rest of the imperial 'Establishment', prepared to work with Nero.[188] Nero found himself with new senior advisers in 62, but these brought continuity, not change.[189] Thus, in 64 Nero showed great 'tact' in working with the Senate in managing the affairs of Crete, one of the provinces nominally under its control.[190] Then there is Nero's later coinage. It had become usual for the base-metal coins of the Principate to bear the legend *EX SC* or *SC* for *Ex Senatus consulto* ('By decree of the Senate'). This was probably to show respect to the Senate for the powers and honours it voted to *principes* to establish them in office. At the start of his principate, Nero did not issue base-metal coins. However, *SC* made a novel first appearance on his silver and gold. When around 63, at the very start of his coinage reform, he began to mint lower denomination pieces, these did not carry the legend *SC*, but his silver and gold continued to do so. *SC* on silver and gold ceased in 64, with the introduction of the full 'reformed' coinage, but now appeared on new, very attractive base-metal pieces. All this suggests that throughout his principate Nero acknowledged

---

[184] Cf. below 66.   [185] Tac. *Ann.* 15.23.5–6. Romm 2014, 147; below 216.
[186] Tac. *Ann.* 16.25.1. Cf. Griffin 1984, 81: how Seneca probably still functioned as an *amicus* even after his withdrawal from court life in 62.
[187] Tac. *Ann.* 16.7.1. Above 19, 25.   [188] Cf. Talbert 1984, 25; below 407.
[189] Cf. Warmington 1969, 42, 136; below 136.   [190] Talbert 1984, 401.

the Senate's conferral of his powers, titles and privileges.[191] In 65, the Pisonian conspirators eventually decided to kill Nero by approaching him in public as petitioners. This very old-fashioned plan (strongly reminiscent of the assassination of Julius Caesar and perhaps even modelled on it[192]) indicates the continuing availability of access by senators to the *princeps*.[193] Furthermore, in the course of the first, targeted, round of prosecutions following the failure of the Pisonian conspiracy, accused senators were given the chance to defend themselves;[194] and Nero, acting the outraged senator, defended himself at what must have been an emergency meeting of the Senate (at this time of the year usually in recess) by presenting a dossier of evidence to prove culpable sedition.[195] Yet he also seems to have been prepared to draw a line under the proceedings. When, just as the first wave of prosecutions appeared to have ended, one senator attempted to revive them, his peers persuaded him to desist from reopening matters now settled, 'in his clemency', by Nero.[196] Nero's honouring of the consular, Petronius Turpilianus, and the praetor-designate, the future emperor Nerva, with *ornamenta triumphalia* is particularly important for demonstrating that there were leading senators on his side throughout the affair.[197] Turpilianus was to be one of the pair of generals entrusted with the defence of Italy for Nero in 68 and did not betray him.[198] Close to the end, in late 67, when Nero proclaimed the freedom of Achaea, he recompensed the Senate for the loss of this province by giving it back Sardinia.[199] At the end, in 68, he asked the Senate to condemn Galba and, as in the case of Turpilianus, relied on senators to defend him.[200] Indeed, a major feature of Nero's principate is the way in which his regime allowed senatorial generals outside the Julio-Claudian family free rein in a manner also reminiscent of the old Republic.[201]

---

[191] *RIC* I² pp. 133–5, 137–41. Warmington 1969, 66–7; Griffin 1984, 57–9, 115–16, 120–5; Talbert 1984, 379–82 (whose suggestion that the absence of *SC* on the base-metal coins of c. 63 reflects Nero's 'impatience' with the Senate at this time strikes me as incorrect); Carson 1990, 14–16; Wiedemann. 1996a, 242; Levick 1999b, 49–50; Malitz 1999, 19; Waldherr 2005, 178–9; Butcher and Ponting 2014, 192; below 360.

[192] Griffin 1984, 166; below 72.   [193] Tac. *Ann.* 15.53.2. Cf. below 254.

[194] Tac. *Ann.* 15.58.3. Cf. below 254.   [195] Tac. *Ann.* 15.73.1. Talbert 1984, 210; below 73.

[196] Tac. *Ann.* 15.73.4: *mansuetudine*. Rutledge 2001, 169.

[197] Tac. *Ann.* 15.72.2. Hohl 1918, 385; Bradley 1978a, 98–9; Cizek 1982, 189–93; below 95.

[198] Below 392–3.

[199] Pausan. 7.17.3; *ILS* 8794. Hohl 1918, 389; Bradley 1978a, 145; Griffin 1984, 280 and n. 127; below 265, 337. Maintaining the number of senatorial provinces was both a matter of courtesy and a means of preserving the number of senatorial governorships: Talbert 1984, 396.

[200] Tac. *Hist.* 1.6; Suet. *Ner.* 41.1; Plut. *Galb.* 5.4; Cass. Dio 63.27.1. Below 397.

[201] E.g. below 145.

1.10   Achievements

There was no comprehensive breakdown in relations between Nero and the Senate, and it is against this positive assessment of Nero's dealings with the Roman political community that we can understand the relative success of the Neronian principate.[202] In late 54, the transfer of power from Claudius to Nero, including the exclusion of Britannicus, was managed without a hitch. The new regime was immediately accepted and in the period 54–55 fully confirmed its authority. Between 55 and 59 it survived the sidelining then murder of its chief architect, Agrippina II. In the period 54–63, it successfully dealt with a foreign crisis in Armenia and a provincial rebellion in Britain. This was despite the fact that in Britain Rome endured early defeat at the hands of a woman, Boudica, and in Armenia suffered further humiliation with the capitulation of Caesennius Paetus. The regime also survived the disappearance of Burrus and Seneca and Nero's tricky divorce of Octavia and marriage with Poppaea in 62, and the death of Poppaea in 65. It weathered domestic disaster – material, moral and even religious – in the shape of the Great Fire of 64; and in 65 it foiled the Pisonian conspiracy, a huge metropolitan scare. Apart from its last days, the principate of Nero may, indeed, be regarded as lucky. Even after the murder of Agrippina and Octavia, the Fire, the Pisonian conspiracy and the consequent run of executions and banishments, it could demonstrate that the gods were still on its side. For, following the agreement of an armistice in Armenia in 64, it could announce world peace; and in 66 it enjoyed the consequent propaganda coup that was Nero's reception of king Tiridates in Rome, rightly projected as a successful settlement of the Armenian dispute. 'Universal peace' was broken by a second provincial revolt, in Judaea in 66, but, thanks to the earlier agreement, there was no Parthian involvement and all indications were that Jews would be suppressed as effectively as Britons. From 63, there was change in the imperial gold and silver coinage, but this was caused by a need for reform, not excessive government expenditure. From the end of 66, when Nero went off to Greece, to the end of 67, when he returned, the regime appears to have feared no major crisis. Crisis did not come until 68, but to begin with was manageable. Sensible measures were taken to counter it, and it is likely that both *princeps* and dynasty could

---

[202] The following summary derives from Drinkwater 2013, 159–60. The points it makes will be substantiated in detail below.

have survived if Nero had taken more decisive action. Nero fell, but even his fall was well-managed, since it avoided all-out civil war.

This has taken us far from the Nero of legend. That Nero was a killer. He was complicit in Agrippina's murder of Claudius: he was a parricide. He was also involved in the murder of Britannicus: he was a fratricide. He was directly involved in the murder of Agrippina: he was a matricide. He instigated the deaths of the 'good' Burrus and Seneca: he was an ingrate. He abused his first wife, Octavia, and finally had her killed; and he caused the death of his second wife, Poppaea, and her unborn child: he was a murderer. Further afield, he was also responsible for the destruction of a large number of leading men of Rome and for the persecution of innocent Christians: he was a tyrant. This Nero was also a mad spendthrift. He ordered the firing of Rome, sang grand opera during the conflagration, and then used the space created to build a magnificent new palace, the Golden House, suitable for a god – himself, as Apollo. And he was sexually depraved: a rapist (he violated Britannicus); a perpetrator of incest (he slept with Agrippina); and a mocker of the institution of marriage (he neglected Octavia and united himself officially with the eunuch Sporus). No good male Roman, instead of campaigning he toured Greece as a professional entertainer and on his return celebrated these activities by parodying the Roman triumph. Depraved, he compelled others to join him in his depravity. Early in June 68, he was forced from power, declared a public enemy and driven to commit suicide in humiliating circumstances. But this bad Nero is the Nero of his enemies, and if we start with him we are tempted to fit all the evidence 'into our preconceived picture of the tyrant'.[203] He deserves to be looked at afresh.

---

[203] Champlin 2003, 51.

CHAPTER 2

Agrippina and Her Legacy

2.1 Introduction

Nero was brought to power by the determination and capability of his mother.[1] We cannot understand him without first understanding Agrippina II, one of the most remarkable figures of early imperial history. Her character and deeds are as much distorted by the source tradition, especially by Tacitus,[2] as are those of Nero, and require as much effort to reconstruct.

2.2 Life and Career to the Accession of Nero

In her childhood and early adulthood Agrippina endured upheaval and danger exceeding anything experienced by the young Nero. Under Tiberius, when she was no more than four years old, her father, Germanicus, died in circumstances which pointed to government involvement. Her mother, the ambitious and headstrong Agrippina I, attempted to exploit these suspicions but this led only to her own destruction and the deaths of Agrippina II's elder brothers, Nero and Drusus. When Agrippina's only surviving brother, Gaius, succeeded Tiberius in 37, she was first honoured but then vilified, terrorised and, in 39, deprived of her property and sent away from Rome and from her toddler, Nero.[3] However, she survived, never forgot her hereditary destiny, and used her tenacity, intelligence and political skill to restore herself to greatness. She returned from exile under Claudius, in 41. Now widowed, her priority will have been to defend herself and Nero against Claudius' wife, Messalina, determined to secure the succession of her newly-born son, Britannicus. Both boys could not grow up to occupy the same supreme position, so Agrippina began the

---

[1] Tac. *Ann.* 13.21.6.   [2] Ginsburg 2006, 9: 'Tacitus' Agrippina is largely a literary construct'.
[3] Barrett 1996, 30–2; 37–9, 46–8; 51–4, 63, 66, 69.

long and perilous game of placing Nero at the top of the Julio-Claudian clan.[4] In Passienus, she quickly found a rich and influential new husband who could act as protector.[5] Passienus soon died, but Agrippina was very lucky in the way that his death was quickly followed by the killing of Messalina, in 48, which created the possibility of her union with Claudius.[6] This Agrippina pursued with success, marrying Claudius in 49, despite the fact that she was his niece, for which there had to be special legal dispensation. To achieve her goal, Agrippina must have depended on powerful court politicians, in particular Pallas and Vitellius I, each with his own agenda. Pallas, for example, was too deeply involved in the removal of Messalina to allow Britannicus to succeed Claudius.[7] More generally, court politicians will have been anxious to ensure stability after the Messalina crisis, in particular by keeping Agrippina and Nero safely within the ruling family.[8] However, once the ball had been passed to her, Agrippina took control of the game. Even before her marriage to Claudius, she secured the engagement of his daughter, Octavia, to Nero, displacing an existing fiancé, L. Junius Silanus. In 50, Claudius adopted Nero and brought him on as heir; and in 53 he gave Octavia to him in marriage. In the meantime, there were changes in Agrippina's team. Pallas remained, but Vitellius I died in 51. From 49, Agrippina closely consulted Seneca, an old intimate, brought in to tutor Nero; and just before the death of Vitellius I, Burrus was made sole praetorian prefect. The group that was to bring Nero to power – Agrippina, Pallas, Seneca and Burrus – was now in place. This reflects Agrippina's raw ambition on the part of Nero; but she also made a positive contribution to the development of the Principate. She was the 'embodiment of the Julian and Claudian lines', sharing Claudius' ancestry through her father, Germanicus, his brother, and descended directly from Augustus through her mother, Agrippina I. Marriage to her therefore helped confirm Claudius' position after his irregular accession, the scandal over Messalina

---

[4] Cf. below 278, 282. Ginsburg 2006, 18, 21 (quotation), 23, 33, 107–12, 115, 123–5) sees Agrippina's remorseless drive 'to secure her own power by putting her son on the throne' as an element in her literary and rhetorical 'construction' by the hostile source tradition: a woman out of control, the sign of a dysfunctional leading family, and so that of a dysfunctional state. However, given her pride in her lineage and the existence of Britannicus as a long-term rival to both herself and Nero, her ambition is entirely plausible.

[5] Below 278.

[6] It was, of course, suspected that Agrippina had murdered Passienus: Griffin 1984, 28, from *Schol. Iuv.* 4.81.

[7] *Schol. Iuv.* (Probus) 1.109; Henderson 1905, 28; Hohl 1918, 315.

[8] Cf. Malitz 1999, 6; Rutledge 2001, 150; Waldherr 2005, 35.

and the fear that Britannicus was not in the best of health.[9] Potential rivalry between Nero and Britannicus could for the moment be passed off as unproblematic. Joint succession had been envisaged by Augustus in Gaius and Lucius Caesar.[10] Claudius could therefore project a positive, Augustan,[11] image of a recreated ideal ruling family, consisting of father, mother and dutiful offspring. Official depictions of Agrippina on coins and in sculpture, frequently associating her with Demeter and Ceres, were probably intended to show her bestowing domestic chastity, fertility, peace and prosperity on the whole Empire.[12] Closer to home, Agrippina, working with Claudius, used 'her enormous reserve of patience and her skill in carefully preparing the ground' to improve the central administration and promote a good relationship between court and Senate. The latter policy may not have originated with her, since Claudius, Vitellius I and Pallas appear to have begun to pursue it before 40. However, she deserves credit for her acumen in adopting and developing the strategy. She needed the Senate initially to legitimise her marriage with her uncle and Nero's with his sister-by-adoption, but she seems then genuinely to have appreciated that it was more effective to work with the grain of the Principate.[13] She and her team cultivated the support of senators in the management of state business, gaining their backing and confirming their belief in the importance of the Senate as an institution.[14] This approach proved unable to dispel the distaste felt for Claudius in certain senatorial quarters, caused by his irregular accession and secret trials and execution of aristocrats. In the thirteen years of his principate, 35 senators and 300 equestrians were killed or forced to commit suicide.[15] Most, however, perished under Messalina.[16] Under Agrippina senatorial deaths fell away. Her good relationship with the Senate may have been a motive for removing Claudius,[17] and was certainly a major contributor to the ease of Nero's accession.[18] Agrippina, indeed, never lost sight of this, her main goal. She destroyed all those whom she perceived as standing in its way;[19] and she worked remorselessly to marginalise Britannicus. The appointment of Burrus as sole praetorian prefect, for example, removed a pair of

---

[9] Barrett 1996, 110–11; Holland 2000, 45; Ginsburg 2006, 91–3 (quotation); Romm 2014, 30.
[10] Ginsburg 2006, 25, 27–8.   [11] Ginsburg 2006, 124–5.
[12] Ginsburg 2006, 57–8, 63, 71, 76, 84, 99, 102–4, 124–5; cf. below 38.
[13] Barrett 1996, 73, 98 (quotation), 101, 103, 105, 112–13; Osgood 2011, 228; Michel 2015, 246–51.
[14] Barrett 1996, 127, 134; cf. above 24.   [15] Holland 2000, 37.
[16] Barrett 1996, 103–5; Michel 2015, 204–6.   [17] Below 171.
[18] Barrett 1996, 144; cf. above 15.   [19] Barrett 1996, 135–8.

commanders considered still committed to him. It was the final element in a programme of transfers and promotions designed to ensure the total loyalty of the Praetorian Guard.[20] Equally important, demonstrating Agrippina's capacity for long-term planning and financial skills, she established a fighting fund to meet the expenses of Nero's accession.[21] She will have taken a major part in preparing him for office, including the choice of Seneca as his tutor; and it can only have been she who planned and directed his accession, which bears 'all the hallmarks of Agrippina's subtle manoeuvring'.[22]

2.3 Long-Term Planning

In October 54 Agrippina dominated the Roman state, but what did she have in mind for the future? Her first priority will have remained Nero. She will have wanted him to become a new Germanicus, but not yet. Agrippina was still not quite forty;[23] he was not quite seventeen. She cannot have contemplated any immediate surrendering of her hard-won position, and must have looked forward to several more years in the driving-seat as the senior partner in a team comprising herself, Pallas, Seneca, Burrus and, now, Nero, in continuing co-operation with the Senate: 'business as usual'.[24] Meanwhile, Nero could be trained up to become a Roman senator and a great *princeps*. There is no reason to doubt Agrippina's sincerity. She had always taken her duty to promote Nero's greatness seriously, for example forbidding Seneca to teach him philosophy because 'an excessive interest in that subject was not considered proper for a Roman senator'.[25] She will, however, have expected Seneca to teach the *princeps*-to-be how to operate within the framework of the Principate.[26] Agrippina was probably fairly close to her son. Though cared for principally by domestic servants, Nero must have seen something of his mother between his birth and her exile two years later. The pair were apart for only just over a year, and Nero was too young to retain any lasting memories of the separation. On her return Agrippina probably gave him as much attention as possible. His childhood was nowhere near as bad as Gaius'

[20] Barrett 1996, 118 and n. 83, 120–2; Bingham 2013, 30. [21] Below 342.
[22] Barrett 1996, 143–4 (quotation), 147; Waldherr 2005, 60; Osgood 2011, 229. Cf. above 16.
[23] Cf. below 176.
[24] Cf. Tac. *Ann.* 12.64. Below 50; Elsner and Masters 1994, 3; Shotter 2008, 47, 65–6; Romm 2014, 65.
[25] Barrett 1996, 6 (quotation). Cf. Tac. *Agr.* 4.3; Warmington 1969, 26–7, 142–3.
[26] Below 160.

after the death of Germanicus,[27] or that of his mother. All this supports
the idea of the development of a relatively positive relationship between
them.[28] Nero appears to have been tractable. While he was being brought
on as heir under Claudius he found himself doing things at which he was
rather good, and liked the attention that this brought; but he exercised no
real power and was probably not hugely interested in government.[29]
Agrippina and the rest of her team can have calculated that this would
continue.[30] Nero had to learn the job, and he had to be toughened up: first
on the streets of Rome,[31] and then on the field of battle. Obedient to his
elders, and with his sporting and artistic interests to divert him, he could
be expected to accept his nominal status as head of state and not resent
others directing the Empire.

But did Agrippina have anything more definite in mind than being just
'senior partner'? She had specific ambitions for Nero; had she any for
herself? Nero's accession represented retribution for the family of Germanicus and Agrippina I: a restoration of the 'dream ticket', succession.[32]
Agrippina, however, appears also to have seen it as a means of creating a
formal position for herself.[33] We can see her ambition at work in the way
she gained and used the titles and distinctions so important in Rome's
'rigorously stratified' society.[34] In 50, in association with his adoption of
Nero and the latter's change of name, Claudius gave Agrippina (no doubt
at her prompting) the honour of being called *Augusta*. This had previously
been granted to Livia after Augustus' death, and to Gaius' paternal
grandmother, Antonia II, on his accession. Agrippina was the first wife
of a living emperor to be so distinguished. Though strictly speaking still a
name, *Augusta* was well on the way to becoming a title.[35] It marked
Agrippina out as the full partner of Claudius *Augustus* and so, using
modern terminology to express its force, 'empress', 'Majesty' for life.[36]
As such, to protect her person, she was given a detachment of praetorians.[37]
In the same year, 50, Oppidum Ubiorum, the town of Agrippina's birth,
was refounded as a Roman colony and renamed in her honour Colonia
Agrippina (in full: *Colonia Claudia Augusta Agrippinensium*: modern

---

[27] Winterling 2007, 34–48.   [28] Below 279, 282.   [29] Above 16; below 283, 286.
[30] Cf. below 81.   [31] Below 134, 297,   [32] Above 14; Ginsburg 2006, 62, 65.
[33] Cf. Waldherr 2005, 65.   [34] Rudich 1993, 143.
[35] It was given to Poppaea on the birth of Claudia in 63 and to the child straight away. Statilia
Messalina received it immediately on her marriage to Nero in 66. Kienast 2004, 99–100; cf.
Waldherr 2005, 227.
[36] Tac. *Ann.* 12.26.1: *cognomen*. Barrett 1996, 108; Malitz 1999, 9; Kienast 2004, 94; Ginsburg 2006,
69–70; Osgood 2011, 216–17; Romm 2014, 42.
[37] Tac. *Ann.* 13.18.4.

Cologne), another signal distinction: 'Never before had a Roman foundation commemorated a woman'.[38] In 51, Agrippina was allowed to ride in a state carriage (*carpentum*) on ceremonial occasions, a privilege normally reserved for priests and holy objects (though one perhaps earlier accorded to Messalina, which Agrippina would have been keen to match).[39] Also in 51, Agrippina's unprecedented status as the near-equal consort of a *princeps* was made manifest in Rome itself, at the ceremony marking the capture of the British leader, Caratacus. Tacitus records that Claudius pardoned him and his family, and

> the prisoners, freed from their chains, paid their homage to Agrippina also – a conspicuous figure on another tribunal not far away – in the same terms of gratitude which they had employed to the *princeps*. It was an innovation, certainly, and one without precedent in ancient custom, that a woman should sit in state before Roman standards: it was an advertisement of her claim to a partnership in the empire which her ancestors had created.[40]

Even if not quite as unprecedented as Tacitus asserts, Agrippina's participation was 'transgressive' behaviour for a Roman woman.[41] Dio states: 'Agrippina often attended the *princeps* in public, when he was transacting public business or when he was giving an audience to ambassadors, though she sat upon a separate tribunal. This too was one of the most remarkable sights of the time'.[42] Though this could be a compressed doublet of the Caratacus ceremony, it rings true because of Tacitus' description of Agrippina's intrusion at the official reception of Armenian ambassadors at the start of Nero's principate, and Dio's further statement that at the start of Nero's principate she then received embassies and 'corresponded with peoples, governors and kings'.[43] Under Claudius she appears to have become accustomed to dealing with provincial and foreign peoples, with a particular interest in Judaean politics.[44] In an age when dress was crucial in advertising rank, in 52 Agrippina appeared at the grand draining of the Fucine Lake wearing a cloth-of-gold *chlamys*. This was more than a matter of fashion or the flaunting of herself as *Augusta*. She accompanied Claudius and Nero, both of whom wore the *paludamentum*, the purple cloak of a

---

[38] Tac. *Ann.* 12.27.1; Drinkwater 1983, 38, 56, 130; Barrett 1996, 114–15; Waldherr 2005, 53–4; Romm 2014, 43–4 (quotation).

[39] Tac. *Ann.* 12.42.3; Cass. Dio 60.33.2[1]; *RIC* I[2] Claudius no. 103. Ginsburg 2006, 28.

[40] Tac. *Ann.* 12.37.5–6 (under the year 50). Barrett 1996, 123–4; Waldherr 2005, 53.

[41] Ginsburg 2006, 26 (quotation), 114; Romm 2014, 42–3.   [42] Cass. Dio 60.33.7.

[43] Tac. *Ann.* 13.5.3; Cass. Dio 61.3.2: *epistolas kai dēmois kai archousi kai basileusin epestellen.* Below 133.

[44] Joseph. *AJ* 20.134–6; Barrett 1996, 124–7.

Roman military commander-in-chief. Britannicus was absent, and Nero was being promoted as the true successor of Germanicus, the vigorous, victorious Julio-Claudian *princeps* to come.[45] To appear or be depicted in military dress was the standard way in which Julio-Claudian males projected their power and legitimacy. Agrippina now did the same. The *chlamys* was much the same garment as the *paludamentum*, so she dressed herself to resemble the *Augustus* and his Caesar and to lay claim to an element of their authority: to create a place for a woman in the male-dominated hierarchy of Roman power.[46] Similar efforts along these lines are discernible in the coinage, in innovations which prepared the way for the remarkable early-Neronian issues discussed below.[47] The advertisement on coins of important individuals and members of their family went back to the late Republic. It was enthusiastically adopted by Augustus and subsequent *principes*, particularly in respect of women.[48] On his accession, Claudius honoured his mother, Antonia II, and his father, Drusus I, on coins produced at Rome.[49] From 51, following his marriage with Agrippina and his adoption of Nero, both mother and son figured in various combinations, she with her title of *Augusta*.[50] However, the process was taken further than before. For example, after 50, while Antonia and Drusus continue to be commemorated we also find the honouring of Germanicus and Agrippina I: their son and daughter-in-law, Claudius' brother and sister-in-law, and Agrippina's father and mother.[51] Again one suspects that the initiative was Agrippina's. More significant is that Agrippina does not just appear alone or in association with Nero. On a coin of the Rome mint her image is paired with that of Claudius, his on the obverse ('heads' side), hers on the reverse ('tails'). 'For the very first time the emperor and his consort appear on the same issue'.[52] An identical association is made on a coin of the imperial mint at Ephesus, accompanied by an even more striking type depicting Claudius and Agrippina together 'jugate' – his bust superimposed on hers – with their names and

---

[45] Plin. *HN* 33, 63; Tac. *Ann.* 12.56.5; Cass. Dio 60.33.3. Barrett 1996. 129–30; cf. below 39, 42.
[46] Ginsburg 2006, 29 and n. 41.
[47] Below 44. In what follows, for the sake of simplicity, I disregard coin metals and denominations and the degree of rarity of types.
[48] Ginsburg 2006, 58–9, 60–1, 64, 70, 74–6, 77, 87–8, 89–90, 92: 71, 99, 102–4.
[49] *RIC* 1^2 p. 116 nos. 65–8, 69–74.
[50] *RIC* 1^2 pp. 116–17 nos. 75, 76–9, 82–3, 103, 107–8. Butcher and Ponting 2014, 189.
[51] *RIC* 1^2 Claudius nos. 104, 109; 102, 105–6.
[52] *RIC* 1^2 pp. 116–17 nos. 80–1. Barrett 1996, 109 (quotation); cf. Ginsburg 2006, 57, 69, 71–2.

Figure 2   Claudius and Agrippina: jugate busts.
Courtesy of the American Numismatic Society

titles (*TI[berius] CLAVD[ius] CAES[ar] AVG[ustus] AGRIPP[ina] AVGV-STA*) on the obverse (Figure 2).[53]

Though such a type was already familiar on coins from local mints in the East, 'the head of an emperor and his wife appearing together on the same face of the coin is a remarkable first for Roman official . . . coinage'.[54] Most eastern mints continued to make frequent use of Agrippina's image, and on coins of Assus she is shown facing Claudius.[55]

Agrippina's projection of herself as a prime political actor is also visible in official statuary of the period. The best known example is a pair of reliefs in a temple and sanctuary complex at Aphrodisias in western Turkey. Known as the Sebasteion, it was dedicated to Aphrodite and the deified *Augusti*. Both reliefs are on panels decorating facing twin porticoes, between which ran the processional path to the temple. One, on the south portico, depicts Claudius, heroically nude as befitting the conqueror of Britain, 'standing clasping the hand of his new wife and crowned by a togate personification of the Roman Senate or People' (Figure 3).

The other, on the north, has Agrippina, associated as in the first with the goddess Demeter, bestowing a crown upon Nero, dressed in the uniform of a general (Figure 4).[56]

The presence of the Senate/People figure on the former points up everything that the Augustan Principate stood for: a 'restored' Republic grateful for the protection of a recently renewed dominant family.[57]

---

[53] *RIC* I² p. 119 no. 119.
[54] Barrett 1996, 109 (quotation); cf. Malitz 1999, 9; Osgood 2011, 216–17.
[55] Barrett 1996, 109; an exception is Pergamum: *RIC* I² p. 120.
[56] Barrett 1996, 109–10, 152–3; Ginsburg 2006, 85–9; Osgood 2011, 219 (quotation), 221, pl. 51, 248, pl. 59. Bergmann 2013, 335–6, 343–4, sees a parallel in a cameo from the Shrine of the Three Magi at Cologne.
[57] Romm 2014, 40–1; cf. above 19.

Figure 3   Aphrodisias: Claudius and Agrippina.
Courtesy of the New York University Excavations at Aphrodisias (M. A. Döğenci)

The latter is usually dated to the beginning of Nero's principate,[58] as an indication of Agrippina's role in the accession. However, though Agrippina did not fall as precipitately as commonly envisaged,[59] the few months of her dominance, between October 54 and February 55, seem hardly sufficient for its commissioning and execution. It is, like the former, better dated somewhat earlier, as part of the political 'spin' of the late Claudian administration, underlining the current power of the woman who was wife to the *princeps* and mother to his designated heir. The association of Agrippina with Demeter allowed her to be depicted wearing the diadem, the headgear of goddesses and kings, the only woman of the Julio-Claudian dynasty to be so represented during her lifetime.[60] An equally powerful message was conveyed by a group of statues, probably contemporary with the Claudian Aphrodisias reliefs, in the Metröon at Olympia (Figure 5). Though interpretation is difficult, it

---

[58] E.g. Cadario 2011, 180. Heil (1997, 97) proposes that it celebrated the Armenian victory celebrations of 58, but concedes that this would allow very little time between its commissioning and the death of Agrippina in 59; cf. below 135 and n. 42.
[59] Below 48.   [60] Ginsburg 2006, 89.

Figure 4   Aphrodisias: Agrippina and Nero.
Courtesy of the New York University Excavations at Aphrodisias (G. Petruccioli)

Figure 5   Olympia: the Metröon grouping. Hypothetical reconstruction
Bol (2013, 181): Octavia, Nero, Claudius, Agrippina II, Livia.
Courtesy of Prof. Dr R. Bol

may consist of Claudius, flanked on the right by Agrippina and Livia and on the left by Nero and Octavia.[61]

It projects the renewed strength of the ruling dynasty after the marriage of Claudius and Agrippina and, particularly, after that of Nero and Octavia. Britannicus is ignored. Nero is again shown in full armour: the dynamic young bridegroom, come late but undisputed heir and guarantor of the future greatness of the dynasty and of Rome.[62] But Agrippina is also in close attendance on both him and his stepfather. Agrippina clearly made a determined effort to advertise her presence and power:[63] she 'put herself about'. Another example of her genius for creating her own public image is her insistence, probably in 53, on accompanying Claudius when he made an appearance at the fighting of a major fire in Rome.[64] Though Dio interprets this negatively, as proof of overweening ambition, modern experience shows how important it is for those in authority to show themselves witnessing and alleviating the distress of ordinary people. A male presence would be appreciated but expected, which explains the attendance of Augustus and Gaius at previous blazes. However, Livia's accompaniment of Augustus and Tiberius had made very strong favourable impressions,[65] and Agrippina must have aimed at the same effect with Claudius. All this did not come to a grinding halt on his death and Nero's accession in October 54. Agrippina continued to carve out a place for herself in the Roman state.

2.4   'Queen Mother'

In principle, women never had a place in the politics of the Roman Republic. This was because they were not allowed to hold *imperium* – the power to command others – and so could not become officers of state. In practice, we can see frequent tension between the nominal powerlessness of all women and the influence exercised by some female aristocrats as relatives, wives and property-owners. The Republic's acquisition of an empire vastly increased the power and wealth of a few aristocratic families, which in turn created a number of 'elite women', both 'good' (e.g. Cornelia, mother of the Gracchi) and 'bad' (e.g. Clodia, sister of Clodius).[66] The change from true Republic to 'restored' Republic brought

---

[61] Ginsburg 2006, 76, 82 and n. 118.   [62] Bol 2013, esp. 180–4; cf. above 17; below 167.
[63] Cf. Waldherr 2005, 52–5.   [64] Cass. Dio 60.33.12.
[65] Malitz 1999, 67; Winterling 2007, 85; cf. below 236.
[66] Milnor 2005, 1, 39, 221–3. I am also very grateful to members of the Sheffield Late Antiquity Reading Group for discussion of this topic.

more opportunities. In theory, very little had altered. Apart from the position of *Augusta*, the only official role that a leading woman could take was that of priestess of a deified emperor.[67] However, with the arrival of autocracy and the development of 'bedroom' politics, wives, mothers, sisters, daughters and mistresses could become agents in their own right by tapping into the power of the *princeps*. They were helped by Augustus' projection of his modest home and happy family as the political, cultural and moral centre of the state. Imperial wives and daughters were represented as traditional helpmeets – pious, obedient, chaste, hard-working and fertile – toiling behind closed doors to support father, husband, and children: an imperial 'first family' incorporating all the values of the brave days of old.[68] When such elite women involved themselves officially in state affairs they did so selflessly, for the general good, dedicating public buildings or helping people to fight fires.[69] Yet the Principate had many paradoxes,[70] and one of these was that palace domesticity encouraged female power. In the Republic, much public life was accommodated in the private sphere of the aristocratic household. This continued under the Principate, and the more so as the Palatine home of the *princeps* became the 'palace' and the heart of a 'court'.[71] The women living on the Palatine found themselves at the centre of politics, with enormous opportunities for the able.[72] They had to tread carefully. An assertive woman was liable to be labelled 'promiscuous', a 'virago'.[73] However, the fact that such accusations were made shows that, underneath, change was afoot. Female status and influence had to be recognised and accommodated. Gaius had honoured his grandmother, Antonia II, and, particularly, his sisters Drusilla, Livilla and Agrippina, giving all three the rights of Vestal Virgins. He also had them included in consular proposals of motions to the Senate, and in oaths of allegiance to him and for his wellbeing. Above all, when he fell seriously ill shortly after his succession, he named his favourite sister, Drusilla, as heir to 'both his property and his power'.[74]

Agrippina is our best example of a 'new woman'. The hostile source tradition deplored the fact that she acquired more privileges than Livia and

---

[67] Ginsburg 2006, 38.
[68] Milnor 2005, 3–4, 10–15, 27, 29–32, 56–7, 84–91; Richlin 2014, 101.
[69] Milnor 2005, 63; Richlin 2014, 84; above 42.   [70] Cf. below 83.
[71] Michel 2015, 11–12, 29–61; below 59.
[72] Milnor 2005, 16, 31–4, 38, 99, 102–6, 139, 149, 183; below 59, 259.
[73] Ginsburg 2006, 106; Richlin 2014, 85, 92.
[74] Suet. *Calig.* 24.1: *bonorum atque imperii*, 15.3; Cass. Dio 59.3.4; Barrett 1996, 52–3; Waldherr 2005, 21–2; Winterling 2007, 56, 62, 80.

Figure 6   Nero and Agrippina: facing busts.
Courtesy of the American Numismatic Society

even then was not satisfied,[75] but this only reflects her success. Highly
intelligent, ambitious, courageous and experienced, Agrippina might well
have thought that she could build on what had happened under Gaius and
what she had encouraged under Claudius, and create a legitimate position
from which she could run the state. This returns us to the earliest
Neronian coin-type, recalling the facing-bust issues of Claudius and
Agrippina.[76] The obverse bears Agrippina's name and titles and facing
busts of Nero and Agrippina; the reverse bears Nero's name and titles
(Figure 6).[77]
     The full legends are:

> Obv. *AGRIPP[ina] AVG[usta] DIVI CLAVD[i coniunx] NERONIS CAES
> [aris] MATER* (Her Majesty Agrippina, consort of the deified Claudius,
> mother of Nero Caesar)

> Rev. *NERONI CLAVD[i] DIVI F[ilio] CAES[ari] AVG[usto] GERM[anico]
> IMP[eratori] TR[ibunicia] P[otestate]* (For Nero Caesar Augustus Germani-
> cus, son of the deified Claudius, imperator, holder of tribunician power)

This coin-type is far more than confirmation of literary accounts of
Agrippina's dominance during the early weeks of the Neronian principate,
before a sudden 'fall'.[78] Its design is extraordinary: 'the first time that a
living imperial woman appeared together with the ruling emperor on the
obverse of a coin' with this emperor never before 'so closely identified with
his mother as opposed to his father'.[79] Agrippina knew how the Principate
worked, and will, well before October 54, have appreciated the threat
posed by Nero's accession, however much she craved this. He, the holder
of supreme *imperium*, would immediately become *princeps* – 'The Boss' –
able to call all the shots. If she was to safeguard her position she must act in

---

[75] Cass. Dio 60.33.12.   [76] Above 39.   [77] *RIC* 1² Nero nos. 1–3.
[78] Cf. Ginsburg 2006, 73; below 53.   [79] Ginsburg 2006, 72, quoting Rose.

advance, making the most of her current authority. It was probably she, therefore, who conceived the facing-bust type, perhaps even before Claudius' death. What did she intend it to convey? Under Claudius it was not unknown for members of the *princeps'* family, male and female, to be named on coins in the nominative case, as if they were responsible for minting them, which they were not.[80] However, in the case of Agrippina and Nero the distinction between Claudius, the *princeps* and coin-issuer, and the relatives he honoured was occasionally made explicit by putting his name in the nominative and theirs in the subordinate dative case, *Agrippinae; Neroni*: 'for Agrippina'; 'for Nero'.[81] Agrippina adopted this convention in the Neronian facing-bust type. Her name and honorifics appear on the obverse in the nominative; Nero's, on its reverse, are in the dative indicating that this was *her* type, minted *for* him, and all the more striking because it appeared after a likely two-year break in the production of new *aurei* and *denarii*.[82] This is Agrippina projecting herself as more than just another high-ranking but powerless female dependant, and even more than as the widow and priestess of Claudius and direct descendant of Germanicus and Augustus legitimising the new ruler.[83] She is, rather, a political actor in her own right, operating independently of Nero's paternal line and, indeed, unlike Claudius on his accession, of any external military support.[84] She leads with her name/title of *Augusta*, still hers despite the death of her husband and still entitling her to a praetorian escort. The following reference to her relationship to the divine Claudius is important, but occluded by its position. What draws the eye most is the third element: 'Mother of Nero Caesar'. Under Claudius, Agrippina had featured on a coin-reverse as *[Mater] Caesaris Augusti* – 'Mother of the Heir'.[85] She also appears as *Mater Augusti* on coin-types from the provincial mint of Caesarea-in-Cappadocia contemporary with the Neronian facing-bust type.[86] Nero issued the phrase *Optima Mater*, 'Best of Mothers', to the praetorians as his first password as *princeps*.[87] In this we may again see the influence of Agrippina. All suggests that while Claudius still lived, Agrippina looked forward to establishing a new position for herself under Nero as *Augusta* and 'Queen Mother'. *Mater Augusti* was a warning to any potential opponent that she could draw directly on the power of her (tractable) son: that she, not Nero, is really in charge. Barrett rightly

---

[80] E.g. *RIC* I² Claudius nos. 66 (Antonia), 103 (Agrippina II).   [81] *RIC* I² p. 125.
[82] Waldherr 2005, 54; Butcher and Ponting 2014, 190; below 356.   [83] *Contra* Ginsburg 2006, 73
[84] Shotter 2008, 55.   [85] *RIC* I² Claudius no. 117.   [86] *RIC* I² p. 148 nos. 607–8, 610–11.
[87] Tac. *Ann.* 13.2.5.

proposes that Agrippina's aims were always to establish Nero as *princeps* and herself as 'a kind of regent'.[88] Augustus had made the *princeps* leader of the state, even though the position was novel, extra-constitutional and gave him no direct supremacy. Agrippina may well have thought that she could do the same with *mater Caesaris*.[89]

She supported theory with practice. Tacitus criticises the way in which Agrippina, having married Claudius, created 'a tight drawn, almost masculine, tyranny',[90] but as a woman she had to act far more forcefully than any man and, in the longer term, needed to create a third sex for herself. This she began under Claudius and continued under Nero. On Nero's accession, the Senate decreed her an escort of two lictors and additional security in the shape of a squad of German lifeguards.[91] The granting of lictors was nominally related to her appointment as priestess of the deified Claudius,[92] but it had greater significance. By giving Agrippina and her sisters Vestal status, Gaius had made them to some degree honorary males.[93] Since Vestals were allowed only one lictor when they left their precinct, Agrippina's two would have further advertised her liberation from the restraints imposed upon her sex and made her look 'as if she were a magistrate', 'a woman who had quasi-official share in the administration of the principate'.[94] She had, indeed, the appearance of a permanent regent. Agrippina and her advisers were no fools. They must have believed that she could succeed. The minting of the joint-bust type, presumably for initial distribution to important praetorians and senators, reflects their belief that there were others in the political community who would tolerate a female at the heart of government (another example of the intellectual vigour of the 'Neronian' age[95]). It is in this context that we may best understand Agrippina's scandalous 'eavesdropping' on senatorial meetings held in a chamber in the Palatine complex, probably in the expanded *Domus Tiberiana* palace.[96] For the Senate to meet here was not unusual. Though increasingly convening in the Curia Julia, it had always been flexible in the choice of its venues and a Palatine location was not unprecedented (though this is the last we hear of). It was also not

---

[88] Barrett 1996, 152.   [89] Cf. above 44.
[90] Tac. *Ann.* 12.7.6: *adductum et quasi virile servitium.*
[91] Tac. *Ann.* 13.2.6, 18.4; cf. 1.14.3. Furneaux 1907, 155; below 61.   [92] Cf. Beard 1980, 17.
[93] Above 43; Beard 1980, 15–18, 25.
[94] Griffin 1984, 39 (quotation); Barrett 1996, 192 (quotation); cf. Romm 2014, 63.
[95] Cf. below 119.   [96] Tac. *Ann.* 13.5.2; cf. below 47, 49, 251.

unusual for interested, male, third parties to attend.[97] Agrippina will always have paid close attention to its business and the more so since, under Claudius, she worked closely with senators. She could not, as a woman, either become a senator herself or observe senatorial meetings, but she might direct senators through correspondence and through allies in the House. Therefore why, under Nero, did she go out of her way to have the Senate meet repeatedly on the Palatine[98] and to listen in on its meetings? Tacitus implies that she did so to intimidate the body, but since senators had only just welcomed the new regime with open arms, and the one measure that Tacitus specifically reports the Senate as having taken under such circumstances, concerning gladiatorial shows, was supposedly contrary to Agrippina's wishes,[99] such an interpretation is implausible. A better explanation is that she was developing her use of the Senate as an instrument of her power while enhancing its status and expressing her respect for its ways. She brought it closer to the centre of government but, by staying decently concealed was 'careful not to offend tradition'.[100] In this we may again see her bending the Principate to accommodate a female leader, while being careful not to break it. The accession had gone well. Nero, as titular head, was now part of her team but in a non-executive capacity. Agrippina was still on top, and intended to stay there for the foreseeable future.[101]

How long did Agrippina maintain her dominance? Tacitus suggests that it ended almost as soon as it had begun. He has her facing criticism of Claudius' principate in Nero's programmatic speech to the Senate;[102] and he follows this with an account of the Senate's exploiting its new-found freedoms by, among other things, annulling a Claudian directive obliging quaestors-designate to pay for gladiatorial games.[103] This Agrippina opposed as 'a subversion of the acts of Claudius', and so 'a serious symbolic assault on her own standing'.[104] Tacitus associates the setback with Agrippina's improper eavesdropping and her outrageous conduct at a reception of Armenian ambassadors, when she attempted to join Nero on his tribunal as joint president.[105] He thus implies that Agrippina's position

---

[97] Talbert 1984, 113–17; Barrett 1996, 150–2.
[98] Barrett (1996, 50) notes Tacitus' repetitive 'used to be called': *vocabantur*.   [99] Cf. below 47.
[100] Barrett 1996, 152 (quotation). Ginsburg (2006, 39) observes that Tacitus stops short of saying that Agrippina interfered directly in senatorial business.
[101] Cf. Elsner and Masters 1994, 3; Barrett 1996, 150; Waldherr 2005, 65.   [102] Above 16.
[103] Above 21.
[104] Tac. *Ann.* 13.5.2: *tamquam acta Claudii subverterentur*; Barrett 1996, 162 (quotation).
[105] Tac. *Ann.* 13.5.3; cf. Cass. Dio 61.3.3–4.

Figure 7   Nero and Agrippina: jugate busts.
Courtesy of RomaNumismatics Ltd. www.RomaNumismatics.com

was resented and reduced before the onset of the Armenian crisis early in
55, his next concern. In short, Agrippina's regency was over before the end
of 54, after lasting for only a few weeks. As coins indicate Agrippina's
dominance, so they appear to reflect her decline. Her image next appears
in a less commanding position on the obverse, jugate, i.e. with Nero's, but
now behind it, with his titles promoted to the obverse and hers relegated to
the reverse (Figure 7):[106]

> Obv. *NERO CLAVD[i] DIVI F[ilius] CAES[ar] AVG[ustus] GERM[anicus]
> IMP[erator] TR[ibunicia] P[otestate]* (Nero Caesar Augustus Germanicus,
> son of the deified Claudius, imperator, holder of tribunician power)

> Rev. *AGRIPP[ina] AVG[usta] DIVI CLAVD[i coniunx] NERONIS CAES
> [aris] MATER* (Her Majesty Agrippina, consort of the deified Claudius,
> mother of Nero Caesar)

She then disappears from the coinage entirely. It is little wonder that the
current *communis opinio* is that soon after Nero's accession a clique led by
Seneca and Burrus marginalised his mother.[107] This does not ring true.
Seneca and Burrus owed their eminence to Agrippina, and had recently
worked closely with her to make Nero *princeps*. They had no obvious
motive to attack her late in 54; and, even if they had been tempted to do so
they will have known that she was more than a match for them. The pair
were not daring and ruthless politicians in the mould of Sejanus or, later
under Nero, Nymphidius Sabinus. We should assume that they remained
basically loyal to Agrippina. (The apparent appearance to the contrary of
Seneca's *Apocolocyntosis* will be considered more closely below.[108]) Considered afresh, the view that Agrippina's power extended into 55 is not

[106] *RIC* 1² Nero nos. 6–7.
[107] E.g. Cass. Dio 61.3.2; Henderson 1905, 56–7; Griffin 1984, 39–40; Rudich 1993, 7, 13; Barrett
1996, 156–7; Holland 2000, 72–3.
[108] Below 104.

contradicted by the jugate type. The relative abundance of the first, facing-bust, coins suggests that these were put into circulation from 54 into 55. Reference to Nero's first consulate on the jugate coins implies that these were prepared for issue from January 55. Though the jugate obverse is a less dramatic indication of Agrippina's commanding position in the state than the facing-bust type, it carries her full titles, in the nominative, and still exalts her as sole *Augusta* (the title was never given to Octavia) and 'Queen Mother'. The reverse type, celebrating Claudius' deification, was a further reminder of her high status. As Barrett says, the coin-type amounted to a huge honour for her.[109] Agrippina's administration may have introduced it to mark a return to normality. Nero, the new *princeps*, was now firmly in position, and could – indeed should – be shown as such. At the same time, however, Agrippina is depicted, literally, as the power behind the throne. The *terminus ante quem* for her loss of authority is 12 February 55, the date of Britannicus' fourteenth birthday, on which he would have come of age and before which he died.[110] I propose that Agrippina's power continued more or less unabated to the end of January, and then suffered a totally unexpected setback.

Tacitus' account of Agrippina's early reverses and errors is best regarded as rhetorical compression, in which events of early 55 are located at the end of 54.[111] It is, for example, difficult to believe that, with so much other business being generated by the change of *princeps*, the Senate could, before the end of 54, have spared time to concern itself with changes in the charges laid on prospective quaestors. What Tacitus puts next, Agrippina's listening in on the Senate and the incident of the Armenian ambassadors, may rather be interpreted as indicating the continuation of her power.[112] In the first three months or so of the new regime – Dio's 'for a long time'[113] – every significant act will have required Agrippina's approval. Such acts included the appointment of Corbulo to deal with the Armenian situation;[114] but they will earlier have comprised Nero's first speeches as *princeps*. These, though carefully crafted by Seneca, must all have been vetted by Agrippina.[115] Tacitus' report of Nero's 'programmatic' speech makes it appear anti-Claudian: a rehearsal of the horrors of the old regime coupled with a promise that these would never happen again.[116] This does not square with Agrippina's current dominance and her capacity for micromanagement.

---

[109] Barrett 1996, 167.   [110] Levick 1990, 55; Kienast 2004, 93.
[111] Cf. below 133, 138; Ginsburg 2006, 36.   [112] Above 46; below 133.
[113] Cass. Dio 61.3.2: *epi polu.*   [114] Below 133.   [115] Cf. Holland 2000, 65.   [116] Above 16.

Criticism by Nero of the Claudian regime would have amounted to
criticism of Agrippina and her team; and pledges of better times for the
Senate are inconsistent with Agrippina's earlier co-operation with it. If
delivered as Tacitus reports, the speech would have enraged her.[117] It is
more likely that Tacitus modified its contents to denigrate Claudius and
expose Nero as a *princeps* who broke his word. Nero, as mouthpiece of the
new administration, probably proposed something different: not change
but continuity, albeit 'enhanced' continuity under a new and better
princeps.[118] Both Gaius and Claudius had made 'Augustan' promises,
which everyone will have known they had not kept. The new administration had to offer something more plausible. Tacitus makes what was
said appear anti-Claudian by having Nero refer to 'recent' causes of
dissatisfaction.[119] These – secret trials, palace intrigue and the power of
favourites – were, however, a feature of the early Claudian court, as they
had been of those of Tiberius and Gaius, and had already been targeted by
Agrippina. Nero therefore probably mentioned them not to make further,
tired promises but to emphasise that recent improvements would be taken
further. In this case, how may we explain that part of Nero's earlier funeral
oration for Claudius, written by Seneca, which by its mention of the
deceased's foresight and sagacity had provoked widespread smirking?[120]
The reaction might have been accidental: the result of natural tension
during a critical time compounded by a rhetorical culture in which audiences were habitually on the alert for daring allusions, intentional or not:
Rudich's *interpretatio prava*; Bartsch's 'doublespeak'.[121] On the other hand,
if we accept that the administration always carefully considered its public
utterances,[122] we need another explanation. It could be that Seneca, soon to
demonstrate a taste for satire in the *Apocolocyntosis*, slipped a small example
of it in the oration;[123] but sly criticism of Claudius would have infuriated
Agrippina, and Seneca was not brave enough to cross her.[124] A more likely
alternative is that the joke was licensed by Agrippina, who wanted to create
a space between the new regime and its predecessor while acknowledging its
dependence upon it.[125] This allows us to appreciate Agrippina's political
abilities. She owed much to the later Claudian principate, which she helped
to shape; and she set great store on Nero's adoption by Claudius, his
marriage to Octavia and his position as 'the son of a god'. On the other

---

[117] *Contra* Barrett 1996, 161.   [118] Cf. above 20.   [119] Tac. *Ann.* 13.4.2: *recens*.
[120] Tac. *Ann.* 13.3.2: *postquam ad providentiam sapientiamque flexit*, nemo *risui temperare*.
[121] Rudich 1993, xxxii–iii; Bartsch 1994, 63–6, 66. Cf. below 87.   [122] Holland 2000, 68.
[123] Below 102.   [124] Below 104.   [125] Cf. Romm 2014, 66–7.

hand, she was aware of the problems caused by Claudius' continuing unpopularity, and was astute enough to take these into consideration in launching the new principate. She therefore commissioned speeches that distanced it from the worst Claudian excesses and put a line under the Claudian administration; and she tolerated some minor 'anti-Claudian' legislation.[126] She demonstrated that she was a pragmatist, not an ideologue: 'a realist' who 'played the political game'.[127] What she did allowed her to retain her political dominance into 55. This was the extended period when Nero 'left to his mother the management of all public and private business', when she 'managed for him all the business of the Empire'.[128]

2.5 The Acte Affair

The only person who could threaten Agrippina's position was Nero, with his inalienable power as *princeps*. He remained dutiful, but he was no fool and no puppet.[129] Although, to the end of his principate, he had no burning desire to take over the running of the Empire and was ready to leave this to others,[130] he needed to feel that he could take charge of his own affairs, which explains his occasional 'break-outs'.[131] An early rumble of thunder came when Agrippina attempted in vain to curb his purported excessive generosity to the freedman Doryphorus.[132] The main storm broke after he had 'slipped into a love affair with a freedwoman by the name of Acte',[133] a tale so human that it rings wholly true. What Nero wanted from the affair was probably initially no more than a close relationship with a woman of more or less his own age of the sort that he had never enjoyed with Octavia. Their marriage was no love-match. It brought them no friendship and no children and may, indeed, never have been consummated.[134] Nero, like any healthy adolescent, wanted 'his own space',[135] but had no thought of quarrelling with his mother, still less of bringing her down. The affair was begun by Nero, aided by two personal friends, Marcus Otho and Claudius Senecio.[136] According to Tacitus, his

---

[126] Above 21; cf. Griffin 1984, 60: that quaestors were relieved only of the obligation to give games: some may have continued to do so anyway.

[127] Cf. Barrett 1996, 161 (quotations), and below 262, on Nero.

[128] Suet. *Ner.* 9: *Matri summam omnium rerum privatarum publicarumque permisit*; cf. Cass. Dio 61.3.2: *panta autōi ta tēi archēi prosēkonta diōikei.* Bradley 1978a, 69; Fini 1994, 117.

[129] Cf. Griffin 1976, 88.　[130] *Contra* Barrett 1996, 156.　[131] Below 164.

[132] Cass. Dio 61.5.4. Barrett 1996, 156–7; below 330, 342.

[133] Tac. *Ann.* 13.12.1: *delapso Nerone in amorem libertae, cui vocabulum Acte fuit.*

[134] Below 189–90; Waldherr 2005, 97; Walde 2013, 15.　[135] Waldherr 2005, 81–2.

[136] Tac. *Ann.* 13.12.1.

male advisers let it run because they thought it would divert Nero from
pursuing respectable women.[137] Agrippina was less happy and soon,
presumably, instructed him to break with Acte. She cannot have done so
out of moral scruple. The sexual morality of the Roman aristocracy was
hardly bourgeois, as Agrippina's own previous liaisons demonstrate.[138] It
was open to Nero, as to any male of his class, to take servile and lower-class
women as his concubines. Such behaviour must, indeed, have been
expected of a youth, even a married youth, to prove his manhood. As with
Nero's street-fighting, 'boys will be boys'.[139] Her concern will have been
that what should have been a brief affair seemed set to become a chronic
infatuation, with Nero treating Acte as his wife.[140] This threatened more
neglect of Octavia, the compromising of the dynastic settlement which had
brought Nero into the ruling family,[141] and even less chance of legitimate
heirs. In the shorter term, however, it also threatened Agrippina's position.
Despite her efforts to create an official position for herself, female power
still depended on intimacy. A mother, especially a 'working mother', could
not expect to have the same influence as a wife or mistress.[142] With
Octavia this was no problem, since she and Nero lived apart. Acte was
very different. and Agrippina reacted badly to her new prominence,
vilifying her as 'her slave-born rival, her daughter-in-law the skivvy'.[143]
This was an overreaction, out of keeping with her usual pragmatism.[144] As
was to happen again in her conflict with Poppaea, with whom she had
more in common,[145] she found it difficult to deal with authentic female
rivals – genuine companions, not mere sex partners – for Nero's affections.[146] Acte, on the other hand, showed herself to be cool-headed,
practical and supremely loyal down to the end of the Neronian principate
and even beyond. She would never have allowed Nero to endanger his
position, which is why, although the matter was discussed, she would
probably never have agreed to a full marriage to him.[147] Agrippina, instead
of letting the affair reach a safe equilibrium, engineered a flaming row
between herself and her son, which drove Nero to threaten to abdicate and
retire to Rhodes.[148] In doing this, Agrippina exposed the basic weakness of
her position: that, for all her attempts to establish herself as *Augusta* and
mater Caesaris, she could not give orders to the *princeps*.

---

[137] Tac. *Ann.* 13.12.2: *ne senioribus quidem principis amicis adversantibus.*
[138] Cf. below 193 and n. 188.   [139] Below 297.   [140] Cf. Tac. *Ann.* 13.13.1.
[141] Cf. Ginsburg 2006, 41.   [142] Cf. Sen. *Clem.* 1.9.3–7, on Livia and Augustus.
[143] Tac. Ann. 13.13.1: *liberta aemula, nurus ancilla.*   [144] Cf. above 51.
[145] Romm 2014, 105–6.   [146] Below 179.   [147] Cf. below 182, 282, 311.
[148] Suet. *Ner.* 34.1. Waldherr 2005, 82.

Nero bore the increasing wrath of his mother 'until' he could take no more and turned to Seneca.[149] This is not surprising, given the closeness of pupil and tutor.[150] 'Until' suggests that Agrippina's criticism of the liaison, like that of Nero's free spending, had begun early in his principate. Nero therefore probably involved Seneca towards the end of January, 55, after which events moved very quickly. The affair was not part of a great scheme by Seneca and Burrus to topple Agrippina, initiated soon after Nero's accession.[151] The prospect of either taking over her position as regent – they had neither the will nor the competence – or of entrusting imperial administration entirely to Nero – he was too young and inexperienced – would have terrified them. They were drawn in only after Nero's appeal to Seneca forced them to choose between himself and his mother. However, in what followed the key person was surely Burrus. Although Seneca had shown an early taste for sailing close to the political wind, he had suffered significantly for this under Claudius and was by now no political martyr. Rudich notes his general 'idiosyncratic dissidence which oscillated between confrontation, compromise and compliance'. Seneca's real self is, indeed, impossible to establish because of his constant inconsistency in attitude and behaviour. His philosophical writings are impossible to square with what he did as a courtier: co-operating with autocracy even as he deplored it; habitually choosing self-preservation over principle; and failing every major test of nerve.[152] As in the case of his recent composition of the *Apocolocyntosis*, he would not have dared sole personal confrontation with Agrippina.[153] With Pallas a dyed-in-the-wool supporter of Agrippina,[154] he must immediately have consulted Burrus. Burrus is usually thought of as junior in the partnership which they now formed and which ran to 62.[155] In this instance, he may be considered senior because, as praetorian prefect, he was the only member of Agrippina's management team able directly to enforce an order given from above, whether by Agrippina ('block Nero's access to Acte!') or Nero ('secure it!'). To borrow a phrase of Tacitus, his power was based on its own strength.[156] Despite being a client of Agrippina,[157] and later an outspoken champion of Octavia,[158]

[149] Tac. *Ann.* 13.13.2: *donec.*   [150] Below 105, 282.

[151] Above 49. Cf. Ginsburg 2006, 37, 40; *contra*, e.g. Henderson 1905, 62; Rudich 1993, 7–8; Holland 2000, 72–3.

[152] Rudich 1993, 14 (quotation), 108; Romm 2014, esp. 113, 151, 180, with: xiii–xv, 14, 16–17, 17–18, 20, 22–3, 26–8, 33–6, 54, 64, 76–7, 91, 92, 105, 116, 127–8, 149–50, 152–3, 157–8, 160, 187; below 157.

[153] Below 104.   [154] Tac. *Ann.* 13.2.3–4.   [155] Rudich 1993, 15–16.

[156] Tac. *Ann.* 13.19.1: *potentia . . . sua vi nixa.*   [157] Tac. *Ann.* 13.20.1: *Agrippinae gratia provectus.*

[158] Cass. Dio 62.13.1–2.

Burrus was renowned for his *virtus*, 'moral excellence'.[159] He would have felt bound by his oath of allegiance to Nero, and could not have ignored a direct plea from the *princeps*, even against Agrippina. Though neither Seneca nor Burrus had deliberately contrived a break with Agrippina, once it had begun they may have found certain of its aspects agreeable. Despite their support of Agrippina's efforts at constitutional change, male cultural prejudice must have made them uncomfortable with petticoat government.[160] More practically, to work for a powerful Queen was much easier than to work for a Queen Mother, which involved an awkward juggling of two chiefs.[161] There was also the problem of the Claudian legacy. Though this could be manipulated to their benefit,[162] they may well have been disturbed by the continuing depth of hatred and the extent to which Agrippina, unfairly, remained associated with its excesses. The longer they remained loyal to her, the more they would be tainted with its crimes.[163] However, they could not have relished the prospect of change, for once they had decided to go with Nero, they had to back him all the way.[164] It was probably then that Seneca persuaded a compliant relative, Annaeus Serenus, to disguise the affair by claiming that gifts lavished on Acte by Nero were from himself.[165] It was probably at this stage, too, that they helped concoct a royal pedigree for Acte and to investigate how Nero might establish a more respectable liaison with her.[166] On the other hand, as Seneca and Burrus had no thought of trying to topple Agrippina towards the end of 54, so they had no plans to remove her in early 55, even after their commitment to Nero. All three had worked together too long to allow this; and their views on the political future remained very similar.[167] Furthermore, Agrippina was simply too strong to be immediately ejected from the political game.[168] Seneca and Burrus probably hoped for a reconciliation, but she loathed their betrayal, which prevented any relaxation of tension.[169] Thus Agrippina's dominance and the unity of the ruling team were irrevocably broken. She soon bowed to the inevitable. Probably in early February 55, she apologised to Nero for her intemperate conduct, offering the couple the use of her own quarters, and promised him her personal fortune (a measure of the grandeur in which she lived and

---

[159] Tac. *Ann.* 14.51. Cf. Rudich 1993, 15.   [160] Cf. Romm 2014, 75–6.
[161] Cf. Barrett 1996, 159–60; Waldherr 2005, 65.   [162] Above 50.   [163] Cf. below 194.
[164] Cf. Romm 2014, 79.
[165] Tac. *Ann.* 13.13.1. So *contra* Barrett 1996, 167–8: that this was much earlier.
[166] Above 52; below 311; Barrett 1996, 101, 112–13.   [167] Cf. Barrett 1996, 159.
[168] Below 174.   [169] Tac. *Ann.* 13.14.6. Malitz 1999, 25; cf. Shotter 2008, 62.

the continuing acrimony between mother and son about his spending habits).[170] But this was too late. A clear sign of Agrippina's losing the initiative was the immediate dismissal of Pallas from his post as *a rationibus* ('minister of finance'),[171] more likely the result of the political machinations of Seneca and Burrus than of any vindictiveness by Nero.[172]

2.6 Legacy

Agrippina's experiment in regency was over, but it had an important legacy, fundamental to my interpretation of Nero. It established the precedent of a team, not, apart from some odd 'break-outs',[173] the *princeps* running the Neronian Empire.[174]

---

[170] Tac. *Ann.* 13.3.2–3 (on *cubiculum* cf. below 77). Above 51.
[171] Tac. *Ann.* 13.14.1. Cf. Table 1 and below 193, 326.   [172] Below 186.   [173] Below 164.
[174] Cf. below 58.

CHAPTER 3

The Establishment Team

3.1 Introduction

The extent to which Nero was personally responsible for what was done in his name, both good and bad, is not a new issue. It appears very early in the source tradition in the assertion, variously expressed – as, for example, in the *quinquennium Neronis* – that Nero did not immediately take charge of the Empire but was guided first by Agrippina and then by Seneca and Burrus.[1] The *communis opinio* has long been against this interpretation, advocating that from the start Nero was his own master. Henderson, for example, sees him not 'as the mere puppet mouthpiece of his ministers, but as the Prince who hearkened indeed gladly to their advice, but had projects and determination and discreet insights of his own'.[2] Griffin similarly argues that Nero, 'a pupil, not a puppet' of his mentors, took 'an active interest in government on his accession'.[3] I, too, dispute a 'docile then dominant' Nero, but for a different reason. I propose that Nero's contribution was always minimal: that from 54 to 68 he remained mainly on the sidelines of the Roman political game.[4] I base my conclusion chiefly on the tension between the many significant achievements of the Neronian principate and Nero's increasing investment of his time and energy in artistic and athletic activities.[5] Soon wearying of the job of *princeps*, he turned his attention to fields in which he believed he could excel.[6] Fortunately for him, by 54 the institution of the Principate had developed to such an extent that it could carry a *princeps* as a passenger, as perhaps it had already shown in the case of Claudius, at least after his marriage to Agrippina.[7] The idea of a disengaged Nero delegating the running of the Empire to others is also not new. Grant, for example, argues that Nero,

---

[1] Above 27; cf. Hohl 1918, 359; Warmington 1969, 44; Barrett 1996, 150.
[2] Henderson 1905, 76.   [3] Griffin 1976, 88; Griffin 1984, 45; cf. Wiedemann 1996a, 246.
[4] Cf. above 12.   [5] Cf. above 30; below 303.   [6] Below 286; cf. Fini 1994, 21.
[7] Cf. Henderson 1905, 14–15; Waldherr 2005, 134; Osgood 2011, 17, 22–3, 27; below 64.

though at the start of his principate very much in charge of affairs, threw himself ever more into artistic activities. When he reached the point of becoming a 'stage professional', he 'must have devoted less and less attention to the problems of empire'.[8] More recently, as we have seen, Elsner and Masters project the possibility of Nero as 'a pawn in other people's political games'.[9] Hurley likewise asks if less personal and less moralising sources might have included 'the depiction of palace intrigue focusing on the contending groups that tried to maintain the upper hand while controlling a young and ultimately detached *princeps* more interested in his own performance as a citharode than he was in the governance or even the politics of Rome'.[10]

My chief inspiration here, however, has been Champlin's portrayal of Nero as an obsessive: a man who, tiring of being *princeps*, put his own interests before those of the state and turned his life into a drama in which he was the sole star.[11] He pursued theatre and sport as a showman: the patron and creator of grand spectacles such as public banquets, the execution of Christians, the reception of Tiridates and the Greek 'triumph'. But he was also a participant, in particular as a citharode or charioteer.[12] Nero took both sets of activities very seriously. It was in his nature to commit himself wholly to any enterprise he undertook. He could not be a spectator, or even an amateur: he had to contribute, at a professional level.[13] Becoming a credible professional musician will have taken up huge amounts of time: to compose the pieces to which he would sing and dance; to hone his stage skills, especially in playing the *cithara*; and to build himself up physically to perform them well in public.[14] His sporting activities will likewise have required strenuous training and practice. Nero's hard work paid off. In music he became more accomplished than the average aristocratic amateur and set high standards for the 'false' Neros who came after him.[15] In sport he was capable of driving a ten-horse chariot team.[16] Nero became obsessive but 'he was not crazy'. No mental disorder caused him to lose touch with reality; he just chose to distance himself from it.[17] The distancing process began around 58.[18] It accelerated in 66–67,[19] and is particularly visible

---

[8] Grant 1970, 15 (quotation), 56, 73–8, 127.   [9] Elsner and Masters 1994, 3; above 12.
[10] Hurley 2013, 42.   [11] Cf. Champlin 2003, 79, 234; below 287.
[12] E.g. Champlin 2003, 65–75, 210, 228–9, 233.
[13] Cf. Henderson 1905, 127: Nero 'must needs be a performer in any pursuit he loved'.
[14] Cf. above 56; below 303; Pausch 2013, 70.
[15] Tac. *Hist.* 2.8. Malitz 1999, 44; Reitz 2006, 21–2   [16] Below 293.
[17] Champlin 2003, 81, 236 (quotation); below 284.   [18] Below 144.   [19] Below 288–9.

just before his fall in 68. The extreme 'role-playing' and 'grand fantasy' that Champlin detects in Nero's later behaviour are not signs of a break with reality but reflect the extent to which he brought his private interests into public life. The roles he played were those of committed artist and sportsman; the fantasy that he entertained was that he was competing like any other entrant.[20] This caused him to neglect his duties as *princeps*, but not to lose touch with life in general. Nero never confused what was going on in the theatre with reality or, when outside the theatre, never distanced himself from reality by making the whole of his life into some sort of perpetual play. He put on grand shows and undertook ambitious personal performances, but never lost himself entirely in them.[21] He had to rely on real-life skills in handling a racing-chariot; he used art to exorcise his personal anguish, but he could still step out of character; and he continued to indulge in court banter.[22] He was not unaware of reality, but chose to ignore aspects of it which he found distasteful. Life for him became a perpetual party.[23]

His neglect of the Empire was bound to damage his historical reputation.[24] In addition, by throwing himself into stage roles that strengthened malicious rumours he helped create the image of himself as a 'monster'.[25] But this was for the future. In the present, serious crises, far and near, often caused reality to intrude uncomfortably into Nero's everyday interests.[26] However, the Neronian principate managed to withstand most shocks. It proved, indeed, to be generally very successful.[27] How may this be explained? If Nero was not in charge, who actually ran the Roman Empire and was responsible for its successes and failures? Implicit in this question is the assumption that, *contra* Millar's model of 'the emperor at work', the central imperial administration did not simply react to events. Like Osgood I believe that a certain degree of initiative was taken by the centre to secure its own survival.[28] If we do not ascribe this success to Nero or any single deputy, we have to identify a group of people – a 'team'. Its chief members are likely to have been few in number. Their achievements suggest that they were capable of flexible thinking and benefited from constructive discussion.

---

[20] Champlin 2003, 55.   [21] *Contra* Champlin 2003, 100; below 88.   [22] Below 118, 290, 291.
[23] Cf. Champlin 177.   [24] Cf. Cass. Dio 63.12.2.   [25] Below 291.
[26] Champlin 2003, 177.   [27] Above 30; below 392; cf. Champlin 2003, 1–3.
[28] Osgood 2011, 25–27; cf. 126–45.

3.2 The Team

The notion of a team should not surprise. Crook complains of the writing of imperial history as imperial biography – 'Tiberius built this road' or 'Vespasian imposed this tax' – and agrees with Dio that imperial rule was a task no *princeps* could undertake single-handed.[29] There is no need to assume that by the mid-first century everything of importance was decided by the *princeps*. 'As long as [the advisers] acted in the name of the *princeps*, and not contrary to his expressed wishes, the system could proceed without friction or disruption'.[30] Early in Gaius' principate the running of the Empire was in the hands of his praetorian prefect and former father-in-law. Later, even when Gaius began to exercise full control, he had to turn to his sisters and brother-in-law for assistance.[31] With regard to Nero, my approach is different from Crook's treatment of advisers, which is primarily synchronic and aimed at demonstrating the continuity that such people brought to the administration, from *princeps* to *princeps* and between dynasties of *principes*.[32] Though this is valuable it ignores particular issues of the day and takes us away 'from the study of the Principate as a political system to study of administrative systems and hierarchies'.[33] I offer a diachronic examination of the wider team behind a single *princeps*, at first treating it as no more than consultative, and then moving to consider how it took over the running of the Empire.[34]

3.2.1 The Court

Who composed this team? I propose, very broadly, the most important members of Nero's 'court', by now, as the *aula Caesaris*, becoming an authentic contemporary term.[35] From the time of Augustus the *aula* had developed within the *domus Caesaris*, 'the 'imperial household', evolving from the standard aristocratic household of the Late Republic.[36] At its beginning, with senior ex-slaves in charge of each major aspect of its

---

[29] Cass. Dio 52.14–40. Crook 1955, 115, 128; cf. Cizek 1982, 182; Michel 2015, 233.

[30] Waldherr 2005, 64: 'Solange sie im Namen des Kaisers und ohne dessen eindeutigen Widerspruch erfolgten, führte dies zu keinerlei systemsprengenden Reibung oder Brüchen'.

[31] Winterling 2007, 59–63, 70.   [32] E.g. Crook 1955, 29, 33–6, 44.

[33] Wallace-Hadrill 1996, 285.   [34] Cf. Michel 2015, 195.

[35] Sen. *Dial.* 2.33.2; Tac. *Hist.* 1.13, 2.94. Winterling 2009, 2–3, 79–103; Mordine 2013, 104. What follows refers frequently to the same people and groupings as Cizek 1982, 173–256, but from a different perspective, with a very different conclusion: *contra*, in particular, 213: 'seul Néron décide'.

[36] Cf. Wallace-Hadrill 1996, 283 and n. 1, and generally 283–308.

activities – food and lodging, wardrobe, accounts, correspondence etc.[37] – this household will have appeared very similar to those of other great aristocratic families. As late as 64, one of the accusations against D. Silanus was that his domestic establishment bore too great a resemblance to that of the *princeps*.[38] However, the importance of the *domus Caesaris* was necessarily much greater. It grew stronger than any of its rivals, and proved a major support to Claudius.[39] Its benefits were both practical and symbolic. Its 'departments' provided the basic components needed to run an administration independent of the Republic; and it created a new, private, space for interaction between people of power away from the Senate and the Forum.[40] The role of the ideal *paterfamilias* of this ideal 'first household' strengthened each *princeps*' claim to direct the Empire.[41] Like the 'restored' Republic, it was an Augustan expediency that proved 'indispensable'.[42]

3.2.2   Intimates

The most important members of Nero's court were those who enjoyed easiest access to him:[43] his mother, his wife or mistress and their senior ladies-in-waiting, and his wider family and personal friends: *familiares, intimi, proximi amicorum*.[44] 'Personal friends' included a relatively wide range of people: intimates who shared his tastes, some (such as Otho, Senecio and Annaeus Serenus) of about the same age and others (such as Piso) older; members of his literary circle, in particular Petronius and Lucan; and trusted mentors, such as Seneca.[45]

3.2.3   Military Prefects

Other close court figures were the equestrian prefects commanding the praetorian cohorts, by now twelve in number, which acted as the *princeps*' main lifeguard.[46] There were usually two prefects, perhaps to dilute their power; perhaps because in the Praetorian Guard's early years it lacked a

---

[37] Cf. Wallace-Hadrill 1996, 298.
[38] Tac. *Ann.* 15.35.3. Below 197; cf. Wallace-Hadrill (1996, 295) on the *princeps*' court as the centre of a 'solar system' of other, lesser, aristocratic, courts; Michel 2015, 130–1.
[39] Crook 1996b, esp. 135–6; Osgood 2011, 23, 39.
[40] Crook 1996b, 136; Mordine 2013, 101–4, 107–8.
[41] Crook 1996b, esp. 135–6; Osgood 2011, 23, 39.   [42] Mordine 2013, 116.
[43] Cf. Calp. *Ecl.* 4.152–9 and below 269.   [44] Winterling 2009, 91.
[45] Cf. Levi 1949, 115–16; Osgood 2011, 194–5; Mordine 2013, 104–5.
[46] Keppie 1996, 393; Bingham 2013, 16, 52–3.

single barracks, making its men harder to oversee; or perhaps because it was felt that there should be a guards-commander on duty day and night.[47] The praetorians proper were not parade soldiers but fighting troops officered by men of ability, many of whom had served in the *vigiles* and the *cohortes urbanae*, and some even in the legions.[48] When, in 69, Otho took them into battle for the first time since Tiberius, they did well.[49] Their prefects, on the other hand, were not usually military men but senior Establishment figures promoted through court patronage.[50] The praetorians were not the only guards. Also part of the innermost circle were the commanders of the 'German' guard. This was a regiment of mounted infantry, 500–1,000 strong. Another inheritance from the days of Augustus, it was raised not from 'free' Germans but from subjects of the Empire, the Batavi of the lower Rhine, and so resembled the many 'auxiliary' regiments of the main army. However, it was not part of the army structure; and being armed but not armoured, it had a paramilitary appearance. Like the praetorian prefects, its commanders were probably two in number and non-military outsiders. They had the rank of *decurio*, the equivalent of praetorian tribune. Under Nero, one of these was his great favourite, the ex-gladiator, Spiculus.[51] Finally in this category, though usually overlooked,[52] were those in charge of the *Augustiani*. This organisation, recruited from handsome young equestrians as a claque for the *Iuvenalia* of 59, expanded to become an additional bodyguard of around 5,000 men, under equestrian officers.[53] One reason for its creation may have been to avoid using praetorians as Nero's cheerleaders after Burrus was 'very unhappy' with the experiment.[54] If so, it is likely that it was the *Augustiani* who were the 'squaddies' found attending Nero's performance at Naples in 64.[55] Likewise, it could have been *Augustiani* who were 'the soldiers stationed among the stands' who both orchestrated applause and terrorised those who could not keep up with it, and 'the units on duty' who encouraged Nero to let the audience hear his 'celestial voice' at the second Neronian Games of 65.[56] The *Augustiani* took a prominent

[47] Cf. Tac. *Ann.* 4.2.1–3. Waldherr 2005, 103; Shotter 2008, 52; Bingham 2013, 20.
[48] Bingham 2013, 60–1; below 62, 241. [49] Bingham 2013, 35.
[50] Cizek 1982, 103; Keppie 1996, 384; Bingham 2013, 19, 28.
[51] Bradley 1978a, 275; Bellen 1981, 34–57 (esp. 44–6), 100–104; Bingham 2013, 16–17.
[52] An exception is Cizek 1982, 186.
[53] Below 302; Bartsch 1994, 8 and n. 15; Waldherr 2005, 123. [54] Tac. *Ann.* 14.15.7: *maerens.*
[55] Tac. *Ann.* 15.33.3: *militum manipuli.*
[56] Tac. *Ann.* 16.5.1; *milites … qui per cuneos stabant*; Suet. *Ner.* 21.1: *[statio] militum, quae tunc excubabat.* Bradley 1978a, 132; Bingham 2013, 102–5. Grant (1970, 212), like Tacitus, distinguishes between the claque and the guardsmen who punished the crowd. However, when

role in Nero's grand return from Greece in late 67, shouting that they were the 'the soldiers of his triumph'.[57] It is likely that they, too, were under two non-military equestrian commanders who owed their position to patronage. We are ignorant of the names of any of these, but given the short duration of the unit this is hardly surprising. Senior officers of the *Augustiani* must, however, have been significant figures at court. Tacitus complains that from the start some equestrian *Augustiani* were 'insolent', some by nature but others out of 'dreams of power'.[58] This suggests that others close to the *princeps* may have come to resent them as rivals, a possible cause of political instability.[59] There were two other substantial paramilitary forces stationed in Rome: a gendarmerie of four *cohortes urbanae*, under a senatorial *praefectus urbi*, and a watch/fire service of seven cohorts of freedmen *vigiles*, under an equestrian *praefectus vigilum*. Both units had strong links with the praetorians as a result of praetorians being seconded to them as centurions. Their commanders must be counted close to the *princeps* either *ex officio* or, as in the case of the *praefectus vigilum* Annaeus Serenus, through both office and friendship.[60] Given the political importance of the Misenum fleet under Nero, a further senior semi-military court figure may have been its commanding equestrian prefect.[61] A final important prefectural courtier was the *praefectus annonae*, in charge of feeding Rome. Though he did not hold a military or semi-military appointment, since his duties were to do with maintaining peace within the City he must have been close to the others and, as in the case of Faenius Rufus, might be promoted praetorian prefect.[62]

3.2.4 Liberti

Equally close to Nero, though debarred from formal recognition as his *amici* by their origin, were the senior *liberti Augusti*, 'household freedmen'. Our accounts of his principate open and close with the activities of Helius;[63] and they are shot through with references to equally influential freedmen – e.g. Doryphorus, Epaphroditus, Polyclitus – and to lesser, but still significant figures – e.g. Anicetus, Acratus, Phoebus (see Table 1 for

Tacitus was writing, the *Augustiani* were long gone, which might have led to confusion; and Tacitus had his own reasons for stressing praetorian involvement: Bartsch 1994, 9.
[57] Suet. *Ner.* 25.1: *militesque se triumphi eius clamitantes.*
[58] Tac. *Ann.* 14.15.8: *procax, in spem potentiae.*   [59] Below 208.
[60] Canter 1932, 288; Griffin 1984, 72–3; Barrett 1996, 120; Waldherr 2005, 210–11; Bingham 2013, 16, 105–7, 110; Michel 2015, 148–50; above 54.
[61] Cf. Romm 2014, 108; below 186, 199, 219, 392.   [62] Michel 2015, 149; below 178.
[63] Tac. *Ann.* 13.1.3; Cass. Dio 63.12.1–3.

Table 1 *Leading* liberti

1. The 'big three' posts (known holders):	
a rationibus (in charge of finance)	Pallas
	Phaon
ab epistulis (in charge of correspondence)	[Narcissus]
	Beryllus
a libellis (in charge of petitions)	Callistus
	Doryphorus
	Epaphroditus
2. Other powerful figures	Acratus
(some probably holding the posts of *ab epistulis Latinis* [in charge of	Anicetus
Latin correspondence], *a cognitionibus* [trials], *a studiis* [patronage],	Atimetus
a memoria [records] etc.)	Crescens
	Graptus
	Halotus
	Helius
	Icelus
	Narcissus
	Paris
	Patrobius
	Pelago
	Petinus
	Phoebus
	Polyclitus
	Ponticus
	Romanus
3. Court cronies	Acte
	Agialus
	Celer
	Pythagoras
	Severus
	Sporus
	Thalamus
	Vatinius

other names and offices). At his death, Nero was attended only by *liberti*: his *a rationibus*, Phaon, his *a libellis*, Epaphroditus, and Sporus/'Poppaea'. These, as his 'chief ministers' and his 'empress', constituted a skeleton administration: he died a *princeps*.[64] There is debate as to the extent to

[64] Below 413.

which the high standing of senior Claudian and Neronian *liberti Augusti* reflects the emergence of a distinct branch of administration: an imperial 'civil service'. Historians currently view the phrase as excessively modern in its connotations, preferring 'household administration'.[65] Yet the fact that the Principate survived the succession of a number of very different Julio-Claudian *principes*, and soon the disappearance of the dynasty itself, indicates that it had become an entity in its own right.[66] The processes whereby power was transferred from Claudius to Nero and from Nero to Galba demonstrate that much of its endurance derived from the co-operation of senior *liberti*.[67] Freedmen were already very powerful under Gaius.[68] Though recent research on Claudius has been keen to reinstate him as an active agent in affairs,[69] it has proved unable fully to dispel the impression of senior freedmen forming a permanent imperial secretariat, 'an increasingly stratified and bureaucratic corps'.[70] The dominance of Agrippina in the later part of Claudius' principate, supported by leading figures in the court circle, including high *liberti*, may have helped to consolidate the position of the last. Very much thanks to *liberti*, the mid-first century appears to have seen the creation of a basic machinery of central imperial government, which Nero inherited in October 54 and which in June 68 continued to function independently of a *princeps*.[71]

Beyond their normal duties *liberti* could be given important special commissions, in the performance of which, as instruments of the *princeps*, they outranked their social superiors. Perhaps the best known of these is Polyclitus' post-Boudican commission of enquiry into the state of Britain; another is Pelago, the freedman eunuch who supervised the execution of Rubellius Plautus.[72] Such responsibilities greatly increased their influence but affronted ancient authors, who mention them only in passing, imprecisely, and usually very critically. A prime example of our patchy knowledge of *liberti* is 'Claudius of Smyrna', who entered imperial service under Tiberius and rose high under Gaius and Claudius. Though not, as is sometimes asserted, appointed *a rationibus* after Pallas (the post probably went to Phaon; see Table 1),[73] by 55, he must have been a senior figure in

---

[65] E.g. Wallace-Hadrill 1996, 297–8; Osgood 2011, 39.
[66] Cf. Malitz 1999, 15; Waldherr 2005, 63–4.   [67] Cf. Barrett 1996, 75–6; below 409.
[68] Winterling 2007, 115–16.
[69] E.g. Barrett 1996, 72, 110; Shotter 2008, 24; Osgood 2011, 198; Gibson 2013, 122–3.
[70] Wallace-Hadrill 1996, 297–8; Mordine 2013, 104 (quotation); Osgood 2011, 257. Cf. Waldherr 2005, 65, 134; Osgood 2011, 40, 204; Hurley 2011.
[71] Cf. Winterling 2009, 116–17; Osgood 2011, 250. Below 407.
[72] Tac. *Ann.* 14.39.1, 59.3. Below 138; cf. Henderson 1905, 217.   [73] Weaver 1972, 289.

the financial administration, though probably stationed away from Rome. He survived Nero and his immediate successors to be promoted *a rationibus* under the Flavians. His career would be lost to history were it not for a poem by Statius, written to console Claudius' son on his father's death at almost ninety; and even then his name remains uncertain.[74] There will have been many other *liberti* working at every level in the *domus Caesaris* and in the provinces: a galaxy – Statius' *ordo*[75] – of imperial office-holders about most of whom we know nothing.[76] This is a classic example of the sources' prioritising the activities of the *princeps* and a few of his circle while ignoring those of other important agents. 'The quiet operation of a vast financial machine was not news like the death of a blue-blood senator'.[77] On the other hand, we should not exaggerate aristocratic prejudice. There must have been many equestrians and senators prepared to work with *liberti*. If not, there would have been neither 'court' nor Principate. They included such figures as Agrippina II and Seneca and earlier, under Claudius, that 'courtiers' courtier', Vitellius I.[78] Though the Neronian administration, conscious of the bad name *liberti* acquired for their influence over Claudius, may have tried to keep them from the public gaze,[79] what they did was essential for good government. We should not, like our sources, despise their influence; but we should not expect too much of senior *liberti* themselves in terms of honesty, neutrality or efficiency. They were probably no better and no worse than the seventeenth and eighteenth century servants of the English crown, such as Samuel Pepys.

3.2.5   *The Outer Circle*

Family, close friends, senior security staff and senior *liberti* were distinguished by their privilege of easy access to the *princeps*. At one remove, in an outer circle with more restricted though still significant rights of approach, were senior senators of the 'restored' Republic. These were, for example, allowed to offer the *princeps* their formal greeting (*salutatio*) at his levée (*admissio*); were, as formal *amici*, unlike the *liberti*, invited by him to banquets; and were expected to entertain him in their turn.[80] The right of the senatorial elite to socialise with the *princeps* as nominal equals according to the conventions of the Republic both sugared the bitterness

---

[74] Stat. *Silv.* 3.3. Weaver 1972, 284–91.   [75] Stat. *Silv.* 3.3.63.
[76] Cf. Weaver 1972, 197–281.   [77] Grant 1970, 54.   [78] Osgood 2011, 88, 154.
[79] Cf. Griffin 1976, 107–8.
[80] For the principle see Suet. *Vesp.* 2.3; Plut. *Galb.* 12.2. Millar 1977, 112, 209–10; Talbert 1984, 68; Wallace-Hadrill 1996, 291–2.

of the rise of lower-class newcomers and served to remind the *princeps* that constitutionally he was neither king nor autocrat.[81] Like the *liberti*, most secondary *amici* are difficult to identify because of the scant attention given to them by our sources. However, we know of some, of whom not all were personally close to the *princeps*.

Under the Republic, aristocratic clients of one great patron could show hostility to his rivals. Under the Principate, however, all had to be 'friends' of the supreme patron, the *princeps*.[82] As a result, some individuals found in the outer circle of *amici* owed their position more to their competence than to intimacy with him. Thus men like Thrasea Paetus and Vespasian may be regarded as Nero's counsellors but not his cronies.[83] Vespasian was a soldier, and because of the sources' interest in warfare we know rather more about the senators who commanded major frontier armies. These will be considered in closer detail below;[84] for the moment it suffices to say that they were substantively different from their fellows because they exercised considerable real power which they used both to defend and expand the Empire and to maintain the Principate and its current head. But this power could be turned against the centre; most recently in 39, by Gaeticulus, commander of the military zone of Upper Germany, against Gaius; and in 42, by Scribonianus, governor of Dalmatia, against Claudius.[85] Though both were soon suppressed, they demonstrated that provincial army commanders could pose a problem.[86] However, so far the Empire had been spared a viable full-blown military coup. Tacitus' 'secret of empire' – that generals had the power to challenge and replace an incumbent *princeps* away from Rome[87] – was as yet undiscovered or, better expressed, known but not yet acted upon.[88] Such reluctance may have resulted from painful memories of the civil wars of the Republic.[89] For the moment, the Praetorians remained the sole military force to be reckoned with.[90]

---

[81] Wallace-Hadrill 1996, 289–90, 299. Cf. below 305.   [82] Winterling 2007, 27–8.

[83] Crook 1955, 24, 27 and n. 6 (Tac. *Ann.* 15.23.5; Suet. *Vesp.* 4.4). Cf. Millar 1977, 111; Wallace-Hadrill 1996, 283–4; below 97.

[84] Below 174.

[85] Barrett 1989, 101–6; Levick 1990, 59–60; Barrett 1996, 61–2, 87; Winterling 2007, 102–4; Osgood 2011, 32, 44; Gibson 2013 128.

[86] Cf. Shotter 2008, 13.   [87] Tac. *Hist.* 1.4: *imperii arcanum*.   [88] Chilver 1979, 48.

[89] Below 111, 162, 269.   [90] Cf. Osgood 2011, 34.

3.3 *Consilium*

None of this was institutionalised.[91] Nero might consult all members of the inner and outer circles, freeborn and freedmen, male and female, formally and casually, in public and in private, singly or in groups, irrespective of status. In a tradition that extended to the later Roman Empire, he may well have sought the views of his barber, Thalamus, or even his shoemaker, and must surely have confided in his personal physician, Andromachus, all of whom were members of the court.[92] Tacitus appears both to confirm and deplore such practice in describing his praetorian prefect and his second wife as comprising 'the *princeps'* privy council in his ferocious moods'.[93] However, the context is one of high tension following the unmasking of major conspiracy, when the thought of being murdered by supposed intimates was enough to put anyone in a bad mood. Tacitus' words suggest that in normal circumstances discussion and resolution of serious state business involved a wider range of *amici*, met more formally in the *Consilium principis*, 'Imperial privy council'.

3.3.1 *Structure and Operation*

Like so many key features of the administration of the Early Empire, the *Consilium principis* owed its existence to Augustus' adaptation of Republican precedents. It was an expanded version of the councils of relatives, friends and acquaintances which the great men of the Republic, original and 'restored', were expected to turn to for advice on the running of their private and public affairs.[94] It was part of Rome's 'immemorial tradition that men in positions of responsibility should not take decisions alone', even if they had the power to do so.[95] This helps explain Galba's creation of a Spanish 'senate' immediately upon his revolt in 68.[96] However, details of its membership, organisation and activities are difficult to establish. This is principally because it was never recognised as an organ of state, and so is treated very summarily by our sources. Its obscurity is compounded by the fact that, as already touched upon, the phrase *amicus principis* – 'friend of

---

[91] Cf. Winterling 2009, 92–3; Michel 2015, 117–18.

[92] Mart. 8.52.2–3; Arr. *Epict. diss.* 1.19.17–23; Amm. Marc. 22.4.9–10. Cf. Mordine 2013, 106, 108–9; Michel 2015, 118, 162–4; below 123.

[93] Tac. *Ann.* 16.61.4: *saevienti principi intimum consiliorum.*

[94] Cf. Tac. *Ann.* 16.25.1: on how Thrasea Paetus consulted his *amici* as to the best course of action following his accusation in 66. Crook 1955, 104–5; cf. Millar 1977, 118–22; Michel 2015, 243.

[95] Crook 1955, 4.   [96] Below 394.

the *princeps'* – was not used solely to distinguish its members but was also given as an honorary title to other important figures in the Empire.[97] Even its name is unknown: *Consilium principis* is a modern labelling.[98] By the time of Nero, the *Consilium* was nominally made up of leading senators who met under the chairmanship of the *princeps* to advise him on matters of state. These also attended him on certain important public occasions, such as the reception of foreign envoys and major trials.[99] However, membership was flexible. Although it was probably not until the early second century that senior *equites* were fully accepted as regular members, it is clear that they attended much earlier. Praetorian prefects were accepted from the time of Tiberius; and under Claudius an experienced procurement official joined the *princeps' potissimi amici* in discussing how to deal with Messalina. It is unthinkable that Nero did not consult Claudius Senecio who, with Otho, helped him in the Acte affair of 55 and remained prominent until the Pisonian conspiracy. The same pragmatism must have permitted the attendance of senior *liberti Augusti.* It would have made little sense if, for example, Polyclitus was not allowed to brief the *Consilium* on the state of Britain after Boudica or if the current *a rationibus*, who was effectively responsible for the totality of state finances, was not on hand to comment on the financial implications of particular decisions.[100] Prefects and *liberti* could not, however, be formally acknowledged as *amici* and so did not as such wait on the *princeps* in public on such occasions as the reception of important foreign envoys. These expected to be greeted by 'old' Rome, i.e. by representatives (including the *princeps*) of the Senate: that 'head of Empire and glory of all the provinces'. We see this exemplified on a grand scale on the coronation of Tiridates.[101] Prefects and *liberti*, though able to play prominent parts in certain judicial processes, for example at Burrus' examination of Agrippina in 55,[102] were also debarred from participation in the trials of senators. Finally, invitations to attend the *Consilium* were apparently extended to them individually as a privilege, not a right *ex officio.*[103]

One remarkable aspect of the loose texture of the *Consilium* is that it might include females. The earliest evidence of this mentions the presence

[97] Crook 1955, 23–6; cf. Millar 1977, 116.   [98] Crook 1955, 104–6; Winterling 2009, 81.
[99] Crook 1955, 32–3, 116; cf. above 378.
[100] Tac. *Ann.* 13.12.1, 15.50.1, 15.70.2. Crook 1955, 36, 42, 61; Millar 1977, 120. *Contra* Wallace-Hadrill 1996, 30; Ginsburg 2006, 18. Cf. Alpers 1995, 143, 147–50; above 60, 64.
[101] Tac. *Hist.* 1.84: *caput imperii et decora omnium provinciarum.* Talbert 1996, 336–7; Winterling 2009, 9–10; below 377.
[102] Tac. *Ann.* 13.21.2; cf. below 74, 177.   [103] Cf. Crook 1955, 62, 65.

of *matronae* (respectable married women) at a *Consilium* held by Claud-ius.[104] That Agrippina was an accepted member of Claudius' *Consilium* is confirmed by her unusually prominent position at his reception of Caratacus, tartly remarked upon by Tacitus. Dio, likewise, makes much of her public attendance on Claudius even when he was receiving foreign envoys.[105] Because the *Consilium* had no place in the constitution of the 'restored' Republic, it should not, strictly speaking, be called a 'privy council'.[106] The senior senators who made up most of its number could never have countenanced the existence of such a body. Their instinctive deference was to the Senate, and they felt that their 'real' jobs were elsewhere in Rome and the Empire in service to the Republic. To acknow-ledge 'privy councillor' as their chief distinction would be to deny the nominal pre-eminence of the Senate.[107] Just as bad, it would have sug-gested that they, like the imperial *liberti*, were professional administrators, not gentlemen amateurs who took on such work out of duty not reward.[108] The term privy council is, however, too useful to abandon.

A further aspect of the *Consilium*'s loose weave was that, unlike the Augustan Senate,[109] there was no formal selection or deselection of its members, no prescribed sessions, no fixed venue or venues, and no specific responsibilities.[110] This did not make its business chaotic or indecisive. Habit must have encouraged order with regard to all of its business; and order was essential for its judicial activities.[111] Though specific procedures for its non-judicial business are elusive, stray references in texts hint at how people believed it was usually conducted.[112] Thus a *princeps* could always convene a *Consilium*, but never arbitrarily. Except in an emergency, members should be given reasonable notice and required to meet at a convenient time of day. A *Consilium* should always be more than 'a caucus, a conclave of those in power'.[113] *Amici* were consulted for their compe-tence and to show that the *princeps* had the full support of all respectable society.[114] They should, therefore, be of different backgrounds and opin-ions, including indeed men who, though dependable, had no great per-sonal liking for the *princeps*. Under Nero these included not only, as we

---

[104] Crook 1955, 43; Millar 1977, 120.   [105] Tac. *Ann.* 12.37.5; Dio 12.37.5. Cf. above 37.
[106] Crook 1955, 62–3.   [107] Cf. Talbert 1996, 321.   [108] Crook 1955, 29–30.
[109] Talbert 1996, 328.   [110] Crook 1955, 26, 107.   [111] Crook 1955, 109–14.
[112] Tac. *Ann.* 14.62.6, 16.61.4; Juv. 4; Suet. *Ner.* 41.2; Cass. Dio 63.26.4. Cf. Crook 1955, 50–1; Michel 2015, 244–5; above 67.
[113] Crook 1955, 113.
[114] Michel 2015, 245–6: 'L'empereur serait plus ou moins obligé d'inviter à son conseil les sénateurs et les chevaliers les plus importants pour ne pas les froisser et s'assurer de leur loyauté, mais aussi pour souligner leur soutien à la politique qu'il mène'.

have seen, Thrasea Paetus and probably Vespasian, but Cassius Longinus, recklessly proud of his descent from one of the killers of Julius Caesar.[115] One suspects that the fact that the *Consilium* was never recognised as an organ of state encouraged candour. If it had been formally constituted, its meetings would have been subject to strict rules of deference, preventing frank discussion.[116] Normal advisory sessions of the *Consilium* will have been in private, usually where the *princeps* was currently resident. In Rome this will have been mainly inside the mixed private, public and religious complex that was the Palatine/Golden House.[117] Its other activities – the reception of foreign envoys and delegations and petitioners from within the Empire, and the holding of trials – normally took place in public.[118] In the case of the first, senatorial members appear to have had no speaking role.[119] With regard to the second, however, senators, praetorian prefects and even *liberti* played an active part.[120]

3.3.2   Legal Business

This takes us to consideration of a charge implicit throughout the main source tradition: that the Neronian administration came to despise the law. The *princeps* was directly involved in the making and execution of laws. This derived from Republican practice whereby any magistrate, attended by *amici* of his *Consilium*, had the right to undertake judicial business. Under the 'restored' Republic, the *princeps* was a perpetual magistrate by virtue of his permanent tribunician and proconsular, and occasional consular, power. His legal work involved the formulation of laws and the holding of trials (*cognitiones*: 'enquiries').[121] His presiding over *cognitiones*, however complex and tedious these might be, was regarded as a prime duty, demanded of him as a matter of course by the public.[122] People in fact preferred the jurisdiction of the court of the *princeps* and his *Consilium* to that of magistrates of the 'restored' Republic, and were enabled increasingly to resort to it by the huge ambiguities in the Roman legal system.[123]

---

[115] Longinus: Tac. *Ann.* 16.7.3; Crook 1955, no. 81; Griffin 1984, 194–5. Crook 1955, 113 (quotation).
[116] Cf. below 116.   [117] Wallace-Hadrill 1996, 286–7; above 46; below 251.
[118] Millar 1977, 119.   [119] Millar 1977, 236.   [120] *Liberti*: below 364.
[121] Millar 1977, 236; Talbert 1996, 333–4; Galsterer 1996, 406, 408.
[122] Crook 1955, 63–4, 83–4; Millar 1977, 119, 240.
[123] Crook 1955, 57; Galsterer 1996, 398, 405–6, 407–8. Cf. above 18, and the failed attempt under Nero to ensure that various cases from Italy and the senatorial provinces went, as they should, to the courts of magistrates, not that of the *princeps*: Tac. *Ann.* 13.4.3, 14.28.2; Suet. *Ner.* 17. Bradley 1978a, 109–10.

The displacement of old Republican by new autocratic instruments was inevitable.[124] *Prima facie* contrary to the trend, the Senate, which had never functioned as a regular court under the Republic, was conceded such a role by Augustus, hearing cases that were held to affect the wellbeing of the state.[125] The characteristic fuzziness of the Roman legal system is again reflected in the fact that senatorial trials appear to have been poorly regulated. In 66, Thrasea Paetus had to write to ask Nero to specify the charges against him.[126] However, since the Senate acted as court relatively infrequently this mattered little, and the existence of the senatorial court did not relieve the growing pressure of legal business on the *princeps* and his advisers.[127] Before Nero was distracted by other interests, he took his general judicial duties very seriously. This is an even better indication of his resolve to act the good *princeps* than his intervention in fiscal matters.[128] Here, his insistence on considering the opinions of his advisers in writing and in private before delivering a judgement will, though expensive in court time, have further encouraged frankness.[129] Crucial to our understanding of the character of the Neronian regime is whether it eventually ignored the established system and took extra-legal and violent action against its enemies, real and perceived.

Secret intracubicular ('bedroom') trials had sullied the name of Claudius and were specifically rejected by Nero at the commencement of his principate.[130] Did he finally resort to these himself? The evidence, though poor, suggests that, albeit often imperfectly, most proceedings were modelled on due process, 'primitive though it may have been', beginning with formal accusation by *delatores*, 'informers'.[131] This is clearest in the first phase of prosecutions following the uncovering of the Pisonian conspiracy, early in 65.[132] Tacitus, though depicting what happened as a reign of terror, with mass arrests and summary justice, says enough to allow us to reconstruct a different set of events. He allows that the accused were brought to the Servilian Gardens 'to plead their cause' before Nero, Tigellinus and Faenius Rufus.[133] His report that one of them delayed in exposing Rufus as a fellow-conspirator also indicates that some were

---

[124] Bowman 1996a, 347, 350; cf. Talbert 1984, 432–3, on the general historical laxness of the Roman constitutional system.
[125] Talbert 1984, 461–4; Rutledge 2001, 17, 21, 28.
[126] Tac. *Ann.* 16.24.1; Talbert 1984, 481, 483–4. Cf. below 216.
[127] Cf. Crook 1955, 31 (Augustus), 43 (Claudius), 48 (Nero).
[128] Suet. *Ner.* 15.1. Bradley 1978a, 93–6; Fini 1994, 43–4; below 351.   [129] Waldherr 2005, 177.
[130] Above 17.   [131] Rutledge 2001, 17, 152–3, 156, 178 (quotation); below 319.
[132] Below 197.   [133] Tac. *Ann.* 15.58.3: *ad dicendam causam.*

brought back for further questioning, i.e. that cases were not dealt with at breakneck speed, with fear and prejudice substituting for evidence and proof. As Rudich says, 'after their leader's suicide the actual conspirators, as well as other suspects ... were given a formal trial and allowed to speak in their defense ... Even Seneca's case was considered *in absentia* ...'[134] Tacitus' later comment, that it was precisely because of the lack of a case, or even a charge, against the consul, Vestinus, that Nero was forced to stop pretending to be a judge and resort to direct action, using 'despotic force', without a trial,[135] therefore deserves particular attention. Tacitus says that Nero resorted to force because he already wished to destroy Vestinus. He had hoped that someone would name him as a conspirator, but since there was no accuser he just sent in the praetorians. Nero purportedly wanted to remove Vestinus first because Vestinus had abused their earlier close friendship by frequent and harshly apposite criticism. More recently, he had angered Nero by marrying the *princeps'* mistress, Statilia Messalina.[136] The first motive is implausible given Nero's usual lack of vindictiveness, the second given his devotion to his current wife, Poppaea.[137] The move against Vestinus is better explained in political terms. Vestinus was a demanding powerhouse of a man. Tacitus notes his 'energetic spirit', together with his extreme Republican utterances and his ambition.[138] Indeed, the Pisonian conspirators excluded him from their plans because they found his 'headstrong and uncooperative nature' made him impossible to work with.[139] At the back of the conspirators' minds was probably precedent. Though the model for their planned murder of Nero was apparently the assassination of Julius Caesar, their model for what was to follow was the assassination of Gaius, adapted to incorporate successful elements of Nero's accession to ensure that their candidate, no other, was put up for approval by the praetorians.[140] The events of 41 would, however, have alerted them to a possible alternative: that after an assassination power might revert to the consuls, and in April 65 the two ordinary consuls were A. Licinius Nerva Silianus and Vestinus.[141] It is therefore likely that the conspirators blackballed the latter in order to impede any intervention by him.[142] As the conspiracy was uncovered, the same thought may well have occurred to the administration: Vestinus was still in a position to strike. His consulship shows that his quarrel with Nero had

---

[134] Tac. *Ann.* 15.66.2. Rudich 1993, 121–2.   [135] Tac. *Ann.* 15.69.1: *vis dominationis*.
[136] Tac. *Ann.* 15.68.4–5. Cf. below 116.   [137] Below 283, 310.
[138] Tac. *Ann.* 15.52.4: *acre ingenium.* Furnaux 1907, 387; cf. below 90.
[139] Tac. *Ann.* 15.68.3: *praeceps et insociabilis.*   [140] Rudich 1993, 88; Waldherr 2005, 190.
[141] Tac. *Ann.* 15.48.1. Liebenam 1909.   [142] Cf. below 210.

not wrecked his social or political career.[143] He lived in a house that overlooked the Forum; maintained a band of young slaves that might be interpreted as some sort of private army; and on the day of the disclosure of the conspiracy was holding a formal dinner party.[144] Such high-profile public activity at the tensest of times might well arouse legitimate suspicion and prompt pre-emptive action. The orders given to the tribune sent to arrest Vestinus were 'to forestall the attempts of the consul, seize what might be termed his citadel, and suppress his chosen corps of youths'.[145] This had echoes of, *inter alia*, the *senatus consulta* that allowed Cicero to eliminate the Catilinarian conspirators and gave Gaius supreme power; of Nero's declaration to the Senate concerning the cases of Sulla and Plautus that he was 'watching with extreme care over the safety of the commonwealth'; and of the sixth provision of the *lex de imperio Vespasiani*.[146] As a senior magistrate of the Republic, Nero had full authority to act as he thought fit to secure the safety of the state, but invocation of this responsibility will have required some sort of due process, even if not full trial.[147] Vestinus might have successfully defended himself before the *princeps*, but he chose to commit suicide.[148] Vestinus may have entertained treasonable thoughts, but if so he had not yet acted on them, and he perished because of the *princeps'* sudden sense of betrayal by many whom, like Lucan and Petronius, he had previously considered his intimates.[149] However, the violence against him, like that against all others involved in the Pisonian conspiracy, was enacted within a judicial framework.

A further indication of proper practice is that proceedings of the cases held before Nero were fully recorded. This is implicit in Tacitus' conviction that his readers would trust him when he claimed to quote Subrius Flavus' 'very words';[150] and it is explicit in his report that Nero collated a complete dossier of the evidence against those condemned and their admissions of guilt, and laid it before the Senate.[151] Proper process in the first round of Pisonian prosecutions allowed certain accused to come close to acquittal because of initial lack of evidence, and others to have the

---

[143] *Contra* Rudich 1993, 121; cf. below 97.　　[144] Tac. *Ann.* 15. 69.1–2: *convivium.*

[145] Tac. *Ann.* 15.69.1: *praevenire conatus consulis, occupare velut arcem eius, opprimere delectam iuventutem.*

[146] Gaius: Suet. *Calig.* 14; *ius arbitriumque omnium rerum*; Nero: Tac. *Ann.* 14.59.5: *sibi incolumitatem rei publicae magna cura haberi*; Vespasian: McCrumm and Woodhead 1961, 1. 17–21. Cf. below 83.

[147] Cf. Fini 1994, 193–4: 'Auch die Einzelheiten der Hinrichtung des Konsuls bestätigen, daß hierfür ein Gerichtsurteil vorgelegen haben muß'.

[148] Tac. *Ann.* 15.69.3.　　[149] Cf. below 201.　　[150] Tac. *Ann.* 15.67.4: *ipsa … verba.*

[151] Tac. *Ann.* 15.73.1: *conlata in libros indicia confessionesque damnatorum.*

case against them dismissed or to be pardoned. There was no great witch-hunt, no reign of terror.[152] Nero in fact intervened to save Seneca's wife, Paulina; and Lucan's mother, Acilia, was left unharmed (Table 2).[153] 'On balance, Nero seems to have handled the crisis reasonably well. The executions he ordered ... were the verdicts of formally conducted trials and appear to have been necessitated by the demands of his own safety; the more numerous sentences of exile were relatively mild, and a number of suspects were evidently given an amnesty. Compared, for instance, with the frenzy of persecution under Tiberius after the fall of Sejanus ... such moderation could even have been seen as clemency'.[154]

If one allows the operation of the machinery of justice in the *princeps'* court in the events of 65, one must expect to detect it at other, less threatening, times. In 55, Agrippina faced charges of treason but was not dealt with clandestinely, being given a fair trial before Burrus (presumably sitting as Nero's deputy) with Seneca and a number of freedmen observers in attendance. This allowed her to defend herself with success.[155] In 62, Octavia faced two formal trials for adultery. In the first, presided over by Tigellinus, successor to Burrus and again, presumably, acting as Nero's deputy, she was denounced by the flute-player, Eucaerus. His charge was supposed to be corroborated by evidence taken under torture from her slave maidservants, but it was significantly compromised by their loyalty.[156] In the second, the accuser was a much more powerful figure, Anicetus, the killer of Agrippina, 'in the presence of friends convened by the *princeps* to play the part of (*velut*: literally, 'as if') his *Consilium*'.[157] 'As if' makes this *Consilium* a judicial sham, but one suspects partisan reporting. Given the seriousness of the accusation, there is no reason to doubt that Octavia was tried by a legitimate court of law.[158] Against this background, the end of Plautus and Sulla, in 62, may not have been as lawless as Tacitus makes out. He recounts how, at the instigation of Tigellinus, Nero simply had them killed. He then has Nero reporting them as enemies of state to the Senate, without informing it of their fate, and the Senate grotesquely expelling them though they were already dead.[159] Tacitus also says that the secret of Plautus' intended murder

---

[152] Cf. below 218.   [153] Tac. *Ann.* 15.64,1; 71.12. 215.   [154] Rudich 1993, 128.
[155] Tac. *Ann.* 13.20.5, 21.2–8. Cf. below 117.   [156] Tac. *Ann.* 14.60.3–4.
[157] Tac. *Ann.* 14.62.6.
[158] Cf. Furneaux 1907, 311: either by Nero's *consilium* or, possibly, by a traditional family council, like the one convened to try Aulus Plautius' wife for adopting 'alien superstition' in 57 (Tac. *Ann.* 13.32.4). Cf. Sen. *Clem.* 1.15.3.
[159] Tac. *Ann.* 14.57–9, esp. 58.5. Below 191.

was less well kept than that of Sulla's, allowing a warning to be sent to him.[160] The reporting of execution after the event to the Senate as conspiracy confounded is not new: this is how the regime handled the death of Agrippina.[161] What is odd here, however, is the long time-gap. The suspicion arises that the pair were tried and found guilty of treason by the *princeps'* court in their absence, after which measures were taken to carry out their sentences and to inform the Senate of what had happened, in a process much more regular than Tacitus narrates.[162] The judicial side of the second wave of post-Pisonian accusations and trials, in 65–6, is more difficult to follow because of lack of information.[163] Tacitus, indeed, now expresses distaste at detailing the fate of the slain.[164] Following the sudden death of Poppaea and a likely subsequent change in Nero's character,[165] this was a tense and dangerous period, in which even Tigellinus found himself accused by a freedman of a possible acquaintance of Petronius.[166] Generally, however, we may assume the continued operation of the *princeps'* court, as in the accusations against Publius Gallus, Publius Anteius and Ostorius Scapula II, Annaeus Mela and Petronius.[167] That Tigellinus actually prevented Petronius from defending himself here suggests that he feared that he may have been able to prove his innocence. Petronius' response was to commit suicide in a grand fashion. Anteius, Scapula and Mela also committed suicide, but in their case the motivating force was the characteristic aristocratic unwillingness to defend oneself in court, which confuses the issue in deciding whether they were offered fair trials.[168] Others were luckier. The senators Vulcacius Tullinus and Cornelius Marcellus and the *eques* Calpurnius Fabatus, implicated as accomplices in charges against L. Silanus and Cassius Longinus, actually benefited from delays in the operation of the legal system. They appealed their cases to the *princeps'* court and saw them dismissed under pressure of more important business.[169] Tacitus' account of the post-mortem senatorial trial of Antistius Vetus and his family, in which he disparages Nero's offer of clemency concerning the manner of their deaths, resembles his treatment of the deaths of Sulla and Plautus.[170] What is remarkable at this time is the significant involvement of the Senate in high-profile trials. In 65, L. Silanus and Cassius Longinus were accused of plotting rebellion in a deposition to the

---

[160] Tac. *Ann.* 14.58.1.   [161] Tac. *Ann.* 14.58.1.
[162] Cf. Fini 1994, 148–9; *contra* Rudich 1993, 70.   [163] Cf. below 215.   [164] Tac. *Ann.* 16.16.
[165] Below 288–9.   [166] Tac. *Ann.* 16.20.2. Rudich 1993, 157–8.
[167] Tac. *Ann.* 16.12.1, 14–15, 17.4–6, 18.5–19.5. *Contra* Rudich 1993, 146.
[168] Cf. below 320; Rudich 1993, 143.   [169] Tac. *Ann.* 16.8–9. Rudich 1993, 139.
[170] Tac. *Ann.* 16.11.6. Above 74.

Senate. This then tried them, found them guilty and sentenced both to exile.[171] Likewise in 65, Antistius Vetus, father-in-law of Rubellius Plautus, was facing trial before the Senate for being a public enemy when he committed suicide, together with his mother-in-law and daughter.[172] The two most famous senatorial trials, presided over by the consuls are those of Thrasea Paetus and Barea Soranus, along with family and friends, in 66.[173] They were accused by senators loyal to the regime, and they were tried and found guilty by senators sitting as judges. Theirs were not show trials, 'the culmination of the Neronian terror',[174] forced on the Senate by a vengeful tyrant. Nero was very much in the background.[175]

One may conclude that throughout Nero's principate those accused of treason were dealt with in the *princeps'* court or by the Senate in accordance with established legal process. Regular process does not, of course, necessarily mean dispassionate and fair trial. The *princeps'* court could, especially in the heat of political crisis, treat people badly, as in the case of Plautius Lateranus. He was sentenced and executed without being given time to bid farewell to his family or 'the usual moment's respite in which to choose his death' (i.e. presumably to opt for domestic suicide).[176] However, there was always the appearance of due process, and so acknowledgement of the existence of proper standards of behaviour:[177] the law was never despised.

Two further points should be made here. The first is that Tacitus was helped to present the *Consilium*'s crisis-*cognitiones* as instruments of tyranny because most senatorial accused would have preferred to be heard before consuls and Senate, not *princeps* and *amici*, and because if they had to go before *princeps* and *Consilium* they would have preferred to do so in public.[178] Intracubicular justice, repudiated by him on his accession, put Nero back in the company of Claudius.[179] Yet there is justification for trials *in camera*. Putting senators before senatorial judges or trying any class of defendant in the presence of an overexcited populace might dangerously increase tension.[180] Furthermore, it is debatable as to when prudently 'secluded' becomes tyrannically 'isolated'. The Romans never rigorously segregated public and private space.[181] Whether a particular venue was scandalous must sometimes have been a matter of opinion. One might,

[171] Tac. *Ann.* 16.7.1–9.1. (Silanus did not go into exile, but was held in Italy and killed there by a centurion in obscure circumstances: Tac. *Ann.* 16.9.2–5.)
[172] Tac. *Ann.* 16.10–11. Above 75; below 85, 346.   [173] Below 216–17.
[174] Rudich 1993, 158.   [175] Tac. *Ann.* 16.21.3–22.1. Rutledge 2001, 116, 116–19.
[176] Tac. *Ann.* 15.60.1: *non illud breve mortis arbitrium*.   [177] Below 215.
[178] Cf. Crook 1955, 106.   [179] Above 71.   [180] Henderson 1905 96; Galsterer 1996, 409.
[181] Below 259.

indeed, question Claudius' culpability. One of his most notorious 'bed-room' trials, in fact the only one that we securely know of, was that of Valerius Asiaticus in 47, supposedly at the instigation of Messalina. Tacitus describes Asiaticus being 'heard inside a bedroom', with Messalina looking malevolently on. This was no kangaroo court but a meeting of Claudius and his *Consilium* in judicial mode, during which Asiaticus almost won his case.[182] 'Bedroom trial' is a very loaded phrase, redolent of the secrecy of the boudoir, but we should not necessarily understand *cubiculum* as denoting a wholly private chamber. Like Cicero, many a *princeps* may have used his *cubiculum* as an office;[183] and '*cubiculum*-as-office' may have led to the extension of the term to any room or set of rooms within the Palatine that was usually private but sometimes a venue for state meetings.

The second point is that *principes* did not stand above the law. The emergence of the Principate increased complexity and ambiguity in the making and execution of Roman law. During the first and into the early second century, this necessitated continual interaction between residual Republican institutions and authorities and *principes*.[184] Nonetheless, it was always the last whose decision was accepted as final. This derived from the statutory right given to a *princeps* on his accession to exercise the power of last resort in the state.[185] However, none of this put the *princeps* above the law. Though he controlled the law, he was, 'trusting to his wisdom and benevolence', expected to observe it, exercising his exemptions only for the good of the state.[186] This reflects Roman perception of the law as the bedrock of the Empire. In the early first century, a prefect of Egypt was criticised for refusing provincials easy access to the law and, after they had access to it, for not respecting its decisions. Even in the very different conditions of the early third century, Septimius Severus and Caracalla could announce that, though they were exempt from the law, they would live by it.[187] Nero, as part of this tradition, never acted, or tried to act, as a matter of course, above the law.[188] The Neronian administration respected the law, and sought not to ride roughshod over its regular functioning. Suetonius reports that Nero, bent on murdering Britannicus, sneered at a hesitant accomplice, 'So I'm supposed to be frightened of the *lex Iulia*?'[189]

---

[182] Tac. *Ann.* 11.2.1–3.1: *intra cubiculum auditur*. Griffin 1984, 53; cf. Bingham 2013, 96.
[183] Cic. *Scaur.* 26.   [184] Crook 1955, 57–8.   [185] Below 83.
[186] Crook 1955, 145: 'the ruler was not, in principle, "above the law"'; cf. Brunt 1977, 113–16 (quotation); Crook 1996a, 84, 121–2; Winterling 2009, 133.
[187] Bryen 2012, 789, 804.   [188] *Contra* Cizek 1982, 73.
[189] Suet. *Ner.* 33.2: *sane … legem Iuliam timeo*. On the precise *lex* see Barrett *et al.* 2016, 47 and n. 12.

Whether Nero killed Britannicus is debatable, and these words occur in a highly tendentious section of Suetonius' 'Life'.[190] If Nero ever uttered them, it is more likely that he did so in a different context in the unbuttoned atmosphere of his court, and that, like many other of his throwaway remarks, they were subsequently maliciously misquoted.[191] More important here, however, is that this particular urban myth indicates the popular conviction that the *princeps* should, indeed, be subject to all laws, that Nero was well aware of this, and that, by implication, for most of the time even he respected the obligation.[192] Tacitus reports that in 59, Nero, on receipt of news of the failure of the first attempt on Agrippina's life, panicked in case she arraigned him for this before the Senate and People.[193] Though the truth of the incident is suspect, it suggests that Tacitus expected Nero to recognise that Senate and People were still the sovereign powers in the Roman state, to which even he had to answer.

Finally, Thrasea Paetus was able to assert the independence of the senatorial court, describing it as being 'under no compulsion' in the making of its decisions when sentencing Antistius Sosianus, found guilty of *maiestas*, in 62.[194] It was its routine compliance with the law that made the regime's irregular legal actions so shocking to contemporaries.[195]

3.3.3   *Inclusivity*

Central to my interpretation of the working of the Neronian court is that, as Nero marginalised himself in pursuit of his own interests, most state business was handled by his counsellors.[196]

Indeed, according to Crook, Nero's principate is of great significance in the history of the *Consilium* because he was more dependent upon it than any of his predecessors.[197] Crook proposes that it was the setting for many of the major debates and decisions mentioned in the sources, in particular:[198]

(a)   the handling of the Armenian crisis, including the initial appointment of Corbulo as commander-in-chief, from 54 to 63

(b)   the power struggle between Agrippina and Seneca and Burrus for control of Nero in 54–5

---

[190]   Below 176, 321; Bradley 1978a, 194; cf. 198.   [191]   Below 118; cf. 296.
[192]   Cf. Crook 1955, 145 and n. 144: '[The remark] illustrates the consciousness of the law in the very moment of flouting it'.
[193]   Tac. *Ann.* 14.7.2. Below 180.   [194]   Tac. *Ann.* 14.48.5: *nulla necessitate obstricto.* Cf. above 28.
[195]   Cf. below 322.   [196]   Below 81.   [197]   Crook 1955, 45.
[198]   Crook 1955, 45–7, 116; cf. Cizek 1982, 215.

(c)   the question of Nero's relationship with Acte in 55
(d)   the indictment of Pallas and Burrus in 55
(e)   the controversy over the privileges of freedmen in 56
(f)   the proposed abolition of indirect taxes in 58
(g)   the decision as to whether to abandon Britain following Boudica's
       rebellion in 60–61
(h)   the 'confession' of Anicetus in 62
(i)   the handling of Vindex's revolt in 68.

The gap between 62 and 68 is striking and perhaps significant for the
notion of the 'disengaged' Nero. I return to it below.[199] Crook puts the
high-ranking 'political' members of the *Consilium*, in particular Seneca and
Burrus, over the 'literary' *amici*, 'who need not detain us'.[200] To some
degree this is justifiable. Roman polite society moved in various discrete
but interlinked circles (domestic, social, economic, political, intellectual
etc.) that centred on a few powerful patrons.[201] As we have seen, there
were occasions when only the most distinguished could be acknowledged
as counsellors.[202] However, the informality of the *Consilium* will have
allowed the participation of a wider range of people, either regularly and
directly, as in the case of the senior *liberti*, or irregularly and indirectly, as
I suggest for particular financial advisers.[203] The literary set will have been
important in helping the regime to project Nero as the worthy heir of
Aeneas of Troy.[204] We must be prepared to accept a relatively high degree
of inclusivity in the working membership of the *Consilium*. None of the
main groups discussed so far – family, friends, security staff, *liberti*, senior
statesmen, generals – was sharply defined, mutually exclusive or highly
restricted as to its activities.[205] There were remarkably few insurmountable
social barriers. Caecina Tuscus, the prefect of Egypt exiled by Nero for
purportedly misusing imperial property, was the son of the *princeps'* wet
nurse;[206] and one of Nero's great favourites, to whom he allowed a huge
degree of licence, was Vatinius, a freedman sprung from a cobbler's shop in
Benevento.[207] Contact with the *princeps* brought senior *liberti* level with

---

[199] Below 393.   [200] Crook 1955, 47.
[201] Henderson 1905, 233–4; cf. Cizek 1982, 219–46, noting *circula* as a contemporary term, though
        overoptimistic as to the extent to which these can be identified and their membership determined,
        and exaggerating the number, cohesion and political ambitions of those of the Neronian period;
        Maes 2013, 324–5; Michel 2015, 155–8. Cf. below 101, 115, 119, 122.
[202] Above 68.   [203] Below 363.
[204] Below 111, 268. Cf. Wallace-Hadrill 1996, 294–5; Buckley 2013b, 133–4.
[205] Cf. Wallace-Hadrill 1996, 301–2.   [206] Suet. *Ner.* 35.5. Bradley 1978a, 215–16; cf. below 221.
[207] Tac. *Ann.* 15.34.3, *Hist.* 1.37; Cass. Dio 63.15.1. Below 117; cf. Fini 1994, 104.

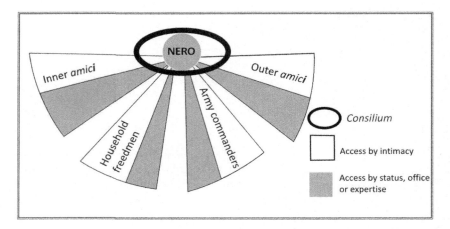

Figure 8   The ruling segments

distinguished senators, at court and even in the field.[208] There could also be close connections between freeborn and freed. The grandson of Callistus, *a libellis* of Gaius, was the praetorian prefect, Nymphidius Sabinus.[209] In assessing the standing and attitudes of those close to the *princeps*, we should take nothing for granted: Vespasian and Faenius Rufus were close and of high status, but hardly Nero's 'friends'; Spiculus was close and of low status, but very probably a 'friend'.

One way of visualising the Neronian court is to represent it as a series of concentric circles, centred on the *princeps*, with these diminishing in influence the further they were away from him. However, this gives the misleading impression that those further 'out' always had to approach the centre through those further 'in' and that only a chosen few might enjoy the greatest influence by acting as members of the *Consilium*, the core 'team'. We must take into account that a number of people gained close access to the *princeps* and membership of the *Consilium* not through personal intimacy but by virtue of their social status, public office or personal expertise. A more accurate representation is, therefore, an adaptation of Michel's 'Greek theatre' diagram (Figure 8).[210]

---

[208] Tac. *Ann.* 14.39.1.   [209] Tac. *Ann.* 15.72.4; Plut. *Galb.* 9.1–2.
[210] For all this see Levick 1990, 53; Michel 2015, 118–21, 158–61, 165–6, 242, 246.

CHAPTER 4

Dissimulation?

4.1 Delegation

In order to argue that Nero left most of the running of the Empire to this team, one must assume that its members were able to operate independently of him. In theory, given the inalienable nature of a *princeps'* powers,[1] this was impossible. The *Consilium* could not meet without him,[2] and so was unable to take the initiative in imperial business. However, the tradition of putting the administration of Rome into another's hands during a *princeps'* absence, exemplified under Tiberius by the vicegerency of Sejanus, under Claudius by that of Vitellius I and under Nero by that of Helius,[3] reveals that there was pragmatic acceptance of delegation of power. More generally, those who brought in the Neronian regime will have been accustomed to indirect rule as a result of their management of Claudius.[4] Whatever their long-term hopes for Nero, they would have expected this to continue for a while yet. We should therefore expect to see Nero's counsellors settling important matters among themselves early in his principate. Thus, in 54, Agrippina took charge of initial decision-making in the Armenian crisis.[5] Likewise in 55, Nero's liaison with Acte was, according to Tacitus, discussed 'by his most important *amici*'.[6] Crook takes this to mean that the affair was debated by the whole *Consilium* including, presumably, Nero himself.[7] Given the delicate nature of the issue, this is unlikely. Discussion will surely have taken place in Nero's absence. Once a pattern of independent action was established we may imagine regular extra-consiliar discussion resolving matters in advance of formal meetings, now necessary only to ratify earlier decisions. Nero, at first inexperienced and then with his interests increasingly elsewhere, would have been happy with such an arrangement. This, in turn, would

[1] Below 84; cf. Bradley 1978a, 225–6. [2] Crook 1955, 62–3. [3] Below 381. [4] Above 64.
[5] Below 133. [6] Tac. *Ann.* 13.12.2: *senioribus . . . principis amicis.*
[7] Crook 1955, 46–7; above 79.

have enabled the decision-makers to discover that it was easier to run the
Empire without him and so, though initially disappointed by his lack of
engagement, to tolerate those interests.[8] Nero's distancing of himself from
the day-to-day running of the Empire began in 58.[9] It ran to 68, as seen in
the notorious meeting of the *Consilium* shortly after Vindex's rebellion
when the main business was despatched promptly, allowing Nero to
devote the rest of the day to water-organs. The long gap in known sessions
of the *Consilium*, from 62 to 68, may confirm that in this period, as Nero's
thoughts turned to other matters, most of its meetings were perfunctory,
rubber-stamping decisions already made.

4.2   Dissimulation and Dissidence?

The question remains as to the extent to which members of the directing
team felt they could speak candidly to each other and to the *princeps*.
I propose that the Neronian court as a whole was never a place where all
were intimidated into dumb acquiescence.[10] In this I challenge a firmly
established conviction. It has long been recognised that the Augustan
restoration was based on a fundamental constitutional contradiction: that
of a 'restored' Republic continuing under an autocratic protector.[11] This
put both sides under pressure. The discomfort of, say, a proud senator
having to serve an authoritarian *princeps* is easy to understand. However,
Julio-Claudian *principes* were themselves always open to challenge; and
although to begin with it was assumed that the main threats would come
from within the family, by Nero the idea had surfaced that if this disappeared or became unworthy the head of another family might assume the
role of protector of the state, thus multiplying the number of potential
rivals.[12] To maintain political stability both senators and *principes* had to
ignore reality and to practise long-term dissimulation. Senators had to
profess loyalty to each *princeps*, however hateful; and *principes* had to show
deference to senators, however suspect. The belief that the consequent
mutual distrust produced a perpetually confused and fearful metropolis is
one of the main supports of the notion of Nero 'the monster'. Recent
scholarship has deepened this impression.

   Senatorial dissimulation – *dissimulatio* – was first addressed in depth by
Rudich.[13] He sees it as being encouraged by a rhetorical culture. The
'pretense and compromise' of the politics of the late Republic combined

---

[8] Above 63; cf. below 193.   [9] Below 144.   [10] Chapter 5.   [11] Cf. above 19.
[12] Cf. Lavan 2013, 69.   [13] Rudich 1993, esp. xvii–xix, xxii, xxxiii–iv.

with the forensic education of the Early Empire to generate a political elite accustomed to saying what it knew was not the truth.[14] Under the Principate, dissimulation helped senators to survive by veiling their hostility – Rudich's multi-faceted 'dissidence': aesthetic; out of ambition; artistic/professional; hereditary; by marriage; moral; political; religious; sexual; and even by 'misadventure'[15] – to the regime. However, it became so ingrained that it caused many to question their own values and actions. This could lead to 'paralysis of will' or 'a condition of mental entropy, capable of perpetuating itself or of becoming self-destructive through a nervous breakdown or even a split personality'.[16] The cause of this malaise was, of course, the 'uneven and awkward symbiosis that was never clearly defined in constitutional terms' between *principes* and Senate.[17] Rudich notes the 'paradoxical' position of the Senate,[18] but closer examination of paradox fell to Winterling.

4.3 Paradox and Confusion?

Augustus established a system in which *principes* used the Senate to legitimise their extraordinary autocratic power. In Winterling's terms, 'egalitarian republican order' and 'imperial patrimonial rule' thus ran in tandem, interdependent but incompatible. This was the fundamental constitutional paradox.[19] Though the paradox had arisen from a desire to create stability, it caused further instability since it prevented any move towards the most practical form of imperial government, 'monarchical legitimacy *sui generis*'.[20] The basic paradox is visible in the senatorial legislation that developed to bestow on each new *princeps* the Republican powers and competencies which gave him the authority to do his job. Each law was no more than a constitutional fig leaf, since by this stage every new incumbent will have had real power given to him by the military. It was, however, the only way in which this power could be legitimised.[21] In essence, all that was required was the passing of a decree allowing the new *princeps* to do everything he felt was necessary to protect the state. Such a

---

[14] Rudich 1993, xxx–xxxi; cf. Williams 2015, 137.   [15] Cf. Rudich 1993, 30 (Montanus).
[16] Rudich 1993, xxii–xxiii; cf. 9 (Britannicus), 113–19 (Faenius Rufus), 171 (Thrasea Paetus), 216 (Verginius Rufus).
[17] Rudich 1993, xvii, xx (quotation).   [18] Rudich 1993, xxi.
[19] Winterling 2009, 43, 156; cf. Winterling 2007, 16–17, 19, 26–7.
[20] Winterling 2009, 110 (quotation), 142–3, 159.
[21] For this and what follows see Brunt 1977, esp. 102; Winterling 2009, 11, 25–7, 134–6. Cf. above 15.

clause exists in the only detailed example of a *lex de imperio* that survives, pertaining to Vespasian.[22] Oddly, however, it is accompanied by a number of others which appear to do no more than elaborate on this provision but which in fact fudge the contradiction that while the law created an omnipotent *princeps* it was the work of an omnipotent Senate. The new *princeps* did not hold sovereign power in the state, which remained with the Senate and People of Rome: he was not a monarch.[23] This led to a subsidiary paradox. If the *princeps* was not a monarch, what was he? There was a contemporary tendency to regard him as 'a kind of holder of magisterial power who simply possesses authority over special administrative structures, assets, a court and a palace, yet otherwise is able to act as a private person in the traditional manner'. But this was not true. A *princeps* was always compelled to be more than a private citizen holding office: once accepted, he was autocrat for life. One proof of this, which caused confusion for Nero and Vitellius, is that a *princeps* was unable to choose bloodless abdication.[24] So paradox spawned paradox. In everyday aristocratic life, for example, there was the paradox of status. Because *principes* operated within the framework of the 'restored' Republic, because this Republic depended on the continued existence of the Senate, and because senators continued to seek status through traditional Republican state office, *principes* had to turn to members of their own household, slave and free, and to equestrians to fill the many new administrative positions generated by *de facto* autocracy. Such people consequently enjoyed power and influence greater than that enjoyed by most holders of traditional magistracies.[25] A prime example is the ex-gladiator and bodyguard, Spiculus.[26] We are back to the court. Yet the court could never become an alternative seedbed of nobility since its positions were not 'honourable'.[27] A new high aristocracy, based purely on service to the *princeps* – composed of what one may call 'kingsmen' – could not emerge. This was not entirely harmful. Without such an aristocracy no new *princeps* was in a position to dismiss all the office-holders of his predecessor, senatorial and non-senatorial, and replace them with his own, making for a high degree of continuity in the central administration.[28] Major changes, such as

---

[22] McCrum and Woodhead 1961, 1. 17–21: clause 6; Brunt 1977, 103, 109. Above 73.
[23] Cf. Brunt 1977, 95–6, 107–8, 116.
[24] Suet. *Ner.* 47.2, *Vit.* 15.4. Winterling 2009, 74–5 (quotation); Flaig 2011, 278–9.
[25] Winterling 2009, 27–32; cf. above 60.   [26] Winterling 2009, 11; above 61.
[27] Winterling 2009, 96–100; Michel 2015, 194.
[28] Above 59; Michel 2015, 194, 201–2, 226–7, 245–6.

Agrippina II's 'reengineering' of the Claudian court,[29] are therefore very noticeable. Broadly, however, the paradox of status and the resulting tension between senatorial and non-senatorial servants of the *princeps* remained an awkward problem. In theory, the *princeps* stood above such bickering, but another subsidiary paradox, that of appointment, might work against him. Within the 'restored' Republic, the 'election' of a candidate to a consulship was in practice the decision of the *princeps* and his advisers.[30] The same team determined the appointment of men of consular rank to administer important border provinces. These provinces were all nominally under the governorship of the *princeps* in his capacity as permanent proconsul. As a result, their governors, however high their rank, did not run them in their own right but only as *legati Augusti*: 'the *princeps'* lieutenants'.[31] There was, however, a second group, smaller in number and essentially non-military but including important provinces such as Asia Minor and Africa. Under the 'restored' Republic, these continued to be the responsibility of the Senate. Governorships were given to ex-consuls, chosen by lot, who held them as proconsuls in their own right, usually for about a year.[32] As with all imperial offices, manifestly suitable candidates could be favoured, and manifestly unsuitable ones excluded, by a *princeps'* making known his wishes.[33] However, prudent *principes* did not wish to appear heavy-handed, and there remained the possibility of a major region falling to an individual not wholly trusted by the administration. In 62, Rubellinus Plautus, living in Asia Minor, was accused of treason and sentenced to death. His father-in-law, Antistius Vetus, resident in Rome, attempted in vain to rouse him to save himself by force.[34] Though this should have ended Vetus' life or, at the very least, his imperial career, by 63–64 he was proconsul of Asia.[35]

In Winterling's view, paradoxes combined to produce unending confusion, frustration and concern. An unsympathetic and unsubtle *princeps* who alarmed significant numbers of senators would, as a senator himself, be well aware of their negativity and so, perhaps, become even more unsympathetic towards them. This made the manner of communication between both sides all-important.[36] *Principes* and senators dealt with the

---

[29] Romm 2014, 40–1 (quotation); Michel 2015, 202–3; above 33.   [30] Bradley 1978a, 98.
[31] Cf. above 17.   [32] Talbert 1984, 145.
[33] Cf. Talbert 1984, 396–400. Corbulo's appointment to Asia is likely to have occurred in this way: below 134, and generally Osgood 2011, 81.
[34] Tac. *Ann.* 14.58. Below 192.
[35] Tac. *Ann.* 16.10.2. Furneaux 1907; Rudich 1993, 68–9, 141; Rutledge 2001, 154–5.
[36] Cf. Flaig 2011, 281–2.

paradoxes by deploying ambiguity. They avoided open conflict by never openly acknowledging the reality of a particular situation or saying what they really thought about it.

4.4 Doublespeak?

Rudich had already reached a very similar conclusion: that the highly rhetoricised culture of the age allowed the crack between what was actually happening and what was being said about it to be papered over by 'a skilful deployment of formal devices affecting both expression in and perception of a text or a speech'.[37] In short, truth was avoided. Writing at the same time as Rudich, but more or less independently of him, Bartsch took a closer look at this 'deployment'.[38] *Principes* and the Roman public had grown used to observing each other sideways, judging each other's mood, and reacting accordingly, in the circus, amphitheatre, theatre etc. This was to continue for centuries, but under Nero the geometry of the relationship was dislocated by the *princeps'* moving himself from auditorium to stage. Bartsch, indeed, locates this new relationship first in the theatre itself, but appears (the qualification is crucial and will be picked up below[39]) to find it occurring beyond. The player-*princeps* now watched all around him as his 'audience'; but this audience, too, must act, deducing and playing out the reaction he required of them. Nero's private life became more and more theatrical: a series of episodes in which those near him found themselves having to react with the spoken, facial and bodily responses appropriate to the plot and characterisation which the watching Nero had decided on. The earliest example of this is the meal at which Nero poisoned Britannicus, at which those present had to accept Nero's portrayal of himself as the shocked and innocent host.[40] What Nero particularly craved from all his audiences was the expression of approval that allowed him to continue in power: the 'performance of consent'.[41] For them to fail to understand that a drama was in progress could lead to disaster. Bartsch cites the case of Julius Montanus, 'punished for violating Nero's script, not for deliberately hitting an emperor'.[42] In the meantime, the *princeps* projected himself from life into theatrical roles and from theatrical roles into life: the real matricide became the stage-matricide, and the stage-matricide then left the stage to act the *princeps*.[43] This led to a massive and debilitating confusion of identity. 'Role prevailed over office',

---

[37] Rudich 1993, xxxi.   [38] Bartsch 1994, 65–6.   [39] Below 88.   [40] Bartsch 1994, 12, 22.
[41] Bartsch 1994, 26.   [42] Bartsch 1994, 19–20; cf. below 317.   [43] Bartsch 1994, 38–9, 42.

making Nero unfit to be emperor. Dio has Nero die, unworthily, in the roles of matricide and beggar.[44] The combination of the theatrical Nero and the confused Nero was terrifying. The senators' solution was continual acting: extreme dissimulation. They resorted to evasive allusion for the benefit of both the autocrat and their peers, flattering the former while signalling to the latter that all this was pretence: 'doublespeak'.[45] But this was no real escape. Both *principes* and audiences, increasingly aware of doublespeak, detected it even where it did not exist. The more tense the situation, the more intently they looked out for subversion.[46]

4.5 A Carnival of Fear?

This impression of a confused and frightened metropolitan society under Nero has proved very influential. Even Miriam Griffin has become much more pessimistic.[47] Maes envisages a Rome in which, in the unreality of a 'restored' Republic, aristocrats parade in a grotesque carnival of fear around the real reality of the autocratic ruler.[48] Practising 'the aesthetics of deviation', they express their concern in literature which presents a world 'turned topsy-turvy'.[49] 'The kind of merry and oppressive lawlessness brought on by the arbitrariness inherent in the rule of the dictator is interiorized by the subject, and hence generalized. This leads to a true reign of terror'.[50] It has in fact become common to detect the hypocrisy and horror of Nero's principate in its literature. This dealt with loss of freedom by introducing 'artificial hyper-realism of descriptions, the unremitting unbalancing of the reader's expectation, the almost morbid obsession with death, the loss of centre and the general disturbance of traditional categories'. Truth is avoided. Instead we find 'cynical or mordant discourse, formulated in such a way that it can never be pinpointed', and 'a poetry of dissimulation'.[51] Nichols suggests that 'Persius may have adopted [his] perplexing, even exasperating, style as a means of illustrating his frustration at the distorted, disfigured society around him'. All of this supports the operation of 'dumb acquiescence' rejected at the start of this chapter. However, such extreme pessimism is open to criticism.

---

[44] Bartsch 1994, 41–3.   [45] Bartsch 1994, 63–6, 66.   [46] Bartsch 1994, 66–8, 79.
[47] Griffin 2013, 471, 479; cf. 1976, 217.   [48] Maes 2013, 322.   [49] Maes 2013, 311.
[50] Maes 2013, 297.   [51] Maes 2013, 312.

4.6   The Problem of the Sources

Rudich's principal weakness is that he simply accepts Nero as 'the monster' of the main source tradition: a 'debauched and pathetic tyrant'.[52] From its beginning the Neronian principate was therefore fated to end in a reign of terror.[53] Very much on the side of Tacitus' 'respectable majority', he is bitterly against the senatorial 'collaborationists' and 'collaborators', especially the *delatores*, who were prepared to work with the regime, giving no thought as to whether the 'majority' might in truth have been a minority, with most senators being prepared to work with the system.[54] His adhesion to Tacitus and his belief in prevalent dissidence and dissimulation cause him to overstate his case. He has, for example, Nero, the 'artistic tyrant', drive Roman aristocrats to despair by insisting on their performance in public, without considering the likely willingness of many to take part.[55] Likewise, while he makes much of *secessio* – the act of retiring from court of one's own volition or as a victim of Nero's formal *renuntio amicitiae* ('withdrawal of friendship') – as an alternative to dissimulation in principle, he has difficulties in handling it in practice, conceding that even Thrasea Paetus' *secessio*, the prime example, 'progressed slowly' as 'he sometimes hesitated as to how he should proceed', and that there was no rush of people ready to follow him along this course.[56] The list of secessionists is remarkably short: apart from Thrasea Paetus and Seneca, only Cassius Longinus, Lucan and Vestinus Atticus, of whom only the first is absolutely certain.[57]

A key point of Bartsch's study, often overlooked, is that neither her 'theatrical' Nero nor her 'confused' Nero should be taken as the historical Nero. 'Theatrical' Nero is very much the creation of Tacitus. In identifying theatre and theatrical behaviour as the location and means of Nero's cold-blooded tyranny, Tacitus reveals how he believed the Julio-Claudian principate operated. However, 'his is not the only understanding of how Nero wielded his power onstage and off'.[58] It is impossible to say whether his theatrical model 'reflects a reality of the Neronian age, a perception of a common source for Suetonius, Dio and Tacitus, a particularly Tacitean outlook that influenced the later historians, or a reaction to the reign of Domitian as evinced by the testimony of the *Agricola* and *Panegyricus*'.[59]

---

[52] Rudich 1993, xxix–xxx.   [53] Rudich 1993, 58.
[54] Tac. *Hist.* 4.43; *multi bonique*. Rudich 1993, xxii–xxiv; below 92.
[55] Rudich 1993, 41–2; below 300.   [56] Rudich 1993, 79–81, 171–2; cf. below 97.
[57] Rudich 1993, 95, 121, 137. Above 28, 72–3; 115, 116.   [58] Bartsch 1994, 22 (quotations), 24.
[59] Bartsch 1994, 191–2.

The result of accepting a grossly theatrical Nero, a Nero who modelled his life on myth and drama, is to identify the theatrical where even the sources do not mention it, for example as a motive for Nero's firing of Rome: 'To offer such a suggestion, I hold, is to follow the sources themselves in using drama to reshape an imperial life, a tempting but pernicious lure ... for interpreters ancient and modern alike ... the power of Nero's role-playing on the stage has exerted a retroactive effect on his life: the actor even when off-stage commits crimes redolent of his roles, and if the roles postdate the crimes they function as it were only as a confirmation of the theatrical impulse that spurred crimes of this nature in the first place'.[60] The 'confused' Nero is the Nero of Suetonius and Dio. These make much less of any teasing interplay between *princeps* and audience in private or public.[61] Instead, they present a more vulnerable *princeps* who acts only to win the praise of his audience. His fault lies not in intimidating people, but in being carried away by his art, confusing stage and life, and so causing great difficulties for himself and others. Their Nero is more 'mad' than 'bad', which led him fatally to neglect his responsibilities as ruler. Their interpretation, like that of Tacitus', is a construct, made up of narratives that are not entirely logical or consistent and explanations that depend on distorted chronology.[62] They, like Tacitus, see events through a 'distorting lens',[63] ground to bring into focus only those 'monstrous' aspects of Nero that each writer expected to see. In short, both the 'theatrical' Nero and the 'confused' Nero are 'NERO', the tyrant of legend, not 'Nero', the historical figure, because both are constructs of the source tradition.[64]

4.7 The Problem of Prejudice: the Strength of the Principate

Modern historians hostile to Nero therefore frequently find it difficult to discover their wholly 'monstrous' *princeps* in the sources. Rudich has to admit that Nero handled the first wave of post-Pisonian prosecutions 'reasonably well'.[65] However, he persists in deploying his many categories of dissidence to propose hatred of the *princeps* everywhere and in everyone, even in Agrippina 'up to the night of her assassination'.[66] Other scholars find enmity throughout Neronian literature.[67] Maes admits the tendency

---

[60] Bartsch 1994, 61–2. [61] Cf. Bartsch 1994, 100–1. [62] Bartsch 1994, 46.
[63] Bartsch 1994, 42. [64] Cf. Maes 2013, 290. [65] Rudich 1993, 123–4, 128; cf. below 218.
[66] Rudich 1993, 17; cf. 11: the Neronian flourishing of the arts in no way excuses the crimes of the regime; cf. below 119.
[67] Cf. above 87.

of researchers to make its interpretation conform to their pejorative view of Nero, but still sees Nero's Rome as 'the land where angels feared to tread'. In similar vein is Connors' characterisation of the Eumolpus of the *Satyricon* as a poet 'in a world where literary brilliance could become a dangerous thing' and his career as reflecting 'the pressures in the increasingly storm-tossed society of Nero's Rome which could end any poet's life and text'.[68] Reading Nero into or out of the literature is, however, just as misguided as reading him into or out of his busts and statuary.[69] One must beware of prejudice. Rudich, making no secret of the fact that his historical analysis was shaped by his experience as a Soviet dissident,[70] gives the impression of a society stretched to breaking point, of a totalitarian state resembling South Africa at the height of apartheid or the former USSR. The Julio-Claudian Empire was not such a society; it lacked the bureaucratic resources to mount a '"Night of the Long Knives" in which political enemies are "liquidated" *en masse*'.[71] If it had, it would have broken apart, taking the Principate with it; but both survived, the latter, in its essentials, well into the third century.[72] The 'belt-and-braces' approach of the *lex de imperio Vespasiani* looks odd to us but reflects Roman pragmatism. Under the 'restored' Republic, nominal sovereignty continued to rest with the Senate and People. Each *princeps*, though expected to obey the law, had therefore to be exempted from normal legal prosecution, which would have paralysed government.[73] The *lex de imperio* was, therefore, a clumsy but effective way of lending sovereignty to the *princeps* of the moment. Though the Republican sentiments of some conservatives, such as Vestinus Atticus,[74] might smack of sedition, these were rare and, as Kimmerle argues, we need to stand back and accept that the expression of Republican sympathies was in principle neither forbidden or dangerous. This was because Augustus had founded the Principate within a 'restored' Republic, and it would have been inconsistent to attack anyone for praising that Republic and its values, even someone like Vestinus Atticus.[75] Moreover, since by the middle of the first century most members of the political community accepted the Augustan compromise as a necessary – albeit,

---

[68] Connors 1994, 232; Gowers 1994; Maes 2013, 290, 300–1 (quotations); Rimell 2015, 127; below 123.

[69] Cf. Kreikenbom 2013.   [70] Rudich 1993, xi.   [71] Rutledge 2001, 178–9 (quotation), 181.

[72] Winterling 2009, 138.

[73] Cf. Rudich 1993, 5. (At p. xxv, Rudich, oddly, has the imperial government abrogating 'any pretense at the rule of law' in dealing with cases of *maiestas*. He appears to have in mind the type of 'kangaroo' trials which I dispute above: 77.)

[74] Above 72.   [75] Kimmerle 2015, 93, 268–9, 273–5, 305.

given the continuing senatorial tradition, sometimes uncomfortable – expedient, praise of the old Republic was no longer automatically taken as criticism of the Principate or of the current *princeps*.[76] What aristocrats desired was that each *princeps* should continue to respect the 'restored' Republic and its implied guarantee of the 'liberty' of senators: no longer that of freedom to practise politics, but that of continued enjoyment of traditional privileges, in particular the exclusive right to hold the highest, Republican, offices of state.[77] One result of this was a lack of pressure on writers. Nothing indicates that Julio-Claudian Rome was a repressive, totalitarian (a wholly anachronistic notion) state in which all criticism of the ruling regime was suppressed as treasonable. In fact, Julio-Claudian *principes* tended to hold back from witch-hunts of purported critics and 'enemies of the state' because such prosecution exposed their autocratic power and compromised the Augustan system. Actions of libel or slander were usually initiated by aristocrats defending their own reputations or trying to curry favour with a *princeps* by overzealously claiming to defend his. *Principes* were then often dragged in as umpires.[78] This is not to say that there were no problems. A degree of leeway in the expression of historical and political judgement did not amount to full licence; one had to be careful what one said about matters touching on the current *princeps*;[79] and the limits of what was acceptable were unknown. Indeed, an opinion tolerated by one *princeps* might find less welcome under a successor.[80] Thus, though Nero was more relaxed than most in his attitude to criticism, common sense dictated that a line be removed from the poetry of Persius in case it was construed as insulting him.[81] In addition, there appear to have been writers unable to resist the allure of an 'edgy' reputation. Seneca I, writing under Tiberius, reprimands those who were 'willing to lose their life rather than pass over a witty double entendre'.[82] Likewise, the orator-turned-dramatist Curiatus Maternus, writing probably under Vespasian, is criticised by Tacitus for insisting on using anti-Establishment allusions to win fame.[83] This suggests that political censure of a regime was considered possible, and therefore looked out for; but most

---

[76] Flaig 2011, 281; Kimmerle 2015, 115, 277, 280–3, 294–5, 298, 308; cf. above 19; below 111.

[77] Kimmerle 2015, 92, 288–90.

[78] Kimmerle 2015, 89–92, 94–99, 99–110, 113, 115–16, 268, 284, 305.   [79] Rutledge 2001, 177.

[80] E.g. Cremutius Cordus: Tac. *Ann.* 4, 34–5; Suet. *Tib.* 61.3. Bartsch 1994, 84–5; Kimmerle 2015, 90.

[81] Below 105; Kimmerle 2015, 101–2, 295.

[82] Sen. *Controv.* 2.4.13: *tanti putant caput potius quam dictum perdere.* Bartsch 1994, 96.

[83] Tac. *Dial.* 3.2, 10.7; Bartsch 1994, 99, 81–2, 101–2, 104, 106–7, 116–18. Cf. Quint. *Inst.* 9.2.66–9. Bartsch 1994, 93–6.

writers will have avoided extremes and remained safe. And all this was
public: there was, as far as we know, no literature of dissidence: no Roman
samizdat.[84] 'Nero's regime was not the kind of dictatorship unable to
tolerate any hint of subversion in its literary figures; and it is not clear
that artists of conscience were compelled to choose between compromise
and death'.[85]

The Principate was not perfect, but it was no arbitrary tyranny. There
was no abrogation of the rule of law.[86] Some individuals stepped out of
line, but most families remained loyal: one 'black sheep' should not be
taken as characterising a whole clan.[87] There was no consequent 'collapse
of values and ... pervasive moral corruption'. On the contrary, the next
generation was to see increased moral strictness.[88] *Dissimulatio* existed, but
it was born of autocracy, not tyranny. Pliny II notes the paradox of even
the 'good' Trajan ordering people to be free.[89] The Principate survived so
long because the majority of the political community, from Roman
senators to leading provincials, wanted it to succeed because it kept the
peace and maintained their own wealth and privileges. The Senate's reward
for legitimising each new *princeps* was the opportunity for its members to
engage in satisfying administrative careers.[90] Even Rudich allows that
many senators enjoyed senatorial work, that new senators recruited by
the *princeps* were likely to be loyal to him, and that positive things may be
said even about *delatores*.[91] It is no wonder that competition to enter the
Senate remained high.[92] Outsiders were keen to join or to be closely
associated with those who were already members: as the low-born
Tigellinus came to the top of Roman politics, he hastened to acquire a
senatorial son-in-law.[93] Furthermore, by admitting wealthy provincials,
the Senate gave these, too, the opportunity to become fully part of the
Empire. A classic example of this is Vindex, who initiated the run of events
that led to the fall of Nero in 68.[94] A particularly satisfying set of responsibilities was given to the governors of the imperial provinces, who had the
opportunity to show their talents as generals, especially under Nero.[95]
Though these were his *legati* and so his subordinates,[96] the term was
Republican and the men concerned pursued senatorial careers and

---

[84] *Contra* Rudich 1993, 59.   [85] Masters 1994, 170.
[86] *Contra* Rudich 1993, xxv; cf. above 77.   [87] Cf. below 225.
[88] Plin. *Pan.* 46.4. Rudich 1993, xxxi; Bartsch 1994, 31–2.
[89] Plin. *Pan.* 66.4: *iubes esse liberos.* Rudich 1993, xxi; cf. Bartsch 1994, 184.
[90] Above 24, below 148.   [91] Rudich 1993, xx, xxi, xxvi–vii 22, 63–4; cf. Winterling 2007, 68.
[92] Above 25; Talbert 1984. 53–65.   [93] Below 187.   [94] Below 389–90.
[95] Above 29; below 145, 227.   [96] Above 85.

participated in campaigns directly comparable to those of the Republic. Hypocrisy and dissimulation existed, but the Principate worked. *Principes* could avoid being seen as hated 'kings' by projecting themselves as high-class senators,[97] and senators could consider themselves as magistrates of the Republic, as both co-operated in the growth of autocracy. This gave the Principate time to develop; and the more people got used to it, the stronger it became. In order to accommodate this positive assessment to the notion of 'paradox' we should not interpret the operation of Roman politics and society too narrowly or legalistically. People can live with rules of behaviour that do not stipulate everything in detail and may contain contradictions. So, with regard to the paradox of status, everyone would have known instinctively that in the long run senior imperial freedmen and prominent *equites* were not, for all their powers, superior to senators. It was this which made *arrivistes* like Tigellinus so eager to get their offspring into the senatorial order. Another example of contradiction is panegyric. Bartsch remarks how, by the early second century, the public eulogy of *principes* was in a state of 'linguistic bankruptcy': praisers, praised and audiences were all aware that what was being said was rarely honest, which led to a huge degree of tension. Yet 'bankrupt' imperial panegyric continued into the Late Empire, which suggests that people thought it had a use. For a senator to lavish praise on a *princeps* confirmed the autocracy; but the constant reiteration of what was expected of a ruler – panegyric as *Fürstenspiegel*, the invention of Seneca[98] – reminded the *princeps* that he was no king, should not play the tyrant, and after his death would face senatorial judgement of his memory. As Bartsch, later more sympathetic in her approach, puts it, 'it is ... the saying which counts'.[99] Most senators were happy to co-operate, serve and succeed within the continuing senatorial tradition.[100] Their co-operation should not be regarded as a 'process of degeneration of senatorial independence',[101] but as Augustus' 'restored' Republic functioning smoothly as the vehicle of *de facto* monarchy.

4.8 Nero and the Senate (ii)

This returns us to the success of the Neronian regime that forms the basis of my interpretation of Neronian government.[102] If one examines the pattern of Nero's principate one may discern a much less strained

---

[97] Cf. Talbert 1984, 163.   [98] Schofield 2015, 69; cf. Rimell 2015, 125–6.
[99] Bartsch 1994, 184–5.   [100] Cf. above 26, 92.   [101] Griffin 1984, 94 (quotation).
[102] Above 30.

relationship between the *princeps* and the leaders of Roman society than
the hostile source tradition proposes. There was never a catastrophic break
with the Senate.[103] At the start of his principate, Nero, benefitting from
Agrippina's political legacy, enjoyed excellent relations with this body.[104]
Though there were problems, this continued beyond proposed ruptures
over reform of indirect taxation, in 58, the end of the 'Quinquennium', in
59, and even the disappearance of Burrus and Seneca, in 62.[105] I have
noted specific examples of the *princeps'* respecting the Senate, from 64 to
68.[106] In addition, Nero's delay in adopting 'Imperator' as his *praenomen*
until the reception of Tiridates in 66 may be seen as a gesture of respect to
the 'restored' Republic. He took it when it might be said that he really
deserved it: 'the highest sign of his identification with Roman tradition'.[107]
Nero perhaps felt that his eastern victories had equalled those of Augustus.
The reception occasioned another Augustan rarity, the ceremonial closing
of the gates of the temple of Janus;[108] and it involved a remarkably
traditional, 'Republican' presentation of the Roman state:[109]

> The emperor, prominent as *imperator* and surrounded by his guard, is
> furnished with the attributes of a magistrate and stands at the head of the
> senate, the most important institution of the Roman polity. Moreover, the
> Roman people are marked out as such by their dress, and they, together
> with the Roman citizen soldiers, play a direct part in the political ceremony
> of the coronation by virtue of the location of its enactment: the Forum in
> front of the speakers' platform.

Generally, the administration took great care over matters that closely
touched senators' interests, such as the distribution of consulships.[110] In a
particular instance, it was prepared to overlook the errant behaviour of the
father-in-law of Rubellius Plautus;[111] and, as we have seen, down to the
early 60s Nero tolerated being the butt of the rough humour of another
leading senator.[112] There is no reason to suppose that most senators did
not accept the relatively few pre-Pisonian conspiracy deaths as unfortunate
but justified by political circumstances,[113] or that they did not see the
Pisonian sentences as something the condemned had brought upon themselves. Circumstances in Rome were undoubtedly tense in 65–6,[114] and
Nero was probably encouraged to journey to Greece to remove himself
from it. Helius' period of control in Rome did not improve matters;[115]

---

[103] Cf. above 26–7; below 148.   [104] Above 15, 17, 20, 34.   [105] Above 24, 27; below 351.
[106] Above 27; cf. below 397.   [107] Malitz 1999, 62.   [108] Below 214; Levi 1949, 206.
[109] Winterling 2009, 10.   [110] Below 144.   [111] Above 85.   [112] Below 117.
[113] Cf. below 195.   [114] Below 372.   [115] Below 228, 230, 380.

and, following Suetonius, some have seen Nero's failure to salute senators with the usual kiss on his departure for and return from Greece, and his exclusion of the Senate from his blessing as he cut the first sod of the Corinth canal, as threatening snubs to this body.[116] Yet there is no sign of the Neronian administration's facing crisis with the Senate at this time.[117] Senators remained loyal; there was no metropolitan or provincial revolt.[118] With regard to the 'snubs', these occur in a very suspect section of Suetonius' 'Life', immediately after a description of Nero's man-eating Egyptian monster.[119] With regard to the missing embraces, Suetonius may, characteristically, have generalised from just one or two incidents; and as for the canal, mistakes in protocol do happen, to become the material for gossip and calumny.[120]

One can find a number of senators prepared to work with Nero. Petronius Turpilianus and Nerva were honoured for their service after the uncovering of the Pisonian conspiracy.[121] In 68, no major senatorial military commander revolted directly against Nero, and Turpilianus, sent to hold northern Italy against Vindex, remained loyal to the end.[122] As loyal civilians one may point to the infamous 'informers': Aquilius Regulus, Cestius Severus, Eprius Marcellus, Nonius Attianus, Paccius Africanus, Sariolenus Vocula, Silius Italicus and Vibius Crispus.[123] Eprius Marcellus' defence of his activities, that like most other senators he had acted under compulsion,[124] looks like a case of 'well he would, wouldn't he?', but hints at the wider co-operation of his peers. This finds some confirmation in the case of the senator and poet, Silius Italicus, who in 68 was rewarded with a consulship for his work as an informer,[125] and in that of 'the amazing A. Marius Celsus', consul designate for 69 and the 'ideal loyalist'.[126] Julius Agricola, father-in-law of Tacitus, probably belongs in the same category, as does Memmius Regulus.[127] More surprising is the extent of the co-operation of 'dissidents' such as Thrasea Paetus. Suffect consul in 56, he was prepared to work with Nero down to 62,[128] was still apparently a senior counsellor in 63,[129] and had to be specifically forbidden to attend

---

[116] Suet. *Ner.* 37.3. E.g. Cizek 1982, 143; Rudich 1993, 207; Fini 1994, 204; Malitz 1999, 89, 94.
[117] Below 389, 407.   [118] Cf. below 230.   [119] Below 321; Grant 1970, 229.
[120] Below 133–4, 99. Cf. Tac. *Ann.* 4.17.1–3.   [121] Above 29.   [122] Below 147; cf. 392.
[123] Below 229–30.   [124] Below 366.
[125] Plin. *Ep.* 3.7.3, 10; Syme 1958, 89; Shotter 2008, 149.
[126] Tac. *Hist.* 1.14, 77. Rudich 1993, 208 (quotations).
[127] Tac. *Agr.* 63; *Ann.* 14. 47.2. Rudich 1993, 54–5; below 190.
[128] Above 27; Liebenam 1909, 13; Rudich 1993, 32–4, 38.   [129] Above 28.

Tiridates' reception in 66.[130] Thus, despite his being accused of gross neglect of senatorial duties, he continued to be considered a member of the Establishment and willing to appear in public as a supporter of the regime.[131] Similarly, it was not until 65 that Nero, by forbidding his attendance at Poppaea's funeral, indicated that Cassius Longinus had fallen out of favour.[132] The force of this is that until then, Longinus, a proud descendant of a regicide and no friend of the regime, was still received at court. With regard to senatorial co-operation with Nero, it is interesting to note what happened on the *princeps'* fall. Turpilianus was killed, but his death was exceptional, and provoked controversy. A little later, action was taken against some of the informers, but this proved difficult because it was feared that these might implicate others:[133] pro-Neronian senatorial interests were strong enough to prevent general persecution of leading loyalists.[134]

One remarkable survivor was Cluvius Rufus, the 'bona fide collaborationist', who survived the fall of Nero and the subsequent civil war.[135] The most remarkable Neronian, however, was Vespasian. Suetonius plays up a quarrel with Nero in Greece, caused by Vespasian's leaving or dozing off during the *princeps'* musical performances which led to his banishment from court in fear of his life.[136] Though the tale is often accepted,[137] it screams fabrication. Vespasian's 'exile' could have been no longer than from October to December 66, when he was appointed commander of the Jewish war: a sign of huge trust in both him and his son, Titus, who accompanied him.[138] Vespasian was an experienced courtier, who had gone out of his way to seek the favour of Gaius at his worst, had done well under Claudius, and fits easily among the loyal Neronians identified above.[139] He was in Greece as one of Nero's senior counsellors and, following the eclipse of Corbulo, was an obvious choice for Judaea.[140] He became *princeps* in 69, the first of a new dynasty that owed much of its legitimacy to its claim that it replaced the jaded Julio-Claudians and their unworthy immediate successors. His Neronian past was an

---

[130] Tac. *Ann.* 16.24.1.   [131] Tac. *Ann.* 16.22.1. *Contra* Rudich 1993, 170.
[132] Tac. *Ann.* 16.7.1; cf. 22.9.   [133] Tac. *Hist.* 1.6; 4.6.   [134] Below 409.
[135] Tac. *Hist.* 4.43. Rudich 1993, xxxiv.   [136] Suet. *Vesp.* 4.4; cf. Tac. *Ann.* 16.5.6.
[137] E.g. Malitz 1999, 44–5; Waldherr 2005, 158.
[138] Below 152, 226, 228; cf. Heil 1997, 189–90.
[139] Suet. *Vesp.* 2.3, 4.1. Griffin 1976, 230; Levick 1999a, 25; Winterling 2007, 107.
[140] Levick 1999a, 28; cf. *contra* Rudich 1993, 194: because of 'the shortage of other available candidates'.

embarrassment, hence the encouragement of a tale which made him a lucky survivor.[141] It could have derived from a piece of banter:[142] Vespasian, known for not sharing Nero's artistic enthusiasms, might have drawn criticism on himself once or twice in the manner described, causing court wits to joke as to how he should be punished.

4.9   Exclusion

Winterling makes much of Vespasian's exclusion from court, taking it as a major example of how this affected aristocrats, 'obliterated in their political and social, and most often also their physical existence'.[143] Such exclusion has been the tool of the despot throughout history, and there is no reason to doubt that it existed under the Principate. However, there is little sign that Nero deployed it as matter of course. It hardly applies to Vespasian and, as already observed, Rudich has difficulties with *secessio*, voluntary or forced.[144] Winterling's other example comes from the principate of Tiberius.[145] With regard to Nero, however, a promising example might be thought to be Otho's removal to Lusitania.[146] The sources offer two versions of its cause.[147] Tacitus' earlier account, in his 'Histories', and those of Suetonius and Dio, have Nero falling in love with Poppaea, the wife of Rufrius Crispinus, making her his mistress, engineering a divorce between her and her husband, and then marrying her off to his friend Otho in order to have access to her until he could divorce Octavia. Otho, however, fell in love with Poppaea, seduced her and quarrelled with Nero when he attempted to keep her for himself. For this he was sent to govern Lusitania.[148] Tacitus' later, longer version, in his 'Annals', has Otho seducing Poppaea and marrying her on his own initiative. He boasted about her at court and Nero, intrigued, had her admitted to his inner circle. She seduced him, and began her long campaign to become his wife. As a result, Otho was 'debarred from his usual intimacy' with Nero, being excluded from his morning *salutatio* and his general company. Then, 'to prevent his acting as Nero's rival in Rome', he was appointed governor of Lusitania.[149] The second version is the more credible. It probably derives from Tacitus' own research and is simpler and more plausible in that,

[141] Cf. Brunt 1977, 101; Levick 1999a, 25: '[On his accession] Vespasian's . . . reputation was indeed dubious'.
[142] Cf. above 25; below 286, 288, 291.   [143] Winterling 2009, 87; cf. 48.   [144] Above 88.
[145] Tac. *Ann.* 6.29.3.   [146] Below 182, 395.   [147] Griffin 1984, 45–6.
[148] Tac. *Hist.* 1.13; Suet. *Otho* 3.1–2; Cass. Dio 61.11.2.
[149] Tac. *Ann.* 13.46.5: *deicitur familiaritate sueta . . . ne in urbe aemulatus ageret.*

given his subsequent strength of feeling for her Nero had to fall for Poppaea very badly, and to instigate the affair.[150] Otho's fate appears at first glance very much like the result of a formal withdrawal of friendship. On the other hand, if the administration felt that he might pose a threat, why did it not simply find an excuse to have him executed? And if Otho was allowed to live, why give him such an important post, for which he was not officially qualified?[151] The whole business clearly puzzled contemporaries and later writers. Suetonius proposes that Nero feared that more radical treatment of Otho 'would make the whole farce public', but then proceeds to show that the affair was anyway soon common knowledge.[152] As for Otho, he will have been dismayed at being sent to the unsophisticated west, and the source tradition is united in seeing him taking revenge on Nero by his energetic support of Galba's revolt. The same tradition also implies, however, that Otho relished his time as an imperial governor;[153] and the fact that he, unlike Galba, initially betrayed Vindex indicates that he was not actively seeking to harm Nero.[154] When he became *princeps* he went out of his way to honour Nero's memory.[155] One must conclude that he suffered no formal renunciation of friendship, which is why Rudich and Winterling exclude him from their examples. Otho and Nero had been unusually close, as reflected in the high level of badinage between them.[156] This familiarity is reflected in Suetonius' story of the unintended farce of Otho's refusing to let Nero into his house to see Poppaea, leaving the *princeps* standing on the street 'alternately threatening and begging to no effect and demanding back the "property" that he had left with Otho for safekeeping'.[157] It seems that Nero, Otho and Poppaea were so close that Nero or Poppaea, or both, felt that neither could be comfortable if, after the threesome had become a twosome, Otho remained in the vicinity. For the same reason, however, he could not simply be destroyed. The only other case that might be adduced, that of Thrasea Paetus, fails because, again as we have seen, Paetus remained close to the centre of political

---

[150] Cf. Griffin 1984, 46 and n. 52; Rudich 1993, 29; Waldherr 2005, 84; below 165.
[151] Furneaux 1907, 215–16.   [152] Suet. *Otho* 3.2.
[153] Tac. *Hist.* 1.13; Suet. *Otho* 3.2, 4.1; Plut. *Galb.* 20.1–2.
[154] Below 395. *Contra* Dawson (1964, 259), I entirely discount the possibility that Agrippina had Otho in mind to replace Nero in 59 since by this time he was in Lusitania. The possible involvement of Otho in this depends on the reliability of Suetonius' notice that he hosted the final party at Baiae. This, however, is questionable since Suetonius also remarks that Otho governed Lusitania for ten years, which would take him out of metropolitan life in 58: Suet. *Otho* 3.1, 2. Griffin 1984, 45–6; cf. Rudich 1993, 35.
[155] Above 10.   [156] Cass. Dio 61.11.2. Cf. below 116.
[157] Suet. *Otho* 3.2: *miscentemque frustra minas et preces ac depositum reposcentem* (trans. Hurley 2011).

action down to 66. The rarity of true exclusion under Nero is in line with the *princeps'* general lack of cruelty and vindictiveness.[158] It was not in his nature to play cat and mouse with people's careers and lives.

4.10 The Power of Gossip

Tacitus' dismissal of co-operative senators as spineless collaborators probably derives from his reaction to the principate of Domitian. Regarded more sympathetically, the Neronian 'quislings' were just getting on with the world as they found it.[159] A number of instances in which a critic might detect Nero's tyrannical direction of a pusillanimous Senate may be more positively interpreted as modifications of existing procedures in which the *princeps* acted rather as a very senior senator.[160] Even unRepublican procedures helped maintain a good working relationship between *princeps* and Senate. On 1 January each year senators had to swear to uphold the acts of past and present *principes*.[161] Thrasea Paetus found himself in trouble when he failed to attend.[162] However, the process also served to reinforce the position of the Senate as a reminder of the indispensable role played by its members in the operation of the Principate. What, therefore, of the tales and rumours which appear to indicate the opening up of a chasm between Nero and Senate? Suetonius declares that, near the end of his principate, Nero, boasting of his limitless power, hinted that he would destroy the Senate and rely on equestrians and freedmen to run the Empire (the context of the 'snubs' noted above). Suetonius likewise reports that by the very end Nero was contemplating the murder of all army commanders and governors, the killing of all exiles and of all people of Gallic descent in Rome, the poisoning of the Senate, and the burning of Rome.[163] Little of this inspires confidence. The 'snubs' have been dealt with.[164] The threatened eradication and destruction may likewise be dismissed as predominantly fictional.[165] There is no indication that Nero refused to give or accept senatorial invitations to eat with him. Indeed, his purported scheme for the destruction of the Senate implies that to the end Nero was still accepting the obligation to dine senators.[166] These accusations probably accrued around some kernel of truth, such as occasional, accidental, lapses in protocol already suggested.[167] Nero's 'boasts' and 'threats' could have resulted from remarks made in private

---

[158] E.g. below 322, 325.   [159] Cf. below 196.   [160] Talbert 1984, 168–9.
[161] Griffin 1984, 170.   [162] Tac. *Ann.* 16.22.1.   [163] Suet. *Ner.* 43.1.   [164] Above 95.
[165] Below 397.   [166] Below 305, 309.   [167] Above 95.

conversations at court, taken out of context by those who wanted to depict him in the worst possible light.[168] They should not be accepted as proof of any alienation of *princeps* and Senate from around 65.[169]

4.11   Dissimulation?

We should be cautious in assessing the novelty and impact of Neronian 'dissimulation'. In every society there is two-way observation and response: 'we all act'. In societies that are not liberal and democratic – historically, the overwhelming majority – this is even more so.[170] Roman society can have been no exception, at any time. In the Roman Republic at its prime, it would have been dangerous for an ordinary person to cross a prince-patron. But these, too, must have put on acts for their social superiors. In Rome, confusion between a person's public office and private authority (*magistratus* and *privatus*), and between their house and court (*domus* and *aula*), began in the late Republic and was only intensified by the emergence of the Principate.[171] The same may be said of the power of freedmen: Chrysogonus was a creature of the dictator Sulla. By the time of the Julio-Claudians, Romans will have been well used to reciprocal observation and social confusion, and will have learned to live with both. The Neronian political community encountered dissimulation, paradox and doublespeak, but was not hamstrung by these. Though society was hardly 'open', those at the top may have enjoyed opportunities for a degree of frankness that provided a welcome change from the worthy but mostly humourless business of the Senate.[172]

---

[168] Below 118.   [169] *Contra* Cizek 1982, 143.   [170] Cf. Bartsch 1994, 10–11; below 286.
[171] Winterling 2009, 58–9, 94–5.   [172] Cf. Talbert 1984, 262–3.

CHAPTER 5

Frankness and Enquiry

5.1 Nero

Neronian frankness was encouraged by Nero's personality and upbringing. As his many interests show, he had a lively mind that craved stimulation. He was not susceptible to flattery and the blandishments of yes-men, as is indicated by his later desire to win the authentic approval of the judges of those contests in which he competed.[1] In his youth a willing pupil, he had reached a high level of education and he became a decent poet.[2] After the death of Agrippina he formed a 'reading circle' of aspiring poets and, perhaps, in the company of Seneca listened to leading philosophers debate their convictions.[3] In Nero's close association with such *literati* there must have been some toleration of outspokenness.

5.2 Neronian Literature

5.2.1 *Petronius, Seneca*

Only this can explain his friendship with Petronius, now generally accepted as the author of that scandalous fictional depiction of contemporary Roman life which is the *Satyricon*, 'one of the wittiest and most entertaining works in surviving ancient literature'.[4] Somewhat older than Nero, of consular rank, Petronius was a rake, but a controlled and

---

[1] Below 292; cf. 285.
[2] Sen. *QNat.* 1.5.6; Mart. 8.70. Charlesworth 1950, 70; Fini 1994, 22; Malitz 1999, 40; Waldherr 2005, 119; below 281.
[3] Tac. *Ann.* 14.16.1–4; Suet. *Ner.* 52. Cizek 1982, 183–4; Griffin 1984, 143–60; Fini 1994, 21; Holland 2000, 91; Hine 2006, 65; Nichols 2013, 258.
[4] Connors 1994, 225; Reitz 2006, 81: 'eines der witzigsten und amüsanten Werke der uns erhaltenen antiken Literatur', and generally 65–81; Berti 2011, 229. Cf. below 295. Though the work should properly be called *Satyricon libri* or *Satyrica* (Reitz 2006, 66–7; Murgatroyd 2013, 241), I keep its usual English title.

authoritative rake, no sycophant. Tacitus remarks on his candour: 'People liked the apparent freshness of his unconventional and unselfconscious sayings and doings'.[5] This allowed him to rib Nero for his lavish personal spending (perhaps on clothes), commenting ironically on his beggarly and penny-pinching appearance.[6] He maintained his independence to the end, committing suicide in 66, having been – probably unjustly – denounced during the second wave of Pisonian prosecutions.[7] Like Petronius, Nero had a developed sense of the ridiculous. As he had a taste for parody,[8] so he had an appetite for satire. This can be seen in his patronage both of Petronius and of Seneca as a satirical writer. That Seneca did make people laugh is demonstrated by the fact that some listeners took elements of his eulogy of Claudius, ghost-written for Nero, as comical.[9] Then, late in 54, soon after the grand state deification of Claudius, his *apotheosis*, Seneca wrote the *Apocolocyntosis*, ridiculing the event as a 'pumpkinification'.[10] Some argue that he added to it after Agrippina's death, but I follow the traditional view that we have it as originally written, probably for the *Saturnalia* (17–23 December) of 54.[11] A sophisticated Menippean satire,[12] it was a very fitting production for this 'Festival of Misrule', which also fell around Nero's birthday. Seneca describes how the established gods of Olympus reject the new deity because of his appearance, personality and earthly deeds. He thus ridicules Claudius, but he also pokes fun at the Roman Senate by couching the Olympian debate in the pompous language of its proceedings and by implicitly questioning the belief that the body had the power to create a god.[13] By having Claudius attempting to enter Heaven on the day of his death,[14] not that of his official deification, he perhaps even suggests that senatorial edicts were of no religious consequence to the Olympians, if they existed at all. For Seneca satirises the gods in general by making their debate scarcely uplifting. In particular, he disregards the usual reverence accorded to the deified Augustus, giving

---

[5] Tac. *Ann.* 16.18.2: *ac dicta facta eius quanto solutiora et quandam sui neglegentiam praeferentia, tanto gratius in speciem simplicitatis accipiebantur*, trans Grant.
[6] Plut. *Quomodo adul.* 19. Barrett *et al.* 2016, 224 and n. 111; cf. below 315. Rudich (1993, 154–5) is surely in error in interpreting this as an indication of Petronius' hidden hostility to Nero.
[7] Above 75; below 215.   [8] Below 313.   [9] Above 50.
[10] This is the usual English translation of the title of the work. Freudenburg (2015, 93–5) prefers 'The Gourd goes to Heaven' or 'The stuttering Bumpkin (i.e. Claudius the fool) goes to Heaven'.
[11] Griffin 1976, 128 and n. 3; Champlin 2003, 113; Reitz 2006, 42–7; 44; Fantham 2013, 22; Mratschek 2013, 50; Whitton 2013, 151–3; Freudenburg 2015, 96; Barrett *et al.* 2016, 45 and n. 7.
[12] Freudenburg 2015, 95–8.   [13] Senec. *Apocol.* 9 (speeches of Diespiter and Janus).
[14] Senec. *Apocol.* 1.

him a speech that parodies his well-known linguistic and sentimental tics.[15] Seneca, the committed Stoic, also makes humorous allusion to the Stoic conception of God.[16] This is not as irreverent as it first may seem. Roman Stoicism was a broad church that allowed some degree of internal criticism, which helped it to adapt to changing times.[17] However, the presence of such criticism in the *Apocolocyntosis* indicates the shotgun blast of the work, sparing nothing and nobody: 'not Augustus' *Res Gestae*, not history, not philosophy, not [*sc.* Seneca's] own *Consolation to Polybius'*. Griffin immediately qualifies this observation by exempting Nero: the *Apocolocyntosis* is 'a farce in which nothing except the young *Princeps* is treated seriously'.[18] However, the *Apocolocyntosis* makes no sense unless it was read by Nero; and to believe that he laughed at everything except its gushing references to himself,[19] which he took seriously, is to underestimate his intelligence. A better interpretation is that the *Apocolocyntosis* pokes fun at him, too. 'The boy emperor's being heralded as a god upon his accession is surely just as ridiculous as the old one's being divinized post mortem'.[20] We should therefore accept Seneca's description of Nero as a 'sun-prince', rising like the sun, under the patronage and in the image of the sun-god Apollo, as the superhuman initiator of a new Golden Age as part of the satirical fun.[21] Towards the end of 54, the notion of the dawning of a new Age of Apollo may have well sparked the poetic and popular imagination.[22] However, there is no reason to believe that either the poets or the court aristocrats for whom they wrote, including Nero, actually believed in an Apolline connection any more than they did in deification.[23] Seneca, desperate for favour, had used similar imagery to grovel to Claudius in his *Consolatio ad Polybium*,[24] but there is no reason to suppose that, under Nero, Seneca found this Claudian guff especially 'mortifying'.[25] Everyone will have recognised it as the sort of flattery expected of leading writers,[26] and Seneca could now, in the *Apocolocyntosis*, deploy the same theme as comic material: 'Apolline' praise of Nero,

[15] Griffin 1976, 131–2, 213.   [16] Senec. *Apocol.* 8. Griffin 1976, 131.

[17] Bryan 2013, 136, 143–5; Mannering 2013, 201; cf. Nichols 2013, 268.

[18] Griffin 1984, 97; cf. Griffin 1976, 131: 'Nothing here is sacred – except Nero'.

[19] E.g. Sen. *Apocol.* 4: the spinning of the thread of Nero's life.

[20] Freudenburg 2015, 104–5 and n. 42.

[21] Sen. *Apocol.* 4; Whitton 2013, 161; *contra* Levi 1949, 46.   [22] Cf. below 268.

[23] Cf. Holland 2000, 70; Champlin 2003, 133; Krüger 2012, 34; Whitton 2013, 157–61; below 269.

[24] Osgood 2011, 140–5; Romm 2014, 28–9.   [25] Osgood 2011, 255.

[26] Cf. Bartsch 1994, 134–5, 144–5; below 108; *contra* Rudich 1993, 12.

deliberately poorly written to point up its parodying of current claptrap, as 'skittish Seneca trashes flash poetastry in hyper mode'.[27]

For this reason, the *Apocolocyntosis* should not be considered as having any great political significance: as, say, forming part of an early initiative to displace Agrippina from her position of dominance.[28] Though critical of Claudius, it makes no direct criticism of Agrippina's personality or political stance;[29] and it satirises Nero along with everyone else. On the other hand, one is bound to suspect that its irreverential attitude to traditional Roman beliefs and institutions, to Claudius' character and, above all, to his deification, the culmination of Agrippina's machinations to secure Nero's succession,[30] would have roused her to fury had she read it.[31] Though, as I have argued above, Agrippina was prepared to accept some ostensible anti-Claudian sentiment,[32] she could never have borne so subversive a work. It is therefore unlikely that the *Apocolocyntosis* formed part of any court entertainment, however exclusive, for the holiday of 54.[33] The work must therefore have been written for furtive circulation between Nero and his closest friends.[34] Seneca, like Petronius, was no robotic 'yes-man'. His earlier affairs with high-ranking Julio-Claudian women, his backing of Agrippina under Claudius, perhaps his writing of drama 'saturate with subversive allusion to the Julian foundation text' (i.e. the 'Aeneid'), and certainly his connection to the Pisonian conspiracy demonstrate that he could be tempted into a gamble.[35] He liked a joke, and in late 54 the deification of Claudius gave him plenty of material. However, he was at heart a survivor, a pragmatist, not a martyr. 'He had never been a man of rigid principle'; and he was inclined to 'compromise, diplomacy and intrigue rather than direct confrontation'.[36] In late 54, Agrippina was all-powerful. Seneca would never have written a word of criticism of the preceding regime had he not been certain that he enjoyed the protection of the one person who had already shown that he could stand up to her, and

---

[27] Henderson 2013, 179 (quotation); cf. Whitton 2013, 162–5; below 269. Though Seneca later refers to a new Golden Age in his *De clementia* (2.1.3–4), this turns out (2.2.1) to be non-mythological: something that will happen only 'in large measure' (*ex magna parte*), i.e. not completely, and be due to the efforts of Nero, not fate. Cf. below 156.

[28] Above 48.   [29] Griffin 1984, 96–7; *contra* Freudenburg 2015, 97.

[30] Cf. above 15; *RIC* 1² Nero nos. 4–5: obv. Claudius as god; rev. ornamental slow *quadriga*.

[31] *Contra* Barrett 1996, 165: that she did read it, and was hurt; cf. Romm 2014, 69.   [32] Above 52.

[33] Griffin 1976, 129–30; Griffin 1984, 96–7.

[34] *Contra* Whitton 2013, 155–6, 161; Freudenburg 2015, 96.

[35] Women: e.g. Barrett 1996, 67–9; Malitz 1999, 8; Holland 2000, 33; Waldherr 2005, 26, 43–4. Drama: Buckley 2013b, 136 (quotation). Pisonian conspiracy: below 199.

[36] Griffin 1976, 135 (quotation); 339; Barrett 1996, 69 (quotation); below 157.

to whom he was personally close: Nero.[37] In short, it must have been with Nero's agreement that Seneca chanced his arm in writing and discreetly circulating the *Apocolocyntosis*.[38] The work was Seneca's and Nero's private joke, the former's birthday- and holiday-treat to the latter, in the uniquely heady atmosphere of the first *Saturnalia* after the death of Claudius.[39]

5.2.2 Critics of Nero

Nero joined in the fun. Having played jokes on Claudius while he was still alive, he now mocked the manner of his death.[40] He also wrote one poem that cruelly libelled Afranius Quintianus and led eventually to his becoming a leading member of the Pisonian conspiracy,[41] and another, *Luscio* ('The One-Eyed Man'), ribbing Claudius Pollio.[42] At first sight, other than in the *Apocolocyntosis*, he appears to have resented being the target of satire. A line in the work of the young poet, Persius, which might have been taken as an insulting reference to the *princeps*, had to be toned down by his tutor and friend, the Stoic philosopher Cornutus.[43] Persius escaped punishment, but others of the upper class suffered apparently for daring to overstep the mark. The year 62 saw the reappearance of the charge of *maiestas* with the prosecution of Antistius Sosianus for having composed and recited scandalous verses mentioning Nero.[44] Later in 62, Nero banished Fabricius Veiento, author of a libellous series of books published as 'My Will' and ordered the burning of the work, even though Veiento had not broken testamentary law.[45] Nero's banishing of the aristocratic intellectuals C. Musonius Rufus and Verginius Flavus in 65 has also been ascribed to their criticism of him.[46] However, the list of Nero's 'victims' is short, and we must be cautious in our judgement of his treatment of them. He could be no ordinary victim of satire. No high Roman aristocrat could ever have allowed *carte blanche* to critics; and Nero, as *princeps*, had to consider the dignity of the state as his own. His detractors had to play the game fairly, which meant a significant degree of self-control. If they did not, he must defend himself, but what we know of his reactions does not

---

[37] Above 51; below 281; cf. Romm 2014, 36–7.
[38] Cf. Griffin 1976, 130: that it was sanctioned by Nero alone; Whitton 2013, 152.
[39] Cf. Henderson 1905, 50–1; Whitton 2013, 153; Romm 2014, 64–5.
[40] Suet. *Ner.* 33.1; Cass. Dio 60.35.4. Griffin 1984, 96.
[41] Tac. *Ann.* 15.49.4. Reitz 2006, 24; cf. below 310.   [42] Suet. *Dom.* 1.1.
[43] Suet. *Pers.*; Berti 2011, 227; Nichols 2013, 266–7.   [44] Tac. *Ann.* 14.48.1. Above 27.
[45] Tac. *Ann.* 14.50. Cf. Furneaux 1907: the right to put such material in wills had been confirmed by Augustus (Suet. *Aug.* 56.1).
[46] Tac. *Ann.* 15.71.9. Cizek 1982, 58–9; Rudich 1993, 125; cf. below 161.

add up to tyrannical repression. Nero appears to have ignored Persius; indeed the fact that his works, albeit tinkered with by Cornutus, were published immediately after his death suggests that, living or dead, the administration made no effort to censor his output.[47] Antistius Sosianus, a notorious firebrand, had brought trouble on himself since he did what he did while praetor, making his remarks a public matter;[48] and prosecution was probably contrived by Tigellinus, not Nero.[49] Furthermore, though Sosianus, once convicted, was protected by Thrasea Paetus, Paetus bitterly criticised him and 'piled praise' on Nero.[50] Fabricius Veiento's libel was not against Nero personally, but 'against the Senate and the priesthoods'; and the administration took an interest in his case not for this but for his charging people for 'favours and the right of official appointments at court'.[51] This, incidentally, puts Veiento very close to Nero as, perhaps, a favourite joker like Vestinus Atticus and Petronius.[52] Like Vestinus, he appears to have gone too far.[53] Both Musonius Rufus and Verginius Flavus must have owed their fate more to their suspected involvement in the Pisonian conspiracy than to their writing. Like Julio-Claudian authors in general, there were probably many more upper-class humorists who teased Nero but who got away with it because they did not abuse privilege.[54]

With regard to his lower-class critics, Nero was famously tolerant. Dio says that in 59 Nero refused to prosecute people reported to be slandering him as a matricide. Suetonius records his patient response to 'those who assailed him with jibes and lampoons'. Apparently there was, towards the end of his principate, a rash of graffiti and jingles attacking him for being a matricide and a parricide, for being a lyre player more than a warrior, and for allowing the Golden House to take over Rome. However, he made no effort to find the authors, and when some of them were denounced he forbade their being severely punished.[55] Bradley explains Nero's failure to prosecute as the result of necessity: he realised that, unlike the authors of upper-class mockery, these would be difficult to find and their punishment would not end the jibes against him.[56] Yet Vitellius was able to track down such people;[57] on at least one occasion Nero knew precisely who those

---

[47] Gowers 1994, 132, 140; Kimmerle 2015, 101–2.   [48] Rudich 1993, 55–6; Fini 1994, 78.
[49] Below 187.   [50] Tac. *Ann.* 14.48.5: *multo cum honore.*
[51] Tac. *Ann.* 14.50: *in patres et sacerdotes . . . munera principis et adipiscendorum honorum ius.* Rutledge 2001, 114–15.
[52] Rudich 1993, 59–60.   [53] Below 116.   [54] Above 91; below 116.
[55] Suet. *Ner.* 39.1–2: *qui se dictis aut carminibus lacessissent;* Cass. Dio 61.16.3. Cf. Henderson 1905, 380; Cizek 1982, 58.
[56] Bradley 1978a, 238.   [57] Suet. *Vit.* 14.4.

concerned were, but still took no action; and when he did act against two named individuals who had subjected him to public insult, the philosopher Isodorus and the actor Datus, he did no more than banish them.[58] Overall, it seems that Nero was fairly relaxed in his reaction to detractors and did not ignore them simply in order to avoid giving substance to their accusations.[59]

5.2.3   Lucan and Cornutus

There remains, however, the question of Nero's fallings out with Lucan and Cornutus. The poet Lucan arrived at court around 59 when he was approaching the age of twenty.[60] With his literary genius and with Seneca as his uncle, he enjoyed immediate success, gaining high office and becoming a close friend of Nero – in fact the only member we can name of the *princeps'* poetic circle.[61] He was chosen to deliver a eulogy of Nero in 60, after which he was further honoured. Not long afterwards, he gave a first public reading of what was to be his major, though never-completed, work, the *De bello civili* ('On the Civil War', i.e. that between Julius Caesar and Pompey), also known as the 'Pharsalia'.[62] At the start of 'The Civil War' Lucan again praises Nero: his apotheosis is already ordained; as a god his job will be to watch over Rome and bring in an age of peace; but to Lucan, he is 'already divine'. Perhaps most striking is the assertion that all the suffering of the war is justified by the fact that it led to Nero's principate: 'it was for you that all this was done'.[63] Subsequently, however, there was a quarrel between Lucan and Nero which resulted in the *princeps'* forbidding the poet to recite or publish his works.[64] Tradition has it that this arose out of artistic jealousy, with Nero resenting Lucan's superior talent, and Lucan responding 'with words and acts of hostility to the prince which are still notorious'. These included insulting off-the-cuff remarks and the publication of a 'scurrilous poem' attacking Nero and his chief advisers. All this, Suetonius concludes, led to Lucan's becoming a major figure – 'almost the standard-bearer' – in the Pisonian conspiracy.[65]

---

[58] Suet. *Ner.* 39.3. Cf. Bartsch 1994, 88.   [59] *Contra* Rudich 1993, xxx; Romm 2014, 119.

[60] Suet. *Vita Luc.*; Vacca *Luc.* (for the sources see Kimmerle 2015, 110 and n. 108). Romm 2014, 122–3

[61] Below 189; Rudich 1993, 94; Fantham 2013, 25.   [62] Reitz 2006, 85; Romm 2014, 125.

[63] Suet. *Luc.*; Luc. 1. 63: *sed mihi iam numen*; 1.45: *tibi res acta est*. Reitz 2006, 82.

[64] Tac. *Ann.* 15.49.3; Suet. *Vita Luc.*; Cass. Dio 62.29.4; Vacca *Luc.*

[65] Suet. *Vita Luc.*: *verbis adversus principem [atque] factis exstantibus … [famosum carmen] … paene signifer.*

Lucan's fatal involvement in the conspiracy has prompted most modern historians to favour the political over the artistic in explaining the rupture, which returns us to the theme of frankness. On this view, Lucan had strong Republican sympathies. His opening praise of Nero is insincere, containing veiled criticism of the *princeps'* squint, obesity, baldness etc.; and as the work progressed he made his views increasingly clear. In Book 4, for example, we find him accusing Julius Caesar, founder of the Julio-Claudian dynasty, of destroying the old Republic and replacing it with a tyranny. In contrast, he praises Caesar's enemies, Pompey and, especially, the younger Cato. This is implied questioning of the legitimacy of the current Julio-Claudian political ascendancy.[66] Nero, eventually unable to bear any more such attacks, muzzled Lucan, who as a result martyred himself for the Republican cause.[67] He thus became another of those critics of the *princeps* who paid the penalty for going too far.

The political explanation is, however, open to question. The opening eulogy may be taken as no more than a manifestation of the courtesy due to a patron from a client, with the 'good' Nero's apotheosis as inevitable, but taking place in the distant future.[68] Lucan was acting *comme il faut*. He did not do it particularly well because his genius was already taking him into new territory. Lucan indeed praised the Republic but this should not, as we have seen, have caused him any problems with the administration.[69] Furthermore, his praise was not uncritical: perception of inconsistencies in the *De bello civili* allows recognition of Lucan's indulging in more than pro-Republican *parti pris*.[70] His final resorting to treason need not indicate a deep commitment to anti-Caesarianism since the Pisonian conspirators had no Republican ambitions and Lucan probably had a less than crucial role among them: he was recruited oddly late for a 'standard-bearer' and, once accused, showed weak resolve. He probably joined an enterprise well under way, in the hope of reward not martyrdom.[71] The *De bello civili* was certainly not part of a growing literary or literary-cum-Stoic 'opposition' to Nero or the Principate. This has been generally discounted; and there is no sign of the work's being regarded as seditious after Lucan's death.[72]

---

[66] Luc. 4.575–9; 4.821–3; cf. 7.638–46; 7.694–6. Cizek 1982, 244–6; Masters 1994, 158–62; Reitz 2006, 85, 91; Buckley 2013b, 139, 142; Hardie 2013, 226; Esposito 2013, 206–7.

[67] Cf. Masters 1994, 15–21; Holland 2000, 183; Hardie 2013, 226.

[68] Reitz 2006, 86; Berti 2011, 228; Hardie 2013, 229; Esposito 2013, 201, 208–11; below 269.

[69] Above 106.

[70] Masters 1994, 151–2, 155–6, 169–70; Hardie 2013, 233–4; Maes 2013, 326; and esp. most recently Kimmerle 2015, 86, 90, 110, 114, 303. Below 111.

[71] Tac. *Ann.* 15.49.3, 15.56.4. Kimmerle 2015, 278–9, 304; below 209.

[72] Griffin 1984, 155–60; Bryan 2013, 137; Kimmerle 2015, 295; below 161.

The *De bello civili* could, therefore have been written by someone still close to Nero. There is no need to assume a growing expression of pro-Republican sentiments that provoked the quarrel with Nero before Lucan had completed the *De bello civili* as we have it, or that Lucan continued to vent his spleen after he had become *persona non grata* at court making the work ever more confrontational. The quarrel could have occurred not long before the uncovering of the conspiracy and Lucan's death early in 65.[73] Closer examination shows that the sources' unanimous statement that its cause was artistic is sufficient.[74]

There was no literary renaissance under Nero. The roots of Neronian literature can be found earlier in the first century, and much of its growth continued later, to blossom fully in the 'Silver Age' of Latin literature.[75] On the other hand, there was what may be termed a distinct 'spike' in quality, sufficient to merit admiration.[76] The spike is characterised by 'neo-Augustanism': a renewed interest in the poetry of two generations before, indicated by frequent referencing of writers such as Virgil and Horace and by a 'galloping consumption of the genres of Augustan poetry – satire, epic, pastoral, panegyric'.[77] One way of exploring Augustanism was to imitate it. The 'Eclogues' of Calpurnius Siculus and the *Carmina Einsidlensia* consciously recall Virgil's 'Eclogues', with an occasional echo of the 'Georgics'. An alternative approach was to react against the Augustan 'classics' and aim at 'modernism'. This, shaped by the practice of *declamatio*, public reading, and steeped in the love of the *sententia*, the pithy remark, exhibited new, rhetorical, styles and language. Constantly seeking out the unexpected and the grand, it was capable of high-mindedness but often undercut it 'by a witty turn of phrase, a dazzling show of irreverent ingenuity'. It depicted the very real in very artificial language.[78] Its practitioners were keen to overtake their predecessors: to 'dare the undared'.[79] Some of this reaction was 'friendly' in the sense that it explored questions raised by Augustan writers. Buckley, for example, sees Seneca, in his *Hercules*, 'evoking and then exploding Virgilian *virtus*' but thereby 'not so much distorting as revealing some of the problems with the nature of *furor*'.[80] Other reaction was more barbed.

---

[73] Kimmerle 2015, 113–14.   [74] Kimmerle 2015, 110–13.   [75] Berti 2011, 220.

[76] Maes 2013, 306, 325; cf. Buckley 2013a, 209; Dinter 2013, 5; Mannering 2013, 189.

[77] Gowers 1994, 131 (quotation); Reitz 2006, 17; Maes 2013, 309–11; Nichols 2013, 263, 269; Ker 2015, 109.

[78] Berti 2011, 220; Maes 2013, 311 (quotation); Murgatroyd 2013, 250–2.

[79] Dinter 2013, 7–8, quoting Sen. *Thy.* 18–20: *inausae audeat*; cf. Buckley 2013a, 216.

[80] Buckley 2013a, 208, 216.

Parody of Virgil (and of Seneca and even Lucan) has been detected in Petronius' *Satyricon* in the depiction of the author and singer, Eumolpus, though this is debated.[81] Clearer is the unclassical brilliance of the *Satyricon* as a whole. Challenging in its constant ambiguity, it is not a work that should be seen as reflecting 'everyday life in Neronian Italy'.[82] Persius' collection of six satires was still unfinished when he died in 62, aged 27. His style is original, complex and obscure. His poems, basically pessimistic about human nature, make no specific contemporary references but contain harsh general criticism of the poets and orators of his day.[83] Nichols plausibly suggests that these are the neo-Augustan imitators of the classics, 'not the canonical poets who originated such practices, but rather the poetasters he likens to magpies and ravens . . . the contemptible mimics who aspire to style, neglecting substance'.[84] This returns us to Lucan: no weak imitator but a 'literary parricide', who embraced Virgil then stabbed him in the back.[85] Lucan's genius lay in his choice of topic and his manner of treating it. Instead of taking a story from the distant past and simply narrating it or giving it an artificial contemporary meaning, Lucan took one from recent history which had real contemporary resonances.[86] The sounding-board of these resonances was Winterling's 'paradox': that of an autocracy which, through the fiction of a 'restored' Republic, legitimised itself as the predestined heir of the real Republic.[87] It was a subject whose time was ripe. The pain of the civil wars had made earlier consideration of the consequent political change impossible, but by the mid-first century, the majority of the political community will have accepted that the old order was gone and that the Principate was there to stay.[88] Lucan 'dared the undared' by attempting a first contact with the paradox. At the heart of the 'restored' Republic is the *princeps*, so Lucan, after announcing the awful theme of the *De bello civili*, directly addresses the current incumbent, Nero,[89] asserts that civil war was a worthwhile price for his rule and proclaims him his muse: 'You are sufficient inspiration for any Roman poet'.[90] Lucan's 'Civil War' thus reveals itself as Virgil's 'Aeneid' turned upside down. There is no divine inspiration, no divine destiny for the

---

[81] Petron. *Sat.* 89. Berti 2011, 229; Murgatroyd 2013, 252–4; Kimmerle 2015, 115; Setaioli 2015, 261; cf. below 112.

[82] Murgatroyd 2013, 241–3, 245–8, 255; cf. below 296.

[83] Pers. 1; Suet. *Pers.* Levi 1949, 69–70; Reitz 2006, 99–101; Nichols 2013, 258, 260–1, 264.

[84] Nichols 2013, 265–6; cf. above 104.   [85] Dinter 2013, 7 (quotation); cf. Masters 1994, 154–6.

[86] Romm 2014, 123; Kimmerle 2015, 270, 276–7, 292, 294.   [87] Kimmerle 2015, 275–6, 292.

[88] Kimmerle 2015, 269, 277–8, 284, 291, 294, 298, 302.   [89] Kimmerle 2015, 294.

[90] Luc. 1.66: *tu satis ad uires Romana in carmina dandas.*

Julian clan: indeed no divine intervention at all. What brings the dynasty to power and creates the Principate is long, bloody, civil strife. Lucan picks up the cardinal Roman virtues – *virtus, pietas, fides* – which Virgil made incarnate in Aeneas, only to depict them piecemeal and misused. The 'Civil War' likewise subverts Virgil's 'Georgics' and 'Eclogues': the world that emerges after the conflict is not the result of the victory of good over bad, and so 'not a new Golden Age, but an eternal age of enslavement to an imperial master', 'a Stoic ordered universe thrown into disorder'.[91] So was the journey from Republic to autocracy worth the price? Having raised the question, Lucan offers no straight answer, no simplistic moral equations: Republic = good, Principate = bad.[92] The horror of 'profoundly unspeakable' civil war, 'the pity of it',[93] clearly stimulated him personally yet it may also have been, along with the Troy theme,[94] part of the Zeitgeist thanks to growing concern about the possible recurrence of trouble as Nero failed to produce an heir.[95] Lucan, along with others, will have been aware that the Republic, for all its genuine aristocratic freedoms, had brought bloodshed and misery, while the Principate, with its restriction of those freedoms, had brought peace and prosperity. Such tension, part of the 'paradox', helps explain his inconsistencies: Caesar has vices and virtues; Pompey and Cato have virtues and vices; *libertas* means different things to different people. The *De bello civili* is, indeed, characterised by 'narratorial unreliability'.[96] Neither Lucan nor his characters offer authoritative judgements. Consistent with the enduring Roman failure to produce a considered analysis of the Principate,[97] both present different views of the conflict. Lucan's view of contemporary politics is, in fact, full of 'confusion, contradiction, ambiguity, and ambivalence'.[98] This made for a very difficult work which many contemporaries, like many modern readers, must have struggled to follow.[99] While staying true to the basic facts, Lucan, like a modern film director, ruthlessly compresses, reorders and rewrites the events of the Civil War to create not a history or a political

---

[91] Bartsch 1994, 182; Dinter 2013, 7; Hardie 2013, 227–8 (quotation), 229–31, 236 (quotation); Maes 2013, 316.

[92] Cf. Kimmerle 2015, 269, 299–300, 305–7.

[93] Kimmerle 2015, 294: 'das eigentliche Unsagbare'; Thomas Hardy, *The Pity of It* (1915), one stanza of which in particular suits the theme of the *De bello civili*: 'Then seemed a Heart crying: "Whosoever they be/At root and bottom of this, who flung this flame/Between kin-folk kin-tongued even as are we,/Sinister, ugly, lurid, be their fame;/May their familiars grow to shun their name,/And their brood perish everlastingly."'

[94] Above 79; below 112.   [95] Cf. below 114, 179.

[96] Kimmerle 2015, e.g. 269, 293, 299, 305.   [97] Above 19.   [98] Rudich 1993, 94.

[99] Cf. Hardie 2013, 234.

tract, but brilliant drama and magnificent, unorthodox, revolutionary, poetry, fully comprehensible only to those who already know what happened.[100]

Nero, as a man of letters, was part of the neo-Augustan wave,[101] as is reflected in his enthusiastic taking up of the Troy story. Scenes from the legend decorated the *Domus Transitoria* and are the dominant element in the mythological decoration of the *Domus Aurea* Pavilion.[102] Nero probably wrote two major works on its theme: the *Halosis*, 'The sack of Troy', part of which he may have declaimed when viewing the Fire; and the *Troica*, 'Troy', a major epic.[103] Though he injected novelty into the story by favouring Paris over Hector,[104] his generally conservative treatment exposed him to criticism from the modernists. As we have seen, there are some elements in the *Satyricon* which may be interpreted as parody of Virgil but which may just as well be interpreted as a dig at Nero: 'Eumolpus', like the *princeps*, writes a 'Sack of Troy', always gets a bad reaction but always comes back for more, except at the end, where he switches to lighter, salacious material and achieves success.[105] More probable is that Nero was among those Persius had in mind when he attacked mediocrity. It has been suggested that the controversial line already noted was not only a personal insult to Nero, but also a parody of his poetry; that his work includes other unflattering allusions to the *princeps*; and that he criticised excessive Hellenism.[106] Lucan, likewise, may have made fun of Nero's work in his infamous exclamation while moving his bowels in a public latrine.[107] Differences between the modernists and the *princeps* were bound to cause tension. In the case of Petronius (if applicable) and Persius, the regime seems to have characteristically laughed off or ignored what was said.[108] To explain away Nero's attitude to Persius and lampooners as 'autistic' is unjustified.[109] Again, this was no police state.[110] The same licence was probably initially extended to Lucan,[111] but then withdrawn. Though the rift was artistic rather than political, it is unlikely to have been

---

[100] Masters 1994, 153–4; cf. Hardie 2013, 237; Kimmerle 2015, 306. Cf. Reitz 2006, 95–6: 'Die Perversität des Bürgerkriegsgeschehens ... Mord, Selbstmord, Massenselbstmord bilden die Anlaß für ekstatische Szenen'.
[101] Gowers 1994, 132–3; Fantham 2013, 27.
[102] Bragantini 2011, 190–1, 196; Lorenz 2013, 375–6; below 242, 248.
[103] Levi 1949, 73; Reitz 2006, 23, 83–4; below 238.
[104] Charlesworth 1950, 70; Malitz 1999, 41.
[105] Maes 2013, 323; Murgatroyd 2013, 252–3; cf. below 114.
[106] Above 105; Rudich 1993, 61–2; Reitz 2006, 24; Dinter 2013, 5; Maes 2013, 310; Nichols 2013, 266–9.
[107] Suet. *Vita Luc.* Reitz 2006, 24.   [108] Cf. above 107.   [109] Gowers 1994, 132, 140.
[110] Above 90.   [111] Cf. Masters 1994, 170.

caused by Nero's childish envy of Lucan's talents and jealousy of his fame.[112] The *princeps* believed that he possessed natural sporting and artistic talents, but was doubtful of their extent. This basic lack of confidence explains his willingness to devote himself to hours of training and practice, and to be sedulous in his observation of competition rules.[113] Nero actually possessed an above-average range of sporting and artistic skills. This permitted him to see the potential in Lucan, whose abilities cannot have been evident to all. There must have been many contemporaries who dismissed his work as modernist rubbish. We should give Nero, helped perhaps by Lucan's similar dislike of bloodshed, disdain for conventional religion, and interest in superstition, credit for taking him on as a client. Above-average is not, however, the same as genius, and as a poet Nero will have quickly found himself inferior to his protégé.[114] A gap will have opened up between them, but again the reason for the ultimate break was probably not simply Nero's petulant artistic jealousy, 'a trivial motive'.[115] Nero did not gag one of the leading literary figures of his day because he could not endure his celebrity.[116] He was not naturally vindictive;[117] and he knew that by muzzling Lucan he would not destroy his superiority.

We should consider Lucan's likely culpability in the quarrel. Two years older than Nero, and possessed of an 'insane self-assurance',[118] he may well have intimidated Nero, making his contempt for his conservatism plain and so hitting the *princeps'* most vulnerable spot, his self-confidence.[119] Lucan's genius allowed him to devise taunts that would have made a saint swear; he cannot have been easy to know.[120] But we should also take into account Lucan's artistic dependence on Nero. His declaration that Nero, not the muses, was his inspiration was his way of advertising that he was embarking upon an unprecedented work.[121] New poetry for a new age – the age of Nero – sounds positive, but has a negative side. Lucan was probably committed to writing about the Civil War even before he came to court. Raised within the senatorial tradition and rejecting the Augustan historical teleology of Virgil, he was, despite his refusal to take sides, bound to judge the conflict badly. The proemium to the *De bello civili* is already

---

[112] *Contra* Rudich 1993, 94.   [113] Cf. below 292.
[114] Cf. Reitz 2006, 85: Nero's verses on the Tigris, subsequently ridiculed by Lucan, may have been intended to outdo *Luc.* 3.261–3.
[115] Masters 1994, 170.   [116] Maes 2013, 308, 326.   [117] Below 186, 219, 283–4, 322.
[118] Graves 1956, 14.   [119] Cf. below 285; Kimmerle 2015, 115.
[120] Cf. above 107; Kimmerle 2015, 112.   [121] Esposito 2013, 208, 211.

framed by pessimistic material;[122] and the work as a whole presents Julius
Caesar and his descendants as something other than the creators and
legitimate protectors of a 'restored' Republic. Though Lucan will have
appreciated Nero's patronage, he will also have seen him as part of the
story, and must have looked for signs that identified the *princeps* as a Julio-
Claudian tyrant. Yet he must also have been frustrated by the fact that
Nero, unlike Caesar, was no worthy villain.[123] Rather, Nero, a poor poet
and an inert ruler, was a *fainéant*, allowing others to rule the world while,
in his childlessness, he let it drift back onto the reefs of conflict. Lucan may
also have seen Nero as an artistic traitor. In a process that ran from 63 into
64 and culminated in Tigellinus' banquet, Nero reinvented himself as a
popular figure.[124] This cannot have gone down well with politically
conservative aristocrats, already alarmed at his growing inclination to act
the professional entertainer.[125] In addition, however, the intelligentsia may
have been dismayed by his switching from intellectual and literary to
melodramatic and popular composition and performance. This began with
his singing of one of his own compositions during the Fire of 64, and
manifested itself fully in 65, just after Lucan's death, in his performing the
part of Niobe, possibly another of his compositions. In this he revealed his
liking for the ever-popular theme of 'the wronged woman'.[126] Melodra-
matically written and executed, these performances were, apparently, a
great hit with the Roman public. Suetonius reports that Vitellius ordered
the public performance of one of Nero's compositions and was 'the first to
jump for joy' at it, which suggests widespread popular approval.[127] 'Songs
demand a special talent and a simplicity far removed from the profusion of
learned allusions of Latin poetry traditionally associated with Nero'.[128]
Since Nero's new direction was a challenge to the intellectuals' monopoly
of culture, Lucan may also have despised a vulgarising Nero drifting away
from him and his kind.[129]

I propose that Lucan, ever more frustrated and dissatisfied with Nero,
used the frankness of his court to goad him into acting out of character. It
is unlikely that Nero ever understood what was going on in Lucan's head,
but he was bound to respond as he did to the venom of his insults,

---

[122] Esposito 2013, 209.   [123] Cf. Hardie 2013, 233–4.   [124] Below 293.
[125] E.g. below 205, 230.   [126] Suet. *Ner.* 21.2. Waldherr 2005, 127; below 238.
[127] Suet. *Vit.* 11.2: *primus exsultans.*
[128] Reitz 2006, 22–23: 'Lieder erfordern ein besonderes Talent und eine Einfachheit, die weit von
     dem gelehrten Anspielungsreichtum der lateinischen Gedichte entfernt ist, die man in der
     Tradition mit Nero verbindet'.
[129] Cf. Cizek 1982, 244.

allowing Lucan to see himself as the injured party. Lucan was pampered, self-centred and self-seeking, at the end committing perjury by naming his own mother as a Pisonian conspirator.[130] He was therefore probably highly sensitive to any slighting of himself, even by himself: he perhaps suffered self-loathing because he recognised his dependence on the *princeps*, both artistic and material. Though he had brought most of this upon himself, he will have bitterly resented Nero's efforts to bring him to heel. With his career threatened, he and his supporters ascribed what had happened solely to Nero's artistic jealousy, a charge that future generations were happy to take up in the creation of Nero 'the monster'. It is no surprise that Lucan, aroused, rash and politically naïf, drifted into membership of an aristocratic conspiracy.[131] Nero's resentment probably ran less deep than his. Generally, he was someone who, having forged a close relationship, tended not to break it.[132] He may well have failed to realise the depth of Lucan's antipathy towards him, and even have hoped for a reconciliation. Lucan's punishment was relatively light: he was prevented from putting what he had written before the public, but not from writing more. Nero's action may even have been protective: 'Nero felt he had to put a stop to his impertinence, which was harmful not only to himself but to his network of friends'.[133] If, at this stage, Lucan had been suspected of real Republican extremism, he would have paid a much higher price. Nero's continuing tolerance would have made Lucan's subsequent betrayal even more of a shock to him.[134]

Similar artistic considerations may explain Nero's banishment of Cornutus for disparaging his projected history of Rome in heroic verse. L. Annaeus Cornutus, probably a freedman of the family of Seneca and Lucan, was a famous Stoic thinker of the day. Immensely versatile, he led one of the intellectual circles already mentioned. He has been proposed as the author of the *Octavia*; and he taught Lucan and Persius.[135] Persius' works are strongly Stoic in tone, and contain praise of Cornutus.[136] Persius was thought capable of poking fun at Nero,[137] and some believe that if he had lived his Stoicism would, like that of other 'imperial dissidents', have caused his destruction.[138] It is therefore tempting to see Cornutus' circle as a likely centre of 'Stoic opposition' and to interpret Cornutus' sentence as state repression of political opponents. This is unlikely. There was no

---

[130] Below 215.   [131] Below 209.   [132] Below 282.   [133] Masters 1994, 171.
[134] Cf. below 211.   [135] Bryan 2013, 136–9; Nichols 2013, 267; above 79.
[136] Nichols 2013, 267   [137] Nichols 2013, 258–9, 265; above 105, 112.
[138] Nichols 2013, 270.

concerted Stoic opposition.[139] Nero took no particular notice of Persius;[140] and there is an alternative explanation for his treatment of Cornutus. According to Dio, Cornutus objected that the projected verse-history would be too long and unattractive. I take this to mean that, like Nero's melodramatic songs, the work would be simply vulgar: a vehicle for his enthusiasms as a popular entertainer, not something of intellectual value. Cornutus, indeed, met the countercharge – that one of his favourite authors, the third century BC Stoic, Chrysippus of Stoli, was excessively prolific – with the observation that Chrysippus' works helped their readers to live their lives, implying that Nero's epic would not.[141] Since the incident is likely to have fallen towards the end of Nero's principate, probably in 65 or 66 (closer dating is impossible),[142] Cornutus may have been made vulnerable by the uncovering of the Pisonian conspiracy and Nero's deep hurt at the duplicity of close friends. Politics may therefore have played a part in his banishment, but his quarrel with Nero was basically literary. There is no cause to use his case as evidence that, as a matter of course, Nero throttled criticism. Like his treatment of the Christians, this was one of those occasions when a rare act of apparently wanton viciousness drew attention.

5.3   Saying the Unsayable

We are left with the impression of a court where people were not afraid to air at least some of their opinions: one in which those close to Nero felt emboldened, with caution, to touch on controversial subjects. Nero's character provoked pointed teasing from his close friends. According to Plutarch, the notoriously spendthrift Otho chaffed Nero and played tricks on him on account of his meanness, apparently much to Nero's delight.[143] Vestinus Atticus, consul *ordinarius* in 65, had earlier done much the same. According to Tacitus, Nero and Vestinus had once been very close, despite the latter's notoriously 'headstrong and difficult' nature, which says much for the *princeps*' general tolerance. However, the relationship eventually soured as Nero came to fear 'the masterful friend who so often mocked him with that rough humour which, if it draws too largely on the truth, leaves pungent memories behind'.[144] Vestinus' death in the wake of the

---

[139] Below 161.   [140] Above 106, 112.   [141] Cass. Dio 62.29.2–3; cf. Nichols 2013, 271.
[142] Cf. Rudich 1993, 150–1; Nichols 2013, 271.   [143] Plut. *Galb.* 19.3. Cf. above 102 (Petronius).
[144] Tac. *Ann.* 15.52.4; 15.68.3–4: *praecipitem et insociabilem . . . ille ferociam amici metuit, saepe asperis facetiis inlusus, quae ubi multum ex vero traxere, acrem sui memoriam relinquunt.* Bradley 1978a, 208–9; above 106.

Pisonian conspiracy is explicable on political grounds,[145] but what may be taken from the story is that Nero had, for a significant period, tolerated penetrating personal criticism from a leading senator. It is likely that Vestinus' barbs had to do with both Nero's character and, given Vestinus' known propensity to profess Republican sentiments,[146] his position as *princeps*. It is reasonable to suppose that Lucan, too, treated Nero to his views on the unhealthy relationship between autocracy and tyranny.[147] But Nero gave as good as he got. A piece of advice in Seneca's *De clementia* of 55, that Nero should bridle his tongue, suggests that a degree of badinage was soon accepted practice. Equally illuminating is Seneca's later revelation in the same work that he was instrumental in broadcasting one of Nero's *sententiae*, even though this 'not intended for others' ears': badinage was taken up and repeated.[148]

Though the Pisonian conspiracy badly rattled the court, there are signs of continuing banter, written and verbal. In 66, in the assault on Thrasea Paetus and his followers, a young poet, Curtius Montanus, was accused of being a 'scribbler of abominable verses' and exiled: another upper-class satirist who had overstepped the mark.[149] More important, also in 66, probably just before Nero's departure for Greece, the prominent freedman Vatinius exclaimed, 'I hate you, Caesar, for being of senatorial rank'. Following Dio, this is normally interpreted as a courtier's toadying remark, appropriate to a time when Nero had turned against the Senate.[150] However, global hostility to senators should not be accepted without question;[151] and Vatinius' words fit the pattern of intimate banter already noted. Tacitus tells us that he owed his influence at court to his 'scurrilous wit' and his acting the clown.[152] Thus Vatinius was the court fool, licensed to say the unsayable. The unsayable, known to all the political community but never formally debated, was that 'restored' Republic and Principate were mutually contradictory institutions. In saying what he did, Vatinius made fun of the contradiction. The loyal servant of an autocratic *princeps*, a 'kingsman', he had the effrontery to address the same *princeps* in his alternative identity as a Republican senator, pointing up the paradox that the *princeps* could not, but did, play both roles. His daring criticism was not of the Senate but of the Principate. Clever banter continued after the

---

[145] Above 72.   [146] Above 90.   [147] Cf. Reitz 2006, 86.

[148] Sen. *Clem.* 1.7.4–8.1, 2.1.1: *nec alienis auribus data.* Below 156.

[149] Tac. *Ann.* 16.28.2: *detestanda carmina [factitans]*, 16.29.4; cf. Elsner and Masters 1994, 3; *contra* Rudich 1993, 177–8.

[150] Tac. *Ann.* 15.34.2; Cass. Dio 63.15.1. E.g. Grant 1970, 179, 228; Rutledge 2001, 115.

[151] E.g. above 99.   [152] Tac. *Ann.* 15.34.3: *facetis scurrilibus.*

Greek trip. According to Dio, Nero asked one of his philosopher friends if he approved his marrying Sporus/'Poppaea', to be told: 'You do well, Caesar, to seek the company of such wives. Would that your father had the same ambition and had lived with a similar consort!'[153]

Acceptance of banter and its dissemination allows a better understanding of certain incidents in the Neronian principate. As Rudich remarks, the fanciful charge made against Agrippina in 55, of plotting rebellion with Rubellius Plautus, may have been based on one of her off-the-cuff remarks.[154] And as Barrett says, Nero's 'flippant comments', especially his remarks about a concubine who resembled his mother, may well have caused talk of incest between the pair.[155] Other sexual banter may lie behind Suetonius' report that according to Nero no man was ever fully chaste, and that he pardoned all other faults of those who confessed their lewdness to him.[156] An exchange of literary quotations between Nero and his intimates may have prompted the *princeps* to indulge his histrionic fancies when viewing the Great Fire.[157] Nero's comment that keeping expenditure within budget was mean and stingy while wasting and squandering took real taste and genius also surely falls in the same category.[158] If accepted, 'banter' takes some of the sting from the most infamous of Nero's utterances. Take, for example, his observation that no previous emperor knew the limits of his power.[159] Gaius had made a similar remark.[160] Recalled by Nero and his friends, this could have formed the basis of a private conversation, part jocular, part serious, about the nature of power in Rome: some exploration of the 'paradox'. Then, however, leaked, taken up by Suetonius and quoted out of context, it could be made to sound like the blood-curdling musings of a tyrant.[161] Court conversation about the realities and problems of the current system may likewise have been the kernel of truth in Nero's purported threats to destroy the Senate and hand government positions over to *equites*, and even, in 68, to kill all exiles and all people of Gallic descent in Rome, to poison the Senate and to fire Rome.[162] Similarly, the praetor Larcius' offer of a large fee to Nero if he would sing for him at a private engagement rings more true as a

---

[153] Cass. Dio 62.28.3a.   [154] Rudich 1993, 19–20; below 177.
[155] Cass. Dio 61.11.4. Barrett 1996, 183 (quotation; cf. 53, on similar accusations against Gaius); below 312.
[156] Suet. *Ner.* 29. Cf. Winterling 2007, 134, on Suetonius' taking Gaius' 'cynical jokes' ('zynische Witzen') too seriously; below 313.
[157] Cf. Holland 2000, 164.   [158] Suet. *Ner.* 30.1. Rathbone 2008, 277–8.
[159] Suet. *Ner.* 37.3: *negavit quemquam principum scisse quid sibi liceret.*
[160] Suet. *Cal.* 29.1: *memento omnia mihi et in omnis licere.* Bradley 1978a, 225.
[161] Cf. Bradley 1978a, 225–6 (more cautiously).   [162] Suet. *Ner.* 36.1, 43.1. Cf. above 99–100.

piece of court banter than as a serious proposition. Tradition hostile to both Nero and Tigellinus, who is supposed to have exacted the fee even though the concert was not given, turned what was said against both, making the first ridiculous and the second rapacious.[163]

Nero, at ease with friends, was imprudently provoking, but where there was an element of free speech he might justifiably expect to enjoy some of this himself.

5.4 Wider Neronian Culture

Some degree of open speech may have been encouraged by the fact that Nero's principate was a time of heightened intellectual activity. Under him, a number of aristocratic social circles were home to significant enquiry by statesmen, philosophers, poets and natural scientists.[164] In Cizek's words, 'During the first century, cultural activity never shone so brightly as it did under Nero'.[165] More recently, Ginsberg has characterised 'Nero and Neronian culture' as being 'thirsty for knowledge and a vibrant milieu for innovation'.[166] The range and originality of Neronian literature have already been explored.[167] The rest may be considered under three broad headings: architecture and art, science and exploration.

5.4.1 Architecture and Art

In architecture there was great innovation in concept, design and execution. This is characterised by a masterly treatment of internal space and light, particularly observable in both stages of the Golden House Pavilion and brought to perfection in its Octagonal Suite, 'one of the most precocious designs in the history of western architecture'.[168] However, it also found expression in many other features of the Golden House complex, for example the revolving domed ceiling of the grand banqueting hall in the *Domus Tiberiana*/Neronian palace, confused by Suetonius with the hall itself:[169]

---

[163] Suet. *Ner.* 21.1; Cass. Dio 63.21.2.   [164] Above 79.

[165] Cizek 1982, 363: 'Jamais au 1er siècle l'activité cultural ne fut aussi brillante que sous le règne de Néron'; generally, 363–74.

[166] Ginsberg 2014.   [167] Above 109; cf. Maes 2013, 323.

[168] Ball 2003, 26, 161–2, 219–20 (quotation), 228, 240.

[169] Suet. *Ner.* 31.2; Bradley 1978a, 180; Elsner 1994, 119; Meyboom and Moormann 2012, 133; Beste and Hesberg 2013, 326. Meyboom and Moormann 2013, 21–2; Quenemoen 2014, 70; below 249, 255.

There were dining-rooms with fretted ceilings of ivory, whose panels could turn and shower down flowers and were fitted with pipes for sprinkling the guests with perfumes. The main banquet-hall was circular and constantly revolved day and night, like the heavens.

Architecture merged with art in finish and decoration. There was the golden gleam of the Golden House Pavilion.[170] Pliny I tells of the use of a transparent stone, newly discovered in Cappadocia, in the refurbishment of the Temple of Fortune. This, like the revolving domed ceiling, showed 'a penchant for surprise and effect' never matched by the Flavians.[171] From Pliny I we also learn of the development under Nero of methods of painting stone to enhance its appearance, and of the invention of a turtleshell veneer that looked like wood.[172] Though Pliny dismisses both as manifestations of an unnecessary craving for luxury, the former reflects the demands of an emerging class of consumers below the aristocracy, and the latter a thrill in experimentation for its own sake. In this respect Bragantini notes the clarity of colour and rapid, nervous style of the wall-paintings of the 'Baths of Livia'.[173] The best known element of Neronian architectural decoration is, indeed, wall-painting. Lorenz identifies significant innovations at the great villa near Oplontis, at Pompeii and in the Golden House Pavilion. These play with reality and perspective merging actual and virtual gardens, making small houses and rooms seem larger; or they depict mythical scenes in ways which require viewers to create meaning for themselves, outside the actual story. All this resulted in 'a hugely complex visual environment', affording 'more audience-led, discursive forms of interaction':[174] a different type of banter. Painting took on a life of its own, becoming more than decoration.[175]

As with literature, Neronian engagement with art and architecture should be regarded as a spike in a longer line of development: a brilliant but short-lived 'firework'.[176] Innovation in wall-painting was founded on advances of the late first century BC and early first century AD;[177] and Pliny I records that the painting of stone began under Claudius.[178] The

---

[170] Below 264.   [171] Plin. *HN* 36.163.1. Beste and Hesberg 2013, 328.
[172] Plin. *HN* 35.3, 16.233.   [173] Bragantini 2011, 191.
[174] Lorenz 2013, 365–6, 367–8 (quotation), 370–1, 375 (quotation), 378–9; cf. Bragantini 2011, 196–7.
[175] Bragantini 2011, 191.   [176] Viscogliosi 2011a, 92.
[177] Moormann 2003, 388; Lorenz 2013, 364, 365–6, 369, 371–3; Meyboom and Moormann 2013, 280.
[178] Plin. *HN* 35.3.

concept of a Neronian architectural 'revolution' likewise needs to be nuanced.[179] The vast amount of building work after the Fire did not provoke but accelerated the exploitation of concrete and 'structural innovation and constructional efficiencies in this medium'.[180] It was this that produced the interior space and light of the Golden House,[181] but 'late first-century architecture was firmly rooted in established conventions', and though innovation flourished under Nero it sometimes led nowhere. It was tamed by the Flavians, before flaring up again under Hadrian and his sumptuous villa at Tivoli.[182] On the other hand, as with the literature, artistic and architectural developments under Nero deserve great respect and should not be crudely characterised as yet 'another symptom of the Neronian interest in perverting reality', or seen as an example of an absolute ruler using architecture to flaunt his 'world domination and immortal status'.[183] 'Innovative and experimental, grandiose in intention and execution ... [their] bold exuberance is anything but the baroque death-throes of an age of madness'.[184] The administration had the courage to give architects, such as Severus and Celer, who designed the Golden House, and artists, such as Famulus, who decorated it,[185] their heads, and generally benefited from such trust.[186] Alongside grand domestic and public architecture and art there were more down-to-earth projects, such as the Campanian navigations and major canals planned in Gaul and Greece.[187] Though most of them were never brought to completion, these too are admirable in their conception and, beyond their immediate usefulness, suggest a widening of horizons that takes us next to Neronian science.

5.4.2   Science

Innovation in building was intimately connected with innovation in science. The evolution of Neronian wall-painting may be seen as experimentation with space;[188] and some ingenious mechanism was necessary for the domed ceiling to revolve in concert with the heavens.[189] More broadly, this was also the time when Pliny I was collecting material that he

---

[179] *Contra* Ball 2003, e.g. 25.
[180] Ball 2003, 24–5, 227, 264, 274–7; Quenemoen 2014, 65 (quotation).
[181] Shotter 2008, 122; Quenemoen 2014, 70–3 and figure 4.2, 75–9.
[182] Ball 2003, 25; Quenemoen 2014, 63–4 (quotation); cf. 71, 74; cf. below 260, 263.
[183] Quenemoen 2014, 68.   [184] Elsner and Masters 1994, 5.
[185] Tac. *Ann.* 15.42.1; Pliny *HN* 35.120. Lorenz 2013, 363.
[186] Tac. *Ann.* 15.42.1. Though cf. below 262.   [187] Below 342.   [188] Lorenz 2013, 374, 378.
[189] Cf. Bradley 1978a, 180; Beste 2011b, 171, 175.

would eventually incorporate into his *Naturalis Historia*, published under the Flavians. Another contemporary writer with a strong interest in the physical world was Seneca, author of *Naturales Quaestiones*, written probably after 62, but researched earlier.[190] Seneca was interested in the natural world because he believed that its study gave human beings codes of morality and behaviour in life and freed them from fear of death.[191] However, though his works contain some odd omissions, for example the Fire of 64, he had a scientific curiosity comparable to that of Pliny I.[192] Hine notes his interest in magnification and refraction, and comments: 'Seneca may have believed that the pursuit of technological innovation is no business of the philosopher ... but he is ready to draw on recent technology when it will help his argument'.[193] He was, perhaps, responsible for Nero's ophthalmic emerald.[194]

A more down-to-earth aspect of contemporary scientific endeavour is the *De re rustica*, written by Columella who, apparently, also moved in contemporary court circles. This is a systematic and detailed handbook of farming, the most important sector of the imperial economy. Though innovatory both in style and content, and strongly moral in character, it is clear in meaning and was plainly written for hard-nosed owners of large-scale, slave-worked, estates, producing crops for the market.[195] It suggests both broad practical knowledge and open-minded reading of Punic, Greek and Roman material.[196] Interest in scientific farming is perhaps also discernible in Calpurnius Siculus, whose second eclogue shows a keen interest in animal husbandry and horticulture, and whose fifth amounts to a detailed summary of the pastoral year, with more than a passing nod to veterinary medicine.[197] Columella presents himself as an expert, in a society of experts, his work ranking 'with treatises on other fields of knowledge, like oratory, science, or even dancing and singing';[198] and this was, indeed, an age of technical handbooks, in both Latin and Greek. The latter have recently been very usefully brought together by Hansen. Hansen notes, for example, the pharmacologist Pedanius Dioscurides, possibly an army surgeon and 'probably the most renowned pagan Greek writer of the Neronian period', whose five volumes on plants and their medicinal uses, the *De materia medica*, were to win high praise from Galen

---

[190] Hine 2006, 49, 66–7, 68–72; Reitz 2006, 35–6, 128–9; Doody 2013, 288; Mannering 2013, 191; Berno 2015, esp. 82–3.
[191] Mannering 2013, 191–3, 196–7; Berno 2015, 83, 85–8.   [192] Romm 2014, xviii, 27.
[193] Hine 2006, 52–3.   [194] Below 304–5.
[195] Milnor 2005, 265; Reitz 2006, 121–8; Reitz 2013.   [196] Reitz 2013, 280–2.
[197] Calp. *Ecl.* 2.36–51, 5.51.   [198] Columella *Rust.* 1, pref. 3–4. Reitz 2013, 282.

and were consulted for centuries to come. Another medical man, Nero's personal physician, Andromachus II, dedicated a long treatise on poisons and their antidotes to the *princeps*. (One suspects that the charge of Nero 'the poisoner' owed much to this.) The best known of such writers today is Heron of Alexandria, whose great works were the *Mechanica* and the *Automata*. Heron, albeit somewhat anachronistically, deserves the title of 'engineer' for his work on machines. Most famous of these is the first we know to have harnessed the propulsive power of steam. Hansen calls him 'an author of handbooks in the best sense of the word', producing material that was innovative and up to date.[199]

Appreciation of the scientific spirit of the age points up the dangers of isolating certain aspects of Neronian life and interpreting them out of context in order to confirm one's own preconceptions. Gowers uses *aqua decocta* – 'boiled-down'/'rendered'/'concentrated' and refrigerated water, supposedly invented by Nero – as metaphor for the boiled-down nature of Neronian poetry: '. . . most Neronians write as though they are conscious that the heat is on, that they will be burnt out all too soon'. The Neronian poets, like the *princeps* himself, lived life fast and grew up fast, but remained immature: 'outgrown adolescents took on themselves too great a task and withered away too soon'.[200] This is to go too far. Pliny I's account of *aqua decocta* comes in a dispassionate summary of a debate about what sort of water was the healthiest to drink, in which boiled, cooled water emerged as the most highly recommended. In inventing – or, perhaps more likely, sponsoring – *aqua decocta*, Nero was exhibiting no absurd personal fancy, reflecting the fevered conditions of his court, but following the best medical opinion of the day.[201] Likewise, the infamous 'water-organ episode' of 68 when, in the middle of a crisis, Nero seemed more interested in the latest musical instruments than in saving his principate, may have hidden depths. In confirming the *princeps*' liking for gadgets, it raises the possibility that, as Hine puts it, 'the emperor was a serious sponsor of technological progress in this area, and perhaps in others as well'.[202]

The technical marvels of the Golden House suggest that experts were available in all fields, drawn to Rome by Nero's many interests. 'Neronian Rome must have possessed for them the same kind of allure as California

[199] Tac. *Ann.* 12.66.4–5, 13.15.4. Hansen 2013, 303, 308–9 (quotation); cf. Maes 2013, 337–8.
[200] Gowers 1994, 133–4.
[201] Plin. *HN* 31.40; Suet. *Ner.* 48.3. Gowers 1994, 131, 133–4; cf. Maes 2013, 290 and n. 14; below 305.
[202] Hine 2006, 66.

for European scientists today. There they might find unlimited resources in money and materials and an enlightened prince who would give them every encouragement to experiment'.[203] This may be reflected in technological advances in Nero's wooden amphitheatre, touched on by Calpurnius Siculus, which made possible, as Coleman suggests, the most elaborate 'fatal charades' and were adopted in the building of the Colosseum.[204] It also probably found effect in the application of science to measures intended to prevent the spread of fire after the disaster of 64 in the design and construction of buildings and, perhaps, the provision of syringe extinguishers and siphons.[205] Science must also have played a part in the pursuit of the great canal projects of the period, in Italy and in the Empire, which also reflect a broadening of geographical horizons.

5.4.3   Geography

In this period began the rise of the Greek novel. A great favourite was Antonius Diogenes' 'Incredible Things Beyond Thule', a tale of travel to exotic places including Scandinavia and even the moon.[206] Closer to reality, Lucan has a digression on north African snakes and their bites, and references to the unknown source of the Nile. Hardie comments on his 'scientific curiosity', and Maes calls the snake excursus, with its mixture of the scientific and the grotesque, 'the most emblematic scene in the whole of Neronian literature'.[207] Under Nero, more was being discovered of the world around and beyond the Mediterranean.[208] This was yet another spike, a jump in interest in geography that had begun under Claudius.[209] In the north, the lure was amber, which had various uses but was especially prized for the decoration of the arena. Pliny I records that a superintendent of Nero's gladiatorial shows commissioned an *eques* – to whom Pliny seems later to have talked directly – to bring back a huge haul of the material from the Baltic. In the process this *eques* established the distance from Carnuntum to the northern sea as *c*. 600 Roman miles (920 km/550 statute miles).[210] In addition, as result of the Bosporan

[203] Dawson 1964, 264.
[204] Cal. *Ecl.* 7.47–53, 69–72. Coleman 1990, 70, 52–3; Bartsch 1994, 54; Rea 2011, 214; below 323, 325.
[205] Tac. *Ann.* 15.43.4: *subsidia repremendis ignibus.* Beste and Hesberg 2013, 314–5. Cf. below 340. Waldherr 2005, 211.
[206] Griffin 2013, 471; Hansen 2013, 304–5.
[207] Luc. 9.700–733; 10.191, 271. Hardie 2013, 237; Maes 2013, 323–4.   [208] Cf. Hine 2006, 52.
[209] Osgood 2011, 107–112.   [210] Plin. *HN* 37.45.

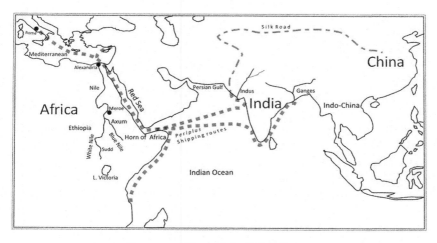

Figure 9   Africa and the Indian Ocean.
After Grant 1970, 133; Wild and Wild 2014, 92 figure 1; Wikipedia Periplus of the Erythraean Sea)

kingdom's being brought firmly within the Roman sphere of influence, Mithridates, the brother of its client-king, Cotys, is likely to have informed Pliny I on conditions around his homeland.[211] However, in the south and east there was an even greater expansion of contemporary Greco-Roman geographical knowledge. The mid-first century is the likely date of publication of the *Periplus Maris Erythraei*. This 'Red Sea Sailing Book' details shipping routes from the Mediterranean down the Red Sea and the coast of East Africa, and across the Indian Ocean to the mouth of the Ganges. Outwards along these routes went an increasing amount of goods from the Mediterranean; more important, ships returned with spices and silk from the East. Pliny I's stern moral disapproval of silk clothing hints at the great extent of the trade, is an interesting example of the divergence between the real and the literary worlds, and is a further indication of the expansion of the Neronian economy (Figure 9).[212]

There was particular Roman interest in the region of the Horn of Africa. Seneca, able to talk to those concerned, reports how two centurions got as far as the middle reaches of the White Nile before being stopped by the massive swamp of the Sudd. His account suggests that they were there for purely scientific purposes, having been sent by Nero, 'a great lover of the

[211] Plut. *Galb.* 13.5. Braund 2013, 90; below 139.
[212] Cizek 1982, 340; Ruffing 2014, 71–2, 76, 78; Wild and Wild 2014, *pass.*; *OCD⁴* 1142. Cf. above 120.

truth' (*veritatis ... amantissimus*), to investigate the source of the Nile. This fits Nero's efforts, while in Greece, to resolve the question of the depth of the Alcyonian Lake.[213] Pliny I, however, declares that they were members of a praetorian military expedition, commanded by a tribune, despatched to reconnoitre the region with a view to an 'Ethiopian campaign' ([*bellum*] *Aethiopicum*). Pliny recounts that the expedition voyaged up the Nile, leaving the Roman Empire at Syene (Aswan) and travelling to Meroë. From Meroë it pressed on to the confluence of the White and Blue Niles (at modern Khartoum) and continued up the White Nile. This is consistent with Seneca's information that it was in contact with, but skirted, the Axumite kingdom of Abyssinia to the east. As it went, it sedulously mapped and measured its progress (giving, for example, an exact figure of 996 Roman miles [*c.* 1527 km/916 statute miles] as the distance from Syene to Meroë) and recorded and noted the lands, peoples, fauna and flora on its route.[214] The apparent contradiction between Seneca and Pliny as to its purpose is not irresolvable: it is redundant to assume two separate expeditions, each with a different agenda.[215] Combined scientific and military reconnaissance expeditions by great powers continue to this day.[216] The Neronian expedition must have been of some size and taken a significant time – say, two to three years – to be planned, assembled, sent out, do its job and return safely. Pliny's statement that an Ethiopian war might be added to the Empire's 'remaining wars' (*reliqua bella*) suggests a date after the suppression of the Boudican uprising in 60–61 but before the ending of the Armenian and Black Sea campaigns in 65/66, after which the Empire was formally, albeit temporarily, at peace.[217] The two centurions were probably interviewed by Seneca some time before his death in 65. The year 61 seems the most likely for the expedition's departure, with its return in 63 or 64, probably the former.[218] Its report of its findings will have caused great excitement in Rome. A consequent 'Ethiopian craze' may be reflected in the games arranged for Tiridates by the imperial freedman Patrobius in Puteoli in 66, during which a whole day was devoted to acts featuring Ethiopians.[219] As Tiridates' visit in 66 may later have enthused Nero to dream of an expedition to the Caucasus,[220] so the Nile explorers may have stimulated him to contemplate emulating Augustus, Germanicus and possibly even Alexander the Great by

[213] Paus. 2.37.5–6.
[214] Sen. *QNat.* 6.8.3–4; Plin. *HN* 6.181, 12.8, 19 (*DCCCCLXXXXVI m.p.*). Braund 2013, 96.
[215] Hine 2006, 63; *contra* Levi 1949, 208; cf. Heil 1997, 166 and n. 41.
[216] Cf. Doody 2013, 297–8.   [217] Below 139, 214; Table 3.   [218] Fini 1994, 74; cf. below 205.
[219] Cass. Dio 63.3.1. Braund 2013, 96–7.   [220] Below 150.

visiting Egypt, by way of Greece, and travelling triumphantly up the river.[221] He certainly ordered extensive preparations for this, including new buildings in Alexandria. All this was probably enough to create the rumour that he had already decided on an Ethiopian war, but there is no good reason to take this seriously and to suppose that troops were actually moved to Egypt for it.[222] Nothing came of the plan. His advisers may have warned him off the trip because of last-minute uncertainty surrounding the death of D. Junius Silanus, but it is likely that, for his own reasons, Nero had already gone off the idea.[223] It may have been his expensive vacillation in this respect, at a time when Egyptian resources were stretched, that provoked a quarrel between him and the prefect of Egypt, Caecina Tuscus.[224] Nero was fickle, and the Egyptian trip may be counted one of his 'break-outs',[225] but it is remarkable that his administration could envisage and launch the original Nile expedition. This was fully justified by the commercial and political importance of the Horn of Africa and the Indian Ocean; and it was probably its negative report of conditions south of Egypt that prompted abandonment of any thoughts of moving on Ethiopia: a rational decision based on good data.

5.4.4   Nero?

The distinction between *princeps* and administration raises the question as to the extent to which Nero was responsible for 'Neronian' intellectual and cultural developments. It is tempting to see him, with his multiplicity of interests, as their main impulse. Gowers, for example, says that he 'provides the inspiration, the context, for [the] prolific output' of the Neronian poets.[226] However, as with administration, while the *princeps* probably had an effect on specific issues on specific occasions, he did not direct everything.[227] Nero engaged closely, as long as it suited him, with particular pet projects, e.g. the *Domus Transitoria*; the Golden House; certain gadgets and scientific investigations; his coin portraits. However, he cannot physically have been involved in everything, even in his favourite fields, and the acceptance of spikes leads to the conclusion that he was not an originator but followed trends that had already developed their own vitality: he was

---

[221] Braund 2013, 96–7.   [222] Cass. Dio 63.8.1. Below 150–1 and n. 176; *contra* Braund 2013, 96.
[223] Tac. *Ann.* 15.36.1–5; Suet. *Ner.* 19.1. Rudich 1993, 83; Malitz 1999, 49; Holland 2000, 150. Below 197, 205, 223, 308.
[224] Suet. *Ner.* 35.5; Cass. Dio 63.18.1. Below 221, 345.   [225] Below 164.
[226] Gowers 1994, 132; cf. Doody 2013, 297; Hardie 2013, 235.
[227] Cf. (on wall-painting) Lorenz 2013, 370, 378.

part of the spirit of the age, adopting the interests and the fashions of the
young Roman 'smart set'.[228] To call a period the 'Neronian', 'Elizabethan'
or 'Victorian' is not to suggest stimulation by a ruler in every field at every
level but rather to identify a time of general excitement, endeavour and
success. Neronians sensed something in the air which was changing their
culture and, positively or negatively, appreciated Nero's role in the
transformation.[229]

All this was the opposite of an age of suffocating repression. Again,
'Nero's regime was not the kind of dictatorship unable to tolerate any hint
of subversion in its literary figures; and it is not clear that artists of
conscience were compelled to choose between compromise and death'.[230]
Petronius has Trimalchio tell the tale of the invention of an unbreakable
glass, which an unnamed *princeps* immediately suppressed in case it
undermined the value of gold. We find very much the same story in Pliny
I who, discussing the spread of glass manufacture in the West, says that the
ruler concerned was Tiberius, but shows little confidence in the authenticity of the incident. However, he adds as a matter of fact that under Nero
two small glass cups, made to look like stoneware, were sold for the
exorbitant sum of HS 6,000. Both the *Satyricon* and the *Naturalis
Historia* suggest that innovation in glassware was a talking-point at the
Neronian court.[231] This court can hardly, therefore, as some have claimed,
been remote from the outside world,[232] but was a place for the reception
and exchange of ideas There was no free speech. This had been restricted
under the Republic by the power of leading aristocrats and the operation of
the patron–client system, and was even more so now that all were clients of
the *princeps* in a *de facto* autocracy.[233] Epictetus makes much of the strain
of being close to the sole ruler of the world: of standing at a lofty height
from which one might suddenly be toppled at the autocrat's whim. Such a
situation would certainly have inhibited the giving of honest advice.
However, Epictetus' moralising gloom is open to question;[234] and one
suspects that a considerable element of the 'strain' was aristocratic affectation, derived from class prejudice and philosophical hostility to tyranny.[235] It was, without doubt, always risky to annoy a *princeps* or those
closest to him. On the other hand, the rewards of proximity to the ruler
were immense,[236] and there was never a shortage of people eager to win

---

[228] Bergmann 2013, 337–9, 355–7; Lorenz 2013, 364, 367–71, 378–9; below 306.
[229] Cf. Hine 2006, 65; Reitz 2006, 1.   [230] Masters 1994, 170; above 92.
[231] Petron. *Sat.* 51; Plin. *HN* 36.194–5.   [232] Cizek 1982, 215; *contra*: Fini 1994, 103–4.
[233] Cf. above 100, 105.   [234] Below 300; cf. Rudich 1993, xx–xxi.   [235] Cf. Millar 1977, 110.
[236] Crook 1955, 27; Millar 1977, 113–14; Winterling 2009, 89.

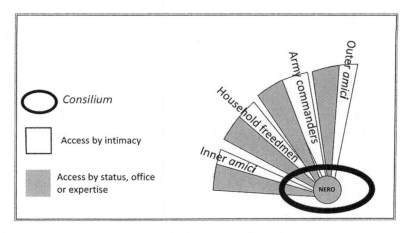

Figure 10   The protecting hierarchy

them. Nero never lacked significant upper-class support.[237] This was anyway, in modern terms, an unhygienic, dangerous world, in which everyone was always no more than a whisker away from death. The position of Nero's advisers was no worse than that of, say, English courtiers under the Tudors and Stuarts, who accepted the possibility of torture and execution, for themselves, their relatives and their clients,[238] along with the opportunity for power and riches as part and parcel of the job. Nero was no great practitioner of arbitrary exclusion from court, and no great killer.[239] When he chose to involve himself directly in state business, his personality will have permitted some degree of frankness from his advisers;[240] and, in his absence, these will have been willing to take this from each other.

5.5   Protected Nero

In the event, Nero, though perfectly capable of being an effective *princeps*, grew bored with the details of administration and began to take a back seat in the day-to-day running of the Empire.[241] Senior courtiers filled the power vacuum and directed affairs, An increasingly disengaged but compliant Nero allowed further progress in this direction, with major decisions being thrashed out by *amici* and their associates and put to the *princeps*

---

[237] E.g. above 29.   [238] Cf. Romm 2014, 46.   [239] Above 99; below 232.
[240] Above 69, 101, 117.   [241] Above 57, below 286.

only for formal approval.[242] This development requires a new perception
of the power relationships within Nero's principate, which can be represented by rearranging the segments of Figure 8 into the much tighter fan-
shape of Figure 10. Here Nero does not sit at the centre of his regime,
directing it, but, tucked into a corner, is protected and to some degree
isolated by it. This leads one to wonder whether Nero's various obsessions,
in particular those to do with the circus, the stage and the *palaestra*, were
entirely of his own making, since the more he was diverted the greater the
political leeway enjoyed by his advisers.[243]

[242] Above 81.
[243] Cf. Malitz 1999, 39; Waldherr 2005, 120 (though both concern themselves here with the early
period: Waldherr 2005, 104).

CHAPTER 6

Warfare and the Generals

6.1 Introduction

Before moving further we must consider events on the periphery of the Empire. Forming the permanent backdrop to the Neronian principate were the succession issue and, oddly for such a pacific *princeps*,[1] warfare. The succession issue has already been touched upon and will be considered further below. Here I deal with warfare. This is important because it both reflected and formed central government thinking. Because it attracted the attention of ancient writers, it provides a window into imperial administration and politics.

6.2 Armenia (i)

6.2.1 Background

Armenia had become a bone of contention between Rome and Parthia in the first century BC. Fresh trouble had arisen in 52 when the Parthian king, Vologaeses, put his brother, Tiridates, on the throne.[2] In 52/53 Vologaeses withdrew from Armenia, but the situation remained unstable.[3] Crisis came in 54 when, just after Nero's accession, news came that Vologaeses had returned to Armenia in support of Tiridates.[4] The government's response was to give Gnaeus Domitius Corbulo an extraordinary military command on the upper Euphrates, based on the provinces of Cappadocia and Galatia (Figure 11).[5] His orders were 'to hold Armenia'.[6] Heil argues that this signified the declaration of all-out war in the East,

---

[1] Below 332.
[2] Tac. *Ann.* 12.50.1. Furneaux 1907, [107]. Tacitus' handling of the Armenian war, in which he discusses events of one year under the date of another, prevents an entirely reliable chronology. Here I follow Heil 1997, 222–3.
[3] Heil 1997, 59–60.   [4] Heil 1997, 60–1.   [5] Heil 1997, 62–4, 207.
[6] Tac. *Ann.* 13.8.1: *retinendae Armeniae.*

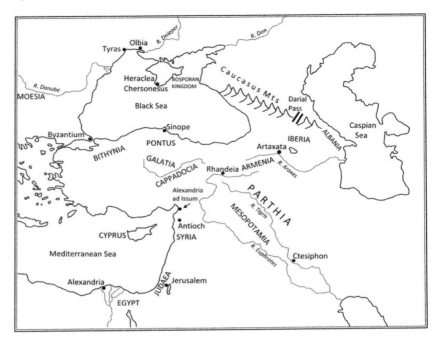

Figure 11   The East.
After Braund 2013, 87, Map 1

aimed at putting Armenia permanently into Roman hands. It was a major
change, since Rome had previously relied on diplomacy stiffened by
sporadic displays of force.[7] The reason was not that Armenia had massive
strategic importance for Rome's eastern policy. Its remoteness meant that
it did not: Roman and Parthian efforts to control it were about symbol not
substance. Likewise, there was no sudden realisation that Parthia under
Vologaeses posed a major threat to the territorial integrity of the Roman
Empire: Parthian internal politics determined otherwise. Rather, Nero
needed *virtus*, in the sense of 'military excellence', to legitimise his new
position.[8] On this basis, Heil argues that Neronian involvement in
Armenia began well but ended badly. The final settlement, advertised at
Tiridates' reception in Rome in 66 as a great victory, had been proposed by
Parthia as early as 61 and put Armenia permanently into Parthian hands.[9]

---

[7] Heil 1997, 64–5: 'eine entschlossene Kriegspolitik'.   [8] Heil 1997, 2, 65–76.
[9] Heil 1997, 104–5, 114, 197.

Heil is correct in seeing the need to interpret Roman foreign policy in the context of central politics.[10] However, his main argument is undermined by a false premise, taken from Tacitus and adopted by most modern commentators: that in appointing Corbulo, Nero acted on the advice of Seneca and Burrus not Agrippina.[11] Tacitus has Seneca and Burrus reacting to news of renewed Parthian intervention by ordering strong countermeasures. Then comes Parthian withdrawal due to civil war and consequent lavish celebration in Rome. Only after this, and implausibly late, do we get the appointment of Corbulo and his journey eastwards. A more credible order of events is: news of trouble; the appointment of Corbulo to deal with it; countermeasures; and early success.[12] Tacitus appears to place these events before the end of 54.[13] This is followed by some historians;[14] others, justifiably, appear less sure.[15] Either way, Corbulo must have been selected late in 54 or early in 55, when Agrippina was still the dominant force in Roman politics.[16] It was she who, showing her customary flexibility and flair, gave Corbulo the eastern command.

She cannot have ordered him to launch all-out war. That Agrippina helped shape Claudian foreign policy is likely given her influence and her habit of participating with Claudius in the reception of ambassadors, seated on her own tribunal.[17] Her close involvement in this field helps us understand her *faux pas* in the matter of the Armenian envoys, who probably came at the beginning of the crisis to win support for the pro-Roman faction in the country.[18] Tacitus presents the incident as a woman wantonly putting herself forward as co-chair of a diplomatic conference, 'showing no regard whatsoever for her son's reputation'.[19] Agrippina was, however, far too canny for this to be credible. The scandal loses force if we suppose that she, well-informed about Armenian affairs, entered the meeting assuming that, as *Augusta* and 'Queen Mother', she would, seated on her own tribunal, play much the same role under Nero as she had under Claudius.[20] But 'Queen Mother' was not the same as wife, giving her no automatic right of attendance.[21] Those in charge of court protocol had, quite properly, provided only one tribunal, for Nero. Agrippina,

---

[10] Heil 1997, 10.
[11] E.g. Heil 1997, 62, 76, 119. Cf. Henderson 1905, 58–9; 164–5; Hohl 1918, 397; Syme 1958, 1.387; Syme 1970, 33, 39; Grant 1970, 70; Griffin 1976, 119; Griffin 1984, 78; Fini 1994, 67.
[12] As Furneaux 1907, [108] cf. [112]; Warmington 1969, 91.   [13] Tac. *Ann.* 13.6–8, 13.11.1.
[14] E.g. Henderson 1905, 58–9, 160–5; Hohl 1918, 358; Levi 1949, 168; Syme 1970, 38.
[15] E.g. Griffin 1984, 226. Cf. Tac. *Ann.* 13.9.7; Furneaux 1907, 164; Heil 1997, 63; above 49.
[16] Above 48–9; cf. Barrett *et al.* 2016, 82 and n. 2.   [17] Cass. Dio 60.33.7. Above 37.
[18] Heil 1997, 62.   [19] Malitz 1999, 16–17 (quotation).   [20] Cf. Osgood 2011, 93.
[21] Cf. above 68.

seeing this too late, attempted to save face by approaching Nero's seat, which only made things worse. She was rescued by a still-loyal Seneca, who got Nero to show deference by rising and coming to greet her.[22] The incident, though embarrassing, was not a sign of Agrippina's overweening arrogance or a reflection of an abrupt decline in her power. Gaffes occur in every age. What matters is if and how they are remembered: in this case, very negatively by a source tradition as hostile to Agrippina as it is to Nero. Agrippina remained in charge and if anyone understood the complexities of the Armenian problem it was she.[23] She will have grasped that embarking upon major hostilities so close to Nero's accession could be disastrous if things went badly or even too well, since victory would bring huge fame to the general responsible who, for the moment, could not be Nero. He needed a military reputation; indeed, his heroic deeds had already been promised.[24] However, he was too young and inexperienced to take the field in person. He had first to be toughened up;[25] and he was needed in Rome to help establish the new regime. Late in 54, realising that previous, even Claudian, policy – 'the dreary series of expeditions into and out of Armenia and the futile installations and expulsions of Roman nominees'[26] – had not worked, Agrippina decided that nominal suzerainty over a Parthian dependency offered more stability than the creation of a Roman vassal.[27] To implement it she needed a competent general who agreed with her assessment of the situation, would stay loyal, and might eventually find himself acting as mentor of Nero on his first major campaign.[28] For this she chose Corbulo.

6.2.2   Corbulo (i)

Corbulo had been under somewhat of a cloud, having had successful campaigning in Lower Germany brought to a sudden end by Claudius in 47.[29] On the other hand, this had occurred before Agrippina had married Claudius, which allowed her to become his patron. His reinstatement by Agrippina occurred probably from around 50.[30] 'Hold Armenia' was conveniently open-ended, allowing Corbulo to act on his own initiative and recognise Tiridates if Vologaeses proved willing to allow nominal

---

[22] Cf. Gibson 2013, 125   [23] Cf. Heil 1997, 100.   [24] Above 42.
[25] Above 36; below 166; cf. Heil 1997, 64.   [26] Charlesworth 1950, 72.
[27] Henderson 1905, 160–3.   [28] Below 166.   [29] Tac. *Ann.* 11.20.3. Malloch 2013, 261–3.
[30] Hohl 1918, 396; Levi 1949, 169; Syme 1970, 38 (though with some caution, having previously (1958, 1.387) described him as simply 'extracted from retirement').

Roman sovereignty.[31] Corbulo was not perfect,[32] but he was no fool. He understood that Agrippina's policy was the best and he adhered to it in the face of subsequent vacillation by the central government. In the long term this brought success, creating a peace that lasted until Trajan and a way of dealing with Armenia that endured until the early fifth century.[33] In the short term, perhaps even as Corbulo was being appointed, the Armenian crisis subsided as Vologaeses again withdrew into Parthia. Though mainly due to internal troubles, this may also have been prompted by news of current Roman mobilisation.[34] This allowed the Senate to grant special honours to Nero: a triumphal robe, an ovation and a statue in the temple of Mars Ultor.[35] These should not be disparaged. *Virtus* had to be taken where it could be found, and this was a lucky windfall.[36] The statue, in particular, confirmed Nero's standing as a worthy successor of Caesar and Augustus.[37] Corbulo did not then exploit Parthian civil discord to go on the offensive.[38] His strategy remained the acceptance of Tiridates as long as he and Vologaeses conceded that Armenia lay within the Roman sphere of influence. Corbulo used the informal armistice to strengthen his command, while famously, as earlier in Germany, acting the martinet.[39] Though, as events were to show, Vologaeses was in principle prepared to accept nominal Roman suzerainty, he was unwilling for Tiridates to be crowned by a Roman, still less for him to travel to Rome for the ceremony, a humiliating sign of subservience.[40] Early in 58, therefore, hostilities began afresh and lasted into 59. Corbulo, making demands on his army and on himself that rivalled those of heroic Romans of old,[41] did well for the regime. Following the taking of the northern capital of Armenia, Artaxata (Figure 11), in 58, his troops hailed Nero as *imperator* and Tiridates fled the country. When news of this arrived in Rome, the Senate confirmed the title and decreed a second round of justifiable celebration, a quasi-triumph.[42] However, those in the know will have realised that

---

[31] Furneaux 1907, [113]; Griffin 1976, 226, 229.   [32] Below 142.

[33] Henderson 1905, 193, 195; Traina 2009, 3. Heil 1997, 186–9 is too negative about the Trajanic intervention: Trajan had his own reasons for ignoring precedent and picking a fight with Parthia.

[34] Parthian civil war: Tac. *Ann.* 13.7.2; Roman show of strength: Furneaux 1907, [108].

[35] Tac. *Ann.* 13.8.1.   [36] Heil 1997, 77–9.   [37] Cf. Drinkwater 2007b, 70.

[38] Heil 1997, 86–9 and n. 13 (following orders from Rome, which does not square with his general argument: above 132).

[39] There was still some fighting: Heil 1997, 86; Furneaux 1907, [112].

[40] Cf. Tac. *Ann.* 15.24.3 (under 63).   [41] E.g. Tac. *Ann.* 14.24.1–2.

[42] Tac. *Ann.* 13.41.5; Dio 63.3.3. Heil 1997, 92, 94; Braund 2013, 91–2; below 331; though cf. Barret *et al.* 2016, 13. Though some interpret Tacitus as saying that Nero was hailed *imperator* in Rome rather than in Armenia (e.g. Levi 1949, 172), this is contrary to the traditional practice of the title being conferred by victorious troops in the field: Tac. *Ann.* 2.18.2, 3.74.6. Cf. Talbert 1984,

Tiridates would soon be back, and that tedious seesawing over the control
of Armenia had to be stopped. For Corbulo, victory was not the end but a
way of persuading Vologaeses to agree to Tiridates travelling as a suppliant
to Rome. However, for the moment Corbulo had done rather too well, for
by expelling Tiridates he encouraged a change in Roman policy.[43] This
was to forget about Tiridates and to put an outsider, the Cappadocian
prince Tigranes, a descendant of Herod the Great, long a hostage in Rome
and so probably known personally to Nero, on the throne as a puppet
ruler.[44] Its attraction was the promise of maximum Roman influence short
of direct annexation,[45] but this 'act of the home government' must have
been against Corbulo's better judgement.[46] Corbulo saw his command
dissolved and himself made governor of Syria, with instructions to support
Tigranes.[47]

6.3   The New Order and Britain

The date of the change in policy is significant. It fell in 60, not long after
the death of Agrippina, at a time when Seneca and Burrus were becoming
increasingly vulnerable. It may be interpreted as the first sign of newcomers exercising political muscle.[48] Chief among these were Poppaea and
probably, even though before his first direct appearance in the source
narrative, Tigellinus. Despite his low birth, he had become a colourful
figure at the court of Gaius. Caught in the crossfire of Gaius' political
attack on his own sisters, Julia Livilla and Agrippina, Tigellinus was
accused of adultery with Agrippina, and perhaps even Julia and both their
husbands, and banished. After Gaius' fall, he returned and restored his
wealth and position by breeding racehorses, which explains how he was

---

363: the Senate conventionally confirmed military salutations of the *princeps* as *imperator*. This was
also the occasion of the attempt to grant Nero a perpetual consulship and other extravagant
honours, most of which were refused: above 22. The Aphrodisias relief depicting an heroically
nude Nero, flanked by Nike and a trophy and grasping Armenia, might well belong to this period,
though not that of Agrippina crowning Nero: Heil 1997, 95–6; Figure 4; cf. Mratschek 2013, 49:
in 55; above 40–2.

[43] Tac. *Ann.* 14.26.1; 15.1.1: *Tiridate pulso.* Furneaux 1907, [114–15]. Cf. below 146, on the effect
that this had on events in Britain.

[44] Tac. *Ann.* 14.26.1. Cizek 1982, 325; Heil 1997, 98–9; Malitz 1999, 58.

[45] Henderson 1905, 178.

[46] Furneaux 1907, [115] (quotation); cf. Griffin 1976, 227. *Contra* Levi 1949, 173–4, 176–80: Nero
sent in Tigranes precisely to check Corbulo's plans for even greater Roman involvement in
Armenia, with Tigranes as his tool.

[47] Tac. *Ann.* 14.26.4; 15.3.1. Heil 1997, 100; below 137.

[48] Cf. Waldherr 2005, 144, though making the 'newcomer' Nero himself; below 188.

able to befriend the chariot-mad Nero.[49] By 60 he was *praefectus vigilum*, in charge of the City's paramilitary fire brigade.[50] However, Poppaea and Tigellinus could not have operated without the support of others: 'The quiet operations of persons superior in birth, rank, and talent might also be surmised'.[51] Poppaea and Tigellinus may be regarded as the leaders in a move to displace Seneca and Burrus, and their tactic appears to have been to enhance Nero's *virtus* and so bolster their position by creating a success in the East: Armenia held by a Roman client looked better than Armenia under a Parthian prince. The initiative, like the appointment of Corbulo, did not come from Nero himself. Freed for the moment from any obligation to show himself in the East,[52] he could concentrate on staging the first 'Neronian' festival.[53] But trouble was brewing. Tigranes immediately pursued an expansionist policy, provoking, in 61, retaliation by Vologaeses which panicked the whole of the Roman East.[54] Corbulo took all measures necessary to defend the region while unilaterally abandoning Tigranes and reverting to seeking a negotiated peace with Vologaeses.[55] But the imperial government also discarded Tigranes. In mid-61, in response to an earlier request by Corbulo to relieve him of military responsibility for Armenia so that he could concentrate on the defence of Syria, it revived his extraordinary eastern command and gave it to Caesennius Paetus, *consul ordinarius* in 61.[56] Paetus was commissioned not to support Tigranes but to subdue and provincialise the country.[57] He arrived in the East in autumn 61. This was a second major policy reversal. Vologaeses' diplomatic advances to Rome, agreed between him and Corbulo, were rejected.[58] For change to come in Armenia in later 61, new ideas on dealing with the country had to have prevailed earlier. This returns us to 60 and the rising ambitions of Poppaea and Tigellinus.

---

[49] *Schol. Iuv.* 1.155; Barrett 1996. 49, 86.

[50] Tac. *Hist.* 1.72; Cass. Dio 59.23.9; *Schol. Iuv.* 1.155. Fini 1994, 142; above 62; below 241. Tigellinus must have been appointed *praefectus vigilum* after Nero had become *princeps* since it appears that one Laelianus held the office *c.* 54/55: Cass. Dio 61.6. 6.

[51] Syme 1958, 387.   [52] Cf. below 166.

[53] Bradley 1978a, 92; below 298; cf. Levi 1949, 175, on 60 as a good year for Nero.

[54] Tac. *Ann.* 15.1–3, 9. Cizek 1982, 326: that imperial government must have sanctioned this – to get rid of him and pursue an alternative policy; Heil 1997, 101–2.

[55] Tac. *Ann.* 15.5.5, 6.1, 7.1; Griffin 1976, 228; Waldherr 2005, 151: Tigranes was 'von Corbulo höchstpersönlich vom Thron gejagt'.

[56] Tac. *Ann.* 14.29.1. Below 145.

[57] Tac. *Ann.* 15.3.2, 15.6.4–6: *se tributa ac leges et pro umbra regis Romanum ius victis impositurum.* Fini 1994, 69; Heil 1997, 106. *Contra* Malitz 1999, 58–9: Paetus pursued his own policy of annexation.

[58] Tac. *Ann.* 15.5.5, 7.1.

Caesennius Paetus was their man, executing their orders.[59] Full annexation was, given the nature of Armenian geography and society, a bad
decision,[60] but Poppaea and Tigellinus had become ever more hawkish.[61]
Expansion of empire could be projected as a greater achievement than the
establishment of a kingdom held by an unreliable client. In addition we
must consider the wider context. The years 60–61 had also seen major
fighting in Britain, where the revolt of Boudica had resulted in massive
humiliation and destruction of Roman life and property, 'the worst
cataclysm yet suffered under Roman imperial rule'.[62] Though the rebellion was suppressed its memory will have persisted, as will the difficulties
of meeting the massive costs of the revolt making new demands on a
fiscal system already stretched by hostilities in Armenia.[63] Furthermore,
during 61 the peaceful settlement of Britain was jeopardised by quarrelling between the two most important Roman officials there, the governor, Suetonius Paullinus I and Julius Classicianus, Nero's financial
agent for the province. This became so fierce that it necessitated intervention by an imperial commissioner, the senior freedman, Polyclitus.[64]
Seneca's name, too, was dragged into the crisis. He was rumoured to have
helped precipitate the revolt by calling in personal loans;[65] and, since
Britannia was Claudius' creation, and Seneca was closely associated with
the Claudian regime, he may also have been seen as representing an
administration that had presented the Empire with a poisoned chalice.[66]
Contemporary court exasperation with Britain and with Seneca and his

---

[59] Above 136; *contra* Heil 1997, 107–8.   [60] Henderson 1905, 157–60.

[61] Cf. Waldherr 2005, 151: 'Alles in allem ist wohl davon auszugehen, dass es im Umfeld des Kaisers
eine Gruppe von Hardlinern gab, die die römische Politik im Osten nach ihren Vorstellungen neu
gestalten wollten. Vergessen wir nicht: Es war die Zeit, als Burrus starb und Seneca sein politisches
Mandat verlor' Though he asserts (153–4) that the main decisions were made by Nero.

[62] Cf. Waldherr 2005, 144–5; Romm 2014, 129 (quotation). Though Tacitus places all the events of
the revolt in 61, current opinion is strongly that it began in 60: e.g. Grant 1970, 111; Frere 1978,
114 and n. 39; Griffin 1976, 231; Cizek 1982, 296; Griffin 1984, 225; Birley 2005, 48–9; Braund
2013, 85 (all generally following Syme 1958, 2.765, himself following earlier scholars, e.g.
Henderson 1905, 206–7). However, there remains a case for 61 as the year of Boudica's
rebellion. After the consular date for 61, which Tacitus gives at *Ann.* 14.29.1, there follows a
summary account of events in Britain down to 60, in which year we can date Suetonius Paullinus'
attack on Anglesey and the following clean-up operations. This allows the Boudican revolt to occur
in 61. See e.g. Carroll 1979, who deals with technical issues arising out of the change of governor,
from Paullinus to Petronius Turpilianus, which some have seen as forcing the date for the beginning
of the rebellion back into 60; Wallace 2014, 25.

[63] The costs: (1) of Boudica's destruction; (2) of subduing the main rebellion; (3) of extinguishing the
embers; (4) of ensuring that it did not happen again: Tac. *Ann.* 14.38. Cf. Warmington 1969, 66;
below 337.

[64] Tac. *Ann.* 14.38.4–39.1.   [65] Dio 62.2.1. Romm 2014, 131–2; cf. below 339.

[66] Cf. Strabo 4.5.3, on the unprofitability of holding Britain.

clique may be reflected in the report that Nero had threatened to withdraw Roman forces from the province.[67] Though the last could have been malicious interpretation of one of Nero's 'flippant comments',[68] the old order was wounded.[69] It would have suited the new to accelerate its death by engineering success elsewhere, hence the decision to annex Armenia.[70]

6.4 The Black Sea

Increased aggression in Armenia fits in with contemporary expansion on the lower Danube and in the Black Sea region. Throughout the 60s there was sustained Roman military activity here. This is ignored by the main literary sources and must be reconstructed from stray references elsewhere. The most important piece of evidence is a Flavian inscription recording the exploits of Ti. Plautius Silvanus Aelianus during a governorship of Moesia (Figure 11) that probably lasted from around 60–66.[71] It relates how Aelianus brought peace and prosperity to his province, internally by settling whole communities of transdanubian barbarians south of the river, and externally, probably around 62, by crushing incoming Sarmatians. He also ensured the loyalty of the leaders of settled border peoples: Bastarnae, Roxolani and Dacians. All this was accomplished despite the transfer of 'a large part of the army' – in fact, one of the three legions under Aelianus' command – to Armenia: direct evidence of the major troop movements of the period.[72] However, all this was still only imperial police-work. What really distinguishes Aelianus' career is his deployment of Roman power far outside his province, along the Black Sea coast. Having made the Greek

---

[67] Suet. *Ner.* 18: *deducere exercitum.* There is debate over the date. Some (e.g. Stevens 1951; Bradley 1978a, 110–137; Fini 1994, 60; Romm 2014, 132; Barrett *et al.* 2016, 124 and n. 1) prefer a time before Boudica, in the period 54–57. The majority of authorities, however, interpret it as a reaction to the Boudican rebellion (e.g. Holland 2000, 120; Birley 2005, 42; Waldherr 2005, 144; Braund 2013, 85–6). News of the near-annihilation of Legio IX (Tac. *Ann.* 14.32.6) was perhaps the stimulus, based on the precedent of the Varus disaster of AD 9. The 'threat' could, however, have been just another instance of misreported badinage: above 117–18.)

[68] Above 118.

[69] Cf. Syme 1958, 2.766: 'the disaster in Britain may have impaired the credit and influence of Seneca, and of Burrus'; Griffin 1976, 233 (referring to Nero and the *deteriores*).

[70] Cf. Heil 1997, 107–8: accepting the need to show strength after the British debacle, but drawing a different conclusion from this.

[71] *CIL* 14.3608 = *ILS* 986 = Smallwood 1967, no. 228. Henderson 1905, 224–6; Grant 1970, 130; Griffin 1976, 244–5, 456–7; Cizek 1982, 334–7; Griffin 1984, 108, 116; Levick 1999a, 22; Braund 2013, 89. There is disagreement as to exact dates, which produces a maximum period of 57–67. I follow Syme 1982, 478.

[72] Henderson 1905, 183, 224; Cizek 1982, 335–6; below 333.

cities of Tyras and Olbia exclaves of Moesia, he advanced beyond the
Dnieper to the Crimea, where he ended a Scythian siege of Heraclea
Chersonesus (Figure 11). The piecing-together of Aelianus' activities in
this region, based very much on the interpretation of local coins, is
uncertain. However, it is likely that though he did not formally annexe
the Bosporan kingdom of the eastern Crimea he brought it firmly into the
Roman sphere of influence.[73] Thus by 66 when, according to Josephus, his
achievements were sufficiently well known to be referred to by Agrippa II,
he had significantly extended Roman interests to the north and east of the
Black Sea.[74] Together with the annexation of the kingdom of Pontus, in
64/65 (Figure 11),[75] this made the Black Sea, like the Mediterranean, a
Roman lake. Conquest was in the air, and Aelianus' was the sort of success
that Poppaea, Tigellinus and their supporters will have hoped for from
Paetus in Armenia.

6.5   Armenia (ii)

Early – from late 61 into early 62[76] – news was good. Though Vologaeses
had moved westwards to counter the Roman change of strategy, Paetus
announced victory in Armenia, and Rome celebrated in style.[77] Corbulo
had successfully defended Syria against Vologaeses but, thanks to Paetus,
his monopoly of major military success was, apparently, broken. Reality
was different. Paetus, perhaps under pressure from the centre to achieve
too much in too short a time,[78] had suffered total defeat. In later 62,
Vologaeses cornered him at Rhandeia (Figure 11) and forced him to
negotiate a humiliating withdrawal.[79] Having fallen back to join Corbulo,
Paetus proposed an immediate counterattack, but Corbulo rejected this
on the grounds that he had received no such orders from Nero and that
his priority was Syria.[80] Corbulo then negotiated his own armistice and
demilitarisation of the war zone with Vologaeses.[81] In line with the terms
of Rhandeia, he also permitted Vologaeses to send an embassy to Nero.

---

[73] Cizek 1982, 338–9; Heil 1997, 152–4; Braund 2013, 89–90, 98; OCD[4] 254.
[74] Joseph. BJ 2.367. Henderson 1905, 226; Cizek 1982, 336. Cf. below 145.
[75] Suet. Ner. 18; Aur. Vict. Caes. 5.2; Epit. de Caes. 5.4. Henderson 1905, 226. Grant 1970, 129;
      Cizek 1982, 321; Griffin 1984, 228; Braund 2013, 86, 88, 90. Cf. below 143.
[76] Cf. Heil 1997, 109–10, 223   [77] Tac. Ann. 15.18.1.
[78] Cf. Henderson 1905, 185; Heil 1997, 110 (on Paetus' high level of aggression).
[79] Tac. Ann. 15.9.2–16.6; Dio 62.21.1. Cizek 1982, 327; Heil 1997, 110–11.
[80] Tac. Ann. 15.17.1–3: non ea imperatoris habere mandata. Below 155.   [81] Tac. Ann. 15.17–5.

The original policy of accommodation with Tiridates was now back in play.[82] Officially, the government did not know about Paetus' defeat until the arrival of the Parthian embassy in Rome at the beginning of spring 63.[83] However, bad news travels fast and Tacitus says that uncertainty about the eastern situation was current in Rome in 62, prompting government action to calm fears about the wheat supply.[84] The administration promptly rejected the terms offered by the Parthian envoys: essentially, that Tiridates was ready to accept his crown from Rome as long as he did not have to travel there personally to receive it. However, the courteous dismissal of the envoys, 'with presents, leaving room for hope that Tiridates would not make the same requests in vain if he brought his suit in person',[85] indicates that the government had also accepted accommodation as long as this included a coronation in the capital: pantomime, but necessary pantomime since it would neutralise Paetus' defeat and reassure the public that Rome still had the upper hand in Armenia. A Parthian change of mind was encouraged by some noisy sabre-rattling, again by Corbulo. He was replaced as civil governor of Syria but retained his military authority there and had this extended to cover the whole of the East. He was also given more troops and resources. Tacitus says that war was decided after the *princeps* had consulted his leading counsellors, which some have interpreted as Nero personally directing foreign policy.[86] However, all that Nero was doing was holding a meeting of the *Consilium* which had managed the Armenian crisis from the outset and which was likely manipulated by Poppaea and Tigellinus.[87] Corbulo launched his campaign in 64. It was remarkably brief. After little heavy fighting and, instead, speedy negotiation with Vologaeses and Tiridates, the Parthians accepted his way of thinking. In 64, Tiridates did public obeisance to a statue of Nero at Rhandeia, the site of Caesennius Paetus' humiliation, and agreed to go to Rome to receive the diadem of kingship from Nero's own hand.[88] Rhandeia II was more than a false Roman victory confected from a Parthian *fait accompli.*[89] It was a real success for Corbulo, who struck a substantive deal with

---

[82] Tac. *Ann.* 15.14.5. Cf. Heil 1997, 104, 112–16: according to him, this was the first time that the solution of nominal suzerainty, proposed, by Vologaeses in 61 after the expulsion of Tigranes, was accepted by Rome, but by Paetus, not Corbulo.

[83] Tac. *Ann.* 15.24.1–25.1.   [84] Tac. *Ann.* 15.18.1–2. Cf. below 333.

[85] Tac. *Ann.* 15.25.4: *cum donis tamen, unde spes fieret non frustra eadem oraturum Tiridaten, si preces ipse attulisset.*

[86] Tac. *Ann.* 15.25.2: *consuluit inter primores civitatis Nero.* E.g. Waldherr 2005, 153–4.

[87] Cf. above 78.   [88] Tac. *Ann.* 15.28.2, 29.1–6 (under 63); Heil 1997, 120, 221.

[89] *Contra* Heil 1997, 122–4.

Tiridates, whether or not this may be called a formal treaty. It was Corbulo, in fact, who proclaimed Tiridates as king by permission of Rome. When Tiridates eventually went to Rome he travelled in state, as monarch, for his coronation not his accession.

6.6   The Generals

6.6.1   Corbulo (ii)

Tiridates' grand reception in Rome, in 66, and the associated ceremonial such as the closing of the doors of the temple of Janus, was the high point of Nero's principate.[90] Tiridates' journey to the capital took some time to arrange, but when he finally set out he was accompanied almost all the way by one of Corbulo's senior officers, his son-in-law Annius Vinicianus, acting commander of legion V *Macedonica*.[91] Corbulo's association of his close family with Parthian royalty is a clear sign of his own immense power and status. He dominated eastern affairs from the time of his appointment by Agrippa, resisting central pressure and imposing her solution on the Armenian problem.[92] From 63 he was the superior of all other eastern governors and the arbiter of the fates of nations. Under him, Damascus was absorbed into Syria, and Pontus into the province of Cappadocia-Galatia.[93] His position was comparable to that of Pompey the Great after his obtaining *imperium maius*, and to Crassus in terms of the *matériel* made available to him.[94] He had broken the ruling family's monopoly of major military commands. His status equalled that of Drusus I and Tiberius under Augustus, and of Germanicus (than whom he was far more successful) under Tiberius. Tacitus portrays him as a flawed hero: a brilliant general, possessing great personal courage and endurance but excessively greedy for glory.[95] Thus, for example, he reports the view that Corbulo could and should have resolved the threat caused by Parthian reaction to Tigranes' aggression in 61 before the arrival of Paetus. 'He preferred to have the war rather than fight it', i.e. he did not want to bring the confrontation to a successful conclusion because this would terminate his command, and he did not want to risk failure because that would

---

[90] Cf. above 94.   [91] Tac. *Ann.* 15.28.4; cf. Cass, Dio 62.23.6. Syme 1970, 37; Griffin 1984, 178.
[92] Above 141; below 155.
[93] Hohl 1918, 378 [in 63]; Bradley 1978a, 114 [*c.* 64]; Griffin 1984, 228; Heil 1997, 144–8.
[94] Tac. *Ann.* 15.25.2–6. Hohl 1918, 405; Levi 1949, 185; Syme 1970, 36; Griffin 1976, 225; Cizek 1982, 328; Fini 1994, 70; Heil 1997, 208–10.
[95] E.g. Tac. *Ann.* 15.3.1, 15.6.1–3, 15.10.7. Heil 1997, 40, 44–8, 51–2; Malloch 2015, 86–8.

damage the reputation he had already acquired.[96] In short, he wanted
Paetus to take the blame for any subsequent failure.[97] Tacitus also asserts
that Corbulo was slow to support Paetus when he came under pressure
because this would 'increase the glory of a rescue'.[98] Both charges are
unfair. Given his many responsibilities in 61, and the fact that he himself
had requested help in dealing with Armenia, Corbulo could do no more
than await Paetus' arrival. And once things had gone wrong in Armenia, he
could afford no hasty action. Yet such criticism contains a grain of truth.
Corbulo was desperately keen to make his name. It was his military
ambition on the Rhine that had caused him to be reined in by
Claudius.[99] On his arrival in the East in 55 he immediately quarrelled
with the governor of Syria, Ummidius Quadratus, each man childishly
jealous of the other.[100] Furthermore, it may well have been Corbulo who
decided on the annexation of Pontus, on the basis that campaigning in
Armenia and Mesopotamia would be aided by access to the Black Sea and
also, perhaps, that there was a need to suppress piracy there. The land
routes were, however, given the topography of Pontus, very much secondary to the maritime routes, and one may suspect that it was primarily
rivalry with Aelianus that made Corbulo stake a claim in the new sphere of
expansion.[101] To many contemporaries he will have appeared every inch a
Roman of old: a fine figure of a man, in physique, character and achievements,[102] but such ambition made him a political risk.

Looking forward in time, his position, with no proximate superior,
closely resembles that of the usurping area-commanders of the third-
century 'Crisis'. To borrow the title of one of these, Corbulo was 'Marshall
of the East'.[103] In putting her faith in him Agrippina made an eccentric
choice; but she had done the same with Seneca, two years earlier. Though
much of Tacitus' mangling of the details of the opening of the Armenian
crisis may be explained by the constrictions of his annalistic framework, he
may also have wanted to avoid showing just how much Corbulo owed
Agrippina.[104] The gamble was typical of her, and paid off. For all his lust
for glory, Corbulo showed undying loyalty to the regime. He stood by
Nero even when he was involved in the death of Agrippina; and he was

[96] Cf. Furneaux 1907, 322.
[97] Tac. *Ann.* 15.3.1: *bellum habere quam gerere malebat*; cf. 15.6.3. Furneaux 1907, 322.
[98] Tac. *Ann.* 15.10.7: *subsidii laus augeretur.*   [99] Tac. *Ann.* 11.19.7; cf. above 134.
[100] Tac. *Ann.* 13.8.4, 9.3–7; Hohl 1918, 397.
[101] Tac. *Ann.* 13.39.1 Heil 1997, 149–56; Braund 2013, 88.   [102] Hohl 1918, 408–9.
[103] Cf. Drinkwater 2005, 45; Heil 2008, 747: Odenathus as *corrector totius Orientis.*
[104] Above 133; cf. Heil 1997, 85, on the sources' reluctance to acknowledge his faithfulness to Nero.

not, judging from the fact that he remained in post, directly implicated in either the Pisonian or even, contrary to general belief, the Vinician conspiracy.[105] He followed Nero's last orders to the letter, even when these led to his own death.[106] Corbulo's career raises questions about his political position. These will be examined further below.[107] For the moment, it suffices to say that he must have had very powerful allies at court, and that he was not seriously threatened until autumn 66. Also however, it raises questions about the relationship between the Neronian administration and its generals.

6.6.2   Consuls and Generals

The period 55 to 60 saw Nero hold four out of the five consulships of his principate.[108] His first, in 55, lasted only three months, but his second, in 57, was for a full year, probably to advertise his growing maturity and distance him from his adolescent street-fighting of 56.[109] Though little of importance is recorded for 57, the experience seems to have been a success. It was continued into the first six months of 58, when Nero took the consulship for which he had been designated by Claudius in 51,[110] and famously contributed to current debate on fiscal matters.[111] Thereafter, however, he seems to have begun to lose interest in imperial administration.[112] His fourth consulship, in 60, is best associated with the first 'Neronian' games,[113] after which he took no more until the crisis of 68. Though showing respect for Republican tradition and hardly excessive in number, the four early consulships reduced the chances of other senators to win the coveted office. However, in this period the regime appears to have ensured that election to a consulship, whether ordinary or suffect,[114] was available to at least four senators per year. Similar care is reflected in the fact that, anticipating that only two senators other than the *princeps* would be consul in 57, six were appointed for 56. Further early sensitivity to traditional senatorial feelings may be seen in the frequent election of ordinary consuls from families which had provided Rome with consuls in the past but had been neglected by Claudius.[115] Then came change.[116] From 61 to 68 there were, apart from the exceptional years of 65 (that of

---

[105] Below 224.   [106] Rudich 1993, 198–9   [107] Cf. below 154.   [108] Above 22.
[109] Below 296; cf. Champlin 2003, 153, on Nero's growing maturity.
[110] Kienast 2004, 96; cf. Barrett 1996, 116.   [111] Below 351.
[112] Cf. above 56; below 288; Talbert 1984, 177–8.   [113] Bradley 1978a, 92; above 137.
[114] Above 22.   [115] Osgood 2011, 199.
[116] For details of what follows see Levi 1949, 146–7; Griffin 1984, 62, 85.

the Pisonian conspiracy, which opened up gaps in the consular ranks which had to be filled in haste) and 68 (that of Nero's fall), generally only two consuls each year, with suffects appointed only as necessary. In addition, the social mix was greater. Some had consular ancestry, but this tended to be more recent. Others, beginning with Caesennius Paetus, in 61, and including Verginius Rufus, in 63, were 'new men', from families which until then had not produced a consul.[117] This, like the rise of relatively lower-class generals, such as Vespasian and Mucianus, at this time should not be interpreted as Nero's aversion to the Senate but as part of cyclical change in the backgrounds of favourites that, down to the Late Empire, was part of the system. Claudius had preferred lower-born men before the early-Neronian administration returned to aristocrats. The later-Neronian regime promoted newcomers, but even then change was uneven: both Aelianus and Fonteius Capito, Verginius Rufus' colleague in Germany, were from the social elite.[118] The administration's intention appears rather to have been increasingly to favour men of administrative and military ability.

Alongside Corbulo, the prominent generals of the period were Quintus Veranius, Suetonius Paullinus, Plautius Silvanus Aelianus, Caesennius Paetus (whose father-in-law was brother to Vespasian[119]), the brothers Scribonii, Verginius Rufus and Vespasian. Corbulo was appointed in 54/55. Quintus Veranius, governor of Britain from 57, was set on an aggressive policy in the west of the province. He died unexpectedly in 58, but a similar policy was pursued by his successor, Suetonius Paullinus, and culminated in his assault on the Druidic stronghold of Anglesey in 60.[120] It was probably from around 60 that Plautius Silvanus Aelianus, governor of Moesia, campaigned around the Black Sea.[121] Caesennius Paetus fought and lost in Armenia in 62. The brothers Scribonii were made governors of Upper and Lower Germany around 63. Though they were not involved in significant fighting there, the entrusting of such an important command to men who were so close to each other that they might almost be considered a single personality is worthy of notice.[122] The possibility of a grand Caucasus expedition, which would have required a senatorial executive commander, arose in 66.[123] Verginius Rufus was appointed governor of Upper Germany late in 66, after the fall of the

[117] Waldherr 2005, 182.
[118] Thus *contra* Hohl 1918, 40; Warmington 1969, 156–77; Syme 1970, 2; Griffin 1984, 178; Fini 1994, 201–2; Levick 1999a, 25. Drinkwater 2007a, 158–9; Osgood 2011, 89.
[119] Griffin 1976, 230.   [120] Below 332.   [121] Above 139.   [122] Below 227.
[123] Below 148.

Scribonii, and defeated Vindex in 68. Vespasian was made commander-in-chief in Judaea early in 67, and was very soon (soon enough to send prisoners of war to work on the Corinth canal[124]) winning victories there. All this reveals an administration generally ready to launch major military expeditions and to appoint commanders who were outside the Julio-Claudian clan. Successful generals gained what the Republican tradition had taught all good Romans to respect, a military reputation.[125] The relatively high number of such commands under Nero demands explanation.[126] Precedent was set by Corbulo. He was appointed because there was no family alternative. His success made him famous and, with the Julio-Claudian monopoly broken, others were bound to press for the same opportunity. Tacitus reports the contemporary view that Suetonius Paullinus was 'a rival of Corbulo, and anxious to equal the laurels of the recovery of Armenia by crushing a national enemy'.[127] The regime was flexible enough to accede and to give its favourites a high degree of trust. Corbulo, frustrated at being restrained from campaigning by Claudius, had exclaimed 'blessed were the Roman generals of old'.[128] Under Nero, the brakes were off. Corbulo's appointment showed 'a career opened to the virtues'; it was 'almost like the glorious old times'.[129] Although the policy was begun by Agrippina, it was continued by Seneca and Burrus and intensified from around 60 as Poppaea and Tigellinus and their circle strengthened their position by promoting men of ability and honouring them with the consulship. An apparent exception that proves the rule is the consulship of 'Suetonius Paullinus', in 66. He was probably not the governor of Britain in 60/61, Suetonius Paullinus I, but his son of the same name. Though tensions after Boudica's rebellion had resulted in the elder Paullinus' removal from Britain, before and during the revolt he had shown military mettle and he was to take a leading role in early conflicts in 69. He remained a considerable political figure, and honouring the son was a way of signalling that the father was still in favour.[130]

The absence of Silvanus Aelianus from the consular *fasti* of 61–68 is puzzling, as is his general absence from history. He is not recorded in any historical text. What we know of his campaigns comes from a single

---

[124] Below 364.   [125] Cf. below 227.   [126] Cf. below 332, 337.
[127] Tac. *Ann.* 14.29.2: *Corbulonis concertator, receptaeque Armeniae decus aequare domitis perduellibus cupiens.*
[128] Tac. *Ann.* 11.20.1: *beatos quondam duces Romanos.*
[129] Tac/ *Ann.* 13.8. 1: *locus virtutibus patefactus.* Heil 1997, 76: 'fast wie in den glorreichen alten Zeiten'.
[130] Birley 2005, 48 and n. 106, 50 and n. 113.

inscription recording the belated award of triumphal honours to him by Vespasian.[131] The lack of honours and consulship could mean that Aelianus had fallen into disfavour under Nero: Griffin observes that he was nephew by adoption of Claudius' first wife, Plautia Urgulanilla, which may have put him under a political cloud.[132] Against this, even Corbulo, who had received triumphal honours for his service in Germany,[133] never received them for his greater success in the East, which makes their being awarded to Turpilianus, Nerva and Tigellinus in 65 for essentially civilian service even more remarkable.[134] The regime's stinginess may have been deliberate, to avoid creating jealousy between field-commanders. Additionally, since the Neronian regime kept Aelianus at a high level for a prolonged period, it could be that there was no time to give him a consulship. His command ran possibly into 67, perhaps with a view to extending it to cover the great Caucasus expedition,[135] and it was soon followed by Nero's fall. Finally, Aelianus' failure to appear in Tacitus, Suetonius and Dio may be ascribed to the dependence of these authors on a tradition which lauded Corbulo and was disinclined to commemorate a significant rival. Tacitus, in fact, made use of Corbulo's war memoirs,[136] and, while conceding that his hero was not beyond reproach,[137] may have sought to enhance his reputation as the precursor of Agricola.[138] However we may explain Aelianus' apparent eclipsing, the overall impression is that the Neronian regime trusted and valued its generals, to the point of never excessively penalising them for well-intentioned failure. Paullinus' career was not ruined by his less than wholly successful record in Britain;[139] and on his return from Armenia Paetus endured no more than a few jokey remarks from Nero.[140] This was rewarded by their loyalty. It is remarkable how many consuls of this second period kept faith with the Julio-Claudian dynasty.[141] In 68, Verginius Rufus, like his colleague in the German military areas, Fonteius Capito, did not desert Nero; and Turpilianus was killed for his loyalty.[142] Historians have sometimes explained the change in the distribution of consulships negatively, as resulting from a deepening division between Nero and the Senate, which would eventually

[131] *CIL* 14.3608 = *ILS* 986 = Smallwood 1967, no. 228; above 139.
[132] Griffin 1984, 194; cf. below 174.
[133] Tac. *Ann.* 11.20.2; Cass. Dio 60.30.5. Heil 1997, 63; Malloch 2013, 295–6.
[134] Tac. *Ann.* 15.72.2. Rudich 1993, 197; above 29.   [135] Below 226.
[136] Tac. *Ann.* 15.16.1–3; Hurley 2013, 34.   [137] Above 142.
[138] Rubiés 1994, 40; esp. Heil 1997, 28–30, 53–4.   [139] Above 146.
[140] Tac. *Ann.* 15.25.7: *facetiis insectari satis habuit Caesar.*   [141] Cf. Levi 1949, 99.
[142] Below 392, 402, 405.

play a major part in his fall. There are no clear signs of such a conflict,[143] and the recruiting of able men to ranks of the upper aristocracy served only to strengthen the senatorial tradition.[144] The promotion to the highest ranks of government and society of people of talent and loyalty is an activity that historians of any other culture and time usually praise as beneficial.

6.7   The Caucasus and Judaea

6.7.1   The Caucasus

The loss of the final part of Tacitus' 'Annals' obscures a major military development, the essentials of which have to be reconstructed from stray references in his 'Histories' and elsewhere. What is clear is that, soon after Tiridates' reception,[145] Nero began to prepare a major expedition to the East, which he would lead and which would take him through the 'Caspian Gates'. As Pliny I notes, these should properly be referred to as the 'Caucasian Gates', since they gave access across the eastern Caucasus southwards into Iberia, an allied kingdom which had aided Corbulo in his campaigns in Armenia. They are usually identified as the Darial pass, linking modern Russia and Georgia (Figure 11).[146] Nero created an elite force, made up of auxiliary regiments and detachments from legions in Britain and on the Rhine and middle Danube, and of a complete legion, XIV *Gemina*, from Britain, now reckoned to be fully pacified after the Boudican rebellion.[147] He also raised a new, crack, Italian legion, I *Italica*, made up of men six feet tall.[148] He may also have sent military engineers ahead to Iberia.[149] On the assumption that it followed on strategically from recent success in Armenia and the Black Sea region, the general aim of the expedition has been interpreted as the securing of the new 'Roman lake'.[150] A proposed short-term, reactive, strategy is the suppression of incursions by Sarmatian Alans, mentioned by Lucan, through the Darial pass into Iberia and Armenia.[151] A proposed long-term, proactive,

---

[143] Above 26.   [144] Above 18; cf. Talbert 1984, 490.
[145] Below 226; *contra* Heil 1997, 164: from 63, after news of Paetus' defeat.
[146] Suet. *Ner.* 19.2; Cass. Dio 63.8.1; Plin. *HN* 6.40. Warmington 1969, 98; Bradley 1978a, 117–18; Griffin 1984, 228–9; Heil 1997, 170, 224–31.
[147] Tac. *Hist.* 1.6; 2.11; Warmington 1969, 78.   [148] Suet. *Ner.* 19.2; Warmington 1969, 98.
[149] Levick 1999a, 169; Braund 2013, 97–8.   [150] Above 140.
[151] Luc. 8.222–3. Braund 2013, 98.

plan is the extension of Roman control beyond the Caucasus.[152] The launching of so large an army solely against barbarian raiders would have been to use a sledgehammer to crack a nut, but professed peace-keeping might indeed have served as a pretext (for Parthian consumption) for extending Roman power towards the Caspian. Either way, both strategies are made much of by those who see Nero as taking an active, traditionally imperialistic, interest in foreign policy, 'being more attentive to the business of empire than the hostile tradition encourages us to imagine'.[153] Yet the notion that he had any such concern, to the point that he 'had a desire to go to the frontiers',[154] is questionable. From start to finish he showed himself no general, never visiting his troops and never taking to the field even when this was his last chance of survival.[155] He could not have endured months, possibly years, of war far from Rome in harsh and dangerous conditions. Those members of the Neronian Establishment who were really interested in foreign affairs can hardly have welcomed what was proposed. Close consideration suggests the lack of any rational war aims.

Though in this period Rome made first contact with Sarmatians and Alans, these posed little direct threat across the Caucasus which, unlike the lower Danube, offered no easy invasion routes. Substitution of Lucan's 'Alans' with Tacitus' 'Albani', specifically referred to by him as the target of Nero's campaign but generally dismissed as a misunderstanding of 'Alani', does not provide a more reasonable strategy. The Albani lived much further eastwards than the Darial pass, on the Caspian Sea, and so would have been an unlikely foe.[156] Above all, a major expedition in the Caucasus must involve Armenia, and so threaten to disturb the recent peace with Parthia.[157] Later, indeed, when Tiridates faced severe northern barbarian raids into Armenia, Vologaeses sought assistance against them from Vespasian. However, this was when the Armenian question had long been settled, and there was a 'climate of peaceful coexistence between Romans and Parthians'.[158] Vologaeses is unlikely to have made such a request of Nero when Parthia needed to show that it was capable of managing its own affairs without further Roman military interference.[159] For the same reason, Vologaeses will not have tolerated a major Roman presence in the

---

[152] E.g. Henderson 1905, 226–7; Bradley 1978a, 118; Cizek 1982, 338, 342–3.
[153] Waldherr 2005, 155; Braund 2013, 89 (quotation), 96–8.   [154] Braund 2013, 99–100.
[155] Below 401.   [156] Tac. *Hist.* 1.6. Chilver 1979, 155; Heil 1997, 170–5.
[157] Cf. Heil 1997, 176–7.   [158] Levick 1999a, 168.
[159] Joseph. *BJ* 7.244–51; Suet. *Dom.* 2.2; cf. Cass. Dio 66.11.3. *Contra* Braund 2013, 98.

Caucasus, threatening Parthia from the north.[160] Even without such potential friction, and under a *princeps* like Vespasian, totally secure at home and with a distinguished military career, the deployment of so large a force into so relatively unknown and hostile an environment at so great distance from Rome would have been a gamble. Under Nero, still reeling from a major metropolitan conspiracy and with no military experience, it would have been a recipe for disaster. The Neronian Establishment will have long wanted Nero to go to war to gain a military reputation,[161] but the Caucasus were too far away and the circumstances too dangerous. For the moment, they preferred to send him no further than Greece.[162] The concept of a Caucasus campaign was misguided, the preparations costly[163] and the risks great.

The most likely explanation for Nero's proposal is that, *pace* Henderson, it was indeed a 'whim':[164] an ill-thought-through 'break-out'.[165] Its stimulus may have been Nero's meeting with Tiridates, which generated a desire to meet his real equal, Vologaeses. According to Dio, Nero had invited the Parthian emperor several times to Rome, but was always refused. Instead, Vologaeses asked Nero to come to see him. Dio has Nero reacting negatively to the rejection, but his account here is epitomised, brief and unsatisfactory. Perhaps enthused by his success with Tiridates and his related adoption of the title *Imperator* as a *praenomen*,[166] Nero nicknamed legion I *Italica* 'Alexander the Great's phalanx',[167] and so perhaps toyed with the idea of following in the great man's footsteps by crossing through though the Caspian Gates (even though, as Pliny I pointed out, the Darial pass was not the one actually used by Alexander).[168] From here he might traverse a land of mystery and myth before meeting Vologaeses, as warrior to warrior, in the East.[169] Troops destined to be sent eastwards were probably identified or raised over the summer of 66 and ordered to move in 67, ready for campaigning in 68/69, after Nero had finished in Greece. Though the Establishment had no choice but to agree, it probably anticipated that, given Nero's track record in undertaking distant, difficult and

---

[160] Cf. Cizek 1982, 342–3.   [161] Above 132, below 166.   [162] Below 380, 382.

[163] Below 333.   [164] Henderson 1905, 227.

[165] Cf. below 333. Heil (1997, 177) makes it a whim of Nero's advisers, another desperate attempt to give him a military reputation.

[166] Above 94.   [167] Suet. *Ner.* 19.2; Warmington 1969, 98.

[168] Plin. *HN* 6.40. Warmington 1969, 98; cf. Bradley 1978a, 118–19. On Nero and Alexander see Cizek 1982, 343; Heil 1997, 178–9.

[169] Dio 63.7.2, with 63.8.1. Giardina 2011, 24.

uncomfortable journeys, he would not take the scheme to completion. Nero was no Alexander and was, indeed, soon diverted by his unexpected enjoyment of his Greek trip,[170] and by a new eastern crisis, in Judaea. As the impulse behind the Caucasus expedition weakened, none of the units destined for it got further than the Balkans, and all were brought back in 68 to face Vindex.[171]

6.7.2 Judaea

The first rumblings of major unrest in Judaea occurred at about the same time as Tiridates' reception in Italy and Rome, in late April/May 66.[172] There were some nasty incidents, but the situation was kept under control and, to begin with, would have seemed no more than an awkward local difficulty: a serious but routine problem of imperial policing. It could be ignored. The settlement of the Armenian question was much more important, and justified the closing of the doors of the temple of Janus to signify that the Roman world was at peace.[173] However, from around late July 66 the Judaean crisis deepened, with the Jewish storming of Masada and rejection of Roman sacrifice in the temple at Jerusalem. A massacre of Roman troops at the end of September, at or near the start of Nero's visit to Greece, revealed that it had got out of hand.[174] The concatenation of the apparent resolution of the Armenian problem, the prospect of increased Roman intervention east of the Black Sea, and growing trouble in Judaea will, in late 66, have generated a complex strategic and tactical situation that demanded action by the Neronian administration on the advice of its generals.[175] An early example of such considered action must be the rapid movement of troops into Egypt, which prevented the Jewish revolt from spilling over into Alexandria and so disrupting grain supplies to Rome. This took place 'two months and more before the Roman government knew that it was faced with a major Jewish rebellion, and about the time of Nero's departure for Greece'. Another example may be the decision not to draw on eastern forces for the Caucasus expedition. Similarly, in the summer or autumn of 66, the Syrian military command appears to have been removed from Corbulo and given to Cestius Gallus, supplemented by the

---

[170] Below 382.   [171] Tac. *Hist.* 1.6, 9. Bradley 1978a, 118, 260; *contra* Braund 2013, 97–8.
[172] Joseph. *BJ* 2.14.4: in the [Macedonian] month of Artemisius.   [173] Below 214.
[174] Joseph. *BJ* 2.17.2, 17.5–10. Waldherr 2005, 158.
[175] Here, *contra* Heil 1997, 159, 167–8, I reject any notion of any sort of Ethiopian campaign at this time: below n. 176.

transfer of a significant proportion of Corbulo's troops, preparatory to action in Judaea.[176] This, however, led only to further Roman military humiliation, which must have revived memories of the Boudican rebellion, in the shape of Gallus' defeat as he withdrew from a fruitless attack on Jerusalem early in November 66.[177]

6.8   Conclusion

There was no imperial 'grand strategy' for the East, or for the Empire as a whole. The administration allowed its generals remarkable licence in devising their own regional strategy and tactics:[178] as in the case of Suetonius Paullinus in Britain, Aemilianus around the Black Sea and, above all, Corbulo in Syria, who pursued his own policy despite decisions made in Rome. The new 'Roman lake' came about by accident, not design. In fact, though the Neronian regime gave some thought to administration in the provinces by proceeding against corrupt imperial officials,[179] its grasp of the wider political and military situation appears to have been weak. It failed to see trouble coming in Britain and Judaea, and, in the end in Gaul. Furthermore, in late 66 'generals and warfare' combined to produce internal difficulties. Corbulo, expecting to be consulted about the current military situation, cannot have been surprised by Nero's polite summons to his winter residence in Corinth, in no way foreseeing that this would lead to his own destruction.[180] This returns us to the court and politics.

---

[176] Chilver 1979, 11 (quotation); above 148. Major troop movements led to a significant increase in the garrison of 'Alexandria' (Joseph. *BJ* 2.494, 3.8; Tac. *Hist.* 1.31, 70). Griffin interprets these as movements of troops bound ultimately for the Caucasus campaign and, perhaps, in parallel, for another proposed Neronian expedition to Nubia. In her view, Nero intended to leave Greece to supervise both campaigns, at first from Alexandria, which explains the construction of the baths building that got Caecina Tuscus into trouble (Griffin 1984, 229; similarly Cizek 1982, 341). However, sending large numbers of troops to Egypt, travelling there oneself, and contemplating additional fighting in Nubia, is strange behaviour if one is set on campaigning in the Caucasus. As Bradley (1978a, 118) says, 'It would make little sense for troops intended for the Caucasus to be sent beforehand to Alexandria'. To this one might add 'and the more so if, at the same time, one is faced by trouble brewing in Judaea'. In addition, it is more likely that the baths building was constructed in 63/64 in preparation for an earlier, aborted, visit, the prospect of which had given rise to false expectations of an Ethiopian war: above 127, below 205, 221, 373. The simpler explanation is that there is confusion in the sources: while some troops were sent to *Egyptian* Alexandria to repress unrest there caused by the burgeoning Jewish revolt, others – including legion XV *Apollinaris* and probably the majority – were despatched to *Syrian* Alexandria (İskenderun, on the Gulf of Issus, north of Antioch: *contra* Heil 1997, 167 and n. 45; Levick 1999a, 29) to join the main force being gathered to pacify Judaea: Henderson 1905, 372; Heil 1997, 191–2 and n. 48; above 141.

[177] Joseph. *BJ* 2.527–55.   [178] Above 29.   [179] Above 23; below 157.   [180] Below 221, 225.

CHAPTER 7

Politics

7.1 Power-Groups

With a relatively open court, even the most influential individual or group could not control everything. This allowed authentic political activity,[1] by which I mean more than the struggle for personal superiority for its own sake that characterises most human associations, especially autocratic governments where all battle to gain the leader's ear.[2] I also exclude social rivalries between senators, equestrians and freedmen,[3] and make no attempt at the politics of prosopography: the reconstruction of alliances and feuds from family relationships and ties of patronage. Aristocratic competition for social dominance certainly occurred. Much attention has been given to the power of 'an interlinked group of families' – the Pomponii, Plautii, Petronii and, especially, the Vitellii – during the middle years of the first century. Though the Vitellian nexus was weakened by the death of its leader, Vitellius I, in 51, by around 60 it had recovered much of its strength. Some see Vitellian backing as having consolidated Corbulo's rise under Claudius, helped Galba gain his Spanish command, and taken Vespasian to the top in Judaea.[4] It will have been behind the rise of Vitellius II, who rebelled against Galba in 69.[5] However, the paucity of data makes the impact of this group difficult to gauge; and, again, it is dangerous to pursue prosopographical politics too far.[6] What concerns me here is not the perennial grinding together of the tectonic plates of Roman aristocratic society, or the clashes of particular titans at its summit, but the detection of specific objectives which allows the identification of influential individuals and groups working not just for their own ends or, still less,

---

[1] Elsner and Masters (1994, 3–4) come close to this conclusion, albeit briefly.
[2] Cf. Winterling 2009, 89–90; Osgood 2011, 212.   [3] Wallace-Hadrill 1996, 301–2.
[4] Syme 1970, 38; Griffin 1976, 454; Syme 1982, 462, 464–5, 480 and n. 108; Levick 1999a, 14–15 (quotation).
[5] Cf. Tac. *Hist.* 1.9.   [6] Below 225.

against the *princeps* personally, but against policies he was currently pursuing on the advice of other advisers: a sort of loyal opposition. Millar proposes as a general rule that *amici* were politically weak because they could not rely on a 'secure base' or 'sectional interest' in any dispute with the *princeps*.[7] Anything that tests this is significant. Power-groups of a sort certainly existed. and can be seen at work in the events surrounding the assassination of Gaius and the accession of Claudius as the Establishment, faced with sudden emergency, sought new ways to maintain the Julio-Claudian line.[8] They are also evident in the fall of Messalina, the rise of Agrippina and the adoption of Nero.[9] Under Nero, one may point, for example, to the likely orchestrated popular sympathy shown to Octavia in 62;[10] and the Pisonian conspiracy was the product of a set of metropolitan alliances.[11] Such groups do not, however, test Millar's rule because, either bent on changing the current *princeps* or his heir or diffuse and short-lived, they do not reflect long-term 'loyal oppositions' operating through the normal power system of shifting court cabals. Competition between such cabals may be glimpsed in the activities of lesser figures caught up in wider struggles for power. One tantalising example is Julia Silana and her circle in 55;[12] but she is mentioned only in passing, with no indication of her backers. What we do have, however, are signs of one particular prominent and long-lasting cabal created by her rival, Agrippina.

Agrippina lost her dominance in 55, but she remained a redoubtable figure until her death.[13] She was helped in this by her formation of an interest group so powerful that it outlived her. Crucial for its construction was a set of key appointments. The first, late in 54, was that of Corbulo to the Armenian command.[14] The second and third, both in 55, were those of Claudius Balbillus as prefect of Egypt and, more significant, of Faenius Rufus as *praefectus annonae*.[15] The initial priority of this group will have been the protection of Agrippina. Its success is visible in the relatively long time she managed to survive. More important here is what followed her death, during the rise to prominence of Poppaea and Tigellinus.[16] Balbillus had been replaced in 59,[17] but both Corbulo and Faenius Rufus survived the change, with the latter being promoted praetorian prefect alongside Tigellinus in succession to Burrus in 62. Given the purported

[7] Millar 1977, 113.   [8] Cf. Barrett 1996, 72; Gibson 2013, 118.
[9] E.g. (Agrippina) Barrett 1996, 127–30.   [10] Tac. *Ann.* 14.60.6–61.2. Below 193, 195.
[11] Cf. Levi 1949, 96; below 201.   [12] Below 178.   [13] Cf. below 181.   [14] Above 133.
[15] Below 177–8. Barrett (1996, 177) adds Publius Anteius' appointment as governor of Syria in place of Ummidius Quadratus.
[16] Above 136.   [17] Cf. below 344.

antipathy shown to him by both Nero and Tigellinus,[18] this is very strange, and the more so because he lasted in post for three years, down to the self-inflicted disaster of the Pisonian conspiracy.[19] Tacitus claims that Nero felt obliged to appoint him because he was popular with the people and the praetorians,[20] but this is unhelpful. Popular favour is so broad an explanation as to be vacuous, and was of no help to Octavia. Praetorian support for Rufus could have come only after his appointment, had already shown itself incapable of saving Agrippina, and would be of no use to Nero. Do we know the whole story? Though a double prefecture had Augustan precedent,[21] Tigellinus must have resented having a colleague after Burrus had served alone. Did Nero favour Rufus more than the sources allow? As joint praetorian prefect he was responsible for the *princeps'* security during his watch, which should have created some bond between them. Or was Rufus promoted and his enemies wary of him because he had other strong backing? Support for the latter explanation is available in the case of Lusius Geta, one of the pair of praetorian prefects whom Agrippina persuaded Claudius to cashier and replace with Burrus in 51. Despite his dismissal, Geta was appointed prefect of Egypt, which suggests that he 'must have been too powerful to drop'.[22] This returns us to divergent 'loyalist' policy and to Corbulo. When in 62 the Parthian victory over Caesennius Paetus threatened the provincialisation of Armenia, Corbulo rejected Paetus' plea for a combined counterattack on the grounds that he had received no orders to this effect from Nero. This was pure casuistry since Paetus was relatively newly arrived in the East and Corbulo will have known that in pursuing provincialisation he was obeying the instructions of the central administration.[23] That Paetus was not subsequently disgraced confirms that this was official policy.[24] Corbulo's turning a blind eye suggests confidence in friends in high places. His main support will initially have been Agrippina, but since he survived her fall he must have been able to rely on others. The Vitellians can be discounted since they appear to have been behind Caesennius Paetus.[25] The most likely candidate is Faenius Rufus, in a situation of mutual support: Rufus watched Corbulo's back at court while Corbulo's reputation gave Rufus the strength to face out Nero and Tigellinus there. Rufus fell in the first wave of prosecutions after the discovery of the Pisonian

---

[18] Tac. *Ann.* 14.51.6. [19] Below 198. [20] Tac. *Ann.* 14.51.5–6.
[21] Cf. Winterling 2007, 62–3. [22] Griffin 1976, 82–3.
[23] Above 138; *contra* Campbell 1984, 352–3 and n. 25. [24] Cf. Fini 1994, 70.
[25] Above 153; Syme 1982, 463.

conspiracy. Corbulo cannot have escaped suspicion of involvement, which would explain Dio's remark that he sent his son-in-law, Annius Vinicianus to Rome with Tiridates 'as a hostage'.[26] However, Corbulo was not arraigned, hinting that he had still other protectors. Wiedemann proposes Vinicianus himself as Corbulo's 'principal supporter',[27] but this is precluded by his relative youth and inexperience. A possible alternative candidate is Poppaea, recognising Corbulo's basic loyalty and prepared to work with the devil she knew.[28] However, that Corbulo survived her death and even the uncovering of the Vinician conspiracy indicates that others at court were still prepared to protect him. Such co-operation may be interpreted as one of the fruits of the Neronian regime's fair treatment of its generals.[29] The identification and support of fitting individuals may have been promoted by loyal interest groups, with commands assigned through a mixture of patronage, favour and, crucially, informed assessment of talent and reliability. Each group benefited from a protégé's success; and no general appointed to a major provincial command revolted.[30]

7.2   Seneca's *De clementia*: Stoicism and Politics

Did such groups seek more than the personal advancement of their members and the continuation of the Neronian principate, i.e. did any pursue a distinct political 'programme'? Improbable in the case of Nero himself,[31] this may also be rejected in the case of his advisers. Much has been made of whether Seneca strove to use his influence to shape policy. There is a strong francophone tradition of him as an ideologue. Cizek, for example, sees him as the leader of a group favourable to the rise of absolutism as long as this was moderate: 'Antonine' (i.e. inspired by Mark Antony), Stoic, Apolline.[32] Anglophone scholarship is sceptical. Grant questions the extent of Seneca's political dominance;[33] and Griffin is cautious in assessing his ideological influence. She sees Seneca as developing a particular interpretation of the nature of the Principate based on Hellenistic kingship, which he expounded most fully in his *De clementia* ('On Mercy'), addressed to Nero and exalting the power of the *princeps*. However, she sees the work as being ignored by a Nero who had no sympathy for or even real understanding of what was being asked of him,

---

[26] Cass. Dio 62.23.6: *eph' homēreiai.* Above 142.   [27] Wiedemann 1996a, 254.   [28] Below 224.
[29] Below 227.   [30] Below 391.   [31] Below 293.
[32] Cizek 1982, 92, 104–12 (esp. 105: 'politologue').   [33] Grant 1970, 57.

and who had already determined to plough his own furrow.[34] Apart from generally good relations with the Senate and attention to provincial government early in Nero's principate, Griffin therefore finds very little that can be directly attributed to Seneca.[35] I favour the non-ideological interpretation. Seneca had no strong practical political ambitions. He was too much of a courtier to be a reformer. Like his fellow *amici*, he enjoyed gaining influence and getting rich.[36] He was a cross between a 'spin doctor' and 'fixer', making no attempt to change the political world around him, but justifying it and seeking to keep it going as it was.[37] In his politics, as in his philosophy, he was capable of holding conflicting ideas, each of which he followed as it suited the moment: he was a pragmatist.[38] But if so, why did he produce the *De clementia*?

The *De clementia* was probably written in 56.[39] Griffin, following a long-established tradition,[40] proposes that its purpose was in part to defend Nero following the death of Britannicus in 55: 'proclaiming Nero's innocence of bloodshed' and attempting 'to reassure the public that whatever struggles Nero might have with his relations, his principles of government would remain the same'. However, she argues that Seneca also aimed it at the educated elite of Rome as an exposition of political reality: the Principate was an autocracy, and a necessary virtue for the *princeps*-autocrat was *clementia*. The work failed because the behaviour of the *princeps* depended on the character of the incumbent which, in Nero's case, was deficient. After some early exercises in clemency, the 'king' became the 'tyrant'.[41] A problem with this interpretation is that, since people remained uncertain whether Nero had murdered Britannicus,[42] even an indirect, defensive reference to his involvement would have been unwise, feeding the rumour storm constantly raging around him.[43] Why run the risk of suggesting that Nero was capable of 'cruel and inexorable anger'?[44] With regard to political reality, Seneca must have realised that conservatives would not accept autocracy because this went against visceral Roman hatred of monarchy (shown, indeed, by himself in other of his works[45]). Griffin proposes that Seneca hoped to avert hostility to his main

---

[34] Griffin 1976, 136, 170–1; 1984, 77–8, 172. Cf. Warmington 1969, 32; Bradley 1978a, 73; Bryan 2013, 144.

[35] Griffin 1976, 68–76.   [36] Griffin 1976, 81, 89–92.   [37] Cf. Griffin 1976, 76–9.

[38] Above 53, 104.   [39] Sen. *Clem.* 1.9.1. Griffin 1976, 1–2, 135.   [40] E.g. Henderson 1905, 67.

[41] Griffin 1976, 135–6, 141–8, 170–1, 202–9; 1984, 77–8 (quotations).   [42] Below 174–5.

[43] Cf. Sen. *Clem.* 1.8.1: *vestra facta dictaque rumor excipit.*

[44] Sen. *Clem.* 1.5.6: *saeva . . . inexorabilis ira.*   [45] Cf. Reitz 2006, 54.

premise by never directly equating Nero *princeps* with Nero *rex*, but even this is 'all very surprising'.[46] An alternative interpretation, by Rudich, takes as its foundation the fact that, after the eclipsing of Agrippina, Seneca and Burrus were 'the government' in a supposedly 'restored' Republic, a circumstance which 'without parallel or precedent, subverted the remnants of Augustan make-believe'. If, however, Seneca could present Nero as a Hellenistic king, advised by a sage – himself – the situation might be made acceptable.[47] The problem here is, again, that even an indirect projection of Nero as *basileus/rex* would run contrary to Roman political tradition. Furthermore, *sophos* or not, as a senior senator and member of the *Consilium* Seneca will anyway have been expected to advise Nero.[48] His position was an accepted part of the system and required no further justification.

A different approach to the *De clementia* is to regard it, like the *Apocolocyntosis*, as indeed 'a personal message to Nero', not a public treatise.[49] Unlike Seneca's moral essays, which employ the rhetorical trick of a dedication to a friend or relative in distress or doubt and introduce their themes gradually,[50] the *De clementia* begins abruptly, as Seneca announces that the work is his own initiative and moves directly to address Nero. The statement that it is intended 'as a sort of mirror' for the *princeps*, in which Nero will be able to scrutinise his own conscience, jolts the reader 'into rapt attention and expectation'. Subsequent tales of court life bring out the intimacy of the relationship between the two.[51] The work is about clemency and kings, to which Seneca, perhaps influenced by his misfortunes under Claudius,[52] had already given great thought. This was not easy, since Stoicism considered raw pity as a redundant emotion, but Seneca's originality enabled him to proffer a solution based, in a very Roman way, on reasoned or 'rational' mercy.[53] His exposition brings out his own basic humanity.[54] On the other hand, it 'deploys many themes characteristic of the existing literature of advice to monarchs', most of which Nero had probably already heard before as Seneca's pupil.[55] But the

[46] Griffin 1976, 141; cf. Schofield 2015, 70.   [47] Rudich 1993, 13–14.   [48] Above 65.
[49] *Contra* Griffin 1984, 77 (quotation); Schofield 2015, 68.
[50] Shotter 2008, 13; Romm 2014, 13.
[51] Sen. *Clem.* 1.1.1: *quodam modo speculi*; 2.1.2. Schofield 2015, 68 (quotation); cf. Rimell 2015, 125.
[52] Schofield 2015, 73.
[53] Sen. *Clem.* 1.3.1. Bryan 2013, 14; Schofield 2015, 71, 75–6. Cf. Konstan 2015, 174; 179–80; Asmis 2015, esp. 230–2.
[54] E.g. Sen. *Clem.* 1.9.1–11.1; 1.12.5, 16.1–5; 1.18.1–2; 1.23.1.
[55] Henderson 1905, 37; cf. 285; Bradley 1978a, 286; Too 1994, 221; Schofield 2015, 71–2, 73 (quotation).

extant *De clementia* dwells particularly on that which makes mercy necessary for Nero: the supreme power of the *princeps*, catching its essence in a succession of resounding phrases. Nero is the 'vicegerent of the gods' and 'arbiter of life and death for mankind',[56] in 'a position of supreme power', 'able to give life, or to take it away'.[57] Indeed, what sticks in the mind from reading the *De clementia* is absolute power rather than forgiveness. Seneca emphasises Nero has such power but is to be praised for using it well.[58] Nero is thus presented, in modern comic-book terms, as 'Superman': capable of doing enormous harm but instead bringing people 'prosperity, security, justice, freedom and forgiveness'.[59] All this must have been hugely attractive to the young *princeps*, with the added bonus that the text told him that he would not have to lead his armies in person: others would do it for him.[60] The political context is the period immediately after the dominance of Agrippina. With her gone, and with Seneca and Burrus possessing little basic inclination to replace her as joint regents, they will have hoped for Nero's early assumption of his duties and encouraged him accordingly.[61] Seneca therefore wrote the *De clementia* to get Nero to grasp the extent of his power and the responsibility that came with this: to 'jump-start' him into acting the fully functioning *princeps*.

The hope was that he would be seen as a second Augustus,[62] but Augustus was no Hellenistic king so why project Nero as *basileus*? Commentators, ancient and modern, have criticised Seneca for not teaching Nero about the Principate.[63] This is mistaken. The Augustan Principate was hugely complex and its essence is still disputed.[64] Seneca's use of 'court' and, indeed, 'principate', demonstrates that he was well aware of the political realities of his day. On the other hand, active under only the third, fourth and fifth *princeps*, he was simply too close to the beginnings of the current system and too personally involved in its operation to make complete sense of it, politically or philosophically.[65] Furthermore Nero,

---

[56] Sen. *Clem.* 1.1.2: *deorum vice . . . vitae necisque gentibus arbiter.*
[57] Sen. *Clem.* 1.11.2: *in maxima potestate*; 1.21.2: *dandi auferendique vitam potens.*
[58] Sen. *Clem.* 1.1.3–4. Schofield 2015, 70.
[59] Waldherr 2005, 105: 'Wohlstand, Sicherheit, Recht, Freiheit und Milde'; Romm 2014, 89.
[60] Sen. *Clem.* 1.4.1. Cf. below 167.   [61] Above 53.
[62] Cf. Rimell 2015, 125. At *Clem.* 1.14.2–3 Seneca makes something of Nero's recent new title of *pater patriae*, a rare direct acknowledgement of the working of the Augustan principate.
[63] E.g. Drinkwater 2013, 157–9. Cf. Griffin 1976, 148; Too 1994, 211–14; Williams 1994, 180–5. Waldherr 2005, 10.
[64] E.g. Winterling 2009, 12–17.
[65] Sen. *Clem.* 1.1.6. Ker 2015, 110; above 59. Cf. Griffin 1976, 238; Williams 1994, 184–9 and n. 29.

soon to show that he had no real interest in imperial administration,[66] would not anyway have responded well to an developed analysis of the Principate or to any direct exhortation to take up its duties. Seneca, knowing him and wanting him to accept these duties, calculated that it was more effective to appeal to him, as 'Superman', to act the merciful king, indispensable and loved by all: to become the Augustus of popular memory rather than the Augustan *princeps*. This went against all Seneca's principles, both political and philosophical. Agrippina would not originally have appointed him as Nero's tutor if she had not felt that his views on the best way to rule the Roman state 'coincided with her own', which was the '"constitutional" form of principate that operated through consensus and the liberalism of the ruler rather than through simple exercise of power'.[67] And 'it was not Stoic doctrine that kingship was the best form of *res publica*'.[68] His advocacy of Hellenistic kingship was meretricious because, in presenting metaphor – the *princeps* was like a king – as fact, he ignored recent history: the *princeps* was never a king.[69] Though Seneca was a pragmatist, such advocacy is indeed 'all very surprising'. If published, the *De clementia* would have upset many senators.

Seneca's wish must have been that, once launched into it and under proper guidance, Nero would grow into the job of Augustan *princeps*, and for a time this appeared to happen. Nero made an effort but his heart can never have been in it, and from 58 his attention was increasingly elsewhere. The year 57 saw the construction of the great wooden amphitheatre and the holding of magnificent games in the Campus Martius. These probably caught Nero's imagination as much as they did that of Calpurnius Siculus' Corydon.[70] In 58, Nero participated in the debate about indirect taxation, but this was his last major intervention in regular administrative issues. In the same year, indeed, Corbulo's victories in Armenia led to the honouring of him as *imperator* but may also have put him under pressure from Agrippina to show himself in the field and encouraged him to turn to Poppaea, who now appears for the first time at court and with whose help Nero might indulge his artistic tastes.[71] From 59, following the death of Agrippina, he was free to act as he pleased.[72] By then his inattention was of little consequence. As it had become clear that he was unwilling to accept the burdens of office, close advisers had taken up the strain and continued the Augustan/Agrippinian Principate on his behalf. Though Seneca could

---

[66] Above 12, 57, 144, below 286.   [67] Barrett 1996, 107.   [68] Schofield 2015, 74.
[69] Griffin 1976, 139; cf. Too 1994, 220–1.   [70] Calp. *Ecl.* 7.23–72. Below 331.
[71] Above 135, below 166, 178, 181.   [72] Below 297.

not have made complete sense of the developing Principate, he knew what needed to be done to keep it running. He composed the first crucial speeches that allowed Nero to win over the Praetorians and the Senate;[73] and he used his 'ascendancy' to keep the wheels on the political cart.[74] His main aims will have been stability and continuity. He was prepared to co-operate with people who had been strong supporters of Claudius (such as the Vitellians) and those who used Stoicism to express their dislike of current developments (such as Thrasea Paetus and his supporters).[75] In short Seneca pursued no political or ideological agenda, and neither did anyone else, making 'loyal opposition', though it existed, rare and muted.

First-century Roman Stoicism demands direct attention. This was a philosophical age. Many leading Romans associated themselves with various schools: Platonism, Aristotelianism, Epicureanism etc. However, to judge from the affiliations of those we know, the most attractive was Stoicism.[76] It is a measure of the Stoic dominance that Petronius, a satirist to the end, spent his final hours in studied 'un-Stoic' fashion.[77] Today, the best known Neronian Stoic is Seneca, but his contemporaries accorded pole position to another 'celebrity' Stoic philosopher, Musonius Rufus.[78] Though one of Nero's Pisonian victims, he was exiled, not executed, played an important part in the civil wars of 69–71, and lived to a ripe old age.[79] Since the Roman version of Stoicism allowed participation in public affairs,[80] we must ask whether Stoics formed political and ideological power-groups. The answer is decidedly 'no'. We can detect no 'Stoic opposition' to the principle of the Principate.[81] A few Stoics may have taken a stand against individual *principes* but, as in the case of Thrasea Paetus and his circle, these used Stoicism to stiffen, not to generate, their conservative political views.[82] And when the political heat was on, Stoicism allowed those who felt they were likely to be burned, such as Rubellius Plautus and even Thrasea Paetus, to shrink from the flame.[83] Again, Stoicism was a broad church, from which people took such teachings as suited them.[84] It is little wonder that there was no Stoic literary opposition, and so no surprise that there 'was no wholesale or consistent persecution of Stoics under Nero'.[85]

---

[73] Above 55, 58.   [74] Griffin 1976, 103 (term).   [75] Griffin 1976, 97–100, 103; cf. 365.
[76] Bryan 2013, 134–6.   [77] Holland 2000, 195.
[78] Rudich 1993, 125–7; Bryan 2013, 139–42; Hansen 2013, 303, 306.
[79] Tac. *Hist.* 3.81. Above 106; below 199.   [80] Bryan 2013, 134–6.
[81] Rudich 1993, 69–70; Bryan 2013, 136.   [82] Below 217.   [83] Below 192, 217.
[84] Above 103; cf. Doody 2013, 289, 291.   [85] Above 108; Rudich 1993, 159.

7.3   Nero's Team and Its Aims

Seneca's lack of any desire for ideological reform was, therefore, not unique. Scrutiny of Nero's close associates reveals others who demonstrated the same understanding of the Principate and who, whatever their personal views, were determined simply to keep it working. Most of the 'politics', including the political deaths, of the period may be subsumed under 'stability' and 'continuity', as the Establishment used every means at its disposal to keep Nero in power.[86] Senior imperial freedmen would not have desired regime change, since a new administration might cost them dear, as the fate of Narcissus at the hands of Agrippina in 54 will have reminded them.[87] *Amici,* especially army commanders, with class memories of the horrors of the late Republic will have wished to avoid internal conflict. It may be significant that, as the Republican civil wars passed out of living memory, we find dread of renewed strife in the literature of the day. Rubellius Plautus' refusal to precipitate provincial rebellion, Piso's rejection of a military *coup*, and Nerva's complicity in the suppression of the Pisonian conspiracy may likewise reflect such fear.[88] Nero's accession will have encouraged hope of long-term stability. He seemed capable; and his youth gave him plenty of time to produce and raise the heir who would ensure the continuance of the dynasty and its supporters. Though Nero lacked enthusiasm for his job, he was biddable. Inner *amici* and freedmen could direct him along the road of stability while keeping him out of public affairs and encouraging him to produce an heir.

However, Nero could never be turned into a mere figurehead. He was not foolish, slothful or passive. He demanded stimulation from those around him, and down to his fall his court was a place of banter and discourse. This meant that he could not just be ignored or managed by crude toadying; and the older he grew the less predictable he was likely to become.[89] His advisers had to watch their words. The courage and skill of the ever-changing supporting cast of the Neronian imperial soap opera[90] – Agrippina, Pallas, Seneca, Burrus, Acte, Poppaea, Tigellinus and the rest – should not be underestimated. As each team disappeared it was replaced. Most principals, especially Poppaea and Tigellinus, are traditionally disparaged. This derives from the common source tradition. Tacitus paints Poppaea as a *femme fatale*, who wheedled and nagged Nero into destroying

---

[86] Cf. Osgood 2011, 39, 212.   [87] Below 193; cf. Waldherr 2005, 33–4.
[88] Tac. *Ann.* 14.58–59.1; 15.59.1–7, 72.2. Above 111, 114.   [89] Cf. below 164.
[90] Cf. Mordine 2013, 111.

Octavia so that he could marry her.[91] Likewise, he depicts Tigellinus as evil incarnate: vicious, grasping, corrupted and corrupting, working on Nero's fears for his own ends.[92] Dio has Poppaea behind Nero's decision to kill his mother, and presents Tigellinus as outstanding in his debauchery and cruelty.[93] Suetonius is oddly reticent in this respect but in Philostratus' 'Life' of Apollonius, Tigellinus appears as the man who taught Nero his cruelty and extravagance and who, with his network of spies, sought constantly to expose and destroy supposed enemies of the regime.[94] Most modern historians accept this negative characterisation more or less as it stands,[95] but to vilify the rise to power – through class or sex – of 'upstarts' reflects senatorial prejudice.[96] Holland is an exception in summing up Tigellinus as more than 'a serviceable villain': 'He was a clear sighted opportunist of undoubted executive ability, who had the brains to analyse correctly the power structures of imperial Rome, and was able to manipulate them for his own benefit through his understanding of the Emperor's character'.[97] Tigellinus indeed served Nero well. If, for example, one reads between the lines of Tacitus' account of the suppression of the Pisonian conspiracy it becomes clear that he was only doing his duty. The sudden intensification of security in Rome was only to be expected and should not be extended to any earlier period. Tigellinus did not make Rome into a 'police state', an anachronistic concept, and such spies as he had did not, apparently, detect the Pisonian conspiracy.[98] Poppaea, too, was no fool, being well known for her expertise in eastern affairs.[99] She and Tigellinus formed a highly successful partnership and deserve recognition of their efforts. Team-rule was jarred but not significantly damaged by the Pisonian conspiracy.[100] In the period of this conspiracy a third generation of top *amici* and advisers began to emerge. As Poppaea and Tigellinus had replaced Seneca and Burrus, so newcomers gradually replaced them. These included Faenius Rufus' replacement as joint prefect, Nymphidius Sabinus, Petronius Turpilianus and Nerva, all honoured for their role in suppressing sedition, and Cluvius Rufus, along with Vitellius II, compère at the *Neronia*

---

[91] Tac. *Ann.* 14.1; cf. below 182.   [92] Tac. *Hist.* 1.72; *Ann.* 14.51.5.
[93] Cass. Dio 61.12.1; 62.13.2.   [94] Philostr. *VA* 4.42–4.
[95] E.g. Henderson 1905, 135–6, 142. 236; Grant 1970, 212–13; Griffin 1984, 100; Rudich 1993, 64–54; Fini 1994, 134.; Holland 2000, 132, 138; Waldherr 2005, 103; Shotter 2008, 84, 129–30.
[96] Cf. Tac. *Hist.* 1.72; *Schol. Iuv.* 1.155. Above 136.
[97] Holland 2000, 133; cf. Grant 1970, 138; Cizek 1982, 196; Fini 1994, 141–2.
[98] Cf. Rudich 1993, 129; below 201.   [99] Cizek 1982, 179; Griffin 1984, 101.
[100] Cf. below 210.

II of 65 and Nero's master-of-ceremonies in 66–67 in Greece.[101] 'A new patterning of power began to emerge': 'shrewder minds', that helped the regime navigate its way through the crisis.[102] The newcomers secured their power after the death of Poppaea. Nymphidius Sabinus gained in influence, probably to the detriment of Tigellinus;[103] and two women became important. The first was Sporus/'Poppaea''s Mistress of the Robes, Calvia Crispinilla.[104] The second was Nero's third wife, Statilia Messalina. Nero married Statilia, a close acquaintance but not his lover, probably early in 66.[105] She was noble, beautiful, wealthy, intelligent and well educated, and not afraid to speak her mind (the scholiast on Juvenal criticises her as an opinionated 'blue-stocking'). Probably older than Nero and already much married, she was in principle more than an adequate replacement for Poppaea as companion and future mother of his children.[106] However, she found herself having to cope with Nero in his chronic anguish at the loss of Poppaea and in his consequent infatuation with Sporus. She must have been a woman of remarkable fortitude both to agree to marry him and, even more, to try to tempt him into having that all-important child with her.[107] Behind the scenes, those who put her in this position, i.e. those who persuaded Nero to remarry so soon after his devastating loss, must have had enormous influence over both. The Establishment was strong, but it could not be certain that things would always go its own way: Nero was always capable of asserting his will.

7.4   Nero's Break-Outs

This was demonstrated from the start by a series of incidents which show Nero acting against the wishes of his advisers, who then had to deal with the consequences. I term these his 'break-outs'.[108] I do not classify as break-outs actions which arose out of political expediency and involved interested third parties. These, explained elsewhere, include, by year:

59 the sentencing to death of Agrippina
62 the divorce from and execution of Octavia, and the removal of Sulla and Plautus

---

[101] Suet. *Ner.* 21.2, *Vit.* 4; Cass. Dio 63.14.3.
[102] Grant 1970, 215 (quotation); Rudich 1993, 128 (quotation).   [103] Cf. below 216, 408.
[104] Below 231, 311, 388.
[105] Below 310, 320; Bradley 1977, 79–80 and n. 1; Bradley 1978a, 208; Kienast 2004, 99.
[106] *Schol. Iuv.* 6.434. Bradley 1978a, 208; Champlin 2003, 104, 145–6, 162.
[107] Cf. Fini 1994, 202.   [108] Cf. Holland 2000, 54.

64   the basic need for the *Domus Aurea*
65–66 the first wave of persecutions and punishments related to the
      Pisonian conspiracy
66–67 the basic idea of a Greek tour and certain of the inducements
      offered to Nero to participate and then return home.

I also exclude incidents branded as follies by the source tradition but which
may be understood in context (such as, in 58, his proposal to abolish all
indirect taxes; and, in 65, the 'African gold' fiasco),[109] and 'crimes' of
which Nero is unlikely to have been guilty (such as, in 65, the murder of
Poppaea).[110] His break-outs, again examined elsewhere, therefore
comprise:

54   his excessive generosity to Doryphorus and subsequently, no doubt,
      others close to him
55   his instigation of the affair with Acte
      perhaps some element of panic at the news of Agrippina's
      supposed treachery
58   his instigation of the affair with Poppaea
      his suppression of proceedings against the son of Suillius Rufus
59   his failure to give Agrippina a proper burial
63   his insistence upon the lifelike portraiture of the reformed coinage
64   his singing in public in Naples
      his contemplating, then cancelling, a trip to Greece and to the East
      his popularist behaviour at Tigellinus' banquet, and his partici-
      pation in 'lewd' theatricals
      his impromptu recital during the Great Fire
      his treatment of condemned Christians
      his unorthodox development of the *Domus Aurea*
65   his first public performance in Rome
66   his enthusiasm for a great expedition to the Caspian Gates
66–67 his playing the professional entertainer in Greece, appearing un-
      Roman in his hairstyle and dress, marrying Sporus, playing
      female roles, risking mutilation and death in chariot-racing,
      and proving hard to recall to Italy
      his exacting promises of a 'triumph' and a grand 'liberation' of
      Greece
67   aspects of this 'triumph'.

[109] Below 343, 351.   [110] Below 219.

One major break-out spanned the whole of Nero's principate: his failure to undertake any sort of military action. Romans always prized military success. Augustus was essentially a legitimised warlord, and it was crucial for each of his successors to be 'a proven military man' in order to be accepted at home and 'command the obedience and respect of foreign powers'.[111] Nero's promoters will have hoped that he would excel as a soldier. Agrippina, in particular, will have been eager for him to emulate his grandfather, Germanicus.[112] Her expectation is evident in sculptures at Olympia and Aphrodisias which depict Nero as the great warrior-leader to come.[113] Claudius had shown his military mettle by conquering Britain. For the honour of fatherland and family Nero must do at least as well, but again not yet.[114] War was dangerous for young Julio-Claudians. Augustus had sent his grandsons, Gaius and Lucius Caesar, overseas and both had perished, the younger in 2, when he was about eighteen, and the elder in 4, when he was about twenty-three.[115] There was every reason for keeping Nero away from fighting.[116] He first had to be toughened up in military exercises and on the streets of Rome.[117] But Nero needed at some stage to win his spurs, and Corbulo's successes in the Armenian campaign would have allowed him to make at least a token appearance in the East. Agrippina may have nagged Nero to go on campaign there in 58 when, approaching his twenty-first birthday, he showed his maturity by giving up his night-time revels on the streets of Rome.[118] Yet in 58 he was still younger than Gaius Caesar had been on his death from wounds received while fighting in Armenia, so it is not surprising that Nero stayed in Rome. He might have gone to Britain in 61/62 after the defeat of Boudica, but the British victory was costly and marred by early failure, and the situation remained tense.[119] The best opportunity offered itself in 64, when Nero was twenty-six and victory in Armenia seemed assured. According to Dio, the idea arose, but was soon rejected by the *princeps* who used a fall sustained while performing a sacrifice to justify his staying at home.[120] The only time that Nero showed any real enthusiasm for war was over his

---

[111] Griffin 1984, 221–4; Barrett 1996, 152–3; Bellemore 2013, 84 (quotation); Braund 2013, 84 (quotation).

[112] Cf. Barrett 1996, 28–30; above 35, 38.   [113] Above 39, 42.

[114] Osgood 2011, 90–105; Braund 2013, 83; above 35.

[115] Kienast 2004, 73–5; Osgood 2013, 27–8, 34–5.   [116] Specifically, in Armenia: above 131.

[117] E.g. Tac. *Ann.* 11.11.5; Suet. *Ner.* 10.2. Cf. below 297.   [118] Below 178, 297.

[119] Above 138. Holland (2000, 123: 'If Nero had possessed even the smallest spark of military spirit he would surely have called for his armour and saddled a horse') is too critical.

[120] Cass. Dio 62.22.4 (assuming that this is not a garbled doublet of Nero's religious experience in the temple of Vesta: below 205, 309).

Caucasus expedition, but this was unrealistic and the project withered on the vine.[121] There was no thought of him involving himself in the Jewish war.[122] Indeed, Nero left Italy only once, to go to Greece, and never showed himself in the field. He did not go because he was not disposed to do so: this was his 'break-out'. He disliked long-distance travel;[123] and temperamentally he was against bloodshed, preferring fishing over hunting, the traditional aristocratic means of honing the skills of war in time of peace.[124] Likewise, it is not surprising that he seems to have had little interest in *venationes*, the slaughter of animals in mock hunts in the arena. At Patrobius' games in Puteoli in 66 it was Nero's guest, Tiridates, who did the killing.[125] His lack of interest in foreign adventure probably manifested itself early. As a boy he may have decided that all that was necessary to emulate Germanicus was to follow his lead as a man of letters and culture;[126] and I propose above that his non-military spirit may be perceived in the *De clementia*.[127]

Nero's break-outs became more frequent from 64 as, approaching the age of thirty, he found his *métier* and began to act the professional entertainer. However, even down to 68 none was disastrous. Nero's generosity, the building of the *Domus Aurea*, and the 'liberation' of Greece were all expensive but did not seriously rend the fiscal fabric of the Empire.[128] Nothing that Nero did caused irreversible metropolitan discontent. The ordinary people of Rome, indeed, seem to have welcomed his popular excesses, including the 'triumph'.[129] At court and in the Senate Nero's break-outs repelled arch-conservatives and probably caused embarrassment to even his closest supporters. Elsewhere, however, the Empire went on as before. In Greece and the East Nero was particularly popular, as testified by Plutarch and Pausanias and by the appearance of 'false Neros' after his death.[130] Above all, on the main frontier armies stayed loyal. This was because even Nero's neglect of his military obligations was not fatal. For ordinary soldiers his youthful street-fighting and adult interest in hard exercise and bruising and dangerous sports proved that he was man enough to be *princeps*. Their officers appreciated the skill and courage of the Neronian Establishment in choosing its commanders and giving them relatively free rein, and rewarded it with fidelity and a string of successes that gave Nero all the prestige of victory.[131] Like Antoninus Pius to come,

---

[121] Above 150; below 392.   [122] Heil 1997, 189.   [123] Below 377.
[124] Suet. *Ner.* 30.3. Below 297, 300, 322; Drinkwater 2001, 141–3.   [125] Cass. Dio 63.3.2.
[126] Cf. Suet. *Ner.* 10.2. Malitz 1999, 37–8.   [127] Above 159.   [128] Below 350.
[129] Above 94, below 347, 375, 384; cf. Malitz 1999, 47, 49–52; Meier 2008, 569–72.
[130] Alcock 1994, 100, 103–7.   [131] Above 135, 150.

he did not need to be greatly military himself. The fact that Nero had fewer imperial salutations than Claudius, twelve to Claudius' twenty-seven, was a sign not of weakness but of the confidence of the Establishment in its *princeps* and its generals. His fall in 68 did not result from any great hostility to him on the part of his armies. Unlike what happened in 69, there were no great military insurrections.[132] What went wrong in 68 was that the need for a demonstration of at least token generalship became suddenly urgent. Nero's refusal to undertake this was his final, and fatal, break-out.

---

[132] Campbell 1984, 42–3; *contra* Grant 1970, 221.

PART II

Assessment

CHAPTER 8

Killer? I: 54–62

8.1 Introduction

Chapters 8 to 13 review the 'Nero of legend' outlined at the end of Chapter 1. Here and in this Chapter 9 I consider Nero the cold-blooded 'killer', examining all significant Neronian deaths apart from those of the Christians of Rome, Julius Montanus, Domitia and the African landowners, dealt with elsewhere.[1]

8.2 Claudius

The source tradition claims that Claudius died by poisoning. Though towards the end of his principate Nero played the parricide on stage, this should not be interpreted as an admission of guilt but as his way of dealing with unsettling episodes in his life.[2] The tradition points the finger of blame directly at Agrippina,[3] and the charge is not implausible. The first coins of Nero's principate suggest anticipation of a regime change.[4] Agrippina may have found Claudius becoming less easy to control. Britannicus, close to adulthood, remained a rival to Nero. Finally, given her senatorial connections, Agrippina may have thought it prudent to get rid of a ruler who, despite her efforts, could not shake off the senatorial hostility of his early years. If Claudius were toppled by others, she and Nero would fall with him.[5] The case is not proven, and some prefer to believe that Claudius died of natural causes,[6] but either way Nero had no direct responsibility for his stepfather's death.

---

[1] Below 244, 317, 346.   [2] Below 290.   [3] Tac. *Ann.* 12.66.2-5; cf. 13.14.4.   [4] Above 44.
[5] Holland 2000, 58–60; above 34.
[6] For discussion (mostly, though not entirely, hostile to Agrippina): Henderson 1905, 42–3; Hohl 1918, 354–5; Levi 1949, 85; Grant 1970, 33; Warmington 1969, 19–20; Bradley 1978a, 195; Cizek 1982, 83; Griffin 1984, 32; Fini 1994, 25–6; Barrett 1996, 138–42; Heil 1997, 62; Malitz 1999, 11–12; Holland 2000, 63; Champlin 2003, 44–6; Waldherr 2005, 58–60; Winterling 2007, 180; Shotter 2008, 53–4; Giardina 2011, 17; Osgood 2011, 242–5; Romm 2014, 57.

8.3   M. Junius Silanus

'The first death under the new principate', Tacitus declares, was the
murder of M. Junius Silanus, proconsul of Asia, just after Nero's accession.
Though Tacitus again makes clear that the deed was solely the work of
Agrippina, he is set on establishing the 'monstrous' character of the whole
incoming regime.[7] This is part of his senatorial invective, but the death
of Silanus is an illuminating example of the difficulties generated by
tension between traditional Roman aristocratic practice and what was
necessary for the survival of a 'restored' Republic: part of the constitutional
paradox.[8]

Aristocratic Republican families welcomed children as a means of maintaining and increasing the greatness of their lines. Boys were destined for
offices of state; girls were married off to secure alliances with other
powerful families. Blood counted. 'Despite a traditional antipathy towards
the notion of kingship, Romans did make considerable allowance for the
principle of heredity in public life.'[9] Dynastic rivalry suited a society in
which office was usually won through election; elections were more or less
regular and fair; and the positions gained were held for only a year or so.
There was a need for a ready pool of competent adult males, of whom
some would always be competing for, holding or resting from office. Yet
'blood' was negotiable. The desire for heirs explains traditional Roman
unconcern for rights of primogeniture and easy acceptance of adoption,
even of adolescents and adults.[10] It was the legal family, its name and
traditions, that came first, not the individual. Any threat to a family's
continuation should be circumvented.[11] An important consequence of
multiple heirs, direct and adopted, was, given the relatively small number
of aristocratic families, the growth of complex genealogies through which
everyone who mattered was in some way related to everyone else.[12]
Augustus, typically, continued Republican practice, but this was more
than just 'idiosyncrasy'.[13] A key element in the evolution of imperial

[7] Tac. *Ann.* 13.1.1: *prima novo principatu mors*; cf. 13.2.1: *ibatur in caedes, nisi* . . .
[8] Above 19, 98.   [9] Barrett 1996, 16.   [10] Above 14.
[11] Cf. Crook 1992, 545, 548–9, 556 and n. 31.
[12] Lintott 1992, 51 (on the difficulties of reconstructing political groupings/factions in this period):
'The links produced by marriages and adoptions produced such a complex network that it becomes
difficult to isolate a stable unit between the microcosm of the individual politician and his intimates
and the macrocosm of the *potentes* (the leading senators) viewed as a whole'. Cf. below 224–5.
[13] So Crook 1996a, 83.

succession was the sentimental attachment of the army to blood heirs.[14] The first couple of generations of Julio-Claudians were therefore encouraged to make the grand aristocratic marriages and have the children that were their traditional meed and due. (Autocratic Romans could not exclude domestic aristocrats from the dynastic equation by marrying exclusively into foreign autocratic families. This went against tradition and, anyway, soon the only available suitable 'royals' were Parthian.[15]) Augustus had attempted to impose order by designating specific heirs, but the lack of a son of his own and the deaths of the earliest designated heirs thwarted his efforts to establish a clear pattern of succession. In AD 4, he was driven back to the Republican expedient of adoption: of his wife's son, Tiberius, and his own grandson, Agrippa Postumus. Postumus was subsequently sidelined, but Tiberius succeeded and there emerged the possibility of a new line of blood heirs through Augustus' grandnephew, and Tiberius' nephew and adopted son, Germanicus, and Augustus' granddaughter, Agrippina I: the 'dream ticket'.[16] Germanicus died before he could become *princeps*, but the ticket remained and inhibited the operation of full blood-succession under both Tiberius and Claudius. Tiberius continued to advance the sons of Germanicus, even though he had a son and grandson of his own;[17] and Claudius' blood heir, Britannicus, lost precedence to his adopted son but direct descendant of Germanicus, Nero.[18] Thus though 'the dynastic goal was still the old one',[19] by the middle of the first century the 'half-baked' Principate had still not established clear rules of succession. As we have seen, *le roi est mort, vive le roi!* was not part of Roman imperial thinking.[20]

In addition, although there was woolly acquiescence to succession by a designated heir, the feeling remained that an incompetent *princeps* or nominated successor might be challenged by an eligible male; and the extended Julio-Claudian family led to a profusion of men with claims to lead the *domus* that rivalled both those of the incumbent *princeps* and of males of other great families who, by virtue of their marriage with

---

[14] Jones 1964, 1.324. Cf. Jones 1966, 13; Osgood 2011: '... however much other groups had to be cultivated, all emperors ruled most fundamentally at the behest of the armies'. Seager 2013, 54 (on *SC in Cn. Pisonem*): significant parts include 'praise of the army's loyalty and devotion to the *domus Augusta* ... and the injunction to the troops to cleave to those commanders who showed the greatest devotion to the name of the Caesars, which guarantees the safety of the city and the empire ...' Cf. above 162.

[15] Cf. Griffin 1976, 244; below 223.　　[16] Above 14.　　[17] Barrett 1996, 32.

[18] Barrett 1996, 96, 98, 102; Holland 2000, 45.　　[19] Crook 1996a, 105.

[20] Cf. Osgood 2011, 215: the system 'still did not openly acknowledge a principle of hereditary succession'; above 12, 14.

Julio-Claudian women, felt they had a legitimate interest in family affairs.[21] A certain amount of blood-letting after Augustus had pruned some of this growth, but thanks, for example, to the marriages of Claudius and his daughters, it soon grew back.[22] 'Nero was faced with a frightening number of potential rivals and heirs'.[23] We shall see the consequences of this in the cases of Rubellius Plautus and Sulla, 'the two men [*sc.* Nero] most feared'.[24] However, particular threat had been perceived in the Junii Silani, a family which, like the ruling *domus*, was descended directly from Augustus.[25] L. Junius Silanus I, for seven years the intended husband of Octavia, brought in and brought on by Claudius to strengthen his line, was pushed aside by Agrippina in 48 and committed suicide on the day of her wedding to Claudius, in 49.[26] It was his eldest brother, M. Junius Silanus, who was killed in 54.[27] Both were cruel deaths but, like most of those to follow, they must be understood as part and parcel of the ruthless politics of the age, not monstrous tyranny. At the start of the new principate, Silanus, a grown man with legitimate family grievances against Agrippina, might justifiably be seen as a potential focus of opposition and dealt with accordingly, without reference to Nero.[28]

8.4   Britannicus

Though Agrippina was down in early 55, she was far from out. With her lineage, her titles, her experience, her clients and her wealth (Nero does not appear to have allowed her to bankrupt herself in the wake of the Acte affair[29]), she remained a major force in court politics. It was probably she who, while accepting Nero's dismissal of Pallas, won him the appearance of voluntary retirement and ensured his indemnity from audit and prosecution.[30] Agrippina's priority will have been to regain Nero's favour. In this she first experienced failure and then, ironically, fatal success. Failure

---

[21] Winterling 2007, 20–21.

[22] See e.g. Griffin 1984, 194, on the resonances of his marriage to his first wife, Plautia Urgulanilla – among other significant relationships, the adopted aunt of the general Ti. Plautius Silvanus Aelianus: above 147. Cf. Tac. *Ann.* 4.3.1, on what faced an ambitious outsider, Sejanus, under Tiberius: *plena Caesarum domus* ('the ruling house was full of Caesars').

[23] Griffin 1984, 193.   [24] Griffin 1984, 99; below 191.

[25] Wiedemann 1996a, 244, 250. There were four males and two females, sisters. One sister, Junia Lepida, married the lawyer G. Cassius Longinus: see above 25; below 216, 321; Syme 1970, 36–7. The other, Junia Calvina, the last of the line, died under Vespasian: Treggiari 1996, 900.

[26] Tac. *Ann.* 12.3.2, 12.4, 12.8.1; Barrett 1996, 99–100; Osgood 2011, 90, 92, 96; above 33.

[27] Tac. *Ann.* 13.1.1–3. Cf. below 178.

[28] Pliny I's casual charge of poisoning against Nero (*HN* 7.59) need not be taken seriously.

[29] Above 54–5.   [30] Tac. *Ann.* 13.14.2. Rudich 1993, 8.

arose from her sudden apparent interest in Britannicus as an alternative *princeps*.[31] Though Tacitus implies that her threats were genuine, his details are overblown and his report that they were made directly to Nero and were accompanied by no clandestine activities indicates that they were feigned, a means of alarming him into a reconciliation: 'merely another stage in her struggle for Nero's soul'.[32] Agrippina would never have wanted Britannicus to eclipse her son, in whom she had invested so much. Furthermore, managing Britannicus as *princeps* would, with no close blood-tie and his resentment at previous wrong, have proved more difficult than managing Nero. In expressing such sentiments Agrippina revealed that she had still not regained her political touch. The source tradition makes Britannicus the victim of her hot-headedness. He died suddenly and dramatically early in February 55, and his death is blamed on a jealous Nero who had him poisoned.

His fate is not surprising. The Augustan partnership put the *princeps* in control. No autocrat can stomach a rival, and the deification of Claudius made Britannicus, as another 'son of a god', even more of a threat.[33] He was doomed from the start.[34] The Roman political community generally appreciated the situation. As it had approved the death of Tiberius Gemellus under Gaius because it brought political stability so, according to Tacitus, it acquiesced in the removal of Britannicus on the grounds that 'autocracy knows no partnership'.[35] But who was responsible and was this really murder? If Britannicus was murdered, the deed might equally have been the work of Seneca and Burrus, afraid both of Agrippina's regaining power and of the political instability that was bound to arise once Claudius' natural heir had reached manhood. His removal would have been consistent with Seneca's philosophy of the end justifying the means.[36] Again, however, they are unlikely to have been capable of such ruthlessness.[37] Though accepted by the source tradition and politically convenient, the killing of Britannicus is, in fact, more disputed by modern scholars than that of Claudius. The current *communis opinio*, supported by the belief that the Romans had only restricted access to fast-acting poisons, is

---

[31] Tac. *Ann.* 13.14.3–6.   [32] Rudich 1993, 9; Barrett *et al.* 2016, 44 and n. 1.

[33] Wiedemann 1996a, 245.   [34] Rudich 1993, 9; Michel 2015, 223–5.

[35] Tac. *Ann.* 13.17.2: *insociabile regnum.* Cf. Winterling 2007, 64, quoting Philo *Leg.* 68, 'Sovereignty cannot be shared, that is an immutable law of nature' (*akoinōnēton archē, thesmos phuseōs akinētos*). Barrett 1996, 55; Winterling 2007, 46.

[36] Cf. below 185. Similarly Henderson 1905, 67; Warmington 1969, 45; Grant 1970, 47; Rudich 1993, 9–10; Wiedemann 1996a, 245 (more noncommittal); Giardina 2011, 14. On Seneca's 'political realism' see Griffin 1976, 135, 148–51.

[37] Above 48.

that he died following an epileptic fit;[38] and if he died from natural causes, Nero was not responsible for his destruction.

8.5   Agrippina

8.5.1   Recovery (55–58)

After the death of Britannicus, Agrippina focused her sympathies on Octavia. For the first time there is also the hint of sedition in reports that she was creating a fighting fund and strengthening her links with praetorian officers and, an indication that she 'was in quest of a leader and a faction', with leading nobles. The suggestion is that she was now bent on finding herself a powerful new husband, inside or outside the Julio-Claudian family.[39] Though still not yet forty, and with Augustan legislation envisaging child-bearing until forty-nine,[40] she could in principle have borne a new Julio-Claudian. However, since Nero was her only offspring, after nine years of marriage and following a difficult breech birth,[41] this is unlikely. The presumed scenario must have been that she would displace Nero but secure the succession by marrying a man with children. As she had re-engineered the ruling family under Claudius, so might she do so again under Nero.[42] Again, however, this is probably no more than the hostile source tradition's prejudiced speculation. Agrippina would have hated putting herself under the authority of a husband, and Nero was still her strongest card. Her more likely offence is, perhaps in the hope of recalling Nero to his duties in maintaining the dynasty, lamenting the wrong the Acte affair was doing to Octavia.[43] Such behaviour made her

---

[38] For the sources see Bradley 1978a, 198. Rudich (1993, 9) and Waldherr (2005, 74–5) are convinced that Britannicus was poisoned by Nero. Henderson (1905, 66–8), Hohl (1918, 360), Griffin (1976, 134–5), Bradley (1978a, 198–9), and Cizek (1982, 53–4) agree but acknowledge problems. Fini (1994, 115–19, 238 and n. 10), Barrett (1996, 171–2), Holland (2000, 80–2), Shotter (2008, 42, 61), Romm (2014, 81–2) and Barrett *et al.* (2016, 43–4) prefer epilepsy. (A toxin was available in water-hemlock [www.youtube.com/watch?v=2xA22TFkkxMNERO], but this is not a Mediterranean species [*Wikipedia*].)

[39] Tac. *Ann.* 13.18.3: *quasi quaereret ducem et partis.* Grant 1970, 76. Cf. in similar vein Tac. *Ann.* 14.61: Poppaea's accusation in 62 that all the rebellious movement in favour of Octavia needed for success was a male leader (*dux*). Cf. Barrett 1996, 33–5, for similar charges against Agrippina I.

[40] Rawson 1992, 31.

[41] Plin. *HN* 7.46. Barrett 1996, 56; Kienast 2004, 94. Alternatively Griffin (1984, 21) suggests that she may have avoided further conceptions for political reasons and to avoid the division of the family's wealth.

[42] Above 39; Romm 2014, 99–100.

[43] Tac. *Ann.* 13.19.3: *quod Britannici mortem lugeret aut Octaviae iniurias evulgaret* – with excessive mourning for Britannicus unlikely.

unwelcome in the main Palatine complex. She was removed to new quarters and lost her praetorian and German lifeguards.[44] However, her reduction in status was only marginal. She was still *Augusta*, *flamen divi Claudii*, *mater Caesaris*. Her new quarters were still on the Palatine, in the mansion of a former *Augusta*, her paternal grandmother, Antonia II;[45] and she was still, presumably, escorted by lictors. In addition, albeit somewhat coolly and perfunctorily, Nero continued to pay her visits of respect.[46] At the height of their quarrel over Acte, Nero had sent Agrippina a present of fine clothes and jewels. Though she chose to interpret this as an insult, it shows a continuing bond between them.[47] Mother and son were too close to desire a permanent break.[48]

Ignoring this, Agrippina's enemies considered her vulnerable. Still in 55, the charge that Agrippina was in search of 'a leader and a faction' reared its head very specifically when Junia Silana accused her of plotting rebellion and marriage with Rubellius Plautus, by birth an obvious rival to Nero.[49] This attempt to compromise both an *Augusta* and a descendant of Augustus will have caused massive excitement. Tacitus has the news breaking late at night and a sleepy and tipsy Nero provoked into blind panic. He was ready to kill Agrippina and Plautus out of hand, and to summarily dismiss Agrippina's client, Burrus, from his post as praetorian prefect.[50] However, in the source tradition drunkenness and panic are presented as characteristic of Nero's 'bad' behaviour throughout his principate. His chronic inebriation is questionable;[51] and one suspects that Tacitus uses it here as a construct, to confirm Nero 'the tyrant' and to prepare the reader for his tyrannical murder of Agrippina. Tacitus in fact, in a rare mention of his sources, observes that they show significant inconsistency.[52] Events probably moved so fast that no-one was subsequently sure of what happened.[53] What is clear is that Burrus quickly took charge of the situation and convinced Nero that he was in no danger. Burrus then won Agrippina a fair trial in her own residence, in the course of which she refuted all accusations, and then, with the help of Seneca, a private audience with Nero which she used to wreak vengeance on her foes: Junia Silana and her helpers were severely punished for having levelled false charges.[54] In recompense Agrippina won important posts for her clients. Faenius Rufus

[44] Tac. *Ann.* 13.18.4–5.   [45] Above 36.
[46] Tac. *Ann.* 13.18.5. Barrett 1996, 173; *contra* Holland 2000, 74.   [47] Tac. *Ann.* 13.13.5.
[48] Cf. below 283.   [49] Tac. *Ann.* 13.19. Below 191.   [50] Tac. *Ann.* 13.20.   [51] Below 305.
[52] Tac. *Ann.* 13.20.2–4.   [53] Cf. Rudich 1993, 19.
[54] Tac. *Ann.* 13.20.5–21.9. Rudich 1993, 19; Waldherr 2005, 79.

was made *praefectus annonae* and Claudius Balbillus *praefectus Aegypti.*[55] These appointments, together with that of Corbulo, meant that three of Agrippina's favourites were now high in the administration and, in the case of Balbillus and Rufus, in positions crucial for the feeding of Rome.[56] Rufus' promotion displaced Seneca's father-in-law, Pompeius Paulinus: 'Patronage is always a useful gauge of power and influence, and by that measure Agrippina would seem to have emerged from the crisis second only to Nero in status'.[57] In a strange coda, a certain Paetus was sentenced to exile for falsely accusing Pallas and Burrus of plotting to make Cornelius Sulla, husband of Claudius' daughter, Antonia, *princeps.*[58] The odd timing suggests that Paetus made his accusation just after that against Agrippina, intending to bring down her allies. Tacitus has Silana acting out of female spite.[59] Though this has been generally accepted,[60] one suspects that she had powerful backers. The fact that these backers were not Seneca and Burrus, who were clearly convinced from the start of Agrippina's inno-cence and not inclined to destroy her,[61] raises important questions about the nature of Neronian court politics.[62] Related to this, and to the theme of 'Nero the killer', the grim fates of failed accusers are not reliable indicators of Neronian tyranny and terror, but just part and parcel of court political life.

Before the end of 55, therefore, things again seemed to be going in Agrippina's favour. Even Suetonius' otherwise questionable report that Nero purposefully strove to make her life a misery by paying people to harass her with lawsuits in Rome and annoy her on her visits to the country indicates that she was no outcast.[63] Though she then disappears from Tacitus' narrative for three years, her continuing influence may be detected in Nero's postponement of legal proceedings against Publius Celer (who, with Helius, had killed M. Junius Silanus) in 57.[64] Indeed, by the end of 58 Agrippina had probably regained much of her old intimacy with Nero,[65] perhaps helped by a cooling-off of the liaison between Nero and Acte.[66] Agrippina's feeling that she was again winning the game may have given her the confidence to remind Nero of his duty to show himself on campaign.[67] It would certainly explain her willingness

---

[55] Tac. *Ann.* 13.22. Cf. above 154.   [56] Cf. Osgood 2011, 182.
[57] Barrett 1996, 177 (quotation); Romm 2014, 53–4.   [58] Tac. *Ann.* 13.23. Cf. below 191, 219.
[59] Tac. *Ann.* 13.19.2.   [60] E.g. Rudich 1993, 18–19.   [61] Cf. Romm 2014, 98.
[62] Above 154.   [63] Suet. *Ner.* 34.1.
[64] Tac. *Ann.* 13.1.3, 33.1–2. Cf. Rudich 1993, 25; Ginsburg 2006, 45; above 174.
[65] Above 160; below 283.   [66] Cf. above 52.   [67] Above 166.

to risk a second major intervention in his personal life.[68] By late 58, Nero's affections had shifted to the rich and aristocratic (albeit not wholly blue-blooded[69]) and so potentially much more marriageable Poppaea.[70] Agrippina made her second major blunder over a woman by opposing the affair. Agrippina's hostility was both a personal and a political error. If Acte was an infatuation, Poppaea was Nero's true love.[71] And if Agrippina believed that in protecting Nero's marriage to Octavia she was safeguarding his Claudian inheritance, which included his adoption and accession, this was now redundant. Octavia had not provided Nero with an heir and was clearly unlikely to do so: a new succession crisis was brewing:[72] Though Seneca and Burrus, the latter particularly sympathetic to Octavia,[73] can hardly have welcomed Poppaea's appearance as a major player, they were now committed to Nero and will have appreciated the need for him to produce a child; and Poppaea had already proved her fertility.[74] Agrippina's intervention was a serious embarrassment, for which she paid the highest price. But did Nero cold-bloodedly order her death?

8.5.2   Destruction (58–59)

Agrippina was killed around 23 March 59, during the holiday of *Quinquatria*.[75] Tacitus and Suetonius, followed by many modern scholars, blame the 'wicked' Nero.[76] Combined, the sources tell a dark story of his continuing strained relationship with his mother; his devising various means of getting rid of her by stealth; his hypocritical welcoming of her to a grand party of reconciliation at Baiae; his even more hypocritical fond farewell to her as she departed, gratified by his attentions, on a smart new warship, designed to bring about her death by breaking apart. In the event, Agrippina was thrown overboard, survived attempts to beat her to death in the sea, and reached dry land. She then feigned ignorance of the patent

---

[68] Cf. Malitz 1999, 29: 'the advice and admonitions of his mother, expressed with her known intensity'.

[69] Malitz 1999, 30; Waldherr 2005, 83–4.

[70] Cf. Rudich 1993, 28; Holland 2000, 96; Waldherr 2005, 83, 86. For more on the date, see below 181.

[71] Cf. above 52; below 311.   [72] Below 190.   [73] Above 54; below 181.

[74] She had a son, Rufrius Crispinus II: Kienast 2004, 99; cf. below 321. For his father see Bradley 1978a, 207–8; Rudich 1993, 148. Cf. also Winterling 2007, 101, on Gaius' choice of Caesonia.

[75] Hohl 1918, 369 (19–23 March); Bradley 1978a, 203 (23–24 March); Barrett 1996, 246 (23–24 March).

[76] Tac. *Ann.* 14.1.5, 3.2; Suet. *Ner.* 34.2. E.g. Henderson 1905, 118–19; Grant 1970, 73–8; Waldherr 2005, 86.

guilt of her son and sent Agerinus, a freedman, to inform Nero of her lucky escape from a 'serious accident'.[77] He then panicked, contrived a false accusation of intended assassination against Agerinus, and ordered Agrippina's execution for treason. Her brutal killing is infamous. Nero's contemporaries threw it in his face,[78] and it still ranks, alongside his purported burning of Rome and persecution of Christians, as one of the major crimes of his principate. However, there is great uncertainty and inconsistency between and within the various accounts of Agrippina's death.[79] Tacitus first mentions the designing of a detachable structure that would drop Agrippina overboard, yet in narrating what actually happened he describes a collapsing lead-weighted deck canopy, which almost worked, followed by the deliberate *dissolutio* – 'breaking-up' – of the ship, which did not. Suetonius provides a confused account of failed attempts to poison Agrippina and to crush her under a collapsing ceiling on land, then of both a collapsible boat and a collapsible cabin at sea. Dio mentions only an abortive *dissolutio*.[80] Tacitus' account, the most detailed, offers a narrative so full of tensions and contradictions that it has been dismissed as a 'sensational novelette', 'a farrago of lies and absurdities': unreliable history.[81] A particular problem is his 'crowded timetable': can all the events he describes be fitted into the hours available?[82] Though some have bravely attempted to reconcile what Tacitus says with itself and with the rest,[83] it is better to ignore the contrived 'shipwreck' and begin with that part of Tacitus' record which, because it is based on a contemporary public document, is likely to be the most reliable. This is the letter, composed by Seneca, which Nero sent to the Senate from Naples, to where he had withdrawn after Agrippina's death.[84] This letter and Tacitus' comments on it tell us that:

(i)   Agrippina had died, with the strong implication that she had committed suicide, because she had sent an assassin to kill Nero.[85]

---

[77] Tac. *Ann.* 14.6.1: *gravis casus.*   [78] Cf. below 234.

[79] Cf. Dawson 1964, 254–6, 259; Barrett 1996, 186–7.

[80] Tac. *Ann.* 14.3.6, 5.2–4; Suet. *Ner.* 34.2; Dio 61.12.2, 13.3.

[81] Dawson 1964, 254 (quotation); Hurley 2013, 35; cf. Ginsburg 2006, 47.

[82] Dawson 1964, 256.   [83] E.g. Barrett 1996, 184, 187–8.

[84] Tac. *Ann.* 14.10.5–11.4; Quint. *Inst.* 8.5.18. Dawson 1964, 253–4; Rudich 1993, 37; Barrett *et al.* 2016, 72 and n. 93.

[85] Tac. *Ann.* 14.10.5: *luisse eam poenas conscientia quasi scelus paravisset.* Furneaux 1907, 245: 'from a sense of guilt . . . as having plotted murder'; cf. Tac. *Ann.* 14.7.7: *pudore deprehensi sceleris.* Dawson 1964, 253, 256.

(ii)   Her death was trumpeted as the salvation of the state and celebrated,
         following Nero's quasi-triumphal return to Rome, by 'Great Games'
         (*Ludi Maximi*) as a conspiracy confounded.[86]
(iii)   The political community and the populace of Rome accepted the
         announcement and the celebrations without demur.[87]

Agrippina's destruction was thus justified as a necessary act of state.
However, questions remain as to whether she was actually plotting against
Nero and the extent to which he personally contrived his mother's execution. In addressing these, I assume that Nero would not have embarked
upon a complex plan to murder his mother and, to aid its completion,
acted the loving innocent to her face. This Nero is the 'monster' of
tradition. I further suppose that Nero and Agrippina were never alienated
from each other as much as the source tradition suggests, and that by early
59 there appeared to be some possibility of a rapprochement: Tacitus'
'rumour' and Suetonius' 'pretence' of reconciliation invert political
reality.[88]

Apart from Nero, the only people in a position both to fear Agrippina
and to bring about her removal were Seneca, Burrus and Poppaea, now, as
Tacitus declares, beginning to play the political game.[89] The former pair
were not natural allies of Poppaea, but desperation makes strange bedfel-
lows since a full reconciliation between Nero and Agrippina would have
left them vulnerable to her wrath. Poppaea's involvement is crucial. It has
become the *communis opinio* to see Tacitus' dating of her intervention in
politics to 58/59 as one of his inventions, derived from her position in 61/
62 and intended to give a 'weak' Nero the motive for matricide.[90]
However, without the early appearance of Poppaea the murder of Agrippina becomes 'inexplicable' unless we assume that Nero was simply
desperate to free himself from 'the psychological domination of his
mother', which is simply another way of blaming his supposed depravity.[91]
There is no reason to dismiss Poppaea's boasting of her fertility in 58/59 as
a doublet of her condition in 62. Such a claim need not have referred to a
current pregnancy but could simply have pointed up that, unlike Octavia,

---

[86] Tac. *Ann.* 14.13.2–3. Shotter 2008, 80.
[87] Tac. *Ann.* 14.12.1. Cf. Smallwood 1967, no. 22.12–13: official thanksgiving for Nero's safety (*ex
s. c. ob supplicationes indictas pro salute Neronis Caesar*).
[88] Tac. *Ann.* 14.4.1: *rumor reconciliationis*; Suet. *Ner.* 34.2: *reconciliatio simulata*. Below 282.
[89] Tac. *Ann.* 14.1.1; cf. 13.45.1, 46.3.
[90] Dawson 1964, 254, 260; Warmington 1969, 47; Grant 1970, 73; Fini 1994, 126 and n. 27; Barrett
1996, 182; Shotter 2008, 76–7.
[91] Warmington 1969, 47; cf. Holland 2000, 111–12.

she had already borne a child.[92] The length of time between Poppaea's pushing for marriage with Nero in 58/59 and her achieving it in 62 is explicable in terms of Nero's shock at the death of his mother and Burrus' continuing opposition to the abandonment of Octavia. Both obstacles were overcome by news that Burrus was failing physically and that Poppaea was pregnant.[93] Finally, if Otho was in Lusitania by the end of 58,[94] Nero's liaison with his wife, Poppaea, which caused the rift between the two friends,[95] must have been well advanced by March of that year.

Though Tacitus does not mention Poppaea's presence, it is likely that she attended the party at Baiae, of the sort given previously by Otho and others of the smart set.[96] This explains the absence of Seneca and Burrus – hardly 'smart' – though they were close by.[97] Seneca and Burrus had tried to deal with the burgeoning rapprochement by getting Acte, still a force to be reckoned with,[98] to persuade Nero to cool his relationship with his mother by not meeting her in private in Rome;[99] but now here he was meeting her in private in Baiae. Though Poppaea, Seneca and Burrus had reason to be glad to see the end of Agrippina, none would have dared to act against her without the authority of Nero, which he would not have given. What remains is that Agrippina's death resulted from an impromptu, last-minute, opportunistic venture, in which all three turned Nero violently against his mother.[100]

The key to its understanding is, again, Seneca's carefully crafted letter to the Senate, 'the most difficult writing assignment of his life'.[101] At its core is the claim that Agrippina died because she had sent an assassin to kill Nero. It also accuses her of being responsible for all the evil that had happened under Claudius and for subsequently seeking sole power. This second set of charges may be regarded as old hat: the sort of thing that Agrippina's enemies must have said about her ever since she gained

---

[92] Tac. *Ann.* 14.1.2. Furneaux 1907, 233; cf. above 179.
[93] Above 54, below 189, 196, 288. Cf. Cizek 1982, 60, 177–8; Wiedemann 1996a, 248; Holland 2000, 103; Waldherr 2005, 86; Ginsburg 2006, 47.
[94] Above 98 n. 154; cf. Dawson 1964, 258.   [95] Above 97.
[96] Taking Suet. *Otho* 3.1 as a mistaken application of one, or several, such earlier events to 59: above 98 n. 154; cf. Barrett *et al.* 2016, 179–80 and nn. 23, 31. 'Smart set': cf. above 60; Romm 2014, 110.
[97] Tac. *Ann.* 14.7.2.   [98] Cf. below 282.   [99] Tac. *Ann.* 14.2.2; 3.1. Cf. Barrett 1996, 183.
[100] Tacitus (*Ann.* 14.7.3) appears to admit the possibility of the involvement of Seneca and Burrus, but 'conveniently fudges the question of whether they were complicit' in the plot: Ginsburg 2006, 50. Dio (61.12.1) makes Seneca the direct accomplice of Poppaea. The *communis opinio* is to consider Seneca and Burrus innocent: e.g. Henderson 1905, 121–4; Warmington 1969, 48; Cizek 1982, 62–3; Barrett 1996, 189. Cf., however, Fini 1994, 239 and n. 28.
[101] Romm 2014, 116.

prominence under Claudius, and which would always have appealed to conservative senators.[102] There is, however, something new: that Agrippina, foiled in her quest for dominance, was the enemy of the troops, the Senate and the People because she opposed the distribution of donatives and largesses.[103] This rings wholly false since Agrippina must always have appreciated the need to keep and retain the support of these groups, and the more so if she was aiming to overthrow Nero. Finally and, as Tacitus himself implies, somewhat oddly, after congratulating the state on its good fortune in the removal of Agrippina the letter refers to a 'shipwreck', stressing that it was 'accidental'.[104] This locates the maritime disaster directly before Agrippina's death,[105] and, presumably, attempts to counter a charge that it had been contrived. Any attempt to flesh out these bare bones requires a high degree of speculation, indeed of historical novel writing,[106] but I offer the following narrative.

By late 58, Nero and Agrippina appeared to be drifting back together. This alarmed Seneca, Burrus and Poppaea but they could do nothing about it. However, all was not lost. Nero's desire to be reunited with his mother did not derive solely from his affection for her. There were two women in his life, Agrippina and Poppaea, both of whom he longed to please. His attempts at reconciliation with the former were undertaken also out of regard for the latter. The position of a son who is an only child, torn between his love for his mother and that for a woman whom his mother detests, and who detests her in return, is unenviable.[107] Nero's hope must have been that by drawing close again to Agrippina he could persuade her to drop her objections to his divorcing Octavia and marrying Poppaea. The party at Baiae was intended to accelerate the process of persuasion. By inviting his mother and going out of his way to honour her, and by bringing mother and mistress together in cheerful circumstances on neutral ground, Nero hoped to encourage both to bury the hatchet. This did not happen. Agrippina relished her restored status but bitterly disappointed Nero by her continued hostility to Poppaea. Her intransigence gave Seneca, Burrus and Poppaea the chance for action against her when the opportunity unexpectedly presented itself. This came with news of a serious marine accident, but probably not a sinking and so, strictly speaking, not a 'shipwreck'. Though he uses the term *naufragium*, Tacitus'

---

narrative indicates, at worst, no more than that Agrippina's ship suffered a
severe heeling.[108] Heeling, however, resulted in the deaths of her attendants. Again contrary to Tacitus' account,[109] it is likely that Nero received
the bad news of these and of Agrippina missing, presumed drowned,
before the good news of her survival. Report of disaster would have arrived
quickly if the incident occurred nearby and close to shore. This seems
likely if, as Tacitus says, Agrippina's ship had not been long under way
before disaster struck.[110] Such reports would have arrived all the quicker if
the incident itself had been caused by an escort vessel accidentally colliding
with the stern of Agrippina's ship.[111] Naval personnel could speedily have
contacted Baiae; and subsequent intense naval activity would have alerted
people on shore, bringing them to the beach to see what was happening.[112]
The location of Agrippina's villa is significant. There is uncertainty in and
between the sources as to how and when Agrippina travelled to Baiae,
where and for how long she stayed in the area before the party, how she got
to it, how she returned to the villa where she was staying, and where she
was killed after the accident.[113] Details of place and time are frequently
difficult to establish even with the best of information, and in this case it is
likely that most of what we are told is as untrustworthy as the story of the
collapsible ship. Here, I follow Barrett in assuming that Agrippina arrived
by ship from Anzio a few days before the party. She was greeted by Nero at
either the naval base of Misenum or the port of Baiae, and accompanied by
him to a seaside villa just south of Baiae, at Bacoli, where she recuperated
(Figure 12).[114]

On the evening of the party she travelled by litter from Bacoli to Baiae,
but to suit herself, not because she had heard rumours that Nero was
planning murder-by-ship.[115] After the party, in the early hours of the
morning, she embarked for the short voyage home. The collision took
place between Baiae and Bacoli. Tacitus reports that Agrippina ended up at
the Lucrine Lake, to the north of Baiae, where she might have obtained
land transport back to Bacoli. However, it greatly eases the 'crowded
timetable' if one assumes that Agrippina was rescued off Baiae by fisher-
men from the Lucrine Lake and conveyed by them to the bay of Bacoli.[116]
On the arrival of news of Agrippina's likely death, Nero summoned Seneca

---

[108] Tac. Ann. 14.5.4–5.   [109] Tac. *Ann.* 14.7.1   [110] Tac. *Ann.* 14.5.2.
[111] Barrett 1996, 188 (moving Suet. *Ner.* 34.2 more plausibly to a later date).
[112] Cf. Tac. *Ann.* 14.8.1, for news spreading quickly.   [113] Barrett 1996, 244–5.
[114] Barrett 1996, 186, 244–5; Keppie 2011, 41–3, 45; *contra* Barrington Atlas, 44.4F.
[115] Tac. *Ann.* 14.4.6; cf. Dawson 1964, 257; Barrett 1996, 245.
[116] Tac. *Ann.* 14.5.7. Cf. above 180.

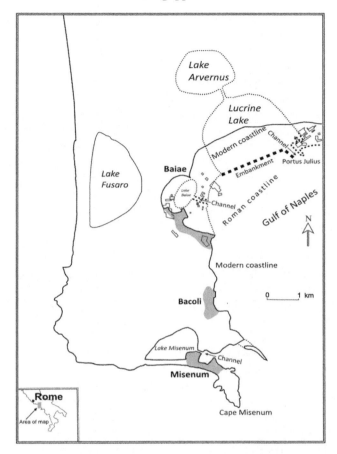

Figure 12   Baiae and its region.
After Keppie 2011, 38, figure 2; Barrett et al. 2016, 60, map 2

and Burrus for advice. Their spirits and those of Poppaea will have risen. Nero will have been shocked, but is bound to have experienced a guilty pang of relief. When it was subsequently reported that she had survived, Seneca, Burrus and Poppaea will have been cast down. Nero will have been relieved, but is bound to have experienced a guilty pang of regret. Then came Agerinus announcing that Agrippina, having survived a freak accident, was now safe in her villa. This was the moment of decision. It was not Nero, but Seneca, Burrus and Poppaea who, thinking on their feet, framed Agerinus by arranging the 'discovery' that he was carrying a sword and accusing him of being an assassin sent by Agrippina to kill Nero.[117] They then used this to work on Nero. Here, once more, the subsequent letter from Naples is important as a likely summary of what Seneca, Burrus and Poppaea put to Nero as well as what he later presented to the Senate. They rehearsed old charges against Agrippina, all of which Nero must have heard many times before,[118] but added new charges. These included the wholly false allegation that Agrippina was accusing Nero of contriving her death by arranging an 'accidental' shipwreck. Nero, already dismayed at the failure of the party and always hugely hurt by betrayal by intimates, would have been in a receptive mood.[119] He would particularly have resented his extraordinary privileging of Agrippina in providing her with transport by warship being interpreted as a plot to kill her. Deeply wounded by the calumny and profoundly shocked by how close the 'assassin' had come to achieving his goal, he turned all the emotion of possible reconciliation against Agrippina: 'Nero now knew the full, unbelievable, wickedness of his mother'.[120] He was won over and, after a summary legal process,[121] sentenced Agrippina to death. Nero was never habitually vindictive.[122] His extreme distress at the supposed treachery of his mother is reflected in the meanness of her burial and the lack of provision of any kind of monument: 'the very heart and sanctuary of his love-feelings had been blasted'.[123]

Burrus warned against using Praetorians to carry out the execution, so responsibility for this was given to Anicetus, Nero's former tutor, now commanding the fleet at Misenum, and a force of marines.[124] Again contrary to Tacitus' main account, but in keeping with the chronology implied by the letter, all this occurred only after the arrival of Agerinus.[125] Agrippina could have been allowed to commit suicide to escape murder, which was more respectable and is what the official report implied. On the other hand, this is unlikely since suicide could have taken time when it suited all involved to be rid of her without delay. She was probably killed, but quickly and therefore perhaps not as brutally as the source tradition says. Seneca used the same case he had put to Nero, based on old prejudice and new accusations, to win over the Roman Establishment. But his

---

[117] Tac. *Ann.* 14.7.7.
[118] Cf. Waldherr 2005, 93: [Seneca] 'fasste in dem Schreiben nochmals alle Vorwürfe, die über die Jahre hinweg gegen die Kaisermutter vorgebracht worden waren, zusammen'.
[119] Cf. Waldherr 2005, 89; above 73, 115.
[120] Dawson 1964, 258 (albeit based on a different reconstruction of events).   [121] Cf. above 73.
[122] Cf. below 283.   [123] Tac. *Ann.* 14.9.2–3; Dawson 1964, 259 (quotation); Barrett 1996, 190.
[124] Tac. *Ann.* 14.3.5, 7.5, 8.2–6.   [125] Tac. *Ann.* 14.7.7.

defence exposed the *princeps* on two counts. The first is that, by having Nero order Agrippina's death, it formally designated him a matricide. The second is that, by raising the possibility that the incident was not accidental, it helped create the urban myth of the 'collapsible ship'. Once the notion was in circulation it was unstoppable. Like Nero's singing at the Fire, it was too good a story to ignore, 'one of the most familiar and colourful incidents of antiquity'.[126] It enjoyed credibility because of Nero's general love of toys and gadgets, and of theatricality since the collapsible ship was bound to bring to mind the sophisticated 'special effects' of the arena.[127] People may, indeed, have confused it with an actual vessel that Nero later had built in Rome.[128] The collapsible ship became closely associated with Anicetus because of his role in the death of Agrippina.[129] The whole thing was false but, since Nero allowed its seed to be broadcast, it is yet another instance of the *princeps'* creating his own 'monstrous' image.[130]

8.6 The Year 62

8.6.1 Burrus?

Seneca and Burrus would probably have preferred to limit Agrippina's power but keep her in play as a counterweight to Poppaea and her allies,[131] but these now took the initiative. The key year was 62. This began well, with Caesennius Paetus' reports of victory in Armenia.[132] Military success may, indeed, have emboldened Tigellinus to get his senatorial son-in-law, Cossutianus Capito, to revive the practice of accusing aristocrats of high treason under the law of *maiestas*.[133] Capito levelled charges of libelling and slandering Nero against Antistius Sosianus, a fiery individual whose quarrel as plebeian tribune with the praetor Vibullius had, in 56, given the Senate the chance to act as if the old Republic were still in existence.[134] However, the accusation appears less 'tyrannical' if we accept the argument that it was intended as a public relations exercise, allowing Nero to demonstrate clemency: the *princeps*, who otherwise had nothing to do with the prosecution, would be brought in to save Sosianus, once

---

[126] Barrett 1996, 184.   [127] Cf. Cass. Dio 61.12.2. Above 124.   [128] Cf. Dawson 1964, 263–6.
[129] Tac. *Ann.* 14.3.5.
[130] Cf. below 291; Bartsch 1994, 42, on the 'distorting lens' of Suetonius' structure.
[131] Cf. Griffin, 1984, 74; Barrett 1996, 189; Romm 2014, 98.   [132] Above 140.
[133] Above 21.   [134] Above 25, 27, 105; Rudich 1993, 55–6, 62.

convicted, from a horrible death by scourging.[135] The incident is, therefore, both the first direct sign of Tigellinus' renewed high standing at court
and a further indication of the extent to which he and Poppaea were now
seeking to control the image and direction of the Neronian principate.[136]
As in their change of policy in Armenia, their inexperience let them down,
for they underestimated the revulsion that the charge of *maiestas* could
generate among senators.[137] The ploy was thwarted by Thrasea Paetus,
who pre-empted Nero's act of mercy by persuading the Senate to sentence
Sosianus only to exile, with which the *princeps* concurred.[138] Another
indicator that Poppaea and Tigellinus were still not entirely on top of
the game is their inability fully to exploit the unexpected death of Burrus.
Rumour said that he was killed by Nero, but this is unlikely. In the front
rank of imperial politics for many years, Burrus will anyway have been
ready for retirement and his death at this time is likely to have been from
natural causes.[139] Tigellinus succeeded him as praetorian prefect, but not
alone, having to accept Faenius Rufus as colleague.[140] However, the
influence of Poppaea and Tigellinus was soon strengthened by Seneca's
embarking upon a protracted withdrawal from political life.[141] Like that of
Burrus, his disappearance was inevitable. Isolated by the death of Burrus,
finding his lifestyle, his ambition and his advanced age the object of savage
criticism, and perhaps already looking forward to his death,[142] he let Nero
discharge him with dignity, though he remained influential.[143] Most
senators would probably have been happy to see Burrus and Seneca go.
Both were, as provincials, social interlopers, and both were strongly
associated with the Claudian regime. In addition, Seneca had refused to

[135] Rutledge 2001, 114; Kimmerle 2015, 105–6.
[136] Above 136. Bradley (1973, 177–9) is right to 'disassociate Nero from personal involvement in the
case' but in error in seeing it as resulting from financial opportunism on the part of Capito. Revival
of accusations of *maiestas* was far too serious to be allowed to come about fortuitously; and, as
Bradley says, Capito was the 'minion' of Tigellinus. However, as Rutledge observes (2001, 114,
176), the prosecution will have helped Capito, recently restored to the Senate following expulsion
for having committed extortion, repair his reputation. Cf. Rudich 1993, 56; Wiedemann 1996a,
249–50.
[137] Cf. Romm 2014, 146.   [138] Tac. *Ann.* 14.48–9, cf. 16.14.1. Above 27, 77.
[139] Tac. *Ann.* 14.51.1–3, leaving the question open; Suet. *Ner.* 35.5 and Cass. Dio 62.13.3: absolutely
sure. Cf. Henderson 1905, 135; Hohl 1918, 304–5; Warmington 1969, 49; Bradley 1978a, 218.
Contra Romm 2014, 134.
[140] Tac. *Ann.* 14.51.5. Above 154.   [141] Tac. *Ann.* 14.56.6; Romm 2014, 136, 144, 148, 170.
[142] Mannering 2013, 202; Romm 2014, 148, 172–6. Rutledge (2001, 115) suggests formal delation,
which is unlikely.
[143] Cf. Tac. *Ann.* 14.52–56; 14.65. Henderson 1905, 136–41; Warmington 1969, 49; Griffin 1976,
171; Waldherr 2005, 103.

be wholly absorbed by the senatorial tradition.[144] Though Seneca understood the place of the Senate in the Principate,[145] with an influential
younger brother, M. Annaeus Mela (father of Lucan), who notoriously
chose to remain equestrian and himself apparently preferring the company
of equestrians, he and his family seem to have remained uncommitted to
the House's traditions or its business.[146] Such reserve might have been
charitably attributed to his convictions as a Stoic philosopher, were it not
for an evidently unreliable moral compass clearly demonstrated in a major
sex scandal that had led to his being exiled by Claudius and, above all, by
his becoming 'super-rich' (Mela had an equally grasping reputation).[147] It
is no surprise that he attracted the charge of hypocrisy.[148] The Establishment accepted the transfer of power to Poppaea and Tigellinus. Their
chance further to consolidate their position came in the middle months of
62 with Poppaea's realisation that she was pregnant by Nero.[149] This
returns us to the succession issue.[150]

8.6.2   Succession

The marriage between Nero and Octavia had been arranged for political
reasons between two very young people: engaged in 49 when Nero was
approaching twelve and Octavia only nine; and married in 53 when he was
still not sixteen and she hardly thirteen.[151] Since both were legally siblings,
it was also of questionable morality.[152] It had never gone well. Tacitus says

---

[144] Above 18.   [145] Above 159.
[146] Griffin 1976, 96 (quotation); 1984, 78–9. For Mela, see below 363.
[147] Compass: above 53. Scandal (purported adultery with Agrippina's sister, Julia): Cass. Dio 60.8.5,
61.10.1; *Schol. Iuv.* (Probus) 5.109. Wealth: Tac. *Ann.* 15.64.6: *praedives*; 13.42.6 with 13.18.1
(the strong implication that Seneca benefited from Britannicus' fall). Tac. *Ann.* 14.52.1; Cass. Dio
61.10.3, 62.2.1 (Seneca and the Boudican revolt). Tac. *Ann.* 13.42.5–6, Osgood 2011, 42 (Suillius
Rufus' bitter attack on Seneca in 58, which included the charge that he had acquired 300 million
HS since the start of Nero's principate); Romm 2014, 100–1. Though such accusations may have
been unjust (cf. Malitz 1999, 21), the fact they could be made suggests that Seneca was not above
reproach. Mela: Tac. *Ann.* 16.17.3 hints that Mela was deeply involved in corrupt deals as imperial
procurator: below 350.
[148] Tac. *Ann.* 13.42.5; Dio 61.10.2; Romm 2014, 101–2. A certain amount has been made of hostility
to Seneca and Burrus arising out of their likely favouring of fellow Spaniards and Gauls, but as
Warmington (1969, 40) argues, this is unlikely because such patronage would have been seen as no
more than what was normally expected of the powerful. For a summary of their activities see
Wiedemann 1996a, 245.
[149] Cf. above 182. The daughter born in January 63 must have been conceived around April 62, with
Poppaea aware of her pregnancy from around June and beginning to show it by July; cf. Waldherr
2005, 101.
[150] Above 52, 179.   [151] Tac. *Ann.* 12.9.1; Cass. Dio 60.32.2. Bradley 1978a, 62.
[152] See Cass. Dio 60.32.2 for how Agrippina circumvented legal prohibition.

that Nero could not even bear to touch his wife,[153] so it is hardly
surprising that the pair had produced no children. The absence of heirs
will eventually have produced stirrings of concern. The succession question first raised its head some time before 59 when Nero, while seriously
ill, had only half-jokingly nominated the venerable Memmius Regulus to
follow him.[154] Agrippina's mistake in 58–59 had been to fail to realise that
it was taking precedence over the Claudian link.[155] The issue was sub-
merged by her death but resurfaced abruptly in 60. The appearance of a
comet and a lightning-strike on an imperial villa while Nero was in
residence, followed by his suffering another serious bout of illness after
swimming in the nearby source of the Aqua Marcia, caused political
uncertainty and stimulated speculation which resulted in Rubellius Plautus' being forced to withdraw to Asia.[156] At the start of 62, there remained
important figures who owed their rise to Agrippina, respected the marriage
as her creation, and feared that divorcing Octavia might raise questions
about the legitimacy of Nero's retaining her political dowry, the
Empire.[157] These included not only Seneca and Burrus, but also Corbulo
and Faenius Rufus.[158] However, time had cemented Nero's independent
claim to succeed Claudius;[159] the succession issue was ever more pressing;
and Nero was anyway anxious to start his own family.[160] He, Poppaea and
Tigellinus might legitimately feel that he had more chance of getting an
heir if he was married to a woman whom he had chosen himself and with
whom he could feel at ease. Born c. 31, Poppaea was around six years older
than Nero, and therefore able to act as mother as well as wife,[161] and she
had already proved her fertility.[162] Poppaea herself, noble, beautiful,

---

[153] Tac. *Ann.* 13,12.2: *uxore ab Octavia . . . abhorrebat.*

[154] Tac. *Ann.* 14.47.1–2. Tacitus recounts this under the year 61, which could mean that he is
referring to the illness of 60, dealt with immediately below. However, his remark that, despite
attracting such potentially dangerous notice, Regulus continued to live his quiet life, suggests an
interval of some years.

[155] Above 179.

[156] Tac. *Ann.* 14.22; Suet. *Ner.* 36.1; Cass. Dio 61.18.3. For Rubellius Plautus see below 191.
Though Tacitus separates the portents from the illness, I follow Henderson (1905, 133–4) in
making them all part of a single run of events, given the close proximity of the places mentioned.
Seneca, presenting a Nero in harmony with Nature, interpreted the comet positively: *QNat.*
7.21.3; 7.17.2; cf. Plin. *HN* 2.92; Doody 2013, 297. On Nero's health in general see below 305;
Bradley 1978a, 284.

[157] Cass. Dio 62.13.1–2.   [158] Above 154.   [159] Above 13–14.

[160] E.g. Tac. *Ann.* 15.23.1–5 for Nero's joy at the birth of his first child, a daughter, which resulted in
the unprecedented bestowal upon her of the title *Augusta* (above 36 n. 35) and huge sorrow at her
early death.

[161] Cf. Warmington 1969, 47; below 281.

[162] Tac. *Ann.* 13.45.4, 14.1.2: she already had a son by the *eques*, Rufrius Crispus, and drew Nero's
attention to her fertility.

intelligent and ambitious,[163] will have realised that she must get Nero to divorce Octavia and marry her to ensure her own long-term success. A new marriage is likely to have been increasingly supported by a significant proportion of the court Establishment in order to avoid the destabilisation of an uncertain succession.[164] By mid-62, Burrus and Seneca had disappeared from the political scene and Poppaea was pregnant. The time had come to act but, since a divorced Octavia, popular and with the potential to remarry, might pose as big a threat as a widowed Agrippina had been,[165] her removal must be carefully planned and ruthlessly executed.

8.6.3   *Rubellius Plautus, Faustus Cornelius Sulla*

First, the residual Agrippinian faction had to be squared. Since Corbulo and Faenius Rufus probably recognised the need of an heir, this was not too difficult; Faenius' prefecture may have been the price of their backing.[166] This allowed the regime to move against two particular potential *foci* of disaffection. Plautus was a great-grandson of Tiberius, which made him grandnephew of Claudius and third cousin to Antonia, Octavia and Britannicus. More important, he was by virtue of Tiberius' adoption by Augustus a great-great-grandson of the latter and so nominally the equal of Nero.[167] In 55 Junia Silana had unsuccessfully accused Agrippina of encouraging him to rebellion.[168] In 60, when portents reawakened concern over the succession, Plautus was banished to Asia.[169] Cornelius Sulla, the proud bearer of an ancient Republican name, was, through the same line of descent as his first cousin, Nero, great-grandnephew of Augustus and great-grandson of Mark Antony.[170] As the husband of Claudius' elder legitimate daughter, Antonia, he was also Nero's brother-in-law and the son-in-law of a god.[171] In addition, he may have been the half-brother of Messalina, and so uncle to Britannicus and Octavia.[172] Thus, though not outstanding in intellect and ambition,[173] he could be seen as a more

---

[163]   Tac. *Ann.* 13.45.1–2. Champlin 2003, 104; Waldherr 2005, 84.   [164]   Above 162.
[165]   Popularity: Tac. *Ann.* 14.60.6–61.2, 64.1. Remarriage: Tac. *Ann.* 14.61.3–7. Warmington 1969, 50; Cizek 1982, 55, 176; Waldherr 2005, 98.
[166]   Cf. above 154; *contra* Shotter 2008, 83–4. Tacitus' (*Ann.* 14.57.1) tale of how Tigellinus soon undermined Rufus' position by branding him a client of Agrippina can hardly be true since this will already have been well known.
[167]   Griffin 1984, 74; *CAH* 10², 991 (*Stemma* 2).   [168]   Above 177.
[169]   Tac. *Ann.* 14.22; above 190.   [170]   *CAH* 10², 991 (*Stemma* 2).
[171]   Kienast 2004, 92; Wiedemann 1996a, 245.
[172]   Zonaras, 11.9: his father termed Messalina's *gambros/gener*. Wiedemann 1996a, 244.
[173]   Though some took his dimness for cunning: Tac. *Ann.* 13.47.1, 4; 14.57.4.

dangerous challenger than Rubellius Plautus, whose Stoic principles encouraged political passivity.[174] He, like Plautus, fell under suspicion in 55, when Burrus was unsuccessfully accused of planning to make him *princeps*.[175] In 58, following the emergence of Poppaea and her implied challenge to Octavia and the Claudian link,[176] he was, for safety's sake, not as the result of any particular charge, exiled to Marseille.[177]

In 62, both men perished because Poppaea and Tigellinus wanted them out of the way before acting against Octavia.[178] Tacitus has Tigellinus working on Nero's fears by arguing that the pair were dangerous because they were near to armies stationed in areas whose inhabitants were likely to have their heads turned by men of illustrious descent.[179] His case is presented as tendentious: Plautus and Sulla, resident in Asia Minor and southern Gaul respectively, were far from regional military centres in Syria and on the Rhine. Yet Tigellinus' counsel contains a grain of truth. By allowing Plautus to settle relatively close to Corbulo the regime had, typically, shown its faith in the latter but still created a potentially dangerous situation. Tacitus reports that in 62 there was a rumour in Rome that, before his killers had been able to reach him, Plautus had revolted and sought the aid of Corbulo. Corbulo was never disloyal, but the scare shows how people imagined he might intervene in metropolitan politics;[180] and though Plautius' revolt was a chimaera, reality was almost as threatening. His father-in-law, Antistius Vetus, warned him of his impending execution and advised him to resist it by force.[181] If Plautus had complied, he might well have sparked unrest in Asia Minor, and perhaps the more so because the current governor of the province may have been Barea Soranus, a known critic of the regime and, as a fellow Stoic, close to Plautus.[182] Likewise, in the case of Sulla, Corbulo's success in Armenia had fired the ambitions of other Roman generals.[183] The regime might reasonably fear that just loose talk of Corbulo's rebelling in the East might tempt emulation by a colleague in the West, using Sulla as a figurehead. Its anxiety over both men is reflected in the Senate's marking their destruction, like that of Agrippina, by ordering acts of

---

[174] Cf. Tac. *Ann.* 14.57.5.   [175] Tac. *Ann.* 13.23.1.   [176] Cf. Wiedemann 1996a, 247.

[177] Tac. *Ann.* 13.23.1; 13.47.1. Rudich 1993, 30.

[178] Cf. Fini 1994, 147, 149; Wiedemann 1996a, 250.   [179] Tac. *Ann.* 14.57.1.

[180] Tac. *Ann.* 14.58.1–2. Cf. below 224.

[181] Tac. *Ann.* 14.58.3. Though Antistius then supposedly changed his mind (Tac. *Ann.* 14.59.2), his relationship with Plautus would have made him unpopular with the regime, and he died in the second round of killings after the Pisonian conspiracy: below 216.

[182] Below 216. Tac. *Ann.* 16.23.1. Furneaux 1907, 457–8; Griffin 1984, 171, 178, 256 and n. 10.

[183] Above 146.

national religious thanksgiving.[184] The way was now clear for the removal of Octavia and Poppaea's marriage to Nero.

8.6.4 *Octavia*

This happened very quickly. Octavia was divorced on the grounds of sterility; twelve days later, Poppaea was married to Nero.[185] Octavia was then charged with previous adultery with a slave. When this failed she was at first fairly well treated but then soon banished to Campania. This resulted in very serious rioting in favour of Octavia and against Poppaea in Italy and Rome, a sign that Poppaea and Tigellinus were still not wholly in control of events. It prompted further trumped-up charges against Octavia: of other earlier adultery with Anicetus (still commanding the Misenum fleet and bribed to bear false witness to his complicity) and treason. She was found guilty, exiled to Pandateria and soon killed.[186]

8.6.5 *Doryphorus, Pallas*

There followed action against prominent opponents of the divorce and remarriage who, unlike Faenius Rufus and Corbulo, refused to move with the times. Tacitus says that Doryphorus, Nero's *a libellis*, perished because he was opposed to Poppaea, and Pallas, the great *a rationibus* dismissed in the wake of the Acte affair, because Nero resented his enormous wealth.[187] Doryphorus' fate is understandable. Pallas, a staunch 'Agrippinian'[188] and so probably also hostile to Nero's divorcing Octavia, is more likely to have suffered for this than for his riches, most of which apparently passed to his family.[189] For leading *liberti*, death was a career risk. They made powerful enemies and were especially vulnerable during major crises. In 54, alongside the death of M. Junius Silanus,[190] Agrippina had engineered that of her old enemy, Claudius' *ab epistulis*, Narcissus, supposedly against the will of Nero.[191]

---

[184] Tac. *Ann.* 14.59.6: *supplicationes*. Talbert 1984, 389.   [185] Tac. *Ann.* 14.60.1; Suet. *Ner.* 35.3.
[186] Tac. *Ann.* 14.60.2–64. Above 186.   [187] Tac. *Ann.* 14.65.1. Above 55.
[188] He was supposed to have enjoyed a sexual liaison with Agrippina: Tac. *Ann.* 14.2.4, with 12.25.1;
cf. *Schol. Iuv.* (Probus) 1.109.
[189] Bradley 1978a, 187.   [190] Above 172.
[191] Tac. *Ann.* 13.1.4: *invito principe*. Barrett 1996, 156; Osgood 2011, 250.

8.7 Conclusion

M. Junius Silanus was the victim of his high birth, and his death was nothing to do with Nero. Both Claudius and Britannicus may have died of natural causes; but if Claudius was murdered, the deed was not Nero's, and if Britannicus was murdered, others may have been involved. Agrippina was certainly murdered, but this may likewise have been forced on Nero by interested third parties. In each case, the disappearance of a major Julio-Claudian was apparently broadly accepted as contributing to the stability of politics and so being for the good of the state. The death of Britannicus occasioned no massive hostility;[192] and it is remarkable how little immediate negative reaction there was to that of Agrippina.[193] Thrasea Paetus was unique in openly objecting to senatorial rejoicing at her end; and even he then continued to work with the regime.[194] The accusation of matricide appears to have surfaced only after the Fire of 64, and particularly in the wake of the Pisonian conspiracy.[195] The rise of Poppaea and Tigellinus and, above all, uncertainty over the succession raised the political temperature. In 62, Burrus probably died of natural causes and Seneca was simply 'let go': their day was done. However, changing circumstances forced Faenius Rufus and Corbulo to compromise, and destroyed Rubellius Plautus, Cornelius Sulla, Octavia, Doryphorus and Pallas. None of this is morally uplifting. Octavia was particularly badly treated. Tacitus notes the gross contradiction between the original charge of sterility and the later accusation that Octavia aborted a child by Anicetus.[196] Yet she, like the rest, passively accepted her fate. The only person showing any spirit was one of her lady's-maids who, cruelly cross-examined by Tigellinus, spat out that her mistress's cunt was cleaner than his mouth.[197]

On the other hand, none of this amounted to murderous tyranny. In particular, the year 62 should not be seen as the time when Nero fell out of the influence of the 'good' Seneca and Burrus and under that of the 'bad' Poppaea and Tigellinus, and first showed himself as 'evil'.[198] The deaths of this year, though cruel, should be regarded as the inevitable outcome of the dangerous politics of the time. The reality of this danger is visible in the metropolitan rioting that followed the banishment of Octavia to Campania. This involved a popular occupation of the Capitol, the Forum and

---

[192] Cf. above 175.   [193] Warmington 1969, 46 (quotation).   [194] Above 27.
[195] Below 234.   [196] Tac. *Ann.* 14.63.1.
[197] Tac. *Ann.* 14.60.4: *castiora esse muliebra Octaviae ... quam os eius.*   [198] Tac. *Ann.* 14.51.5–6.

even part of the Palatine complex, and considerable damage to public property. Some person or group must have been set on causing mischief.[199] Poppaea must have been terrified by the proximity of a hostile mob, and her subsequent assertion that the trouble might have produced a 'leader' willing to challenge Nero in the name of Octavia may have contained a germ of truth.[200] Fortunately for the regime, matters did not get out of hand. The mob was dispersed with minimum force and without serious casualties. However, unrest on such scale should have been prevented; that it occurred is a third sign of the new administration's difficulties in asserting total control. Its reaction was probably to increase its ruthlessness hence, probably, the elimination of Doryphorus and Pallas. Their strength, both personally and as members of the Establishment, had allowed them to survive the new marriage but the suspicion may have arisen that they were in some way associated with the rioting.

In 62, hard decisions had to be made, and these and their execution were not 'tyrannical' but the work of a new set of advisers, personally ambitious but essentially steadfast servants of the incumbent *princeps*. From 54 to 64 political killings were, in fact, relatively few and probably all accompanied by some form of legal process.[201] At least to begin with, more of those found guilty were exiled than executed; and it took eight years for the regime to remove Plautus and Sulla.[202] What we see is the precise targeting of people seen as political threats, not indiscriminate blood-lust or greed. This is supported by the fact that no Silani are found alongside Plautus, Sulla and the other victims in 62; that, despite fears to the contrary, the regime did not take action against Plautus' family;[203] and that, as noted, most of Pallas' wealth apparently passed to his family. Even aspects of the killings that strike us as atrocious are explicable. Though the corpses of Plautus, Sulla and Octavia were decapitated and the heads taken to Rome,[204] this should not be taken as wanton mutilation. In an age without easy proof of distant death, and so of unsettling posthumous 'doubles' – earlier, of Agrippa Postumus, later of Nero himself[205] – a severed head was the best proof of an enemy's decease. The same grisly convention had been followed by Agrippina II, under Claudius. Ruthlessness ensured peace. This must have been the particular aim of leading *liberti* for whom change threatened trouble.[206]

---

[199] Above 154.   [200] Tac. *Ann.* 14.61.4: *dux.*   [201] Above 71, 74; *contra* Fini 1994, 149.
[202] Fini 1994, 145.   [203] Tac. *Ann.* 14.59.1–2:
[204] Sulla: Tac. *Ann.* 14.57.1; Plautus: Tac. *Ann.* 14.59.4; Octavia: Tac. *Ann.* 14.64.4.
[205] Grünewald 2004, 140–4, 151–4.   [206] Above 162, 193.

They were not inclined to revolution and, after the deaths of Doryphus and Pallas, *liberti* are conspicuous for their loyalty to the Neronian administration. It is significant that no important imperial freedmen appear to have been involved in the Pisonian conspiracy; and some paid the price for their allegiance on Nero's fall.[207] Other members of the political community will also have feared civil strife.[208] Though Tacitus berates the Senate for slavishly accepting, even celebrating, the 62 killings, those involved were just political pragmatists. As Warmington notes, the disturbances surrounding the removal of Octavia were short term, and stability was soon restored to government.[209] The switch of partner appeared justified. Poppaea bore Nero a daughter, Claudia, in January 63. A clear measure of the importance of the occasion is that both mother and child were given the title of *Augusta*. Poppaea had been brought up to the same level as Livia; and this was the first time that *Augusta* was applied to an infant.[210] The baby died soon afterwards, but her parents were still young and by 65 Poppaea was again pregnant, restoring hope in the future.[211]

The Neronian regime has been criticised for ridding itself of potential rivals: morally, because it was wrong to do so; and practically, because it left itself with no supporting family allies. The first is unrealistic: family values do not apply to monarchs.[212] With regard to the second we must bear in mind that Nero died young. If he had enjoyed a normal lifespan and produced several children, the removal of blood-rivals would have ensured security for his heirs. These deaths and those like them do not, therefore, make Nero a 'killer'. The vast majority of early Neronian killings are attributable to the court Establishment acting out of necessity.

---

[207] Below 409.   [208] Above 162.   [209] Tac. *Ann.* 14.64.5–6. Warmington 1969, 51.
[210] Tac. *Ann.* 15.23.1. Barrett *et al.* 2016, 186 and n. 55.   [211] Tac. *Ann.* 15.23.1–4; below 219.
[212] Giardina 2011, 14, 17.

CHAPTER 9

Killer? II: 62–68

9.1 Introduction

This chapter continues the theme of Chapter 8 and examines all remaining Neronian deaths, with particular attention to those of the Pisonian and Vinician conspirators and of Corbulo.

9.2 D. Junius Silanus

There were no major deaths between 62 and 64, but early in 64, the middle Silanian brother, D. Junius Silanus, was charged with plotting rebellion and forced to commit suicide.[1] The fact that he died ten years after his eldest brother suggests that he was basically harmless. However, certain of his actions had been indiscreet;[2] and he perished after the death of Nero's baby daughter in 63 and before Poppaea's second pregnancy in 65: an awkward time when people may have again looked to the Silani as potential heirs, and when the Establishment therefore decided that he should die.[3] Nero's protest that had Silanus gone to trial he would have allowed him to live indicates that the *princeps* was not the prime mover in the affair.[4]

9.3 The Pisonian Conspiracy

9.3.1 Introduction

Killings increased dramatically following the unmasking of the Pisonian conspiracy. The plotters were betrayed in April 65, on the eve of an attempt to assassinate Nero. However, before considering their fates, we

---

[1] Tac. *Ann.* 15.35; Cass. Dio 62.27.2.   [2] Rutledge 2001, 82; above 60.   [3] Cf. above 127.
[4] Tac. *Ann.* 15.35.5. Cf. above 76.

must first establish how an intended metropolitan coup squares with the idea of Nero's being protected by a loyal Establishment, set on maintaining the Julio-Claudian line.

9.3.2 Membership

The conspirators included some significant Establishment figures. Their nominee to replace Nero, Piso, was, despite Tacitus' criticism of his character,[5] someone to be reckoned with. Of noble descent, he had been treated badly by Gaius but was restored by Claudius and flourished under Nero, frequently entertaining the *princeps* at his Baiaean villa. Here, Nero enjoyed a relaxation of security and absence of formality that indicate trust in a host who shared his artistic interests.[6] Piso has, in fact, been tentatively identified as the 'Meliboeus' of Calpurnius Siculus' Ornytus,[7] and is generally accepted to be the addressee of the *Laus Pisonis*. This praises him as a forensic orator, a declaimer of literature, a poet in his own right, a composer for the lyre, an athlete, and adept at the military board-game 'Little Soldiers' (*ludus latrunculorum*).[8] As such, he was, like Nero, a man of his time.[9] Unlike Nero, however, he indulged his artistic interests in private, otherwise acting the responsible and active public figure in the best Roman tradition.[10] This made him a plausible candidate: 'In a certain way he embodied the Neronian zeitgeist in a way that was acceptable even to those of stricter dispositions'.[11] Rudich surmises that his claim to power may also have derived from his descent from Pompey the Great.[12] Another conspirator who was an intimate of Nero was Claudius Senecio who, along with Otho, had helped him begin the Acte affair.[13] Together with Piso, other artistic plotters were Lucan, Afranius Quintianus and Antonius Natalis. The most powerful courtier by far was Faenius Rufus, the first praetorian prefect known to have taken an active role in a plot against his *princeps*.[14] A link between the intellectual and political sides of court life may have been provided by Seneca. Tacitus gives the impression that Seneca was wrongly accused of participation in the conspiracy,[15] while providing sufficient information to suggest the contrary. Dio names him as

---

[5] Tac. *Ann.* 15.48.4.
[6] Tac. *Ann.* 15.52.1. Above 60; Waldherr 2005, 186. Cf. Henderson 1905, 261; Rees 2013, 96–7. For the likely location of the villa see Keppie 2011, 39.
[7] Calp. *Ecl.* 1.94. E.g. Rudich 1993, 93.   [8] Green 2010; Rees 2013, 102–3.
[9] Cf. below 301.   [10] Below 374.   [11] Malitz 1999, 80 (quotation); Waldherr 2005, 186–7.
[12] Rudich 1993, 91–2.   [13] Tac. *Ann.* 13.12.1, 15.50.1. Above 51.   [14] Bingham 2013, 62.
[15] Tac. *Ann.* 15.60.3.

a senior plotter, alongside Faenius Rufus.[16] While most historians give Seneca the benefit of the doubt,[17] some indeed see him as the *éminence grise* of the affair.[18] In support of his complicity is that Piso and Seneca were in contact with each other towards the end of 64; that, despite his retirement, Seneca was close to Rome on the scheduled date of the assassination; and that there was even credible talk of Seneca's replacing Piso once Nero had been disposed of.[19] At the very least one is bound to suspect that Seneca was aware of serious metropolitan disaffection, did not reveal it to the authorities, and so was an accessory before the fact.[20] Other key Establishment figures, important because of their proximity to the *princeps*, were senior praetorians, in particular Subrius Flavus and Sulpicius Asper, a tribune and a centurion respectively. Tacitus, indeed, calls this pair 'the most committed', which suggests that they were the instigators of the plot.[21]

Then, roughly in the order in which they occur in Tacitus, we find lesser figures: a broad spectrum of idealists (Plautius Lateranus with, perhaps, the reformed rake Flavius Scaevinus); 'chancers' (Cervarius Proculus, Vulcacius Araricus, Julius Augurinus, Munatius Gratus, Marcius Festus); and praetorian officers (Gavius Silvanus, Statius Proxumus, Maximus Scaurus, Venetus Paulus) and privates (... Pompeius, Cornelius Martialis, Flavius Nepos, Statius Domitius) recruited or ordered to join the plot to give it muscle. Around them was a penumbra of associated civilians either denounced by the rest (Acilia, Glitius Gallus, Annius Pollio) or – a much larger number – considered suspect because of their links with them (Novius Priscus, Rufrius Crispinus, Caedicia, Verginius Flavus and Musonius Rufus, Caesennius Maximus and, perhaps, Cluvidienus Quietus, Julius Agrippa, Blitius Catulinus, Petronius Priscus and Julius Altinus). An outlier to this collection of freeborn aristocrats is the freedwoman Epicharis, who attempted to suborn the fleet at Misenum. Two others appear to have been caught in events: the consul Vestinus Atticus and, a little later, Claudius' daughter, Antonia.[22]

Tacitus and modern scholars pronounce on the likely guilt or innocence of these people but, apart from those who were undeniably involved and

---

[16] Cass. Dio 62.24.1.
[17] E.g. Grant 1970, 214; Griffin 1984, 155, 174; Rudich 1993, 106–8; Malitz 1999, 82.
[18] E.g. Fini 1994, 187–90.
[19] Tac. *Ann.* 15.45.5, 60.7, 65. Below 202; cf. Rudich 1993, 107–8; Holland 2000, 191.
[20] Cf. Henderson 1905, 280–3, Cizek 1982, 59, 262–3, Griffin 1984, 174; Rudich 1993, 109; Waldherr 2005, 192; Romm 2014, 180.
[21] Tac. *Ann.* 15.49.1: *promptissimi.*   [22] Above 72; below 220.

those who escaped formal punishment at the time (Gavius Silvanus,
Acilia), for most, as for Seneca, this is impossible to establish with confidence. What is undeniable is the difference between the membership of
the conspiracies of 65 and 68. The main Pisonian conspirators, preponder-
antly freeborn, upper-class males, were far from the mongrel crew
described by Tacitus: 'a mixture of rank and classes, ages and sexes, rich
and poor'.[23] However, apart from Faenius Rufus, they included no Establishment heavyweights: no senior *liberti*, no prominent political lawyers
and no frontier-generals. Very few, in fact, belonged to the 'protecting
hierarchy'/*Consilium*.[24] In short, though connected with the court Establishment (even Epicharis may have been the mistress of Seneca's brother,
Mela[25]), most conspirators did not belong to its most powerful interest
groups. It is, indeed, remarkable how few conspirators came from old
aristocratic families, and how many had strong literary interests.[26] The
conspiracy did not reflect or provoke any crisis in the regime's relations
with the Senate.[27]

9.3.3   Course

Tacitus provides two direct chronological references. The first is that the
conspiracy began in 62, when Piso grew fearful following an unsuccessful
accusation of Seneca by one Romanus.[28] This has been accepted by some
historians,[29] but Tacitus later declares that though he is unsure who started
the conspiracy, it was certainly not Piso and other civilians whom he
names.[30] Some have found confirmation that the conspiracy was under
way before 65 in Tacitus' report that Subrius Flavus felt tempted to attack
Nero while he was on stage, or while he was rushing about trying to save
the burning *Domus Transitoria* during the Fire of 64,[31] but this is unlikely.
The upsetting stage performance was surely no earlier than Nero's first
public performance in Naples not long before the Fire.[32] This was at least a
year before the disclosure of the conspiracy and so, like Tacitus' starting-
date of 62, does not square with his second direct chronological indication:

---

[23] Tac. *Ann.* 15.54.1: *diversi generis ordinis, aetatis sexus, ditis pauperes.*
[24] Above 130; *contra* Grant 1970, 214. Cf. Winterling (2007, 91) on the involvement of leading men
    in the conspiracy of 39.
[25] Griffin 1984, 174.   [26] Rudich 1993, 92–3; Reitz 2006, 12.
[27] *Contra* Warmington 1969, 136; cf. above 94.   [28] Tac. *Ann.* 14.65.2.
[29] Rudich 1993, 76, 91; Holland 2000, 181.   [30] Tac. *Ann.* 15.49.1. Cf. Rudich 1993, 76.
[31] Tac. *Ann.* 15.50.6. E.g. Cizek 1982, 308; Fini 1994, 154.
[32] Below 298. For a likely date in March cf. below 389 with Cass. Dio 63.26.1.

that the plot was 'no sooner hatched than fully grown' at the start of his account of 65.[33] In addition, Tacitus says that Subrius Flavus held back during the Fire because he did not want to commit murder, however justified.[34] Flavus was a stickler for military discipline, even down to the digging of his own grave.[35] He liked to work within a command structure: like Cassius Chaerea, who struck the first blow against Gaius and was also a praetorian tribune, 'a man who was to the end someone who carried out the commands of others'.[36] The fact that he could contemplate individual action suggests that he was not yet part of a plot.

It is probably best to treat the date of 62 as 'an absurdity',[37] ignore the Fire story, and assume that the plot got under way only towards the end of 64. This fits Tacitus' second chronological indication and his notice of contact between Piso and Seneca after the latter's final withdrawal from public affairs at this time.[38] Tacitus then says that, though the conspiracy was under way, a final decision as to how and when to strike was subject to delay.[39] A little later, he reports that the plotters did not act until they were sure that they could enlist Faenius Rufus. Since context and language suggest that those concerned were now both praetorians and civilians, and since Rufus was soon to show himself a weak reed, one may conclude that Flavus and Asper had not involved him in their initial of scheming. Rather, they first enrolled civilians whom they judged to be sympathetic and who might provide a plausible candidate, and only when these showed them-selves reluctant to act without more powerful backing did they recruit Rufus, whose conversation had led them to believe that he could be turned against Nero.[40]

This raises the question of whether there was one conspiracy or a constellation of conspiracies. The latter was the case under Gaius and usual with most late Republican and early imperial plots. Epicharis' scheme was, at best, semi-detached. From a different background to the rest, and working with different accomplices, she formulated a wholly different plan: to do away with Nero at sea.[41] This was a recipe for disaster since anyone planning to get rid of Nero had to do so in Rome in order to stay in control of consequent political upheaval.[42] Tacitus says that she was

---

[33] Tac. *Ann.* 15.48.1: *coepta simul et aucta.*   [34] Tac. *Ann.* 15.50.7.   [35] Tac. *Ann.* 15.67.6.
[36] Cf. below 202; Winterling 2007, 168; 'Er war und blieb jemand, der Befehle anderer ausführte'.
[37] Griffin 1984, 85 (quotation); cf. Rutledge 2001, 166–7; Kimmerle 2015, 105.   [38] Above 199.
[39] Tac. *Ann.* 15.51.1. Cf. below 209.
[40] Tac. *Ann.* 15.50.5: *ubi coniuratis praefectum quoque praetorii in partes descendisse crebro ipsius sermone facta fides.*
[41] Tac. *Ann.* 15.51.3.   [42] Henderson 1905, 267; cf. Holland 2000, 187.

driven to devise it by the reluctance of the rest to act, but one suspects that she acted alone throughout and her name became associated with the Pisonians only after all had failed. The latter comprised two very different groups of soldiers and civilians,[43] each with its own grievances and agenda. No man of action and socially and intellectually close to Nero, Piso himself was probably brought in as no more than an aristocratic figurehead.[44] Tacitus recounts, without denial, the rumour that Subrius Flavus and the centurions secretly planned that once Nero was dead they would kill Piso and replace him with the already complicit Seneca.[45] A little later, Tacitus has Subrius Flavus initially deny involvement in conspiracy on the grounds that, as a man of arms, he 'would never have shared so desperate an enterprise with unarmed effeminates'.[46]

After initial indecision, the conspirators decided to kill Nero on 19 April, during the *Cerealia* festival, as he left the Circus Maximus after a chariot-race.[47] However, last-minute nerves led to their betrayal,[48] and it was the praetorians who failed the civilians, The latter, accused, first held back from exposing their military partners in the hope that these might still kill Nero.[49] Especially guilty was Faenius Rufus, who restrained Subrius Flavus from killing Nero during the first round of trials.[50] Yet Flavus himself bears some blame for characteristically following the orders of his prefect; and, once denounced, he at first pleaded innocence. Similarly, when Gavius Silvanus asked Rufus if he should carry out the sentence of death on Seneca, expecting the answer no, he accepted the prefect's order to proceed.[51] Rufus' direction of his subordinates indicates that he could easily have seized the initiative.[52] Rudich's explanation for his strange inaction is a 'nervous breakdown',[53] but sudden loss of nerve does not fit with his long survival at the top of the administration. Tacitus has Rufus, unlike other condemned praetorians, die very badly, a fitting reward for his weak conduct. However, he also mentions a change of will,[54] which suggests that Rufus had proved that he was never wholly engaged in the plot. Allowed to speak, he might have protested that he did not start the conspiracy, indicated those occasions when he prevented its success, and informed on others.[55] His collaboration won

[43] Cf. Rudich 1993, 98; Holland 2000, 185–6; Waldherr 2005, 186.
[44] Cf. Barrett *et al.* 2016, 192.   [45] Tac. *Ann.* 15.65. Above 199; Holland 2000, 185–6, 188.
[46] Tac. *Ann.* 15.67.1: *inermes et effeminati.*
[47] Tac. *Ann.* 15.53.1. Hohl 1918, 385; Waldherr 2005, 190.   [48] Tac. *Ann.* 15.54.1–55.1.
[49] Tac. *Ann.* 15.66.1.   [50] Tac. *Ann.* 15.58.4.   [51] Tac. *Ann.* 15.61.6.
[52] Bingham 2013, 63.   [53] Rudich 1993, 113–19.   [54] Tac. *Ann.* 15.68.2–3.
[55] Cf. Waldherr 2005, 192.

him permission to commit suicide and so spared him both public humiliation and the impoverishment of his family.[56] The praetorians thus
showed lack of resolve, but the civilians were almost as bad. Piso, fearful
and indecisive, wasted chances to retrieve the situation and went down
without a fight.[57] Accusation and trial brought out the worst in many
others who quickly accused their colleagues.[58] There was no thought of
heroic martyrdom. Even Seneca, typically, appears to the end to have
hoped for clemency from Nero.[59] Tacitus declares that fate had made
cowards of them all,[60] but this is too hard; it fails to appreciate that the
conspirators never enjoyed the mutual loyalty of a single group with
strong common aims.

9.3.4 Motives

The conspirators' motives were, indeed, 'contradictory and confused'.[61]
Precisely what Tacitus thinks terrified Piso in 62 is obscure and perhaps
purely rhetorical, to convey the impression of a rising tide of upper-class
hatred against Nero.[62] Epicharis' activities reflect hostility to Nero, but
what she had in mind when she condemned Nero's 'many crimes' and who,
if anyone, else was behind her – though surely not Mela – remain
unknown.[63] She certainly played on personal motives in her attempt to
recruit the naval captain, Volusius Proculus.[64] Faenius Rufus acted out of
personal motives. Tacitus tells us that he joined the conspiracy not because
he hated Nero but because he felt that Nero was giving too much credence
to the constant accusations made against him, as a favourite of Agrippina,
by Tigellinus.[65] Though, thanks to Corbulo, Rufus' place at court was
probably stronger than Tacitus suggests,[66] by late 64 the war in Armenia
was over, Tigellinus more powerful and Corbulo's influence on the wane.[67]
Personal motives were probably also behind the adherence of many *literati*.
Friction between the *princeps* and his fellow artists was the price paid for
court banter,[68] and, compounded by disappointment at Nero's intellectual
change of course, is the best explanation for Lucan's participation.[69] Piso
was perhaps drawn in as a *literatus*. However, he may also have resented

---

[56] Below 319.   [57] Tac. *Ann.* 15.52.1–2, 59 *pass*.   [58] Cf. Tac. *Ann.* 15.56.2.
[59] Romm 2014, 188.   [60] Tac. *Ann.* 15.67.1; 61.6: *fatali omnium ignavia*. Cf. below 234.
[61] Rudich 1993, 16.
[62] Tac. *Ann.* 14.65.2. Cf. Rudich 1993, 91; Barrett *et al.* 2016, 195 and n. 4.
[63] Tac. *Ann.* 15.51.4: *omnia scelera*. Rudich 1993, 100–1; cf. below 206.   [64] Tac. *Ann.* 15.51.3.
[65] Tac. *Ann.* 15.50.4; cf. 14.57.1.   [66] Above 155.   [67] Above 30.   [68] Above 105.
[69] Above 114.

Nero for his appropriation of land for the *Domus Aurea* and for the character of this complex,[70] and been tempted to make his mark on history.[71] All this amounts to no more than the inevitable stresses and strains among a relatively small metropolitan 'polite society' which need not have resulted in conspiracy. Something must have happened in late 64 to stimulate an odd collection of praetorians and civilians to combined action. What was it?

There must have been some level of background concern among high aristocrats. The deaths of 62 and of Silanus will have been unsettling; and the fact that government was being directed by Poppaea, Tigellinus and leading freedmen was hardly in line with the Augustan programme of the start of the Neronian principate. As for Nero himself, conservatives will have been disquieted by his excessive interest in sport and entertainment.[72] This was not just a matter of morality. Charioteering was a young man's game. Anyone still competing in his late twenties was celebrated.[73] Nero, now approaching twenty-seven, might be judged irresponsible in risking himself in this way, especially while there was still no heir. On the other hand, if he had gone to war he would have put his life at risk; and none of this general concern should have resulted in conspiracy. The most likely event to stimulate particular concern early in 64 is, rather, Nero's first professional appearance, in Naples.[74] This made a huge impression on him. His rapturous reception encouraged him to accept his vocation as a performing artist,[75] which he clearly regarded as a major turning-point in his life. Naples became very important for him. It was where he chose to receive Tiridates in 66,[76] and from where, as one of his 'birth-places', he began his triumphal progress of 67.[77] The Naples experience immediately impacted on his actions as *princeps*. In 63 he had thrown a set of gladiatorial games in Rome so magnificent that they won the grudging approval of Tacitus.[78] Part of their splendour must have been their bloodiness. It might appear that the previously fastidious Nero was beginning to act the normal *princeps*.[79] A more significant pointer in this direction is that preparations were also being made for him to go on a grand foreign tour, travelling to Greece and then to Egypt.[80] There was gossip of a possible campaign into Ethiopia, and of a journey into Syria to

---

[70] Below 262.   [71] Cf. Rudich 1993, 91.   [72] Below 374.
[73] Mart. 10.53, on Scorpus, who died at 27.   [74] Tac. *Ann.* 15.33.2; Suet. *Ner.* 19.1. Below 298.
[75] Below 308.   [76] Below 218.   [77] Below 383.   [78] Below 298.   [79] Below 322.
[80] Though Tacitus (*Ann.* 15.34.2, 36.1) reports these as two separate, impulsive schemes on the part of Nero, given the extensive preparations for the Egyptian leg (cf. below 221) they are better treated as a long-conceived plan.

join Corbulo and finish the Armenian campaign. Though the former is improbable,[81] the latter should not be dismissed out of hand.[82] All this would have made it appear that in 64 Nero would at last act the imperial *princeps*. Though Nero himself may have initially proposed the trip,[83] all came to nothing. After his performance at Naples, he set out eastwards but got no further than Benevento before returning to Rome and cancelling the undertaking. His excuse was religious,[84] but it is more likely that, once on the move, he reverted to his characteristic lack of enthusiasm for long-distance travel and, fired by his experiences in Naples, conceived a desire to pursue his own, very personal, version of his principate: 'Greek' in the sense of being unmilitary, artistic and popular, but aimed at Romans and Italians.[85] Instead of going to Greece and beyond, Nero appeared as guest of honour at Tigellinus' banquet.

This probably led to a high level of disappointment in the political community, even at the centre of government. Poppaea and Tigellinus must have approved the Grand Tour and been dismayed by its cancellation. More generally, down to 64 the extent of Nero's artistic leanings and his unorthodox view of his job as *princeps* will probably have been known to relatively few: though he had performed previously, he had done so in private, as at the *Iuvenalia*.[86] His public appearance at Naples seems to have been spontaneous, catching the Establishment off guard.[87] Given their prejudices,[88] news that the *princeps* had played the professional entertainer will have come as a shock to traditional aristocrats. They will have judged this as excessively Hellenic, and so scandalous, behaviour by a man who was in one person a high Roman noble, a senior magistrate of the Republic and the head of its most important family. 'Emperors simply should not be professional performers. Amateur indulgence in an art or sport might be pardonable; obsessive dedication was not.'[89] Conservatives will have feared that there was worse to come, perhaps in the forthcoming *Neronia* II.[90] To make matters worse, Nero's populist, local (Roman/Italian) behaviour at his Naples performances and at Tigellinus' banquet may have resulted in fear of incipient demagogy. The people of Rome, perhaps resentful of Nero's first revelation of his true self to those of Naples,[91] and concerned about the loss of patronage that his absence would bring, will have been delighted with his decision to remain in the

---

[81] Above 127, 152 n. 176.   [82] Cass. Dio 62.22.4. Cf. above 166.   [83] Above 127.
[84] Below 309.   [85] Below 293, 309, 375.   [86] Tac. *Ann.* 15.33.1. Below 288.
[87] *Contra* Champlin 2003, 76; cf. below 206.   [88] Below 299.   [89] Champlin 2003, 81.
[90] Malitz 1999, 79–80.   [91] Holland 2000, 149.

City and celebrate this with a great feast. Both Greek and Roman history taught that a leader who obtained the favour of the mob might use it against the upper classes and so unbalance the established social order, the preservation of which was one of a *princeps'* major responsibilities.[92] 'Over-generosity to the *plebs*, or even worse, personal participation in performance ... although it might delight the commons, contravened a variety of upper-class norms, incurred a variety of aristocratic frowns, and consequently cost, rather than earned, aristocratic esteem'.[93] Milnor categorises Nero's behaviour as 'publication': 'the desire to share with the populace at large what ought to have been kept private'. The more people saw of their *princeps* the more they would want to see of him and the more he would be tempted to comply. This amounted to 'a kind of prostitution: he and his audience appear as co-conspirators, mutually destructive of each other's morals'.[94] Such a ruler might well be seen as a class traitor, a potential tyrant or king. The real scandal of Tigellinus' banquet was Nero's encouragement of the participation of the mob.[95] Associated with the fear of demagogy is likely also to have been fear that Nero was beginning too closely to resemble Gaius, who too had shown great interest in sport and entertainment, and whose feasting had become extensive, unorthodox and unusually socially inclusive.[96]

The year 64 commenced, in fact, with the start of a major run of Nero's 'break-outs'. After Naples and Tigellinus' banquet came the Great Fire, and further unease about certain of Nero's actions.[97] Nero again showed a populist approach in his personal efforts to contain the Fire and his measures to relieve its victims. The same attitude may be seen in his conception of the Golden House, especially its Pavilion.[98] The novelty of his approach is reflected in the fact that he could subsequently be suspected of arson: by mid-64, even the Roman people, whose favour he cherished, were uncertain as to what to make of this new Nero.[99] Once generated, distrust of the *princeps* meant that many of his acts could be interpreted as criminal: the beginning of the hostile source tradition and an explanation for Epicharis' accusations.[100] In these circumstances, even Seneca, probably shocked by Nero's blatant public advertisement of his artistic and sporting interests, which amounted to an abrogation of his responsibilities as *princeps*, whether Augustan or Hellenistic, was ready to reject his pupil. In addition, and more personally, Seneca may have

[92] Cf. Edwards 1994, 87   [93] Lendon 1997, 124.   [94] Milnor 2005, 296–7.
[95] Cf. Champlin 2003, 159.   [96] Suet. *Calig.* 54; Cass. Dio 59.5. Winterling 2007, 75, 78–9.
[97] Above 165.   [98] Below 248–9.   [99] Below 243.   [100] Above 203.

resented Nero's acceptance of his second offer of the bulk of his fortune – the first had been made and rejected in 62 – to help pay for building work after the Fire, even though this hardly left him destitute.[101] Borne down by the *acedia* of old age and feelings of failure, he abandoned any duty of care towards Nero, leaving it to fate to decide what happened to him. Yet the Neronian regime quickly recovered its credibility. The Fire was well handled, Nero's related peccadillos forgotten, and domestic misfortune balanced by foreign success as Tiridates recognised Rome's sovereignty over Armenia and the Black Sea region was taken firmly into the Roman sphere of influence.[102] Conservative dismay alone was not, therefore, sufficient to produce conspiracy. Conservatives will have realised that they lacked the support of the wider political community; and anyway, as we have seen, the main civilian Pisonians were hardly typical aristocratic 'conservatives'. What was missing was real conviction and power, especially that of the military. The frontier armies were too distant and too loyal. Epicharis turned to the navy, but was betrayed. The catalyst was a group of senior praetorians.

Gaius had fatally alienated one of his praetorian tribunes by acting the workplace bully,[103] but we hear of nothing similar from Nero: this was not his style. When Subrius Flavus broke under questioning, he told Nero that he hated him as the murderer of Agrippina and Octavia, as the perpetrator of unbecoming conduct in the circus and on the stage, and as an arsonist.[104] Concerning the first of these charges, Flavus' attitude must have been that of a minority of praetorians, since the majority had accepted these acts and remained loyal to Nero until almost the end.[105] Furthermore, after the conspiracy was revealed there was no witch-hunt among the praetorians. The administration's use of recruits to make arrests was no more than prudence, given the unexpected threat from serving praetorians; and some officers, though charged, were not executed but reduced in rank, pardoned or even acquitted.[106] Flavus' third charge is, as we shall see, most unlikely: a wild shot.[107] However, the accusation of unbecoming conduct explains why some senior praetorians, like some aristocrats, judged Nero

---

[101] Tac. *Ann.* 14.54.4, 56.3; Cass. Dio 62.25.3. Romm 2014, 169–70; Barrett *et al.* 2016, 211 and n. 59.

[102] Above 140, 141; 235–6, 247.   [103] Joseph. *AJ* 19.29–31. Winterling 2007, 166–7.

[104] Tac. *Ann.* 15.67.3. Below 234.   [105] Cf. Griffin 1984, 167–8; below 411.

[106] Tac. *Ann.* 15.59.7 (probably mistakenly putting this before the revelation of praetorian involvement). Table 2; Waldherr 2005, 193. (Reduced: ... Pompeius; Cornelius Martialis; Flavius Nepos; Statius Domitius. Pardoned: Statius Proxumus. Acquitted Gavius Silvanus.)

[107] Below 234.

unfit to be *princeps*.[108] After a good start, he had profoundly disappointed them by indulging in ever more un-Roman activities. Their dismay will have grown gradually. Most praetorian officers must always have looked askance at the more extreme 'artistic' elements of Nero's behaviour, manifested early in his principate. However, these will have been indulged in privately, and when he began to give them a more public airing, praetorians could have accepted them as 'traditional'. Thus they could have tolerated *Neronia* I as Nero establishing Greek-style games in Rome, as Augustus had established them in Naples,[109] and Nero was not yet a professional competitor. At *Neronia* I, though he accepted prizes for rhetoric and poetry, he did not compete for these; and though he played and sang, he refused the prize for lyre-playing.[110] In short, he was still acting the amateur. In the early years, too, Nero's artistic eccentricities will have been adequately balanced by his sporting prowess. This demonstrated that he was no weakling or coward and so worthy of respect by the military.[111] The turning-point for the most disaffected praetorians was, again, his professional performance at Naples early in 64. The Neapolitan games themselves cannot have repelled them since, again, they were Augustan, and the praetorians must have already known them from Nero's probable attendance in 56 and 60.[112] Alongside the *Augustiani* they will have accompanied him there as they accompanied him at the *Iuvenalia* and *Neronia* I in Rome.[113] The problem was Nero's novel conduct: his 'break-out'.[114] Instead of remaining in the audience as head of state he went on stage as performer. And when not performing he turned up at the theatre to dine and banter with the audience.[115] Apart from this 'degradation of the authority of the imperial position',[116] Nero's consorting with crowds must have been a nightmare for senior praetorians charged with guaranteeing his safety. Their nerves may have been further frayed by officers of the *Augustiani* beginning to conduct themselves as their equals,[117] and, as Nero changed his mind about his grand progress, by uncertainty as to whether or not they should prepare for overseas service. On top of everything came an earthquake. Subsequent stress might have resulted from the sudden need to provide security for the *princeps* at Tigellinus' banquet.[118] The bulk of the praetorian rank and file, like the bulk of the Italian and Roman populace, probably enjoyed Nero's antics, but a large

---

[108] Cf. Brunt 1959, 533.   [109] Below 298, 377.
[110] Tac. *Ann.* 14.21.8; Suet. *Ner.* 12.3; Cass. Dio 61.21.2.   [111] Below 304.
[112] Cass. Dio 63.26.1 suggests that they were held every four years (here, in 68, four years after 64).
[113] Above 61.   [114] For the following see Tac. *Ann.* 15.33.3–34; Suet. *Ner.* 20.2–3.
[115] Cf. below 309.   [116] Warmington 1969, 137.   [117] Above 62.   [118] Above 205.

proportion of senior officers lost patience with him. (Seven of the twelve serving tribunes eventually faced charges of participation in the Pisonian conspiracy. Of the remaining five, only two were clearly not involved.[119]) Thus Subrius Flavus turned against Nero on the grounds of 'personal ethics', not political ideology or philosophy. It was a matter of honour. He saw his loyalty to the *princeps* as being outweighed by his duty to tradition.[120] A final straw may have been news of Poppaea's pregnancy, which threatened to secure the Julio-Claudian principate whatever Nero did. Once the praetorian officers set the ball rolling, others, for very mixed reasons, joined in.

9.3.5 Assessment

The most striking aspect of the Pisonian conspiracy, crucial for any judgement of the regime's treatment of the plotters, is how close it came to killing Nero. Because the *princeps* did not pursue a policy of seclusion, he constantly ran the risk of attack both in public and in private.[121] His safety depended upon his lifeguards, especially the praetorians, and if these were compromised he was vulnerable. Too wide a choice of opportunities to destroy him caused the conspirators problems in deciding where and when to act.[122] Assassination must have seemed easy. Certainty of success explains why some, like Lucan, with no death wish but rather expecting great reward, were tempted to join, and others, like Scaevinus, in sharpening his dagger, and Seneca, in moving back to Rome, were careless in their behaviour.[123] However, general security was not 'lax in the extreme'. The conspiracy was disclosed only through the last-minute nerves of one of the main plotters.[124] Such discretion is even more remarkable if, as Green proposes, the *Laus Pisonis* was written for secret circulation in support of Piso's claim to rule.[125] Even after their betrayal, some conspirators endured cruel questioning by their accusers. Similarly, despite Tacitus' implication to the contrary, though there seems to have been some indecision, there was probably no excessive delay.[126] If the conspirators came together towards the end of 64, an attempted coup in spring 65 was reasonably fast progress. Furthermore, though the assassination itself was to be on the 'Caesarian' model, with the first blows struck

---

[119] Rudich 1993, 127; Bingham 2013, 63.
[120] Rudich 1993, 113 (quotation); *contra* Cizek 1982, 259–60.
[121] Above 198; below 254; cf. Barrett *et al.* 2016, 190.   [122] Tac. *Ann.* 15.52.1–2.
[123] Cf. Romm 2014, 177, 181.   [124] Tac. *Ann.* 15.54. *Contra* Barrett *et al.* 2016, 191 (quotation).
[125] Green 2010, 522.   [126] Above 201.

by a senator,[127] their plan for what was to follow shows that they had
learned from the death of Gaius and the accessions of Claudius and
Nero.[128] They harboured no dreams of restoring the old Republic but
simply wanted a new *princeps*: proof of the political community's acceptance of the Augustan settlement.[129] Piso's accession was to be secured by
his presentation to the praetorians by one of their prefects. The pill of
revolution was to be sugared by Piso's public association with Claudius'
sole surviving legitimate offspring, Antonia, probably without her prior
approval.[130] The Pisonian conspiracy failed only by chance, and even after
its initial disclosure it could have been rescued by the praetorians or Piso.
Instead, there was dithering and disaster.[131] Yet even if the conspirators
had managed to kill Nero and elevate Piso, they were bound to fail in the
long term. They were not typical of their society, and represented no
widespread political opposition to the Neronian regime. Nero, despite his
recent break-outs, posed no threat to the upper classes *en masse*, an attitude
rewarded by their continuing loyalty to him.[132] The notion that he,
'suspicious and easily frightened', was through Tigellinus beginning to
create a police state is an anachronism.[133] If the Pisonians had killed Nero,
they would have found themselves facing significant opposition leading to
their destruction and even civil war.[134]

9.3.6   Punishment

Their betrayal resulted in the greatest concentration of accusations, condemnations, deaths and banishments of Nero's principate. Our sources
describe what happened as a reign of terror, when the tyrant turned against
the aristocracy as if to destroy it root and branch.[135] In the spirit of the
famous last words of Seneca and Subrius Flavus, Nero is depicted as evil
and the conspirators as good or, at least, well-intentioned.[136] Tacitus,
probably drawing on official senatorial documents,[137] records a total of
thirty-four executions or forced suicides and eighteen banishments of

---

[127] Tac. *Ann.* 15.53.3. Above 29.   [128] Above 72; below 211.

[129] Wiedemann 1996a, 230; Malitz 1999, 80; Barrett *et al.* 2016, 191. Cf. above 72, 117.

[130] Below 220.   [131] Cf. Waldherr 2005, 188–91.   [132] Cf. below 230.

[133] *Contra* Grant 1970, 212–13 (quotation); Fini 1994, 183; Holland 2000, 194. The praetorian
speculatores were scouts, couriers and, by extension, 'spies' (Bingham 2013, 89–91), but never a
Roman Stasi: above 90; below 366.

[134] Cf. Henderson 1905, 265–6.

[135] Cf. Hohl 1918, 386: 'Es schien, als ob Nero die Edelsten der Nation systematisch ausrotten
wollte'; above 71.

[136] Tac. *Ann.* 15.62.2–3, 67.2–3.   [137] Tac. *Ann.* 15.74.3. Hurley 2013, 37; below 236–7.

named persons (Table 2).[138] This is appalling, but we should appreciate the horror Nero must have experienced as the details of a conspiracy which came close to causing his death and those of his family and supporters and plunging Rome into chaos came to light.[139] Under attack, the Neronian regime had as much right to defend itself as did later those of Vespasian, Domitian, Nerva, Trajan and Hadrian;[140] and we might expect just desire for punishment to be accompanied by a craving for revenge.

As we have seen, after the upsets of 64, things appeared to be returning to normal for the Neronian administration, and Poppaea was again pregnant.[141] The regime, having eliminated most of its likely dynastic rivals,[142] must have felt very confident. As Tacitus observes, Nero had taken no precautions against a coup.[143] When this came, it was an enormous blow, and the more so because it was a metropolitan and court conspiracy, involving a number of people whom Nero had previously trusted. There was also the shock of a novel challenge to the Julio-Claudian principate, aimed at elevating the leader of a different *domus*.[144] The regime's relief at its escape from total destruction is reflected in subsequent official rejoicing, and in the renaming of the month of April

---

[138] These numbers, and others given below, are my own. They differ slightly from those found in Henderson's (1905, 486) much-cited (e.g. Fini 1994, 190–2) analysis; cf. below 214 n. 147. They do not include the deaths which must have followed the disclosure of the Vinician conspiracy: below 218, 223.

[139] Tac. *Ann.* 15.73.3.   [140] Cf. Griffin 1984, 196; Holland 2000, viii; Michel 2015, 204–6.

[141] Cf. Levi 1949, 198.

[142] Most, but not all, since L. Junius Silanus II was still alive, though under suspicion: Tac. *Ann.* 16.7; below 215.

[143] Tac. *Ann.* 15.59.3: *nihil adversum haec Neroni provisum.*

[144] Cizek 1982, 51. For the importance of the ruling *domus* see Tac. *Ann.* 13.17.5: after the death of Britannicus, Senate and People were enjoined to cherish Nero as 'the one survivor a family born to the heights of power' (*qui unus superesset e familia summum ad fastigium genita*). In this respect, though Osgood (2011, 9) identifies the period immediately following the death of Gaius, in January 41, as the first time that consideration was given to such candidates, the dire circumstances of those involved in the debate, and their almost immediate trumping by the accession of Claudius, show that the choice was never real. Osgood generally (e.g. 2011, 102) also makes too much of Claudius as an incompetent and unsuitable outsider. Though his earliest, 'manifesto', coins, do not claim legitimacy from the *domus Augusta* but from the praetorians (Gibson 2013, 117), his relationship to Germanicus put him firmly in the imperial family, especially in the minds of soldiers who did not have the complex pedigrees of the high Roman aristocracy to heart: so Joseph. *AJ* 19.217–19 (Gratus, the praetorian who discovered Claudius, exclaims 'here's a Germanicus!' (*Germanikos men houtos*) and urges him to act 'to take the throne of your ancestors' (*kai tōn progonōn apolambane ton thronon*). And even if Messalina aimed at overthrowing Claudius in 48, it has to be remembered that she was a great-grandniece of Augustus. The Julio-Claudians were remarkably resilient. Cf. Gibson 2013, 117, on Claudius' status and influence, especially among his fellow-*equites*, by 41, and the Senate 'would be well aware that Claudius was neither a simpleton nor a renegade'.

Table 2 *The Pisonian conspirators, actual and alleged*

PHASE 1: 65

	Name	Tac. *Ann.* 15	Status	Fate	Date
1	Gaius Piso	48, 59	Senator	Suicide	65
2	Subrius Flavus	49, 67	Praetorian tribune	Executed	65
3	Sulpicius Asper	49, 68	Praetorian centurion	Executed	65
4	Annaeus Lucanus [Lucan]	49	Senator	Suicide	65
5	Plautius Lateranus	49, 60	Senator	Executed	65
6	Flavius Scaevinus	49, 70	Senator	Executed	65
7	Afranius Quintianus	49, 70	Senator	Executed	65
8	Claudius Senecio	50, 70	Eques	Executed	65
9	Cervarius Proculus	50, 71	Eques	Pardoned for informing	65
10	Vulcacius Araricus	50, cf. 71	Eques	Executed?	65
11	Julius Augurinus	50, cf. 71	Eques	Executed?	65
12	Munatius Gratus	50, cf. 71	Eques	Executed?	65
13	Antonius Natalis	50, 71	Eques	Pardoned for informing	65
14	Marcius Festus	50, cf. 71	Eques	Executed?	65
15	Gavius Silvanus	50	Praetorian tribune	Acquitted (but still committed suicide)	65
16	Statius Proxumus	50	Praetorian tribune	Pardoned	65
17	Maximus Scaurus	50, 68	Praetorian centurion	Executed	65
18	Venetus Paulus	50, 68	Praetorian centurion	Executed	65
19	Faenius Rufus	50, 66, 67	Praetorian prefect	Suicide?	65
20	Epicharis	51, 57	Freedwoman	Suicide under torture	65
21	Vestinus	52	Senator	Suicide	65
22	Annaeus Seneca [Seneca]	54, 60	Senator	Suicide	65
23	Acilia	56, 71	Mother of Lucan	In the end ignored	65
24	Glitius Gallus	56, 71	Senator	Exiled	65
25	Annius Pollio	56, 71	Senator	Exiled	65
26	... Pompeius	71	Praetorian tribune	Deprived of rank	65
27	Cornelius Martialis	71	Praetorian tribune	Deprived of rank	65
28	Flavius Nepos	71	Praetorian tribune	Deprived of rank	65

(*cont.*)

	Name	Tac. *Ann.* 15	Status	Fate	Date
29	Statius Domitius	71	Praetorian tribune	Deprived of rank	65
30	Novius Priscus	71	Senator	Exiled	65
21	Rufrius Crispinus	71	Senator	Exiled	65
32	Verginius Flavus	71	Senator	Exiled	65
33	Musonius Rufs	71	Senator	Exiled	65
34	Cluvidienus Quietus	71	? Senator	Exiled	65
35	Julius Agrippa	71	? Senator	Exiled	65
36	Blitius Catulinus	71	? Senator	Exiled	65
37	Petronius Priscus	71	? Senator	Exiled	65
38	Julius Altinus	71	? Senator	Exiled	65
39	Caedicia	71	Wife of Scaevinus	Exiled	65
40	Caesennius Maximus	71	Senator	Exiled	65

PHASE 2: 65/66

	Name	Tac. *Ann.* 16	Status	Fate	Date
1	Cassius Longinus	7, 8	Senator	Exiled	65
2	L. Junius Silanus II	7, 8, 9	Senator	Exiled then executed	65
3	Lepida	8	Wife of Cassius; aunt of Silanus;	?	65
4	Vulcacius Tullinus	8	Senator	In the end ignored	65
5	Cornelius Marcellus	8	Senator	In the end ignored	65
6	Calpurnius Fabatus	8	Eques	In the end ignored	65
7	Antistius Vetus	10, 11	Senator	Suicide	65
8	Sextia	9, 11	Mother-in-law of Vetus	Suicide	65
9	Pollitta	9, 11	Daughter of Vetus	Suicide	65
10	Publius Gallus	12	Eques	Exiled	65
11	Publius Anteius	14		Suicide	66
12	Ostorius Scapula II	14, 15	Senator	Suicide	66
13	Pammenes	14	Soothsayer	?	
14	Annaeus Mela	17	Eques	Suicide	66
15	Anicius Cerealis	17	Senator	Suicide	66
16	Rufrius Crispinus	17	Eques	Exiled in 65' now suicide	66
17	Titus Petronius (Arbiter)	17–18, 19	Senator	Suicide	66

(cont.)

	Name	Tac. *Ann.* 16	Status	Fate	Date
18	Silia	20	Wife of senator	Exiled	66
19	Minucius Thermus	20	Senator	Executed	66
20	Thrasea Paetus	21–2, 21, 33–4	Senator	Suicide	66
21	Barea Soranus	21, 23, 30, 33	Senator	Suicide	66
22	Helvidius Priscus	28, 33	Senator	Exiled	66
23	Paconius Agrippinus	28, 33	Senator	Exiled	66
24	Curtius Montanus	28	Senator	Termination of career	66
25	Servilia	30, 33	Daughter of Barea Soranus; wife of Annius Pollio	Suicide	66
26	Cassius Asclepiodotus	33	?	Exiled	66
27	Antonia	15.52; Suet. *Ner.* 35	Daughter of Claudius	Executed	65/66

as 'Neroneus'.[145] Associated with this may be the coin-reverse depicting universal peace: the temple of Janus with its gates closed and the legend 'Peace won on land and sea'. The temple gates were formally closed in mid-66 on the occasion of Tiridates' visit, but the related coin-type appears to have been put into circulation in 65, perhaps to reassure the public that all was under control.[146] The regime had been shaken to the core, and it would not have been surprising if Nero and his supporters had indulged in an orgy of revenge. It is crucial in assessing the notion of Nero 'the killer' to accept that this did not happen. 'Pisonian' did not become a catch-all accusation that spelled immediate arrest and probable death. The regime's initial response was in fact to target ringleaders and close accomplices: eighteen named persons, including Seneca and Lucan, were probably killed or took their own lives; thirteen were exiled; and four praetorian officers were demoted.[147] The accused were taken before Nero and his counsellors

[145] Tac. *Ann.* 15.74.1–2, 16.12.3; Suet. *Ner.* 55.

[146] *PACE P R TERRA MARIQVE PARTA*: *RIC* 1² p. 140; Suet. *Ner.* 13.2; Tac. *Ann.* 15.46.2 (on 64): *haud alias tam immota pax* ('a time of unprecedented peace'). Cf. Griffin 1984, 122; Carson 1990, 16.

[147] For details of the individuals concerned see Table 2, Phase 1. The number of suicides would be increased through the inclusion of that of Gallio, brother of Seneca, recorded in Jerome's 'Chronicle' under 66. Unlike Henderson (1905, 486), I exclude Antonia's death from these

at his quarters in the Servilian Gardens. As already observed, there was at least the appearance of due legal process: accusers offered evidence of guilt and accused were allowed to defend themselves.[148] Time may also have been allowed for the interrogation of members of their households.[149] When Epicharis was betrayed, she was imprisoned but not executed because there was no evidence against her. Later, she was cruelly tortured and committed suicide,[150] but three other accused were pardoned and two (one of whom was Acilia, mother of Lucan, denounced by her own son[151]) let go. Seneca's wife was prevented from committing suicide with her husband on the grounds that Nero had no quarrel with her – a sign of his continuing lack of vindictiveness.[152] Finally, when for personal reasons, a senator attempted to revive and widen the first phase of prosecutions by launching an attack on Seneca's brother, Junius Gallio, he was dissuaded by the full Senate on the grounds that the *princeps* had decided that the matter was now finished.[153]

The regime's actions appear less restrained in the second wave of prosecutions that began later in 65 and persisted into 66. There were more named deaths (fifteen) and banishments (six), and one termination of a senatorial career (Table 2). At first glance these accusations, unlike those that preceded them, seem entirely arbitrary, with Nero reacting 'blindly, like a wounded beast' to denunciations arising more out of the malice of the accusers – usually associated with Tigellinus – than with any real involvement in plotting by the accused.[154] One especially nasty aspect of this was the destruction of the last of the Silani, L. Junius Silanus II, son of Marcus, on a charge of incest.[155] On closer consideration, however, we can discern a pattern and establish a context. With regard to pattern, there is a relatively small group of courtiers considered guilty of complicity in the Pisonian conspiracy either by association with those condemned in the first wave or with each other. These were Publius Gallus (linked to Faenius Rufus), Annaeus Mela (Lucan), Anicius Cerealis (Mela), Rufrius Crispinus, a former husband of Poppaea (Mela), Titus Petronius

---

figures, putting it instead in the second wave of prosecutions: below 215, 220; cf. above 211 n. 138.

[148] Tac. *Ann.* 15.51, 55, 58. Above 71.   [149] Cf. Rutledge 2001,169.

[150] Tac. *Ann.* 15.51.8, 15.57.

[151] Tac. *Ann.* 15.56, 71. Though Grant (1970, 215) dismisses Lucan's involvement, it is not out of line with his selfish personality: above 115.

[152] Tac. *Ann.* 15.64.1: *at nullo in Paulinam proprio odio.*

[153] Tac. *Ann.* 15.73.4. *Contra* Cizek 1982, 265–6. Cf. below 363.

[154] Waldherr 2005, 194 ('blindwütig wie ein waidwundes Tier'), 196–7.

[155] Tac. *Ann.* 16.8.2. Rudich 1993, 139; cf. below 312.

(Scaevinus) and Silia (Petronius). Much larger was a collection of prominent figures long regarded as unfriendly. These were L. Junius Silanus II and his family and associates (Cassius Longinus the jurist,[156] Lepida, Vulcacius Tullinus, Marcellus Cornelius and Calpurnius Fabatus); the family of Rubellius Plautus and his circle (Antistius Vetus, Sextia, Pollitta; Barea Soranus, Servilia, Asclepiodotus); and Thrasea Paetus and his family and circle (Helvidius Priscus, Paconius Agrippinus and Curtius Montanus). Finally, there were stray political *personae non gratae* of the regime: Publius Anteius, Ostorius Scapula II, Minucius Thermus and, presumably, the astrologer Pammenes.[157] As for context, in mid- 65, not long after Nero had drawn a line under the first Pisonian prosecutions, Poppaea and her unborn child died, allegedly as the result of a violent quarrel with Nero.[158] Her death deprived the *princeps* of his closest friend and most important counsellor, and caused him intense grief and self-condemnation. His misery will have been compounded by the fact that his fortunes had again appeared to be on the mend, with the birth of an heir and the great state visit by Tiridates to look forward to.[159] More widely, the death of Poppaea reopened the succession issue at a time when, following the disappearance of the Pisonian courtiers, the regime's power-structure had to be rebuilt and consolidated.[160] Above all, Tigellinus had to assert his dominance, which may have not been straightforward given the promotion of the Nymphidius Sabinus as joint praetorian prefect in place of Faenius Rufus. Well connected (he was grandson of the imperial freedman, Callistus, powerful under Gaius and Claudius), clever and ambitious (he played a key role in the fall of Nero[161]), Sabinus may have represented elements at court that were not entirely behind Tigellinus.[162] Renewed feelings of insecurity in later 65 can only have been increased in 66 when, as seems likely, Nero was again seriously ill.[163] In the heightened political tension of the time, Tigellinus' destruction of all perceived threats, whether residual Pisonians, potential heirs and their associates or known troublemakers, appears, if not forgivable, then at least understandable, and the more so if preparations had already begun to take the court to Greece.[164]

More as to context may be won from closer consideration of the fate of Thrasea Paetus and Barea Soranus. Paetus was the leader of an awkward circle of critics of the regime. Though these made much of their Stoic

---

[156] Above 25.   [157] For details of the individuals concerned see Table 2, Phase 2.
[158] Below 219.   [159] Cf. above 142; below 343.
[160] Cf. Osgood 2011, 214, for similar damage limitation following the fall of Messalina in 48.
[161] Cf. below 408.   [162] Cf. above 164.
[163] Suet. *Ner.* 51. Bradley 1978a, 284; cf. above 190; below 305–6.
[164] Below 380; cf. Malitz 1999, 87.

philosophy, their criticisms were not those of all Stoics, who were many and varied in their political views.[165] Their standpoint was very much that of fellow senatorial arch-conservatives. Like Thrasea Paetus, they did not have to have long pedigrees: the senatorial tradition could make members of relatively newly promoted families more reactionary than many a scion of an ancient Republican line.[166] While accepting the necessity of the Principate, they were determined to maintain traditional aristocratic status and rights, and so inclined to find fault with individual *principes* who appeared to threaten these. They used Stoicism to bolster and articulate their support of the *mos maiorum*.[167] They were thus very different from Stoics such as Seneca who, albeit grudgingly, were prepared to work within the current autocratic system.[168] They expressed their disapproval in words and, *in extremis*, in withdrawal.[169] However, criticism was resented and secession was tantamount to desertion. A *princeps'* power depended on *imperium* and *auctoritas* (authority or – perhaps more understandable today – 'charisma'). He obtained *imperium* from the Senate at the start of his period of office,[170] but his *auctoritas* had to be constantly renewed, through the approval of his actions by Senate, people and army. Under the Julio-Claudians, it was the first of these that was nominally the most important.[171] Senators' approval had to be unambiguous. For example, while conscientious attendance of the Senate was required of senators, on its own it was not enough: they had openly to express their support of the *princeps*. While 'curt assent' was tolerated, 'silence was always open to interpretation as rebellion'.[172] Quietism was not an option. 'Dumb insolence', whether inside or outside the House, could be construed as malevolence, *animus nocendi*; and in times of strain it could be interpreted as outright hostility.[173] The 'Stoic' group was a constant irritation; even the 'good' Vespasian was to act against them.[174] Under Nero, Thrasea Paetus first irked the administration by showing disrespect to the *princeps*, and then by withdrawing (albeit gradually and not entirely) from state business, in particular from attendance at the Senate and various state ceremonials.[175] In an 'empire of honour' this 'posed an unbearable threat to the emperor's *dignitas*'.[176] However, it does not fully explain why, in mid-May 66, the administration scheduled Paetus' trial

---

[165] Reitz 2006, 98; cf. above 103.   [166] Malitz 1999, 85; above 18.

[167] Grant 1970, 219; Rudich 1993, 162; Malitz 1999, 85; Bryan 2013, 137.

[168] Waldherr 2005, 195; above 157.   [169] Cf. above 192.   [170] Above 21.

[171] Cf. Talbert 1984, 22, 68–72, 134–6; Osgood 2011, 197.

[172] Talbert 1984, 134–7, 252–3 (quotation), 255 (quotation).

[173] Talbert 1984, 136–7; Rudich 1993, xxxii, 23, 165; cf. below 407.   [174] Levick 1999a, 89, 192.

[175] Tac. *Ann.* 16.22.1–2. Talbert 1984, 201–2; Rudich 1993, 78, 165, 167–8, 174; Waldherr 2005, 195–6; above 88.

[176] Lendon 1997, 144.

immediately before Tiridates' reception under the tightest security. Praetorians and German guards had been put on the streets of Rome and neighbouring communities on the discovery of the Pisonian conspiracy, but had, presumably, in the meantime been stood down. In mid-66, praetorians were again stationed in strength around the Forum.[177] Far from burying bad news in the excitement of Tiridates' arrival, as Tacitus would have it,[178] this surely drew attention to it when all eyes were on the capital and suggests another recent bad scare. The highly charged language of the accusers, depicting Thrasea Paetus as Cato to Nero's Julius Caesar and calling him a 'traitor' and an 'enemy of the state', reflects real alarm.[179] I propose that the scare was the uncovering of the 'Vinician conspiracy' in late April or early May: not, as is usually thought, well in advance of its being sprung but only just before it was due to be put into action, while Nero was receiving Tiridates in Naples.[180] Investigations lasted into June.[181] In absolute terms, the Vinician may be regarded as being no more than a less extensive, more hastily put together, more quickly discovered and so much less dangerous aftershock of the Pisonian conspiracy.[182] However, it was another totally unexpected threat to the life of the *princeps* from someone in whom he had shown great trust and which, if it had succeeded and caught up Tiridates and his entourage, might have precipitated war with Parthia. It therefore provoked the Establishment to act with speed against those whom it saw as its general enemies – Thrasea Paetus and his circle – as well as those it could connect with the plot – Barea Soranus and his circle (since Annius Vinicianus, the probable ringleader of the Vinician conspiracy, was brother-in-law to Soranus' daughter, Servilia).[183] This is, again, tragic but understandable. In the second, as in the first wave of Pisonian prosecutions, the Neronian regime destroyed its enemies, real and imagined, but little more.

9.3.7   Conclusion

'Reign of terror' is a wholly inappropriate description of what happened in the aftermath of the Pisonian conspiracy. The phrase was coined to describe ghastly events in revolutionary France, in which thousands perished throughout the country. The Neronian regime never embarked upon a campaign of indiscriminate slaughter.[184] It reacted savagely against specific perpetrators in Rome but, knowing that it could rely on the loyalty

[177] Tac. *Ann.* 15.58.1–2, 16.27.1. Rudich 1993, 105.   [178] Tac. *Ann.* 16.23.3.
[179] Tac. *Ann.* 16.22.2; 28.3: *proditor . . . hostis.* Rutledge 2001, 116.   [180] Below 221, 223.
[181] Below 223–4   [182] Cf. below 223.
[183] Tac. *Ann.* 16.21–35. Griffin 1984, 179; Rudich 1993, 173; Rutledge 2001, 119.
[184] Griffin 1984, 168; Fini 1994, 190–2; Holland 2000, 193; above 74. *Contra* Cizek 1982, 43.

of the bulk of the praetorians, of the Misenum fleet and of the frontier armies, went no further. Its destruction of the plot must have been a relief to the majority of the political community, whose priority was stability.[185] There was a political crisis in 64, but it was not general.

9.4 Poppaea

The main source tradition is unanimous in recounting that, after *Neronia* II in early summer 65,[186] Nero and the pregnant Poppaea had a heated argument. Suetonius says that it was over his late return home from chariot-racing. Nero gave Poppaea a savage kick, inducing a miscarriage from which, already unwell, she died.[187] Given the private location of the incident and the social position of those involved, what really happened can have been known to only a few, and its details were hushed up. Later writers, convinced that Nero was capable of any wickedness, were willing to pin the blame on him.[188] However, even they are inconsistent, representing him as the perpetrator of either an act of mindless violence or premeditated murder.[189] Judgement is difficult. Nero was neither habitually vindictive nor, by this time, much given to drink.[190] Furthermore, he was desperately in love with Poppaea and with the idea of fatherhood.[191] On the other hand, as a youth he showed that he liked to use his fists;[192] and to the end he had occasional moments of violence.[193] On balance, it is plausible that Poppaea and the baby died as the result of a matrimonial row that got out of hand, but if so Nero was at worst guilty of manslaughter. He paid a huge price – Champlin's 'flash of a temper . . . eternity of sorrow'[194] – and his remorse significantly disturbed his mental state.[195] The deaths of mother and unborn child were not crazed acts of murder by a psychopathic tyrant.

9.5 Antonia

According to Suetonius, after the death of Poppaea Nero proposed to Antonia, the older stepsister of Britannicus and Octavia, was refused, and

---

[185] Cf. above 162.
[186] There is some uncertainty over the time of *Neronia* II. I follow Champlin 2003, 74 and 289 (with Griffin 1984, 161, 280); *contra* Bradley 1978a, 129–31; Reitz 2006, 13–14; Meier 2008, 586.
[187] Tac. *Ann.* 16.6.1; Suet. *Ner.* 35.3: *gravida et aegra*; Cass. Dio 62.27.4. *Neronia* II: below 343.
[188] Suet. *Ner.* 35.4: *nullum adeo necessitudinis genus est, quod non scelere perculerit.* Cf. below 295.
[189] Tac. *Ann.* 16.6.1: recounting but rejecting a charge of poisoning. Cf. Bradley 1978a, 212.
[190] Cf. below 305, 322.
[191] Tac. *Ann.* 16.6.1: *liberorum cupiens et amori uxoris obnoxius.* Above 230.   [192] Below 296.
[193] Below 410.   [194] Champlin 2003, 105.   [195] Above 216, below 288, 294.

in revenge had her executed on a charge of plotting revolution.[196] Though some accept the story,[197] the idea that Nero desperately wanted Antonia for his wife and destroyed her out of spite is unconvincing. Again, revenge was against his nature and the importance of the Claudian connection had diminished. The prime need was for Nero to produce his own heir and to achieve this he must marry a woman in whose company he found pleasure. Antonia was an unlikely choice since she was now relatively old (certainly older than Poppaea) and, as the sister of Octavia and the widow of Cornelius Sulla, both victims of the regime,[198] probably not well disposed to Nero. Statilia Messalina (probably somewhat younger than Poppaea), already being groomed for the job, was a much better bet.[199] Behind the tale lies the sad truth that Antonia had become another loose cannon. She was actually destroyed for her association with the Pisonian conspiracy. Tacitus records the belief that she was to accompany Piso to the praetorian barracks where he was to be hailed as *princeps* in order to give his coup an appearance of legitimacy and then marry him. The former is possible, the latter, as Tacitus himself declares, not, even though it came from Pliny I, since it would have been highly distasteful to both parties.[200] It is significant that nothing happened to Antonia in the first, highly targeted, wave of accusations.[201] Her destruction fell in the second round against more widely perceived enemies. One is therefore bound to doubt the extent of her involvement with the Pisonians. At most, participation was to be forced on her at the last minute, without her prior consent. More likely, however, is that the charge of treason was retrospectively confected by a new Establishment seeking to rid itself of a potentially unreliable princess in an unsettled period.[202] It was a 'pretext'.[203]

9.6   The Last Killings

9.6.1   Introduction

The loss of the final part of Tacitus' 'Annals' makes it difficult to reconstruct events from mid-66 to the end of Nero's principate. However, other

---

[196] Suet. *Ner.* 35.4; cf. *Schol. Iuv.* 8.213. Bradley 1977; 1978a, 213; Cizek 1982, 56, 180–1.
[197] E.g. Waldherr 2005, 226.   [198] Kienast 2004, 92–3; above 191.
[199] Kienast 2004, 100; below 372.
[200] Tac. *Ann.* 15.53.4–5. Barrett *et al.* 2016, 202 and n. 25. *Contra* Grant 1970, 215; Bradley 1978a, 214; Waldherr 2005, 190–1.
[201] Cf. Rudich 1993, 102.   [202] Above 216.
[203] Furneaux 1907, 388 (quotation); Holland 2000, 204.

sources indicate more deaths. Suetonius' 'Vinician conspiracy', has long been accepted as a plot led by Corbulo's son-in-law and senior subordinate, Annius Vinicianus, in early summer 66. Since Vinicianus drops out of the picture after its uncovering, it is likely that he and his accomplices were executed.[204] According to Dio, once Nero had reached Greece he summoned Corbulo to his side but, after the latter had landed at the port of Corinth, ordered him to be killed. Corbulo, realising what was about to befall him, cheated his killers by seizing a sword and stabbing himself.[205] Suicide was also chosen by the brothers, P. Sulpicius Scribonius Proculus and P. Sulpicius Scribonius Rufus, commanders of the military districts of Upper and Lower Germany respectively, likewise summoned to Greece by Nero but then subjected to political attack and denied the opportunity to defend themselves before him.[206] Dio intensifies the gloom of his account by reporting that Caecina Tuscus, prefect of Egypt, was banished for using a bath building specially built for Nero after he had proposed a visit to Alexandria, presumably in 64.[207] In the meantime, Nero's representative, the *libertus* Helius, ruled Rome with a rod of iron. He put to death Sulpicius Camerinus and his son for refusing to give up their ancestral title of 'Pythicus' on the grounds that this showed disrespect for Nero's current victories at the Pythian games.[208] Dio gives the impression that one reason why Nero turned on the Scribonii was for their wealth, which receives some support from a notice by Tacitus in his 'Histories'.[209] In the same place, Dio suggests that, while in Greece, Nero brought about the deaths of 'many' nobles on account of their fortunes or family.[210] Earlier, he observes that Nero devastated Greece as if waging war, killing many people after forcing them to make generous bequests to himself and Tigellinus.[211] Dio continues that Nero confiscated incalculable amounts of property from the living, and votive offerings from temples in Rome, and that he took leading men to Greece just to kill them.[212] According to

---

[204] Suet. *Ner.* 36.1. Bradley 1978a, 220–1; Griffin 1984, 178–9; Wiedemann 1996a, 254; below 223.

[205] Cass. Dio 63.17.5–6. The epitomator is obscure here, and some scholars (e.g. Henderson 1905, 388; Griffin 1984, 117; Fini 1994, 201) have Corbulo being presented with Nero's order to kill himself, and obliging with his own sword.

[206] Cass. Dio 63.17.2–4; *CIL* 13.11806 (=*ILS* 9235), with Speidel 1994. Above 145.

[207] Cass. Dio 63.18.1; Tac. *Ann.* 15.36.1; Warmington 1969, 100; Bradley 1978a, 114–15, 128–9 (a decision was made in spring 64 to prepare for a visit in the summer of this year, or later). Cf. above 205; below 373.

[208] Dio 63.18.2; cf. 63.10.1. For Helius' rapacious associates, see Cass. Dio 63.12.3 on the *libertus* Polyclitus and Tac. *Hist.* 4.42, 1.48, Plin. *Ep.* 1.5.3, with Griffin 1984, 178 and below 230 on the informer Aquilius Regulus.

[209] Cass. Dio 63.17.1–2; Tac. *Hist.* 4.41.   [210] Cass. Dio 63.17.2.   [211] Cass. Dio 63.11.1–2.

[212] Cass. Dio 64.11.3; cf. Tac. *Ann.* 15.45.2.

him, Nero also slew the dancer, Paris, out of artistic frustration and jealousy.[213] Are such events proof of Nero's finally becoming a tyrannical killer?

9.6.2   The Vinician Conspirators

In 66, Tiridates reached Italy. He had travelled as far as possible by land, and entered the peninsula from the north. It is likely that he arrived early in April, as soon as his escort was sure that the Ljubljana–Aquileia (Figure 1) road would be free from snow or snow-melt. Then, presumably, he travelled down the Adriatic coast before crossing into Campania. Here, probably from late April, he was formally welcomed and entertained by Nero before being escorted by him to Rome for the main ceremonies scheduled for mid-May.[214] He arrived in Rome soon after the start of the trials of Thrasea Paetus and Barea Soranus.[215] Since he took nine months for the journey, he must have set out in September 65.[216] For most of the way he was under the protection of Vinicianus.[217] Vinicianus must have known of the Pisonian prosecutions of 65–66. As a senior army officer serving in a major theatre of operations and personally and professionally close to the commander-in-chief, he will have had access to official communications and will have been able to send and receive personal letters through the military post.[218] Then, from September 65, as commander of Tiridates' escort, he will have had his own communications network which allowed him to keep Tiridates in touch with the East and manage the logistics of the massive diplomatic caravan (which included Tiridate's own honour guard of 3,000 Parthian cavalry[219]) as it moved westwards. With each day his contact with Rome grew easier. On his entry into Italy he could hardly have been so startled by news of the second wave of Pisonian prosecutions that he turned to conspiracy.[220] For most of his journey reports from Rome had probably stretched Vinicianus' loyalty to Nero but not yet broken it. Though he will have known Tiridates' visit would give the *princeps* glory unequalled since Augustus, he persisted in his duties. It is more likely that he was tempted into sedition only after he had reached Italy, was increasingly relieved of the myriad responsibilities he

[213] Cass. Dio 63.18.1.
[214] Cass. Dio 63.2.3, 63.7.1. Šašel Kos 1986, 35; Griffin 1984, 178 and n. 75. His route may have been dictated by Zoroastrian religious scruples, which prevented him from being more than a day at sea: Fini 1994, 71 and n. 21.
[215] Tac. *Ann.* 16.23.2; above 218.   [216] Cass. Dio 63.2.2.   [217] Cass. Dio 62.23.6.
[218] Cf. Kolb 2000, 286–9.   [219] Cass. Dio 63.2.1.   [220] Thus *contra* Griffin 1984, 179.

had borne so far, and was now in close touch with family and friends under threat.[221] He then seems to have acted precipitately.

Suetonius, in his unique, fleeting, mention of the *coniuratio Viniciana*, says that it was 'both kindled and uncovered at Benevento'.[222] It has long been assumed that the reference to Benevento indicates that the plotters aimed to attack Nero while he was *en route* for Greece later in the year.[223] Since he had stayed in Benevento on his first, aborted, trip to Greece in 64,[224] it is reasonable to assume that he passed through it again in 66. However, the organisation of an assassination so far ahead when Nero's travel arrangements were still being finalised and that, given his track record,[225] might be changed or cancelled at the last minute, seems unlikely.[226] An alternative chronology is that Vinicianus determined to take action much earlier, while Nero and Tiridates were still in Campania. Here he could exploit his physical closeness to Tiridates, and so to Nero, before his mission came to an end. In addition, he might calculate that here Nero would be more than usually vulnerable to attack. In a 'holiday' area,[227] resident in his favourite city, Naples, and indulging in that rare pleasure for *principes*, social intercourse with autocratic equals in the shape of Tiridates and accompanying family (his wife, sons and nephews), the *princeps* would probably have insisted on minimal security.[228] Benevento lies not far from Naples, and Vinicianus and Tiridates may have stayed there as they crossed the Apennines through Samnium into Campania (Figure 1).[229] It would have been a convenient rendezvous for the conspirators, but it was not the place of assassination. Vinicianus' snap decision to undertake murder was, however, quickly followed by the detection of the plot. This reconstruction fits the detection of criminal *consilia* (so, aspirations, not deeds) in late April or early May and the celebration of this by the Arval priests around the middle of the latter month.[230] A second round of celebration by the Arvals in mid-June suggests that, diverted by Tiridates' visit and the trials of Paetus and

---

[221] Above 218; cf. Rudich 1993, 124.   [222] Suet. *Ner.* 36.1: *Beneventi conflata atque detecta est.*
[223] E.g. Hohl 1918, 388; Bradley 1978a, 221; Griffin 1984, 178–9; below 379.
[224] Tac. *Ann.* 15.34.2.   [225] Cf. below 226.   [226] *Contra* Griffin 1984, 179.
[227] Cf. Wallace-Hadrill 1996, 288, on the 'relative *otium*' of the bay of Naples.
[228] Cf. above 198.
[229] Levi (1949, 207) has Tiridates travelling down the eastern Italian coast only as far as Ancona, 'per poi percorrere in corteo trionfale con Nerone la strada da Ancona a Roma'; but this is to ignore Dio's account that king and *princeps* met in Naples. Waldherr (2005, 228) has him going as far as Picenum, but this is still rather far north for a crossing to Campania and Naples.
[230] Smallwood 1967 nos. 25, 3–4; 26, 20–21 (*ob detecta nefariorum consilia*). Griffin (1984, 178 and n. 75), perhaps aware of the problems involved in supposing a plot against Nero so far ahead of his visit to Greece, proposes a later chronology.

Soranus, the administration first eradicated the ringleaders and their suspected allies and only later dealt with the rest. There is no reason to believe that the plot caused Nero to become significantly more anti-senatorial,[231] but it must have come as another great shock.[232] It is strange that in the extant 'Annals' Tacitus makes no mention of it in its proper place but, given its ephemeral nature, it may be that he preferred to prioritise more important events. He might have referred to it in the lost chapters of Book 16,[233] but, given its dismal failure, the crisis that its success might have caused with Parthia, and the proximity of its leader to Corbulo, he may well have passed over it in silence.

9.6.3   Corbulo (iii)

This raises questions as to the extent to which Corbulo was involved in the affair and threatened by its failure. By recording that Corbulo had volun-tarily despatched Vinicianus to Rome as both an escort to Tiridates and as hostage to Nero, Dio hints both that the general was becoming fearful of the *princeps* and that he was complicit in the conspiracy.[234] It has, for example, been frequently proposed that he was Vinicianus' choice as successor to Nero,[235] which implies some prior agreement on his part. But Corbulo's involvement to any degree is most unlikely. Ancient and modern writers read his mind in the knowledge of the revolts against Nero in 68 and, especially, the full-scale civil war of 69–70, when field-com-manders developed a taste for intervention in metropolitan affairs; but this was yet to come.[236] Corbulo had remained steadfastly loyal to the Julio-Claudian family,[237] and his loyalty had brought him a level of success which he would have been unwilling to endanger. His advancement of Vinicianus should be taken as no more than due performance of social obligation. Patronage of family members was the duty of every Roman aristocrat. Since the complexity of their family relationships, evident in the

---

[231] *Contra* Griffin 1984, 179; cf. above 117.   [232] Above 218.

[233] Tacitus' flexible chronology has been observed above, 131 n. 2, 138 n. 62. Rudich (1993, 136) notes that he fails to mention the senatorial deification of Poppaea in its right place, only later saying that Thrasea Paetus absented himself: Tac. *Ann.* 16.21.2.

[234] Cass. Dio 62.23.6.

[235] E.g. Henderson 1905, 387; Warmington 1969, 156; Grant 1970, 221; Syme 1970, 37–8; Cizek 1982, 268; Holland 2000, 207–8.

[236] Cf. above 66.

[237] Cf. Tac. *Ann.* 11.20.1; Dio Cass. 60.30.4–5, 62.23.6. Hohl 1918, 409; Rudich 1993, 197–9; above 143.

case of Corbulo himself,[238] meant that many aristocrats were related to each other,[239] nepotism was so extensive that, without corroboration, specific acts of favour cannot be taken as indicating political deals. 'Prosopographical' politics should not be pushed too far.[240] Individual aristocrats had very different characters and ambitions: they did not instinctively hunt in family-packs.[241] It would have been unfair and socially disruptive for Roman administrations automatically to consider patrons as being involved in the misdeeds of all their clients. Black sheep existed and had to be accepted.[242] As Corbulo continued in office after the first round of Pisonian condemnations, which had taken down his father-in-law, Cassius Longinus,[243] so he continued after the Vinician conspiracy which, devised without his knowledge,[244] took down his son-in-law, Vinicianus. However, other factors were in play.

By 66, Corbulo will have been in a difficult position, Vinicianus or no Vinicianus. Everyone will have known that the glory of Tiridates' visit was owed to him. Once the Armenian confrontation was over, strains were bound to develop between general and Establishment, increased by Corbulo's loss of court champions through the Pisonian conspiracy and, perhaps, the death of Poppaea.[245] Around June 66, though he was as yet in no immediate danger his future will have been uncertain. The regime could not tackle the 'Corbulo problem' until Tiridates was safely back in Armenia, and the king was in no great hurry. He left Italy by sea, sailing from Brindisi to Dyrrachium (Figure 1), and spent time visiting the cities of Asia. With his customary large entourage, now swollen by Roman workmen (some hired for him by Nero, some by himself), he can again have travelled only very slowly.[246] However, even before he crossed the imperial frontier there began a sequence of events which would destroy Corbulo. From mid-66, revolt flared in Judaea and by the end of the year the province was in turmoil.[247] Corbulo, reasonably expecting to be consulted about this and other military matters, complied promptly with Nero's courteous summons to Corinth and showed his confidence in his role as trusted *amicus* by travelling without a full escort.[248] One of his major concerns must have been the proposed Caucasus expedition, which he is likely to have opposed for reasons already discussed and because,

---

[238] Syme 1970, esp. 31–2, 37.   [239] Above 172.
[240] Cf. Rudich 1993, 26, 201; Barrett 1996, 75; above 153.
[241] Syme 1970, 32 (about Corbulo's family): 'The sons of Vistilia are a collection rather than a group. Discord is as likely as harmony'.
[242] Cf. Michel 2015, 200.   [243] Griffin 1984, 178.   [244] Rudich 1993, 196, 199.
[245] Above 154.   [246] Cass. Dio 63.6.6–7.1   [247] Above 151.   [248] Cass. Dio 63.17.6.

distinguished by the presence of Nero, it would actually be led by his rival, Aelianus.[249] He might well have been arguing that the Judaean crisis must lead to the postponement of all other major undertakings; and, given Nero's habit of cancelling foreign ventures, he might well have believed that his case would prevail. However, late in 66 Nero's dream of an eastern campaign was still very much alive. The annual celebration of the official commissioning of legion I *Italica* fell on 20 September. This indicates that preparations for the Caucasus campaign were put in hand quickly over the summer of 66. If, as is usually accepted, Nero left for Greece in late September, the formal commissioning of the brigade may have been his last major public duty before his departure, signifying his close interest in the project.[250] A second point of contention between Corbulo and the *princeps* is likely to have been the Judaean command. Whatever was decided for the Caucasus expedition, Corbulo must have expected that he, the Middle East expert, would be entrusted with suppressing the Jewish revolt.[251] Vespasian, the eventual commander-in-chief, had a lesser reputation, was of inferior social status, and (though whether he was in disgrace at this time is questionable[252]) ranked lower as an *amicus*.

But Corbulo's past was catching up with him. Though he was not destroyed by his association with Vinicianus, the fact that he did not, as governor of Syria, as a matter of course impose order on Judaea at the start of the troubles, and indeed that he may have lost command of substantial numbers of troops, suggests that he was put under some sort of restraint after the conspiracy, and would confirm its dating to spring/early summer 66.[253] In addition, despite his expertise and his proximity, Corbulo could not be given command of Judaea or even allowed to support Roman campaigning there, because this would further increase his status. Finally, approaching the age of seventy, there must have been legitimate doubts about his capacity to lead heavy fighting.[254] On the other hand, he could not be brought back to retirement in Italy where, having acquired 'glory and prestige too great for a senator and subject',[255] he would have presented an embarrassing contrast to the non-military Nero. By late 66, there was no

---

[249] Above 147, 149.
[250] *CIL* 3.7951 = *ILS* 2295; Chilver 1979, 10. September: Hohl 1918, 388; Smallwood 1967 nos. 25, 26; Griffin 1984, 229; Holland 2000, 217–18; Waldherr 2005, 234. *Contra* (departure in August) Bradley 1978a, 118, 137; Bradley 1978b, 61–2; Halfmann 1986, 173. Cf. below 379.
[251] Cf. Malitz 1999, 94.   [252] Suet. *Vesp.* 4.4; cf. Tac. *Ann.* 16.5; Levick 1999a, 25.
[253] Above 223; Heil 1997, 191; Holland 2000, 218.
[254] Syme 1970, 30: 4 BC–AD 1. Vespasian was thus about ten years his junior.
[255] Syme 1970, 39.

alternative to his elimination. However, it is again unlikely that he was killed out of hand.[256] He was probably accused of treason, tried, found guilty and condemned to death *in absentia* in Nero's court then, on his landing in Corinth, given formal notice of sentence and allowed to commit suicide. The Establishment would have had no difficulty in finding accusers. Tacitus notes the rumour that Arrius Varus, who had served with distinction under Corbulo in Armenia and who later played a prominent role in the events of 69, 'in secret conference with Nero brought serious charges against Corbulo's good character', and was rewarded by promotion to a senior centurionate.[257] Likely accusations are that Corbulos' criticism of the Caucasus expedition amounted to *lèse majesté* and, perhaps now for the first time, that he was involved in the Vinician conspiracy. The malicious accusation of a leading general would explain Mucianus' words in urging Vespasian to seize power before it was too late: 'Have you forgotten the murder of Corbulo?'[258] However, it should be acknowledged that Corbulo's destruction resulted from a combination of his own ambition and harsh political necessity, not from Nero's general blood-lust or specific distrust of established military men. With no institutionalised set of *viri militares* – no 'general staff' or 'officer corps'[259] – the removal of a top commander is more likely to have been seen by the rest as the creation of career opportunities than as an attack on them all.

9.6.4   The Scribonii

All this should be taken into account in explaining the fate of the brothers Scribonii. Far from being nervous about its generals, the Neronian regime had appointed the best to commands that allowed them to gain what Roman aristocratic males traditionally craved: a military reputation.[260] The Scribonii had benefited greatly from this. In 58, the brothers had, most unusually, been put in charge of a praetorian cohort, 'the first and only time under the Julio-Claudians that a contingent of the guard was given over to the command of men of consular rank',[261] in order to suppress rioting in Puteoli. Then, from no later than 63, they exercised what was effectively a joint command over Upper and Lower Germany, the location of a huge force of seven legions and associated auxiliary regiments.[262] This is a mark

---

[256] Cf. above 76.

[257] Tac. *Hist.* 3.6: *secretis apud Neronem sermonibus ferebatur Corbulonis virtutes criminatus.*

[258] Tac. *Hist.* 2.76: *An excidit trucidatus Corbulo?* Heil 1997, 186–7.

[259] Campbell 1984, 325–47.   [260] Above 145.   [261] Bingham 2013, 88.

[262] Hohl 1918, 365; Cizek 1982, 322–3; Eck 1985, 27, 125–8; Speidel 1994, 213,

of the regime's confidence in their loyalty, as is the fact that they were left
in post following the uncovering of the Pisonian and Vinician conspiracies.[263] By late 66 it will have become clear that a major effort was needed
to suppress the Jewish rebellion. The regime needed the best advice it
could get. The Scribonii must already have been consulted on the sending
of troops from the Rhine to the Caucasus,[264] so it is likely that they were
summoned to Greece to discuss Judaea. A crucial issue remained the
appointment of a commander-in-chief. In the end, late in 66 or early in
67, the job was, with typical Neronian latitude of powers, given to
Vespasian.[265] However, just before this, with Corbulo dead and Aelianus
probably still destined for the Caucasus, it must have struck other senior
generals, including the Scribonii, that they were in with a chance. Instead
the Scribonii were forced to kill themselves. What went wrong? Dio
implies that the breakdown between the brothers and the *princeps* was
not immediate: unlike Corbulo, the Scribonii first gained access to Nero.
Only later were they denied it, and denounced to Nero by the senatorial
courtier, Paccius Africanus.[266] It may have been that, as the conjoined
twins of the Roman Establishment, they proved ever more difficult to
employ as they rose up the military ladder – 'job-sharing' was not a normal
form of appointment – and that, rejected for Judaea, they made their
resentment known. If so, it would have been difficult to return them to the
Rhine or retire them to Italy, and much easier simply to remove them.
Their deaths, like that of Corbulo, should be interpreted as resulting from
the expediencies of court politics, not Nero's tyrannical fear and greed;[267]
and like Corbulo's, their fate was probably decided in some sort of trial.

9.6.5   *The Victims of Helius*

In assessing Helius and his activities we must avoid the revulsion of ancient
and many modern historians at the spectacle of a freedman playing the
tyrannical *princeps* in Rome while the tyrannical *princeps* was playing the
professional entertainer in Greece.[268] Helius, a Claudian freedman, was no
fool. He was involved in the removal of M. Junius Silanus at the start of
Nero's principate and maintained his high position to its end. It was
he who travelled to Greece late in 67 to persuade Nero to return to

---

[263]   *Contra* Cizek 1982, 271–2. Cf. Eck 1985, 127: that Proculus probably set up the Mainz Jupiter
column, with its inscription *pro salute Neronis Caesaris Aug.* in 65, to celebrate the foiling of the
Pisonian conspiracy.
[264]   Above 148.   [265]   Cf. Levick 1999a, 29.   [266]   Tac. *Hist.* 4.41; Griffin 1984, 180.
[267]   Cf. below 346.   [268]   Cass. Dio 63.12.2; Griffin 1984,179–80.

Italy.[269] In 66–67, however, he was not Nero's regent in the capital.[270] The principle that 'Rome is where the emperor is' was established very early.[271] All the main elements of Nero's court – his wife, Statilia Messalina; Sporus/'Poppaea'; their personal attendants; his senior praetorian prefect, Tigellinus; his freedman secretaries; and his closest *amici* – accompanied him to Greece and administered the Empire from there.[272] However, the smooth running of Rome, the sentimental heart of the Empire, home to an enormous, unruly population, and the resort of the many senators who had not been invited to Greece,[273] had to be secured in the *princeps'* absence. This was the responsibility given to Helius, acting in collaboration with the court, still relatively near.[274] Why the position was given to him is considered below.[275] His appointment, with authority over people of every social class,[276] is a measure of the trust that the administration placed in him: the civil equivalent of that which it accorded its generals. To make it work, he and his team of fellow freedmen[277] could not act alone but needed the support of the metropolitan political community. Helius will have had to respect any resident consuls, but his prime ally must have been Nymphidius Sabinus, whose praetorians provided the ultimate sanction for his commands.[278] Co-operation between the two may have been helped by their similar backgrounds. Sabinus was the grandson of Callistus, *a libellis* of Gaius, and so sprung from the freedman court circle.[279] After the Pisonian conspiracy Sabinus had, in the company of two senior senators and Tigellinus, been given exceptional honours, in his case *consularia insignia*.[280] Though left in Rome, he will have enjoyed the highest standing. We may suppose that Helius likewise worked with the senatorial *praefectus urbi*, who controlled the urban cohorts, the city's gendarmerie, and his subordinate, the equestrian *praefectus vigilum*, in charge of the paramilitary watch and fire service.[281]

---

[269] Suet. *Ner.* 23.1; Cass. Dio 63.12.2, 19.1–2. Above 174.

[270] Cf. below 381; *contra* Rudich 1993, 201.

[271] *Pan. Lat.* 3(11).12.2 [Gallet.]: *ibi ... esse sedes imperii videretur quo ... venerat imperator.* Cf. Michel 2015, 97–111, on the mobile court that accompanied Claudius on his British expedition.

[272] See e.g. *ILS* 8794; Cass. Dio 63.13.1. Among the most prominent *amici* was Cluvius Rufus, part of a new set that emerged following the suppression of the Pisonian conspiracy: Cass. Dio 63.14.3; above 163. For the court in general see above 59. *Contra* Malitz 1999, 89; Mratschek 2013, 54.

[273] Cf. Griffin 1984, 180.   [274] Cass. Dio 63.11.4. Rudich 1993, 201.   [275] Below 380.

[276] Cass. Dio 63.12.1.

[277] Polyclitus and probably, since Galba destroyed them together, Patrobius and Petinus: Tac. *Hist.* 1.49; Plut. *Galb.* 17.2; Cass. Dio 64.3.4.

[278] Holland 2000, 206, 221.   [279] Tac. *Ann.* 15.72.4; Plut. *Galb.* 9.1–2. Above 80.

[280] Tac. *Ann.* 15.72.3; cf. above 29.   [281] Above 62.

He must also have had the backing of individual equestrians and senators. We know of a number of high-ranking supporters of the Neronian regime at this time, thanks to their subsequent vilification as 'informers'.[282] These are the *eques* Annius Faustus and the senators Aquilius Regulus, Cestius Severus, Eprius Marcellus, Nonius Attianus, Paccius Africanus, Sariolenus Vocula, Silius Italicus and Vibius Crispus.[283] A number of these will have been in Rome during Helius' stewardship: Aquilius Regulus was a prime figure in the destruction of the Camerini and also, in this period, of the consulars M. Licinius Crassus Frugi and Ser. Salvidienus Orfitus.[284]

Helius needed strong backing. Later denigration of him as a jumped-up, power-crazed pocket-tyrant ignores his serious problems. These cannot have included early intimations of Vindex's rebellion:[285] there was a long a gap between Helius' pleas to Nero to return to Italy in autumn 67 and Vindex's rebellion in March 68, during which life appeared to return to normal.[286] His troubles lay rather at home. He will have faced difficulties in dealing with the city population. Romans never liked a *princeps*, as guarantor of the corn dole and provider of entertainments, to be absent long,[287] and freeborn citizens probably resented being governed by a freedman.[288] Helius probably encountered even more resentment in certain senatorial circles. Though the number of senatorial adherents to the Neronian regime in both Greece and Rome indicates that there had been no massive rift between it and the upper classes, a significant minority of senators will have been hostile as a result of the Pisonian prosecutions and what followed. As the months progressed, their dislike of Nero will have been deepened by reports from Greece of the deaths of Corbulo and the Scribonii, and of the *princeps'* enthusiastic adoption of the role of professional performer. These may have begun to test Helius' authority. Ancestral republican badges of status could be taken as a challenge to *principes*, as Gaius indicated in 40.[289] In 67, the Camerini may have been flaunting their ancient title as a reproach to Nero;[290] and Camerinus'

---

[282] Rutledge 2001, 22; below 365.

[283] Annius Faustus: Tac. *Hist.* 2.10. Aquilius Regulus: Tac. *Hist.* 1.48, 4.42; Plin. *Ep.* 1.5.1–3. Cestius Severus: Tac. *Hist.* 4.41. Eprius Marcellus: Tac. *Hist.* 2.53; 4.6–7. Nonius Attianus: Tac. *Hist.* 4.41. Paccius Africanus: Tac. *Hist.* 4.41. Sariolenus Vocula: Tac. *Hist.* 4.41. Silius Italicus: Plin. *Ep.* 3.7.3; 3.7.9–10. Vibius Crispus: Tac. *Hist.* 2.10; 4.41. Rutledge 2001 nos. 9, 26, 38, 64, 68, 85, 90, 103.

[284] Rudich 1993, 201–3; Rutledge 2001, 33.

[285] *Contra* Grant 1970, 232; Cizek 1982, 389; Waldherr 2005, 251; cf. Rudich 1993, 207.

[286] Below 387.   [287] Tac. *Hist.* 15.36.6; Yavetz 1969, 125–6.

[288] Meier 2008, 596; Waldherr 2005, 243 (though I reject the idea that at this time arrears in pay caused general disapproval of the regime among the army: below 341).

[289] Winterling 2007, 136.   [290] *Contra* Rudich 1993, 201.

point-blank refusal to obey a direct order from Helius certainly suggests a dangerous weakening of discipline. In using his authority to remove a few troublemakers, Helius was just doing his duty by Nero, but this took the latter's principate into dangerous waters.[291]

9.6.6 Deaths in Greece

Tales of greed and murder in Greece need to be handled with similar circumspection. The Greek tour was the first foreign progress of Nero's principate, indeed the first since Claudius' British expedition. The imperial entourage was massive.[292] From Nero's viewpoint, the main attraction of the Greek trip was cultural: the opportunity to compete as artist and sportsman at all the major festivals.[293] We know that he fretted over the details of his public appearances, which included his equipment and his backing acts.[294] Therefore alongside the court and its usual praetorian escort there will have been the full *Augustiani*, Nero's 'part bodyguard, part club of enthusiasts ... and part claque',[295] together with performers, riggers and general theatrical and sporting hangers-on. These, mostly young and excited, will have found themselves in a sophisticated, albeit somewhat run-down, part of the Empire, from which they expected novelty and good living. They would have been an enormous burden on their hosts.[296] On top of this, some visitors practised direct extortion. The most notorious was Calvia Crispinilla, the wardrobe mistress of Sporus/ 'Poppaea', but there must have been more.[297] Nero was tarred with the same brush and, additionally, accused of pursuing his greed to the point of murder. But his victims are unnamed, and Dio's indictment finds no confirmation in Plutarch or Pausanias.[298] Nero was, in fact, hugely popular among ordinary Greeks. The upper classes will have found him a demanding guest, and will certainly not have relished the activities of his hangers-on, but there is no reason to think that they suffered 'arbitrary terror'.[299] Contradicting his purported rapacity are accounts of Nero's acting as an open-handed patron. The story that he subsequently demanded the return of money that he had given Greek cities, if true, fits a much later period – the crisis following the revolt of Vindex[300] – and reflects the extent of his original generosity. He was certainly guilty of

---

[291] Below 364.   [292] Cass. Dio 63.8.3, 10.2. Fini 1994, 203.   [293] Below 378.
[294] Below 398.   [295] Warmington 1969, 115 (quotation); below 302.
[296] Cf. Michel 2015, 97–9.   [297] Cass. Dio 63.12.3–4.   [298] Hohl 1918, 389.
[299] Rudich 1993, 187–8.
[300] Suet. *Ner.* 24.2, 32.3; Cass. Dio 63.14.2. Bradley 1978a, 193; see also below 367.

appropriating the best of Greek art, but powerful Romans had done this before and would do it again, out of aesthetic admiration as much as greed.[301] Furthermore, Nero's appropriation began with his building of the *Domus Transitoria* and then the 'Golden House', and so antedated his sojourn in Greece.[302] Likewise, the execution of Paris, which Dio puts at about this time but dissociates from goings-on in Greece, and which Suetonius reports only as rumour,[303] could well have been due to reasons other than artistic jealousy. Nero was not greatly interested in Paris' artistic speciality,[304] and though an entertainer, Paris was deeply involved in court politics. In 55 he was among those who schemed unsuccessfully against Agrippina, escaping her wrath only because he was protected by Nero.[305] In the tense circumstances of 65–66, he could well have perished through association with Pisonians.[306]

9.7   Conclusion

The verdict of this chapter must be like that of Chapter 8: that, where they occurred and are not simply invented, most Neronian killings after 62 were due to political necessity and managed by the Establishment. Nero the cold-blooded 'killer' is a construct. Determined to wring this from whatever evidence was to hand, 'the second-rate writers of later ages enjoyed themselves greatly'.[307]

---

[301] Cf. below 257, 346. Cf. Plin. *HN* 34.84: Vespasian did not return Nero's stolen artworks, but placed them in the Temple of Peace, but see below 257 n. 230.
[302] Tac. *Ann.* 15.45.3, 16.23.1; Plin. *HN* 34.84. Bradley 1978a, 172.   [303] Suet. *Ner.* 54
[304] Barrett *et al.* 2016, 247 and n. 30; below 377.   [305] Tac. *Ann.* 13.22.3.
[306] Cizek 1982, 209.   [307] Henderson 1905, 381 (quotation).

CHAPTER 10

Arsonist, Persecutor and Ruthless Property Developer?

10.1 Arson: The Case For

The Great Fire of Rome broke out late on 18 July 64.[1] It burned for six days, died down and then flared up again to rage for another three days.[2] It affected most of the City, especially those parts not shielded by the Tiber or the Servian wall.[3]

Tacitus reports:

> None ventured to combat the fire, as there were reiterated threats from a large number of people who forbade extinction, and others were openly throwing firebrands and shouting that they had their authority – possibly in order to have a free hand in looting, possibly from orders received.[4]

According to Suetonius:

> [Nero] . . . pleading displeasure at the ugliness of the old buildings and the narrow, crooked streets, set fire to the city so openly that several men of consular rank did not dare to lay hands on senior members of his personal staff although they caught them on their properties with tow and fire-brands, while some granaries . . . whose site he particularly desired, were demolished by engines of war and then set on fire, because their walls were of stone.[5]

Similarly, according to Cassius Dio:

> Nero set his heart on accomplishing what had doubtless always been his desire, namely to make an end of the whole city and realm during his lifetime . . . Accordingly he secretly sent out men who pretended to be drunk or engaged in other sorts of mischief, and caused them at first to set

---

[1] Tac. *Ann.* 15.41.3. I am grateful to Drs Werner Lütkenhaus and Simon Malloch for their comments on this chapter.
[2] Tac. *Ann.* 15.40.1–2; *ILS* 4914; cf. Suet. *Ner.* 38.2. Bradley 1978a, 232.
[3] Tac. *Ann.* 15.38–41, esp. 40.4: of the fourteen Augustan districts of the city, three were levelled, seven badly damaged and only four unharmed. Panella 2011a, 82; Shaw 2015, 78, n. 29.
[4] Tac. *Ann.* 15.38.8: *esse sibi auctorem.*   [5] Suet. *Ner.* 38.1–2.

fire to one or two or even several buildings in different parts of the city, so that the people were at their wits' end, not being able to find any beginning of the trouble or put an end to it . . .[6]

That Nero was in some way guilty of arson seems to be confirmed by references elsewhere in Tacitus' 'Annals', in the anonymous *Octavia*, and in Pliny I's 'Natural History'.[7] Champlin emphasises the first of these, a verbatim account of Nero being denounced as an 'incendiary' by the praetorian tribune Subrius Flavus, on trial in 65 for involvement in the Pisonian conspiracy: 'the words of an eye-witness' make it look 'as if Nero was indeed responsible for the fire from the beginning' because 'he wanted to rebuild the city'.[8]

10.2   Arson: The Case Against

That Nero was to blame is unlikely. Tacitus, providing the most detailed extant account of the Fire,[9] records the suspicion that it was the work of the government,[10] but, though himself no lover of Nero, prioritises accidental cause and describes the accusation as no more than 'widespread suspicion'.[11] As for what Subrius Flavus said, one is bound to retort, 'Well he would, wouldn't he?' At first, fighting for his life, he had strenuously denied any association with the conspiracy. Then, closely questioned by Nero, he changed tack and sought to inflict maximum damage on the *princeps'* reputation by hurling in his face every possible major accusation.[12] These ranged from fact (of killing Agrippina and Octavia) to opinion (of conduct unbecoming a *princeps* in the circus and on stage) to rumour (of setting fire to Rome). The last was his weakest weapon, and the more so because by 65 the regime had achieved success in shifting blame to the Christians.[13] Tacitus admired Flavus, but ignored his allegation of incendiarism in his discussion of the cause of the blaze, as he did with the charge against the Christians which he also plainly disbelieved.[14]

---

[6] Cass. Dio 62.16.1–2.   [7] Tac. *Ann.* 15.67.3; Ps.-Sen. *Oct.* 831–3; Plin. *HN* 17.5.
[8] Champlin 2003, 185, 191.   [9] Below 237.
[10] Tac. *Ann.* 15.38.1: *an dolo principis incertum*; 38.8: *seu iussu*; 44.3: *iussum incendium*.
[11] Tac. *Ann.* 15.38.1, 8; 44.3: *infamia*.
[12] Cf. above 207. Similarly Seneca, in his death speech, threw the charge of matricide against Nero, in a manner meant for general consumption: Tac. *Ann.* 15.62.7–63.1. This is ironical, given his own direct involvement in the event.
[13] Tac. *Ann.* 15.44.8; below 247.
[14] Tac. *Ann.* 15.44.3. Below 244. Dr Lütkenhaus has pointed out that the close similarity between Tacitus and Dio at this point suggests that the whole encounter between Flavus and Nero was to be found in the common source tradition, and that it was this that disinclined Tacitus from

(Tacitus also makes no mention of arson as a motive in his earlier account of Flavus' contemplating the murder of Nero during the Fire.[15]) The notices in the *Octavia* and Pliny I are similarly questionable,[16] and it is significant that Nero is not blamed by the contemporary or near-contemporary Josephus, Martial and Juvenal.[17]

Consideration of a range of other points produces a strong circumstantial case in that Nero's favour. The night of 18/19 July 64 – at the height of an Italian summer, bringing out crowds seeking relief after the heat of the day, short, and with the moon only just past full[18] – was not the ideal time for large-scale fire-raising. The Fire did not start in the area that Nero took over for his wider Golden House. Indeed, beginning by the Palatine,[19] it destroyed his own recent major new project, the *Domus Transitoria*, linking the Palatine with the Gardens of Maecenas on the Esquiline, in which he had placed a great collection of works of art.[20] Similarly, the second outbreak of the Fire began as an outlying blaze, to the west of the main conflagration area, on property belonging to Tigellinus.[21] Nero liked the dramatic, and liked to be in engaged in what he did. If he had caused the Fire, he would have been on hand from the start, but he heard of its outbreak *c.* 60 km (36 statute miles) away in Anzio, where he too was probably escaping the summer heat.[22] Suetonius, pushing rumour much further than Tacitus, describes imperial chamberlains going about torch in hand, and substantial buildings destroyed 'by war-engines' – presumably rams and grabs rather than artillery.[23] Dio likewise complains that the military was in action not saving houses but spreading the blaze.[24] However all this has long been interpreted very differently: either as the work of looters, some perhaps seeking protection by dressing themselves in court livery;[25] or as popular misunderstanding of the necessary creation of

---

transposing the former's accusation back to his discussion of the causes of the Fire. This, however, underestimates Tacitus' skill as an historian: below 244.

[15] Tac. *Ann.* 15.50.6. Above 200.   [16] Bradley 1978a, 231.

[17] E.g. Bradley 1978a, 231, 269; Fini 1994, 151–2.

[18] Full moon was on 17/18 July: Hohl 1918, 381. Cf. Warmington 1969, 124; Bradley 1978a, 230; Griffin 1984, 132.

[19] Tac. *Ann.* 15.38.2; below 237.

[20] Suet. *Ner.* 31.1. Bradley 1978a, 171; Griffin 1984, 127–8; Chaisemartin 2003, 158–9; below 242.

[21] Tac. *Ann.* 15.40.3. Panella 2011a, 82 and figure 10a.

[22] Tac. *Ann.* 15.39.1. Waldherr 2005, 12; *contra* Bradley 1978a, 230.

[23] Suet. *Ner.* 38.1: *bellicis machinis*. I owe this observation to Dr Lütkenhaus.

[24] Cass. Dio 62.17.1.

[25] Hohl 1918, 381 (citing Sievens, 1870, on historical parallels with the great Hamburg fire of 1842); Fini 1994, 157; below 241. Routine looting during fires may be reflected in Suetonius' description of Afranius' (fl. later second century BC) play, 'The Fire': *Ner.* 11.2; Bradley 1978a, 84.

the fire-breaks that finally brought the blaze under control.[26] Nero, characteristically, hastened to Rome,[27] threw himself into a vain attempt to save the *Domus Transitoria*,[28] and then arranged emergency accommodation and cheap food for the victims of the Fire.[29] Though he may well also have sung of the sack of Troy,[30] it is striking that he did not later explore this theme in his favourite stage roles, which suggests that he felt no direct emotional involvement in the blaze.[31] Finally, Nero liked being liked, and in 64 had already commenced a scheme of endearing himself to the population of Italy and Rome by making his first public stage appearance at Naples and throwing the City open as his own on the occasion of Tigellinus' banquet.[32] He would not have risked the infamy of being discovered an arsonist.[33] It is not surprising that most modern historians have proposed that the Great Fire was an accident, not an act of criminality.[34] It was just one of the many chance blazes that plagued Rome and all big pre-industrial cities with their narrow and rambling streets, densely packed jerry-built wooden-framed buildings, and primitive firefighting techniques.[35] Rome had suffered major conflagrations before, both under the Republic[36] and under the Julio-Claudians, the most recent in AD 6, 27, 36 and 53.[37] The fundamental difference between that of 64 and the rest was how badly it got out of hand.[38]

10.3   Why Nero?

If Nero was innocent of arson, why did people subsequently believe him guilty?[39] For the pertinent details we rely mainly on Tacitus. Though comparison between Tacitus, Suetonius and Dio indicates, as usual, their employment of a common source, Tacitus, as we shall also see later in his treatment of the Christians, offers additional information indicating

---

[26] Tac. *Ann.* 15.50.1. *OCD*[4]; Wiedemann 1996a, 251. For a very positive assessment of Nero's fire-control operation see Fini 1994, 156–7.

[27] *Contra* Malitz 1999, 67.   [28] Tac. *Ann.* 15.50.6

[29] Tac. *Ann.* 15.39.2–3. Fini (1994, 157) is again very positive here.   [30] Below 238.

[31] Cf. below 290.   [32] Above 206.   [33] Fini 1994, 154.

[34] So Hohl 1918, 382: 'Man wird also mit Wahrscheinlichkeit den Brand auf einen Zufall, nicht auf einen verbrecherischen Willensakt Neros zurückführen'. Cf. Warmington 1969, 124; Bradley 1978a, 230–1; Griffin 1984, 132; Rudich 1993, 85; Fini 1994, 160; Wiedemann 1996a, 250; Holland 2000, 163; Beste and Hesberg 2013, 324.

[35] Canter 1932, 270, 279–84; Panella 2011a, 79–80.   [36] Canter 1932, 271–3.

[37] 6: Cass. Dio 55.26.4; 27: Tac. *Ann.* 4.64.1; 36: Tac. *Ann.* 6.45.1; 53: Suet. *Claud.* 18.1. Canter 1932, 274–5; Levick 1990, 112.

[38] Griffin 1984, 129: 'there was nothing routine about this blaze'; below 237.

[39] Cf. Romm 2014, 168.

personal research.[40] Thus, for example, unlike Suetonius and Dio, he does not dwell on the number of deaths caused by the first phase of the blaze, and observes that its second phase was more notable for destroying buildings than for taking lives.[41] This seems strange, and Tacitus sought to explain the latter as resulting from a lower density of population in the affected areas. Low mortality is, however, characteristic of big fires in pre-industrial cities because these did not produce large amounts of poisonous fumes and gases and were usually slow-moving enough to allow people to escape. The casualty list of the Great Fire of London 1666 was 'tiny'.[42] On the other hand, Tacitus' highly compressed narrative requires expansion in order to reconstruct the proper sequence of events. For example, though at first he says that no-one dared fight the Fire, he later states that its first phase was ended by the creation of a huge fire-break below the Esquiline.[43] This is probably best understood as indicating that the initial blaze was unusually fierce and fast. It broke out among the highly combustible stock of shops built into the eastern end of the Circus Maximus. From here, fanned by a strong east wind, it sped westwards, with the open circus complex acting as a flue and its dry wooden superstructures further feeding the flames. It ran north around and into the Palatine and on to the Forum. It continued further north and northeastwards, spread by the scattering of embers over a wide area.[44] Its ferocity probably paralysed those who should have directed the fight against it. Both contemporaries and historians are unanimous in laying much of the blame for the spread of the Great Fire of London on the Lord Mayor, Sir Thomas Bludworth, for his early refusal to demolish buildings to create a fire-break.[45] A further lesson from 1666 is the subsequent importance in the work of controlling the Fire of James, Duke of York (the future James II).[46] It could have been that in 64 it was only after the flames had somewhat abated, and after Nero and his staff had arrived to rally people's courage and authorise firefighting methods involving the destruction of property, that effective efforts were made to tackle the blaze.

---

[40] Below 244.
[41] Tac. *Ann.* 15. 38.7 (emphasis on the plight of refugees and the *suicide* of survivors), 40.2.
[42] Tinniswood 2003, 131–5. Holland (2000, 163) makes the point that the London fire 'burned for only half as long a time, and was confined to a smaller area with a lower population'. But a large multiple of a very small number still produces a small number.
[43] Tac. *Ann.* 15.38.8, 15; 40.1; above 233.
[44] Tac. *Ann.* 15.38.2, 43. Canter 1932, 276; Holland 2000, 160; Waldherr 2005, 211; Tomei 2011, 125, 129; Panella 2011a, 82–5 and figure 10a.
[45] Tinniswood 2003, 44, 187.   [46] Tinniswood 2003, 111.

Similar unpicking of Tacitus' narrative helps explain how Nero came to be branded an incendiary. Tacitus implies that the process began with reports of Nero's singing to the flames, which aroused hostility even as the *princeps* strove to aid the victims of the disaster.[47] Tacitus, Suetonius and Dio have different versions of the *princeps*' bizarre performance. The best known is that of Suetonius: that Nero ascended the Tower of Maecenas in his gardens on the Esquiline (Figure 13) and in full view and full stage costume sang 'The sack of Ilium'. Though this smacks of a story still growing in the telling, and Tacitus reports the incident as rumour, that Nero viewed the Fire from somewhere and sang something is very plausible.[48] Such behaviour is consistent with his character and interests. Nero loved the theatrical, and loved to perform as a singer, accompanying himself on the *cithara*, the 'professional' version (heavier, more complex and so more difficult to master) of the lyre.[49] The Fire at its peak must have been a magnificent spectacle, too stimulating an experience for a performer to waste.[50] There will have been the visceral sight and sound of huge, multicoloured, flames, collapsing buildings – many ancient and sacred – and human beings in distress. Comparison with the fall of Troy (thanks to Virgil's 'Aeneid', from the time of Augustus automatically connected to the history of Rome and the Julian dynasty, and in the Neronian period again very much in the air[51]) was unavoidable. Nero might well have performed an extract from his own epic on the Trojan war,[52] and the extract might well have contained his observation, quoted critically by Dio, that Priam, king of Troy, was fortunate in seeing his country and his throne destroyed together. If so, this is another instance of his words being used against him out of context.[53] Nero's singing, the consequent spread of disapproval and the transformation of resentment into outright blame must have occurred well after the outbreak of the Fire. Only after he had done all he could to fight the blaze and organise help for its victims would the *princeps* have time for 'aesthetic glee',[54] and only after

[47] Tac. *Ann.* 15.39.2–3, 15.44.2. Grant 1970, 151; Fini 1994, 155–6.
[48] So Grant 1970, 152: 'it is all too probable that Nero did give such a display'; cf. Holland 2000, 164; *contra* Maes 2013, 296–7.
[49] Holland 2000, 70 n. 8; Waldherr 2005, 118; Pausch 2013, 52.
[50] Henderson 1905, 239: 'The scene was a temptation that no impressionist artist could resist'.
[51] Below 268.
[52] Suet. *Ner.* 38.2–3; Juv. 8.221. Cf. Tac. *Ann.* 15.39.3: in a private theatre in palace gardens; Cass. Dio 62.18.1: publicly, on the roof his palace. Bradley 1978a, 234; Warmington 1969, 124; Cizek 1982, 45–6. Griffin 1984,132; Fini 1994, 154–5; Reitz 2006, 23–4; Fantham 2013, 26; above 112.
[53] Cass. Dio 62.16.2. I owe this observation to Dr Lütkenhaus; cf. above 118.
[54] Griffin 1984, 132.

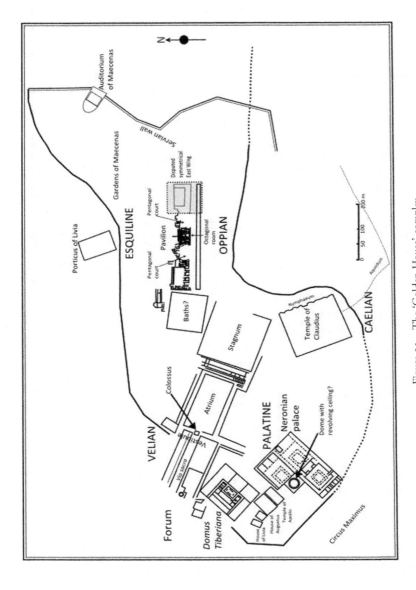

Figure 13 The 'Golden House' complex.
After Claridge 1998, 268; Chaisemartin 2003, 157; Carandini 2011, 238; Panella 2011b, 161; Perrin 2016, 242–3

he had sung could people have begun to resent his singing. Tacitus seems in fact to date the rumours that Nero, intent on the creation of a new Rome, was actually responsible for setting and spreading the Fire, to after its renewed outbreak.[55] How long after he does not say, but that hostility to Nero took some time to show itself may be inferred from the tenor of Tacitus' accounts.

Fire broke out and caused distress, but the Neronian regime kept its head, extinguished the flames and cared for the victims. Unlike the Great Fire of London, we hear of no popular unrest due to shortages of food or shelter.[56] There was suffering but not despair; no immediate rush to find someone criminally responsible for the disaster. The prescription of age-old expiatory ceremonies suggests the establishment of a senatorial commission to investigate the religious implications of the Fire.[57] We may surmise from the operation of an earlier enquiry into indirect taxation that it did a thorough job of work.[58] It could not, therefore, have overlooked the secular side of the disaster, and alongside its religious recommendations it was probably also responsible for the drafting of new regulations concerning the layout and fabric of new buildings in Rome, the use of the public water supply, and the provision of firefighting equipment (probably fire-blankets, buckets, axes, ladders, hooks, shovels, perhaps syringes, and maybe even siphons – early fire-engines).[59]

Tacitus' chronology, however, appears confused here, since he puts the rites after a relatively lengthy discussion of the secular measures. The commission's work could not have begun until the Fire had been fully extinguished and order fully restored. With so much to do, it must have been the end of the summer, at the earliest, before it promulgated the verdict that the Fire was accidental: Tacitus' *forte*: 'by chance', the opposite of his *iussum incendium*: 'premeditated arson'.[60] This was surely the time for the religious ceremonies appropriate to 'an act of God', including vows to Vulcan, the god of fire,[61] after which came implementation of the secular regulations. The report ended the matter,[62] but not before an ugly period of witch-hunting had resulted from the drawing of a very different conclusion.

---

[55] Tac. *Ann.* 15.40.3; above 235.   [56] Tinniswood 2003, 103–7.
[57] Tac. *Ann.* 15.44.1–2. Griffin 1984, 132–3; Closs 2016; cf. Talbert 1984, 386–91 on the continuing importance of senators in religion in this period
[58] Below 352.
[59] Note that Tacitus (*Ann.* 15.44.1) puts the secular measures before the religious. Tac. *Ann.* 15.43.4. Canter 1932, 288; Waldherr 2005, 211; above 124. Cf. Tinniswood 2003, 48–9; Closs 2016, 115.
[60] Tac. *Ann.* 15.38.1, 44.3.   [61] Tac. *Ann.* 15.44.1–2. Cf. below 247.   [62] Below 247.

In large pre-industrial towns, minor and medium fires were common-place. In imperial Rome there may have been around 100 per day.[63] Occasionally, small blazes turned into much larger outbreaks, but there was no immediate fear that these would end in disaster. Because fires were frequent, communities devised ways of dealing with them, involving both private and public initiatives.[64] Julio-Claudian Rome, provided with a professional watch and fire service (the *vigiles*) and gendarmerie (the *cohortes urbanae*), and a large standing garrison (the Praetorians) ready to support these two agencies as needed, was more prepared than most.[65] People would have expected the Fire of 64 to be contained. That it was not must have left the city population – with many, even those not directly affected, suffering what we might call post-traumatic stress disorder[66] – increasingly feeling betrayed by the authorities and ready for someone to blame.[67] A few, guilty about their own poor behaviour (e.g. panicking in the face of danger, resorting to profiteering and looting etc.[68]), may have been especially ready to attack others. There was probably early disquiet at Nero's singing. This was irrational given his earlier firefighting efforts, but as the conviction grew that the administration had failed them, people would have accepted continuing gossip that its head had indulged in personal amusement. Actually moving to blame the *princeps* for the blaze was a greater step, but justification was on hand in another rumour: that the Fire had spread not from a single source but through multiple acts of incendiarism.[69] This would have encouraged people to believe what they had begun to want to believe. Accident and inattention, and the effect of wind-blown embers,[70] could be discounted: the Fire was the work of conspiracy. But who were the conspirators? In September 1666, culprits were conveniently to hand. Britain was at war with Holland and France and was doing badly. Accusations of arson could therefore almost imme-diately be directed at resident citizens of these countries and their alleged English accomplices.[71] In July 64 Rome had no foreign bogeymen to blame. The Gauls and the Carthaginians had been defeated,[72] and the

---

[63] Bingham 2013, 107.   [64] Cf. Tinniswood 2003, 46–51.
[65] Canter 1932, 287–8; Holland 2000, 161–2; Bingham 2013, 106–9; above 62.
[66] Cf. Tinniswood 2003, 141, 143: '[London's] citizens were haunted by demons'.
[67] Cf. Hohl 1918, 382; Griffin 1984, 132; Shaw 2015, 91.
[68] Cf. above 235; Tinniswood 2003, 67–8, 106, 119, 130, 136.
[69] The charge is implicit in Tacitus (*Ann.* 15.38.6) and Suetonius (*Ner.* 38.1), and explicit in Cassius Dio (62.16.2). Cf. Tinniswood 2003, 58, 119.
[70] Cf. above 237.   [71] Tinniswood 2003, 51, 58–9; 66; 109; 145–8.
[72] Though note Tacitus' report that some observed that the Fire had begun on date of capture and burning of Rome by the Senones: *Ann.* 15.41.3.

Germani were yet to come. The only external power that could pose a threat was Parthia: distant; with probably few of its citizens resident in Rome; and, with the settlement of the Armenian question, no longer hostile. However, gathering resentment had to find someone who had both the motive and the capacity to fire-raise on a grand scale, and this left only Nero and his grand plans for a New Rome.

Ultimate responsibility rested, anyway, with the *princeps*, the great patron, answerable for the welfare of all.[73] Nero had played the role well. Though he incurred negative gossip through his association with the deaths of Britannicus, Agrippina and Octavia, this had not developed into any serious hostility in the capital.[74] Such tolerance may be ascribed to the popularity of his accession and general recognition that these deaths, however regretful, were politically necessary. Between 62 and the Fire, indeed, there is every indication that Nero had regained the backing of the *plebs* after their demonstrations in support of Octavia.[75] Acceptance of his marriage to Poppaea (and, with this, of the rise of Tigellinus) will have been eased by the birth and sad death of Claudia Augusta.[76] The prestige of the regime was increased by success in Armenia and by its adept handling of a rumoured food shortage in 62.[77] The *plebs* were treated to great gladiatorial games in 63 and to 'Tigellinus' banquet' early in 64.[78] Nero probably also helped himself by his relaxed attitude to ordinary people, for example in the way in which he reacted to critical graffiti.[79] One might expect that additional unease would have been caused by Nero's *Domus Transitoria*, 'The House of Passage', begun around 60. This flouted convention by cutting across the ancient centre of Rome to connect the Palatine and Esquiline.[80] It was probably no single structure but a suite of buildings and gardens, old and new, around 1 km/0.6 statute mile in extent. By July 64 it was taking shape at both ends (on the Palatine with the so-called Baths of Livia, and on the Esquiline with a fairly standard villa[81]). In between there must have been at least one useable substantial property: the mansion, perhaps the townhouse of Nero's paternal birth family, the Domitii Ahenobarbi, and the home of his art collection, which Nero tried to save from the Fire.[82] However, the *Domus*

[73] Wiedemann 1996a, 251; Waldherr 2005, 212; Shaw 2015, 91; cf. below 315–16.   [74] Above 175.
[75] Above 193.   [76] Above 196.   [77] Tac. *Ann.* 15.18.2. Above 141; below 333 n. 73.
[78] Below 298.   [79] Cf. above 107.   [80] Carandini 2011, 140. For its purpose see below 251.
[81] Ball 2003, 95; Beste 2011a, 153–4; Tomei 2011, 123–4.
[82] Tac. *Ann.* 15.39.1: *domus eius, qua Palatium et Maecenatis hortos continuaverat.* Above 160; Bradley 1978a, 171; Ball 2003, 2–3, 135–6; Moormann 2003, 382, 386–7; Carandini 2011, 140; Panella 2011a, 78; Beste and Hesberg 2013, 322–3; Perrin 2016, 230–33 and figure 1.

Transitoria seems to have provoked little direct contemporary or historical criticism, perhaps because most of it was built on land already controlled by the Julio-Claudians or purchased fairly on the market, and because, with large parts open to public access, it did not greatly disrupt city life.[83] (The contemporary Temple of Claudius was set in a large garden, which suggests that it was government policy to give residents more recreative space.[84]) There is no reason to suppose that, by the time of the Fire, Nero was unpopular in the capital, but this makes it all the more remarkable that he could be thought capable of grand arson.[85] Popularity is fickle. Increased exposure to the public gaze can generate both speedy fame and speedy infamy. The Roman people may have become unsure as to what to make of the new, 'popular' Nero as manifested in his 'coming out' as a public performer at Naples,[86] his sudden decision not to leave Italy and Rome to visit Greece and Egypt,[87] his appearance at Tigellinus' banquet,[88] and his participation in 'lewd' theatricals.[89] Nero's initial absence from the fight against the Fire may have caused resentment, along with the rumour that he left Anzio only on news of the threat to his *Domus Transitoria*.[90] What he did after he arrived generated suspicion. People find it easier to blame authority when that authority has had a part in the events concerned. In 1666, James, Duke of York, doing sterling work in leading the firefighting, provoked enduring mistrust when it was thought that he, a suspected Catholic, was rescuing 'guilty' foreigners caught by the mob.[91] Nero's singing caused distrust and, once this was aroused and word got about that the authorities had put their energies into spreading the blaze, not containing it, other details could be thrown in as proof of government arson, such as the interpretation of the creation of fire-breaks as fire-raising.[92] It is possible that aristocrats later to involve themselves in the Pisonian conspiracy were not averse to encouraging such gossip.[93] Finally, the precedent of the *Domus Transitoria* will have helped convince people of the seriousness of Nero's grand architectural plans. Thus, probably not immediately but well before the publication of the findings of the senatorial commission, Nero was accused of incendiarism.[94]

[83] Griffin 1984, 128; Ball 2003, 96–7; Beste 2011a, 154; Perrin 2016, 231. *Contra* Waldherr 2005, 207–8, 218–19; Viscogliosi 2011b, 157–8.

[84] Cf. Hesberg 2011, 110–12.   [85] Rudich 1993, 85; Romm 2014, 166.

[86] Below 298. Cf. Meier 2008, 584: 'the "*coming out* des Künstlers"', though dating this from 59.

[87] Below 309; cf. Fini 1994, 156.   [88] Cf. above 205–6.   [89] Below 313.

[90] Tac. *Ann.* 15.39.1. Waldherr 2005, 213.   [91] Tinniswood 2003, 157–8.

[92] Above 235–6; Bingham 2013, 109.   [93] Waldherr 2005, 215; above 201.

[94] Cf. Rudich 1993, 85; Holland 2000, 166. I am grateful to Dr Malloch for his comments on this point; my conclusion is, of course, my own.

10.4   Christians as Scapegoats

To quash such rumours the administration took action which led to local prosecution of Christians.[95] There are problems in reconstructing what happened. First, while the main literary tradition is unanimous in suggesting that some contemporaries thought Nero guilty of arson,[96] Tacitus alone has him scapegoating Christians. Second, Nero 'the arsonist' is not found in the earliest Christian tradition; full portrayal of Nero as 'the great persecutor' developed only from the later second century;[97] and even then no writer, pagan or Christian, has Nero blaming Christians for starting the Fire. One explanation for the tension between Tacitus and the rest is that this results from a later insertion into his text. This is now generally, if not entirely, rejected.[98] A more recent alternative is that Tacitus retrojected growing concern at the spread of Christianity around 100 into events of the 60s. Shaw proposes that the Neronian administration punished people for arson, but because those punished were not Christians, persecution of Christians 'never happened'.[99] The real victims of government attention, the 'certain persons . . . denounced by the common people of Rome as responsible for setting the fire', were 'Jewish sectarians'.[100] This is, however, to underestimate Tacitus' capacity for personal research, evidenced in both the 'Histories' and the 'Annals'.[101] Though his culture and education encouraged him to treat his material rhetorically and morally – he was no dispassionate historian – this never, as Shaw himself says, drew him into 'outright invention'.[102] If we accept Tacitus' rediscovery of a forgotten historical fact, that the Neronian administration had accused a group of residents of Rome of setting the Great Fire and punished them accordingly,[103] we should also accept his identification of these as Christians. This is all the more so because he had a personal interest in religion, domestic and foreign. Early in his senatorial career he had been a committed *quindecemvir sacris faciundis*, a very senior priestly office 'that would have involved a fairly high degree of sophistication about religious matters';

---

[95] Tac. *Ann.* 15.44.3. Below 322–3.   [96] Above 233.

[97] Stevenson 1967, 3, 5–6, 168; Fini 1994, 151–2; Waldherr 2005, 9; Holland 2000, 172–5; Maier 2013, 388–92; Shaw 2015, 83–5, 96.

[98] Shaw 2015, 79–80; Barrett *et al.* 2016, 164–5.

[99] Shaw 2015, 74 (quotation), 85–9, 92, 94, 96.   [100] Shaw 2015, 84 (quotation), 86, 94.

[101] E.g. Tac. *Hist.* 5.2–10; *Ann.* 13.20.3, 14.2 *passim*; 15.74.3. Syme 1958, 280–1, 289–98, 378; Heil 1997, 30, 36–9, 54; *FRHist.* 2013, 1.541–5, 2 no. 82; above 147, 237.

[102] Syme 1958, 298–301; Shaw 2015, 82, 92 (quotation), 96; above 9.   [103] Shaw 2015, 92.

and in the 'Histories' he shows himself knowledgeable about the Jews.[104] From this, from accounts of contemporaries and probably also from his own experience as governor of Asia *c.* 112,[105] Tacitus will have been able to recognise Christians when he came across them in the records.[106] But who were these, if they were not recognised by the developing, still predominantly eastern,[107] Christian tradition? Shaw's 'Jewish sectarians' points in the right direction. There is a long-established view that the Roman Christians of 64 may have been on the margins of Christianity and Judaism: converted Jews.[108] Jews were soon to be thought capable of firing Antioch, but this was in the context of a savage war.[109] Though Romans had long experienced exasperation and uncertainty in dealing with Judaism, they broadly respected the faith as ancient, public and respectable. In 64, there was no reason for branding Jews in general as arsonists. On the other hand, as they grasped that local Christianity, despite its dependence on Jewish converts, amounted to something very different, they will have grown particularly suspicious of its novelty, social seclusion, and supposedly impious and immoral practices.[110] For scapegoating to work, it has to pick on plausible villains: like enemy aliens in seventeenth-century London,[111] immediately identifiable,[112] already suspect, and ideologically and physically capable of the actions of which they are accused. Metropolitan Romans may well have become distrustful of a breakaway group, relatively small but, thanks to its errant behaviour and strange language, easily recognisable and, perhaps, beginning to proselytise.[113] These made good scapegoats in Rome but went unrecorded in the eastern Christian tradition because they were not part of it.[114] They had probably already been labelled *Christiani/Chrestiani*, and described as such in the City records read by Tacitus. Though the term is not literary before the second century, its use by Tacitus for the Neronian principate is not necessarily anachronistic. In Tacitus' words, it was vulgar usage, which would have taken time to be adopted by educated writers.[115] Tacitus glossed their

---

[104] Tac. *Ann.* 11.11.1; *Hist.* 5.2–10. Barrett *et al.* 2016, 166 (quotation); Malloch 2013, 185–7 and personal communication.
[105] Cf. Shaw 2015, 91 n. 84: perhaps at the same time as Pliny II was governing Bithynia.
[106] Stevenson 1967, 3; Barrett *et al.* 2016, 166.   [107] *EEC* 2, 671; Shaw 2015, 89.
[108] E.g. *EEC* 2,671; Holland 2000, 175; Malitz 1999, 70.   [109] Joseph. *BJ* 7.44. *EEC* 2.671
[110] Warmington 1969, 126; Bradley 1978a, 104–5; Fini 1994, 167.   [111] Above 241.
[112] *Contra* Shaw 2015, 89.   [113] Below 323.
[114] For the alleged martyrdoms of SS Peter and Paul, see below 323.
[115] Tac. *Ann.* 15.44.3: *vulgus Christianos appellabat.* Shaw 2015, 80–1, 84, 85–9; Barrett *et al.* 2016, 167 n. 40; Dr Malloch, personal communication.

beliefs as a new 'pernicious superstition',[116] thus suggesting that they were
the direct forerunners of eastern Christians of the early second century.
This was mistaken, but his mistake should not be taken to mean that they
were not authentic followers of Christ. Confirmation of this may be found
in Suetonius. He, perhaps drawing on Tacitus' findings, likewise has Nero,
rightly, punishing *Christiani*, 'a class of men given to a new and mischiev-
ous superstition'.[117] However, he also records that Claudius expelled the
Jews from Rome because they were continually causing public disturbances 'at the instigation of Chrestus'.[118] Both statements have provoked
debate, but it is not unreasonable to interpret the latter as a confused
reference to apostatising converts to Christianity causing unrest in the
Jewish community in Rome and to suppose that the same people, abhor-
rent to Jews and pagans alike, returned to be blamed and punished as
arsonists under Nero.[119]

    Therefore, as popular suspicions of Nero mounted and with the senat-
orial commission yet to report, the administration established its own
enquiry, set on finding a person or persons to blame. As in 1666, when
'everyone on the margins of society ... became legitimate targets',[120]
Christians living in Rome were brought in for questioning. Interrogation
can generate false confessions. In 1666, one Robert Hubert brought about
his own execution by admitting to arson and continuing to assert his guilt
in the face of all the evidence and the opinion of the English legal
establishment. Such behaviour usually results from a desire for celebrity,
possibly exacerbated by mental illness,[121] but in 64 it could well have been
prompted by profound religious conviction. One can easily imagine how
some Christians appeared to confess to arson by expressing grim satisfaction at God's punishment of the heathen City and by eagerly anticipating
imminent Armageddon: 'The incendiary language of the Christian fanatic
must have given rise to strange misconceptions and misunderstandings'.[122]
Some, indeed, by failing to explain their language or even to deny the
accusation, may have wilfully courted martyrdom.[123] This would have
been good enough for an administration bent on countering the rumour
that Nero was to blame. Initial success then prompted the investigators to
extend the period of their enquiries[124] and to sweep more victims into

---

[116] Tac. *Ann.* 15.44.4: *exitiabilis superstitio.*
[117] Suet. *Ner.* 16.2: *genus hominum superstitionis novae et malificiae.* Below 248.
[118] Suet. *Claud.* 25.4: *impulsore Chresto.*   [119] Bradley 1978a, 103–5; cf. Shaw 2015, 84.
[120] Tinniswood 2003, 148.   [121] Tinniswood 2003, 163–8.
[122] Henderson 1905, 251 (quotation); Holland 2000, 171–2, 177.   [123] Cf. Grant 1970, 161–2.
[124] Fini (1994, 166) suggests to two months.

their net by association – first with those already condemned and then by simple religious affiliation – making all local Christians to blame for arson and, as we shall see, treating them very badly.[125] The government's stratagem evidently worked well: most inhabitants of Rome appear to have been persuaded that Christians set the blaze, though some were unhappy over the manner of their punishment.[126] With this, but not before, the feeling probably arose that the gods had punished Rome for harbouring non-believers and that matters had now been set straight. Tacitus' statement that the Christians had suffered directly because of their 'superstition' and their 'hatred of the human race' is, indeed, probably a reflection of second-century Roman prejudice.[127]

Though the administration succeeded in passing the blame for the Fire of 64 on to Christians, apart from in Tacitus' account, Christians as fire-raisers then drop out of the historical picture.[128] Why? Generally, time moves on, tempers cool and even alleged arsonists are forgotten,[129] especially when the real causes of blazes are discovered and accepted. The Fire of London was eventually attributed to carelessness at a bakery, and suspicion of foreigners and of James, Duke of York disappeared from folk memory. In 64–65, the senatorial commission finally declared that the Fire of Rome was accidental. When Domitian officially called the disaster to mind, he made much of restoring grand altars and annual ceremonies in honour of Vulcan, generic god of fire, vowed by Nero as a defence against future outbreaks but never fully established.[130] These measures suggest provision against mischance, not crime; that Nero made his vow following the report of the senatorial commission; and that its verdict had been broadly accepted. Misgivings over Nero will have been further assuaged by the economic activity generated by his building programme, the excitement of *Neronia* II, the prospect of an heir, Tiridates' visit and the Greek 'triumph'.[131] Popular sympathy for the *princeps* may also have been restored by his narrow escape from the Pisonian conspirators, and the death of Poppaea. In 65, Subrius Flavus might maliciously draw on rumour in a last-ditch condemnation of Nero as an arsonist, but even then, less than a year after the Fire, few would have believed him. The process of forgetting Christian involvement will have been further accelerated by another serious fire in 80, under Titus. This, though human

---

[125] Below 323.   [126] Tac. *Ann.* 15.44.8; below 324.
[127] Tac. *Ann.* 15.44.5: *odium generis humani.* Cf. Holland 2000, 165; Tinniswood 2003, 180–1, 186.
[128] Above 234.   [129] Cf. Canter 1932, 274, 280.
[130] *ILS* 4914. Shaw 2015, 90–1; Closs 2016, 103, 110–11.   [131] Cf. below 343.

agency appears to have been considered (perhaps a lingering memory of 64[132]), was finally ascribed to broad divine displeasure, unprovoked by the actions or failings of any individual or group.[133] The verdict both avoided the turmoil of widespread recriminations and took pressure off the incumbent *princeps*, the figure of ultimate human responsibility.[134] Thus towards the end of the first century the official line was that the fires of both 64 and 80 were not due to any criminality and certainly not to any *princeps*.[135] However, in this period when the historical image of the 64 fire and of Nero was being fixed, there persisted a contrary view that fed the developing tradition of Nero 'the monster'.[136] Christian arson was forgotten but 'the image of a ruler "fiddling while Rome burned" is far too potent, and useful, ever to be discarded from popular imagination'.[137] Subsequent *principes* were ready to tolerate an unofficial charge of arson against Nero, the vicious foil to their own virtues. This explains Suetonius' severing of Tacitus' connection of Nero's punishment of Christians with the Fire. It allowed him 'unequivocally' to blame the *princeps* for the latter,[138] while listing the former among the *princeps'* positive measures to 'safeguard public order and restraint'.[139] Christians were, anachronistically, seen as having been punished for their religion, not for arson.[140]

10.5   The Golden House

Like his involvement with the Fire, Nero's subsequent construction of a new residence in Rome – the *Domus Aurea* or 'Golden House' – has long provoked debate. He planned a collection of buildings, architectonic features and parkland stretching from the Palatine to the Viminal in the north and the Caelian in the east (Figure 13).[141]

Its most famous structure, east of the Palatine, is now known as the Golden House having erroneously been given the name of the entire complex.[142] Archaeologists prefer to call it the 'Pavilion'. The Pavilion looked south down the slope of the Oppian and up that of the Caelian hill, over the area now occupied by the Colosseum. What we know of it derives

---

[132] I owe this point to Dr Lütkenhaus.
[133] Cass. Dio 66.24.1–3: *to kakon ouk anthrōpinon alla daimonion egeneto*. Canter 1932, 276.
[134] Above 242; cf. Closs 2016, 116–17.   [135] Cf. Closs 2016, 110.
[136] Cf. Closs 2016, 118–19.   [137] Warmington 1969, 124 (quotation); cf. Tinniswood 2003, 176.
[138] Stevenson 1967, 4.   [139] Bradley 1978a, 103.
[140] Suet. *Ner.* 16.2. Bradley 1978a, 103–4; above 247.
[141] Suet. *Ner.* 31.1. Meyboom and Moormann 2013, 133, 274.
[142] For an overview: Panella 2011b; Ball 2003, 6; Beste 2011b; Tomei 2011, 131; Viscogliosi 2011b, 137.

from literary texts and archaeological research.[143] It is conventionally
shown as two great peristyle wings, hinged by a 'large octagonal hall,
probably roofed with a massive cupola'.[144] Of 'enormous' size, with an
overall frontage of *c.* 370 m, it was built in the style of a portico-villa, 'with
the main rooms in the façade which, through a portico and terrace before
it, had a fine view on the landscape park lying in front ...'[145] It was
inventively designed, magnificently fitted out with the latest architectural
and technological novelties and lavishly decorated.[146] The Forum to the
west was connected to the Golden House complex by an extended *via
Sacra*. At the top of the *via Sacra* Nero planned to erect a great bronze
statue (Colossus), according to Suetonius, 120 Roman feet high (*c.* 35 m;
116 statute feet).[147] To the east, behind the statue, on the height of the
Velian saddle, an extensive forecourt and ornamental lake (*Stagnum*) gave
on to the Pavilion and a wide, wooded estate. South of the lake, Nero
turned the uncompleted temple of Claudius into an extravagant water-
feature.[148] To the west of this, on the Palatine south of the *via Sacra*, was
another set of grand new buildings, adjoining a repaired *Domus Tiberiana*.[149] Though somewhat clumsy, it is useful to think of both as the
'*Domus Tiberiana*/Neronian palace' complex.[150] The full Golden House
complex covered an area estimated at between 50 and 80 ha (125–200
acres), potentially twice that of the Vatican City.[151] Though the Pavilion
was taken to an advanced stage of construction, there are indications that
neither it nor the Golden House complex as a whole was ever fully
completed.[152] The complex must have been used to impress Tiridates,

[143] Suet. *Ner.* 31.1–2; Bradley 1978a, 169, 173–81; Griffin 1984, 138–9; Chaisemartin 2003,
156–60; Meyboom and Moormann 2012, 131–3; Beste and Hesberg 2013, 322–8; Meyboom
and Moormann 2013, 16–17.

[144] Figure 13; but cf. below 258.

[145] Griffin 1984, 134–5; Fini 1994, 176; Chaisemartin 2003, 158; Meyboom and Moormann 2012,
131, 133 (quotations); Meyboom and Moormann 2013, 22, 70, 79.

[146] Grant 1970, 173; Fini 1994, 177–8; Waldherr 2005, 220; Beste and Hesberg 2013, 326;
above 119.

[147] Suet. *Ner.* 31.1; Cass. Dio 66.15.1 (100 feet). Bradley 1978a, 177; Meyboom and Moormann
2012, 133; cf. below 274.

[148] Moormann 2003, 383–4; Meyboom and Moormann 2013, 17.   [149] Below 250.

[150] Cf. Perrin 2016, figures 2, 3. Carandini 2011, 143 prefers the rather confusing *Domus Augustiana*
to 'Neronian palace'.

[151] Griffin 1984, 137–9; Chaisemartin 2003, 156–9; Moorman 2003, 385; Beste and Hesberg 2013,
324; Meyboom and Moormann 2013, 16 and n. 31. Perrin 2016, 236 and figures 2, 3 would make
it much larger by including imperial gardens beyond the Servian wall.

[152] Grant 1970, 173; Bradley 1978a, 173, 181; Beste and Hesberg 2013, 324; Meyboom and
Moormann 2013, 16; below 259.

perhaps by showing him its sculptures and dining-room with revolving ceiling.[153] However, given its unfinished state and its lack of grand ceremonial features,[154] it is no surprise that the main events of his reception were staged elsewhere.[155] On Nero's death everything changed. The Flavians restored parts of the Golden House complex, such as the temple of Claudius, to their original function. Others they neglected or demolished and built over. Their great architectural legacy was the huge amphitheatre, now known as the Colosseum, built on the site of Nero's lake. Subsequent *principes* followed their lead. Hadrian, for example, replaced the forecourt complex with a temple of Rome and Venus. Most famous is the fate of the Pavilion. Under the Flavians it was probably downgraded to accommodate workmen constructing the Colosseum. It was badly damaged by the fire of 104, slighted, and its remains sealed under the new Baths of Trajan until their rediscovery in the fifteenth century.[156]

Such cavalier treatment is unusual. *Principes* usually tolerated important constructions of their predecessors, as the Flavians maintained Nero's luxurious baths, built for *Neronia* I.[157] Why was the Golden House treated differently? In principle, a major Neronian building programme was not unnecessary. The adornment of the City had been accepted as an obligation by the main political contenders of the late Republic, especially Julius Caesar.[158] Augustus had enthusiastically followed suit and bequeathed the responsibility to his successors.[159] Because, however, no other *princeps* until Nero was particularly active in monumental building,[160] the time was ripe for development. There was a particular need to rationalise the 'palace' structure that had grown up on the Palatine. Here, private aristocratic homes and public buildings had been taken over and amalgamated piecemeal to house the leaders of the Principate and those who served them.[161] A spacious, purpose-built complex would benefit the state. Tiberius and Gaius had made tentative moves in this direction with the so-called *Domus Tiberiana*, occupying the whole of the western Palatine and overlooking the Forum.[162] This was expanded by Claudius, perhaps

---

[153] Below 255.   [154] Below 266.   [155] Below 266.
[156] Bradley 1978a, 173; Claridge 1998, 113, 269; Panella 2011b, 168–9; Meyboom and Moormann 2012, 133; Beste and Hesberg 2013, 325; Meyboom and Moormann 2013, 1–2.
[157] Below 298, 331. Suet. *Ner.* 12.3; Mart. *Epig.* 2.48, 7.34. Bradley 1978a, 87–8; Moormann 2003, 378.
[158] E.g. Pompey, in his building of his theatre. Cf. Griffin 1984, 131; Drinkwater 2007b, 70.
[159] Cf. Elsner 1994, 112–13; below 315.   [160] Chaisemartin 2003, 137; Viscogliosi 2011a, 94.
[161] Griffin 1984,128; Wallace-Hadrill 1996, 287; Beste and Hesberg 2013, 322; Meyboom and Moormann 2012, 132.
[162] Suet. *Calig.* 22; Chaisemartin 2003, 154–5; Winterling 2007, 73; Viscogliosi 2011b, 94–6.

encouraged by Agrippina II,[163] and was probably where Agrippina listened in on the Senate and tried to receive Armenian ambassadors.[164] However, without exploitation of the eastern Palatine, still probably in private hands,[165] space was short.[166] Nero had begun promisingly with the temple of Claudius, a grand wooden amphitheatre, a new market and the baths-cum-gymnasium.[167] Lack of space on the Palatine may explain his *Domus Transitoria*: not so much a 'House of Passage' as the 'Palatine Annexe'.[168]

The Fire of 64 increased the necessity and created the opportunity for action. An additional stimulus was Tiridates. In later 64, Nero and his advisers will have been aware that the new king of Armenia would soon arrive in the imperial capital and have to be impressed by what he saw there. After the Fire, however, Rome's centre was a wreck, requiring the speedy replacement of both government buildings and residential and commercial properties.[169] As for the former, there was something to be said for adopting contemporary models: in the case of the *Domus Tiberiana*/Neronian palace, those of Hellenistic royal administrative complexes, for example that of Alexandria; and in the case of the Pavilion, those of great private houses, especially in Campania, which had produced many architectural and artistic advances.[170] With regard to the latter, there was a pressing need for building regulations to prevent the outbreak of fires and, if they occurred, to help their suppression. Regulation worked. The measures Nero introduced won the grudging approval of Tacitus and Suetonius;[171] and, though they still broke out, big fires were much less frequent after Nero.[172] The new 'palace' failed. For this, Rome had to wait for Domitian.[173]

The anti-Neronian tradition, ancient and modern, attributes the failure of the Golden House to its being the wrong structure in the wrong place at

---

[163] The chronology of the *Domus Tiberiana* is disputed, with some attributing it wholly to Nero. Given the time needed for its construction, Agrippina's abilities and Nero's other interests as *princeps*, I prefer an earlier date for its inception. Barrett 1996, 110–11; Claridge 1998, 121, 123; Winterling 2009, 83 and n. 19; Meyboom and Moormann 2012, 132; Beste and Hesberg 2013, 322; Meyboom and Moormann 2013, 16; Michel 2015, 39–44, 54–7.

[164] Above 46, 133; *contra* Carandini 2011, 137: in the old House of Augustus.

[165] Cf. Tac. *Ann.* 15.69.1: Vestinus' house 'overlooking the Forum' (*imminentis foro aedis*); Carandini 2011, 138; above 73.

[166] *Contra* Ball 2003, 1–2, 135.   [167] Below 331.   [168] Above 235.

[169] Cf. Bradley 1978a, 172–3.

[170] Griffin 1984, 138; Ball 2003, 5–6, 135; Chaisemartin 2003, 156–7; Lorenz 2013, 374–5; Meyboom and Moormann 2013, 18.

[171] Tac. *Ann.* 15.43.1–2 (cf. 15.41.2, on the 'striking beauty' [*tanta pulchritudo*] of the new city); Suet. *Ner.* 16.1. Canter 1932, 286–7; Griffin 1984, 129–30 (noting Nero's plans for 'a Rome of spacious avenues' and for a great 'Rome-Ostia' complex); above 240.

[172] Canter 1932, 276–8; Bingham 2013, 110; above 247, 250.   [173] Chaisemartin 2003, 178–82.

the wrong time. It was the wrong structure because the eye-catching Pavilion took the 'Campanian villa' model too far. 'A lavish rural villa ... in the heart of Rome' was totally out of keeping with the surrounding townscape.[174] It made the Golden House complex as a whole flout a convention, established by Augustus and persisting until the Late Empire, whereby the ancient heart of Rome was a huge national heritage centre, used to distil 'the collective memory of Republican Rome' for the benefit of the Julio-Claudians and all their successors.[175] The convention favoured monumental public structures, in particular orthodox temples and fora.[176] Nero maintained it more or less (i.e. excepting the unusual topography of the *Domus Transitoria*) until 64,[177] but then appears to have sacrificed public utility to private gratification.[178] As Martial observes, 'one house took up the whole of Rome'.[179] In the eyes of aristocratic traditionalists most aspects of the complex, such as its desecration of Claudius' temple,[180] will have appeared as anti-Augustan, anti-senatorial, popularist and so, in every sense of the term, profoundly vulgar. It was in the wrong place because it took up too much room. What our sources report about the complex is, as much as its luxury, its extensive grounds: a massive parkland cheek-by-jowl with the Forum.[181] The typical pre-industrial reaction to major urban fires was to get back to normal as soon as possible by permitting existing owners to occupy former sites in former ways on former streets. Grand plans of reform prevented this, and so were usually pruned or abandoned. But Nero drove ahead with his designs, forcing many people to move. Martial states baldly that the 'arrogant park' had robbed the poor of their homes.[182] Resentment may have been increased by the failure to implement plans for the creation of a 'Greater Rome', extending to Ostia, which might have helped house the dispossessed.[183] In any case, people's lives will have been severely disrupted by the centre of Rome's becoming a giant building site,[184] and perhaps the

---

[174] Elsner 1994, 121.

[175] Chaisemartin 2003, 128: 'la mémoire collective de la Rome républicaine'.

[176] Drinkwater 2007b, 71.   [177] Griffin 1984, 128.

[178] Cf. Bradley 1978a, 229: that the Fire destroyed many old public monuments, 'to which the construction of a personal residence by Nero on an unprecedented scale made a sharp contrast'.

[179] Mart. *Spect.* 2: *unaque iam tota stabat in urbe domus*. Cf. the lampoon quoted by Suetonius, *Nero* 39.2: *Roma domus fiet* – Rome is becoming one house'.

[180] Cf. Waldherr 2005, 220.

[181] Tac. *Ann.* 15.42.1. Bradley 1978a, 169, 170; Griffin 1984, 137; Malitz 1999, 76; Chaisemartin 2003, 139, 155–6; Waldherr 2005, 220.

[182] Mart. *Spect.* 2: *superbus ager*.

[183] Suet. *Ner.* 16.1. Griffin 1984, 130, 133; cf. Bradley 1978a, 100–1, proposing an earlier date.

[184] Cf. Griffin 1984, 139–41.

more so because, given the precious materials and objects that went into the Pavilion's construction,[185] large parts of the site were subject to tight security. All this would have given an impression of intended exclusivity that could later be turned against the building as a 'tyrant's lair'.[186] Finally, the Golden House was built at the wrong time because its massive cost increased already excessive government overspending and so encouraged the fiscal oppression that would play a major part in Nero's downfall.[187] Suetonius complains that after the Fire Nero's financial demands almost bankrupted provinces and private individuals alike.[188]

Yet, as always, one must be wary with the anti-Neronian tradition. As we have seen, the political system was still plastic.[189] Though the role of each *princeps* was shaped and constrained by that of his predecessor, 'and the more predecessors there are the stronger this constraint gets',[190] Nero was still only the fifth such ruler. There were people alive, like Nero's immediate successor, Sulpicius Galba, born in 3 BC,[191] who had grown up under Augustus. Though both Tiberius and Gaius had suffered from refusing to follow the full Augustan script,[192] Nero might have more success in giving Rome a new sort of Principate. There is no doubt that he had different, albeit relatively narrow, ideas about how a *princeps* should behave, exhibited in his non-military interests, his promotion of the arts and sport, and his readiness to mix with people of all classes.[193] He certainly had the common touch. Thanks to a 'extrovert, exuberant' character, he enjoyed being in public, revelled in popular company, attention and applause and in turn interacted easily with those he encountered, rarely forgetting a face and making a point of addressing individuals by name.[194] His love of chariot-racing (a massive professional sport with established teams: Nero supported the Greens) and its star performers gave *princeps* and people a common interest and a common topic of conversation, which could never have been forced. Unlike many a modern politician feigning interest in soccer, Nero was a true fan.[195] In addition, the

---

[185] Meyboom and Moormann 2012, 141; 2013, 28; below 258.   [186] Below 254, 263.

[187] Below 341–2.

[188] Suet. *Ner.* 38.3: *provincias privatorum census prope exhausit.* Cf. Romm 2014, 168–9.

[189] Above 38. Cf. Milnor 2005, 4; Osgood 2011, 21–2 (on the accession of Claudius): 'The political culture of the principate was still very much developing – indeed in a sense, it always was, but especially so now'. Cf. Bergmann 2013, 353: 'a permanent experiment'.

[190] Vout 2013, 64.   [191] Kienast 2004, 102.   [192] Vout 2013, 59 (quotation), 61, 65, 74.

[193] Cf. below 293, 375.

[194] Fini 1994, 56 ('extrovertiert, überschwenglich'), 96–7; Holland 2000, 130. E.g. Suet. *Ner.* 10.2, 20.2, 24.2, 53.

[195] Suet. *Ner.* 22.1, with Cass. Dio 63.6.3, Plin, *HN* 33.90; Bradley 1978a, 135; Malitz 1999, 46; Waldherr 2005, 114–15, 203–4; cf. below 304.

melodramatic side of his singing gave it a wide appeal.[196] Nero had been welcomed by the people of Rome at the start of his principate, enjoyed his positive reception by them, and would have been very unwilling to cut himself off from them in some sort of 'Forbidden City'.[197] Though modelled on the contemporary rural or seaside villa, the Golden House Pavilion, like its immediate predecessor in the *Domus Transitoria*,[198] could hardly have acted as a secluded retreat. The noise and heat of the surrounding City will have made it quite unlike Subiaco or Oplontis.[199] It was a working structure, with one main function.

The first half of the year 64 had witnessed Rome's great 'City-Fest' that was Tigellinus' banquet;[200] and, again, it is unlikely that Nero then showed disdain for his public by setting fire to the place. Generally, as with his gymnasium and baths, he built for the people.[201] In line with his popularising inclinations, the Pavilion was not built for personal gratification or exclusivity, whether as a residence or for autocratic administration. Study of its remains has produced no sign of private quarters or official public rooms.[202] In the grand octagonal hall under the cupola there was space for large-scale entertainments.[203] However, here, as throughout the building, emphasis was on dining, by large numbers of people from a range of backgrounds.[204] The main aim of the Pavilion was to make Nero more, not less, accessible. The full Golden House complex, as Nero's *Domus Transitoria* restored and extended, must have allowed generous public access.[205] It is mistaken to see a desire for retreat in Tacitus' report that the Pisonian conspirators had to use the festival of Ceres to get close to Nero because otherwise he 'rarely left home and secluded himself in his palace or gardens'.[206] The conspiracy was probably launched towards the end of 64,[207] early in the construction of the complex, when buildings and parkland were unsuitable for occupation. Tacitus actually suggests that Nero was currently resident in another 'ancillary palace' in the Servilian Gardens, perhaps to the southwest of the Palatine in the direction of

[196] Suet. *Vit.* 11.2; Reitz 2006, 22; above 114.
[197] Cf. Griffin 1984, 139–40; Milnor 2005, 48–9, 301–2; Beste and Hesberg 2013, 329; Kimmerle 2015, 287; *contra* Fini 1994, 56; Chaisemartin 2003, 155–60.
[198] Below 258.   [199] *Contra* Ball 2003, 2; Viscogliosi 2011a, 97.   [200] Below 293, 298–9.
[201] Beste and Hesberg 2013, 328–9; below 331.   [202] Meyboom and Moormann 2013, 17–19, 22.
[203] Meyboom and Moormann 2013, 70.
[204] Meyboom and Moormann 2013, 69; cf. Hesberg 2011, 114, on a similar role as meeting-point for Nero's baths/gymnasium.
[205] Suet. *Ner.* 31.1: *quam primo transitoriam, mox incendio absumptam restitutamque auream nominavit.* Perrin 2013, 236, 238; above 243.
[206] Tac. *Ann.* 15.53.1: *rarus egressus domoque aut hortis clausus.* Fini 1994, 184; Malitz 1999, 81.
[207] Above 201.

Ostia.[208] Tacitus' first observation should therefore be interpreted as showing not that Nero was being stand-offish but rather that he was, with typical enthusiasm, throwing himself into the creation of the complex, alongside his architects, builders and craftsmen: state business which he could undertake with gusto.[209] Here and elsewhere, moreover, Tacitus reveals that he had in no way become a recluse, since he regularly attended the circus and 'frequently' visited Piso's villa at Baiae without his guards.[210] The conspirators' decision to kill him at the *Cerealia* games probably had less to do with any problem in approaching him than with their desire to do the deed in Rome on a public occasion, emulating the tyrannicides of 44 BC and AD 41 and placing themselves close to the levers of power.[211] The Golden House complex, with its twin nodes of the Pavilion and the *Domus Tiberiana*/Neronian palace, was a combined residence, administrative centre, pleasure garden and open-air theatre, enabling the *princeps* to live in due state, receive his ministers and entertain on a huge scale. Though extensive, it was malicious exaggeration to say that it took up the whole City.[212]

We must look beyond the Pavilion. The *Domus Tiberiana*/Neronian palace, 'rising above the Forum' on the Palatine, the eternal centre of Roman sentiment and power,[213] offered generous residential and administrative space and will have been 'the core of the *Domus Aurea* ... the area where Nero ... spent most of his time'.[214] It would always have been superior to the Pavilion for staging grand receptions, even if the latter had been completed.[215] Current thinking locates Nero's famous dining-room with a revolving ceiling here;[216] and it may have been the location of Nero's second collection of sculptures.[217] It was probably the topping-out of this palace, not the Pavilion, that prompted Nero to quip that he was at last beginning to be housed like a human being.[218] But private and public

[208] Tac. *Ann.* 15.55.1. Cizek 1982, 305; Meyboom and Moormann 2013, 18 (quotation); Barrett *et al.* 2016, 203 n. 32; below 256.

[209] Cf. above 56.   [210] Tac. *Ann.* 15.52.1: *crebro*. Bingham 2013, 83–5.

[211] Griffin 1984, 166; Rudich 1993, 100.

[212] Panella 2011b, 160; Perrin 2016, 245. The fine impression of the Golden House complex as whole given by Viscogliosi 2011b, 158 figure 2 indicates how limited was its extent.

[213] Meyboom and Moormann 2012, 132 (quotation).

[214] Ball 2003, 4, 135 (quotation); *contra* Carandini 2011, 145: the *Vestibulum* complex.

[215] Cf. Panella 2011b, 166; Tomei 2011, 123, 135; Meyboom and Moormann 2012, 132–3 (quotation); 2013, 15–17, 69; below 262.

[216] Panella 2011b, 161; Tomei 2011, 131; Viscogliosi 2011b, 158 figure 2; *contra* Beste 2011b, 71; cf. above 119.

[217] Cf. Moormann 2003, 381; Meyboom and Moormann 2013, 70.

[218] Suet. *Ner.* 31.2: *quasi hominem tandem habitare coepisse.*

business could have been done at other locations, for example in the baths attached to the Pavilion (later absorbed into the Baths of Trajan).[219] The parkland in which all were set was no great novelty. The creation of such space by amalgamating existing 'ancillary palaces' and their gardens already owned by the Julio-Claudians can be seen in the *Domus Transitoria*, itself simply an extension of an established pattern of urban development within the old Servian walls beyond which the modern City was fast expanding.[220] The Golden House followed Roman metropolitan precedents, as well as those of Hellenistic royal palaces and Campanian seaside villas, and so was hardly alien.[221] Finally, the Colossus might have become, like the Eiffel Tower, the London Eye or, indeed, the Flavian amphitheatre by which it was later dwarfed, a popular icon of the new-look Rome.[222] The prevailing impression is of a complex that looked outwards as much as inwards. 'As part of his general reconstruction of Rome Nero could have had the idea of embellishing the central area with parks, groves and fountains. Here in his complex of buildings he could hear audiences and do business, while his people would have had access to him and some of his buildings and grounds, such as the restored Temple of Fortune, in wonderful transparent stone. Nero's *comitas* and *popularitas* must be remembered: he was not a man to deprive his public'.[223] Yet, though built with access in mind, the complex cannot have been intended to be permanently wide open. Government needs some privacy, and Nero's grand dinners and spectacles would have required planning, preparation and rehearsal. The *princeps* would also have avoided the risk of being taken totally by surprise, out of character, costume and make-up. Some areas must have been always out of bounds, and others capable of temporary closure,[224] but he will have wanted his 'installations' to be frequent and generous.

Acceptance of the Golden House complex as a combined private/public facility has implications for judgement of its cost. It is impossible to say how much Nero spent on it, but at least some idea of scale may be obtained from a modern comparison. In 2010, an international

---

[219] Meyboom and Moormann 2012, 133; cf. Michel 2015, 70–6.
[220] Moormann 2003, 382–3, 386–7; Meyboom and Moormann 2012, 132; Michel 2015, 64–70; cf. above 242.
[221] Above 252.   [222] Cf. below 275.
[223] Griffin 1984, 139–40 (quotation); cf. Cizek 1982, 155; Shotter 2008, 63, 121; Meyboom and Moormann 2013, 17 (oddly *contra*); Plin. *HN* 36.163; Panella 2011b, 160; Mordine 2013, 115; above 120.
[224] Cf. Perrin 2016, 136.

engineering group estimated that to build a replica of Buckingham Palace, 'the most expensive home in the world', to the highest standards would take three and a half years and cost £320 million. Land costs of £440 million for the 16 ha (40 acre) site would bring the final bill to £760 million.[225] The same structure, set in urban parkland of about the same area (50–80 ha) as the Golden House complex, would therefore cost between £1.7 billion and £2.5 billion. There are factors which will have made the Golden House cheaper.

There is no sign of any large-scale compulsory acquisition of land for the Golden House.[226] Substantial plots, such as the *Domus Tiberiana*/Neronian palace, the temple of Claudius and the Gardens of Maecenas and Lamia, were already in state hands. Though Nero bought additional land, it is likely that prices were relatively low compared to central London, and the more so because much of the Pavilion was constructed on what had been a poorish area.[227] As for costs of construction, labour charges, servile and free, will have been lower than in modern London, and the celebrated Pavilion, an exercise in 'lateral' architecture, had only two storeys, of which the upper was lightly constructed and more of a belvedere than a full floor.[228] It was much smaller overall than Buckingham Palace, with around 240 rooms and corridors as against 19 state rooms, 78 bathrooms, 52 principal bedrooms and 775 separate areas including hallways and staircases.[229] A significant part of the complex's decoration will have been at a bargain price since Nero acquired many valuable works of art from the provinces, presumably *gratis* or at a substantial discount.[230] A further consideration is that there are indications that the *Domus Aurea* was built with a view to economy. Throughout there was careful extraction of reusable materials (e.g. columns, cornices, marble and statuary) from fire-damaged buildings; and not all remaining débris was taken from the City, as Tacitus implies, with some consolidated on site to form foundation terraces.[231] The western wing of the Pavilion has been interpreted as the Esquiline terminal

---

[225] atkinsglobal.   [226] Perrin 2016, 234–5; below 347.

[227] Griffin 1984, 133; cf. Moormann 2003, 382; 385–6 (a useful list of *horti* in possession of the state); Meyboom and Moormann 2012, 132–3; 2013, 17; Perrin 2016, 232, 238, 241.

[228] Ball 2003, 10–11; Viscogliosi 2011a, 99 (quotation); Meyboom and Moormann 2013, 18–19, 70–1.

[229] The lower figure comes from Meyboom and Moormann 2012, 131; the higher from the assumption that the extant structure is *c.* 60 per cent of the whole, but see below 258.

[230] Above 231–2; Waldherr 2005, 238. Grant (1970, 179–80) is sure that Nero's agents paid for what they took, though against this is Chaisemartin's (2003, 159) observation that the Flavians returned some works of art to their rightful owners.

[231] Tac. *Ann.* 15.43.4. Panella 2011a, 86.

of the *Domus Transitoria*, itself constructed over demolished buildings but designed to make the best use of their remains. Damaged but not destroyed by the Fire, it was repaired and skilfully integrated into the larger new structure.[232] This itself is now thought by many to have been less extensive than previously thought, with its new eastern wing consisting only of the central Octagonal Suite, standing between two pentagonal courts.[233] This reduces the length of the whole from *c.* 370 to *c.* 280 m. Further efforts to avoid expenditure have been detected in, for example, the reuse of existing structures in new building on the Palatine,[234] and in the creation of the ornamental lake: not excavated in depth in an existing marsh but formed simply by leaving a space, no more than 4 m (13 feet) deep, in compacted fire débris.[235] On the other hand, consolidation and sophisticated terracing still cost money;[236] and the Pavilion was embellished with expensive marbles, gold, precious stones and, probably, rare woods and ivory on a scale far more lavish than that seen in Buckingham Palace.[237] There was also the expense of restoring and enhancing the *Domus Tiberiana*/Neronian palace, building the forecourt and the baths next to the Pavilion, landscaping the whole site etc. One can only guess, but let us assume that the cost of the Golden House fell near the middle of the proposed range of £1.7–2.5 billion: for the sake of arithmetical convenience, around £2 billion at 2010 prices.

How does this translate into Roman money? We may begin by giving £2 billion a gold-value, first for 2010, then for a period when gold coins were still in circulation in the UK, and finally for early imperial Rome. At the 2010 average price of £188 per sovereign, £2 billion is the equivalent of 10,638,298 gold sovereigns. The 1870 edition of William Smith's *Smaller Latin Dictionary* values an *aureus* at 18s 5d, i.e. 0.92 of a Victorian sovereign.[238] Thus 10,638,298 sovereigns would be equivalent to 11,563,367 *aurei*, or HS 1,156,336,700, making the Golden House complex cost in the region of HS 1.2 billion. But this needs adjustment, since it is the estimated cost of the complex as a whole which, as touched upon, was never taken to completion. Many of the Pavilion's rooms were

[232] Ball 2003, 8, 10–11, 95–6, 130, 156–7. 160–1, 182, 220. *Contra* Beste 2011b, 172; Meyboom and Moormann 2013, 20.
[233] E.g. Ball 2003, 10, 13–14; Beste 2011b, 170 figure 1; Carandini 2011, 137 figure 1; Viscogliosi 2011b, 157 figures 1–3. *Contra* Hesberg 2011, 109 figure 2; Meyboom and Moormann 2013, 19.
[234] Tomei 2011, 125.   [235] Ball 2003, 9; Panella 2011a, 90; 2011b, 166–7.
[236] Ball 2003, 6; Panella 2011a, 90–1.
[237] Champlin 2003, 131; Meyboom and Moormann 2013, 28–9; cf. below 259.
[238] This is consistent with Henderson 1905, 281 (17s 6d/£0.875), 481.

fully finished, but others were left undecorated and, very oddly given its principal function, it lacked latrines and kitchens.[239] Galba stopped work on the Golden House; Otho granted it HS 50 million; but Vitellius and his wife complained that it was still not luxurious enough, a remark surely to do with a still unfinished *Domus Tiberiana*/Neronian palace, given that the Pavilion was 'not for living in'.[240] Nero's expenditure on the place was therefore probably less than HS 1.2 billion: say (assuming that it would have cost twice Otho's HS 50 million to bring it fully up to scratch), HS 1.1 billion. Such expenditure would be impossible for a private individual. Cicero spent HS 3.5 million (0.0035 billion) on his Palatine house in the mid-first century BC;[241] even in today's much richer world, the 2010 report notes that the most expensive private residential property to date was the Villa Leopolda, on the Côte d'Azur, built for a Russian oil-billionaire at a cost of £390 million – the equivalent of *c.* HS 0.25 billion.

However, as touched on above, the Golden House complex, particularly the Pavilion, was far more than a private dwelling.[242] The homes of Roman aristocrats were always used for public business. *Principes* followed suit, albeit on a much greater scale.[243] It is this which explains the Palatine complex's becoming a seat of imperial government.[244] With regard to the wider Golden House complex, hybrid use may be assumed for both the *Domus Tiberiana*/Neronian palace and even the Pavilion which, though built for private banquets,[245] must also have encouraged public business. Marble revetments were conventionally a feature of public, not private structures. The public areas of certain private houses were, however, indicated by the use of marble finishes.[246] This occurs on a grand scale in the Pavilion, where Meyboom and Moormann have identified a 'hier-archy' of rooms in graded levels of decoration, in particular, different proportions of marble wall-panelling, the most superior being in the central octagon.[247] Such luxury implies very important guests who, brought together in such quasi-public surroundings, were bound to discuss public as well as private business. It may have been public activity more suitable for the Palatine complex being conducted within a nominally

[239] Meyboom and Moormann 2012, 133–4; 2013, 20, 69.
[240] Suet. *Otho* 7.1; Cass. Dio 65.4.1–2. Panella 2011b, 168; Lorenz 2013, 374; Meyboom and Moormann 2012, 133 (quotation); 2013, 1.
[241] Cic. *Fam.* 4 (V. 6).2. Milnor 2005, 81.   [242] Above 254.
[243] Milnor 2005, 18, 65–6, 72; Mordine 2013, 115.   [244] Cf. Winterling 2007, 71–4.
[245] Meyboom and Moormann 2013, 69–70.
[246] Moormann 2003, 388; Beste and Hesberg 2013, 328–9; Meyboom and Moormann 2012, 133; Meyboom and Moormann 2013, 69.
[247] Meyboom and Moormann 2013, 70–3.

private building – a 'retreat designed for cultivated leisure'[248] – which exposed the Pavilion to the charge of being the home of a 'tyrant' and, worse, of a 'king'.[249] The Golden House complex was not a worthless product of Nero's self-indulgence and so, like many of his supposed private extravagances,[250] had a legitimate claim on state funding at a level far beyond the means of a private individual. Even so, *c.* HS 1.1 billion may seem unaffordable given that the Roman administration's annual tax income was only around HS 1 billion.[251] However, Pliny I reports that Claudius' two aqueducts cost HS 0.35 billion;[252] and the cost of the Baths of Caracalla has been put at around HS 0.6 billion.[253] The Golden House, though expensive, still falls on the same financial spectrum.[254] Furthermore, as we shall see, the Roman state had ways of meeting current account deficits.[255] Expenditure of HS 1.1 billion, spread over several years, would have been heavy but not back-breaking. It could be managed, as something similar must have been managed later in the building of Hadrian's Tivoli.[256]

HS 1.1 billion is, indeed, only a fraction of what was spent on war during Nero's principate, in Armenia (the minimum amount of which I put at HS 4 billion[257]), in Britain and in Judaea. If provincials suffered severe fiscal pressure – which is questionable[258] – it was surely as a result of this, not the Golden House. 'It seems doubtful … that Nero's building policy in itself was financially ruinous'.[259] However, such a sum would have attracted attention even if it had been for an undeniably utilitarian project, and the feeling that the *princeps* had spent too much on the Golden House complex for his own benefit appears to have provoked outrage, but from whom and how? There are no signs of popular hatred of Nero from 64, allowing probably Galba and certainly Otho and Vitellius to occupy the complex in 68–69.[260] Most people were prepared to acquit Nero of arson and tolerate his building programme. With regard to the poor, Griffin proposes that this was because the programme provided paid

---

[248] Mratschek 2013, 51–2.   [249] Meyboom and Moormann 2013, 74–6; below 262.
[250] Below 315.   [251] Below 326.   [252] Plin. *HN* 36.122; Osgood 2011, 174.
[253] Jongman 2007, 597, 611.
[254] Though the greater wealth of the industrial world is evident in the greater costs of the largest current public building projects, even these may be seen as falling on this spectrum. The BBC radio programme 'More or Less' of 22 April 2016 listed these as the Hinckley C Nuclear Power Station: £18 billion; the renovated Grand Mosque, Mecca: £16 billion; Hong Kong airport: £29 billion; the International Space Station: £80 billion. Expressed in 2010 values (*c.* 0.825 of those of 2016) and converted to the first-century Roman unit of account, they amount to HS 8.9 billion, HS 7.6 billion, HS 13.8 billion and HS 38.2 billion respectively.
[255] Below 348.   [256] Cf. Giardina 2011, 18.   [257] Below 334.   [258] Below 347.
[259] Bradley 1978a, 171; cf. below 314–15.   [260] Giardina 2011, 19; above 259.

work; Perrin notes that, as tenants, these would not have suffered loss of rental income due to the Fire or state acquisition of land.[261] Furthermore, though they had lost their homes, they may have found shelter on the projected parkland, which was probably never laid out in full, still less allowed to reach any stage of maturity.[262] The better-off may have felt gratitude to Nero for paying for the building of the new design of porticoes (for use as firefighting platforms), for the clearing and making good of sites, and for rewarding those who rebuilt quickly.[263]

Just before his death Nero thought of appealing over the heads of a treacherous Establishment to the *plebs*.[264] Suetonius presents the notion as delusional, and adds that Nero rejected it because he feared he would be killed before he could make his case. However, as we shall see, other schemes to rescue the *princeps* at this time merit attention, and it could well be that the idea was founded on Nero's continuing popularity with the people, demonstrated by his favourable reception on his return from Greece and by the cultivation of his memory after his death.[265] This was not a *princeps* who had fallen out of popular favour through the building of a palace. This leaves the upper classes as the most likely source of moral outrage over the Golden House complex. Some must – as always – have simply accepted the project; and some, for example the landowners who provided the wood, bricks, tiles etc. necessary for new construction in Rome, must have welcomed it as a means of lining their pockets.[266] Reasonable criticism might have been that the Pavilion, with an area of marble revetments calculated at over 1 ha (2.5 acres),[267] was far too self-indulgent; and that the Colossus, whoever it was meant to represent,[268] was a potential eyesore. An additional justifiable complaint may have been that, despite Nero's initial zeal, he did not give enough attention to the project, in particular the Pavilion. Nero left Italy in autumn 66 and did not return until December 67. He landed at Naples and journeyed to Rome to celebrate his 'triumph'; but his triumphal route did not take in the Golden House, and he then returned to Naples.[269] It would not be out of character if, after the shock of the Pisonian conspiracy in 65 and the death of Poppaea and her unborn child in 66, Nero lost his initial enthusiasm for the building and turned to embellishing the Theatre of Pompey, repairing

---

[261] Griffin 1984, 133; Perrin 2016, 241, 246.   [262] Cf. Meyboom and Moormann 2013, 17.
[263] Tac. *Ann.* 15.43.2–4, Suet. *Ner.* 16.1. Cf. above 124.   [264] Suet. *Ner.* 47.2
[265] Cf. below 411; Yavetz 1969, 123–9; Rudich 1993, 40.
[266] Levi 1949, 201; Moormann 2003, 377; Quenemoen 2014, 66.
[267] Meyboom and Moormann 2012, 141; 2013, 74.   [268] Below 274.
[269] Above 226; below 383–4, 389.

the Circus Maximus and restoring the *Domus Tiberiana*/Neronian palace for the reception of Tiridates.[270] The Pavilion's lack of latrines and kitchens, already noted, suggests later absence of oversight. Inattention to the Pavilion may have added to its expense. The Pavilion was built at speed, down to June 68, with no decline in the quality of its materials or workmanship.[271] Lax supervision may, after the economy of its architects,[272] have encouraged its decorators to excess. However, there will have been an influential minority of aristocrats whose opposition to the project went beyond criticism to anger: perhaps at the way that Nero had taken over most of the remaining private houses on the Palatine,[273] but probably most of all at his flouting of both architectural and political tradition in building something that in their eyes rendered visible 'a more monarchical conception of the Principate'.[274] Related to this would have been the *princeps*' apparent intention to institutionalise popular feasting in the Pavilion, which smacked of demagogy.[275] This would have been mistaken: Nero had no great ideological designs:[276] he did not create the Pavilion as an instrument of demagogy or monarchy, or to raise himself above senators by outspending them.[277] A new palace complex was essential, but Nero's fall made his creation a hostage to fortune.

Later Flavian 'spin' could combine reasonable criticism and minority outrage.[278] Had Nero and the Julio-Claudian dynasty survived, the Golden House might have been seen as 'nothing prodigal', and praised not abused.[279] Even under Otho or Vitellius it might have enjoyed a better fate. The Flavians, however, sought to sell Nero 'the tyrant'. The upper classes were relatively easy to convince by allowing them to adopt the outrage of the minority, and so giving them an excuse for both tolerating and destroying the last of the Julio-Claudians. The people of Rome were a harder nut to crack, but Vespasian met the challenge. The Golden House complex had promised entertainment on a grand scale, but in a somewhat unusual – Hellenic, 'arty' – fashion; and, since it was never finished, its buildings and parkland could not be remembered as the venue of great events. The Flavian amphitheatre, on the other hand, built over its lake, promised and quickly delivered good, solid, old-fashioned Roman spectacle. Further, in condemning the *Domus Aurea*, it appears that the Flavians emphasised its possession of what the *Domus Transitoria* never

[270] Cf. Moormann 2003, 378.   [271] Meyboom and Moormann 2013, 20–1.   [272] Above 257.
[273] Cf. above 250.   [274] Griffin 1984, 133; cf. Michel 2015, 58; Perrin 2016, 237, 245, 241.
[275] Cf. below 309.   [276] Below 293.
[277] Holland 2000, 198; Meyboom and Moormann 2013, 17 n. 48 (*contra* Perrin).
[278] Elsner 1994, 118.   [279] Elsner 1994, 123.

had: great extent and clear cohesion, both made possible by the Fire. Even if people accepted that Nero had not caused the Fire, and that most additional land had not been gained by confiscation or compulsory purchase,[280] the complex had an ill-omened past which could be manipulated against Nero's memory. It was all this that, perhaps based on an architect's model of the finished structure that included the Gardens of Maecenas,[281] allowed the projection into popular imagination of Nero's palace as fully completed, sprawling, exclusive and threatening: a tyrant's lair, the ostentatious dwelling of a 'cruel king' who selfishly put private indulgence before the public good, and so, like that of its creator and his line, fully deserving its annihilation.[282] Vespasian could therefore win over the people by promoting himself as the simple soldier, the agent of the *plebs*, restoring to them 'what they should have by right' and owe to no master.[283] The accusation was taken up by the source tradition, allowing subsequent generations, those of Tacitus, Suetonius and Dio, who had never set eyes on the complex,[284] to embroider the tale in its telling. Thus Suetonius described the relatively modest and shallow ornamental lake (similar to the Pecile at Hadrian's Tivoli) as some sort of inland sea.[285] The Golden House estate was made to appear unnatural and so immoral, and, as a representation of the world in miniature, as 'a grand symbol of how Nero wished to treat the entire Empire, as an extension of his personal space, an enormous playground in which he might indulge his egomania and idiosyncratic whims'.[286]

---

[280] Above 257.   [281] Cf. Beste and Hesberg 2013, 324; below 275.

[282] Martial, *Spect.* 2: *ferus rex*. Cf. Henderson 1905, 243 and n. 2 (on the legendary 'sylvan charms' of the Golden House): 'The rapid growth of the "silvae" is perplexing. Perhaps the popular imagination grew as fast'; Griffin 1984, 137–9; Elsner 1994, 122–3.

[283] Griffin 1984, 207 (quotation); Meyboom and Moormann 2012, 133.

[284] Meyboom and Moormann 2013, 15.

[285] Suet. *Ner.* 31.1: *maris instar*. Meyboom and Moormann 2013, 16; above 258.

[286] Milnor 2005, 302.

CHAPTER 11

Divinity, Madness, Acting, Ideology, Burn-Out

11.1 Divinity

11.1.1 Nero-Apollo?

One aspect of Nero 'the monster' closely related to the Fire and the Golden House is Nero 'the god'. Many have proposed that he was driven to build his *Domus Aurea* by his growing conviction that he was divine. This is in turn related to the common belief that he suffered from 'imperial madness': he was insane.[1] In support of this much has been made of the 'solar imagery' of the complex. Nero was clearly very taken with Apollo, the divine master-musician and charioteer, closely associated with the sun. From 59 he made frequent reference to the god. The *Augustiani* hailed him as Apollo; and at the same time, he declared his voice to be 'celestial', and expected sacrifices to be offered for its good. From 62, he issued a coin-type which depicted him as Apollo, singing to the lyre. In 64, his acting the charioteer on the occasion of the punishment of Christians suggests that he was presenting himself as Apollo. Near the end, in his 'triumph', he dedicated his success to Apollo, not Capitoline Jupiter.[2] From this it is not difficult to see the Pavilion as the residence of Nero-Apollo, a god on earth and the founder of a new solar monarchy. Gilded within and without by gold and by the southern sun, and overlooked by an equally glittering,

---

[1] Bergmann 2013, 353; cf. Winterling 2007, 8; above 8.
[2] *Augustiani*: Tac. *Ann.* 14.14.2, 15. 8–9; Cass. Dio 61.20.4; Champlin 2003, 113; above 231, below 302. Voice: Tac. *Ann.* 14.15.9, 16.22.1; Suet. *Ner.* 21.1; cf. Cass. Dio 62.26.3. Coins: *RIC* 1² Nero nos. 73–82, 121–3, 205–12 [Rome mint 62–68], 380–1, 384–5; 414–17, 451–5 [Lyon mint 64–67]; Bradley 1978a, 151–2; Griffin 1984, pl. 31; Champlin 2003, 117. Christians: Champlin 2003, 125. Triumph: Champlin 2003, 118. Generally: Bradley 1978a, 131; Griffin 1984, 163; Champlin 2003, 112–17, 143–4; below 382.

radiate-crowned, colossal statue of Nero as Helios-Apollo, it celebrated the start of a new Golden Age.[3]

Such thinking was first formulated by L'Orange in 1942. It immediately attracted strong criticism,[4] but has persisted and evolved and continues to attract support.[5] The Golden House as the residence of Nero-Apollo is particularly championed by Cizek, who sees Nero's Apollinism as 'extolling royal virtue and solar theocracy'.[6] The 'Apolline' interpretation appears to be confirmed by Greek honouring of Nero as the 'new Helios'. Solar theocracy has likewise been related to Parthian thinking. Thus, in 66, Tiridates initiated Nero into the cult of Mithras, and the 'Golden Day' of his double coronation by Nero, at sunrise in the Forum and then in the newly gilded Theatre of Pompey,[7] recalled the crowning of Mithras by the Unconquered Sun.[8] A variation of this is to link the Golden House with Nero's worship of the Dea Syria, and see it as an exclusive, eastern-style 'paradise', befitting his status as a despot.[9] Nero 'the divine' likewise explains his wish to rename the Peloponnese ('the island of Pelops') as Neronosnesus ('the island of Nero') and Rome ('the city of Romulus') as Neropolis (the city of Nero').[10] The 'authentic note of megalomania' has also been identified in Nero's proclamation of the freedom of Greece, made in Corinth at the end of November 67,[11] a grand gesture that elevated him far above his puny subjects and encouraged them to exalt him as quasi-divine. As is usual with Nero, further reflection produces less dramatic conclusions.

---

[3] Ps.-Sen. *Oct.* 624–5; Plin. *HN* 33.54; Mart. *Spect.* 2.3. Champlin 2003, 131 (orientation). Bradley 1978a, 173, 179; Griffin 1984,137. Resplendent roofs were probably very prominent in low-rise cities, and Romans always credited them with great powers to impress: cf., for example, Symmachus (*Orat.* 2.13) on the red roofs of Valentinian I's trans-Rhine bases which, according to him, had a huge effect on barbarous *Germani*. Sen. *Ep.* 115.13–14 ('The Sun-god's palace, set with pillars tall, and flashing bright with gold') has been seen as criticism of the Pavilion, but this is disputed by Rimell (2015, 132–3), and must anyway have been written before the building had been properly begun; cf. Meyboom and Moormann 2013, 28–9. For extant gilding in the remains of the *Domus Tiberiana*/Neronian palace see Tomei 2011, 124.

[4] E.g. Charlesworth 1950, 71.   [5] E.g. Tomei 2011, 131.

[6] Cizek 1982, 88: 'il exalte la vertu royale et la théocratie solaire'; 130.   [7] Below 266.

[8] 'Golden day': Cass. Dio 62.6.1; Champlin 2003, 126–7. Mithraism: Cass. Dio 62.5.2; Bradley 1978a, 90, 175; Cizek 1982, 146; Griffin 1984, 216.

[9] Bradley 1978a, 90; Chaisemartin 2003, 159; Waldherr 2005, 224.
    Bergmann 2013, 353, and Beste and Hesberg 2013, 326–7, give useful outlines of these, and the following, interpretations. For Nero's lack of ideology see below 293.

[10] New Helios: Bradley 1978a, 146; Griffin 1984, 216 and n. 46; Champlin 2003, 117. Peloponnese: Hohl 1918, 389 (citing *ILS* 8794, in which Nero refers to 'the former' (*heōs nun*) Peloponnese); Rome: Tac. *Ann.* 15.40.3; Suet. *Ner.* 55; Chaisemartin 2003, 160. Cf. below 271.

[11] Warmington 1969, 118; date: below 383.

We should be wary of reading ideology into or out of the Golden House complex.[12] We know very little of the layout and appearance of the *Domus Tiberiana*/Neronian palace, but the Pavilion was clearly a place for feasting: no residence for man or god. There was no grand entrance, no internal processional way or imposing staircase to a throne-room,[13] no space for large-scale spectacles. Communication between the Octagonal Suite and the rest was, indeed, remarkably restricted.[14] In short, there was no place for a sun-king to sit in dazzling state. In this respect it is significant that the new Pavilion complex was on no ceremonial route linking it to the rest of the City so it played no central role in the reception of Tiridates or Nero's 'triumph'.[15] As for Apollo, the decoration of the Pavilion contains no Apolline or solar imagery, or any ideological representation of power.[16] If the Golden House complex, including the Pavilion and the Colossus, had been intended to convey a politico-religious message, one might expect some or all of its elements to have appeared on the new 'reform' coinage, from 64, but this is not the case. Buildings are shown, but these are new, or newly restored, traditional constructions elsewhere.[17] As for eastern influence, Nero eventually turned against the Dea Syria, even urinating on her image,[18] and the Golden House complex was conceived and begun a good two years before Tiridates' arrival in Rome.[19] Whatever Tiridates may have believed, or later related,[20] his coronation is more likely to have been decoratively golden than profoundly Mithraic.[21] There were practical reasons for the 'goldenness' of the Golden Day. Again, in mid-66 it is likely that the centre of Rome was still a building site,[22] but Tiridates' visit was too important to postpone. He could be received in some rooms of the *Domus Tiberiana*/Neronian palace, but nothing there was suitable for the grandest events. These were therefore scheduled for venues, such as the Theatre of Pompey, which had survived the Fire but which needed to be extensively restored, with much use of gold, for the purpose.

---

[12] Above 254; cf. below 358.
[13] Cf. Ball 2003, 10–11, 141, 139 and figure 44 on the impressive, but severely functional, western staircase.
[14] Viscogliosi 2011a, 99; Meyboom and Moormann 2013, 78–9.   [15] Above 255; below 384.
[16] Charlesworth 1950, 71; Meyboom and Moormann 2013, 16.
[17] Moormann 2003, 379–80; Meyboom and Moormann 2013, 14.   [18] Suet. *Ner.* 56.
[19] Meyboom and Moormann 2013, 16.   [20] Charlesworth 1950, 72.
[21] Bradley 1978a, 91, 289–90; Griffin 1984, 216–7.   [22] Cf. above 249.

11.1.2 Golden Age?

Meyboom and Moormann downplay Nero-Apollo and make more of the Golden House as advertising the beginning of a new Golden Age, harking back to mythological and Augustan precedents.[23] Similarly, Mratschek proposes that on the Golden Day Nero emphasised 'the radiance of the sun' in order to show predictions fulfilled: the Golden Age forecast at the beginning of his principate by poets inspired by Apollo was now at hand.[24]

This returns us to the beginning of Nero's principate.[25] In Julio-Claudian Rome, poetry, its patronage and production, had become a respectable aristocratic activity, as demonstrated by the appeal of the anonymous author of the *Laus Pisonis* to his patron, 'Calpurnius Piso', usually taken to be the Piso of the conspiracy.[26] From the equally anonymous author of the *Carmina Einsidlensia* and from Calpurnius Siculus in his 'Eclogues', however, it appears that earlier, under Claudius, poetry had found no *princeps*-patron.[27] At the start of his principate, Nero demonstrated his interest in the genre by giving regular public recitations.[28] Though the works he read were not necessarily his own,[29] this would have marked him out as a potential sponsor, stimulating ambitious poets to urge powerful backers to obtain his support for them.[30] The poets' 'Age of Peace' fits this very early period, when war in Armenia was threatening but had not yet broken out.[31] Anticipation of a new *princeps*-patron may well, however, have occurred even before Claudius' death. While Calpurnius Siculus' 'prophecy' of Nero's accession, set in the early autumn of 54,[32] would have been treasonable if published before 13 October, it has an immediacy which suggests that such thinking was current and, when the moment came, ready to be expressed. Hopes of Nero as the super-patron led to excess. He was extolled as the equal of Homer and the superior of Virgil,[33] and, in looks and talent, as the equal companion and even the superior of Apollo: indeed, as a

---

[23] Meyboom and Moormann 2012, 133; 2013, 14–16. Cf. Cizek 1982, 310–11; Bradley 1978a, 175–6; Griffin 1984, 216; Mratschek 2013, 51.

[24] Mratschek 2013, 53.   [25] Above 16–17.

[26] *Laus Pis.* 209–61. Cf. Pausch 2013, 48, 63; below 373.

[27] Stover's proposed redating of both to the later fourth century (above 17 n. 83) has much to commend it. Yet, if correct, these poets possessed hugely exceptional skills in escaping the culture of their age since, as Dr Lütkenhaus observes (in personal communication), their works give a totally convincing impression of an early imperial *princeps* operating in an early imperial society.

[28] Suet. *Ner.* 10.2.   [29] Pausch 2013, 48 and n. 14.

[30] Cf. Calp. *Ecl.* 4.29–49, 84–9, 152–9; above 79.

[31] E.g. *Carm. Einsid.* 2.15–38; cf. above 131, 135.   [32] Calp. *Ecl.* 1.1, 33–88.

[33] *Carm. Einsid.* 1.43–49.

'new Apollo', divine.[34] Often taken as further evidence for the early development of an ideological projection of Nero as Apollo,[35] this is better understood as poetic licence. For 'Nero-Apollo' was not part of contemporary official thinking.[36] The earliest coin-types, though novel in featuring Agrippina as much as Nero, carried a conservative message: that what was happening was a return to the Julian normality, to the 'dream succession'. It promised continuity, not ideological change.[37] Calpurnius Siculus, indeed, appears to refer to Nero's 'Augustan' accession speech.[38] The same message may have underlain Nero's pre-accession plea for tax exemptions for Troy, in which he enlarged upon the history of the place as the ancestral home of Aeneas and the Julian clan, also picked up by Calpurnius Siculus.[39] The significance of the Troy story perhaps, indeed, showed itself even earlier, in Agrippina's pushing Nero into a leading role in the 'Troy battle' of the Secular Games of 47.[40] Increasing evocation of the Aeneas legend perhaps stimulated the revived interest in Troy and Virgil that is a feature of Neronian literature.[41] The concept, found in the *Carmina Einsidlensia*, that the fall of Troy was a price worth paying for the present happy age,[42] could have emerged from this programme and inspired Lucan's similar justification of the bloody civil wars of the later first century BC: that their fruit was the principate of Nero.[43]

'Nero-Apollo' was not part of official policy in 54–55 and should be treated as a rhetorical turn of phrase. In the Greco-Roman religious tradition there was much less of a distinction between mortal and divine than in the Abrahamic, and so less sensitivity to blasphemy.[44] In Calpurnius Siculus, an attractive but incompetent singer can jokingly be declared 'worthy of the name "Apollo", if only he did not sing'.[45] More positively, a countryman glimpsing Nero in Rome can report, 'I thought that in one face the looks of Mars and Apollo were combined'.[46] Likewise, the 'Piso' of the *Laus Pisonis* is praised for his talent as a lyre player with the words 'well may we believe that you learned under Phoebus' tuition'.[47] Rather more

---

[34] E.g. *Carm. Einsid.* 1.36, 2.38: *tuus iam regnat Apollo.* Cf. Reitz 2006, 115 (on Calp. *Ecl.* 4's praise of Nero as a prince of peace): 'Seine Nähe zu den olympischen Göttern und das beinahe Verschmelzung seiner Person mit Phoebus Apollo wird besonders breit ausgemahlt'.

[35] E.g. Cizek 1982, 88–9.   [36] *Contra* Meier 2008, 587; cf. Bergmann 2013, 342–3.

[37] Cf. above 16.   [38] Calp. *Ecl.* 1.54–72: *afflictum aevum*; above 17.

[39] Tac. *Ann.* 12.58.1; Calp. *Ecl.* 1.44–5.   [40] Tac. *Ann.* 11.11.5; cf. Malitz 1999, 5–6.

[41] Above 79, 111–12.   [42] *Carm. Einsid.* 1.37–1.41.

[43] Luc. 1.33–46: *quod tibi res acta est.* Cf. above 108.   [44] Winterling 2007, 140.

[45] Calp. *Ecl.* 6.14–16: *qui posset dici, si non cantaret, Apollo.*

[46] Calp. *Ecl.* 7.83–4: *in uno et Martis vultus et Apollinis.*

[47] *Laus Pis.* 166–8: *te credibile est Phoebo didicisse magistro.*

seriously, panegyrists were committed to treating *principes* as divine. They must declare that a *princeps* was 'good', with the implication that he was, and would continue to be, worthy of deification on death. Since his deification was, therefore, inevitable, the gods must already be preparing to receive him. This makes a living *princeps* divine, so why not address him as such: 'you are a god!'?[48] Even Pliny II, after congratulating Trajan for rejecting excessive praise, has him rivalling the gods in power, and 'later still, Trajan has all but metamorphosed into Jupiter himself'.[49] An incumbent *princeps* is 'very god';[50] and, by extension, where he lives can be characterised as divine: in Nero's case, the 'inner shrine of the Palatine Phoebus'.[51] This was the language of rhetoric, 'comparative and panegyric', not any sincere perception of divinity, to which educated people, including *principes*, cannot have given much literal credence, and which Seneca cruelly satirised in his *Apocolocyntosis*.[52] Once started, however, the concept had an unstoppable momentum: if Nero is destined for divinity, his deceased infant daughter must, even before his own death, be considered divine.[53]

In addition, however, though the 'Golden Age' was basically an intellectual conceit, Nero's new principate may well have generated sentiments which made the welcoming of an 'Age of Apollo' unusually appropriate. The civil wars that brought about the Principate were still in the public consciousness. Galba, Nero's successor, whose grandfather's generation will have been born around 60 BC, will in his youth have talked to men who had witnessed them first hand.[54] Tacitus imagines Romans remembering their horrors in 69.[55] The Principate was relatively new. No-one could have known that it would last for centuries, and be robust enough to survive many series of savage civil wars.[56] After the assassination of Gaius, disastrous contention between rival claimants for power had been averted by the accession of Claudius. However, the supporters of continuity and peace had been lucky to be able to find such a replacement at short notice; and even Claudius was an improbable and irregular *princeps*:[57] He was a stop-gap, and as he grew older people will have feared that disorder might

---

[48] Calp. *Ecl.* 4.144: *es enim deus*; cf. Luc. 1.63: *sed mihi iam numen* ('to me you are already divine').
[49] Plin. *Pan.* 4.1–4, 80.3–5; Bartsch 1994, 163.
[50] Calp. *Ecl.* 1.46–7; 1.84–8; 4.144; 4.*165*: *deus ipse* etc; cf. 4.84: *praesens numen*; 7.6: *iuvenis deus*; 7.76: *venerandum . . . numen*.
[51] Calp. *Ecl.* 4.152–9: *sacra Palatina penetralia . . . Phoebi*.
[52] Henderson 2013, 179; Bergmann 2013, 341–2 (quotation); above 103. Cf. Winterling 2007, 143; Nichols 2013, 266; *contra* Holland 2000, 143–6.
[53] Tac. *Ann.* 15.23.4.   [54] Below 395.   [55] Tac. *Hist.* 1.50.   [56] Cf. above 253.
[57] Osgood 2011, 21–2, 30, 30–1.

threaten again. Agrippina's clever political footwork avoided all this, and Calpurnius Siculus' 'prophecy' of change that would not result in civil war exudes relief.[58]

'Golden Age' imagery was a feature of the very start of Nero's principate, before his main display of enthusiasm for Apollo, his conception of a new palace complex and his reception of Tiridates. It was a poetical conceit that fitted the politics of the day, not a permanent ideological prop, and explains neither the Golden House nor the Golden Day.

11.1.3   Hellenistic Kingship?

Another ideological/religious explanation for Nero's Apollinism and creation of the Golden House is that he aimed to establish a full, Hellenistic, monarchy. Realising that he had 'absolute power' over the Empire, he sought to establish and display it on the model of recent Greek god-kings: 'there was more ideology behind Nero's pretensions and projects than mere megalomania'.[59] Nero sought to found a personal autocracy on a new form of *auctoritas*, derived not from service to the state but from a unique intimate association (*comitatus*) with Apollo, who would then bless and legitimise his rule.[60] A secular version of this is that Nero never believed that he was Apollo or close to Apollo, and may even have doubted the existence of this god. Rather, like Gaius, who had also worn Apolline costume without regarding himself as divine, he acted Apollo to advance his plans for a new style of government: no longer the Principate, but outright autocracy. This was a matter of ideology, not of theology, and 'however monstrous or bizarre or even irrational his behavior might appear, there was a purpose to it'.[61] According to Champlin, Nero's move towards Apolline autocracy began on the death of Agrippina, and was well under way by 60.[62] It ran at full speed from 64,[63] when we can see Nero developing his Apolline role in his reaction to (and possibly even in his setting of) the Great Fire of 64;[64] in his building of the Golden House, 'the house of the Sun';[65] in his reception of Tiridates, in 66;[66] and in, in 67, the 'triumph' celebrating his artistic successes in Greece.[67] To the same

---

[58] Calp. *Ecl.* 1.49–51, 78, 83–8; cf. Reitz 2006, 114; above 111.
[59] Meyboom and Moormann 2012, 131, 133 (quotation), 142 (quotation).
[60] Warmington 1969, 118; cf. Levi 1958, 197, Bradley 1978a, 289; Griffin 1984, 218–19; above 217.
[61] Champlin 2003, 132–3, 135, 236–7 (quotation); cf. Bergmann 2013, 346–7.
[62] Champlin 2003, 113–15.   [63] Champlin 2003, 113–15.
[64] Champlin 2003, 121–6, 186–91; cf. above 234.   [65] Champlin 2003, 127–32.
[66] Champlin 2003, 117–18.   [67] Champlin 2003, 117–18.

end, from around 66 we see him experimenting with the roles of Hercules, Romulus, Camillus, Mark Antony, Augustus and, above all, Periander of Corinth.[68] This reflected 'a daring new conception of Roman power' as Nero, not like a god but like a hero of legend, 'raised himself above the level of ordinary action and responsibility' to become 'a great tyrant'.[69] Both '*comitatus*' explanations, religious and secular, are attractive, because they would be an early indication of where the politics and ideology of the Empire were headed: from the Principate to the Dominate and, in the early fourth century, to the *comitatus* of Constantine I with Christ.[70] They break down, however, because, as will be argued below, Nero displayed no significant ideological leanings towards Hellenistic kingship.[71] Furthermore, if Nero was resolved to be a secular Apolline sun-king, why experiment with other semi-divine or even mortal roles? There is no mention of his emulating Periander in the sources;[72] and though Periander's military reputation would have appealed to a traditional Roman, it would have been less attractive to Nero, whose interests were artistic and who craved public acclaim and affection, not fear.

The hunt for signs of *principes* inclining to towards Hellenistic monarchy is, in fact, a sterile field of Julio-Claudian studies. Gaius, infinitely more politically aware than Nero, has frequently been accused of this, with no justification.[73] Holland sees Nero's embalming of Poppaea's body as indicating the extent of his adoption of Ptolemaic monarchy, but this overlooks his great love for his wife: he simply did not wish to lose her to the flames.[74] If Nero's mind had been moving in this direction he would have planned a grand tomb for them both. A *princeps*' awesome powers caused some, particularly in the eastern provinces, accustomed to royal ideology, to regard him as divine. This explains Nero the 'new Helios' and 'the island of Nero', etc.[75] Elements of eastern cult practice had spread westwards and resulted in the bestowal of divine honours on 'worthy' rulers after their death[76] and in an inclination on the part of some of the political community to propose these for living *principes*.[77] However, moves to treat the *princeps* as a living god were always officially rejected, as Nero did in 65.[78] The Principate was not travelling towards Hellenistic

---

[68] Champlin 2003, 107–11, 135, 139–44, 171–6, 199–200.   [69] Champlin 2003, 111.
[70] Cf. Winterling 2009, 117, on Gaius' attempt to use religion to resolve the paradox of the Principate 250 years too early.
[71] Below 374, 376.   [72] Champlin 2003, 107.   [73] Winterling 2007, 144–5.
[74] Holland 2000, 196; below 312.   [75] Above 265; Bradley 1978a, 290–1; Griffin 1984, 215, 217.
[76] Osgood 2011, 139–40; Winterling 2007, 139–41; Mratschek 2013, 49.   [77] Above 265.
[78] Tac. *Ann.* 15.74.3–4.

monarchy. It was *sui generis*. Once established, it remained the political benchmark for over two centuries; and though it then changed into the 'Dominate', it did not become a full monarchy before the fall of the West.[79] Gaius and Nero, like other Romans before them, occasionally acted the divine because this was expected of them by sycophantic underlings or because it suited them to do so,[80] but were never set on being god-kings. If Nero had ever intended to declare himself Nero-Apollo, he would have done so in Greece, which he did not. He visited Delphi for its games, not Apollo, whose shrine he robbed;[81] and he returned to Rome as a human victor, not a god.[82]

II.1.4   Nero the Mortal

I argue below that Nero took on the role of Apollo because this empowered him to break from that of *princeps*.[83] This allows a secular explanation for Nero 'the divine'. A secular interpretation of the *Domus Aurea* must be correct for, as many have observed, conclusive proof comes from Nero's declaration that the place at last allowed him to be housed like a human being.[84] And as he lived like a human being, so he was portrayed as a human being, competed as a human being, and died as a human being, with no reference to any divine status.[85] The inevitable conclusion – that Nero had no religious delusions, and certainly never thought of himself as divine – is neatly expressed by Miriam Griffin: 'We do not need to follow scholarly flights of fancy and see ... hints that the *Domus Aurea* was planned to symbolise the rule of Nero the new Sun-god ... The evidence ... does not seem to point to a serious attempt on Nero's part to introduce divine monarchy'.[86] On this argument, the claque's cries and reference to the 'celestial voice' were flattery and affectation: a simile not an equation.[87] The Apolline coin-type is striking in its persistence (it spans the great reform), but it was restricted to bronze issues and was subject to no further development. Though accepted by Sutherland and Carson as depicting Nero-Apollo, it is now usually regarded as representing only the god.[88] It reflects no more than Nero's very Augustan high regard for

---

[79] Above 271.   [80] Winterling 2007, 139–41, 144; cf. below 273.
[81] Champlin 2003, 133; cf. above 103.   [82] Below 273, 384.   [83] Below 287.
[84] Above 255; Charlesworth 1950, 71; Bradley 1978a, 181; Champlin 2003, 132.
[85] Above 113; below 302, 413.
[86] Griffin 1984, 138, 218. Cf. Warmington 1969, 121; Bradley 1978a, 151, 288–9. below 287.
[87] Cf. Charlesworth 1950, 71; Bradley 1978a, 131; cf. below 285.
[88] *RIC²* p. 156; Bergmann 2013, 347, though cf. Barrett *et al.* 2016, 257.

Apollo (intervening *principes* had not advertised him on their coinage). That it showed Nero as the god is a post-Julio-Claudian interpretation, an early example of reading Nero out of or into contemporary artefacts.[89] If Suetonius had not drawn attention to it as such,[90] it is unlikely that modern historians would have seen it in this way. (Suetonius actually gets the date of the coin-type wrong, postponing it to fit Nero's triumphal return from Greece.) This is likely also to apply to Suetonius' reference to supposedly contemporary Apolline statues of Nero.[91] Nero probably acted the Apolline charioteer during the punishment of Christians because he derived confidence from the role.[92] There are grounds for interpreting his 'triumph' as traditional and Augustan rather than radically Apolline.[93] Nero's proclamation at Corinth may be viewed not as an act of megalomania but as a piece of theatre in which he played the part of Flamininus, the famous 'Liberator of Greece' of 196 BC.[94] What followed from this – Nero the 'new Helios', other associations of him with gods, and the renaming of cities in the eastern part of the Empire[95] – was no more than Nero's toleration of the conventions of a Greek East used to adulating its rulers.[96] He gave his audience what they wanted, if *de haut en bas*: despite his Greek artistic leanings, Nero, always very mindful of his Roman aristocratic descent,[97] will always have looked down on contemporary Greeks.[98] As a Roman noble he will also have been sensitive to religious convention. At the commencement of his principate he had refused semi-divine and divine honours in Rome and the Empire.[99] After the Pisonian conspiracy, he had conspicuously rejected a senatorial proposal that a temple be dedicated to him as *divus* because *principes* were not thus honoured until after their death.[100] Nero's supposed desire to rename Rome 'Neropolis' has been denied as part of the denigration that grew out of suspicions of his ordering the Fire and, perhaps, given its Greek form, out of popular misconceptions of 'Nero's absurd philhellenism'.[101] However, he may well have considered that, following the Fire, he was creating a new Rome and so toyed with the idea of the new City's being named after him. If so, this derived from excessive enthusiasm and ill judgement, not aspirations to

---

[89] Above 266; cf. Cadario 2011, 182.   [90] Suet. *Ner.* 25.2.
[91] Suet. *Ner.* 25.2. Bergmann 2013, 347; cf. 347–9: that the numismatic depiction of Nero as a 'world ruler' in 64–68 (with radiate crown and the globe and aegis of Zeus) reflects a senatorial honour and has Augustan precedents.
[92] Below 287–8.   [93] Below 384.   [94] Cf. Hohl 1918, 389: 'ein blosser Theatercoup'.
[95] Griffin 1984, 217.   [96] Above 271.   [97] Suet. *Ner.* 41.1. Shotter 2008, 38.
[98] Cf. below 373, 375.   [99] Tac. *Ann.* 13.10. Griffin 1984, 216; cf. above 269.
[100] Above 271; Bradley 1978a, 176–7.   [101] Bradley 1978a, 291; Griffin 1984, 131 (quotation).

divinity. Throughout Nero's principate, his motives were personal, not ideological: 'of any deliberate and calculated religious policy, or of any constitutional design, I see no certain trace'.[102] Nero the 'divine' is another aspect of the creation of the 'mad, bad' Nero, along with 'Nero the murderer', 'Nero the arsonist', 'Nero the spendthrift' etc.

11.1.5   The Colossus

This leaves us with the question of the Colossus, still frequently interpreted as a depiction of Nero as the Sun and cited as manifesting Nero's ambitions of god-kingship.[103] This is unlikely. Pliny I and Suetonius, whom one might expect to have been ready to record any possibility of Nero's presenting himself as semi-divine or divine, state only that the Colossus was a representation of the *princeps*.[104] What they criticise is its massive size, which smacked of 'self-glorification' even for a ruler of Rome.[105] Such images were usually reserved for the gods: the Colossus 'exceeded what was deemed appropriate in matters of imperial self-portraiture'.[106] Again, however, its size was probably more to do with Nero's overenthusiasm and ill judgement than with any politico-religious policy. Its creator, Zenodorus, renowned for his colossal statue of Mercury at Clermont-Ferrand, built big.[107] Furthermore, working in a tradition in which it was not unprecedented for living *principes*, including Augustus, to be represented 'theomorphically', i.e. with divine attributes,[108] Zenodorus could well have given the Colossus a radiate crown, the attribute of Apollo as the sun. In this he may have been encouraged by current developments, as the Senate extended the privilege of being shown wearing a radiate crown from the dead – it had already been used on coin representations of the deified Augustus – to the living *princeps* in honour of his victory in Armenia and, perhaps, to acknowledge that though not yet deified himself he was, as the 'good' *princeps*, already destined for Olympus. The contemporary use of the radiate crown on Nero's reformed coinage may have been

---

[102] Charlesworth 1950, 72, 74; below 293.
[103] E.g. Holland 2000, 199; Cadario 2011, 184–8; Dinter 2013, 11. Cf. above 265; Bradley 1978a, 175–6 (for the debate); Bergmann 2013, 346, 351 (drawing: p. 350);
[104] Plin. *HN* 34.45: *destinatus illius principis simulacro colossus*; Suet. *Ner.* 31.1: *colossus . . . ipsius effigie.* Bradley 1978a, 176.
[105] Griffin 1984, 131 (quotation), 216. This confirms that, as now usually accepted, the structure was a huge statue of Nero (like the Statue of Liberty), not (*contra* Shotter 2008, 122) a large statue of him on a pillar (like Nelson's Column).
[106] Bergmann 2013, 351.   [107] Plin. *HN* 34.45. Bradley 1978a, 177.
[108] Bergmann 2013, 341 for the term.

related to this, but probably its main purpose was, by referencing Augustus, to underline that the new coins marked no great break with the past by giving them a comforting 'Augustan aura'. Subsequently, as a characteristic of the imperial bronze two-*as* piece, the *dupondius*, the radiate crown became no more than a mark of value.[109] The Augustan precedents are crucial. Early acceptance of theomorphic representation is a nice example of the political community's employing Hellenistic ways of exalting a *princeps* without radically changing the Principate. The radiate crown should not be interpreted as ideologically significant. On the Colossus it would have signified at most the continuation of the Augustan conceit that the *princeps* was *comes* to Apollo. In commissioning the statue Nero had simply bought big and bought what was on offer, making an artistic decision and aiming at an architectural tour de force. A massive statue, erected by personal choice at so public a location was unprecedented and ill-judged,[110] but the gesture carried no political message.[111]

Yet the fact that the source tradition criticises the Neronian Colossus only for its size, not for any of its details, raises the question as to whether it was ever erected under Nero. It has long been suspected that Suetonius' ambiguous wording – that the new forecourt at the head of the *via Sacra* was so large that a Colossus 'stood'/ 'might stand' there – hints that it may not have been erected in Nero's lifetime.[112] This is plausible. The designing of such a monument and its modelling, manufacture of casts and armature, assembly of casts on the armature, and finishing is no easy task. The seventeenth-century colossus of San Carlo at Arona on Lake Maggiore, at *c.* 24 m (79 statute feet) tall, excluding its pedestal, smaller than the Colossus, took 84 years to complete. The Statue of Liberty, taller, at *c.* 46 m (151 statute feet), but built with industrial technology, took eleven years.[113] Pliny I's giant linen-portrait of Nero, at 120 Roman feet high perhaps a final full-scale preparatory drawing for the Colossus, displayed in the *Horti Maini*, would in itself have been a major undertaking.[114] Nero's onsite patronage would have given maximum speed to the project. But if, characteristically, his interest waned and work was then interrupted by civil war, one may doubt that it was ever finished. Vespasian probably inherited an expensive construction kit: probably a base, part of the armature and an incomplete set of castings. Unwilling to waste

---

[109] Griffin 1984, 217–18; Bergmann 2013, 344–51 (quotation); above 269.
[110] Cf. Fantham 2013, 22.　　[111] Bradley 1978a, 177; cf. below 285.
[112] Suet. *Ner.* 35.1: *staret*. Bradley 1978a, 177; Coleman 2006, 20.
[113] Models: Plin. *NH* 34.46; San Carlo: visitor centre; Statue of Liberty: Wikipedia.
[114] Plin. *HN* 35.51. Elsner 1994, 119; Holland 2000, 199; Moormann 2003, 382.

money, he decided to finish the project, and the Colossus was first 'set up' in 75.[115] Vespasian probably removed Nero's features but retained the solar attribute of the radiate crown, added that of the world-tiller and dedicated it to the Sun.[116] The fact that he accepted its erection on its intended site (it was Hadrian who had it moved next to the Flavian amphitheatre[117]) shows that in the event it was not considered an eye-sore.[118] Pliny I, indeed, says that it became an object of admiration.[119]

11.2   Madness?

11.2.1   Psychoanalysing Nero?

If Nero did not believe that he was divine, why did he sometimes act Apollo? [120] Is this indicative of a different, but still significant, psychosis? Was he 'mad'?[121] We shall never know Nero's mental state. He is unavailable for direct analysis, and historians are not clinicians. For this reason, some scholars have warned against speculation. However, it is impossible for historians and archaeologists to engage fully with the Neronian principate without taking some view of the mental condition of the *princeps*.[122] Some do this directly. Holland, for example, refers to the 'series of psychological shocks in infancy' suffered by Nero. These, he believes, resulted in levels of emotional mistrust which 'make it hard to maintain genuinely close personal relationships'. Later, albeit cautiously, he draws on modern psychological studies to observe that the possession of great power does not preclude feelings of inferiority, in Nero's case in the presence of Agrippina.[123] For Waldherr the Golden House was the result of an 'immature and unbalanced' personality that craved attention and vented infantile frustration whenever baulked; for Carandini it reflects Nero's 'spectacularly megalomaniacal policy'.[124] Even Meier, having declared that Nero's innermost thoughts 'will remain forever closed to

---

[115] Cass. Dio 66.15.1: *hidruthē*.   [116] Suet *Vesp.* 18; Bradley 1978a, 176; Bergmann 2013, 349.
[117] HA *Had.* 19.12.   [118] Cf. above 261.   [119] Plin. *HN* 34.45: *venerationi*.
[120] I am considerably indebted to Dr Oliver James for his prompt and generous help with this section. I was also given valuable initial advice by Professor David Clarke and Dr Alan Sunderland. The responsibility for all I say here remains, of course, entirely mine.
[121] Above 8.   [122] Cf. Beste 2011b, 175; Cadario 2011, 182.
[123] Holland 2000, 13, 22–3, 111.
[124] Waldherr 2005, 225: 'unreifen und unausgeglichenen'; Carandini 2011, 146: '[la] politica spettacolarmente megalomane di Nerone'.

us', attempts to reconstruct these from his activities as *Kaiserkünstler/Künstlerkaiser*.[125] Others simply tacitly assume that Nero was sane. The study of Nero demands the gamble of psychoanalysis.

11.2.2   Degrees of Irrationality

Since modern clinical psychology emphasises the absence of a clear distinction between 'sanity' and 'madness', this amounts to deciding whether Nero was significantly more irrational than the majority of his contemporaries. His state of mind has to be located on a scale ranging from 'super realism' through 'average realism', 'minor illness', and 'personality disorder', to 'major delusion (major depression/schizophrenia)'.[126] Though we cannot put him on the analyst's couch or in a functional MR scanner,[127] we may be able to derive some understanding of his character from what we know of his personal relationships, viewed other than through the distorting lens of Nero 'the monster'.

Though Suetonius derives the worst aspects of Nero's character from his infamous paternal forebears, it is now generally accepted that 'nurture' is as important as 'nature' in the formation of personality.[128] Neglectful or unsympathetic treatment of a child may lead to Freudian extremes. Excessive correction may produce a 'punitive' conscience, characterised by inhibition, conformity and diligence to a degree that 'crushes personality and allows little space for instincts'.[129] Deficient attention produces a 'weak' conscience, characterised by rebelliousness, self-indulgence, intrigue, vindictiveness and a liability to 'random promiscuity and unstable relationships'. A weak conscience goes with a weak sense of self, which can result in lack of empathy or even psychopathy. A very weak sense of self has also been proposed as a cause of schizophrenia. The best upbringing is one between excess and deficiency of attention, producing a child with a 'benign' conscience.[130] *Prima facie*, Nero's upbringing exposed him to both excessive and deficient attention. Born into the ruling family under a *princeps*, Gaius, who had yet to produce an heir and whose official

---

[125] Meier 2008, 574: 'wird uns für immer verschlossen bleiben'; cf. below 372.

[126] James 2007, 273–4.

[127] Editorial comment 2011; Lanius *et al.* 2011. I am grateful to my friend and colleague, Professor A. T. Barker, of the Medical Physics Department, Royal Hallamshire Hospital, Sheffield, for guidance on fMR scanning.

[128] Suet. *Ner.* 1.2–5; cf. Cizek 1982, 28. James 2007, 5–7, 12–13, 93–7, 138–9. Cf. Fonagy and Luyten 2009, 1356; Lanius *et al.* 2011, 333.

[129] James 2007, 93–4, 110 (quotation).

[130] James 2007, 87, 96, 122 (quotation), 123, 125, 200–6.

successor, Tiberius Gemellus, was soon eliminated, Nero must from the start have been the object of intense court interest. Late in 39, when Nero was approaching his second birthday, his mother fell victim to court intrigue and was exiled. Nero's father then died, and he was put into the care of his paternal aunt Domitia (much older sister of Domitia Lepida, the mother of Messalina), a woman notorious for her miserliness.[131] Agrippina returned from exile in 41, following the murder of Gaius and the accession of Claudius, but had to find a new husband – who turned out to be Domitia's husband, Crispus Passienus – to protect herself against continuing intrigue. This was orchestrated by Claudius' wife, Messalina, in favour of herself and her son, born in 41, and against which Nero's *de facto* role as reserve heir to the sickly Britannicus would have offered little protection.[132] Following Passienus' death and Messalina's downfall, Agrippina contrived her own marriage to Claudius, which took place in 49.[133] Nero's first six years of life, from late 37 to late 43, were therefore years of potential emotional stress. Throughout the ages, upper-class parents have tended to distance themselves from their young children. Roman aristocrats were no exception; and with his father dead and his mother a high-level player in court politics Nero would have seen even less of his parents than the majority of his peers. For the most part, he would have been brought up by servants, slave and free.[134] Cizek, in a rare extended attempt at a considered psychological assessment of Nero, has this upbringing generate a personality which, though never 'mad', was profoundly 'unbalanced', as reflected in his hypocrisy, mistrust and immorality,[135] the imbalance deriving from a childhood lacking in affection that left Nero with a profoundly weak conscience. By about the age of seven he had no self-discipline but controlled his passions only by following the instructions of those in charge of him, in order to win their approval. He had learned to distrust those around him, hide his true feelings and lie to suit

---

[131] Suet. *Ner.* 6.3; cf. Suet. *Ner.* 34.5, Cass. Dio 61.17.1–2. Historians, ancient (cf. Tac. *Ann.* 12.64.6) and modern, have great difficulties in distinguishing between these two women, with many (e.g. Shotter 2008, 41) naming Domitia Lepida as Nero's guardian. Here I follow Barrett 1996, 45–6, 70, 137, 175. Cf. Hohl 1918, 355; Bradley 1978a, 57–8, 207; Griffin 1984, 27–31; Malitz 1999, 11; Waldherr 2005, 29, 39–40.

[132] *Contra* Holland 2000, 39.

[133] For all this, see Barrett 1996, 45–6, 51–91. For further on Domitia see below 340.

[134] See e.g. Bradley 1992, 220 on 'a certain distancing' between upper-class parents and children; and 1991, 38, 56–8 on the role of the *familia* in the day-to-day care of upper-class children and on the strains on upper-class family life.

[135] Cizek 1982, 27, 28: 'déséquilibre psychique'; cf. 35.

his purposes. Soon he would learn to hate his cool, cruel and controlling mother.[136] Lacking internal control, Nero, once *princeps*, simply pleased himself. This produced a 'double personality': when times were good, Nero was a 'laid-back' sensualist; when they were bad, he became an anguished megalomaniac.[137] Cizek's Nero is impulsive and unreliable, intent only on gratifying himself, and cowardly, vindictive and highly superstitious.[138] His interpretation appeals because it confirms the traditional interpretation of Nero as 'monster'. However, since it is likely that it was shaped by this tradition, we should ask if Nero's childhood experiences were really so damaging.

Nero was brought up by substitute parents, but substitutes can do a better job than the real thing. 'If a physically absent mother may be one potential cause of insecurity, a loving, consistent substitute can not only compensate for the absence but may actually be better for the child than the original'.[139] That Nero had a relatively happy childhood may be detected in his close relationship with his nurses and teachers – the all-important 'trusted other'.[140] Nero's first close physical and emotional contact would have been with his wet nurse not his mother, another aspect of aristocratic parental aloofness. Suckling a child is intrusive, and can be messy and exhausting. By the late Republic, wet-nursing was taken for granted among the Roman upper classes.[141] The name of Nero's wet nurse is uncertain, but the fact that her son, Cornelius Tuscus, rose high under him suggests a continuing warm relationship between all three.[142] Nero and Tuscus must have been almost exactly the same age, and so may well have been playmates. After weaning, Nero would have been cared for by other nurses. Two of these (one of whom may have been his original wet nurse[143]), Egloge and Alexandria, helped deposit his ashes.[144] Their loyalty again suggests a strong and lasting bond between all three, which has parallels in other periods of Roman history.[145] As a toddler, Nero was not

---

[136] Cizek 1982, 28, 32, 35. Cf. Waldherr 2005, 82; James 2007, 33–4, 138; below 282.

[137] Cizek 1982, 33: 'Lâche et jouisser, angoissé et mégalomane, très vite Néron révèle le double aspect de sa personalité'.

[138] Cizek 1982, 34–5.   [139] James 2007, 170 (quotation); cf. 219.

[140] Fonagy and Luyten 2009, 1357; cf. Griffin 1984, 46: 'From a psychological point of view it is interesting to observe here the tendency of Nero to remain attached to those who looked after him in early youth'.

[141] Bradley 1992, 201, 215–16; cf. Waldherr 2005, 39.   [142] Suet. *Ner.* 35.5; above 79, 221.

[143] Cf. Bradley 1992, 20, 25–6.

[144] Suet. *Ner.* 50. Cizek 1982, 28–9. Though Suetonius calls both *nutrices*, and *nutrex* usually means wet nurse, the term is also used of nurses whose responsibilities were only 'custodial': Bradley 1991, 13–14.

[145] E.g. Bradley 1992, 221, on Pliny II and his nurse.

devoid of male attention. Though Suetonius' sneer that during his time
with Domitia Nero was entrusted to the care of a 'dancer and barber' defies
easy explanation, it may refer to the services of *nutritores*, male nursery
nurses. These were not unusual in Roman upper-class homes, usefully
complementing female *nutrices*.[146] The phrase 'dancer and barber' might
refer to these men's other skills but, since dancers and barbers were known
for 'corruption and debauchery', it could equally be a typical Suetonian
rhetorical twist, pointing up that Nero was very early encouraged along the
path to evil.[147] In fact the established system probably did its job of
neutralising 'dislocating circumstances that rendered minimal the anticipation of a stable domestic environment'; i.e. Nero's child-minders, female
and male, 'provided the emotional and physical relationship in the life of
the child which was not always present in the parent-child relationship'.[148]
Nero next appears to have formed similar strong affection for his *paedagogi*
(first teachers), Beryllus and Anicetus. The former became his *ab epistulis
Graecis* (Secretary for Greek Correspondence); the latter was later
appointed commander of the fleet at Misenum and was closely involved
in the deaths of Agrippina and Octavia. Nero would hardly have given
them such responsibilities if he had not completely trusted them.[149]

Yet it should not be said that Nero's early life caused him to prefer the
company of slaves and freedmen.[150] Like all Roman aristocrats he used these as
required, from high-ranking counsellors to court fools and castrated par-
amours, but the people closest to him in spirit, such as Seneca, Poppaea,
Petronius and Lucan, were all of senatorial rank. Earlier, the young Nero seems
to have been close to at least two high-ranking adults other than his parents.
Despite her fearsome reputation as a battle axe, there are signs that his aunt
Domitia was genuinely fond of him, continuing to indulge him to the end of
her life.[151] And in the very first months of his principate, Nero honoured his
guardian, Asconius Labeo. Normally, he would have remained under the
protection of his father until he reached the age of majority. However, since
his father died before this, male guardians were found for him from his family,
including Passienus. When Passienus died, the responsibility passed to Labeo,
with whom Nero appears to have forged a strong link.[152]

---

[146] Suet. *Ner.* 6.3: *nutritus est sub duobus paedagogis saltatore atque tonsore.* Bradley 1991, 37–55.
[147] Too 1994, 212 (quotation); cf. Barton 1994, 51–2.
[148] Bradley 1991, 58 (quotation), 60 (quotation).
[149] Beryllus: Joseph. *AJ* 20.183–4; Table 1. Anicetus: above 187, 193. Cizek 1982, 28–9.
[150] *Contra* Holland 2000, 54; cf. Walde 2013, 13.   [151] Barrett 1996, 70, 175. Cf. below 340.
[152] Tac. *Ann.* 13.10.1; *CIL* 5.2848. Bradley 1978a, 50–1; Griffin 1984, 46; Barrett 1996, 86; Barrett
et al. 2016, 32 and n. 20.

Nero's was not a perfect upbringing. The slaves and ex-slaves who surrounded him for most of the time were his social inferiors and so could not have afforded to be totally candid with him.[153] And one wonders what, despite the affection of Labeo, the effect of the absence of his father, and so of a strong male role-model, had on him. Is this, for example, at least part of the explanation for his preference for older, more confident, women?[154] On the other hand, this absence at least freed him from the often oppressive awareness of a successful father or grandfather.[155] If we can forget Nero 'the monster' and resist the temptation to infer his mental state from his supposed misdeeds, we may glimpse someone who had early problems but who was not left mentally unbalanced. That he enjoyed a relatively contented childhood may also be reflected in his acquisition of a good education. Children tend to want to please those who raise them, usually their parents,[156] but for Nero these were his nurses and teachers. The latter gave him an education which was 'rich, erudite, complex and meticulously planned'.[157] After the *paedagogi* he appears to have extended his affections to his higher-level tutors – as *grammatici*, the philosophers Alexander of Aegae and Chaeremon of Alexandria; and as *rhetor*, Seneca.[158] Seneca was, as a senatorial politician, hardly the average professor.[159] On the other hand, keeping close to his equestrian roots, and with a real genius for philosophy and drama, he was not a typical senator. Seneca knew how to please, and was especially good at pleasing the young.[160] In his dealings with Nero he may well have appeared attractively unorthodox, not standing on his dignity, and willing to encourage Nero to laugh at his mother behind her back. Having recently lost his only child, a son, in infancy he may well have viewed Nero as a substitute.[161] There is every reason to suppose that the two were genuinely close, even if they eventually grew apart.[162] Another interesting, newly proposed aspect of Nero's relationship with educated males is that he appears not to have capriciously

---

[153] Cf. Walde 2013, 13.
[154] Poppaea certainly was certainly older than Nero (above 190), and Acte is very likely to have been. Statilia Messalina (born 30–40: Kienast 2004, 100) may well have been chosen to replace Poppaea in part because she, too, was older than Nero. Cf. Holland 2000, 23, 76.
[155] Cf. James 2007, 117–18, 141; cf. 75: violent fathers often (through their behaviour, not their genes) produce violent sons.
[156] James 2007, 99–102.
[157] Cizek 1982, 28–9: 'erudite, complexe et minutieusement programmé'; cf. Holland 2000, 52–3.
[158] Cizek 1982, 30–1; Barrett 1996, 107; Osgood 2011, 47.
[159] Hohl 1918, 352; Warmington 1969, 29; Bradley 1978a, 285; Shotter 2008, 51; Bryan 2013, 142; cf. Romm 2014, 4.
[160] Rimell 2015, 123–4; cf. above 105.   [161] Romm 2014, 26.
[162] Cf. Romm 2014, 50–1; above 188, 194.

interfered in the actual construction of the Golden House Pavilion. Once its plans had been agreed, he trusted his experts to execute them.[163]

A well balanced personality is capable of authentic and lasting relationships with people of both sexes, and Nero appears to have inspired affection in women. Acte was loyal to him beyond his death, accompanying Egloge and Alexandria in depositing his ashes.[164] That he once cherished her is indicated by his wish to marry her and by his persisting in the relationship in defiance of Agrippina.[165] Wiser counsel, perhaps even that of Acte herself, prevailed, the idea of marriage was dropped, and Nero moved to a more socially equal affair with Poppaea.[166] However, Acte was not tossed aside and was still influential in 58/59.[167] The Poppaea affair appears to have been a real love-match. From the start it was fraught with difficulties since both parties were married: Poppaea to Nero's close friend, Otho, and Nero to Claudius' daughter, Octavia. Nero eventually got his way, and the two wed in 62. Nero doted on Poppaea and was devastated by her death, the more so because he may have precipitated it and that of their unborn child.[168] He had longed to be a father, as he had already demonstrated by his joy at the birth of his first child, Claudia, by Poppaea, and his sorrow at her early death.[169]

Nero's best known relationship with a female is, of course, that with his mother. This broke down in 55 because of his continued liaison with Acte,[170] but there is a case for a later rapprochement. Agrippina's relationship with her son may never have been as cool as commonly supposed.[171] Immediately Nero was born he was important as a potential heir, and he became even more significant as an ever rarer direct descendant of Augustus.[172] Throughout her political intrigues, Agrippina could never have afforded to forget him. It is likely that, immediately on her return from exile under Claudius, and perhaps jealous of 'substitute parents' such as his paternal aunts and Anicetus,[173] she actually fussed over his care. Indeed, during this period Agrippina, battling the hostility of Messalina, was probably particularly attentive to Nero, removing him from Rome perhaps even as far as Asia Minor. Later rumours of their supposed incest suggest that, though mother and son had their difficulties, they remained close and

---

[163] Ball 2003, 96, 115.   [164] Above 279.   [165] Below 311.
[166] Her senatorial pedigree was mixed: Waldherr 2005, 83; above 179.
[167] Tac. *Ann.* 14.2.2; cf. above 182.   [168] Above 219.   [169] Above 190, 219.
[170] Above 51.   [171] Cf. above 36, 278–9.   [172] Barrett 1996, 55; cf. above 174.
[173] Cf. Tac. *Ann.* 12.64.6, 14.3.5. Above 278.

demonstrated mutual affection.[174] This expectation of closeness makes it possible that by late 58 the two had come together again.[175] On Nero's birthday on 15 December of that year, the Arval priests honoured Agrippina in association with Concordia. 'The choice of Concordia instead of the usual Juno probably refers to the ideal of harmony between the empress-mother and Nero, and the fact that the Genius of Nero figures after the Concordia of his mother publicly manifests the good relationship between the emperor and his mother in the last year before her death'.[176] Gossip that Agrippina's sexual advances were causing Nero to avoid meeting her in private and to praise her when she took a holiday away from him may be regarded as malicious, made possible by the busy schedules of both.[177] A developing rapprochement would explain Nero's warm reception of Agrippina – real, not feigned – and her pleasure at it on the day before her death.[178] Their closeness was probably the product of their earlier voluntary internal exile, when Nero became no 'spoilt brat' but 'an energetic, but watchful and sensitive child, who had known from infancy that some people wanted to kill him – and that a false move on his part might result in a disaster both for him and his mother'.[179] Equally positively, in the mid-40s Agrippina's political concerns may have prevented her from outwardly expressing too many hopes for her son and so from turning him into a 'dominant goal depressive' – expecting too much of himself – in later life.[180] Nero's initially very successful assumption of the roles of heir-presumptive, heir-apparent and *princeps* is explicable in terms of a good relationship with Agrippina: as he had been eager to please his teachers so he was now eager to please his mother.[181]

Finally, another *fil rouge* of this study, in an age of vindictiveness (one has only to think of the machinations of Agrippina or the plots of Senecan tragedies[182]) there is no sign that Nero was especially vindictive, or encouraged vindictiveness in others. This is not to say that he never acted out of spite: few do. His dismissal of Pallas after his victory over his mother in the Acte affair was mean but is the exception that proves the rule. At the time, Nero was under extraordinary stress; and he must have almost immediately relented to a degree since Pallas was not executed but allowed

---

[174] 'Incest': Tac. *Ann.* 14.2; Suet. *Ner.* 28.2; Cass. Dio 61.11.3–4. Barrett 1996, 88–9, 183; Holland 2000, 23, 25, 35–6; Waldherr 2005, 41, 102; below 312.
[175] Holland 2000, 100. [176] Smallwood 1967, 21.32–3; Erker 2013, 121–2 (quotation).
[177] Tac. *Ann.* 14.3.1. Ginsburg 2006, 48. [178] Tac. Ann. 14.4; cf. above 183.
[179] Holland 2000, 49. [180] Above 32–3; James 2007, 63–4 (quotation).
[181] *Princeps*: above 12, 16; pupil: above 281; cf. Holland 2000, 49. [182] Dinter 2013, 9.

to go into retirement.[183] Otho, whose continued presence at court would have been an embarrassment after the marriage of Nero and Poppaea, was likewise not killed or exiled, but appointed to a respectable governorship on the Iberian peninsula.[184] Plutarch pays a back-handed compliment to Nero's lack of malice in observing how 'odd' it was that because of his marriage to Poppaea Nero killed 'his own wife and sister' (i.e. Octavia) but spared Poppaea's previous husband.[185] Generally, as we have seen, Nero did not encourage political witch-hunts.[186]

Nero's good relations with people explains his hurt when he felt himself betrayed by those he trusted.[187] This caused him to lash out, but such a reaction is hardly abnormal. The tradition of Nero 'the monster' sees madness in (roughly in order of notoriety): the murder of his mother; the firing of Rome; the persecution of Christians; the deaths of Claudius, Britannicus, Octavia and Poppaea; the murders of senators; depraved sexual acts; the building of the Golden House; the Greek tour; and his final impractical reaction to rebellion. As I have argued above and will argue further below, most of these and other 'outrages' may be explained on the grounds of political necessity or dismissed as hostile invention. There is nothing in Nero's behaviour to indicate profound mental unbalance: that his conscience was excessively 'punitive' or 'weak'. His creativeness, spontaneity, capacity for enjoyment and lack of vindictiveness are against the first; his ability to form stable relationships is against the second. His conscience fell probably in the middle of the range: 'benign', with some elements of 'weak'. He owed its positive elements to his relatively secure childhood. Its negative ones are likely to have been intensified by stressful experiences in his twenties.[188] The 'non-monstrous' Nero that we may detect despite the prejudice of the sources was not habitually addictive or prone to bingeing on sex or alcohol or food.[189] He did not set out to debauch himself or others.[190] He was not usually mistrustful of those around him.[191] He was not a 'control freak'. Though prepared to be unconventional, he was not a novelty-seeking risk-taker.[192] He had a keen taste for parody and satire, which he permitted to include himself.[193] His extrovert character caused him to enjoy being in public and

---

[183] Above 55, 174.   [184] Tac. *Ann.* 13.46.5; above 97.
[185] Plut. *Galb.* 19: *paralogon ēn ... tēn gunaika kai adelphēn. Contra* Rudich 1993, 30 (that Nero killed Otho's wife and sister).
[186] Tac. *Ann.* 13.43. 7. Above 29; cf. 207; Rudich 1993, 28.
[187] Above 186 (Agrippina); 73, 115 (Lucan etc.).   [188] Below 288.
[189] Cf. below 305. This and many of the following criteria are developed from James 2007, 200, 204.
[190] Cf. below 307.   [191] Cf. above 58.   [192] Below 293.   [193] Cf. above 102.

mixing with people of all classes and tastes.[194] Keen on sport and entertainment, though against traditional public blood-letting,[195] he threw
himself into activities in which he was interested. In his chosen fields he
was highly competitive because he longed for genuine praise.[196] However,
he was genuinely uncertain of his abilities, veering between uplifting
aspiration and depressing self-doubt. He therefore derived real delight at
being declared a victor, since each victory was won through unremitting
human effort, not divine aid.[197] On the other hand, uncertainty led to his
being obsessive in his artistic and athletic training.[198] Though he was
capable of close friendship and great generosity, he could give the impression of being self-centred.[199] In extremes of fortune, good and bad, he was
capable of impulsive behaviour that might seem excessive and selfish,
perhaps even hostile and frightening. He appears to have inherited some
inclination to violence under pressure, but he kept it in check and revealed
it only rarely.[200] He was vain about his appearance.[201] He knew his own
mind, and could be extremely stubborn – hence his 'break-outs', many of
which were expensive and made work for others.[202] Nero was far from
perfect and must, at times, have been difficult to know. But he was not
vastly irrational: on the scale of disorder he perhaps straddled 'average
realism' and 'minor illness'. He had his faults, but he was neither 'mad' nor
(relative to his time, class and rank) especially bad and dangerous to
know.[203] Overall, his main problem was not any crazed inclination to
tyranny but, especially at the end, a lack of engagement with the office of
princeps.[204] It might, indeed, have been better for him if he had been more
'disordered', since 'disorders' (remorseless drive, lack of empathy etc.)
often help people at the head of large organisations.[205]

Nero's 'madness' is, like so much else, the result of post-mortem
defamation, and appears relatively late in the source tradition. The Nero
of the *Octavia* is icily sane in his assessment of the realities of power.[206]
Tacitus, in describing Nero's despatching of his mother to her death, calls
him 'brutal' but not mad. And though Suetonius uses the word *furor* of
Gaius' mental condition, in Nero's case he associates it with Nero's
extravagance and so confines it to its more usual meaning of 'excess'.[207]

---

[194] Above 236, 253.   [195] Cf. below 418.   [196] Cf. above 101.   [197] Cf. below 383.
[198] Below 292.   [199] Cf. below 293.   [200] Suet. *Ner.* 5.2, 47.1; above 282., below 410.
[201] Cf. below 306.   [202] Above 164.   [203] So Holland 2000, 197.   [204] Below 407.
[205] James 2007, 242–3.   [206] Cf. above 159.
[207] Tac. *Ann.* 14.4.8: *ferus animus*; Suet. *Calig.* 50.2, *Ner.* 31.4: *impendiorum furor*; cf. Joseph. *BJ*
2.250. Winterling 2007 150, 176–7; 2009, 104; cf. Buckley 2013a, 206.

This returns us to the question posed at the beginning of this section. If Nero did not believe that he was divine, why did he act Apollo?

11.3 Acting

Modern historians make much of Nero 'the actor',[208] but acting alone does not condemn him: we all create a range of characters with which to face life. This is not necessarily bad. It can be used to cover embarrassment, make friends or to bolster confidence in situations of uncertainty and so generally benefit our mental health. James cites Oscar Wilde on authenticity – complete frankness, to ourselves and others – being available only through acting or pretence.[209] Nero, like everyone else, was bound to act, and the more so because, as a Roman aristocrat, he would have been permanently on display in a period when the educated class placed great emphasis on life, and death, as drama.[210] In addition, as an Augustan *princeps* Nero was both the Roman aristocrat writ large and a ruler compelled to veil his autocratic position by acting as a magistrate of a continuing Republic.[211] This was not beyond his capabilities. As a child he acted the willing pupil to please his teachers; as an adolescent he acted the *princeps*-to-be to please his mother and Claudius; and as a young adult he acted the 'good' *princeps* to please Agrippina, Seneca and Burrus. His performances brought him the approval of others and probably, for a while, genuine satisfaction for himself. Gradually, however, he grew uncomfortable with the very difficult role of *princeps*.[212] He craved release from administration and politics, and looked to participation in sport and art where he could earn authentic praise for his own accomplishments. However, even though he had recognised his *métier*, his society, the position he occupied within it, his upbringing and recent history all made it impossible for him to be entirely himself: despite his growing alternative interests he must continue to act the *princeps*. The 'restored' Republic demanded a 'chief citizen', and as head of the Julio-Claudian house Nero was bound by the expectations of his relatives and dependants to fill the role. That he saw that all this was an act is reflected in his characteristic banter. Mockery of the imperial office that in the *Apocolocyntosis* was a secret joke between him and Seneca continued more openly in

---

[208] E.g. Bartsch 1994, 12, 22; above 86.
[209] James 2007, 55–56, 217–18, 270–1, 273; 2007b, 418–24.
[210] Cf. Bartsch 1994, 55–6; Connors 1994, 227–30; below 300.   [211] Above 19.
[212] Cf. above 70.

conversation between himself and his close friends.[213] His heart was not in the job which is why, 'always playing a role – but never the right one', the one part he found he could not play was 'that of Caesar'.[214] But why did he act Apollo?

It has been suggested that, by moving close to Apollo, Nero was following the lead of Augustus and that his later Apolline programme was an extension of the Augustan propaganda of the start of his principate.[215] Though simple continuation of Augustan tradition may have appealed to some of his advisers, it does not ring true for Nero himself, no slave of convention. He was never keen on formal state religion – we are back to his blasphemous treatment of the Dea Syria[216] – in the end putting all his trust in a small statue of a girl which he worshipped as an all-powerful deity.[217] The construction of temples was therefore 'not a hot item in the Neronian building policy'.[218] Augustan-style state religion, indeed, continued undisturbed,[219] further proof that Nero was not set on religious revolution. So why was Nero so drawn to Apollo that he sometimes appeared to act Apollo? We must look to Nero 'the actor', not Nero 'the god': to 'the increasingly audacious self-dramatization of an indefatigable artist and performer'.[220] However, while Champlin's actor is set on a determined ideological course, mine acts only for temporary relief and has little idea of where he is headed. This Nero acts Apollo in order to justify his means of escaping for a while from the role of *princeps*. 'Apollo' was loaded with cultural resonances which the educated classes would instantly have appreciated.[221] Apollo was a god to be both loved and feared: one of war as well as peace. He had made singing holy, and charioteering the sport of kings.[222] In playing 'Nero-Apollo' the *princeps* was expressing his interest in sport and art but not thereby abdicating his position as autocrat. This gave him the authority and confidence to follow alternative interests

[213] Above 104; below 291. This was not unique: one is reminded of Vespasian's 'Oh dear, I think I'm turning into a god' (Suet. *Vesp.* 23.4).
[214] Edwards 1994, 92–3 (quotations); cf. Meier 2008, 589–90; above 16, 57; below 294.
[215] Grant 1970, 207; Cadario 2011, 184; above 272.   [216] Above 266.
[217] Suet. *Ner.* 56 (*summum numen*); Bradley 1978a, 292. Nero's reverencing of this image fits with what Pliny I says (*HN* 30.15, 17) about Nero and Mithraism: that Nero was alerted to Mithras by Tiridates, and drawn to his worship because he believed that through this he would be able to control the gods; but he gave it up when he when he found he could not do so. Cf. Cizek 1982, 351–2.
[218] Moormann 2003, 379.   [219] Erker 2013, 118–25.
[220] Champlin 2003, 234. Cf. Elsner 1994, 113; Buckley 2013b, 133.
[221] Cf. Champlin 2003, 93–4.   [222] Waldherr 2005, 120; Braund 2013, 85, 95.

and, for a short time, be more of himself: authenticity through acting, part of his coping strategy.[223] He played the role and then laid it aside.

Yet why did he throw himself so enthusiastically into alternative activities in the first place? Though Nero had long been interested in the arts and sport, and probably began to tire of the duties of a *princeps* in 58,[224] he showed a particular enthusiasm for games relatively late, in 59 with the *Ludi Maximi* and the *Iuvenalia*.[225] He did not perform in public until 64, and indulged in large-scale performance only from later 66, after his arrival in Greece. This suggests that his turning away from the role of *princeps* was not only enabled but also accelerated by the death of Agrippina: by his making himself a matricide.[226] We should not assume that, though never 'mad', he remained mentally the same throughout his life. Disturbing events can affect personalities. Complex Post-Traumatic Stress Disorder (CPTSD) has been linked to 'repeated interpersonal trauma occurring during crucial developmental periods'.[227] These periods are usually those of early life, but Nero was subject to considerable stress a number of times as a young adult: on the deaths of Agrippina (59), Octavia (62) and his first child (63); on the Great Fire (64) and the Pisonian conspiracy (65); and on the death of Poppaea and her unborn baby (65). That, whatever his degree of responsibility for it, he was profoundly affected by Agrippina's killing is adequate explanation for the long delay in his divorcing Octavia and marrying Poppaea.[228] Such major calamities may also have stimulated him increasingly to seek relief in sport and art. He put on the mask of Apollo to justify these diversions. After Poppaea's death, such relief became even more necessary. That he was plunged into an abyss of sorrow is reflected in his treatment of her corpse and his obsession with her double, Sporus.[229] However, again, Nero never became 'mad'. In the post-Poppaea period there are no signs of his displaying the most acute symptoms of CPTSD, such as a fragmented, emotionally unregulated and self-loathing personality, emotional numbness and lack of empathy.[230] On the contrary, he maintained close friendships and retained his ability to banter and his common touch. On the other hand, he may have suffered some lesser mental disturbance, which caused him to turn even more obsessively to the roles of sportsman and actor, exposing himself to new

---

[223] Cf. above 286. I was alerted to clinical 'coping strategy' by Dr Sunderland; cf. James 2007, 85.
[224] Above 144.   [225] Below 297.   [226] Above 187.   [227] Lanius *et al.* 2011, 332.
[228] Above 182; cf. Waldherr 2005, 183.   [229] Below 312.
[230] Editorial comment 2011, 329; Lanius *et al.* 2011, 333–4.

and challenging circumstances, both real and 'virtual', in order to come to grips with all his painful experiences.[231]

'Disassociation' is a psychological condition in which unhappy memories and unwanted situations detach people from society, and which they attempt to deal with by playing a range of parts: 'We may feel most real when pretending to be someone else'.[232] Nero will have been aware of rumours: that his mother had contrived the death of his stepfather; that his stepbrother had died no natural death, and that he was involved in the murder; and that he had slept with his mother. On top of these he actually knew that he bore some responsibility for the deaths of Agrippina, Octavia and, though unintentionally, Poppaea. It appears that Nero could not shake all this from his mind and that, though again never 'mad', his dwelling on it, especially while in Greece, caused him to suffer a form of CPTSD and disassociation. There is general acceptance of a link between the charges and Nero's choice of stage roles.[233] He sang the parts of Oedipus, who killed his father, married his mother, and blinded himself;[234] of Orestes, who killed his mother and stepfather on the orders of Apollo of Delphi;[235] of Alcmeon, another matricide;[236] of Thyestes, who devoured some of his children, and had a son by his daughter; and of Hercules, who killed his children and their mother while mad.[237] In the 'climaxing' of his activities as a performer, Nero also sang female parts:[238] of Niobe (his first, in 66[239]), who caused the deaths of her fourteen children by boasting about them to Leto, the mother of Apollo and Artemis; of Antigone, who killed herself and brought about the deaths of her fiancé and his mother; and of Melanippe, who suffered because of a secret pregnancy. Perhaps most touchingly, he sang as Canace, who had a child by her brother, born despite attempts to abort it only to be killed by its grandfather, who then ordered Canace to kill herself.[240] Champlin interprets these performances as Nero's facing up to the accusations levelled against him, admitting them and attempting to explain and justify them to audiences able to pick up every nuance of his performance. His defence was political necessity or temporary imbalance of mind.[241]

---

[231] Champlin 2003, 55; above 57–8.   [232] James 2007, 210.
[233] For the following see Suet. *Ner.* 21.2 (Niobe), 21.3 (Oedipus, Orestes, Canace, Hercules); Cass. Dio 63.9.4 (Oedipus, Orestes, Alcmeon, Canace, Thyestes, Hercules), 63.10.2 (Canace); Juv. 8.228–9 (Thyestes, Antigone, Melanippe).
[234] Champlin 2003, 101–2.   [235] Champlin 2003, 97–8.   [236] Champlin 2003, 98–9.
[237] Champlin 2003, 107.   [238] Meier 2008, 587: 'Zuspitzung'.
[239] Waldherr 2005, 127; Meier 2008, 585.   [240] Champlin 2003, 103–6.
[241] Champlin 2003, 92–8, 103.

Thus playing the matricide allowed him to defend the murder of Agrippina as the removal of someone who owed her final power to the suspicious death of her husband, who as a woman had no right to run the state,
and who was threatening the rightful heir, himself.[242] Nero did this on his
own initiative, not in reaction to rumour, in order to take the attack to
Agrippina, but it rebounded against him by creating, or at least confirming, stories about him.[243] But such self-justification lacks the emotion and
drama which Nero craved, and Champlin is forced to go beyond it to
conscience: the central point is that it was Nero and not his enemies who
chose to mythologise the murder of his mother. 'By presenting Orestes as
one of his favourite roles, by underscoring the predilection with Alcmaeon,
by dramatising the torment of the conscience in his life off-stage, by
performing the matricide on stage in a mask that bore his own features,
Nero framed the terms of the debate over his own guilt'.[244] Raw emotion
must, in particular, have largely formed his portrayal of Canace, which he
played wearing a stage-mask bearing the features of Poppaea.[245] I propose
that his performances were not a means of political self-defence but
another coping strategy. Seeing parallels between his own life and Greek
tragedy,[246] he chose to act certain roles because these allowed him to
identify and explore a number of unusually difficult experiences. He may
have sensed that the death of Poppaea had taken him to the edge of
madness;[247] and he may indeed have become addicted to the lash of
conscience.[248] As today:

> By identifying with fictional characters in films and novels we can experi-
> ence our emotions more intensely than in reality . . . Escape into fiction and
> a regaining of power over otherwise inescapable reality is a prime motiv-
> ation of creative artists. In all the arts there is an element of controlling
> other humans by engaging their emotions and forcing them to feel those

---

[242] Champlin 2003, 97–8, 102.   [243] Champlin 2003, 99–100, 110.   [244] Champlin 2003, 99.
[245] Cass. Dio 63.9.5, 10.2. Suetonius' claim (*Ner.* 21.3) that he wore masks of his current lovers is
surely a characteristic derivation of a series from a single instance.
[246] Meier 2008, 592.
[247] Cf. Reitz 2006, 48, on Seneca's tragedies, with which Nero must have been very familiar, as
'Psychoprogramme', allowing the reader/spectator to peer into an abyss of unavoidable and
insoluble evil; cf. Reitz 2006, 60, concerning Seneca's *Phaedra*, and the attention it gives to
madness, and its link to love: '*Furor* und *libido* sind nahe beieinander'.
[248] Cf. Henderson 1905, 125–6, on Nero as Orestes, relating this both to his fears, after the death of
his mother, of being pursued by the Furies, and his rejoicing in such a fate: 'To be the prey of the
Furies' cruel chase was a mark of no small distinction. Even an artist-prince may boast of it and
fearfully rejoice in it, when by repetition of the savage tale he comes to accept this new gift of the
Tragic Muse, the belief not only in his own certain guild, in the incredible penalty as well'.

that are difficult or moving – most often, the ones that the artists cannot cope with themselves.[249]

As an artist, Nero may have believed that he could create the best art from such experiences: he was inspired by them.[250] However, his obsession with the past prevented him from moving on to accept his full responsibilities as *princeps* and encouraged others to believe in the rumours of his involvement in evil deeds. Other aspects of the behaviour of mythological matricides, such as their sexual relations with their mothers, then came to be attached to him, exerting 'a retroactive effect on his life'.[251] Stage-incest and stage-murder combined with gossip and spite to 'confirm' real incest and real murder, for example, concerning the 'collapsible' ship: "'Ah, that's how he got rid of his mother then'".[252] Allusion-hungry audiences would have been sensitive to such perceived admissions of guilt: '... if the roles postdate the crimes they function as it were only as a confirmation of the theatrical impulse that spurred crimes of this nature in the first place'.[253] Performing such roles in public anyway grossly contravened Roman aristocratic good taste.[254] It was therefore easy for Nero's enemies when, for other reasons, his political position weakened and after his fall, to brand him as the insane and heartless perpetrator of atrocious crimes, the 'debased endpoint' of the gens Iulia.[255] But this was in the future. As far as Nero was concerned, the roles were just roles. He never lost himself within them; he never became totally disassociated from society; he always returned to reality. When assessing the story of the young recruit who ran to 'free' Nero from his stage-chains, we must recognise that it was the soldier, not the *princeps*, who confused fiction and fact.[256] Though contemporaries may not have fully appreciated the distinction, Nero knew when he was in character and when he was not, i.e. when he was acting.[257] He adopted other personalities only when he was on stage; and when he left it he was himself again.[258] Renewed banter over the nature of his power signalled his taking up the role of *princeps*.[259] As he acted the *princeps* so he acted the actor.

[249] James 2007, 213.   [250] Cf. Lenz 2013, 282
[251] Bartsch 1994, 61 (quotation); Champlin 2003, 110, 138; Meier 2008, 592–3.
[252] Dawson 1964, 261–5.   [253] Bartsch 1994, 61–2 (quotation), 79–80.
[254] Waldherr 2005, 128–9.   [255] Buckley 2013b, 135, 139 (quotation).
[256] Suet. *Ner.* 21.3; Cass. Dio 63.10.2.
[257] According to Green (2010, 504), in principle the Romans had no concept of being in character. In another instance, however, Nero showed that he did: below 318. *Contra* Griffin 2013, 476; cf. Bartsch 1994, 46, 61–2, 190; above 58.
[258] *Contra* Buckley 2013b, 133.   [259] Cf. above 97.

Acting the actor and sportsman began before Nero's first public stage performance, in 64, and peaked during his time in Greece, in 66–67.[260] Such behaviour invites the suspicion of hypocrisy: that Nero went through the motions of competition knowing that the prizes would be awarded to him anyway. This is unfair. Despite acting Apollo as musician and charioteer, Nero never insisted on any unjustified appreciation of 'divine' excellence. On the contrary, he always behaved like an ordinary competitor. Though many performing artists are open to the charge of narcissism, craving recognition to override their low self-esteem,[261] this does not ring true of Nero. His upbringing in the hands of people who cared for him and for whom he cared, and his awareness of his exalted background, Domitian and Julio-Claudian,[262] will have forestalled any sense of worthlessness. Likewise, it is unlikely that he suffered utterly profound doubt about his abilities. He appears to have had genuine poetic ability and perhaps not too bad a voice;[263] and his reported last-minute contemplation of abdication in favour of a career as a citharode makes sense only if both he and the creators of the anti-Neronian tradition were aware of his abilities.[264] His problem was that he knew he was good but, anxious for authentic praise, had genuine doubts as to precisely how good he was and whether he could produce a first-rate performance on the day.[265] To achieve success, he subjected himself to a harsh regime of exercise, diet and training;[266] and during competitions, in order to avoid disqualification and defeat, he sedulously, in a manner unbefitting a Roman aristocrat, let alone a *princeps*, kept strictly to the rules, obeyed officials and abhorred mistakes.[267] Competition judges must have found his public fawning and private complaining very difficult to handle.[268] Likewise, his acting the ordinary competitor even while off-stage, casually dressed and heedless of his personal safety among the crowds, will have been a nightmare for those in charge of protocol and security.[269] A slighting remark in Dio hints that he may actually have lost some contests;[270] but his clear ambition must have disturbed those competitors capable of beating him. In his envy, he is supposed to have attempted to undermine their confidence, buy them off

[260] Above 288.   [261] Cf. James 2007, 214.   [262] Above 279.

[263] Suet. *Ner.* 20.1, 52; Mart. *Epig.* 8.70; *contra* Tac. *Ann.* 14.16.1–2. Cf. Bradley 1978a, 123–4; Fini 1994, 22; Holland 2000, 115; above 101.

[264] Cass. Dio 63.27.2.

[265] Tac. *Ann.* 16.4.2. Fini 1994, 99; *contra* Cizek 1982: 'il se tenait pour le plus grand artiste de son temps'.

[266] Suet. *Ner.* 20.1; Cass. Dio 63.9.1. Below 303–4.

[267] Suet. *Ner.* 23.2, 24.1; Cass. Dio 63.9.2. Cf. Tac. *Ann.* 16.4.2.   [268] Suet. *Ner.* 23.3.

[269] Suet. *Ner.* 20.2; Cass. Dio 63.9.1–2.   [270] Cass. Dio 63.21.2.

and even destroy the memory or contrive the deaths of the best of them.[271] Yet he was not vindictive, and such charges, like most against Nero, were probably exaggerated or fabricated. Thus his alleged jealous killing of Paris rings false because pantomime was not part of Nero's professional repertoire.[272] Nero was, in his own eyes, a genuine competitor but he was simply uncertain of his 'world professional ranking'.

11.4   Ideology

I deal with Nero's ideology in more detail below.[273] Here it suffices to repeat that, far from aiming at divine kingship or ever-greater secular autocracy, or at effortless and unquestioned stardom, he had no clear notion as to where he was going as *princeps*, sportsman or public entertainer, or how well he was progressing *en route*. After the death of Agrippina he moved from acting the *princeps* to acting the sportsman and artist. Thus engaged, he could have given little thought to deep political issues. A major obstacle was simply one of time. He devoted hours to preparing himself as singer and musician. Probably even more went into charioteering: he cannot have worked his way up to driving a ten-horse team without constant physical training and the acquisition of complex skills.[274] This has significant implications for the identification of those who actually ran 'Nero's' principate for most of his reign.[275] Once his principate was running as he wished, with him taking a back seat in its administration,[276] Nero appears to have conceived a more active desire to alter Roman society: to make it more relaxed – more 'Greek', with the *princeps* closer to the people – and less militaristic. A crucial turning-point appears to have been Tigellinus' 'banquet' of 64.[277] In all this, however, his ambitions were relatively narrow, very personal and vulnerable to disruption by contingent events. He made no serious effort to reform Roman state religion;[278] and, more important, he never sought to abandon the military foundation of the Principate. On the contrary, he gave his generals, campaigning under his auspices, free rein.[279] He left the routine administration of the Empire to others; he had no ambitions for advanced autocracy; he followed no philosophical school;[280] he had no overarching ideology.[281] Near the end, his Greek 'triumph' was self-indulgent and

---

[271]   Suet. *Ner.* 23.2, 24.1; Cass. Dio 63.8.5, 63.9.2, 63.18.1.
[272]   Suet. *Ner.* 54; Cass. Dio 63.18.2 Above 232; Bradley 1978a, 143; Fantham 2013, 20.
[273]   Below 373.   [274]   Below 304.   [275]   Above 130.   [276]   Cf. Mordine 2013, 112–13.
[277]   Below 308.   [278]   Erker 2013, 131.   [279]   Above 145.   [280]   *Contra* Holland 2000, 55.
[281]   Cf. Griffin 1984, 219: 'Nero concentrated on exhibiting his superiority as an artist'; below 309.

self-centred but ideologically unfocused in its strange mixing of the novel and the old-fashioned.[282]

11.5   Burn-Out?

Even Nero's limited ambitions were doomed to failure. He could pursue them only as long as the court Establishment was prepared to support him. His fall in 68 was not the result of delusion, but of obstinacy, of refusing to do what was expected of a *princeps*, of playing the part, but not to the full.[283] But here a final aspect of the relationship between Nero's personality and ambitions requires consideration. In 66, Nero had gone to Greece while under the strain of the Pisonian conspiracy and the death of Poppaea.[284] His experience there seems to have enabled him to come to terms with these and earlier troubles, and even to enjoy himself. The visit came to a magnificent climax late in 67, with the declaration of the freedom of Greece at Corinth. Nero then returned to Rome in style, but after this, and especially from March 68, events moved quickly to destroy him.[285] The strong impression is that Nero was disinclined to save himself.[286] It could be an artefact of the sources that we find no reports of the planning or holding of any major games,[287] but if authentic this is unsurprising and significant. The Greek visit, the Italian progress and the Roman 'triumph' must have left Nero in acute need of physical and mental recuperation. More important, they may have left him emotionally burned out. He had scaled the heights of success in sportsmanship and the performing arts. The 1,808 victory-crowns that he exhibited as his spoils marked him out as the supreme athlete and entertainer: 'world Number One'. There was nothing else for him to achieve.[288] Furthermore, through his acting, he had faced and overcome most of his deepest anxieties. Though he was still in denial about the death of Poppaea, he could at least relax in the company of the ever-attentive Poppaea-substitute, Sporus.[289] It may well be that from early 68 Nero fell into a torpor, not the best condition for what was about to follow.[290]

---

[282] Below 384.   [283] Below 407.   [284] Holland 2000, 197; above 288.   [285] Below 389.
[286] Cf. below 393.   [287] Cf. below 302.
[288] Suet. *Ner.* 25; Cass. Dio 63.21.1. Cf. below 338; Meier 2008, 597–8, 600–1.   [289] Below 311.
[290] Below 389.

CHAPTER 12

Depravity?

12.1 Introduction

The popular perception of Nero is that he was not just mad but also hopelessly depraved. Having complained that 'there is no shameful act that all too lurid fantasy has not heaped upon Nero's Borgia-like character', even Hohl succumbed to describing how, in 64, Nero threw himself into sensuous orgies in which Rome became a new Sodom.[1] 'Fantasy' is, of course, the stock-in-trade of the anti-Neronian source tradition in which senatorial misrepresentation was amplified by the stricter morality of the next generation of Romans.[2] How 'bad' Nero is painted will always depend on contemporary attitudes. Twenty-first century concepts of 'depravity' are neither those of ancient Romans of any age nor those of earlier modern historians. Henderson, for example, excoriates Petronius' *Satyricon* as 'impossibly indecent', 'outside the imagination or the experience of the modern reader'.[3] On the other hand, we should not cheerfully welcome the 'liberal' morality of the *Satyricon* as authentic Neronian morality of *princeps,* court or society at large. The Roman intellectual elite always fretted about a decline in values, even under 'good' leaders.[4] Thus, although Pliny II was more optimistic under Trajan, Tacitus' praise of the noble barbarian in his *Germania* and gloomy moralising in his *Annales* show that he could not see any significant improvement.[5] In addition, the elite harboured many misconceptions about the 'immoral' lives of the rest of the population.[6] Petronius could exploit this to confect a tale of ubiquitous vulgarism and debauchery, in a world represented by such

---

[1] Hohl 1918, 368: 'Es gibt eben keine Schandtat, die von einer allzu lebhaften Phantasie nicht auf die Borgianatur Neros gehäuft worden wäre'; 379; cf. below 298–9, 308.
[2] Above 7, 88. Tac. *Ann.* 3.55. Bartsch 1994, 29–32; Milnor 2005, 293; Griffin 2013, 474–5.
[3] Henderson 1905, 327–8; cf. above 101.   [4] Doody 2013, 295.
[5] Plin. *Pan.* 46.4. Cf. Bartsch 1994, 30.   [6] Erker 2013, 129–30.

characters as Encolpius ('in crotch') and Ascyltos ('shagged out').[7] He wrote fiction that probably contained little truth, and may in fact be inverted to reveal the boorish Trimalchio as a hard-working, self-made man doing well for himself and helping to maintain the relative good health of state finances.[8] For us to use the *Satyricon* to reconstruct Neronian morality would be like using Pope's *Dunciad* to reconstruct that of Georgian England. The best approach is to consider Nero's alleged vices head on, under Suetonius' categories of 'indiscipline, lust, extravagance, avarice and cruelty'.[9] Much of what Suetonius says derives from the common source tradition, but he shapes this material to imply that each type of vice led inevitably to the next and so make Nero solely responsible for his criminal principate and its failure.[10] Many of Suetonius' criticisms have already been dismissed; the remainder do not stand up to close scrutiny.

12.2   Indiscipline

Suetonius begins with the misdeeds of Nero's first years as *princeps*, in particular his nightly wandering of the streets of Rome in disguise, drinking, stealing and beating up passers-by and being badly beaten up by them. This finds similar mention in Tacitus and Dio; and Pliny I remarks on an ointment used by Nero to treat bruises sustained in brawls. Tacitus adds that his behaviour encouraged imitators which increased the scale of disorder.[11] In one notorious incident, Nero suffered at the hands of the young senator, Julius Montanus. After this, he was protected by a squad of soldiers and gladiators. During the daytime he revelled in encouraging fighting in the theatre between rival mime actors and their supporters, viewing the mayhem from a safe vantage.[12] Yet this behaviour is hardly surprising. Youth, especially highly privileged male youth, has always sought excitement in such ways: Gaius is purported to have done the same on Capri.[13] There is no need to interpret it as a desire to test popular opinion.[14] In some societies such pursuits may even be regarded as commendable indicators of the daring and physical fitness expected in future military leaders.[15] Those whom Nero sought to please in this

---

[7] Murgatroyd 2013, 241 (quotations), 245.   [8] Murgatroyd 2013, 254; cf. below 364.
[9] Suet. *Ner.* 26.1: *Petulantiam, libidinem, luxuriam, avaritiam, crudelitatem ... exercuit.*
[10] Bradley 1978a, 153–4.   [11] Tac. *Ann.* 13.25.2. Holland 2000, 95; Winterling 2007, 47.
[12] Sen. *Clem.* 1.8.2; Suet. *Ner.* 26.2; Tac. *Ann.* 13.25, 13.47.2–3; Cass. Dio 61.8–9; Plin. *HN* 13.126; cf. below 317.
[13] Winterling 2007, 47.   [14] Bradley 1978a, 155.   [15] Cf. Holland 2000, 95; below 303–4.

period, Agrippina and Pallas and Seneca and Burrus,[16] may well have encouraged him. The set-to with Montanus and its consequences will have embarrassed them, and they would not have wished Nero to come to serious harm, but their provision of 'minders' shows that they did not stop his adventuring.[17] Champlin's suggestion that in all this Nero was playing the boy-'King of Saturnalia' (*rex Saturnalicius*) and then the adult-'Prince of Saturnalia' (Nero: *princeps Saturnalicius*) is questionable.[18] However, his point that Nero's rowdy behaviour lasted only from his accession in to 58, when he turned 21, is instructive. It may be understood as 'youthful folly', 'boys will be boys'.[19]

Suetonius continues his tale of how Nero's innate lack of manners turned into degeneracy by dwelling on his participation in great banquets on land and on water. These were inordinately long and depraved, in particular in their debasing of respectable Roman married women:

> Whenever he drifted down the Tiber to Ostia or sailed about the bay at Baiae, arranged along the shores and banks were taverns with private chambers, notorious for dissipation and infamous for their proprietors, who were matrons pretending to be dancing girls and who urged him to step ashore on one side or the other.[20]

Nero's banqueting and humiliation of women is part of a wider aspect of his alleged ill-manneredness: his debauching of others and of himself. Suetonius first touches on the corruption of others earlier in his 'Life' of Nero, in his description of the *princeps'* insistence on upper-class participation in *spectacula* – public entertainments.[21] Though Suetonius appears little concerned by this, it was properly a violation of the conventions of Roman aristocratic society and is given scandalised attention by Tacitus and Dio.[22] In 55, *equites* hunted wild animals and fought as gladiators.[23] In 57, senators and equestrians fought each other and wild beasts, and served as attendants in the arena.[24] In 59, the *princeps* celebrated Agrippina's death by staging the *Ludi Maximi*.[25] These for the most part amounted to an extended variety performance, comprising popular dramas and entertainments, staged throughout the City, in which senators and equestrians took leading parts. One featured an *eques* riding a

---

[16] Above 286.   [17] Romm 2014, 93–4; cf. below 317.
[18] Champlin 2003, 150–60; cf. below 313.   [19] Champlin 2003, 152–3.
[20] Suet. *Ner.* 27.3 (trans. after Hurley 2011).   [21] Suet. *Ner.* 11.2.
[22] Cf. Cass. Dio 61.17.4–5.   [23] Cass. Dio 61.9.1; Champlin 2003, 68.
[24] Tac. *Ann.* 13.31.1; Suet. *Ner.* 12.1.   [25] Cf. above 181.

tightrope-walking elephant. Dio also mentions upper-class participation in charioteering, the fighting of wild beasts and gladiatorial contests.[26] In the same year, Nero held the *Iuvenalia*, a family event made semi-public,[27] to celebrate the first shaving of his beard. The *Iuvenalia* were also mainly theatrical and musical, involving upper-class participants of both sexes and all ages. Tacitus expresses particular horror at this:

> Neither rank, nor age, nor an official career debarred a man from practising the art of a Greek or Latin stage-performer, down to attitudes and melodies never meant for the male sex. Even women of distinction studied indecent parts.

Elsewhere, he tells of Fabius Valens, later a senatorial commander in the civil war of 69–70, who appeared in mimes. Another named noble performer is the octogenarian dancer, Aelia Catella. Nero allowed no performers to wear masks. The *Iuvenalia* concluded with an event that recalls Suetonius' lascivious matrons. Tacitus describes how, around the *Navale Stagnum*, an artificial lake built by Augustus as the venue for mock naval battles,

> ... little hidden rendezvous and drinking-dens sprang up, and every incentive to voluptuousness was exposed for sale ... Hence debauchery and scandal throve; nor to our morals, corrupted long before, has anything contributed more of uncleanness than that herd of reprobates.[28]

Nero's first full Greek-style games, the *Neronia*, held in 60 and scheduled to take place every five years thereafter, featured musical, gymnastic and equestrian competitions. These were, on the Greek model, aesthetic, ascetic and indeed sacred. However, while conceding that they ended 'without any glaring scandal', Tacitus again criticises them for compulsory upper-class involvement and for their endorsement of degenerate foreign ways.[29] The next great spectacle we know of occurred in 63, and consisted of gladiatorial contests which Tacitus describes as having been as magnificent as any in the past, while deploring the way in which even more women of standing and men of senatorial rank 'were disgraced in the arena', which must mean that they took part.[30] In 64, Nero appeared for the first time in public as a singer and charioteer, in Naples; and then came

---

[26] Tac. *Ann.* 14.14.5; Suet. *Ner.* 11.2; Cass. Dio 61.17.2–5; Bradley 1978a, 84; Champlin 2003, 70.
[27] Waldherr 2005, 121.
[28] Tac. *Hist.* 3.62; cf. 1.7; Tac. *Ann.* 14.15.1–4; Suet. *Ner.* 11.1; Cass. Dio 61.19–20.
[29] Tac. *Ann.* 14.20–21 (21.7: *nullo insigni dehonestamento*); Suet. *Ner.* 12.3. Warmington 1969, 115; Champlin 2003, 72–3.
[30] Tac. *Ann.* 15.32.3: *per arenam foedati*. Champlin 2003, 73.

'Tigellinus' banquet' in Rome, 'the party of the century'.[31] Though
Tigellinus was the organiser, Nero was clearly the host and, according to
Tacitus, 'treated the whole city as if it were his house'.[32] Festivities centred
on the *Stagnum Agrippae* in the Campus Martius.[33] This was an another
artificial lake, enclosed by parkland and connected to the Tiber by a canal.
Built under Augustus, it had been incorporated by Nero into his luxurious
new gymnasium complex.[34] Here, seated on a great raft, drawn around by
boats rowed by male prostitutes, Nero and his guests dined in splendour.
They were watched by great crowds, attracted by the imperial show, free
gifts, a small zoo and lakeside brothels, filled with noblewomen and
opposite which professional prostitutes paraded naked. Dio gives details
of the raft and adds that the brothels were filled with women of every
degree, unable to refuse any man who wanted them.[35] Both authors
describe drunken debauchery lasting from day into brightly-lit, rowdy
and, for some, fatal night.

I will consider 'banquets' and 'brothels' more closely below.[36] To what
extent did Nero degrade the Roman upper classes by making them
perform for the masses? Henderson had no doubts, describing Nero as
'corrupting others ... till even Roman Society sickened at the sight'.[37]
A modern response is 'probably very little'. The source tradition adopted
traditional Roman aristocratic prejudice against public entertainers. Moralising post-Neronian writers, in particular, loathed them as social outcasts
whose calling nevertheless gave them a public platform outside the control
of the political elite.[38] Abhorrence on principle was probably increased by
embarrassment at practice: Roman aristocrats demonstrated an ineradic-
able inclination to be public performers themselves.[39] Post-Neronians
strove to replace the 'glamour' of performance with 'shame',[40] but in
Nero's time 'glamour' was still ascendant. There are very few signs of
inordinate pressure being put on members of the Neronian upper-class to
perform in public.[41] Though some aristocrats will have detested the idea,
even Tacitus has to concede that others volunteered. He explains this as

---

[31] Tac. *Ann.* 15.37; Cass. Dio 62.15; Champlin 2003, 153 (quotation). For Henderson (1905, 236),
 this was no 'party' but 'vice, open, unrestrained', which he cannot bring himself to describe in
 detail.
[32] Tac. *Ann.* 15.37.1: *totaque urbe quasi domo uti.*
[33] Tac. *Ann.* 15.37.1–7, with Champlin 2003, 153–4.   [34] Gymnasium: below 331.
[35] Cass. Dio 62.15.   [36] Below 302, 307.   [37] Henderson 1905, 236.
[38] E.g. Plin. *Ep.* 4.22.7. Edwards 1994, 83–6.
[39] Tac. *Ann.* 1.77.5. Cf. Furneaux 1907, 356 on Tac. *Ann.* 15.32.3; Bradley 1978a, 87.
[40] Edwards 1994, 84 (quotations), 90.
[41] E.g. Bradley 1978a, 84; Champlin 2003, 65, 71, 76–9, 115.

the combination of substantial financial inducements and implied threats; but elsewhere he admits that at least one of the conscripted, Fabius Valens of the *Iuvenalia*, grew to relish the experience.[42] Likewise Dio declares baldly that although some equestrians and senators competed in the *Iuvenalia* against their will, others were ready to do so.[43] Neither writer suggests that conscription was more prevalent than volunteering. Though Epictetus appears to confirm extreme compulsion, this is probably better interpreted as standard Stoic anti-tyrannical, and standard Flavian anti-Neronian, rhetoric.[44] Aristocrats' readiness to perform will have been encouraged by the fact that for them life was 'almost always played out in an at least semi-public space': performance was what they did.[45] Under the Republic, great families borrowed from theatre in staging grand public funerals,[46] but the starring role craved by every ambitious males was that of *triumphator*. Aristocrats learned how to construct *personae* appropriate to each occasion in the rhetorical studies of their youth.[47] Performance continued under the 'restored' Republic as aristocrats acted constantly before dependants, peers and *principes*:[48] *Principes* themselves went further. They extended the traditional triumph with, for example, Claudius taking the lead in a *Buffalo Bill's Wild West Show*-like re-enactment of his conquest of Britain. They also presided on grand occasions such as Nero's reception of Tiridates, staged twice to meet public demand and made to look very much like a triumph.[49] Performance for public entertainment was not vastly different and was no Neronian innovation. The fact that nobles could, as 'brilliant amateurs',[50] put on creditable public shows at relatively short notice indicates significant prior experience. Hunting, weapons training and active service would have prepared young men for animal-hunts in the arena, under Nero as they had under Gaius.[51] Those who participated would have done so because they enjoyed the experience, with no grudge against a non-participating Nero who had his own known preferences.[52] Aristocratic participation in pantomimes and plays was probably rooted in what we might call amateur theatricals.[53] Senators

---

[42] Tac. *Hist.* 3.62; cf. Tac. *Ann.* 14.21.1 on majority, presumably educated-class, approval of *Neronia* I. Above 298.

[43] Cass. Dio 61.17.3.   [44] Arr. *Epict. diss.* 1.2; Bradley 1978a, 84; Champlin 2003, 287–8.

[45] Pausch 2013, 65: 'fast immer in einem zumindest halböffentlichen Bereich abspielte'.

[46] Littlewood 2015, 166.   [47] Littlewood 2015, 162–3   [48] Winterling 2007, 137–8.

[49] Suet. *Claud.* 21.6. Osgood 2011, 92; Barrett *et al.* 2016, 243 n. 23; above 265. Dio's (62.23.4) statement that, following Rhandeia II, Nero was saluted as *imperator* and held a triumph 'contrary to precedent' (*para to nenomismenon*) seems to refer to this reception; cf. Payne 1962, 181.

[50] Cizek 1982, 124; 'de brillants amateurs'.   [51] Cf. Winterling 2007, 77.

[52] Cf. Rea 2011, 211–12.   [53] Suet. *Calig.* 54.2. Holland 2000, 24–5.

performed in dramas associated with traditional festivals in their home towns;[54] and the recitation of verse texts – classed together with song as *carmina* – was a regular aristocratic diversion. Domestic 'concert' productions of extracts from Seneca's dramas are thus very likely.[55] Dio reports *didaskaleia* ('schools') of entertainment which prepared aristocrats for the *Iuvenalia*.[56] These are unlikely to have been new. Gaius had been a keen dancer;[57] and pantomime – properly, 'ballet' – was currently all the rage.[58] The broader context is, of course, 'a world about to turn Greco-Roman'.[59] The Hellenisation of Roman culture began under the Republic, strengthened under the Julio-Claudians and flourished in the second century in the 'Second Sophistic'.[60] Educated Romans of the mid-first century rode the cultural new wave.[61]

Many aristocrats were, therefore, not averse to public performance, and probably the more so because, with the rise of the *princeps* as the ultimate patron, traditional aristocratic display was restricted. *Spectacula* were well established,[62] and participation in them would have brought aristocrats into contact with famous professional entertainers who, though of low status, were not vastly dissimilar to themselves in terms of wealth and celebrity: so, with people with whom they might to some degree relax. Conservatives fought to prevent aristocrats from fighting as gladiators (presumably in non-lethal exhibition bouts[63]) and, generally, from appearing in shows (a senatorial decree of 19 explicitly bans this), but to no avail.[64] As praetor and consul, Nero's grandfather brought Roman knights and matrons on the stage to act a farce.[65] Nero's new principate, coming like a breath of fresh air to those who had experienced the stultifying and often frightening years of Tiberius, Gaius and Claudius,[66] will have raised expectations of licence. A likely 'bright young thing' of the period is Ummidia Quadratilla, who died at almost seventy-nine under Trajan. A close contemporary of Nero, she offended the strait-laced tastes of the early second century by continuing to maintain her own freedman *corps de ballet*; and there is even the hint that she too had, in her time, trod the boards.[67] Nero's ban on the wearing of masks could not have

---

[54] Tac. *Ann.* 16.21.1: Thrasea Paetus.
[55] Reitz 2006, 21, 49, 60; Buckley 2013a, 211; Maes 2013, 289–90. Cf. Suet. *Ner.* 10.2: on Nero's 'respectable' reading of his poems at home (as opposed to in the theatre).
[56] Cass. Dio 61.19.2.   [57] Suet. *Calig.* 54: *saltator*
[58] Grant 1970, 84, elaborating on Sen. *QNat.* 7.32.3.   [59] Dinter 2013, 3.   [60] Below 373–5.
[61] Cf. Winterling 2007, 67, 76–7.   [62] Furneaux 1907, 250; Champlin 2003, 62–55.
[63] Cf. Beste and Hesberg 2013, 318.   [64] Levick 1983, esp. 105–10, 115; Talbert 1984, 46–7.
[65] Suet. *Ner.* 4.1.   [66] Cf. Rudich 1993, 43; Shotter 2008, 81; above 267.
[67] Plin. *Ep.* 7.24.4–7.

humiliated such people. Professional actors were masked for comic and tragic performances, but not for mimes; the amateurs were just following suit.[68] The same air of excitement explains the success of the *Augustiani*. These were created for the *Iuvenalia* of 59 as Nero's special corps of attendants. Perhaps inspired by the games of 55 and practices of the Alexandrian theatre, they were at first raised from dashing young *equites*.[69] From 64, however, they comprised large numbers of commoners under equestrian officers.[70] Part Roman *iuventus*, part band of Hellenic 'companions', they wore 'a sort of uniform, with thick hair, dandified dress and their left hands bare of rings',[71] privileging the non-senatorial young and encouraging their self-identity. Membership must have been voluntary and fiercely competitive.

We cannot condemn Nero for debauching Roman aristocrats by coercing them into public performance. He 'could count on considerable sympathy among the leaders of society' for this when it was in full swing.[72] Then, typically, he apparently lost interest in it. Though there were other grand entertainments after Tigellinus' banquet, there is no mention of aristocratic participation, apart from that of Nero himself.[73]

So did Nero debauch himself? This returns us to his banquets. Scholars have long seen corroboration of literary accounts of Nero's self-debauchery in his 'reformed' currency, introduced in 63 and circulated in full from 64. It had many significant changes, among which were a more imaginative conception and better execution of its obverse and reverse types.[74] In Hellenistic fashion, the obverse types portray a very realistic, very human Nero, whose fleshy features seem to confirm the sources' tales of excess (Figure 14).[75]

Thus Barrett, for example, compares the handsome young Nero with 'the gross specimen that self-indulgence would create in a few short years'; and Bergmann accepts 'a life of indulgence ... visually expressed through fatness, a double chin, and small eyes sunk into the surrounding flesh'.[76]

---

[68] Cf. Reitz 2006, 23.   [69] Cizek 1982, 186; Meier 2008, 585.

[70] Tac. *Ann.* 14.15.8; Suet. *Ner.* 20.3, 25.1; Cass. Dio 61.20.4; Warmington 1969, 114–115; Bradley 1978a, 82, 127–8; Cizek 1982, 186–8; above 61. (*Contra* Bradley and Cizek, I do not believe that it began as early as 55.)

[71] Suet. *Ner.* 20.3. Levi 1949, 160; Champlin 2003, 60. Cf. above 62.   [72] Champlin 2003, 66.

[73] Tac. *Ann.* 15.44.7. Suet. *Ner.* 21.1. 46.3; Cass. Dio 63.1,6.3, 21.1.

[74] Warmington 1969, 66; cf. above 28; below 341, 354.

[75] *RIC* I² Nero no. 60. Cf. Warmington 1969, 66: '... no effort is made to make his person transcendent in any way'; above 272.

[76] Barrett 1996, 143; Bergmann 2013, 336. Cf. e.g. Griffin 1984, 30, 121; Carson 1990, 15; Fini 1994, 15; Romm 2014, 161.

Figure 14   Fleshy Nero.
Courtesy of RomaNumismatics Ltd. www.RomaNumismatics.com

Figure 15   Fleshy Vespasian.
Courtesy of RomaNumismatics Ltd. www.RomaNumismatics.com

However, viewed dispassionately, the coins (and similar contemporary statuary) hardly show a collapse into grossness: an interpretation surely determined by the hostile literary tradition. Vespasian's coin portraits show equally fleshy features, but these are usually accepted as being owed to years of hard campaigning (Figure 15).[77]

Given his artistic and sporting interests Nero must have been unusually fit and strong. If he wanted to be a first-rate citharode he needed to master the *cithara*. This, the instrument of the professional musician, was heavier and harder to play than the lyre, the instrument of the aristocratic amateur. Its mastery required long hours of taxing practice. Nero will also have needed continuous, intensive voice-training. The latter is directly reported by Suetonius:

> [He neglected] none of the exercises which artists of that kind are in the habit of following, to preserve or strengthen their voices. For he used to lie on his back and hold a leaden plate on his chest, purge himself by the syringe and by vomiting, and deny himself fruits and all foods injurious to the voice.[78]

---

[77] *RIC* 2² Vespasian no. 756. Günther 2013, 128–9.
[78] Suet. *Ner.* 20.1. Waldherr 2005, 118; Reitz 2006, 20, 22; Fantham 2013, 20–4; Pausch 2013, 52.

Thus Nero 'worked out', which would also have helped him to sustain demanding stage roles which involved dance as well as song.[79] If he wanted to be a first-rate racing-charioteer he needed similar taxing fitness training and practice.[80] While in Greece in 67 he was learning how to race a ten-horse team. Since chariots were usually drawn by four horses, our response to this should indeed 'be one of astonishment'.[81] Charioteering was, no matter the number of horses driven, a hugely demanding and dangerous activity, even for bystanders.[82] To race chariots in the circus was the peak of daring, which explains why leading charioteers were accorded great fame and wealth. Racing-chariots were basically coracles on wheels, offering no protection to their drivers, who showed huge nerve in simply boarding them.[83] To direct them required immense strength and stamina. In each horse team, only the innermost pair, controlled by reins, were attached to the chariot-shaft. The rest, usually two but sometimes up to eight in number, were harnessed to these and controlled by traces. Charioteers needed powerful hands, arms and upper bodies to manage reins and traces. Furthermore, they had to have powerful torsos and hips because reins and traces were fixed to a belt round their waist. This assemblage was all they had to steer their rigs around the twin fearsome left-hand turns of the course; and in an emergency drivers could not escape their vehicles until they had cut themselves free from it. Powerful legs and feet were required to maintain a balance on the interwoven leather straps that made up the floor of the chariot and was its only suspension. Driving a team on its own at any speed round a course was an achievement in itself. Racing with others was massively more demanding, given the need to maintain a high speed, overtake, avoid crashing and avoid crashes. Charioteers needed first-rate eye–brain coordination to anticipate changes and dangers in the shifting field of competition. The idea that Nero's looks – his 'scowl' or 'blinking, half-closed eyes' – reveal a profound short-sightedness is therefore as questionable as their reflecting a lack of fitness.[84] References to his myopia are found in Suetonius and Pliny I, with the latter also recording that Nero watched gladiatorial contests with the aid of an emerald.[85] However, the form and likely optical effectiveness of the emerald device

---

[79] Reitz 2006, 20 (Canace, Hercules, Oedipus, Orestes), 23.   [80] Cf. Waldherr 2005, 116.
[81] Suet. *Ner.* 24.2. Champlin 2003, 59 (quotation).   [82] Suet. *Ner.* 5.1, *Vit.* 17.2.
[83] I owe many of the following points to Dr Fear.
[84] Henderson 1905, 413 (quotation); Grant 1970, 19 (quotation).
[85] Suet. *Ner.* 51.1: *oculi … hebetiores.* Plin. *HN* 11.144: *Neroni … at, nisi cum coniveret ad prope admota, hebetes*; 37.64: *Nero princeps gladiatorum pugnas spectabat in smaragdo.*

are very unclear;[86] and severe short-sightedness would have prevented Nero racing a chariot team of any size. His eye problem was probably minor, or an affectation (he liked his gadgets[87]), or a combination of both. It was exaggerated by later critics as yet another indication of his unfitness for office: *principes* were supposed to be as physically perfect as possible, which made Claudius such an oddity. Nero's racing-chariots in real, not exhibition,[88] performances is testimony to a fine physical condition and a strong nerve. It is significant that at the same time as he was racing a ten-horse team he was contemplating entering high-level competitive wrestling.[89]

But if Nero did not allow himself to run to seed, how does this square with his love of banquets, as claimed by Suetonius and demonstrated in his construction of the Golden House Pavilion? I deal with the association of banquets with popularism below.[90] Here the issue is the extent to which these encouraged him to gluttony and drunkenness. In principle banqueting was just another aspect of aristocratic performance. A *princeps* was duty-bound to host and attend banquets as a means of promoting unity within the established social hierarchy, in particular because these allowed him to show due deference to magistrates and senators as nominal social and political peers. Augustus, Gaius and Claudius had thrown such feasts; Otho, Vespasian and Domitian would follow suit;[91] Nero was simply maintaining the tradition.[92] If he extended the self-discipline he showed in musical and sporting training to rationing what actually passed his lips, he could have 'feasted' regularly without ruining his health. Some historians have, indeed, denied that he was an habitual glutton and drunkard, citing his invention of a famous non-alcoholic drink, 'Nero's distilled water'.[93] Suetonius, in fact, states explicitly that Nero was unusually healthy, being ill only three times during his principate.[94] His qualification – that Nero remained well despite his 'indulging in every kind of notorious excess' and his refusal to give up his 'wine or usual habits' when ill – rings false. Likewise, Tacitus' description of Nero being drunk in the

---

[86] Grant 1970, 195, suggests that the jewel may have been used as a mirror or reflecting stone rather than as a lens.

[87] Suet. *Ner.* 41.2; cf. above 123–4, 249.   [88] Cf. Cass. Dio 59.74 (Gaius).

[89] Suet. *Ner.* 53. Champlin 2003, 80–1.   [90] Below 309.

[91] Goddard 1994, 68–71; Winterling 2009, 85–6.   [92] Cf. above 99.

[93] [*Aqua*] *Neronis decocta*: Suet. *Ner.* 48.3; Plin. *HN* 31.40. Henderson 1905, 413; Cizek 1982, 37–9; Fini 1994, 110; cf. Gowers 1994, 131 and above 123. Grant (1970, 106, 193), inconsistently, has Nero being both fit and gluttonous.

[94] Suet. *Ner.* 51, presumably the illnesses of *c.* 54–60, 60 and 66: Bradley 1978a, 284. Cf. above 190; below 372. Barrett (1996, 113) proposes an earlier illness, in the period 50–54.

small hours of the morning when he heard of Agrippina's supposed plot against him in 55 may be read as the *princeps'* spinning out his drinking, not his indulging in an all-night 'binge'.[95] His excessive, 'depraved', behaviour here, as elsewhere, may be seen as a later construct: 'the inevitable part of the image of the tyrant'.[96] So what did the new portraiture of the reformed coinage aim to portray?[97]

Nero was always careful of his appearance. This is shown in his changing hairstyles. Traditional Roman morality disparaged male interest in coiffure as time-wasting and effeminate.[98] However, Nero's official portraits – on statues, busts and coins – show him abandoning the simple traditional Julio-Claudian hairstyle immediately after the death of Agrippina and experimenting with others.[99] By 64 he had adopted an elaborate style, described by Suetonius as 'stepped' (i.e. 'crimped', 'permanently waved') and, along with his later switch to shoulder-length hair, deplored by his biographer as making him 'utterly shameless'.[100] Nero's crimped style should not be taken to indicate a Hellenising ideology, or of a popularist copying of stage entertainers and charioteers. It was rather his adoption of a fashion of the time. Nero was thereby distancing himself from the dowdy past by depicting himself as a member of the metropolitan smart set.[101] (One suspects that the 'thick hair' of the *Augustiani* was dressed on much the same lines.[102]) His growing of a light, 'designer stubble' beard probably also resulted from a wish to keep up with fashion.[103] Keenly aware of his appearance, even if he had allowed his physique to collapse it is most unlikely that Nero would have allowed this to be shown on his own coins. But he remained fit, and I propose that the new obverses advertised physical developments that Nero was proud of. In line with the Hellenistic model of his coin portraiture, his embonpoint would have suggested not self-indulgence but the opulence expected of the supreme patron.[104] More specifically, with his modish hairstyle, it projected the youth and fitness that allowed him to succeed in his chosen roles of singer and sportsman. Portrait-artists may, however, have unconsciously picked up consequent problems:

[95] Tac. *Ann.* 13.20.1: *provecta nox erat et Neroni per vinolentiam trahebatur.*
[96] Goddard 1994, 68.
[97] Cf. above 302; below 354, 362; Grant 1970, 200; Griffin 1984, 121–2; Reitz 2006, 16.
[98] Bergmann 2013, 338–9; Richlin 2014, 193.   [99] Bergmann 2013, 336.
[100] Suet. *Ner.* 51: *coma … in gradus formata … pudendus.* Bradley 1978a, 284; Bergmann 2013, 336–7; below 388.
[101] Bergmann 2013, 338; cf. above 128; below 373.
[102] Suet. *Ner.* 20.3: *pinguissima coma.* Above 302.   [103] Bergmann 2013, 337 (quotation), 339.
[104] Cf. Cizek 1982, 36–7; Reitz 2006, 16 ('Uppigkeit').

Such activities could conceivably result in some hypertrophy of muscles in his upper torso, arms and possibly his neck. You only need to look at some wrestlers and boxers on the TV to see this.

And:

Of course, another possibility is that he might have developed goitre (swelling of the thyroid gland in the neck caused by iodine deficiency). His habit of purging himself by syringe and vomiting and avoiding certain foodstuffs is something that could give rise to mineral or vitamin deficiencies.[105]

Nero may not have been as fit as he believed because, in his search for perfection, he had gone too far. But this was due to characteristic over-dedication, not gourmandising.

If Nero did not debauch aristocrats by coercing them into public performance, or himself by excessive feasting, did he still debauch upper-class women by forcing them into brothels as Suetonius' lascivious matrons? Suetonius' accusation looks very much like his typical extrapolation of a bad habit from one or two particular instances: here, the parties around the *Stagnum Navale* in 59 and, especially, the *Stagnum Agrippae* in 64.[106] Nero's 'depraved' entertainments were therefore not non-stop. Furthermore, it is likely that the level of depravity on these two occasions was lower than the sources claim. We must again make allowance for later prudishness and for the influence on us of Hollywood-style, no-holds-barred 'orgies'. As we have seen, upper-class participation in public entertainment was not new.[107] Aristocrats probably performed short, somewhat low-brow, 'turns' or 'sets'.[108] Waldherr proposes that many sets in the *Iuvenalia* were drawn from *fabula togata*, the traditional comedy form, in which an elderly elegant woman not infrequently told of the troubles of her youth and, with witty cynicism, of the travails of true love. Such a part would have been ideal for a Roman matron who wished to perform.[109] In addition, professional 'dancers or mimes, individually or in groups, would give performances of an erotic nature ...'[110] One can well envisage how a number of those involved – especially women, bound by heavy social restraints – might have taken a moment of relative freedom too far, both on stage and off. In this they could have been encouraged by bawdy 'fringe' entertainers: Tigellinus' banquet may have run alongside the

[105] Gleeson in personal communication (2008).
[106] Above 298–9; Bradley 1978a, 158–9; cf. Champlin 2003, 154–55.   [107] Above 301.
[108] Cf. above 297.   [109] Waldherr 2005, 122.   [110] Holland 2000, 154–5.

festival of the *Floralia*, from 28 April to 3 May, which featured the participation of prostitutes.[111] But all of this involved a small minority, and was temporary. It was not part of the mass prostitution of noble freeborn women or of any grand social breakdown. On the other hand, tales of celebrity high jinks were bound to have spread and expanded in the telling, causing distress to conservatives and giving future writers much juicy material.

If Nero's spectacles and banqueting were not about coercion and debauchery, how should we understand them? The key is to be found in Tigellinus' banquet of 64. As already observed, large-scale public banqueting by *principes* was not unprecedented. Gaius threw a great 'City-Fest' in 37;[112] and Tacitus states that Tigellinus' banquet was only one of many at which Nero treated Rome as his private house.[113] In 64, however, Nero went much further than before with, indeed, 'the party of the century' and a key stage in his development. After difficulties in 62, from 63 the regime had begun to do well, with Corbulo firmly in charge in Armenia and respectable activity in the civil field.[114] It is surely no coincidence that it was then that the administration had the confidence to decide on a complex coinage reform.[115] Nero, Poppaea and Tigellinus were proving to be a good team; and emotionally Nero was probably more settled than he had been for many years. His traumatic involvement in the death of Agrippina was well behind him;[116] and he was happily married to Poppaea. There will have been popular sympathy for him and Poppaea for their loss of the baby Claudia, early in 63.[117] It was now, too, that he finally embraced his *métier*.[118] Early in 64 he made his first public performance as citharode in Naples, and was thrilled by the experience.[119] There was then some political tension. Claudia's death will have revived concern about the succession, which probably led to the death of Junius Silanus.[120] However, with Nero's second marriage having proved fertile, after this there would have been widespread hopes for a new heir and political stability. It was in these favourable circumstances that Nero used Tigellinus' banquet to advertise the sort of *princeps* he wanted to be: Hellenic, promoting sport and art rather than war, and accessible to all his people. He had long displayed his love of

---

[111] Bradley 1978a, 159. The *Floralia* were also the occasion of games: see Suet. *Galb.* 6.1 for the youthful Galba's presentation of a tightrope-walking elephant at these.
[112] Cass. Dio 59.7.1. Winterling 2007, 57.   [113] Tac. *Ann.* 15.37.1.
[114] Tac. *Ann.* 15.32. Furneaux 1907, 356; above 28, 143.   [115] Above 302; below 354.
[116] Cf. above 182.   [117] Above 196.   [118] Cf. above 204.
[119] Cf. Waldherr 2005, 126; Meier 2008, 585.   [120] Tac. *Ann.* 15.35. Above 197.

Hellenism, above all in the *Iuvenalia* and *Neronia* I,[121] but what is crucial here is the narrowness of his horizons.

Tigellinus' banquet was about personal fulfilment, not principles of government. Content to leave the running of the Empire to others,[122] Nero made no effort to reshape the Roman socio-political system; he wanted to change *his* principate, not *the* Principate.[123] Even his Hellenism did not embrace the traditional Hellenistic world: the 'people' he wanted to engage with were those of Rome and Italy.[124] Before Tigellinus' banquet he had toyed with the idea of going to Greece and Egypt, but rejected it, so it was said, on the grounds of a religious experience in the temple of Vesta and of not wanting to abandon the people of Rome.[125] His main intent was now just to play the ruler in the Italian peninsula.[126] Later, in 66–67, having been pressured to travel to Greece,[127] he enjoyed the experience and was reluctant to leave; but he greatly relished his triumphal return to Italy and Rome, and subsequently showed no desire to depart. Such localism explains why, in 64, Nero was thrilled to make the City his house, open to all. He was to pursue this ambition further with his Golden House Pavilion, but it was perhaps already manifest in the *Domus Transitoria*, taking shape at the time: as a great art gallery it presented the glories of Greece to the Roman populace.[128] Nero's games and banquets will have caused dismay among a number of upper-class Romans, and so helped create the anti-Neronian source tradition.[129] In the shorter term, fear of incipient demagogy surely contributed to the formation of the Pisonian conspiracy, unmasked early in 65.[130] Yet any notion that Nero was bent on a 'tyrannical' inversion of social status would have been misguided.[131] There is no sign that from 64 he went out of his way to ostracise the upper classes.[132] The high point of Tigellinus' banquet was the sight of Nero dining in state with his usual close acquaintances: the public was allowed the privilege of viewing the *princeps'* party close to, not of joining it.[133] Likewise in Naples, earlier in 64, though he had eaten in public, the public were not at table with him.[134] We see a similar reserve later in the Golden House Pavilion, with its hierarchy of dining areas.[135] Nero did not corrupt others or himself, or aim at revolution. Conservatives

---

[121] Cf. Cizek 1982, 123–5.   [122] Above 12, 56.   [123] Above 293; below 376.
[124] Above 205.   [125] Tac. *Ann.* 15.36.1–6; Suet. *Ner.* 19.1. Above 221.   [126] Above 204.
[127] Below 378.   [128] Above 235; below 378.   [129] Above 308; cf. Hurley 2013, 39–40.
[130] Above 197.   [131] Dio 61.4.5–61.5.2. *Contra* Goddard 1994, 77, 72–9 (quotation).
[132] Cf. Suet. *Ner.* 27.3: criticism of Nero for attending lavish banquets given by his *familiares*. Cf. above 65, 95, 117, 305.
[133] Tac. *Ann.* 15.37.3.   [134] Suet. *Ner.* 20.3; above 208.   [135] Above 256, 259.

may have complained at his antics, but the majority of the political community will have known that no moral or political line had been crossed.[136] However, it has to be conceded that the events of 64 probably enabled the Pisonian conspiracy by breaking the loyalty of a key group of praetorian officers, and may also have been looked at askance in the western provinces.[137]

12.3 Lust

According to Suetonius, Nero sexually abused freeborn boys, seduced married women, debauched the Vestal Virgin Rubria, all but married Acte, and castrated and married Sporus, whom he then took round Greece as his wife. He ends by claiming that, despite court opposition, Nero committed incest with his mother.[138] His accusations appear to find corroboration in what Petronius did before his suicide in 66, which included ensuring that his will contained a full catalogue of Nero's sexual 'perversions'.[139]

With regard to the boys, Suetonius' statement may be accounted for as more generalisation from just two allegations: that Nero misused Britannicus and the younger Aulus Plautius before killing them.[140] Furthermore, the two may be reduced to one since supposed violation of Aulus Plautius looks like a doublet of that of Britannicus.[141] So how credible is Nero's alleged rape of Britannicus? Aristocratic Roman males faced no great social censure in participating in homosexual behaviour, as long as, as here implied of Nero, they were the active partners.[142] But this is little mitigation and, given the paucity of evidence and his obvious interest in women, a better approach is to doubt whether Nero ever had any significant homosexual appetite.[143] I follow Champlin in interpreting Nero's alleged sexual attack on Britannicus as either fictional, along the lines of what a monstrous tyrant was expected to do or, less likely, if it occurred, as the ritual humiliation of a defeated enemy not the outcome of lust.[144] Nero's seduction of married women may be interpreted as a generalisation from his premarital affair with Poppaea. (That Nero had a serious relationship with Statilia is highly improbable while he still had his precious Poppaea.) Further in Nero's defence, it can be said that in pursuing Poppaea he was

[136] Cf. above 94.   [137] Above 207; below 389.   [138] Suet. *Ner.* 28.
[139] Tac. *Ann.* 16.19.5: *flagitia.*
[140] Britannicus: Tac. *Ann.* 13.17.3: *stupro*; Aulus Plautius II: Suet. *Ner.* 35.4: *per vim conspurcasset.*
[141] Cizek 1982, 41; cf. below 320.   [142] Tac. *Ann.* 11.2.2; above 105.
[143] Above 289; cf. Holland 2000, 205.
[144] Champlin 2003, 164–5. Cf. Bradley 1978a, 198, 215; Rudich 1993, 30; below 320.

driven by an authentic and lasting passion for the woman, not bare lust.[145] The accusation that Nero debauched Rubria is strange because it is repeated nowhere else, while a Vestal scandal under Domitian left a 'substantial literary record'.[146] It is likely to be so overblown as to be 'extremely unlikely'.[147] However, Acte, Sporus and Agrippina take us into better known territory. Here, Suetonius tries to persuade his reader of the truth of his allegations of Nero's sexual misbehaviour by moving from the true to the misunderstood to the false. Nero was no libertine, having only one significant female, apart from his mother, in his life at a time. Of these, he married three – Octavia, Poppaea and Poppaea/'Sporus' – and did his best to formalise his relationship with the fourth, Acte.[148] There is no doubt that Acte and Nero were very close and so every likelihood that he wished to make her more than just a concubine. As both will have realised, because of Acte's servile origin this could not be achieved through full marriage, but they were probably content to settle for the lesser but respectable long-term union, later enjoyed by Vespasian and Caenis, known as *contubernium*. Suetonius' statement that Nero 'almost' made Acte his wife is, therefore, plausible, as is his report that the *princeps* – always solicitous of her – also honoured her with a concocted royal pedigree.[149] With Sporus we move from the true to the misunderstood. Dio confirms that Nero took Sporus to Greece, married him under both Greek and Roman law, and then insisted that he be treated as his wife and equal.[150] Dio also records that while in Greece Nero gave Sporus/'Poppaea' his own household with, as wardrobe mistress, the redoubtable Calvia Crispinilla. Tacitus calls the latter Nero's 'instructress in depravity',[151] but the term should be taken with a pinch of salt since it implies long-term influence. Given her strong personality and political daring,[152] it is likely that Calvia did not hold the post under Poppaea but was instead taken on after her death to deal with a very difficult and now permanent situation – Suetonius states that Sporus continued to be treated in this way after Nero's return from Greece[153] – perhaps with the agreement of Nero's new official wife, Statilia.[154] There is no reason to explain the *princeps*' use of Sporus by

[145] Tac. *Ann.* 13.45–6, with Tac. *Hist.* 1.13; Suet. *Otho* 3; Plut. *Galb.* 19.2–20.1; Cass. Dio 61.11.2.
[146] Bradley 1978a, 160.   [147] Champlin 2003, 163 (quotation); likewise Cizek 1982, 40.
[148] Cf. Fini 1994, 107; below 314.
[149] Suet. *Ner.* 28.1: *paulum afuit*; *Vesp.* 3; Cass. Dio 66.14.1–4. Bradley 1978a, 160; Grant 1970, 43; Cizek 1982, 40; cf. above 182, 281. *Contra* Waldherr 2005, 76.
[150] Cass. Dio 62.28.2–3; 63.12.3–13.2; cf. Dio Chrys. *Or.* 21.6–7. Champlin 2003, 146–9.
[151] Cass. Dio 63.12.4; Tac. *Hist.* 1.73: *magistra libidinum*.
[152] Cf. above 164, 231; below, 388, 400.   [153] Suet. *Ner.* 28.2.   [154] Above 164.

reference to him as a mindless 'love-machine', with intense, complex and continual bisexual needs.[155] Again, he was a 'one-woman man'. Similarly, his impatience with formal religion rules out the explanation that the Sporus marriage was part of his initiation into a mystery religion.[156] The best solution is to link the relationship to Nero's grief at the loss of Poppaea. As he could not bear to part with her body (he had it embalmed, not cremated[157]), so he could not bear to lose her company and, in the anguish of love, filled the void with Sporus, the best available lookalike, albeit of the wrong sex. Their bond was sentimental, not erotic, and may never have been consummated.[158] Nero coped with the loss of Poppaea, as he did with other stresses, through drama. He kept her close by 'marrying' her afresh and by wearing masks with her features on stage.[159] Agrippina takes us from the misunderstood to the false. Nero's suspected incest with his mother traditionally runs a very close second to his killing of her as the most perverted act of his principate, but did it happen? Tacitus provides a summary of a contemporary debate. He says that according to his sources it certainly did, the only disagreement being as to whether intercourse was instigated by Agrippina or Nero. However, he refuses to take sides and even proposes that the whole thing might be just rumour, based on Agrippina's poor character.[160] Dio is even more suspicious of the story, though he records that Nero kept a concubine who closely resembled Agrippina, and that in talking about her used to say that he had sex with his mother.[161] Modern historians remain divided.[162] The charge is best interpreted as more scurrilous invention,[163] in a period when the accusation of incest, easy to make and relatively easy to get social inferiors to corroborate, was 'part of the stock-in-trade of political invective'.[164] Helped by the *princeps'* undoubted closeness to his mother, even down to 59, and by his later recreation of himself, as he acted out the roles of the mythical matricide and tyrant, it could easily be levelled against 'Nero the monster'.[165]

---

[155] Cizek 1982, 39–41: 'Une machine d'amour?'; Fini 1994, 109–10.
[156] Bradley 1978a, 162; Cizek 1982, 41; above 287.   [157] Tac. *Ann.* 16.6.2.
[158] Champlin 2003, 147; cf. Holland 2000, 157, 196–7, 204–5.
[159] Cass. Dio 63.9.5. Champlin 2003, 145–7; Barrett *et al.* 2016, 188 n. 67; above 290.
[160] Tac. *Ann.* 14.2.   [161] Cass. Dio 61.11.4.
[162] For belief in the charge see, for example, Grant 1970, 36; Fini 1994, 126 (of Agrippina only). For a review of the debate see Bradley 1978a, 162–4.
[163] E.g. Barrett 1996, 183; Holland 2000, 102; above 78, 282.
[164] Cf. Tac. *Ann.* 16.8.2. Above 215; Ginsburg 2006, 118–20 (quotation).
[165] Cf. Hohl 1918, 368; Cizek 1982, 40; Champlin 2003, 138; above 291.

Suetonius further illustrates Nero's disgusting erotic behaviour by describing a game in which he played the wild animal, sexually molesting defenceless males and females. In this he was aided by one Doryphorus, to whom he was married as a virgin bride. The existence of the game appears to be confirmed by Dio, who describes how Nero, dressed in the hide of a ravening beast, assaulted naked boys and girls, fastened to stakes.[166] Generally, according to Suetonius, Nero believed that no man was chaste or pure; and he pardoned the faults of those who confessed their lewdness.[167] With regard to the 'marriage', Champlin accepts the identification of 'Doryphorus' with the Pythagoras who, according to Tacitus, played the male to Nero's female in a wedding that took place just after Tigellinus' banquet, and modern interpretation of the event as part of a rite of initiation into an eastern cult. However, he proposes that the ceremony was not authentic ritual but theatrical parody, in which Nero would not have let himself be penetrated. Champlin interprets what happened as Nero's playing the *princeps Saturnalicius* in a rebellion against convention, but in the absence of any great ideological plan this is unlikely.[168] 'Drama', however, is very plausible. Nero's parodying of eastern religion fits his love of satire,[169] and the 'wedding' sits easily in the festivities of Tigellinus' banquet: just another entertainment in which Nero acted the blushing bride.[170] 'Drama' also helps explain the 'lewd game' which, staged within the framework of regular 'amateur theatricals',[171] was perhaps some parody of, say, another religious initiation or Nero's treatment of Christians,[172] or, more generally, as Champlin proposes, of a common public execution. Passionate about the stage and about understanding life through drama, Nero might have desired to experience what it was like to be a ravening animal and fulfilled his wish in a re-enactment of an established element of the arena programme in which condemned criminals suffered death by wild beast.[173] In this 'bizarre pantomime' both beast and criminals were actors: the former Nero, the latter professionals. Though Champlin accepts that Nero performed oral sex on the 'criminals', this is as much a likely distortion as anything else reported of him. Probably no-one was seriously hurt or humiliated.[174] His flippant attitude

---

[166] Cass. Dio 63.13.2.   [167] Suet. *Ner.* 29.
[168] Tac. *Ann.* 15.37.8–9. Cizek 1982, 42; Fini 1994, 110; Champlin 2003, 160–1 (*contra* Bradley 1978a, 164–5: that Doryphorus was the *libertus* Tib. Claudius Doryphorus, Nero's *a libellis*), 166–9, 171–2; above 293, 297, 309.
[169] Above 102.   [170] Holland 2000, 158–9.   [171] Above 300–1.
[172] Bradley 1978a, 164; Cizek 1982, 42.   [173] Cf. below 323.
[174] Champlin 2003, 169–70; cf. Holland 2000, 158.

to chastity and purity may, like much else, be attributed to unfriendly misquotation of his asides.[175]

However, 'lewd' theatricals were bound to attract the disapproval of conservatives and, just before the Fire, shake the confidence of the urban *plebs*.[176] They must be classed among Nero's 'break-outs'.[177] Yet: 'If we could separate fact from innuendo, Nero's sexual life – but for Pythagoras – might appear disconcertingly regular for a Roman, despite its flamboyance. For a man who believed that everyone was completely corrupt, he lived a life of remarkable restraint'.[178] Nero had concubines but, apparently, used them for other than just sexual gratification: for show (the Agrippina lookalike), as a psychological prop (the Poppaea lookalike) or as the supporting cast in some piece of theatre (the 'Amazons' with whose help he hoped to defeat Vindex[179]). He was no complex, voracious, bisexual libertine. To Petronius' denunciation one may retort, as to that of Subrius Flavus, 'Well he would, wouldn't he?'[180] Probably falsely accused of involvement in the Pisonian conspiracy,[181] and given no opportunity to defend himself,[182] Petronius hit back in the only way available. Malicious wills were not unknown.[183] Petronius, probably not directly involved in what he described,[184] spun the gossip of a close friend into cutting invective. His denunciation was probably no more an accurate account of Nero's sexual activities than his *Satyricon* is one of everyday life in Rome and Italy, which is to say very little.[185]

12.4   Extravagance and Avarice

Suetonius quotes Nero as declaring that no gentleman counted pennies and describes how he wasted money on a grand scale, in his reception of Tiridates and in his presents of substantial estates to Menecrates, the lyre player, and Spiculus, the gladiator. To Paneros, nicknamed 'Monkey', a notorious money-lender, he gave huge urban and rural properties and an almost regal burial.[186] Nero was a gambler, and never stinted his personal spending, frequently changing his clothing and owning a gold- and purple-threaded fishing net and mules shod with silver, driven by men dressed in the finest woollen garments. It is under 'extravagance' that Suetonius deals with Nero's building activities, declaring 'there was nothing, however, in

---

[175] Above 77, 118.   [176] Cf. above 206.   [177] Above 164.   [178] Champlin 2003, 161.
[179] Champlin 2003, 163–4.   [180] Above 234.   [181] Above 102.   [182] Above 75.
[183] Cf. Tac. *Ann.* 14.50.1. Rudich 1993, 59.   [184] Tac. *Ann.* 16.20.1. Fini 1994, 109.
[185] Cf. above 101.   [186] Suet. *Ner.* 30 (30.2: *cercopithecus* ['long-tailed ape']).

which he was more ruinously prodigal'.[187] In this, he criticises not only the Golden House but also the Misenum to Arvernus basin and the Arvernus to Ostia canal. Much rings true. Nero loved beautiful and costly possessions. According to Pliny I, he spent HS 1 million on a myrrhine loving-cup and HS 4 million on soft furnishings for his dining-room.[188] Beautiful and costly possessions probably included Poppaea, recorded by Dio as taking a daily bath in asses' milk,[189] and a keen sportsman is also likely to fancy a bet. Nero was a free spender, which has implications for his finances, examined further below.[190] Here, however, I restrict myself to considering whether his spending amounted to 'depraved' extravagance and led to 'depraved' avarice. Against depravity in spending is, first, that Suetonius confuses Nero the man with Nero the *princeps*, including in his personal expenditure that – much more substantial – of the state. The latter includes the cost of Tiridates' reception and of major capital investments such as the redevelopment of Rome after the Fire, which were necessary, and of the Campanian 'navigations' which, by promising a safe inland waterway from Puteoli to Rome, were a potentially valuable commercial investment.[191] Suetonius' confusion will have been shared by many contemporaries.[192] The distinction between the property and income of the state and those of the *princeps* was blurred from the time of Augustus and soon effectively disappeared.[193] Related to this, in criticising the personality of Nero Suetonius here, unlike earlier in categorising of Nero's provision of games under his 'good' actions,[194] shows no appreciation of his responsibilities as head of state. Nero, as an aristocratic Roman, as head of his house, and as Augustan *princeps*, will have been expected to make ambitious proposals for public buildings, following a tradition begun by Julius Caesar.[195] He will also have been expected to put on an imposing personal show – in deportment, dress, accoutrements and companions – whenever he appeared in public.[196] Romans liked their *Augusti* to look like *Augusti* and behave like *Augusti*. Gifts to important individuals, as well as gifts showered on the public during entertainments,[197] were expected of the

---

[187] Suet. *Ner.* 31.1: *non in alia re tamen damnosior.*
[188] Plin. *HN* 37.20.4–5; 8.196.9–10. Millar 1977, 144; Griffin 1984, 206   [189] Cass. Dio 62.28.1.
[190] Chapter 13.   [191] Below 331, 342; Bradley 1978a, 181–2; Keppie 2011, 39–40.
[192] Cf. Winterling 2009, 96.
[193] Below 336. Cf. Osgood 2011, 180, on Claudius' advertisement of his personal funding (*sua impensa*) of aqueducts.
[194] Suet. *Ner.* 11.   [195] Cf. Osgood 2011, 169–70; cf. Warmington 1969, 127; 336.
[196] Cf. above 300.
[197] E.g. Tac. *Ann.* 14.15.3 (on the those of the *Iuvenalia*). Cf. Griffin 1984, 200 (on Augustus): 'Liberality was expected of and praised in the Princeps'.

greatest *patronus* of the Empire.[198] But the patron–client relationship was reciprocal, so there would have been some return on a patron's investment. 'Friends' treated Nero to expensive banquets,[199] and imperial dependants mounted costly games for him.[200] Local aristocrats must have helped to feed and accommodate the imperial train on its progresses in Italy and Greece; and if Nero had ever met Vologaeses in Parthia, he would probably have enjoyed the same scale of hospitality as that with which he had honoured Tiridates.[201] Suetonius' charge of criminal extravagance should be regarded as yet another *topos*: what was expected of any 'tyrant'.[202]

Suetonius next recounts how extravagance led to avarice. He touches on the 'Bassus affair', when Nero grew foolishly excited at the prospect of recovering the ancient treasure of Dido of Carthage,[203] and then proceeds to list the measures that he took to escape the consequences of his financial fecklessness. The *princeps* resorted to false accusation and robbery, and even delays in military pay and benefits for retiring soldiers.[204] He made new laws which extracted more in bequests from his own family freedmen and punished those who did not make bequests to him, and their lawyers. He extended the charge of *maiestas*.[205] He recalled the donations he had made to Greek cities in thanks for prizes conferred upon him, and he introduced laws against the use of luxury dyes.[206] He expected kick-backs on appointments to offices, and he stripped many temples of their treasures 'and melted down the images of gold and silver, including those of the Penates, which however Galba soon afterwards restored'.[207] Suetonius' case appears to be supported by the Bassus affair, as recorded in detail by Tacitus.[208] In 65, Caesellius Bassus, a minor Carthaginian aristocrat, was inspired by a dream to persuade Nero that he might recover Dido's golden treasure. An official expedition was despatched, but returned empty-handed. Nero, anticipating its success, had already spent the booty. However, like most of Suetonius' criticisms, the affair was probably misrepresented by the hostile source tradition.[209] It is considered further below.[210] Here it is enough to say that history is full of confidence tricksters and that the prospect of recovering Dido's treasure would have stimulated the avarice of any Julio-Claudian *princeps*, whatever his financial situation. Otherwise, Suetonius' catalogue of Neronian acts of greed

---

[198] Cf. below 337.   [199] Suet. *Ner.* 27.3: *familiares*. Also, of course, Tigellinus' banquet.
[200] Tac. *Ann.* 14.34.2; cf. above 80, 117.   [201] Cf. above 150; below 342, 348.
[202] Cf. Bradley 1978a, 165–6.   [203] Suet. *Ner.* 31.4.   [204] Suet. *Ner.* 32.1.
[205] Suet. *Ner.* 32.2; above 21.   [206] Suet. *Ner.* 32.3.   [207] Suet. *Ner.* 32.4.
[208] Tac. *Ann.* 16.1–3. Bradley 1978a, 183.   [209] Cf. Bradley 1978a, 185.   [210] Below 342.

amount to a ragbag of vague and questionable assertions. Again, I deal with the most serious in detail below.[211] Of the remainder, the recall of donations, the prohibition of luxury dyes, and the insistence on kickbacks, are relatively petty, probably misunderstood, and in many cases an established part of an administrative machine in which 'corruption' was always an essential lubricant.[212] This leaves Nero's alleged theft of temple treasures. Bradley associates it with his art thefts and, perhaps, his decoration of Golden House.[213] However, works of art were not acquired to be melted down, and Suetonius hints strongly that the sacrilege took place in Rome. The 'theft' could therefore be a garbling of state acquisition of bullion from artefacts melted down by the Fire of 64 or, more likely, of action taken in 68 to meet the emergency of revolt, in neither case evidence of the *princeps'* sustained personal avarice.[214] Despite Nero's expensive tastes, this was anyway unnecessary, since Neronian state finances were on a much sounder footing than the source tradition suggests.[215] For the same reason, there is no cause to propose that fiscal weaknesses led directly to his fall.[216]

12.5 Cruelty

Suetonius justifies his condemnation of Nero as 'cruel' by cataloguing his murders: of relatives, non-relatives and, in the Fire, Rome itself.[217] Most of these matters have been dealt with and Nero generally exonerated from the charge of being a cold-blooded killer. The death of his aunt, Domitia, will be considered below, in discussion of his finances.[218] Of the rest, the fate of the young senator and *quaestor designatus*, Julius Montanus, touched on by Suetonius in an earlier section and fleshed out by Tacitus and Dio,[219] repays close consideration.

In 56, Nero and a gang of youths assaulted Montanus and his wife on the street in Rome. Montanus, in response, gave the *princeps* two black eyes. After this, apparently, all involved returned home. There the matter might have rested since, so Dio says, 'Nero thought the violence had been all an accident and so was not disposed to be angry at the occurrence'. However, Montanus then wrote to the *princeps* to apologise for his action,

---

[211] Chapter 13.
[212] Cf. Bradley 1978a, 192–3 (suggesting, for example, that the legislation concerning dyes may have constituted an attempt to establish an imperial monopoly on their sale).
[213] Bradley 1978a, 194.   [214] Cf. Tac. *Ann.* 15.45.2; below 368, 397.   [215] Cf. below 341–2.
[216] Below 348.   [217] Suet. *Ner.* 33–8.   [218] Below 340, 346.
[219] Suet. *Ner.* 26.2; Tac. *Ann.* 13.25.2; Cass. Dio 61.9.3–4. Above 296.

prompting Nero to utter the chilling remark, 'so he knew he was striking
Nero'. Montanus then committed suicide.[220] The source tradition clearly
intended to convey an impression of Nero as the 'depraved' tyrant,
terrorising the inhabitants of his capital and destroying anyone who stood
up to him.[221] As usual, this does not convince. Nero may have been
annoyed by Montanus' letter not out of feelings of *lèse majesté* but because,
in line with his developing theatrical interests,[222] he went about in disguise
and in character.[223] If he was convinced that he was acting the part of
street-hooligan to perfection, recognition would represent harsh criticism
of his acting skills, and remove much of the fun from the game.[224]
Furthermore, and given his initial forbearance with Montanus, it is difficult to believe that Nero then pressured him to commit suicide. One
suspects the involvement of others.[225] By striking in one person both a
princeps and a magistrate of the Republic, Montanus had, indeed, committed *maiestas* on two counts. This might have been overlooked if he had
stayed quiet, but by writing to Nero he put the affair into the public
domain and invited prosecution.[226] On the other hand, for the legal
process to begin there had to be a prosecutor, and if the *princeps* was
thought to be reluctant it would have taken a brave *delator* to level the
charge.[227] In addition, the dominant political figures were still Seneca and
Burrus, who would probably not normally have been keen to pursue
Montanus through the courts for personal reasons and because the charge
of *maiestas* was currently anathema.[228] Furthermore, if the case did come
before the Senate, it was bound to reveal embarrassing details of Nero's
nocturnal wanderings; and, anyway, the pair probably took the view that
in his street-fighting Nero deserved what he had got and would be better
for it.[229] Yet the affray had flagged up a real danger: that if anyone stood
up to Nero, for whatever reason (given the current crimewave, Montanus
may well have begun by believing he was fighting a Nero-imitator[230]), the
princeps might be seriously injured or killed. At this time it may also have
been feared that uncontrolled street-fighting could provide cover for
assassination, a concern that was to justify the exiling of Sulla in 58.[231]
Nero's gallivanting had to be both encouraged and curtailed; and the
Montanus incident, though awkward, provided the Establishment with

---

[220] Cass. Dio 61.9.4: *ho gar Nerōn ek suntachias allōs hubristhai nomisas oudemian orgēn epoieto . . .
oukoun ëidei Nerōna tuptōn.*
[221] Cf. above 83.   [222] Cf. Tac. *Ann.* 14.14.1.   [223] Suet. *Ner.* 26.1; Cass. Dio 61.9.2.
[224] Cf. Bartsch 1994, 17–19.   [225] Cf. above 130, 183.   [226] Holland 2000, 95.
[227] Below 366.   [228] Above 21, 187.   [229] Above 297.
[230] Above 296; cf. Bartsch 1994, 18–20.   [231] Tac. *Ann.* 13.47.2–4. Holland 2000, 96; above 192.

the opportunity to bring this about. I propose that it was not Nero but his chief advisers who, despite personal misgivings, harassed Montanus into committing suicide in order to warn off potential attackers of any station, and that the same advisers insisted on Nero being accompanied by bodyguards on his nocturnal adventures.[232]

Montanus' death indicates a propensity to worry that made him susceptible to suicide, but it also demonstrates a general lack of confidence among members of the senatorial order in dealing with the Principate however much they appreciated its political necessity.[233] More specifically, it underlines the debilitating effect of a privilege formally ratified under Tiberius.[234] In the Early Empire those suspected of serious criminal acts were, apparently, first 'denounced' to a magistrate in his capacity as judge and, in the most serious cases, as one sufficiently senior to summon the Senate.[235] If he decided that there was a case to answer, he laid an official accusation after which the accused were brought to trial. If found guilty, they were sentenced to exile or death and the confiscation of their possessions by the state as *bona damnatorum* – 'the property of the condemned'.[236] Senators and, presumably, senior equestrians,[237] might, however, expect to be treated more leniently. These were not normally arrested, compelled to attend trial or expected to offer any sustained legal defence.[238] If found guilty and sentenced to death, some, considered the most dangerous, were killed as soon as possible by military executioners.[239] Most, however, were given time to commit suicide. They were, it seems, warned by word or deed that they had been, or were likely to be, found guilty before being formally apprised of the verdict.[240] This gave them time to kill themselves and avoid the humiliation and pain of execution. In addition, since they died notionally uncondemned, they were able to bequeath their property in the normal way, except that they were now expected to make a new will naming the *princeps* and perhaps certain of his intimates as co-benefactors. The convention also spared the accuseds' senatorial peers the embarrassment of confronting them as judges, and permitted the condemned to utter a few fine last words.[241] Some hardy souls refused to take advantage of the concession. Petronius changed his

---

[232] Above 297.   [233] Above 91.   [234] Rutledge 2001, 42–3.
[235] Rutledge 2001, 17; cf. above 70; below 365.   [236] Millar 1977, 163; below 340.
[237] Cf. Barrett *et al.* 2016, 32 n. 23.   [238] Talbert 1984, 481, 484.
[239] E.g. Tac. *Ann.* 14.57.6 (Sulla); 14.59.3 (Rubellius Plautus). Above 74.
[240] Cf. Rutledge 2001, 43.
[241] Tac. *Ann.* 16.26.3. Rudich 1993, 171–2; Rubiés 1994, 40; Edwards 2007, 119–21; Bingham 2013, 91–3.

will only to insult Nero and smashed a precious piece of tableware to prevent it being confiscated.[242] L. Antistius Vetus also refused to participate in the bequest game and, with his daughter and his mother-in-law, committed suicide 'in the grand old style'.[243] Most, however, complied. Tacitus berates Piso, the leader of the conspiracy, for such behaviour, but makes Seneca's suicide a fine example of the good aristocratic death.[244] In an age of drama,[245] this was all nicely dramatic, but it stifled another form of drama. There developed no tradition of accused persons making grand public assertions of their innocence, or of opposition to the actions or policies of a *princeps*, in the Senate as assembly or high court.[246] As the autocratic tendencies inherent in the Principate grew more evident, such people might well have felt that resistance was futile,[247] but with none prepared to fight for a more equal partnership between Senate and *princeps* this was never tested.[248] Thrasea consulted his personal *consilium* and, in the face of conflicting advice, decided not to attend his trial. He was found guilty and sentenced *in absentia*, and committed suicide at home.[249] Montanus did not even wait to be accused. Self-execution could be cited by a *princeps* as proof of guilt, but it made it much easier to brand him a depraved murderer.[250] Barea Soranus was unusual in turning up for his trial, but the nearest the age got to a John Hampden was his daughter, Servilia. She, accused (not unreasonably, according to the beliefs of the time) of dabbling in magic, defended herself with outstanding spirit and courage.[251]

Returning to Suetonius' catalogue of Nero's murders, the accusation that he killed the consul Vestinus Atticus to gain access to his wife, Statilia Messalina,[252] is simply incredible. Though Tacitus records a dalliance between the two,[253] it is most unlikely that Nero had a serious relationship with Statilia before the death of Poppaea, or much interest in anyone else but Sporus after it.[254] Vestinus probably fell for political reasons in the aftermath of the Pisonian conspiracy.[255] Similarly implausible is the charge that Nero raped and killed Aulus Plautius II.[256] The dates of both crimes, their authenticity and even the precise identity of the youth

---

[242] Tac. *Ann.* 16.19.5; Plin. *HN* 37.20. Above 310; Rudich 1993, 155: a 'fluorspar wine-dipper'.
[243] Tac. *Ann.* 16.11.2. Above 216; Rudich 1993, 142 (quotation), though cf. below 346.
[244] Tac. *Ann.* 15.59.8; 15.62–3. Cf. also Tac. *Ann.* 16.14.5, 16.17.6; *Hist.* 1.90; Cass/ Dio 63.11.3. Bradley 1978a, 187; Griffin 1984, 204–5.
[245] Cf. above 286.   [246] Cf. above 112: the exception of literary criticism.
[247] Talbert 1984, 478.   [248] Cf. above 23.   [249] Tac. *Ann.* 16.25.1–26.5; 33.2; 34–5.
[250] Cf. Romm 2014, 21–2.
[251] Tac. *Ann.* 16.30.3–32.1. Cf. Rudich 1993, 161; Rutledge 2001, 120.   [252] Suet. *Ner.* 35.1.
[253] Tac. *Ann.* 15.68.5.   [254] Above 164, 312.   [255] Above 73.   [256] Suet. *Ner.* 35.4.

concerned are all uncertain.[257] Suetonius' subsequent statement, that Nero ordered the drowning of Poppaea's son by an earlier marriage, Rufrius Crispinus II, is equally suspect. The boy's death probably occurred around the time of Nero's marriage to Poppaea, when she was pregnant, allowing Suetonius to imply that Nero cold-bloodedly removed a potential rival of his unborn child. This is plausible because Crispinus may have been about the same age as Nero had been when adopted by Claudius.[258] Yet, given Nero's love for Poppaea, it is hard to believe that he would have acted in this way.[259] It could well be that in the cases of Plautius and Crispinus the hostile historical tradition attached to their premature natural or accidental deaths motives and details taken from Nero's supposed murder of Britannicus. Suetonius' brief report of the mass banishment or murder of the children of those condemned for treason is implicitly contradicted by other sources.[260] His story that Salvidienus Orfitus was executed for letting three shops that formed part of his house near the Forum to certain foreign communities may, like that of Vestinus, be related to the suppression of the Pisonian conspiracy and to Nero's justifiable new-found fear of former intimates.[261] Cassius Longinus, the jurist, whom Suetonius has executed for preserving the death mask of his ancestor, the tyrannicide Gaius Cassius, likewise suffered from Nero's post-Pisonian insecurity, but was – unlike L. Silanus II, with whom he was accused – exiled, not executed.[262] The prosecution of Longinus may also have been a way of attacking his wife, who was one of the Silani, but again it should be noted that it did not lead to her death.[263] Overall, Suetonius provides no hard evidence to support his characterisation of Nero as a multiple killer. His retailing of the rumour that Nero liked to throw men alive to a fearsome Egyptian monster is, indeed, 'curious and far fetched', and shows how far the anti-Nero tradition was willing to purvey fiction as fact.[264] It is not surprising, and equally unconvincing, that by the end Suetonius has Nero declaring that 'no prince had ever known what power he really had', and hinting that he would destroy the Senate and hand over the running of the

---

[257] Bradley 1978a, 214–15; above 310.
[258] Suet. *Ner.* 35.5; Tac. *Ann.* 13.45.4. Bradley 1978a, 215; Kienast 2004, 99: Poppaea's marriage to his father lasted from *c.* 47–51 to 58.
[259] Grant 1970, 147, Cizek 1982, 57.
[260] Suet. *Ner.* 36.2; cf. Tac. *Ann.* 15.71.7. Barrett *et al.* 2016, 223 n. 110.
[261] Suet. *Ner.* 37.1; cf. Cass. Dio 62.27.1. Bradley 1978a, 222. (He was accused by Aquilius Regulus: Tac. *Hist.* 4.42; cf. above 95).
[262] Suet. *Ner.* 37.1; cf. Tac. *Ann.* 16.7.3. Bradley 1978a, 223–4; above 216.
[263] Cf. Cizek 1982, 56–7; cf. above 174 n. 25.
[264] Suet. *Ner.* 37.2. Bradley 1978a, 225 (quotation).

Empire and the army to *equites* and freedmen.[265] Though some take these
and similar remarks seriously, as indicating a breakdown of relations
between *princeps* and Senate,[266] they are best interpreted as court
badinage, quoted inaccurately and out of context.[267]

Suetonius ignores another Nero who, measured by the standards of his
day, was unusually averse to cruelty.[268] His favourite, Greek, interests of
music, drama and sport were not centred on death. Roman spectacles
were, and Nero, as *princeps*, dutifully paid for and attended these. However, despite his love of attention,[269] when he did attend he rarely presided
and at first observed contests through a curtain. When giving games, he
seems to have had no great liking for gladiatorial contests.[270] Those we
know of are few in number, and when he did stage them he sometimes
ordered that there be no deaths, not even those of condemned criminals
(perhaps taking as precedent bloodless bouts between aristocrats).[271]
A number of historians have attributed this to the humanitarian teaching
of Seneca but, given Seneca's relatively late appearance in Nero's life, it is
likely that his dislike of blood-letting was among those characteristics not
acquired but rooted in his character.[272] In contrast, he watched plays in
full view, from above the performance area, from where he also observed
the brawling of the actors.[273] The latter is significant since it shows that, as
with wrestling, he was ready to view physical violence as long as it did not
lead inevitably to death. However, given the conduct of tyrants through
the ages, perhaps most striking is Nero's lack of vindictiveness. He had
been prepared to forgive Montanus his assault and, even more remarkable,
having been made to seem foolish by Bassus in the 'Dido's treasure' affair,
he is said not to have had him humiliated, tortured and killed but, making
allowance for his delusional state, to have allowed him to commit suicide
or, in another version, to have even released him after confiscating his
property.[274] Such consideration makes those rare occurrences when even
contemporaries felt that Nero had acted cruelly, against Octavia and the
Christians, so shocking.[275]

I have explained Octavia's fate as the consequence of both high passion
and political necessity, not brute cruelty.[276] Here I consider the second,

---

[265] Suet. *Ner.* 37.3: *negavit quemquam principum scisse quid sibi liceret*; 36.1.
[266] E.g. Meier 2008, 577.   [267] Cf. above 99, 116, 118; below 397.
[268] Rudich 1993, 49–54; Holland 2000, 5.   [269] Above 285.   [270] Waldherr 2005, 205.
[271] Suet. *Ner.* 12.1. Henderson 1905, 129; Grant 1970, 64; Bradley 1978a, 85; above 301.
[272] E.g. Crook 1955, 119–22; Grant 1970, 58, 64. *Contra* Griffin 1976, 67, 72, 281. Cf. above 284.
[273] Suet. *Ner.* 12.1 (*e proscaeni fastigio*), 26.2.   [274] Tac. *Ann.* 16.3.2. Fini 1994, 81.
[275] Cf. above 78.   [276] Above 189; cf. Fini 1994, 113.

still very much remembered thanks to *Quo Vadis?*[277] Christians were found guilty of firing Rome and the condemned were put to death in Nero's circus and gardens on the Vatican. There they were either clad in animal skins and mauled to death by dogs, or crucified and then, as dusk fell, set alight to act as human torches. Large crowds attended the event, and Nero, dressed as a charioteer, walked or drove among them on a racing-chariot.[278] Most of this would not have seemed especially sadistic to contemporary Romans. Following a judicial tradition that sought to fit the punishment of criminals to their social status and the nature of their crimes, poor, low-ranking Christians paid the appropriate – degrading and painful – penalty for committing grand arson. That their deaths were made a public spectacle also followed the Roman custom of making the execution of common criminals part of the programme of shows in the arena, and of producing them theatrically for the amusement of the crowd: Coleman's 'fatal charades'.[279] Christians suffered due punishment for their criminality, not their religion.[280] Yet their suffering was, in Christian terms, very marginal and certainly without wide-reaching consequences. Scholars have long agreed that there was no great pan-imperial pogrom.[281] It was eastern Christians who later invented both the 'apocryphal' (the great persecutor) and the 'apocalyptic' (the Anti-Christ) Nero.[282] They claimed that SS Peter and Paul had been martyred in Rome under Nero, but the details of these martyrdoms are obscure, there is controversy as to their date (in the early or late 60s?) and doubt as to whether St. Peter ever came to Italy to be martyred at all.[283] Their deaths formed the basis of a gradual confection of events, amounting to historical fiction, that 'projected Nero onto an increasingly fantastic stage with improbably dramatic results':[284] Nero 'the monster'. Crucial for Nero's supposed cruelty here is the number who perished in Rome. Tacitus refers to a 'great multitude',[285] and there had to be sufficient followers of *Chrestos/Christus* for the authorities' accusation of mass arson to be credible[286] and for their collective fate to have aroused the sympathy of spectators.[287] However, since the local

---

[277] Above 244.   [278] Tac. *Ann.* 15.44.6–7. Waldherr 2005, 120–1.
[279] Coleman 1990; Rudich 1993, 86; Shaw 2015, 91–2; above 313.
[280] Waldherr 2005, 217; above 247.
[281] E.g. *EEC* 2.671; Henderson 1905, 352–3; Hohl 1918, 383; Stevenson 1967, 6; Warmington 1969, 125–7; Grant 1970, 154–62; *EEC* 1992, 593; Clarke 1996. 869–71; Maier 2013, 388–90.
[282] Above 8; Shaw 2015, 95.
[283] *EEC* 2.675; Warmington 1969, 125; Fini 1994, 167 and n. 55; Clarke 1996, 871; Erker 2013, 126; Maier 2013, 390; Shaw 2015, 74, 76–8, 93–4.
[284] *EEC* 2.675–6; Maier 2013, 390 (quotation).   [285] Tac. *Ann.* 15.44.5: *multitudo ingens.*
[286] Above 245.   [287] Below 324.

Christian community cannot have been extensive,[288] we should not think of thousands, or even many hundreds, of victims. Fini's proposed maximum of *c.* 300 is itself probably excessive;[289] around 100 individuals would have been enough for the administration, not Nero, in its search for scapegoats.[290] Again, to suppose that he, as the 'real' arsonist, maliciously accused the Christians to deflect blame from himself is to fall into the trap of unthinkingly classifying him as a monster.[291] Nero was not responsible for the Fire, nor did he act against Christians for politico-ideological reasons, setting his *philanthropia* against their *misanthropia* – their 'hatred of the human race'.[292] Tacitus himself does not believe that the Christians had committed arson, but relates that a number of people in Rome were persuaded of their guilt. On the day of their punishment, there was a strong feeling abroad that the accused were getting what they deserved. However, despite this, spectators felt some pity for the victims, 'due to the impression that they were being sacrificed not for the welfare of the state, but to the ferocity of a single man'.[293] This appears to give us Nero 'the monster', but what may have lain behind such public revulsion is the feeling that the manner of the *princeps*' punishment of Christians was in some way inappropriate. This cannot have included any thought of excessive cruelty. Again, what happened was standard practice. Nero generally showed no bloodthirsty traits; with no strong religious conviction of his own, he is unlikely to have singled out Christians for special torture.[294] Rather, his critics may have disliked his self-indulgence. First, though the Vatican gardens (perhaps thought appropriate because they had been used to house refugees from the Fire[295]) were thrown open for the event, they were Nero's personal property and not a normal place of public execution. Second, Nero obtruded too far into the proceedings, using them to focus attention on himself as, for the first time, he appeared as a professional charioteer, perhaps deriving confidence from being costumed as Apollo.[296] Third, Nero's critics are likely to have included members of the Roman aristocracy who saw this occasion, like 'Tigellinus' banquet', as one on which he made himself far too accessible to the ordinary people of Rome.[297] Though the Neronian administration's condemnation of Christians for starting the Fire was successful, at least in the

---

[288] Cf. above 245; Barrett *et al.* 2016, 165.   [289] Fini 1994, 166; cf. Holland 2000, 168, 172–5.
[290] Above 246.   [291] Cf. Bradley 1978a, 104.
[292] Fini 1994, 170–3. Cf. above 56, 309–10; Meier 2008, 575–8.
[293] Tac. *Ann.* 15.44.8: *tamquam non utilitate publica sed in saevitiam unius absumerentur.*
[294] Cf. above 287; Fini 1994, 169–70.   [295] Tac. *Ann.* 15.39.2.
[296] Above 287–8; Champlin 2003, 125.   [297] Above 308; cf. Griffin 1984, 140.

short term,[298] the *princeps* made a personal error in arranging a punishment that was theatrical, not judicial. Knowing that he was not responsible for the Fire, and seeing that the majority of the City population now accepted this, he cheerfully accepted the guilt of the convicted and, with no thought as to how this might look to others, threw himself into producing and starring in a grand, personal 'fatal charade' to deal with them.

The messiness of the deaths of Octavia and the Christians, like the removal of Agrippina, demonstrates that killing was not Nero's strong point.[299] There is no sign that he, unlike so many authentic tyrants of history, ever committed regular and heartless acts of cruelty for his own selfish benefit or amusement.[300]

---

[298] Above 247.   [299] Cf. Warmington 1969, 163; Fini 1994, 134–5.
[300] Fini 1994, 76, 79–80.

CHAPTER 13

Finance

13.1   Introduction

All governments depend on access to the resources of the people they aspire to control, usually through taxation. Without taxation there is no control, no government and, very likely, no state.[1] The Principate was no exception; indeed its main business has been described as the collection of taxes and tribute.[2] This gave those who understood finance the opportunity to gain great influence. Tacitus describes Pallas, freedman *a rationibus* and so *de facto* imperial minister of finance under Claudius, as being 'more or less in control of the realm'.[3] Phaon, Pallas' probable successor under Nero, was important enough, despite their close association, to survive his master's fall,[4] a fall which, moreover, is frequently linked to Nero's financial problems.[5] Nero's finances therefore merit close attention,[6] though in what follows 'Nero' should usually be read as shorthand for 'the Neronian regime'.

It is first essential to gain some understanding of the income and expenditure of this regime. Financial statistics are rare and difficult to deploy. I proceed on the assumption of a mid-first century annual imperial budget of around HS 0.8 billion, accepted by many historians.[7] This was

---

[1] Cf. Rathbone 2008, 277; Osgood 2011, 37.   [2] Osgood 2011, 196.

[3] Tac. *Ann.* 13.14.1: *velut abitrium regni agebat.* Alpers 1995, 142–4; above 68; below 336.

[4] Above 64; below 412; cf. Cizek 1982, 206.

[5] E.g. Levi 1949, 196–7, 201–4; Brunt 1959, 556–8; Warmington 1969, 63, 68–70; Bradley 1978a, 189–90; Cizek 1982, 299–302, 383–5; Griffin 1984, 197–207; Rudich 1993, 209; Wiedemann 1996a, 251–2; Levick 1999a, 36–7; Fantham 2013, 27; Mratschek 2013, 57.

[6] Cf. Levi 1949, 117: 'Le questioni di carattere finanziario avevano un grande peso nelle direttive generali della politica'.

[7] E.g. Levick 1999a, 95; Champlin 2003, 227; Rathbone 2008, 253. Cf. Osgood 2011, 37: *c.* HS 0.711 billion under Claudius; Scheidel 2015, 231 and notes 4–5, 242–3: rising to over HS 1 billion in the second century, or 5–7 per cent of GDP.

drawn from the gross domestic product (GDP) of the Roman Empire. The most recent attempts to quantify imperial GDP produce a range of HS 9–20.9 billion.[8] There is agreement that, whatever its size, only a very small proportion of GDP, between 3 and 10 per cent, was taken by the imperial government, and that it spent the lion's share of this income, probably around 40 per cent, on the army.[9] An imperial GDP of HS 16.0 billion, nicely in the middle of the estimated range of HS 9–20.9 billion, results from estimating the government's income of HS 0.8 billion at *c.* 5 per cent of the total. To put such figures into perspective, HS 400 was sufficient to keep the average family in wheat for a year, and under Nero the annual pay of a legionary was HS 900.[10] A respectable mid-first century lifetime's fortune was HS 200 million, the value of the estate left to Agrippina by her second husband, Passienus.[11] These amounts lie within a wide spread ranging from the HS 115 calculated as being the annual minimum subsistence income during the High Empire, through the HS 1.2 million reckoned to be the annual income of Pliny II, a 'middling senator' early in the second century, to the HS 300–400 million regarded as excessive short-term accumulations by Pallas and Seneca.[12] For most people, HS 1,000 (= 250 silver *denarii* or ten gold *aurei*) was a large sum of money.

13.2   Problems

13.2.1   Potential Stress

As we have seen, the Augustan fiscal system tapped only a very small proportion of GDP. In the East, indeed, and especially in Egypt, there was probably a decrease in taxation relative to Hellenistic levels.[13] The system was also unable to respond quickly to change.[14] Both flaws derived from traditional Roman conservatism, which generated 'a defensive ideology of fiscal minimalism (no new taxes, no increases to old ones)'.[15] This attitude had been strengthened by the Republic's profitable expansion into the Mediterranean region, which allowed it to minimise domestic taxation.[16] From their relatively modest fixed income, *principes* had to pay for the

---

[8] Lo Cascio 2007, 622.
[9] Campbell 1984, 164; Rathbone 1996, 309–12; Lo Cascio 2007, 622, 632, 638.
[10] Holland 2000, 87; Lo Cascio 2007, 637.   [11] Suet. *Pass.*; above 33.
[12] Jongman 2007, 598–601; Tac. *Ann.* 12.53.5, 13.42.6; Juv. 1.108–9; Cass. Dio 61.10.3, 62.14.3.
[13] Scheidel 2015, 233–4.   [14] Scheidel 2015, 254.   [15] Rathbone 1996, 312.
[16] Scheidel 2015, 230–1.

defence and administration of the Empire and act as open-handed public benefactors: 'most emperors were big spenders; it went with the job'.[17] However, traditional 'defensive ideology' made them disinclined to increase regular taxation.[18] They shunned increases in direct taxation and, although they occasionally increased indirect taxes, they usually rescinded the rises in the face of popular unrest.[19] To meet fiscal shortfalls they looked elsewhere. On accession, a *princeps* gained control of all state finances but lost his private fortune, immediately absorbed by the *domus Caesaris*, 'the imperial household'.[20] As a result, all his subsequent spending was, in effect, 'public'. However, a notional distinction between private and public income and expenditure was maintained by each being put through different accounting systems.[21] As *princeps* succeeded *princeps*, this resulted in the accretion of a store of wealth which both permitted *principes* to balance the books and allowed them to show 'personal' liberality; but it discouraged radical fiscal reform. Undertaxing of the whole Empire does not mean that there was no overtaxing of parts. There were different local taxes, and the imperial pattern was uneven.[22] While the Three Gauls escaped relatively lightly, Egypt, though continuing to pay less than under the Ptolemies, was kept under significant fiscal pressure.[23] Pressure was necessary. At times, imperial administrations struggled to cover their commitments even when drawing on all available resources. In the Late Empire the problem was solved through major changes in the taxation system which allowed the acquisition of a much greater portion of imperial GDP.[24] First-century rulers, however, appear to have lived hand-to-mouth. Again, the problem was that 'emperors were meant to spend generously and tax sparingly'.[25]

Principes, such as Gaius, who spent well beyond their means attracted criticism; but so did those, like Tiberius and Galba who, by aiming at a surplus, were accused of being stingy. The unspoken expectation was that

[17] E.g. Levi 1949, 117–18; Lo Cascio 2007, 631; Rathbone 2008, 252 (quotation): Gibson 2013, 123. Cf. above 128, 301, 306, 315–16.

[18] Griffin 1984, 200–1.

[19] E.g. Suet. *Calig.* 40–41. Rathbone 2008, 254–5, 276; Günther 2013, 106–9; below 351.

[20] Wiedemann 1996a, 200–2, 221, 232–3, 239; cf. Wiedemann 1996b, 262–3, 269; Osgood 2011, 38; Mordine 2013, 102–4.

[21] Below 334–6.   [22] Lo Cascio 2007, 624.

[23] Drinkwater 1983, 65; Scheidel 2015, 248, 251; above 327; below 344.

[24] Bransbourg 2015, 266.

[25] Rathbone 2008, 253, 276 (quotation). Scheidel (2015, 247, 253) reaches much the same conclusion, though starting from a much more positive assessment of first- and second-century fiscal situation: 'the scope of genuinely discretionary spending was modest', 'overall margins were slim'. For the force of 'appear' see below 348.

principes should just balance the books.[26] This fiscal life on a knife-edge will have been made more uncomfortable by high levels of corruption. Many leading imperial administrators practised extortion; and all expected expensive gifts from the *princeps*, their subordinates and petitioners. The wealth of senior Claudian and early-Neronian court freedmen was notorious, and towards the end of Nero's principate other *liberti* incurred similar criticism.[27] In the provinces, the imperial government probably tolerated large-scale tax avoidance and evasion by the local aristocrats on whom it had devolved much political and fiscal power.[28] Since most money went to the army, the opportunities for diverting the military budget will have been especially great. Slave *dispensatores* – quartermasters- or paymasters-general, so the actual handlers of cash – were held to be particularly crooked. To limit their depredations they were not given their freedom until after retirement, but this was not greatly effective. Suetonius relates that Otho received HS 1 million from an imperial slave for obtaining him a post as *dispensator*; Pliny I notes the wealth of Drusilianus, *dispensator* in Spain under Claudius; and he observes not so much the misdemeanour, which was only to be expected, as the extraordinary extent of peculation by a *dispensator* of the Armenian war.[29] The differences between the amounts which taxpayers were supposed to pay, those which they actually paid and those which were finally disbursed by the government must have been substantial.[30] Like conservatism, corruption will have significantly reduced room for fiscal manoeuvre, especially in difficult times.

This brings us to the problems of the Neronian administration. Claudius' principate had been careful but costly, given the expenses of his accession, of invading and holding down Britain, of various public works and even of bringing on Nero.[31] *Prima facie*, in 54 there can have been few reserves,[32] yet the administration had immediately to pay out a huge accession donative of *c.* HS 15,000 per man (five times the standard salary), a total of *c.* HS 180 million, to the Praetorians.[33] There were

---

[26] Scheidel 2015, 251 (quotation); Griffin 1984, 202–3; Lo Cascio 2007, 623.

[27] Cf. above 193. Barrett 1996, 133; Osgood 2011, 189, 191; cf. Scheidel 2015, 236. Below 364.

[28] Scheidel 2015, 235, 249, 251.

[29] Plin. *HN* 33.145; Suet. *Otho* 5.2; Plin. *HN* 7.129. Millar 1977, 136; Osgood 2011, 40; below 333.

[30] Scheidel 2015, 230.   [31] Osgood 2011, 34–6, 228–30, 235–6.   [32] Griffin 1984, 203–4.

[33] Cass. Dio 61.3.1, with Suet. *Claud.* 10.4. Josephus (*AJ* 19.247) has HS 20,000; Griffin 1984, 204; Barrett 1996, 144; Holland 2000, 30; Osgood 2011, 35–6; above 15. The total is calculated from an assumed strength of *c.* 12,000: Bingham 2013, 52–6 and n. 31; above 60. It seems odd that Nero did not make payments further afield, in particular to the frontier troops. Gaius is reported to have given the Praetorians HS 2,000 per man, the urban paramilitaries HS 500 per man, other troops HS 300 per man, and the citizen body HS 300 per man with an additional lump sum of HS 45 million:

further bonuses to the Praetorians: in 59, following the murder of Agrippina; and in 65, after the Pisonian conspiracy, of HS 2,000 per man, a total of *c.* HS 24 million together with a grain allowance.[34] A similar donative may also have been given to the German guards.[35] In addition, Nero was generous to the people of Rome. In 57 he gave HS 400, a total of *c.* HS 80 million, to each registered resident male citizen. Though this is the only directly recorded *congiarium*, there are signs of another, either in 54, for the accession, or in 60, on the occasion of the *Iuvenalia*. In 59, he showered gifts on the crowds attending the *Ludi Maximi*,[36] and we may assume more such liberality at other of his spectacles. Nero also supported impoverished members of the upper class, in 58 awarding an annual pension of HS 500,000 to one individual, with other pensions probably as generous.[37] And, famously, he lavished gifts on his friends. Close associates were richly rewarded for their support after the death of Britannicus, the most notorious beneficiary being Seneca.[38] Nero's extravagant gifts to lesser favourites is criticised by Suetonius in his catalogue of imperial vices.[39] Other instances include: the HS 20 million given to Doryphorus very early in the principate; estates in Italy and Sardinia granted to Acte; estates given to Locusta; Anicetus' generous pension; and Sporus' dowry.[40] Tacitus, giving a rare figure, records that such gifts amounted to HS 2.2 billion, and that Galba tried, with little success, to recover them from their recipients.[41] In this respect, Suetonius and Plutarch refer specifically to action against actors and athletes,[42] but one suspects that this indicates that Galba put real pressure only on those he thought socially vulnerable, 'the lowly'.[43] The HS 2.2 billion therefore probably gives us an idea of the value of Nero's gifts to people at all levels

Cass. Dio 69.2.1–3. Though the first two of these gifts amount to *c.* HS 30 million, paltry in comparison to Nero's, the last two may be calculated as amounting to at least HS 130 million, another large sum, though one that does not seem to have attracted comment by modern historians. It may have been the size of this that encouraged Claudius and Nero to concentrate on those who mattered most.

[34] Cass. Dio 61.14.3; Tac. *Ann.* 15.72.1; Suet. *Ner.* 10.1; Bradley 1978a, 77.

[35] Bellen 1981, 88–9; cf. above 61.

[36] Tac. *Ann.* 13.31.2, 14.15.3; Suet. *Ner.* 10.1, 11.2; Cass. Dio 61.18.1–2; *RIC²*, p. 139; Hohl 1918, 363; Bradley 1978a, 75–6; Barrett *et al.* 2016, 34; above 315.

[37] Tac. *Ann.* 13.34.2; Suet. *Ner.* 10.8; Hohl 1918, 364. Cf. above 23.   [38] Tac. *Ann.* 13.18.1–2.

[39] Above 314.

[40] Doryphorus: Cass. Dio 61.5.4; Locusta: Suet. *Ner.* 33.3; Anicetus: Tac. *Ann.* 14.62.6; Sporus: Cass. Dio 62.28.3; Acte, and generally: Bradley 1978a, 167–8.

[41] Tac. *Hist.* 1.20.   [42] Suet. *Galb.* 15.1; Plut. *Galb.* 16.2–3; Bradley 1978a, 167.

[43] Griffin 1984, 206 (quotation).

of society. Finally, as we have seen, though not insanely profligate, Nero never stinted himself.[44]

More widely, Nero did not shrink from lavish spending on great events: 'he was as big on projects as he was on presents'.[45] These included games, such as the *Ludi Maximi* and *Iuvenalia*,[46] and associated entertainments, such as banquets.[47] They also comprised great state occasions, such as Tiridates' reception of 66, Nero's Greek trip of 66–67, and his Roman 'triumph' of late 67.[48] Just the direct cost of the first of these – for travel, accommodation, presents and subsidies – may be estimated at *c*. HS 350 million.[49] With regard to the Greek trip, Nero's grand proclamation of the freedom of Greece had a price because it spelled the ending of Greek tribute payments. Even though Greece was a relatively poor province, Vespasian was quick to restore the status quo.[50] And again 'there was nothing, however, in which he was more ruinously prodigal than in building'.[51] Most of Nero's structures, completed, semi-completed or projected, have been mentioned already. These comprise: the temple of Claudius (from 55); the huge, superbly decorated and equipped wooden amphitheatre in the Campus Martius (57); the grand arch celebrating victory in Armenia (58–62); the *Macellum* (59); the gymnasium and baths for *Neronia* I (60); the *Domus Transitoria* (from 60); the Misenum to Arvernus, Arvernus to Ostia, and Ostia to Rome navigations (probably from 62); the rebuilding of Rome and the grand schemes for the development of Rome and Ostia (from 64); and the Corinth canal (from 67).[52]

---

[44] Above 314.
[45] Cass. Dio 63.17.1: *kai megalopragmōn kai megalodōros* (trans. Rathbone 2008, 252).
[46] Tac. *Ann.* 14.15.3; Cass. Dio 61.18.1.   [47] Above 305.   [48] E.g. below 383.
[49] Suet. *Ner.* 30.2; Dio 63.2.2, 63.6.5. For travel alone, Champlin (2003, 227) proposes HS 200 million, though I make this a little more, at *c*. HS 216 million. Cf. Bradley 1978a, 166.
[50] Henderson 1905, 389; Griffin 1984, 206; Fini 1994, 208–9. Cf. below 337.
[51] Suet. *Ner.* 31.1. Above 314.
[52] Generally, Hesberg 2011. Temple: Suet. *Vesp.* 9.1; Beste and Hesberg 2013, 316–17; above 249. Wooden amphitheatre: Calp. *Ecl.* 7.23–4, 44–6; Tac. *Ann.* 13.31.1; Suet. *Ner.* 12.1. Beste and Hesberg 2013, 318; above 251. Arch: Tac. *Ann.* 13.41.5, 15.18.1. Champlin 2003, 216–7; Beste and Hesberg 2013, 317. Macellum: Cass. Dio 61.19.1. Waldherr 2005, 207; Beste and Hesberg 2013, 315–16. Gymnasium and baths: Tac. *Ann.* 14.47.3; Suet. *Ner.* 12.3; Cass. Dio 61.21.1. Warmington 1969, 128; Bradley 1978a, 87–8; above 299. Waldherr 2005, 60; Beste and Hesberg 2013, 319–20. *Domus Transitoria*: Tac. *Ann.* 15.39.1; Suet. *Ner.* 31.1. Cizek 1982, 304; above 235, 242. Campanian navigations: Tac. *Ann.* 15.42.2–4; Suet. *Ner.* 31.3. Warmington 1969, 132; Bradley 1978a, 71, 181–2; Cizek 1982, 305–6; Beste and Hesberg 2013, 316, 321; above 315. Rome: Tac. *Ann.* 15.43.2–3, Suet. *Ner.* 16.1. Grant 1970, 163; Cizek 1982, 310. Ostia: Suet. *Ner.* 16.1; above 315. Corinth canal: Suet. *Ner.* 19.2; Cass. Dio 63.16.1. Warmington 1969, 133; Bradley 1978a, 115–16.

He also completed Gaius' circus on the Vatican and its access bridge over the Tiber.[53] Most costly of all, of course, was his Golden House.[54]

The Neronian regime had also to cope with substantial unforeseen expense and loss of income such as that caused by the Fire;[55] but the largest outgoings were on war.[56] For a *princeps* little interested in military matters, Nero presided over a remarkably high level of conflict: in Armenia, Britain, Judaea and around the Black Sea.[57] The Armenian conflict was waged on a grand scale. In 55, local units were brought up to strength; others were transferred in from outside, including a whole army group from the Rhine; and client kings were called upon for men and *matériel*. Corbulo soon commanded an exceptionally large and diverse force.[58] Major fighting began in 58, and although Tacitus reports minimal casualties in the storming of one stronghold,[59] prolonged combat in difficult conditions must have led to significant losses overall. When Tigranes was put on the Armenian throne in 60, he was given substantial military support.[60] The renewal of hostilities in 62 saw further major troop movements and fighting, and defeat at Rhandeia.[61] Before peace could be gained, in 63–64, another full legion had to be brought in from Pannonia.[62] In the meantime, from 60 to 61, there was widespread conflict in Britain. Even before Boudica's revolt, Suetonius Paullinus, emulating Corbulo, had been campaigning in Wales.[63] Then came the Icenian rebellion. In military terms, this resulted in the loss of at least part of legion IX *Hispana* and the drafting in of troops from Germany.[64] Fiscally, extensive destruction of lives and property diminished provincial taxability. There was a spell of peace from 63,[65] which allowed Nero to close the gates of the temple of Janus, but in late spring of 66 began the Jewish revolt. This provoked more extensive troop movements that gave Vespasian command of almost 50,000 men and lasted into his principate.[66] Throughout most of Nero's principate there was military activity around the Black Sea;[67] and though there is no reason to suppose that he moved troops to Egypt in preparation for a major campaign up the Nile

---

[53] Shotter 2008, 114; Hesberg 2011, 115.   [54] Above 248.   [55] Champlin 2003, 180.
[56] Levick 1999a, 37.
[57] Cf. Plin. *HN* 6.181. *Contra* Holland 2000, 89, 91–3. Cf. Plin. *HN* 6.181.
[58] E.g. Tac. *Ann.* 13.35.4: army group; 13.40.3–4: complexity. Cf. above 131.
[59] Tac. *Ann.* 13.39. 6.   [60] Tac. *Ann.* 14.26.3. Cf. above 136.   [61] Cf. above 140.
[62] Tac. *Ann.* 15.25.5.   [63] Tac. *Ann.* 14.29. Cf. above 138.
[64] Tac. *Ann.* 14.32, 38.1. Barrett *et al.* 2016, 134 n. 35.
[65] I assume that a successful outcome in Armenia, won early in 64, was well in prospect by the end of 63: above 141.
[66] Levick 1999a, 31; cf. above 151.   [67] Above 139.

around 64 or 66,[68] in 66 he ordered a major concentration of forces for an expedition to the Caucasus.[69] All this must have been a massive drain on imperial resources. While troops were on permanent station, their huge demand for food, fodder and fuel could be met for the most part by requisition and purchase from surrounding areas. Once they were on the move their needs will have been more difficult and expensive to satisfy, and there must have been resort to official foraging and unofficial scavenging.[70] The imperial economy will have been disrupted, and the more so since it did not comprise a single elastic market able to cope with temporary fluctuations in demand, but a network of relatively inflexible local and regional trading-areas.[71] The situation will have been made worse by the fact that most Neronian fighting was against opponents from whom could be wrung no huge amounts of booty.[72] The picture is not entirely gloomy. On the Danube, the transfer of population will have increased agricultural production and so tax yields in cash and kind. Aelianus' inscription boasts specifically that he was the first governor of the province to send large amounts of grain to Rome. Roman policing of the Black Sea must also have encouraged trade and so generated more wealth. But both benefits were long term, with little significant immediate financial gain to the state.[73] Furthermore, Aelianus' success resulted in the creation of that most expensive of weapons in the pre-industrial armoury, a permanent war fleet: the *classis Pontica*, stationed at Sinope (Figure 11).[74]

Though the sources give no costings of military expenditure, it may be possible to obtain something from what we have. Calculated at 40 per cent of HS 0.8 billion, the standard annual cost of maintaining the army would have been HS 0.32 billion.[75] Fighting a major war would have significantly increased this sum, say by 100 per cent: HS 0.64 billion. We are told that the slave *dispensator* of the Armenian expedition was able to siphon off HS

---

[68] Above 127, 152 n. 176.   [69] Cf. Malitz 1999, 95; above 148.   [70] Cf. Rathbone 1996, 310.

[71] Rathbone 1996, 319; Drinkwater 1997, 512. For the massive complications and costs involved in feeding a Byzantine army – men and animals – on the move, see Lee 2007, 96. Haynes (2013, 121) observes that Rome did not regularly move auxiliaries around the Empire, probably because it involved too much effort.

[72] Levi 1949, 195–6; Fini 1994, 54; though cf. below 364.

[73] Levi 1949, 192, relates the extra grain supply to Tacitus' account (*Ann.* 15.18.2) that in 62, while celebrations of Paetus' 'victory' in Armenia were under way, Nero, aware that this was not the truth, had old, spoiled, public grain thrown into the Tiber to show that there was no threat to the supply, i.e. he was confident that there were supplementary supplies. However, this was surely too early for these supplies to have had any significant effect.

[74] Joseph. *BJ* 2.367; cf. Tac. *Hist.* 3.47. Levick 1999a, 114; Haynes 2013, 114.   [75] Above 327.

13 million to buy his freedom.[76] If, following Roman hearsay, he needed three times HS 13 million – to free himself, to pay off the obligations he had incurred in gaining his position and making his money, and to create a personal fortune – we are looking at a total peculation of HS 39 million. If we further suppose that this HS 39 million amounted to between 0.1 and 1 per cent of the value of the money passing through his hands, we reach HS 3.9–39 billion, say HS 4–40 billion, as the basic cash cost of the Armenian conflict. Over nine years (55–64), this would average c. HS 0.44–4.4 billion per annum. The low end of this scale, HS 0.44 billion, lies between the standard annual cost of HS 0.32 billion and the likely maximum of HS 0.64 billion proposed above and so seems a reasonable figure to work with. On this basis I have constructed Table 3, taking the Armenian conflict as the most expensive and estimating the outlay of the fighting in Judaea, Britain and the Black Sea at 75 per cent, 50 per cent and 25 per cent of its cost, respectively. I include the other expenditure outlined above, locating it either throughout Nero's period of office or when we know it fell. The final figure for Nero's gifts has been adjusted to bring the total to HS 2.2 billion. The overall cost of the aristocratic pensions is estimated at six times that of the largest known single payment. Important expenditure which is difficult to quantify is that on construction other than the Golden House. Assuming that spending on discrete structures such as Claudius' temple and the baths/gymnasium was, though hardly parsimonious, small relative to the imperial budget, I offer only two speculative costings of larger commitments: of the Campanian navigations and the rebuilding of Rome. Both are multiples (× 1 and × 2 respectively) of the HS 0.35 billion spent by Claudius on two aqueducts.[77]

Not included are the large subventions made by Nero to the *Aerarium*. In 57 he gave it HS 40 million, and in 62 claimed that he was paying it HS 60 million every year.[78] I omit them because they may be regarded as having no financial significance.[79] First, set against an annual imperial income of c. HS 0.8 billion these amounts are tiny.[80] Second, though actual movement of bullion and coin between state strongrooms was not unknown, it was a very rare, usually emergency measure.[81] Nero's 'transfers' were probably only on paper. Finally, and related to this, as already noted any practical difference between the state's resources and those of the *princeps* had long vanished.[82] Augustus established a legal distinction

---

[76] Plin. *HN* 7.129; above 329.   [77] Above 260.   [78] Tac. *Ann.* 13.31.2; 15.18.4.
[79] Below 336.   [80] Rathbone 2008, 253.
[81] E.g. Cass. Dio 59.1–3 (Gaius). Osgood 2011, 29, 37.   [82] Above 328.

Table 3 *Estimated main extraordinary annual Neronian expenditure (HS billions)*

Year	Armenia/Tiridates	Black Sea	Britain	Judaea	Tacitus' gifts	Donatives/congiaria	Tacitus' pensions	Domus Aurea	Campania/Rome	Total
54	0	0	0	0	0	0.18	0.003	0	0	0.183
55	0.44	0	0	0	0.16	0	0.003	0	0	0.603
56	0.44	0	0	0	0.16	0	0.003	0	0	0.603
57	0.44	0	0	0	0.16	0.08	0.003	0	0	0.683
58	0.44	0	0	0	0.16	0	0.003	0	0	0.603
59	0.44	0	0	0	0.16	0	0.003	0	0	0.603
60	0.44	0.11	0.22	0	0.16	0	0.003	0	0	0.933
61	0.44	0.11	0.22	0	0.16	0	0.003	0	0	0.933
62	0.44	0.11	0	0	0.16	0	0.003	0	0.175	0.888
63	0.44	0.11	0	0	0.16	0	0.003	0	0.175	0.888
64	0	0.11	0	0	0.16	0	0.003	0.22	0.175	0.668
65	0	0.11	0	0	0.16	0.024	0.003	0.22	0.175	0.692
66	0.35	0.11	0	0.33	0.16	0	0.003	0.22	0.175	1.348
67	0	0	0	0.33	0.16	0	0.003	0.22	0.175	0.888
68	0	0	0	0.33	0.12	0	0.003	0.22	0.175	0.848
Total	4.31	0.77	0.44	0.99	2.2	0.284	0.045	1.1	1.225	11.364

between his personal possessions and income and those of the state. The latter continued to be the responsibility of the old Republican *Aerarium*. The former, his *patrimonium*, were managed within his household by a sort of private bank which came to be called the *Fiscus Caesaris*, though in common parlance *patrimonium* and *Fiscus* became interchangeable. Into the second century, all *principes* attempted to maintain the distinction but, given their undisputed autocracy, the growing number and power of officials in their service, and the pragmatism of an Establishment which knew where real authority lay, the interests of the *Fiscus* were bound to prevail. Thus in cases where assets from reversions and confiscations should have gone to the *Aerarium* they were diverted to the *Fiscus*.[83] Under Nero, *Aerarium* and *Fiscus*, both directed by the *princeps*, were 'hardly distinguishable'.[84] *Principes* directed imperial expenditure from within their household using both public and 'private' funds, which explains the rise of the *a rationibus*.[85] Though the *Fiscus* soon eclipsed the *Aerarium*, it never formally replaced it because the *Aerarium*, like the Senate, was both part of the 'restored' Republic and remained a useful working institution, handling income which would be awkward to divert elsewhere, such as the proceeds of indirect taxes which financed the military superannuation fund (*Aerarium militare*). Much effort was put into maintaining the *Aerarium*'s reputation for reliability.[86] Nero's 'transfer of funds' from *Fiscus* to *Aerarium* was a double book-keeping exercise – there was no movement of cash and the *princeps* kept control over the money – undertaken, as Tacitus puts it, to 'maintain public confidence' in the *Aerarium*.[87] Transfer might be in the opposite direction, as when in 67 the Senate is supposed to have granted Nero an annual allowance of HS 10 million.[88] The reliability of this very late reference is, however, suspect; and it should not be taken to indicate that the Senate granted the *princeps* an annual recurrent grant from the *Aerarium*.[89] Like Nero's 'subventions' to the *Aerarium*, such generosity would anyway have been fiscally

[83] Below 348. So Petronius' destruction of property to save it from Nero: Plin. *HN* 37.20; above 320.

[84] For the above see esp. Alpers 1995, 1–165, e.g. (principle) 42–3, 94–5, 118–19, 141, 161–2; (personnel) 48, 131–3; (diversion) 50, 71–3; direction 162–4. Also Millar 1977, 189–90, 197–200; Griffin 1984, 56–7, 199–200; Talbert 1984, 375–8; Levick 1999a, 97; Lo Cascio 2007, 630; Scheidel 2015, 235. Quotation: Sutherland, from Alpers 1995, 165 n. 53. Cf. Cass. Dio 71.33.2, on Marcus Aurelius' referring of fiscal matters to the Senate as being out of courtesy, not necessity.

[85] Talbert 1984, 377–8; Scheidel 2015, 235; above 326, 328.   [86] Below 351.

[87] Tac. *Ann.* 13.31.2: *ad retinendam populi fidem.* Cf. Warmington 1969, 63–4; below 351.

[88] Jer. *Chron. ad ann.* 67 [211th Olympiad]: *Neroni in expensas centies centena millia decreto senatus annua subministrantur.*

[89] Cf. Talbert 1984, 377.

meaningless, being miniscule and involving no additional expenditure or income for the state as a whole. Tacitus' verdict on the transfer of property confiscated from Sejanus under Tiberius from the *Aerarium* to the *Fiscus* hits the nail on the head: 'as if it made any difference'.[90] But there was a real purpose in the 'generosity' of *principes*. The ostensible shifting of funds from the *Fiscus* to the *Aerarium* allowed a *princeps*, cast by Augustus as the supreme patron of the state, to demonstrate *liberalitas* and *indulgentia*.

Nero's giving up of the tribute of Greece was, on the other hand, a real loss.[91] The transfer of Sardinia to senatorial jurisdiction in compensation helped only to balance the books of the *Aerarium*. There must have been a decrease in taxation income that had to be made up from the *Fiscus*. Since the amount involved is impossible to assess, I have not included it in Table 3, but the *Fiscus'* ability to withstand such additional strain will be explored further below.[92]

Table 3 is hugely speculative. None of its figures should be quoted as actual, and its annual totals should not be interpreted as net additions to normal expenditure since large amounts under all heads (e.g. soldiers' pay) will have been met from the regular budget. It is intended to give an idea of the main extraordinary spending areas and trends, and of their cost implications relative to each other and to the imperial budget. Principally, it demonstrates the expense of warfare: 58 per cent of total extraordinary expenditure, against 22 per cent on gifts and pensions and 20 per cent on construction. Also telling is that in every year except 54 the annual total comes close to or exceeds the proposed HS 0.8 billion of the regular budget. It rose to a very high level in 60–61 because of Boudica's revolt. It fell back a little after the suppression of Boudica and the ending of the Armenian conflict but rose again on the outbreak of the Jewish war. There seems, indeed, to be a strong case for the Neronian regime's experiencing chronic and increasing fiscal stress.

13.2.2 *Signs of Stress?*

Roman governments under fiscal pressure did not normally borrow against future revenues to increase income.[93] Instead, they did one or more of the following: increasing standard taxation; increasing extraordinary taxation; increasing confiscation of personal property. They might also auction off *principes'* personal possessions.[94] In times of heavy warfare, more rigorous

---

[90] Tac. *Ann.* 6.2.1: *tamquam referret*; Griffin 1984, 199.   [91] Above 331.   [92] Below 348.
[93] Rathbone 2008, 253; but cf. below 363.
[94] Millar 1977, 48: Gaius, Nerva, Marcus Aurelius, Pertinax.

enforcement of standard state demands also included extension of compulsory conscription. Increases in standard and extraordinary obligations are often revealed by general unrest. Confiscation provoked complaint from those most affected, the upper classes. A clear sign of fiscal malaise was reduction in the weight and fineness of the currency, often evident in the coins themselves and sometimes referred to in literary sources. The alternative strategy was retrenchment, with *principes* reducing army pay and donatives and gifts to the Roman people, and economising on state building projects. The first two might be reflected in military or metropolitan unrest; the third is sometimes mentioned by the sources or revealed by archaeology. Mismanagement of finance by one *princeps* was often pointed up by the ostentatious parsimony of his immediate successor or successors.

Concerning income, we know of no increases in standard direct taxation (anyway very difficult to achieve[95]) under Nero. There was a change in the manner of collection of a standard indirect tax on the purchase of slaves, but this appears to have been intended to improve bureaucracy, not raise income, and the tax itself was local to the city of Rome.[96] As for extraordinary taxation, at the start of his principate Nero actually refused to follow Augustan precedent in demanding 'crown gold' (*aurum coronarium/stephanikon*) from provincial communities.[97] Towards the end, however, he brought back 1,808 crowns presented to him as victor in the Greek games. Though traditionally woven from the cuttings of wild bushes, one suspects that many of these were rendered in precious metals.[98] Nero's premature spending of 'Dido's treasure' probably involved borrowing money and not repaying creditors, and purchasing goods and services and not paying suppliers, both of which may have been regarded as extraordinary state demands.[99] Another irregular exaction was certainly Nero's use of individuals and communities to provide accommodation and entertainment in Italy and Greece.[100] Prolonged warfare caused at least two forced levies in the provinces, in 58 and 65;[101] Tacitus, Suetonius, Dio and Plutarch report Nero's cruel financial harrying of Italy and the Empire, especially the Gallic provinces, after the Fire: 'he nearly bankrupted the provinces and exhausted the resources of

[95] Above 327.
[96] Tac. *Ann.* 13.31.3; Cass. Dio 55.31.4. Furneaux 1907, 194; Günther 2013, 113–14; below 431.
[97] Krüger 2012, 45.
[98] Suet. *Ner.* 25.1–2; Cass. Dio 63.20.2, 21.1; cf. *Carm. Einsid.* 2.29, 31. Bradley 1978a, 150; Cizek 1982, 92; Holland 2000, 222; Osgood 2011, 101.
[99] Tac. *Ann.* 16.3.1; above 316.   [100] Above 316.   [101] Tac. *Ann.* 13.35.4; 16.13.4.

individuals'.[102] Imperial rapacity, indeed, figures frequently as a significant cause of revolt. In explaining Boudica's rebellion, Tacitus adduces Roman confiscation of the whole of her deceased husband's estate and kingdom, which in his will he had divided among his two daughters and Nero,[103] and the dispossession of leading Iceni. Dio paints a general picture of Roman greed in Britain, describing how the provincial procurator insisted on the repayment of loans made by Claudius to leading Britons, and how Seneca likewise brutally recalled loans of HS 40 million. Elsewhere, he declares that from around 66 oppressive taxation increasingly unsettled both Britons and Gauls.[104] The year 66 is significant because it came after the Fire and witnessed the act that sparked the Jewish revolt: the forced withdrawal by the governor of Judaea of the equivalent of around HS 400,000 in gold from the Temple treasury in part payment for arrears of tax.[105] Gaul is significant because it was here that Vindex began the movement that would topple Nero in 68. Dio has him addressing an assembly of Gauls resentful at the *princeps'* forced levies of money.[106] *Prima facie* the most explicit evidence for fiscal pressure on the provinces to generate income under Nero comes from Egypt. In an edict dated 6 July 68, i.e. very early under Galba, the prefect of Egypt, Tiberius Julius Alexander, deplores 'new and unjust exactions' and 'the most pressing abuses' [Prologue] suffered by the people of the country at the hands of those in charge of its taxation.[107] In his list of these abuses, those suggesting extreme fiscal pressure are: [1] compulsion of people to undertake farming of taxes and leasing of (imperial) estates; [4] ignoring of established tax exemptions; and [10]: new demands on farmers for foodstuffs and cash. This, and related evidence, has led to general agreement that deepening economic crisis in Egypt throughout the principate of Nero provoked increasing insistence on the full payment of taxes.[108]

As for nefarious acquisition of the property of the upper classes, complaints span most of Nero's principate. The earliest known instance

---

[102] Tac. *Ann.* 15.45.1; Suet. *Ner.* 38.3: *provincias privatorum census prope exhausit*; Cass. Dio 62.18.5, 63.22.2; Plut. *Galb.* 4.1.

[103] Holland 2000, 120: 50 per cent to Nero, 50 per cent to his daughters; cf. below 340.

[104] Tac. *Ann.* 14.31.1–3, 6; 14.35.2. Cass. Dio 62.2.1; 62.3; 63.22.1a. Cf. above 138; below 344.

[105] Joseph. *BJ* 2.293, 405. Wiedemann 1996a, 251; Levick 1999a, 26.

[106] Cass. Dio 63.22.2. Below 389.

[107] 'Year 1 of the emperor Lucius Livius Sulpicius Galba, Caesar, Augustus, Epeiph 12'. *Kainai kai adikoi eispraxeis; hai engista genomenai epēreiai*: *SEG* 15, 873; McCrum and Woodhead 1961, no. 328; Braund 1985, 221–6 (translation).

[108] Bell 1938; Levi 1949, 140; Bradley 1978a, 216; Wiedemann 1996a, 249; Osgood 2011, 136–7.

is from 59, when Nero is alleged to have poisoned his aunt Domitia in order to seize her substantial fortune.[109] The Augustan convention that all metropolitan rich, and their lawyers, might remember the *princeps* in their will, became formalised in this period, with the implication that deviation could be punished.[110] It spread to the periphery of the Empire. The case of Boudica's husband, Prasutagus, around 60, suggests that provincial testators, anxious to protect dependants from state interference and guarantee them some inheritance, began as a matter of course to make significant bequests to the *princeps*.[111] Then there is Nero's execution of six landowners who, through their creation of huge estates purportedly owned half the province of Africa Proconsularis.[112] The most likely period for this is 64–65, after the Fire and when Nero's attention was directed to Africa by 'Dido's treasure'. In 65–66 Nero pursued those implicated in the Pisonian conspiracy. Many were wealthy, and the state will, through bequest or confiscation, have acquired the property of the condemned.[113] From 66 to 67 there were Nero's antics in Greece through which, according to Dio, he devastated the country as if 'sent out to wage war'. First (in perhaps a garbled example of the provincialisation of metropolitan testatory practice) he killed many people after forcing them to make generous bequests to himself or his favourites. Then he simply killed people and seized the whole of their estates.[114] Dio continues that Nero confiscated incalculable amounts of property from the living and votive offerings from temples in Rome, and that he took leading men to Greece just to kill them.[115] He adds that, while in Greece, Nero, short of money and fearful of opposition, brought about the deaths of 'many' Roman nobles on account of their wealth or family.[116] By way of example he recounts the deaths of Corbulo and the Scribonii.[117] That Nero turned on the Scribonii at least in part to acquire their riches appears to receive support from Tacitus' notice that Paccius Africanus was later condemned for suggesting to Nero the ruin of these men, 'eminent for their fraternal concord and their wealth'.[118] Meanwhile, Helius, in charge of Rome, was responsible for the murders of notable persons, including the Camerini, father and son,[119] whose property will also have fallen to the state.

---

[109] Suet. *Ner.* 34.5. Above 278.
[110] Suet. *Ner.* 32. Millar 1977, 153–6; Griffin 1984, 204–5. Cf. above 316.
[111] Above 319, 339; though cf. below 344.   [112] Plin. *HN* 18.35.5–6.
[113] Bradley 1978a, 189; above 319.   [114] Cass. Dio 63.11.1–3: *hōsper epi polemōi staleis.*
[115] Cass. Dio 63.11.3–4; cf. Tac. *Ann.* 15.45.2 and above 317.   [116] Cass. Dio 63.17.1–2: *polloi.*
[117] Cass. Dio 63.17.2–6.   [118] Tac. *Hist.* 4.41: *concordia opibusque insignis.*
[119] Cass. Dio 63.12.1. Cf. above 221, 228.

Finally, with regard to income, from 64 there was a reduction in the weight of the gold *aureus* and in the weight and fineness of the silver *denarius*. The current view is that the number of *aurei* minted from one Roman pound of gold had been set at forty under Augustus. It subsequently underwent a slight increase, so that by the beginning of Nero's principate it stood at forty-three. In 64 it was raised to forty-five, a reduction in the weight of each coin of *c.* 4 per cent. Likewise, the number of *denarii* struck from one pound of silver, set at eighty-four by Augustus but risen to eighty-nine early under Nero, was raised to ninety-six and taken from a metal that was more copper-rich, resulting in a total loss in silver content of *c.* 7 per cent.[120] There was also a 5–10 per cent reduction in the weight of the lower denomination, base-metal coinage.[121]

With regard to expenditure, early problems in funding the Armenian war and expensive capital projects such as the gymnasium and baths for *Neronia* I and the *Domus Transitoria* may be reflected in the calling-in of state loans to leading Britons.[122] Suetonius accuses Nero of postponing the payment of military salaries and benefits due to retiring soldiers, implying misuse of the *Aerarium militare*.[123] The date is uncertain, but the most likely is also around 60.[124] Securely dated is the suspension of free grain distributions in Rome after the Fire.[125] Finally, Nero was followed by two *principes* renowned for their thrift, Galba and Vespasian, classic examples of prudent rulers struggling to balance the books of a profligate predecessor.[126]

All this strengthens the conclusion that Nero was habitually overspending. Striking is that, though the cost of the Golden House was hardly inconsiderable, it is not the largest item in Table 3. Nero's 'generosity', at *c.* 20 per cent of total expenditure, accounts for twice as much. Yet he should not be blamed for depraved profligacy – for acting like his uncle Gaius.[127] The main drain, at *c.* 58 per cent, was war, and this alone gives the impression that the Neronian administration was living well beyond its means. There appear to be good grounds for accepting that its finances were always problematic, deteriorated profoundly as time progressed and

---

[120] Griffin 1984, 122, 198; Carson 1990, 14; cf. 4; Cf. *RIC* 1² p. 135: a reduction in weight of the *aureus* of *c.* 2 per cent, and of the *denarius* of *c.* 7 per cent.

[121] *RIC* 1² pp. 139–40; Griffin 1984, 124.   [122] Cf. below 352.

[123] Suet. *Ner.* 32.1; above 316.   [124] Bradley 1978a, 184; below 347.   [125] Cass. Dio 62.18.5.

[126] Galba: Tac. *Hist.* 1.18 (*parcus senex*), 49 (*suae parcus, publicae avarus*); Plut. *Galb.* 16.1. Vespasian: e.g. Suet. *Vesp.* 8.2.

[127] Above 316. *Contra* Griffin 1984, 205: 'the financial system can hardly be blamed for the fact that Nero inclined more and more towards the extreme example of Gaius, who had erected extravagance into a guiding principle'.

were a key element in the unrest that toppled the regime. Though the causes of the provincial 'explosion' that destroyed Nero 'were complex and overwhelming', 'the most important [was] the ever-increasing shortage of cash that was forcing [him] to squeeze every penny he could from the provinces'. Rapacity led to provincial unrest which encouraged provincials to 'share the political and moral grievances' of the disaffected metropolitan upper class.[128]

13.3   Solutions

13.3.1   Introduction

In financial matters, as in everything else, Nero 'the monster' owes much to myth and wilful misunderstanding, The details of his excessive gift to Doryphorus seem to derive from a story about Mark Antony.[129] The 'Campanian navigations', maligned by the sources, are commercially defensible. Similar schemes were much in vogue in this period, with canals begun, though never completed, in Greece and Gaul.[130] The assumption that the Neronian regime was on shaky financial ground from the start reckons without Agrippina. Always mindful of the political importance of money, from 41 to 54 she created at least two substantial personal fighting funds.[131] Her expertise in finance explains her close acquaintanceship with Pallas, with whom she prepared for the accession of Nero: by building her first great fighting fund.[132] The expenses of Nero's accession appear, therefore, more bearable and instances of consequent financial stress less compelling, especially when charges of private profligacy are tempered by appreciation of the benefits of spending for the public good.[133] There is no sign of Nero's resorting to auctioning his personal property. He used his victor's crowns for personal gratification and display to favourites, not for spending.[134] Some wealthy may have regarded the burdens imposed upon them by imperial progresses as unwarranted extraordinary taxation, but the many to whom proximity to the court brought status and favours probably

---

[128] Levick 1999a, 36–7.   [129] Above 330; Plut. *Ant.* 4.7–9; Millar 1977, 149.

[130] Tac. *Ann.* 13.53.3. Nero was following a Claudian utilitarian tradition: Henderson 1905, 220; Alcock 1994, 102. Cf. also Hohl 1918, 389; Elsner 1994, 119; Shotter 2008, 90; Osgood 2011, 174; Barrett *et al.* 2016, 143–4 and n. 53; above 121, 315.

[131] Tac. *Ann.* 12.7.7 (cf. *Schol. Iuv.* 4.81); 13.13.3, 18.3.

[132] Cf. Cass. Dio 60.32.3. Levi 1949, 107 and n. 2; Barrett 1996, 130–2, 145–6; Osgood 2011, 22, 235.

[133] Above 315.   [134] Suet. *Ner.* 25.2.

regarded them a reasonable price to be paid. They certainly provided the administration with a means of recovering part of the money spent on gifts. Communities may have been pressured to contribute to the cost of rebuilding Rome after the Fire, but the Great Fire of London shows that one of the regular ways in which developed pre-industrial metropoleis coped with disaster was by appealing as a matter of course for help from other towns – local, national and international. Such an appeal in 64 cannot have been unexpected, and most donors probably responded willingly in expectation of future reciprocal help. In the one case we know of, Lyon gave HS 4 million but got it back when it needed it.[135] Likewise, a case can be made that even Nero's obsession with 'Dido's treasure' arose out of more than mere greed. In 65, Bassus must have contacted him after the suppression of the Pisonian conspiracy but before the death of Poppaea. This was at a time when the *princeps* had escaped assassination and could look forward to *Neronia* II and his first public appearance as an entertainer in Rome,[136] and the birth of his second child,[137] i.e. when he was feeling shaken but lucky. His sense of good fortune may have been strengthened by the replenishing of the state's coffers by the Pisonian confiscations,[138] and by the beginning of a significant decline in military expenditure: Table 3. Nero could well have considered that he was back 'on a roll', making optimism, not avarice, the main stimulus for his belief in Bassus' claims. His confidence may have been further strengthened by sycophantic rhetoric, associated with the holding of *Neronia* II, which picked up these claims and made much of the earth putting up gold.

The extent to which taxation provoked provincial revolt is also debatable. Suetonius' accusations are general and vague. Those that Tacitus and Dio put into the mouth of Boudica and Vindex are patently rhetorical: the stock-in-trade of an historiographical tradition hostile to 'tyranny'.[139] Likewise, Plutarch's report of Galba's claim that he was moved to revolt by the plight of provincials again provokes the reaction 'Well he would say that, wouldn't he?', since it sounds more like how Galba subsequently justified rebellion than a secure indication of conditions in Spain and Gaul.[140] On the other hand, the confiscation of Prasutagus' kingdom and the general calling-in of loans in Britain have a ring of truth. The Claudian administration could well have given compliant British leaders unsecured, low-/no-interest loans of undefined duration. If so, with a

---

[135] Tac. *Ann.* 16.13.5. Tinniswood 2003, 168–75; Romm 2014, 157.
[136] Cf. Waldherr 2005, 127.   [137] Above 247.   [138] Cf. above 340.
[139] Cf. Brunt 1959, 533–4.   [140] So, *contra* Bradley 1978a, 190.

grand new baths building to be paid for and work starting on the *Domus Transitoria*, but most of all with the Armenian war already well under way and the Black Sea campaign just beginning, the Neronian regime would have had good reason to recoup what it was owed. The financially hard-nosed Seneca, and perhaps other astute 'insiders', fearing that this would make British debtors a bad risk, may in turn have withdrawn their private loans, creating a disastrous evaporation of credit.[141] It is possible that Prasutagus was one of those who owed money to the Roman state, that he hoped that making Nero a substantial beneficiary in his will would settle the debt, and that the imperial procurator in Britain decided that this was not enough. If so, the main problem in Britain was not so much chronic fiscal rapacity – indeed, very much the opposite, since Britons appear to have become accustomed to being treated relatively lightly – as administrative mismanagement. In Judaea, the arrears involved were sig-nificant and, again, the Roman state had the right to demand payment. However, at a time when Romano-Jewish relations were rapidly approach-ing their nadir, as in Britain it let itself down not by chronic greed but by poor management: first in letting the debt accumulate, and then in insisting on instant repayment.

Even the Egyptian case is open to doubt. Most of Tiberius Julius Alexander's catalogue of abuses concerns persistent problems arising out of an easily administered country's being habitually treated as a milch cow by those who ran it. 'Abuses and complaints of the kind described in Alexander's edict are by no means confined to this era'.[142] This is exempli-fied in mention of officials buying up debts and then using state force to compel debtors to settle them [2] and of the nefarious activities of state accountants [8, 9, 11]. The few novel grievances comprise restriction of some immunities and extraordinary demands on farmers which may have arisen out of the sudden needs of the conflict in Judaea at the very start of Alexander's prefecture,[143] and so did not result from established Neronian rapacity. Overall, indeed, the edict suggests Neronian concern. Alexander shows a favourable attitude to two previous Neronian prefects, Balbillus (55–59) and Vestinus (59–62) [4],[144] but omits Vestinus' successor, his own predecessor, Caecina Tuscus (*c.* 62–66),[145] and is somewhat guarded about his own early activities, referring to the compulsion that had

---

[141] Cass. Dio 62.2.1. Griffin 1976, 232; Waldherr 2005, 136; cf. below 363.
[142] Bowman 1996a, 365; 1996b, 691 (quotation). Cf. Osgood 2011, 190–1, 200.
[143] Joseph. *BJ* 2.494–7; Griffin 1976, 95; Levick 1999a, 27–8.   [144] Balbillus: cf. above 154.
[145] Tuscus' dates are somewhat uncertain: Bradley 1978a, 114; Cizek 1982, 200.

occurred over the previous five years as if this were nothing to do with him [10]. The omission of Tuscus is understandable given his political disgrace in 66,[146] very possibly the result of misdemeanour more serious than misuse of government property,[147] perhaps gross mismanagement, exacerbated and exposed by the rise in tension in the region. Perhaps after a spell of short-term, emergency administration under an imperial freedman, Ponticus,[148] the government appointed Tiberius Julius Alexander, a well-connected and experienced local candidate to put the country to rights.[149] His edict of 68 may therefore be interpreted as not just a piece of administration but also as a defence of his work to date. Its message is that things are going well. Where there are problems, officials, not prefects, are mainly to blame. He had experienced some difficulties in getting started, mainly due to the single, bad, unnamed prefect and the pressures of war, but now has the situation well in hand. The measure is more about chronic exploitation of Egypt in general, and the late-Neronian strategic situation in the East in particular, than any ongoing economic or fiscal 'crisis'. Though dated by the principate of Galba, the edict must have been drafted under Nero. Its stated date of promulgation, 6 July 68, gives insufficient time for the news of Nero's death and replacement by Galba on 9 June to have arrived from Rome. A number of historians have therefore postulated that Alexander was a secret supporter of Galba, had prior knowledge of his revolt, and published his edict under Galba's name in anticipation of his accession. As will be argued below, there is a simpler explanation.[150]

Likewise with regard to income, there are few deaths and exiles of the rich that can be attributed to Neronian 'rapacity'. Suetonius is misleading in suggesting that the regime used *maiestas* to make money.[151] Trials under this charge were brought back relatively late, in 62, for political not fiscal reasons: to allow Nero to show clemency.[152] Charges of *maiestas* were frequent after the uncovering of the Pisonian conspiracy. Their intention was hardly to display clemency, and the *Fiscus* will have received the *bona damnatorum*.[153] However, the principal motivation for both accusation and penalty was, again, political not financial.[154] Indeed, convention limited the extent of confiscation. Earlier, even Pallas, whose huge wealth is supposed to have caused Nero to have him killed, was able to pass most of this on to his family.[155] Now, those found guilty were given time

---

[146] Above 221.   [147] Bradley 1978a, 215–16.   [148] Cizek 1982, 200.
[149] Cf. Levick 1999a, 28–9.   [150] Below 391.   [151] Suet. *Ner.* 32.2. Above 316.
[152] Above 187.   [153] Above 340.   [154] Cf. Griffin 1984, 205.   [155] Above 195.

to amend their wills in favour of Nero in order to secure at least part of
their estate for their heirs. And though Petronius and Antistius Vetus failed
to comply, even their wills were allowed to stand.[156] Scaevinus, the senior
plotter who made a number of generous gifts on the eve of the initiation of
the Pisonian conspiracy,[157] was excessively pessimistic about what would
happen to his estate if he failed. As for normal customary bequests to the
princeps, fortune-hunting was part of upper-class life. With no tradition of
primogeniture and entail, bequests might benefit a wide circle of relatives
and acquaintances, exciting many great expectations. No sooner had
Agrippina escaped drowning than she, as a likely heir, ordered a search
for the will of the friend who had just died in her place.[158] The metropolitan elite probably accepted naming of the *princeps*, like the provision of
entertainment, as a part of the social order.[159] The provincial rich may
have resented it as another form of indirect tax, but how common was it
beyond the centre? What happened to Prasutagus is not the best ground
for assuming a totally generalised practice, since the king may have been a
state debtor. The new testamentary demands on imperial freedmen may be
seen as a reasonable penalty on those who had improperly assumed this
status; and they were also probably of short duration.[160] The truth of
Nero's depredation of Greece has already been questioned.[161] Here, as
elsewhere, sources misrepresent Nero's enthusiasms. His passion for collecting classic works of art was driven by his love of fine things, not by
greed. Following Augustan precedent,[162] he may have given tax exemptions to donor communities. The fall of the Scribonii may be ascribed to
politics, not greed.[163] The changes in the imperial coinage should not be
seen as resulting from or contributing to acute fiscal crisis, as will be
explained further below.[164] This leaves the supposed poisoning of
Domitia and the fate of the six African landowners. The former is suspect
because it is not confirmed by Tacitus, because it falls before the peak in
expenditure of Nero's principate [Table 3], and because, given Domitia's
age and state of health and the good relationship she had with her nephew,
there was no need for him to resort to crime to be sure of his speedy
inheritance of her estate.[165] The tale may have been spun from talk about
Nero's recent involvement in the death of his mother.[166] Pliny I's reference to the latter, 'the most celebrated statement' of bloody Neronian

---

[156] Above 319, 340; Bradley 1978a, 191–2.   [157] Tac. *Ann.* 15.54.2.
[158] Tac. *Ann.* 14.6.2; Furneaux 1907, 240.   [159] Above 342–3.
[160] Above 316; Bradley 1978a, 190–1.   [161] Above 231.   [162] Cf. Millar 1977, 145.
[163] Above 228; cf. Bradley 1978a, 188.   [164] Below 358.
[165] Above 280; Bradley 1978a, 186; Barrett 1996, 137.   [166] Hohl 1918, 370.

greed, is, as Bradley argues, vague, comes from a hostile source, and bears little close examination. The most we can say is that Nero probably acquired land in Africa, but this was over a period of time and through various means (including legitimate inheritance), not as part of a policy of large-scale confiscation.[167]

As for reduced expenditure, military unrest over pay and conditions does not figure in the record, not even of the events that led to Nero's overthrow. The alleged irregular treatment of retirement benefits could refer to events in 60 when, as part of an ill-starred attempt to repopulate parts of Italy, veterans received land in lieu of cash bonuses.[168] The suspension of free grain distributions in Rome in 64 occurred under exceptional circumstances and was temporary; and, as far as one can see, there was no great popular resentment of Nero in the capital, once the Fire was past and the construction of the Golden House well under way. Indeed, after the initial rejoicing at Nero's fall, the poor bitterly lamented.[169] Galba's economic prudence derived as much from natural miserliness as from the pressures of a financial crisis. His successors in Rome, Otho and Vitellius, found money to spend on a truly Neronian scale.[170] Vespasian was also naturally careful, and his efforts to bring order to the fiscal chaos he found on taking over the Empire, though legendary, came some time after the fall of Nero and followed a hugely damaging round of civil war.[171] The only 'stress measures' that cannot be qualified are the forced levies of troops, and these were inevitable in a period of prolonged fighting.

Nero never embarked on a programme of arbitrary, selfish, illegal confiscation of property to fund his own spending, meet a fiscal deficit or break the power of the aristocracy. Property was confiscated but this was usually the consequence of justifiable political prosecutions. When, for example, building land was needed it was purchased legally (while accepting that those in the know may well have manipulated the market for their own ends).[172] Although the Neronian regime experienced significant fiscal and financial problems, this is the lot of all large administrations. To its credit, it kept control of the situation and did not allow the development of a major crisis. Against the current *communis opinio*,

---

[167] Bradley 1978a, 185–6; Griffin 1984, 187.   [168] Tac. *Ann.* 14.27.3–4. Bradley 1978a, 184.
[169] Tac. *Hist.* 1.4.1. Below 375.
[170] Suet. *Galb.* 12.3; *Otho* 7.1; *Vitell.* 13. Levick 1999a, 96; Rathbone 2008, 25.
[171] Levick 1999a, 95, 103.   [172] Perrin 2016, 229–31, 233–5, 237–8, 245; cf. above 257, 344.

financial difficulties should not be seen as constituting the principal factor in Nero's fall, for which we must look elsewhere.[173]

13.3.2   Income

How did the regime overcome its financial challenges? Most sources perceive fiscal crisis because they misunderstand or misrepresent events. Thus Suetonius judges Nero the imperial patron on moral, not socio-political, grounds. Furthermore, as already noted, the great patron had great clients who were expected to return his favours. There must have been a regular 'churn' of money and services as gifts were made then – as presents, accommodation, entertainment, bequests, confiscations etc. – returned to or reclaimed by the *princeps*, only to be made again.[174] Millar talks of the equalising effect of 'the endlessly resented acquisition of property by the emperor on the one hand, and his distribution of benefits on the other'. All a *princeps* had to do to stay ahead as super-patron was to manage the marginal shortfall that resulted from his obligation to give rather more than he received.[175] And he could stay ahead, both as patron and *princeps*, because of income, only hinted at by the sources, which made his financial life less of a hand-to-mouth existence than earlier suggested.

This income came from gifts, inheritances, bequests, reversions and confiscations. Gifts, some with a market value and others that were simply curiosities, came from foreign peoples and private individuals.[176] Under Nero, some individual gifts, such as those by Agrippina (offered during the Acte affair) and of Seneca (offered on his semi-retirement), were huge. Though it is uncertain whether Nero actually took these (in Seneca's case initially unlikely, though he may eventually have done so to meet the expenses of rebuilding after the Fire), they suggest that others were made and accepted.[177] Inheritances and bequests came to Nero from rich relatives, such as Britannicus, Agrippina, Domitia, Octavia and Poppaea. Non-family bequests have already been touched upon.[178] As the practice spread, it produced a steady stream of capital and income. We know that Augustus received HS 1.4 billion in this way, and this will have increased appreciably under his successors.[179] Reversion involved *bona vacantia* and *bona caduca*. These were properties that fell to the state because their

---

[173] Cf. Fini 1994, 216; below 368.   [174] Above 316; cf. Rathbone 2008, 252.
[175] Millar 1977, 139, 143 172 (quotation).   [176] Millar 1977, 139.
[177] Tac. *Ann.* 13.13.3; 14.54.4; cf. 14.55.7; Cass. Dio 62.25.3. Griffin 1976, 93.   [178] Above 340.
[179] Suet. *Aug.* 101.3. Millar 1977, 154.

ownership had become invalid or because their legal owners had died intestate.[180] They will have been another steady source of wealth. However, probably the most significant were the *bona damnatorum*. We tend to associate these with sensational political cases, as after the failure of the Pisonian conspiracy. However, during the first century AD the penalty spread across the Empire and was used against convicted felons of all types, at all social levels, becoming 'one of the primary sources of the reserves of land and property which the emperors acquired'.[181] These comprised agricultural estates, mines, quarries and such enterprises as brick-works. The amount of money that they contributed to each *princeps'* income must have been enormous. Historians have rightly emphasised the crucial role of these properties in imperial finances with Griffin, for example, declaring them 'the dynamic element in the resources that maintained public services and benefits'.[182] They grew steadily over the centuries, encouraging the displacement of the *Aerarium* by the *Fiscus*.[183] The amount of extraordinary income from all sources was reflected early, in Augustus' public advertisement of the large sums he was able to disburse from it.[184] On this basis, Millar can talk of 'the immense scale of . . . imperial wealth'.[185]

However, acquired property cannot be the sole explanation for the avoidance of a fiscal crisis under Nero. Historians often give the impression that emperors gained such wealth at a strong steady pace, and retained most of what they won, generating a huge patrimony that was passed down from *princeps* to *princeps* and dynasty to dynasty.[186] This is unlikely. If imperial wealth had grown at the speed envisaged the state would eventually have owned practically everything in the Empire, which it did not. There will have been irregularities in the rate of acquisition; and throughout history 'crown property' (an anachronistic but handy term) has been notoriously liable to diminution through alienation. Alienation appears to have been a Julio-Claudian weakness.[187] The Paetus who foolishly accused Pallas and Burrus in 55 was notorious for buying up confiscated estates from the treasury, one presumes at knock-down

---

[180] Millar 1977, 158–60; above 336.
[181] Millar 1977, 165–70, 174 (quotation). Cf. Bowman 1996b, 365.
[182] Griffin 1984, 200. Cf. Millar 1977, 175–200, esp. 181, 186–7; Cizek 1982, 300; Thompson 1987, Levick 1999a, 104; Lo Cascio 2007, 630, 642, 645.
[183] Above 336.
[184] Millar 1977, 191–2; cf. Scheidel 2015, 246 (10–25 per cent of total income?), 253.
[185] Millar 1977, 197. [186] Millar 1977, 165, 176–7; Levick 1999a, 104–5. Cf. above 328.
[187] Thompson 1987, 560.

prices.[188] Under Nero, imperial wealth was threatened by both customary expectation of generosity and his natural open-handedness. His prompt and lavish gifts of property and land to his friends after the death of Britannicus have already been mentioned;[189] and no sooner had Rubellius Plautius been removed than his estates were given to Octavia.[190] If Bradley is correct in supposing that Menecrates and Spiculus were given property confiscated from the estate of Corbulo,[191] we have another case of estates being on the books of the *Fiscus* for only a very short time before being passed on to favourites. Imperial wealth, handled by either the *Fiscus* or the *Aerarium*, might also be eroded by systemic inefficiency and corruption. Tacitus illustrates how provincial state land could be lost to squatters, hints at routine financial malpractice at the expense of the public purse, and suggests that Seneca's brother, Mela, made much of his money in shady deals involving imperial property.[192] Thus, whatever its size, imperial wealth might still have failed to meet the peaks in spending of Nero's principate.

13.3.3   *Management*

I propose that the main reason why the Roman state was not bankrupted in this period and, indeed, why Nero was never criminally profligate, was that both were subject to a high degree of control. 'For most of his reign [Nero] managed to run a balanced budget while appearing to reduce the impact of taxes and to spend generously, so successfully that he gained the reputation of prodigality'.[193] However, it was not the *princeps* himself who was calling the shots. Rather, the freedman-based fiscal machine built up under Claudius and brought to perfection by Agrippina and Pallas continued to function;[194] and the Neronian regime, like the Claudian,[195] included people who were interested in the financial and fiscal situation and who exercised sufficient influence to keep it in order. The relatively frequent mention of taxation and finance in the sources could be fortuitous, but it is equally likely that such concerns were very much in the air at this time: 'It is Tacitus who provides evidence that Nero and his advisers had a serious interest in financial matters and saw careful management of them as part of their responsibilities'.[196]

---

[188] Tac. *Ann.* 13.23.2. Cf. below 351.   [189] Above 330.
[190] Tac. *Ann.* 14.60.5. Cf. above 191.   [191] Suet. *Ner.* 30.2. Bradley 1978a, 166; above 314.
[192] Tac. *Ann.* 14.18.2–4; 13.23.2; 16.17.3.   [193] Rathbone 2008, 277–8.
[194] Cf. Osgood 2011, 40; Scheidel 2015, 229.   [195] Above 342.   [196] Griffin 1984, 197.

A long-running problem was the operation of the old, but irreplaceable *Aerarium*.[197] The regime seems to have been concerned about the unpopularity of some of the taxes collected by this body, and about complaints about the efficiency and fairness of its operation, both of which threatened to reduce its income stream.[198] In late 54 it tackled the first problem by continuing Claudius' revocation of hated indirect taxes introduced by Gaius.[199] As for the second, from 54 to 57 it reduced fees paid to informers by the *Aerarium*, which both won the treasury public approval and saved it money.[200] In 55, the Paetus affair led to the cancellation of old debts.[201] In 56, a squabble between senatorial magistrates and tribunes led to a reduction in the powers to impose fines, the proceeds of which went to the *Aerarium*, enjoyed by both tribunes and aediles.[202] Also in 56, after Helvidius Priscus had exposed abuse of the *Aerarium*'s procedures, came major reform of the institution which transferred authority from quaestors to older and more 'experienced' senatorial prefects. Nero's transfer of HS 40 million to the *Aerarium* in the following year was probably aimed at inspiring confidence in the new officials. The change, in fact, worked well, enduring until the fourth century.[203] The year 57 also saw the alteration in the taxation of the sale of slaves.[204] This left the rate of taxation the same but helped the *Aerarium* by making it easier to collect by switching the obligation to pay from the many buyers to the fewer sellers. By getting the *Aerarium* off their backs, it will also have been popular with buyers though, no doubt, the sellers just added the tax to their prices.[205] Major progress had been made, but that problems still persisted with the *Aerarium* is indicated by later developments, in particular in 58 with Nero's famous proposal to abolish all indirect taxes following public agitation against tax-farmers, presumably in the circus and in the arena.[206]

Historians have given Nero's proposal much attention,[207] with interpretations ranging from a popularising wish to curry favour with the mob, through precocious economic inspiration (in encouraging internal imperial free trade), to the start of Nero's ideological divergence from his early policy of co-operation with the Senate and his first step along the road to

---

[197] Above 336.   [198] Günther 2013, 112.
[199] Suet. *Calig.* 40–41.1. Rathbone 2008, 254–5; Günther 2013, 106–7.
[200] Rathbone 2008, 258.   [201] Tac. *Ann.* 13.23.4. Rathbone 2008, 258; above 349.
[202] Tac. *Ann.* 13.28.3–4. Rathbone 2008, 256.
[203] Tac. *Ann.* 13.28.5–29: *experientia probati*. Rathbone 2008, 256–7; above 336.
[204] Above 338.   [205] Rathbone 2008, 258; Günther 2013, 113.
[206] Tac. *Ann.* 13.50–51. Rathbone 2008, 260–1; cf. below 353.   [207] Cf. Bradley 1978a, 74.

theocracy.[208] Given the regime's careful attention to financial affairs, a better explanation is that Nero, still doing his best to act the good *princeps*, attempted to contribute to current debate: there were people about who were seriously interested in tax and finance, and he sought to join them. His idea was rejected, but his interest is not to be disparaged, since it led to major fiscal improvements. Tacitus follows his report of Nero's proposal with a somewhat unclear description of a raft of commendable legislation which followed. This may be understood as, in respect of indirect taxation: the publication of regulations for tax-farming; the setting of a time limit for the pursuit of alleged cases of tax evasion by officials of the *Aerarium*; the acceleration of court cases against *publicani* (tax-farmers) in Rome and the provinces; the clarification of the exemptions enjoyed by serving soldiers; and the suppression of 'illegal surcharges' made by *publicani*, possibly by manipulating the rates of conversion from local into imperial weights, measures and currency. With regard to direct taxation, there was a relaxation of obligations on taxpayers to transport tax-grain to government depots, the inconvenient designation of which by officials was a long-standing means of extortion; and the declassification of merchant ships as taxable property.[209] In the context of his good relations with the Senate, it is important to note that Tacitus says that Nero was persuaded of the impracticality of his own idea by senators, either in debate or in an advisory capacity.[210] Similar advice is perhaps also detectable in the recalling of British debt which, though it had disastrous consequences, may be set in a context of the need to recall long-standing state loans in order to meet growing costs elsewhere.[211]

We can name some senatorial experts. Insight into fiscal activity and expertise, and the sheer complexity of imperial administration, under Nero is provided by the 'Custom law of Asia' (*lex portorii Asiae*, also known as the *Monumentum Ephesenum*), promulgated in early July, 62.[212] This surely resulted from the legislation of 58 requiring publication of regulations for tax-farming.[213] It gives the names of three ex-consuls who comprised the extraordinary commission set up by a decree of the Senate to deal with the province of Asia. These *curatores vectigalium publicorum* were (listed in order of seniority[214]): A. Pompeius Paulinus, L. Calpurnius Piso, and A. Ducenius Geminus. Roman taxation of Asia went back to

[208] Henderson 1905, 82; Crook 1955, 120; Syme 1958, 416–7; Grant 1970, 60; Cizek 1982, 136–7 (cf. above 196); Holland 2000, 88; Rathbone 2008, 276; Günther 2013, 121.
[209] Tac. *Ann.* 13.51.2: *exactiones illicitae*. Rathbone 2008, 261–7.   [210] Above 23.
[211] Above 341.   [212] *SEG* 39, 1180. Cottier *et al.* 2008.   [213] Above 352.
[214] Cottier *et al.* 2008, 93–4.

Republican times. The commissioners' work must have involved careful consideration of long practice and consequent contentious issues. It is therefore likely that it began significantly before July 62. Though many of its recommendations are unclear they, with the other Neronian fiscal reforms, appear to have been successful in that they allowed greater central control of tax-farming throughout the Empire.[215] Though he does not mention the Asian commission, Tacitus names the same three consulars as being charged by Nero with oversight of the delivery of tax revenues to the *Aerarium* somewhat later in 62.[216] I therefore propose that the proven expertise of the commissioners (whether long established or newly acquired[217]) caused them to be entrusted with a new, wider task relating to the entirety of income due to the *Aerarium*.[218] The clear distinction between the two appointments is significant.[219] Rathbone sees most Neronian fiscal legislation as designed to demonstrate, in the best Augustan fashion, 'fiscal probity, primarily to the benefit of the elite in tune with Nero's accession promise of good and open government with proper involvement of the senate'. Thus Nero's proposal of 58 was 'a staged masterpiece of political propaganda'.[220] The Senate 'spluttered', and the *princeps* 'respectfully deferred' to senators' advice. 'At the end of the show, the Senate had enjoyed the *libertas* of discussing the Empire's finances, while Nero had enhanced his popular image as the emperor who would have abolished *vectigalia* but for the timidity of the senate, and he issued an edict, his own *beneficium*, to restrict abuses, which was probably all he and his advisers had intended to do anyway'.[221] Likewise, in 62, the *lex portorii Asiae* involved no move to increase taxation but was 'an important practical benefit to taxpayers';[222] 'Nero's reforms of *vectigalia* were attempts not to increase fiscal revenues to meet a budgetary deficit but to reduce abuses inherent in their collection by private enterprise; if anything, they suggest budgetary stability'.[223] Such a positive assessment of Neronian policy fits the suggestion made above of a well-ordered fiscal administration and, indeed, Suetonius' judgement of Neronian taxation: 'the more oppressive indirect taxes he either abolished or moderated'.[224] The Neronian reforms were well-intentioned, reasoned, practical and effective.

---

[215] Günther 2013, 116–21.   [216] Tac. *Ann.* 15.18.4: *vectigalibus publicis praeposuit.*
[217] Cf. Cottier *et al.* 2008, 94; Rathbone 2008, 269–70.   [218] Cf. Rathbone 2008, 269.
[219] *Contra* Rathbone 2008, 268–70, 272–3.   [220] Rathbone 2008, 260.
[221] Rathbone 2008, 251 (quotations), 253, 258–9, 263–4, 275.   [222] Rathbone 2008, 274–5.
[223] Rathbone 2008, 253.
[224] Suet. *Ner.* 10.1: *graviora vectigalia aut abolevit aut minuit.* Günther 2013, 110, 122–3; above 351.

They were not driven by lunacy, profligacy or populism.[225] Yet more was going on than political window-dressing or the tweaking of a system that was otherwise working well. It was in 62 that Nero drew attention to his HS 60 million annual subvention to the *Aerarium*, probably again to maintain confidence in the body.[226] This suggests that there were still problems with it, probably as a result of current high costs of warfare. Real concern about its operation led to the appointment of the three commissioners to recommend measures to keep the ship of state well off the reefs of fiscal ruin.

The year 62 was also that of the death of Burrus, the start of Seneca's withdrawal from public life, and the consequent dominance of Poppaea and Tigellinus, under whose influence Nero is supposed to have grown increasingly self-indulgent.[227] Tacitus' references to financial issues as a regular element in political discourse and action now, indeed, come to an end. On the other hand, Levick concludes from what happened immediately after Nero's fall that someone at court must have been a very careful book-keeper, 'for Nero's gifts could be totted up and pursued'.[228] The maintenance of *rationes imperii* ('state accounts') was in the best Julio-Claudian tradition,[229] and I propose that, whatever Nero's behaviour, it was this continuing financial expertise that prevented the mass alienation of imperial property and kept the regime from bankruptcy. Such expertise may be discerned in the care taken to control the cost of building both the *Domus Transitoria* and, initially, the *Domus Aurea*;[230] and it is particularly visible in the reform of the imperial coinage.

13.3.4   Coin Reform

The reform involved significant modification of the metal content of the gold and silver coins and of the appearance of the *aes* (base-metal) issues. Across the range there was the introduction of a much more realistic and eye-catching style in Nero's obverse portraits and bold new reverse types.[231] The larger flans of the *aes* coins, however, permitted some unusually fine designs, making much of new or newly restored buildings in and around Rome and including a remarkably innovative 'bird's eye view' of the harbour-basin at Ostia.[232] There was also a short-lived attempt

---

[225] Cf. Günther 2013, 121–2.
[226] Tac. *Ann.* 15.18.4. Table 3; Rathbone 2008, 252–3, 269; above 334, 351.
[227] Above 187; Griffin 1984, 104.   [228] Levick 1999a, 103; cf. above 330.
[229] Cf. Winterling 2007, 65–6, on Gaius.   [230] Above 257.
[231] *RIC* I² pp. 133, 137, 139; Griffin 1984, 120–1; Carson 1990, 15–16.
[232] *RIC* I² Nero nos. 178–83, pl. 18.182; Carson 1990, 16; Perassi 2002; above 266.

Table 4 *Roman coin tariffs*

Aes	Silver	Gold
as		
sestertius (HS)		
[= 4 *asses*]		
	denarius [= 4 *sestertii*	
	16 *asses*]	
		aureus [= 25 *denarii*
		100 *sestertii* 400 *asses*]

to switch the composition of the *aes* coins from both brass (*orichalcum*, a copper/zinc alloy) and copper to wholly brass. All this will have drawn attention to the new coinage: the administration was not set on hiding change from the public, despite its lowering of the precious-metal content. Furthermore, thanks to the work of Butcher and Ponting we now have a much more positive explanation for this reduction.[233]

Down to Nero's coin reform there was no decline in the fineness of the *aureus* or the *denarius*. On the contrary, *principes* strove to maintain the purity of the gold or silver of each denomination.[234] However, during this period the *denarius* declined slightly but steadily in weight, from *c.* 3.9 g under Caesar to *c.* 3.79 g under Claudius (i.e. from *c.* 1/84 to 1/90 lb Roman). The *aureus* underwent a similar slight decrease, from *c.* 8.03 g to *c.* 7.7 g (i.e. from 1/40 to 1/42.5 lb Roman).[235] The reason for the slippage was probably the nature of the imperial coinage system, introduced by Julius Caesar in 46 BC.[236] This consisted of coins struck in three metals: gold, silver and copper/copper alloy: *aes*. The main denominations were tariffed against each other as shown in Table 4.

All *aes* coins were fiduciary, i.e. HS 1 did not contain metal actually worth $^1/_4$ *denarius* or $^1/_{100}$ *aureus*. However, gold and silver coins were now linked to the market value of each other's metal.[237] Thus each *aureus* should on average contain a weight of gold nominally worth the weight of silver in twenty-five *denarii*, and vice versa.[238] The assumed market ratio of the value of gold to silver was 1:12. In other words (rounding the Caesarian weights), one *aureus* at *c.* 8 g weight per coin equated to

[233] Butcher and Ponting 2014. [234] Silver: Butcher and Ponting 2014, 167–8, 187, 189, 199.
[235] Butcher and Ponting 2014, 168–9, 172–3. 158, 434.
[236] Butcher and Ponting 2014, 234, 434. [237] Butcher and Ponting 2014, 237.
[238] For the qualification see below 356.

twenty-five *denarii* at *c.* 4 g weight per coin: 8/100.[239] The problem was that this bimetallic system ignored the huge mass of Republican *denarii* left in circulation. These made up the bulk of imperial silver coinage as late as Vespasian, and many were so worn as to be significantly under-weight relative to the Caesarian standard.[240] This meant that twenty-five *denarii* did not usually comprise a weight of silver worth the weight of gold in one *aureus*, either newly minted or already in circulation (since *aurei* were usually subject to much less wear than *denarii* they retained more of their original weight[241]). People's ability to purchase full-weight *aureii* with worn *denarii* increased the value of silver, producing a real-world market ratio of gold to silver of *c.* 1:10.[242] Successive *principes* therefore decreased the weight of new *denarii* to match the wear of coins already in circulation; and in pursuit of the ratio of 1:12 they also reduced the weight of new *aurei*. Gold followed silver down.[243]

By the middle of the first century, the cumulative weight loss of *aurei* and *denarii* was still moderate, and the expedient seemed to work. But weights could not be driven down for ever, and the consequent increased market value of silver may have made production of the *denarius* unprofitable. This was because it increased the cost of minting and reduced the profit that pre-industrial minting authorities always strove to make on the manufacture of coins by ensuring that each one contained slightly less value of metal than its face-value.[244] This helps explain the gradual reduction in the minting of *denarii* which reached a peak under Claudius when, between 52 and his death, there was no minting of these coins. There was also a cessation in Claudian minting of *aurei*. These, relatively profitable to produce, had previously been minted in abundance. Perhaps helped by the financial acumen of Agrippina, the authorities may have realised that excessive minting of gold drove up the price of silver.[245] The reduction and suspension of the minting of *denarii* will have been of concern since for 'the convenience of the public ... the state was very much interested in providing a medium of exchange suitable for a wide variety of transactions, from small to large'.[246] A further worry in this respect will have been a shortage of *aes* coins. Physically difficult to mint, producing only a small profit per piece and absorbing large quantities of

---

[239] Butcher and Ponting 2014, 434.   [240] Butcher and Ponting 2014, 37–8, 157, 173, 237, 435–6.
[241] Butcher and Ponting 2014, 437.
[242] Butcher and Ponting 2014, 235: 'The gold to silver ratio was about 1:9$^{1}/_{2}$'.
[243] Butcher and Ponting 2014, 168–73, 198–9, 234–5, 434–6, 437–9, 687–8.
[244] Butcher and Ponting 2014, 191, 237, 439–40.
[245] Butcher and Ponting 2014, 190, 439; above 35.   [246] Butcher and Ponting 2014, 25.

working-metal, these were, throughout history, subject to neglect by pre-industrial governments. A decline in production had led, under Claudius, to a grave shortage in the western Empire, which people met by using imitations.[247] It is not surprising, therefore, that, though Nero produced no *aes* coins until 62–63, at the start of his principate he recommenced production of both *aurei* and *denarii*, the latter virtually pure silver,[248] though still not produced in any great quantity. The problems involved in their minting clearly still had to be overcome. Then came change.

First, the minting of gold and silver coins was moved from Lyon (Figure 1), where it had been from the late first century BC, to Rome, which had retained minting in *aes*. Rome and Lyon subsequently began minting reformed *aes* in quantities which extinguished the need for imitations.[249] Next came abandonment of the bimetallic system, making the *denarius* 'a kind of token coinage', i.e. its intrinsic value in silver was below the rate at which it could be exchanged for *aurei*, which therefore supported its nominal value.[250] This was achieved by a severe debasement of the *denarius*, from virtual bullion down to *c.* 80 per cent fine. The other 20 per cent, mainly copper content was enough to require treatment to give the new coin the appearance of full silver.[251] There was also a moderate reduction in the weight of both *denarius* and *aureus*, of *c.* 4 per cent (reducing an average coin to *c.* 3.45 g, $^1/_{45}$ lb Roman) and *c.* 5.75 per cent (to *c.* 7.35 g/ $^1/_{96}$ lb Roman), respectively.[252] Taking into account the weight of the new *aurei*, if the new *denarii* had been pure silver the ratio of gold to silver would have been about 1:12 and so, with the silvered surface, perhaps another comforting cosmetic maintenance of tradition.[253] However, the combination of debasement and weight loss resulted in a decrease in the silver content of each *denarius* of about 25 per cent, a reduction 'greater than any other single change to the *denarius* until the Severan debasement in AD 194'.[254] By detaching *denarii* from the price of gold, the reform brought down the price of silver, thus restoring profit to the minting of *denarii*.[255] Furthermore, by enabling the silver content of *denarii* to be reduced further without triggering public alarm, it

[247] *RIC* 1² pp. 114–15.   [248] Butcher and Ponting 2014, 193–5, 216–17.
[249] Butcher and Ponting 2014, 24, 175–6, 68–9; *RIC* 1² pp. 115, 136. 142; *contra RIC* 1² pp. 103, 106, 116: the move took place in 37.
[250] Butcher and Ponting 2014, 190, 235 (quotation), 444–5.
[251] Butcher and Ponting 2014, 218.   [252] Butcher and Ponting 2014, 235, 443, 690.
[253] Butcher and Ponting 2014, 444.
[254] Butcher and Ponting 2014, 201, 203–6; 215 (quotation), 217, 218.
[255] Butcher and Ponting 2014, 235.

permitted the Neronian coinage system to last more or less unaltered for a century to come, and its effects still to be felt over 200 years later.[256] An additional, and perhaps equally intentional, benefit of the change was that it brought the imperial *denarius* more into line with the provincial Greek *drachma*, which can only have benefited the economy of the eastern Empire.[257]

In financial terms, the motivation for and the effects of the reform were indeed benign. As with Neronian literature and art, one must never read a *princeps'* character into or out of the coins.[258] Butcher and Ponting avoid hypotheses based on *principes'* 'perceived characters', including the view that the Neronian reform resulted from a fiscal crisis made inevitable by accumulating excessive expenditure and triggered by the Fire: that the regime was thereby 'short of money', in 'straitened economic circumstance', and needing to 'achieve more with the same resources'.[259] If the administration had just wanted to produce masses of inferior *denarii* to pay its debts, it need not have bothered with fine differences in silver content and weight, but simply substantially reduced the weight of each coin.[260] One strong indication that there was no previous inflated spending is that the reform did not result in the immediate mass production of new *denarii* to cover government debt.[261] Reformed *denarii* were minted in moderate numbers, with little impact on the overall composition of the pool of circulating silver.[262] New 'bad' *denarii* did not chase out earlier 'good' coins.[263] Some users showed a preference for pre-reform *denarii*, for example for trade with Parthia and southern India where post-reform *aurei* and *denarii* are rare. However, this is only to be expected in areas outside the Empire where such precious-metal coins circulated as bullion. Tacitus notes that contemporary neighbouring *Germani* preferred Republican *denarii*. Harl equates the German with the Indian attitude, but it was apparently much older and probably reflected social conservatism not calculation of the precious-metal content of the pieces. Within the Empire most people seem to have happily accepted both old and new *denarii*, probably mainly out of convenience. Differences between alloys were hard to detect without resorting to time-consuming assay. This explains users'

---

[256] Butcher and Ponting 2014, 45, 238, 444.
[257] Butcher and Ponting 2014, 229, 235, 444–5, 678–80, 699.   [258] Above 90.
[259] Butcher and Ponting 2014, 19, 230, 233. Wiedemann 1996a, 252; Carson 1990, 14; Griffin 1984, 198.
[260] Butcher and Ponting 2014, 233.   [261] Butcher and Ponting 2014, 45, 208, 238, 261–2.
[262] Butcher and Ponting 2014, 210, 447.
[263] Butcher and Ponting 2014, 49, 449; cf. Levi 1949, 194.

failure to exploit a strange temporary raising of the fineness of *denarii* in 68.[264] Within the Empire *aurei*, too, were a partially fiduciary currency because, whatever their condition (and wear would eventually have taken its toll even on these), their value, like those of the rest, was set by the state. As Epictetus says, 'For the banker is not allowed to reject Caesar's coins, nor the seller of herbs, but if you show the coin, whether he chooses or not, he must give what is sold for the coin . . .'[265] Elsewhere he appears to indicate unease with the Neronian *aes* coinage: 'What is the stamp on this *sestertius*? The stamp of Trajan. Present it. It is the stamp of Nero. Throw it away: it cannot be accepted, it is counterfeit'.[266] However, this may be interpreted as indicating rather that counterfeiters, knowing that people actually preferred Neronian pieces, used them frequently as models.

The reformed coinage looked good, was accepted, and functioned well. It resulted in no significant inflation and so was not the harbinger of the currency collapse of the third-century 'Crisis'.[267] It was not a reaction to fiscal meltdown, but a considered, sophisticated and ultimately successful adjustment of the contemporary coinage system to deal with the differential wear of gold and silver coins.[268]

Reform was complex and could not be enacted overnight.[269] There are, indeed, signs of earlier attempts to devalue the *denarius* late under Claudius and into the principate of Nero, in which one again suspects the influence of Agrippina.[270] The main Neronian reform was carried out in two main stages and a third, very late, subsidiary stage which resulted in a rise in the fineness of the *denarius* to *c.* 90 per cent and removed the need to treat the surface of the coin.[271] This is strange since the failure of the 'improved' coins to be selected by hoarders indicates that the improvement was not appreciated by contemporaries.[272] Furthermore, if Nero now wanted to put more silver into his *denarii*, why did he not simply raise their weight? I return to the issue further below.[273] The precise dating of the two main stages is unclear. The commonly accepted starting-date of 64 derives from the conception of a spendthrift Nero running into massive debt as a result of the Fire, the rebuilding of Rome and the expense of the

---

[264] Tac. *Germ.* 5.5. Jones 1956, 30; Harl 1996, 91 (I owe the latter reference to Professor Silver); Butcher and Ponting 2014, 50–2, 226–9, 448–50; below 359.
[265] Arr. *Epict. diss.* 3.3.3.   [266] Arr. *Epict. diss.* 4.5.   [267] Butcher and Ponting 2014, 40–1, 201.
[268] Butcher and Ponting 2014, 45, 444. Cf. Carson 1990, 14; Rathbone 1996, 317, 319.
[269] Butcher and Ponting 2014, 211, 233.
[270] Butcher and Ponting 2014, 169, 190, 195–9, 200, 234–5; cf. above 34.
[271] Butcher and Ponting 2014, 216–19.   [272] Butcher and Ponting 2014, 228.
[273] Below 364.

Golden House.[274] The coin evidence alone produces a range of dates from 62 to 66, with no particular reason to prioritise 64.[275] With regard to Nero's supposed bankruptcy, he continued to mint *aurei* (from 64 to 66 in remarkably high numbers) and, whatever its cause, the introduction of the finer *denarius* in 68 indicates no 'notable shortage' of silver bullion.[276] As Butcher and Ponting observe: 'The idea of Nero with a reserve of silver does not sit well with his image as a spendthrift, though a reserve might well help explain how Nero was able to introduce *denarii* at a higher fineness in AD 68, and how Otho in 69 could mint a huge coinage on the same standard'.[277] As for the literary evidence, references to the Neronian coin reform are scarce and difficult, and none links it to increased expenditure, even from 64.[278] Butcher and Ponting do not rule out reform beginning in 63,[279] which is probably the most likely date for the reform of the gold and silver coinage, as well as that of the low-denomination *aes* pieces.[280]

As we have seen, the Neronian administration at first produced no *aes* coins. Its resumption of base-metal minting over the full range of coins (from *sestertius* to *quadrans*)[281] is therefore remarkable. Minting began in 62/63 with two trial issues, recognisable by their omission of the legend *[EX] SC* which from the time of Augustus had been a standard feature of imperial base-metal coinage.[282] The first issue was fairly conventional. The second marked 'a radical change', and was in fact, with its switch to *orichalcum* and improved obverse portraiture, the first step in full coin reform.[283] The first trial series suggests that the impulse to resume the minting of base-metal denominations was purely practical: to remedy the shortage of small change. It was successful, suppressing the production of western imitations.[284] The innovative nature of the second trial series suggests that the first had made the Neronian administration realise that it could do more with the coinage. If base-metal minting resumed in 62–63, planning must have begun earlier. Given the difficulties involved in base-metal minting, reflected in technical uncertainties in both trial issues,[285] this is likely to have been significantly earlier, say in 61–62 when

---

[274] Butcher and Ponting 2014, 690; cf. above 326, 358.
[275] Butcher and Ponting 2014, 211, 230–4, 442, 690.
[276] Butcher and Ponting 2014, 201–3, 229 (quoting *contra* Sutherland), 230.
[277] Butcher and Ponting 2014, 236–7.
[278] E.g. Plin. *HN* 33.47. Butcher and Ponting 2014, 203–5.
[279] Butcher and Ponting 2014, 232–3.   [280] Butcher and Ponting 2014, 232–3, 442–3.
[281] *RIC* 1² pp. 114, 136.   [282] Above 28; Griffin 1984, 125.
[283] *RIC* 1² pp. 133, 138–9 (quotation); Carson 1990, 15.   [284] *RIC* 1² pp. 15, 140, 142–3, 146.
[285] *RIC* 1² p. 138.

Seneca and Burrus were being eclipsed by Poppaea and Tigellinus.[286] The improved appearance of the second *aes* trial series hints that the newcomers grasped that they could use the imperial coinage to 'rebrand' the Neronian principate to their advantage. Once close consideration had begun to be given to the *aes* coinage other, more important, aspects such as abolishing the troublesome bimetallic system and bringing the *denarius* in line with the *drachma* might quickly have come to mind. The second trial series of base-metal minting therefore probably coincided with the first stage of the reform of gold and silver coinage in 63.

Although financial gain was not the prime purpose of the Neronian reform, in restoring profit to the minting of silver and making gold go further it gave the regime extra cash.[287] This would have been welcome in the early 60s when spending was high as a result of fighting in Armenia, around the Black Sea and Britain (Table 3). Consequent fiscal strain is indicated by a rise in the number of *officinae* ('workshops') in operation in the mint of Rome from perhaps one to as many as three by 60/61.[288] If we assume some delay between the onset of strain, its perception by the fiscal authorities and government measures taken to relieve it, we again find ourselves in 62 when finance was very much in the air.[289] This strengthens the case for 62 as the year when the Neronian regime both decided upon a 'new-look' *aes* coinage and realised that it could fruitfully extend reform to gold and silver issues, introduced in 63.[290] Though the change was not provoked by the Fire,[291] it will also have proved useful in defraying its costs. The Fire certainly caused more fiscal strain. The number of precious-metal *officinae* in the Rome mint, reduced from three to two in 63/64, rose to six in 64–65; and the production of all lower denomination coins in *orichalcum* ended by early 65, with brass being again confined to the higher value *sestertii* and *dupondii*.[292] But six was the peak of precious-metal *officinae*. There were four by 65/66 and three from 66 to 68.[293] Thus, though the Fire had added to the regime's problems, its finances were apparently soon stabilised. It was not long before the gift made by Lyon to Rome following the Fire was returned after the donor city suffered an identical calamity;[294] and there is no reason to suppose that Florus put financial pressure on the Jews to help meet the expense of the conflagration.[295] Despite lavish spending on Tiridates and the outbreak of the

---

[286] Above 188, 137.   [287] Butcher and Ponting 2014, 445–6.   [288] *RIC* 1² pp. 133–4, 145.
[289] Above 354.   [290] Above 361.   [291] *Contra RIC* 1² pp. 135–6, 140; Griffin 1984, 123.
[292] *RIC* 1² p. 140; Carson 1990, 16.   [293] *RIC* 1² pp. 145–7.   [294] Above 343.
[295] *Contra* Holland 2000, 216; above 339.

Jewish War, both of which added considerably to imperial expenses from 66 (Table 3), there was no significant inflation, no further debasement and no inevitable fiscal crisis.[296]

A sophisticated coinage stimulates economic activity, but badly managed it can undermine monetary, economic, social and even political stability.[297] Good management and, even more so, effective reform requires expert knowledge.[298] In the Neronian reform we should appreciate both the high level of technical skill required to fine-tune the precious-metal content of *denarii*,[299] and the general consideration given to the needs of coin users. It is improbable that inspiration and guidance came from Nero.[300] He must certainly have formally approval the new system, types and legends, including the continued use of *SC*, though now on the base-metal coins.[301] In addition, given his artistic bent he may well have been personally involved in deciding the appearance of the new coins, i.e. in the 'golden' *orichalcum* of the lower denominations, and the new obverse portraits and reverse types.[302] However, with his many other interests from around 63,[303] he is most unlikely to have been responsible for details such as the introduction of marks of value on the *orichalcum* pieces (which, because of their more valuable zinc content, were smaller in size,) or the fine-tuning of the bullion content of *aurei* and *denarii*.[304] In particular, it can hardly have been Nero who initially perceived the need for the resumption of minting of low value coins. Others 'with the appropriate knowledge' must have decided this.[305]

We return to the importance of general financial expertise: the positive contribution of those with 'shrewder minds' and 'a good financial brain' to all fiscal policies of the Neronian principate.[306] As to their identity, there were the members of the three-man board in charge of the minting of coin, the *tresviri monetales*, who had the delicate task of presenting a *princeps* with coin-types and legends that would please him, be in line with tradition and be acceptable to the general public: a ticklish 'tripartite relationship'.[307] These were, however, only junior magistrates. Of greater importance will have been the 'older and more experienced' senatorial prefects given charge of the *Aerarium* in 56;[308] the *senatores/seniores* who advised Nero over his proposals for changes in indirect taxation in 58;[309]

---

[296] Cf. Harl 1996, 91, 274.   [297] Butcher and Ponting 2014, 26–9, 39, 42.
[298] Butcher and Ponting 2014, 19.   [299] Butcher and Ponting 2014, 443.
[300] *Contra* Butcher and Ponting 2014, 237.   [301] Above 28.   [302] Griffin 1984, 120–2, 124.
[303] Cf. above 288.   [304] Cf. *RIC* 1² pp. 139–40; Griffin 1984, 123.
[305] Butcher and Ponting 2014, 19.   [306] Rudich 1993, 128; above 350.   [307] Levick 1999b, 57.
[308] Above 351.   [309] Tac. *Ann.* 13.50.2.; above 23, 78.

and, of course, the members of the Asian and *Aerarium* commissions of 62. These were experts in a society that valued expertise,[310] and they cannot have been alone. The foundations of the fiscal competence of the Neronian regime had been laid by Pallas and Agrippina.[311] By the mid-60s, both had disappeared but there were others who could fill their shoes. Claudius of Smyrna, for example, bridged the generations by serving as an imperial freedman from Tiberius to Domitian. Massively experienced, some identify him, not Phaon, as succeeding Pallas as *a rationibus.*[312] In addition, down to 62 and perhaps some time later, Seneca must have been an influential financial adviser, his skill in this regard being the positive side of his avarice. There were also members of Seneca's family and circle, such as his younger and elder brothers, Mela and Gallio respectively, the latter termed *amicus* by Claudius in an inscription and possibly the 'our Gallio' of Columella's handbook on farming.[313] Other candidates are more shadowy. Suetonius' reference to Paneros the money-lender gives the impression that he was just a crony of Nero, maybe the man who bankrolled his gambling debts.[314] However, his reward, not alienated property but a sort of state funeral, points to a much grander figure, perhaps a trusted financial adviser of the regime and even one of its bankers. (We should note that early in the principate of Vespasian, and so possibly looking to Neronian precedents, the Senate considered borrowing HS 60 million from individuals.[315]) Another influential Neronian financier may have been one Hipparchus.[316] Though the Roman state never came close to creating a National Debt,[317] appreciation that it was in the market for substantial loans may have been an additional factor in causing the removal of private funds from Britain around 60.[318] Experts were available and their influence was for the most part constructive.

Illuminating harmful interference by non-experts may, on the other hand, be detected in the introduction of finer *denarii* in 68. These are associated with unusually militaristic 'eagle and standard' issues. The current consensus is that 'the intended recipients may have been the rebellious Rhine armies'. These armies were not, however, rebellious until very late in Nero's principate; and the military issues do not feature in

---

[310] Warmington 1969, 66; Hine 2006, 67; above 352. Cf. above 122, 282.
[311] Osgood 2011, 202; above 342, 356.   [312] Above 64.
[313] Mela: above 189, 350; Gallio: Columella *Rust.* 9.16.2; Griffin 1984, 71; Reitz 2006, 123, 279–80.
[314] Cf. Cizek 1982, 290: perhaps an old *libertus* made good.
[315] Tac. *Hist.* 4.47; Griffin 1984, 206.   [316] Suet. *Vesp.* 13.3; Cizek 1982, 383.
[317] Cf. Bang 2008, 48 (I owe this reference to Professor Silver); Scheidel 2015, 254 and n. 87.
[318] Cf. above 344.

contemporary Rhenish hoards.[319] An alternative explanation is that they were produced as part of preparations for a war against Vindex, to be led by Nero at the head of an army assembling in northern Italy.[320] In either case, their purpose was political not financial, and if their higher silver content was intended to impress it was a failure. The coins' absence from hoards indicates that users were not sufficiently informed of the improvement, did not believe what they were told, or were not in a position to test it.[321] They were probably the brainchild of politicians not experts, and just wasted a huge amount of silver.

13.4 The Legacy of Helius

The optimism of late spring 65 turned out to be ill-founded, and the more so because of the outbreak of war in Judaea one year later. However, at least some of the Jewish hostilities were profitable. War was waged in a populous and developed country. Under the Flavians, the loot from Jerusalem paid for most of the Colosseum.[322] Under Nero there was already some useful booty, including the 6,000 prisoners of war enslaved and sent to work on the Corinth canal.[323] By 67 the financial position of the Roman state was hardly dire; indeed the outlook may, as in early 64 and early 65, have again looked promising. Yet something must have happened to enable the source tradition to confect a wickedly profligate and rapacious Nero. I propose that this can be found in events in Rome from 66 to 67, and in emergency measures taken to face rebellion in 68.

The second wave of Pisonian condemnations continued after Nero's departure for Greece.[324] Helius, left in charge in Rome, was held responsible for some infamous killings and confiscations. In this he was associated with the high-ranking informers already mentioned.[325] These made their accusations in the Senate or, thanks to Nero's delegation of powers, in the court of the *princeps* over which Helius now presided.[326] A feature of the Roman legal system was that successful prosecutors won a share of the property of the condemned.[327] The sources imply that Helius and the informers exploited this to line their own pockets, and that they shared their prey with Helius' senior freedmen colleagues: Polyclitus and

---

[319] Butcher and Ponting 2014, 219–20.   [320] Below 392.
[321] Butcher and Ponting 2014, 228; cf. 450.   [322] Levick 1999a, 128.   [323] Joseph. *BJ* 3.540.
[324] Above 215; cf. Griffin 1984, 205.   [325] Above 230.
[326] Cf. Talbert 1984, 45, 481; above 70.
[327] Tac. *Ann.* 16.33.4; *Hist.* 4.42. The usual rate was 25 per cent of defendants' property: Bradley 1978a, 266; above 319, below 365.

Patrobius appear in the sources as spectacularly grasping.[328] The impression given is that few, if any, of their victims were guilty but were destroyed for their wealth. After Nero's fall, both freedmen and aristocratic informers were vilified by contemporaries and historians.[329] Nero was held responsible for what they did, which permitted history to brand him as criminally avaricious. We must, however, appreciate the position of those concerned.

In attempting to do a difficult job properly (we find no direct charge of rapacity against him) Helius found himself increasingly out of his depth. Primarily, he faced insolent non-co-operation by certain aristocratic families.[330] The more the upper classes showed him disrespect, the more he reacted against them, provoking more non-co-operation and more denunciation. He strove to get Nero back to Rome not to face developing conspiracy there or in Gaul but to restore order in the capital.[331] Likewise, in judging the 'informers' we must avoid the prejudice of the sources and preconceptions derived from contemporary liberal values.[332] These, reviled by the source tradition as the bane of the aristocracy, were no newly created instrument of Julio-Claudian tyranny but a direct product of Republican custom and practice. Furthermore, the leading *delatores* were not low-born outsiders but relatively new or would-be senators, striving to establish their careers using forensic oratory and the ties and values of patronage (*fides, beneficium* etc, now most strongly owed to the *princeps*), in the best 'senatorial tradition'.[333] Financial reward could, indeed, be great. After the condemnation of Thrasea Paetus, Cossutianus Capito and Eprius Marcellus each received HS 5 million.[334] However, such rewards were also rooted in the Republic, and granted by all *principes*, 'good' and 'bad'; and they were sporadic, risky and had to be shared among each prosecution team. We should not generalise from a few infamous windfalls. Chief *delatores*, including Helius' lieutenants, probably acted for political and social, not financial, gain: to survive and progress.[335] Beyond this, in the absence of state prosecution and intelligence services they were an indispensable part of the judicial and political system, playing a key role in, for example, reform of provincial administration and, more fundamentally, in safeguarding civil peace.[336] For *principes* always had to face the possibility of real enemies, capable of precipitating damaging civil war.[337]

---

[328] Tac. *Hist.* 1.37, 2.95; Cass. Dio 63.12.3.   [329] Rutledge 2001, 29, 122–6.   [330] Above 221.
[331] *Contra* e.g. Shotter 1975, 61.   [332] Rutledge 2001, 4, 6, 13, 83–4, 136, 176, 180.
[333] Rutledge 2001, 23–4, 26–7, 46, 48–9, 52–3, 85–6, no. 67; above 18.
[334] Tac. *Ann.* 16.33.4. Rutledge 2001, 41.   [335] Rutledge 2001, 36–7, 42, 40, 44.
[336] Rutledge 2001, 15–16, 52–3, 55, 83.   [337] Cf. Drinkwater and Lee 2015, 211.

Under Nero, these were always in a minority,[338] but the Pisonian conspiracy had revealed how dangerous they might be and in this respect a number of the 'victims' of Helius may indeed have had a case to answer. *Delatores* of all ranks safeguarded stability by exposing them.[339] *Delatores* did not, however, act as a proactive secret service (an anachronistic concept).[340] Most of their cases resulted from accusations of aristocrats by aristocrats, for genuine reasons or because they, too, sought to curry favour with the incumbent *princeps*, who was then drawn in to resolve matters.[341]

Mention has been made of prosecution teams, and denunciation cannot have begun and ended with the senatorial or equestrian advocates who took cases to court.[342] Here it is helpful to stress a distinction, available in English but not in Latin, between 'informer' and 'prosecutor'.[343] The prosecutors needed evidence, and this they obtained from informers of all social classes who, presumably, were given a share in any spoils.[344] Informers fell into various categories.[345] They could be people who, as a one-off, for their own reasons, denounced suspect aristocrats to the authorities, as in the case of the freedman Milichus and his wife, who exposed the Pisonian conspiracy.[346] There were probably also career informers, sniffing out likely victims, assembling evidence against them and passing it on to prosecutors. Tacitus seems to envisage these threatening aristocrats who broke the law against celibacy.[347] Some career informers may have been hired by prosecutors, the precursors of the private detective.[348] Rathbone, indeed, proposes that 'specialist *delatores* must have often worked closely with the *Aerarium*'.[349] Finally, particularly significant for the understanding of Rome under Helius, high officials acted as informers, briefing advocates about individuals they wished to see removed and commissioning them as prosecutors.[350] An interesting question here is how much inducement or pressure was necessary to persuade a barrister to undertake such a prosecution. Tacitus twice allows a glimpse of how Neronian state-briefed barristers later defended their actions. Aquilius

---

[338] Above 28.   [339] Rutledge 2001, 6, 9, 113, 116–17, 171–2, 178.

[340] Rutledge 2001, 19, 22, 176; above 90, 210.   [341] Above 76, 91, 197.

[342] For an equestrian, albeit aspiring senator, see Rutledge 2001, 48–9, and no. 67 (Ostorius Sabinus).

[343] See e.g. Tac. *Ann.* 4.30.4–5; 12.59.1, 4; 13.21.8–9 for the interchangeable application of *delator* and *accusator*. Modern writers, e.g. Syme 1958, 1.100, 326–7, have inconveniently adopted the same approach, but see now Rutledge 2001, 9.

[344] Cf. Rutledge 2001, 36.   [345] Cf. Rutledge 2001, 9–12, 17.

[346] Tac. *Ann.* 16.54–5; cf. 3.49, for a likely similar denunciation under Tiberius.

[347] Tac. *Ann.* 3.25.2. Rutledge 2001, 9, 56–60.   [348] Cf. Tac. *Ann.* 12.59.1.

[349] Rathbone 2008, 257.   [350] Rutledge 2001, 30–33.

Regulus claimed that he had been forced to do what he did by Nero: refusal would have led to loss of property, freedom or life.[351] Eprius Marcellus, in a 'virtuoso performance', treated his audience 'to a sensible, albeit brief, instruction in political science', observing that one had to take *principes* as one found them – praying for the best but putting up with the rest. Under Nero he, like everyone else in the senatorial class, had accepted a common servitude.[352] Both imply a high degree of compulsion, but this is unlikely. Prosecutors were set on advancing their careers, and what Regulus and Marcellus claimed is a common defence of those, usually the majority in a society,[353] determined to create a decent life for themselves whatever the current political system. They act *comme il faut*, doing what society approves and rewards and adopting a stance of moral 'presentism'.[354] In fact, their forensic skills and contacts made top accusers redoubtable figures, immensely useful to the state: too big to fail.[355] Hence many, like Eprius Marcellus, survived to serve a new regime: natural 'kingsmen'.[356]

Nero's return from Greece, indeed, restored order,[357] but then came the insurrections of Vindex and Galba. The regime faced the first full-scale attack on Italy for generations. Its reaction was robust but expensive,[358] and money had to be raised in in a very short time. It therefore levied its first new regular taxes, resorted to extraordinary taxation on income and rents, and sold Galba's property.[359] This was probably also when Nero attempted to recover some of the generous gifts he had made to Greeks,[360] and when he laid hands on temple treasures, recovered after the Fire or by new appropriation. None of this would have been popular: 'easy to twist against Nero later'.[361] The source tradition depicts most of it as at best inept and at worst tyrannical. However, the situation was serious, and the seizure of Galba's assets, as Galba then seized state assets,[362] was entirely justifiable; and the use of temple treasures was a time-honoured

---

[351] Tac. *Hist.* 4.42. Rudich 1993, 204–5.

[352] Tac. *Hist.* 4.8: *bonos imperatores voto expetere, qualiscumque tolerare . . . qui simul servierit.* Rudich 1993, 184 (quotations).

[353] Cf. Tac. *Hist.* 4.6: how the senate divided when Helvidius Priscus prosecuted Eprius Marcellus on the grounds that 'if Marcellus fell it was the ruin of a host of the guilty'. Rudich 1993, 184: 'an outcome demonstrating the strength of his position and reflecting the fears, vanities and guilty consciences of his colleagues'; Rutledge 2001, 122.

[354] Rudich 1993, 183; Rutledge 2001, 122.   [355] Cf. Rudich 1993, xxvi–xxvii, 25, 201, 206.

[356] Syme 1958, 1.101; Rudich 1993, 186, 206; Rutledge 2001, 51–2, 126; above 84.

[357] Below 387.   [358] Below 392.

[359] Suet. *Ner.* 44.2; Plut. *Galb.* 5.4–5; *contra* Cass. Dio 61.5.5. Rathbone 2008, 253.

[360] Suet. *Ner.* 32.3. Bradley 1978a, 193; above 231.   [361] Rathbone 2008, 252.

[362] Plut. *Galb.* 5.5.

practice.[363] However, together with the activities of Helius, this permitted
Nero's enemies and future rulers and historians wrongly to brand him as
doomed to destruction by fiscal incompetence: 'Leaving aside the fire of
AD 64 and the panic of 68, there is no hard evidence for any financial crisis
in Nero's reign'.[364] But if bankruptcy did not destroy Nero, what did?
This returns us to politics.

---

[363] Above 317, 340; Millar 1977, 146.   [364] Rathbone 2008, 252.

PART III

End

CHAPTER 14

Entr'acte: Greece

14.1 Introduction

Directing Nero was never straightforward since his powers were inalienable: he must always, however nominally, make the final decision.[1] When his counsellors wished to guide him they could do so openly, by directly advocating a particular action and so gaining his approval in advance, or obliquely, by setting in train what needed to be done and then getting him to agree to this, if necessary with irresistible inducements. While Nero did his best to play the 'good' *princeps*, they went for the direct approach. After this, and especially after the murder of Agrippina when Nero increasingly immersed himself in his real interests, the latter was the more effective tactic.[2] The appearance and even participation of Seneca, Burrus and other imperial dignitaries at the *Iuvenalia* of 60 was therefore less a matter of humiliating resignation and extraordinary *dissimulatio* than part of a process which kept Nero happy while members of the *Consilium* ran the state.[3] There was no sudden change in the pattern of administration from 62, when Tigellinus and Poppaea took up the reins.[4] Indeed, in 64 Nero's open acknowledgement of his *métier* accelerated his absorption by artistic and sporting pursuits and ensured that proxy government lasted to the end of his principate.[5] Some adjustment resulted from the unmasking of the Pisonian conspiracy, which took away many favourites, and the death of Poppaea.[6] By 66, Tigellinus, alone, headed a fresh team which included his new colleague as praetorian prefect, the highly ambitious Nymphidius Sabinus.[7] This continued the deft handling of *princeps* and politics, though it should be remembered that no *nomenklatura* acted in isolation. In the

---

[1] Cf. above 81.   [2] Above 160.
[3] Tac. *Ann.* 14.15.7; Cass. Dio 61.20.1–3. Cf. Grant 1970, 56; Malitz 1999, 42: 60; Waldherr 2005, 125; *contra* Rudich 1993, 42.
[4] *Contra* Waldherr 2005, 183; cf. above 27, 136.   [5] Above 308; cf. Bergmann 2013, 357.
[6] Above 210–11, 215.   [7] Cf. Fini 1994, 194.

second wave of post-Pisonian prosecutions there was, for example, always strong senatorial support.[8] However, as a result of the Vinician conspiracy post-Pisonian tension returned in strength; and other factors may have caused serious concern. At the end of 65 plague killed around 30,000 in Rome;[9] and Nero's third, and last, significant illness may have fallen in 66.[10] The administration will have been relieved that, riding on the success of Tiridates' visit,[11] it could implement a long-maturing plan to remove Nero and his new wife, Statilia Messalina, hopefully soon to present him with an heir, from Rome and Italy.[12] In addition, it would now have suited Tigellinus, intent on securing his position, to get Nero to himself.

14.2   Greece

A good place for them to go to – not too near but not too far, and with enough to engage Nero's interests – was Greece. A long-standing conviction is that by visiting Greece Nero was both fulfilling a lifetime dream and, now projecting himself as the ideal ruler-artist, seeking out a place where this would be fully appreciated.[13] Yet throughout his life Nero showed himself no enthusiastic long-distance traveller. There is a possibility that around 42–43 he accompanied Agrippina and Passienus Crispus during the latter's governorship of proconsular Asia, but if so the experience could have left little clear impression on the mind of a five-year-old.[14] After this, and prior to the Greek trip, there is no sign that Nero (unlike his uncle, Gaius, with whom he is frequently compared[15]) ever left Italy. Even in the early part of his principate, when he acted the good *princeps*, Nero never, as he should have done, visited his frontier troops.[16] Later, in 64, there are signs of the commencement of a grand eastern tour, taking in Greece, Egypt and, perhaps, even Syria, but this came to nothing.[17] The same fate awaited the much more ambitious expedition to the Caucasus, which Nero was contemplating as he set out for Greece in 66.[18] Finishing as he had started, in 68 Nero never, still more as he should have done, led

---

[8] Cf. above 75.   [9] Tac. *Ann.* 16.13.1–3; Suet. *Ner.* 39.1. Hohl 1918, 386.
[10] Above 305; Bradley 1978a, 284.   [11] Cf. Malitz 1999, 63, 88.
[12] Cf. above 164. 229; below 380.
[13] E.g. Henderson 1905, 380–1; Hohl 1918, 388; Cizek 1982, 147; Rudich 1993, 187; Waldherr 2005, 232; Meier 2008, 561, 592, 594.
[14] Barrett 1996, 85; Holland 2000, 35–6; Waldherr 2005, 31. Cf. above 282.
[15] Cf. Winterling 2007, 22, 84–5.   [16] Above 166.   [17] Above 127, 166, 205, 221.
[18] Above 148, below 392.

his troops from Italy into Gaul.[19] All this indicates that Nero was basically not keen on visiting foreign parts. It is significant that when he finally got to Greece, he did not do the usual Grand Tour of Athens, Eleusis and Sparta. Ancient and modern authors have proposed a variety of explanation for this, religious, moral, administrative and political.[20] The simplest solution is, however, to accept that he went to Greece reluctantly, and with a very restricted agenda: 'In practice, his vaunted "philhellenism" was sharply limited'.[21]

14.3 Philhellenism

There can be no disputing the authenticity of Nero's philhellenism.[22] This is evident in his early artistic and sporting pursuits, his establishment of the *Neronia* and, above all, his commitment to Greek values at the banquet of 64.[23] His basic interest was normal for a Roman of his class and age. Nero did not create a hellenising movement; as in many other, things he just followed fashion.[24] Despite conservative opposition, public appreciation and even practice of the Hellenic arts had become accepted parts of aristocratic life, especially that of the gilded youth of Rome as it sought new outlets for energy once expended in the political cut-and-thrust of the old Republic.[25] A keen practitioner was the honorand of the *Laus Pisonis*.[26] Britannicus sang, as did his friend, the future *princeps*, Titus. Nero called another future *princeps*, Nerva, the 'Tibullus' of the age. To judge from his epitaph, Verginius Rufus was no mean versifier. Even Thrasea Paetus performed in ancestral games at Padua.[27] Nero's Hellenism, the armature of his literary, architectural and scientific interests, was part of the spirit of the age but also significantly amplified by his own tastes, by his Greek tutors and probably, despite his reservations about modern trends, by Seneca.[28] Nero's problem was that his artistic activities differed from those of the respectable young not in quality but in degree.[29] Traditional Roman

---

[19] Below 401.
[20] Suet. *Ner.* 34.4; Cass. Dio 63.14.3. Hohl 1918, 388; Cizek 1982, 151–2; Alcock 1994, 105; Fini 1994, 131; Malitz 1999, 35; Meier 2008, 565.
[21] Champlin 2003, 54–5; cf. Meier 2008, 55, 569 n. 30.
[22] Charlesworth 1950, 75; Griffin 1984. 119; Alcock 1994.   [23] Above 293, 308–9.
[24] Cf. above 306; Bergmann 2013, 338, 357.
[25] Waldherr 2005, 110–12; Bergmann 2013, 355–6; Pausch 2013, 51–2, 63–5, 68.
[26] Above 267.
[27] Tac. *Ann.* 13.15.3, 16.21.1; Suet. *Tit.* 2.1–2; Mart. 8.70; Plin. *Ep.* 9.19.1. Cizek 1982, 392; Rudich 1993, 129; Cadario 2011, 182; Pausch 2013, 67–8, 70; below 404.
[28] Sen. *Dial.* 12 [*De brev.*].4. Levi 1949, 93–4, 148; Cizek 1982, 29–30.   [29] Meier 2008, 578–9.

views persisted: educated youth must not take its Hellenism too far. The
author of the *Laus Pisonis* treads carefully around Piso's lack of military
experience, suggesting that it is compensated for by his skill as a sportsman
and a player of board-games.[30] He is, however, on safer ground with Piso's
duties as a busy barrister, a conscientious mentor of legal pupils, and a
regular and respected speaker in the Senate. Piso's artistic interests serve as
diversions from hard work.[31] Nero, in contrast, made his the centre of
attention and so was diligent but unproductive with regard to his public
duties: Seneca's *iners negotium* ('aimless activity').[32] For a long time
significant resentment against Nero's *iners negotium* was restricted to the
conservative minority,[33] but eventually his neglect of his responsibilities
led to his downfall. Nero, in fact, gave the performing arts such a bad name
that it was not until Hadrian that they recovered any respectability.[34]
Hadrian, the *princeps*-hellenophile par excellence, 'did almost everything
Nero had done' and was respected for it, which suggests that Nero was
simply ahead of his time.[35] But Hadrian undertook proper *negotium*, and
he was a soldier.

14.4   Ideology

The key questions are whether Nero's obsessive philhellenism made him
long to visit Greece and whether it fostered any ideological intent.[36] Some
see the visit as Nero's response to the call of the East as the home of
autocratic theocratic kingship: Cizek's 'Neronism', the beginning of a
'massive reformation of values' through which the *princeps* sought to create
an international theocracy.[37] Others interpret it as Nero's reaction to
growing hostility in Rome and Italy: he went eastwards to win support
elsewhere. His aim was to integrate the Greek East fully into the Roman
Empire, make it the equal of Rome, Italy and the Latin West, and so
become 'the Hellenistic monarch of a Romano-Greek empire'.[38]
His short-term success is reflected in the popular 'false Neros' who
appeared in the East after his death.[39] His long-term success is reflected

---

[30] *Laus Pis.* 185–209.
[31] *Laus Pis.* 25–64, 84–8, 99; 65–71; 139–58. Waldherr 2005, 108, 112–13.
[32] Sen. *Dial.* 12.4. Cf. Mratschek 2013, 46.   [33] Cf. below 401.   [34] Pausch 2013, 69.
[35] Bergmann 2013, 358.   [36] Above 287, 293; cf. Rudich 1993, 57.
[37] Cizek 1982, 26, 48, 61: 'vaste réforme axiologique', 71, 74, 84–5, 88, esp. 121–65; above 265.
[38] E.g. Levi 1949, 211; Alcock 1994, 105; Malitz 1999, 91; Waldherr 2005, 240–2; Mordine 2013,
114 (quotation).
[39] Above 10; Mratschek 2013, 56.

in second-century Greek writers judging him positively in the context of an extraordinary revival of Greek culture: the 'Second Sophistic', which had a huge impact on Classical, Christian and Byzantine culture.[40] A narrower explanation is *Kulturpolitik*. Nero's innate pacificism caused him to prefer the Greek artistic/sporting *agon* over the Roman militaristic *certamen*. The Greek trip and its competitions was the culmination of his campaign to switch aristocratic priorities from the community and military achievement to the individual and the ways of peace: echoing Cizek, but for a much more restricted constituency, 'to change the value system of the Roman aristocracy'.[41] An extension of *Kulturpolitik* is *Kulturrevolution*: the spreading of secular Hellenic culture beyond the aristocracy to the people of Rome, perhaps to win local support to balance a decline in senatorial backing. This would explain his great homecoming 'triumph'.[42]

None of these proposals is wholly convincing. The case for Nero's being bent on religious revolution and the establishment of an Apolline, theocratic kingship has already been rejected.[43] The argument for his attempting to build an alternative support-base in the Greek East is equally questionable. There was no major break with the Senate; and Nero always went out of his way to please the Roman *plebs*. There is no sign that in 66/67 he faced widespread domestic enmity, whether aristocratic or popular.[44] Once arrived in Greece, he did not show particular respect to its inhabitants. He disrupted the ancient Games; he battened on many of the upper class; his unconventional behaviour must have disturbed most; and for the general population his 'liberation' will have brought little major practical advantage.[45] Indeed, with regard to his great 'liberation' speech, 'some Greeks would have resented his tactless and condescending contrast of contemporary and classical Greece'.[46] As for the Second Sophistic, although there was important writing in Greek under Nero, none matched that of the Latin works of the period. The best, produced by such as Epictetus, Dio Chrysostom and Plutarch, came after Nero: 'Greek-speaking authors, it seems, had only waited for the poet to leave the throne'.[47] The proposition that Nero aimed to change the value system of the Roman

---

[40] Plut. *De sera* 32. Charlesworth 1950, 72–3, 75; Malitz 1999, 93; Griffin 2013, 472.

[41] Levi 1949, 124–6, 158–60; Fini 1994, 55, 73, 77; 83–84, 89–90; Griffin 1984, 43–5, 113–14; Dinter 2013, 3; Bergmann 2013, 355 (quotation); Littlewood 2015, 165–6.

[42] Fini 1994, 13–14, 32–4, 42, 54, 75–7, 83, 89–90, 180, 203–4, 216–17; Waldherr 2005, 209; below 384.

[43] Above 266, 272, 287, 293.

[44] Meier 2008, 569–72. Aristocratic: above 93–4; popular: below 401.

[45] Meier 2008, 568–9, 595; cf. above 273.   [46] Griffin 2013, 472.

[47] Above 122; Hansen 2013, 303, 312 (quotation).

aristocracy has more appeal. Such changes had occurred in the past, for
example in the later Republic when the rise of forensic oratory allowed
Cicero to become a great statesman. Nero probably aspired to elevate
virtuosity in art and sport, particularly as displayed in the most competitive
form of Hellenism, the *agones*, to a point where it might contribute to
aristocratic *dignitas*, and so his own *auctoritas*. As Pausch puts it, he sought
a new, cultural, way of emphasising his special position as *primus inter
pares*.[48] On the other hand, there is no sign of Nero's contemplating a
root-and-branch transformation of Roman aristocratic attitudes. Thanks to
the senatorial tradition, the *mos maiorum* remained strong and continued
to support martial values: real success remained military success. The
Neronian regime made no attempt to alter this, and gave free rein to its
generals:[49] again, for a *princeps* who disliked bloodshed, Nero's principate
was remarkably bellicose. Likewise, there is no sign of Nero's ever seriously
attempting to change the attitude of the Roman *plebs*. Despite his distaste
for bloodshed, he continued to present great gladiatorial contests.[50]

The best explanation for Nero's cultural interests and his eventual
enjoyment of the Greek trip is that these gave him personal gratification.
What he did, especially from 64, was for himself, not the imperial system
as a whole. As sportsman and entertainer, he led the life he wanted and was
otherwise content to let the world proceed as ever. In short, once more,
Nero wanted to change his principate, not the Principate.[51] Nero's aims
were not ideological because he was not sufficiently engaged in Roman
political life to even contemplate alternative ideologies. He was not interested in establishing an advanced autocracy, religious or secular.[52] In
training, rehearsal and performance, he had far too many other things to
do.[53] He had 'no revolutionary forms of rule or world vision'; his concern
'was not primarily with concepts of power but with lifestyle in the widest
sense'.[54] Nero had little notion of where he was taking the Principate.[55]
Though he may well have wished to convince his fellow aristocrats that his
superior artistic skills conferred as much *dignitas* and *auctoritas* upon him
as success in politics and war, he did not wish to transform the entire
aristocratic value system. His aim was, rather, to insinuate his own skills
within it, and so derive benefit for the praise he received for them.[56] Nero's
genial relationship with the *plebs* did not make him a demagogue, bent on

---

[48] Pausch 2013, 66: 'seine Sonderstellung als primus inter pares auch kulturell zu unterstreichent'; cf.
Rudich 1993, xxxi; below 384. Cf. above 205.
[49] Above 29, 293.   [50] Above 298; cf. Rudich 1993, 42.   [51] Above 293, 309.
[52] Above 293.   [53] Above 293.   [54] Bergmann 2013, 357.   [55] Above 287, 293.
[56] Above 286.

crushing the Senate and on basing his authority on popular approval.[57] The clearest proof of this is that on the one occasion when an aspiring demagogic leader would surely have tried to 'work' the crowds, Nero adhered to the best Augustan tradition, receiving Tiridates as the leader of the Roman Republic.[58] And even his final 'triumph', though it had strong Hellenic elements and included various other eccentricities, basically followed Republican and Augustan precedent.[59] Nero liked ordinary people, got on well with them and wanted to be more accessible to them.[60] On the other hand, having grown out of his nocturnal wanderings,[61] he did not want to be part of them. His Golden House complex allowed the controlled, not spontaneous, interaction of *princeps* and people, as his public banqueting put him in sight of but not among them.[62] Nero performed in public because he craved recognition of his artistic expertise and because he needed the stimulus to explore extremes of human suffering through music and song.[63] It is significant that he was apparently less keen on the very popular pantomime, perhaps because he doubted his abilities in this field.[64] Though his changing of his repertoire gave it a wider appeal,[65] his aim was never mindless applause for a 'celebrity' appearance. The narrowness of his view has led some to brand him a debased Epicurean: hedonistic, narcissistic, egocentric.[66] This is to go too far. Nero cannot be categorised as the follower of any philosophy. His purported Epicureanism derives from the mistaken view that he wilfully flouted convention and responsibility, and his 'narcissism' is open to question.[67] He may have appeared egocentric, but this was inevitable given his position in society and his overenthusiasm for his interests.[68]

Down to 64 Nero, despite toying with plans to the contrary, was happy to pursue his philhellenism at home. When he wanted to immerse himself in things artistic he had no need to go abroad. On his doorstep was southern Italy, where Roman participation in Greek culture had long been sanctioned by custom and usage. The Greek games in Naples, at which Nero first sang in public in 64, had been instituted in honour of Augustus in 2 BC, the first on Italian soil.[69] His 'aesthetic culture' was not that of

---

[57] Above 26, 99, 110, 205, 321–2; *contra* Mordine 2013, 115.
[58] Above 68; Waldherr 2005, 229, 231.   [59] Cass. Dio 63.20.3. Below 384.
[60] Above 16, 253, 293, 308–9.   [61] Above 297.   [62] Above 256, 309.
[63] Mratschek 2013, 50–1; above 114, 289.
[64] Tac. *Ann.* 13.25.4. Mratschek 2013, 51; Barrett *et al.* 2016, 247 n. 30; above 232.
[65] Above 114.
[66] Cizek 1982, 351–2, 366; Fini 1994, 13, 88, 97; Malitz 1999, 45; Holland 2000, 182.
[67] Cf. Holland 2000, 55, 135; above 292.   [68] Cf. Bergmann 2013, 357; above 285.
[69] Suet. *Aug.* 98.5. Reitz 2006, 14.

Greece but of the Bay of Naples, where his family had estates. Probably stimulated by this concert, he was then delighted to realise that he could practise his calling of public performer in Italy and Rome.[70] His inclination to remain in Italy fits with his search for Greek works of art for the *Domus Transitoria* and the *Domus Aurea*. Instead of travelling to Greece, he brought Greece to Rome.[71] His construction of the Golden House complex, indeed, encapsulates his reluctance to travel. Hadrian, who had toured his world, was to make that world accessible to him in miniature outside Rome at Tivoli.[72] Nero, who had not, built the Golden House to live like a human being in the capital. From this it follows that Nero did not decide on the Greek trip to satisfy a personal desire or to advance an ideology.

14.5   Inducements

I propose that, although Nero's capital was unsettled in 66, he did not decide 'to escape from Rome' and flee from danger into make-believe.[73] Those who directed him persuaded him to do so for his own good, offering two powerful inducements. First, Greece was sold to Nero as the place where his talents would be most appreciated. There is a ring of truth in Suetonius' story of Nero's deciding to go to Greece immediately after a visit by representatives of those Greek cities that hosted music contests. Treated to private concerts, they applauded him rapturously which caused him to declare that 'only Greeks had the right ear for his music and only they were worthy of him and his efforts'.[74] The delegation smacks of an Establishment ploy.[75] An indispensable part of the scheme was to reschedule the main games within a space of about twelve months so that Nero could compete in them all, and to alter their format to accommodate his particular interests and skills.[76] The inducement was, therefore, competition not assurance of victory. When he was in Greece, Nero always believed that he was good enough to win but was never certain of success. Thus when he won he believed that victory and applause were genuine, not the result of flattery.[77] The second inducement, lesser as far as Nero

---

[70] Waldherr 2005, 126; Mratschek 2013, 47; above 309.   [71] Above 235, 257.
[72] SHA *Had.* 26.5. Quenemoen 2014, 68.
[73] Bradley 1978a, 139; *contra* Griffin 1984, 233 (quotation).
[74] Suet. *Ner.* 22.3: *solos scire audire Graecos solosque se et studiis suis dignos.*
[75] Cf. Mratschek 2013, 54–5.
[76] Suet. *Ner.* 23.1. Bradley 1978a, 140–1; Malitz 1999, 90; Meier 2008, 568; below 382.
[77] Cf. above 292; Fini 1994, 99.

was concerned but still powerful because it appealed to another of his interests,[78] was the construction of the Corinth canal. Suetonius describes how, at the sound of a trumpet, Nero personally cut the first sod.[79] We know that in September 67 Vespasian sent 6,000 Jewish prisoners of war to work on the project.[80] Since the enterprise cannot have been predicated on the availability of such labour, it probably began earlier and by early autumn 67 was sufficiently advanced to make best use of so many hands. Nero perhaps inaugurated the project in spring 67, following his first winter in Corinth, with work commencing in earnest that summer.[81] The workforce will have consisted of the usual mix of slaves and criminals deployed by the Roman state. This explains the tale that the banished Musonius Rufus was seen working in a chain-gang there.[82] Though Suetonius says Nero 'called together the praetorians and urged them to begin the work', these should not be taken as part of the regular labour force. Their role was to mark the start of work, not to do it themselves (for which, anyway, they would have been too few in number).[83] They may have paraded along the planned course with each man simultaneously cutting his own first sod as part of the theatre of the occasion. Their involvement should not be seen as causing them any humiliation and resentment that later contributed to Nero's fall.[84]

Greece was not one of Nero's priorities, but once there he revelled in the success of his artistic activities and used them to explore emotions of guilt and redemption.[85] It is not surprising that in 67 he proved very reluctant to return to Rome.

14.6 Chronology

Nero travelled to Greece in the autumn of 66 but, given his complicated programme, both the decision to go and the start of preparations for the successful delivery of the two inducements must have occurred much earlier.[86] The administration needed, for example, to work out a practical timetable for the reordered games, and to survey the route and plan the construction of the canal. Associated details were the cutting of

---

[78] Cf. above 342.   [79] Suet. *Ner.* 19.2.   [80] Joseph. *BJ* 3.10.10. Cf. above 364.
[81] Cf. Bradley 1978a, 116.   [82] Philostr. *VA* 5.19. Rudich 1993, 126–7; above 105.
[83] Suet. *Ner.* 19.2: *praetorianos pro contione ad incohandum opus cohortatus est.* Bradley 1978a, 116–17.
[84] *Contra* Cizek 1982, 387; Waldherr 2005, 240.   [85] Above 290.
[86] Above 226; Waldherr 2005, 234.

Alexandrian coin-dies advertising the festivals at which the *princeps* was competing,[87] and the building of accommodation for him at the heart of Olympia.[88] Officials could refer to earlier arrangements, made when Gaius expressed interest in building a Corinth canal and, more recently, for Nero's projected foreign trips in 64. However, the former did not result in significant excavation, and the latter concerned Egypt more than Greece.[89] Furthermore, manpower and resources would have been stretched because of the need to rebuild Rome and prepare for Tiridates' visit. The administration needed time, albeit not in inordinate quantity: an autocratic empire did not have to answer to planning authorities, refractory taxpayers or 'nimbies'. Sufficient time was available because of Tiridates' visit, since Nero could not have left for Greece before his guest's own departure. For everything to have been ready in late 66/early 67, work must have started no later than late 65.[90] This falls before Nero's marrying Statilia Messalina. Given his likely unwillingness to remarry at this time, the inducements that were used to get him to Greece may also have served to persuade him back into the marriage-bed.[91]

14.7   Helius

A final question is why, when Nero went to Greece, Helius was left in charge in Rome. This cannot be dismissed as Nero's simply taking 'tyrannical' revenge on the Senate.[92] With almost all major figures of the Neronian administration away,[93] particular care had to be taken for the running of the capital. Under normal circumstances, in the absence of the *princeps* oversight of the City fell to the consular *praefectus urbi*.[94] The current prefect was the capable and popular T. Flavius Sabinus, brother of the future emperor Vespasian, in office from 61 and *prima facie* an ideal candidate.[95] That he was not appointed may have been due to a feeling that this might give too much influence to a rising family, but it was more likely the consequence of the extraordinary length of Nero's projected absence. There was precedent for two forms of action when there was no close family member to represent a long-absent *princeps*. In

---

[87] Bradley 1978a, 139; Malitz 1999, 89.
[88] E.g. Hohl 1918, 388; Bradley 1978a, 115; Cizek 1982, 153; Malitz 1999, 89; Reitz 2006, 14; Meier 2008, 572; Bol 2013, 158.
[89] Suet. *Calig.* 21. Bradley 1978a, 115, 129, 139; Winterling 2007, 85; above 126–7.
[90] Above 372.   [91] Above 164.   [92] Cf. above 26; Waldherr 2005, 233.   [93] Above 228.
[94] Cf. Cizek 1982, 287; cf. Millar 1977, 465.   [95] Tac. *Hist.* 1.46.1. Syme 1982, 478.

the period 26–31, following his retreat to Capri, Tiberius entrusted Rome to his praetorian prefect, Sejanus. In 66 Nero left behind his junior praetorian prefect, Nymphidius Sabinus. Why not name him his formal deputy? The answer is simple. Sejanus' stewardship had proved disastrous; the experiment could not be repeated. From late 39 into 40, Gaius was on the Rhine and in Gaul.[96] He appears to have entrusted Rome to the consul, Domitius Afer.[97] Shortly afterwards, in 43–44, it is clear that during Claudius' five-to-six month absence on his British campaign he left Vitellius I, his fellow consul, as vicegerent.[98] It is this delegation of power to a senior senator that one might expect in 66. Even if Flavius Sabinus was out of the running, there were other loyal senators to call upon, such as those who supported Helius or Fonteius Capito, consul *ordinarius* in 67.[99] But this did not happen. Grant proposes that this was because Tigellinus' departure with Nero removed the Establishment's 'guiding spirit' and so its ability to make its own decisions.[100] Given the ready availability of advisers proposed above, this does not ring true. A negative explanation is that, still unsettled by the Pisonian conspiracy, the regime was unwilling to give special powers to any senator. A more positive one is that the length of Nero's planned absence – at least twice that of Claudius – made it awkward for a senator to be put in charge. Vitellius I's terms of appointment imply that the main administration remained in Rome, requiring senior but short-term supervision. Nero's Greek trip was for much longer, and the machinery of government went with him,[101] leaving any representative with only City and Italian business. This made him a 'super-caretaker', the steward of a vast estate. As such, the post may have been distasteful to traditional senators. Its assignment to a leading *libertus*, acting not as himself but as the instrument of the *princeps*, may have been unavoidable. Helius was just a larger version of his colleague Polyclitus when he headed the commission of enquiry into the Boudican disaster. This also had power to determine the fate of *equites* and senators, the nominal social superiors of its president. Again, however, Helius could not have worked alone: he did not exercise autocracy.

---

[96] Halfmann 1986, 170–2.   [97] Barrett 1989, 98.
[98] Suet. *Claud.* 17. 2; *Vitell.* 2.4; Cass. Dio 60.23.1. Crook 1955, 41 and no. 352; cf. Levick 1990, 142; Osgood 2011, 88.
[99] Above 229, below 394.   [100] Grant 1970, 229.   [101] Above 229.

14.8 'Triumph'

Nero's intended trip was unusually long, but not open-ended. The rescheduling of the games suggests that it was expected to last no longer than about a year.[102] There was no intention of proceeding to Egypt and the East.[103] Nero should have returned to Rome by the end of 67. A problem was his sudden desire for a Caucasus expedition in 66.[104] However, his advisers must have had a shrewd idea that this was another flash in the pan. At heart Nero was no Alexander. Despite the glamour of the great man's name, he would have had little appetite for the hardships of long-distance travel, still less for those of campaigning. His Greek experience reinforced his civilian interests,[105] and by 67 he wished to go no further.[106]

With the games held out of order and at the wrong times of the year, there was bound to have been some logistical slippage; and Nero's new-found enthusiasm will have made this even worse since he will not have allowed his enjoyment to be spoiled by haste. The last of the major games, the Isthmian, held at Corinth, appear to have suffered major delay. Usually held in April or May, in 67 they took place in late November.[107] Nero's reluctance to leave Greece and the increased dangers of winter sailing must have made many wonder if he could be got back to Italy on time. Helius, fast losing control of the situation in Rome,[108] was desperate for the court's return. Dio suggests that in the end he panicked Nero into movement with rumours of a 'great conspiracy' in Rome.[109] This is not found in Suetonius and is probably an erroneous inference from Vindex's rebellion to come. More likely is that Helius, along with the wider Establishment, sensing that Nero was minded to delay, tempted him to return with additional inducements, both probably at the *princeps'* own suggestion, and both to be classed among his 'break-outs'.[110] The earlier is likely to have been that of his 'triumph'. Preparations for this would have taken time (simply embarking the *Augustiani*, transporting them back to Italy, giving them time to recover from sea-sickness, and rehearsing them for their major role in the event would have been a huge undertaking).[111]

---

[102] Above 378.
[103] Above 152 n. 176; *contra* e.g. Malitz 1999, 95; Waldherr 2005, 156, 233, 242; Ebbing 2009, 6.
[104] Above 150.   [105] Cf. Cizek 1982, 160–1; Heil 1997, 180.
[106] Cf. Meier 2008, 573; *contra* Fini 1994, 210.
[107] Suet. *Ner.* 24.2. Bradley 1978a, 144–5; Halfmann 1986, 174.   [108] Above 365.
[109] Cass. Dio 63.19.1: *megalē epiboulē*.   [110] *Contra* Brunt 1959, 533; above 165.
[111] Cf. Malitz 1999, 96.

On the other hand, specific planning could not have begun very early, since Nero would not have 'known' that he would be so successful and therefore deserving of a triumph.[112] In addition, particular 'triumphal' elements need only to have been added to arrangements already made for the usual grand *adventus* ('ceremonial entry') into Rome.[113] According to Suetonius, when Helius first appealed to Nero to return, making no mention of a conspiracy but simply reminding him that his presence was required in Rome, the *princeps* put him off, saying that he should return 'worthy of Nero'.[114] This suggests that Nero felt that he still had important work to do, which in turn suggests that the appeal was made and the 'triumph' proposed and accepted after the completion of most of the games, say, in late summer 67. The second inducement, that Nero should 'sign off' from Greece in a grand manner by personally announcing its 'liberation' to a packed audience after the holding of his final, Isthmian, games, was probably settled in the early autumn.

The 'liberation', declared in late November 67,[115] was probably an additional factor in delaying the Isthmian Games, but once it had been made Nero could be got back home. He left Greece around the beginning of December 67.[116] He did not, apparently, return via Brindisi, but sailed to Puteoli, the port of Naples.[117] This was a longer and, particularly in the winter season, more dangerous sea-route: it is no wonder that he was almost shipwrecked.[118] However, it allowed the immediate commencement of festivities. He made a grand entrance into Naples, then Anzio, his Alban villa (on the site of Alba Longa of old)[119] and finally Rome. The notion of 'homecoming' is indicated by his choice of route: 'he moved from the city where he had been born as an artist to the city where he had actually been born, then to the city of his ancestors, finally to the city where he lived and ruled'.[120] He entered all these places in the manner of a victor at one of the major Greek games: dressed in a Greek cloak, wearing the Olympic victor's crown and carrying the Delphic, and riding through a breach in the walls (the honorific *eiselasis*) on a chariot drawn by white

---

[112] Cf. above 378.   [113] Cf. Michel 2015, 107–8, on Claudius' return from Britain.

[114] Suet. *Ner.* 23.1: *dignus Nerone.*

[115] Meier 2008, 595; Dinter 2013, 4; Mratschek 2013, 54. There is controversy over the date of the 'liberation', with some scholars putting it in 66. Here, however, I follow the *communis opinio*. See e.g. Henderson 1905, 390–1; Bradley 1978a, 144–5; Halfmann 1986, 175–7; Alcock 1994, 103.

[116] Bradley 1978a, 249; Meier 2008, 566 n. 23.

[117] For this and the following: Suet. *Ner.* 25.1–3; Cass. Dio 63.20; Griffin 1984, 163; Champlin 2003, 210–34.

[118] Cass. Dio 63.19.2; cf. Suet. *Ner.* 40.3.   [119] Champlin 2003, 229, 232.

[120] Champlin 2003, 232–3.

horses: 'the entry ... of a *hieronikes*, the victor in one of the great sacred games of old Greece'.[121]

Once in Rome, his 'triumph' was unusual. His route (Porta Capena → Circus Maximus → Velabrum → between Capitol and Palatine → Forum → Palatine → Temple of Apollo) was wholly unorthodox (Figure 16);[122] he was attended not by a slave, reminding him of his mortality, but by Diodorus the famous citharode, one of his defeated opponents; those processing kept shouting grand praises of Nero in chorus; and the final temple was not that of Jupiter of the Capitoline, but of Apollo on the Palatine. On the other hand, it included elements which gave the proceedings something of the look of the traditional triumph. Thus Nero gave primacy to Rome;[123] rode into the city on Augustus' triumphal chariot; wore the gold-spangled purple robe of a *triumphator*; did not travel alone in his chariot; was preceded by a procession of men carrying his crowns of victory as plunder and *tituli* ('placards') indicating where and how these had been won; was followed first by his 'troops', the *Augustiani*, and next by praetorians, *equites* and senators; and finished the parade at the temple of one of the great gods of Rome, which was also adjacent to Augustus' 'modest and unpretentious house on the Palatine'.[124] The occasion was used to stage another spectacular city-wide party, reminiscent of 'Tigellinus' banquet', with garlands, lights, costly perfumes and multiple sacrifices. 'Now the very streets of Rome were for a time one vast theatre, and Nero was the star performer'.[125] Nero meant his 'triumph' to be taken very seriously. It was no crude parody of what had gone before. He may have devised its untraditional route actually to point up the difference between it and the ancient military triumph: an unprecedented celebration of the successes of peace through a combination of Greek and Roman ceremonial.[126] Typically non-ideological,[127] it reflected the importance which Nero attached to his achievements in Greece: he had gained his crowns against tough competition and deserved appropriate recognition. This would win him his own non-warlike *auctoritas*.[128] What resulted was a new 'triumph of an artist'.[129] Yet Nero also showed that even at his most liberated and imaginative, and for all his Greek leanings

---

[121] Champlin 2003, 231 (quotation); Barrett *et al.* 2016, 258 n. 44.
[122] Makin 1921, 31–33; Bradley 1978a, 151; Champlin 2003, 231.
[123] Cf. Winterling 2007, 122, on Gaius' antics elsewhere.   [124] Milnor 2005, 9.
[125] Champlin 2003, 229–30, 233–4 (quotation).
[126] Bradley 1978a, 148–9; Cizek 1982, 158–9; Champlin 2003, 233.
[127] *Contra* Mratschek 2013, 57–8.   [128] Above 376.
[129] Griffin 1984, 163;' cf. Champlin 2003, 234.

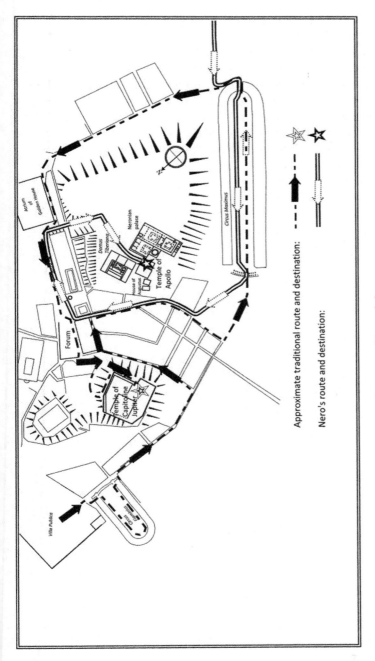

Figure 16   Triumphal routes.
After Makin 1921, 25; Payne 1962; Beard 2007, 334; Carandini 2011, 238

Approximate traditional route and destination:

Nero's route and destination:

and however much he relished the 'performance art' of his creation,[130] he still regarded the Roman triumph as the standard against which all other forms of accolade were to be measured. His grand parade, like his reception of Tiridates,[131] was firmly rooted in the Republican and Augustan past. With full triumphs now very rare (the last was held in 44 to celebrate Claudius' conquest of Britain) it is likely very few appreciated the extent of his divergence from tradition. Most ordinary Romans would simply have enjoyed the grand party; and the court Establishment would have been relieved that Nero was now safely back in the City.

[130] Mratschek 2013, 58.   [131] Above 377.

CHAPTER 15

Fall

15.1 Introduction

Nero returned to Italy in triumph late in 67. Less than a year later he committed suicide in the basement of a villa on the outskirts of Rome. A major difficulty in understanding what happened is the disappearance of the closing books of Tacitus' 'Annals', covering the remainder of 66–68. We have to make do with Suetonius' 'Lives' of Nero, Galba, Otho and Vitellius, Plutarch's 'Lives' of Galba and Otho, what remains of Cassius Dio's 'History' and what we can glean from the extant books of Tacitus' 'Histories', all part of the anti-Neronian source tradition.[1] However, what we have contains valuable nuggets of information;[2] used carefully, it allows a fair explanation of Nero's fall.

15.2 The Lull Before the Storm

The court Establishment will have been pleased that the Greek tour had served its purpose of temporarily distancing Nero from a Rome unsettled by the Pisonian conspiracy.[3] Indeed, at first sight things looked much better for the regime in late 67 than they had in mid-66. Although Nero had to be persuaded to journey to Greece, he had enjoyed his visit and his victorious homecoming. Helius had experienced some aristocratic indiscipline in the capital, but there was no budding conspiracy there and order was restored on the *princeps'* return.[4] And there was no growing financial crisis.[5] Yet Nero's advisers could not have felt entirely happy. The Greek trip had encouraged Nero further to play the professional athlete and actor in a manner unbefitting a *princeps,* and revulsion at such behaviour had been a major force behind the Pisonian conspiracy.[6] Then there was

---

[1] Above 10. [2] Cf. Bradley 1978a, 243. [3] Above 372. [4] Above 230, 364–5, 367, 382.
[5] Above 364–5; *contra* Mratschek 2013, 56–7. [6] Above 208.

Nero's appearance. Appropriate clothing and demeanour were expected of everyone. The public dress of a senator, for example, was a tunic decorated with a broad purple stripe over which went a white toga and red or black sandals.[7] While in Greece, Nero embarrassed conservative senators by receiving them in a short tunic embroidered with flowers, and a loose neck-cloth.[8] He had also abandoned his 'permanent wave' and, in the manner of a professional citharode, grown shoulder-length hair.[9] He probably maintained this relaxed dress code on his return. More substantively, the Greek trip had forced some awkward fiscal changes;[10] and it may also have created court tension by increasing the influence of leading *Augustiani*.[11] Above all, however, the trip had threatened the long-term prospects of the dynasty by allowing Nero to fall into a habit of endless remorse for Poppaea and a consequent interminable infatuation with Sporus/'Poppaea',[12] so diminishing the prospect of a child with Statilia Messalina. It was perhaps around now that Calvia Crispinilla, with her intimate knowledge of Nero's bedchamber, began to lose faith in his survival.[13]

Yet at the start of 68 the positive outweighed the negative. Nero's return generated widespread popular support, burying bad memories of Helius' administration and confirming his position as the darling of the *plebs*, and there was no sign of disaffection among the praetorians. Despite raised eyebrows at the *princeps'* behaviour, there was no prospect of a second major metropolitan conspiracy; and the loyalty of Neronian generals, dread of civil war and lack of precedent will have made successful provincial revolt seem equally unlikely.[14] Late-Neronian coin-types celebrating the army are therefore better associated with the assembling of a force in northern Italy later in 68 than with any worry about army loyalty in the wake of the executions of Corbulo and the Scribonii from 66.[15] Despite Nero's lack of military experience and despite, indeed, his passion for acting (the 'unmanly' 'inverse of fighting'[16]), as long as his generals did their duty and brought him glory he was safe. Indeed, with no surviving Julio-Claudian rivals, he must have appeared unassailable.[17] There was, of course, always the danger of another run of disturbing 'break-outs', but by

---

[7] Talbert 1984, 216–19   [8] Cass. Dio 63.13.3.
[9] Suet. *Ner.* 51. Bradley 1978a, 285; above 306.   [10] Above 331.   [11] Above 62.
[12] Above 294.   [13] Above 164, below 400.
[14] *Contra* Griffin 1984, 117–18; Heil 1997, 181, 199. Cf. above 66, 147, 227.
[15] *Contra* Kraay 1949, 133–5. Cf. *RIC* 1² p. 147; Butcher and Ponting 2014, 213, 219–20; above 364.
[16] Edwards 1994, 86, 90 (quotations).   [17] Cf. Henderson 1905, 395–6; Malitz 1999, 99.

early 68 Nero appears to have been physically and emotionally exhausted.[18] The intense experiences of 65–67 had probably caused him some sort of nervous collapse, without making him 'mad'.[19] He threw himself into his triumph but then withdrew from Rome to his favourite city, Naples.[20] Long unenthusiastic about his duties as *princeps*, he now simply ceased to care about them. Though this boded ill for the begetting of an heir or dealing with any new political challenge, it meant that he was not inclined to slip the traces. The Neronian Establishment faced no immediate crisis and could hope to muddle along as before.[21]

15.3 Vindex

Nero's downfall began, out of the blue, with a revolt by Julius Vindex, governor of one of the provinces of Gaul, probably Lugdunensis. Vindex declared himself in the period 9–12 March 68, following secret preparations which included fruitless overtures to other provincial governors, including Galba, in charge of the Spanish province of Tarraconensis.[22] Galba did not denounce Vindex, but the others did. After he had rebelled, Vindex openly invited Galba to lead the insurrection, this time with success. Vindex was no Gallic nationalist. Though of distinguished Gallic background, his upbringing, education and career had fully integrated him into Roman culture and, especially, into the senatorial tradition. In declaring against Nero, he saw himself as a Roman senator, acting for the Republic,[23] i.e. the 'restored' Republic of Augustus. His intention was to begin a process that would lead to the deposition of a *princeps* no longer worthy of his position and his replacement by a better man. He rose not against Rome, 'but against Nero'.[24] Nor was Vindex some politically inexperienced colonial backwoodsman.[25] To win the governorship of a major province he must have pursued an active and successful senatorial career against strong competition, funded probably by the notorious personal wealth of Gauls.[26] In the course of this career he will have made

[18] Above 294; cf. Meier 2008, 598–600.
[19] Cf. Winterling 2007, 79–80, for similar behaviour, under similar circumstances, by Gaius.
[20] Cf. above 294, 383.
[21] *Contra* Cizek 1982, 382–3; Griffin 1984, 166; Wiedemann 1996a, 250.
[22] Plut. *Galb.* 4.2. Shotter 1975, 64: 'about March 11th'.   [23] Brunt 1959, 546–7.
[24] Kraay 1949, 130, 132; Brunt 1959, 531 (quotation), 534, 543–53. Cf. Cizek 1982, 390; Drinkwater 1983, 40–1; Rudich 1993, 211; cf. above 310.
[25] *Contra* Waldherr 2005, 251: 'auswärtiger, ehedem barbarischer Fürstensohn außerhalb des römischen Adels-Netzwerkes'.
[26] Above 25; Drinkwater 1979; cf. Talbert 1984, 53–65.

many metropolitan acquaintances. This gave him a sense of Roman constitutional niceties that made him something of a semantic pioneer. After revolting, he issued coins which show him devising a legitimate means of challenging an incumbent *princeps* from the periphery. Coin-legends (with associated types) – such as *SPQR OB C[ives] S[ervatos]* ('The Senate and People of Rome. For citizens rescued from death'), *SIGNA P [opuli] R[omani]* ('The military standards of the Roman people'), *SALVS GENERIS HVMANI* ('The salvation of the human race'), and *MARS VLTOR* ('Mars the avenger') – signify that he was not acting in his own name, or even Galba's, but in that of the Republic and its armies and leaving the final decision as to a new *princeps* to the Senate and People. This tactic would be adopted by Galba and other rebels and quasi-rebels (Macer, Verginius Rufus) in 68, and initially by mutinous troops of the Upper German army in 70.[27] Vindex's constitutional self-effacement extended to his not putting his own name on his coins as moneyer, even though this was a good Republican tradition. The practice was copied by Galba but not by Macer.[28] Such caution must be taken into account in reconstructing all Vindex's actions. It was required because he should never have revolted. We do not know what drove him to take action. It could have been some triviality, perhaps a personal grudge.[29] In any case, Vindex's rebellion was a huge gamble because his immediate search for an alternative candidate shows that from the start he knew that he was not a plausible replacement *princeps* – 'a Gaul could not hope to usurp that dignity'[30] – and because he lacked the military strength to challenge praetorians and frontier armies. As governor of Lugdunensis, he commanded no legionary or auxiliary units. He should have been able to call upon the detached cohort of the Roman urban watch guarding the Lyon mint, but this was small and only paramilitary, and since Lyon turned against him even its support is unlikely.[31] His challenge to Nero became dangerous only after he called up local irregulars: the militias of communities throughout Gaul, in particular the Aedui of Lugdunensis, the Arverni of Aquitania, the Sequani of Belgica and, perhaps, the

[27] *RIC* 1² pp. 198–9; cf. Plin. *HN* 20.160; Cass. Dio 63.24.4a; Zonaras 11, 13, p. 41, 12–19 D [in Loeb Cassius Dio, pp. 176–7]. Kraay 1949, 130–1, 133–6, 137–9; Brunt 1959, 534, 537; Townend 1961, 337; Carson 1990, 18–20; Butcher and Ponting 2014, 304–5. Cf. below 394, 400, 405 (Galba, Macer, Verginius Rufus); Tac. *Hist.* 1.56. (Given Vindex's highly Augustan stance, I reject Rudich's (1993, 212) suggestion, deduced from a late garbled account by John of Antioch (Mueller fr. 91), that his ultimate aim was some sort of control over Gaul, in the manner of a 'breakaway' emperor of the third-century 'Crisis'. Cf. below 400.)

[28] Galba: Butcher and Ponting 2014, 271; Macer: below 398.   [29] Syme 1953, 34.

[30] Brunt 1959, 535.   [31] Tac. *Hist.* 1.65; Drinkwater 1983, 42, 96; Carson 1990, 19.

Allobroges of Narbonensis, all under fellow Gallic nobles.[32] This gave him muscle but made his rebellion look Gallic, and Romans had never forgotten the Gallic sack of Rome in the early fourth century BC. With the *terror Gallicus* etched deeply in their race-memory, Vindex's use of pan-Gallic levies would have made many suspect that 'a Roman senator from Gaul was still a Gallic baron', a prejudice that was to prove disastrous in his reception by the Rhine army.[33]

Despite Vindex's marginality, some modern historians see his rebellion as quickly spreading empire-wide. Noting that Tiberius Julius Alexander published his edict in the name of Galba on 6 July 68, before news of the deposition of Nero could have reached him from Rome,[34] they propose that he had become part of the plot against the *princeps*.[35] This is unnecessary. There was no early warning of Vindex's rebellion; and Alexander's support is unlikely given that the majority of military governors stayed loyal to Nero.[36] Assuming instead that Alexander, like the rest, remained loyal to Nero to the end, the 'Galbian' dating of his edict may be explained by taking into account that the text we have is a copy, set up in the Thebaid Oasis on 28 September 68, when the accession of Galba would have been known there for several weeks.[37] Though it was finalised at the start of July, the edict probably suffered substantial delay in its dissemination and publication as a result of the mass of urgent business soon caused by the change of ruler. When it arrived in the Oasis, the local *strategos* (district commissioner) faced an awkward decision: whether to publish it under its original dating, by the regnal years of the now already vilified Nero, or to amend this to the first year of Galba. Since the document professed to be about imperial concern and positive reform, he could choose the latter.[38] Egypt was too distant. Vindex desperately needed strong local backing and will not have wasted time and run greater risk of betrayal by advertising his cause throughout the Empire.[39] Those he approached were probably close neighbours: the Gallic and Spanish governors and the German army commanders.

---

[32] Joseph. *BJ* 441; Brunt 1959, 532; Drinkwater 1983, 41–2.

[33] Tac. *Ann.* 11.1.3, 1.27. Syme 1953, 34 (quotation); cf. 29, 31; Matthews 1975, 349–50; Drinkwater 1983, 7, 17, 29, 37, 42; Drinkwater 2007a, 22–6; below 402.

[34] Kolb 2000, 325–6.

[35] Above 339; e.g. Turner 1954, 60 (citing Wilcken); Brunt 1959, 536–7; Shotter 1975, 63; Bradley 1978a, 259–60; Cizek 1982, 385–6.

[36] Bradley 1978a, 259–60; cf. Bradley 1978a, 256: the possibility of opposition to Galba as close as Baetica.

[37] Barrett 1996, 143 n. 2; Cf. Kolb 2000, 325.   [38] Cf. Brunt 1959, 558.

[39] As Suet. *Galb.* 10.3.

The latter are crucial. With his acknowledged military and political experience,[40] Vindex would never have contemplated rebellion if he had not anticipated the support, or at least the acquiescence, of the Rhine generals. In this respect he showed poor judgement and, perhaps, revealed a sense of provincial prudery at Nero's conduct never shared by the majority of the political community.[41] After declaring, he was forced to call out the Gallic militias because the generals had failed to respond to his plea, but even then he probably hoped to bring them in; and he would have had his hopes confirmed by the lack of any immediate hostile action by the German commanders, especially Verginius Rufus, in charge of Upper Germany and so the nearer to Lugdunensis.[42] His rebellion was, therefore, not part of any pan-imperial movement against Nero. Since it was relatively minor, the regime will have expected it to fail and, moreover, be a good way of jolting Nero back into acting the 'good' *princeps*. Memories of the *terror Gallicus* made Vindex a worthy enemy, whose defeat would redound to the credit of the man who led it: Nero. The fact that a 'formidable army' was ready in northern Italy by Nero's death suggests that the complex process of assembling it must have begun almost immediately upon news of Vindex's revolt.[43] Its core comprised legions XIV *Gemina* and I *Italica*, and legionary detachments and auxiliary regiments from Britain, the Rhine and the middle Danube previously committed to the now-defunct Caucasus expedition and now stranded from Italy to Pannonia.[44] The northern Italian army may have been further strengthened by other detachments from the Danube;[45] and units were recalled from as far away as Egypt, though whether these arrived before Nero's death is unclear.[46] In addition, as part of the major preparations garbled by Suetonius, there was the raising of a new legion, I *Adiutrix*, from freedmen crews of the Misenum fleet.[47] The army was commanded by Petronius Turpilianus and Rubrius Gallus. Turpilianus was an experienced and capable soldier and administrator, as reflected in his appointment to the governorship of Britain after the revolt of Boudica. Though now elderly, he was no geriatric, being not much older than Corbulo had been on his death. He was a leading member of the Establishment, awarded triumphal honours for his part in suppressing the Pisonian

---

[40] Cass. Dio 63.11.1[2]. Drinkwater 1983, 40.   [41] Cf. above 310.   [42] Below 394.
[43] Syme 1937, 11 (quotation).
[44] Tac. *Hist.* 1.6, 2.11; Suet. *Ner.* 19.2. Syme 1937, 10–11; above 126, 148, 150–1, 166–7.
[45] Tac. *Hist.* 1.9.   [46] Tac. *Hist.* 1.31, 70. Syme 1937, 11.
[47] Tac. *Hist.* 1.6; Suet. *Galb.* 12.2; Plut. *Galb.* 15.3–4. Cf. Bradley 1978a, 265; Griffin 1984, 181; Champlin 2003, 3.

conspiracy and executed by Galba for being a 'Neronian general'.[48] Gallus,
who became influential under Otho, Vitellius and Vespasian, must also
have been a prominent court figure.[49]

Nero, still resident in Naples, learned of Vindex's rebellion soon after 19
March. At first, for over a week, he supposedly did nothing to counter the
threat.[50] The hostile tradition recounts that then, stung by Vindex's edicts
denouncing him as a poor lyre player and as a Domitian, not a Julio-
Claudian, he wrote to the Senate exhorting it to avenge him and pleading a
throat complaint to excuse his not speaking in person.[51] Initial indolence is
usually accepted and explained as resulting from Nero's loss of contact
with reality and 'delusions of grandeur',[52] but this ignores the brisk
military preparations. More likely is that the Establishment immediately
geared up for action while keeping Nero in Naples. There was no need for
him to attend the Senate, because this body had no direct say in the affairs
of Lugdunensis, and because in late March it was soon to begin its long
spring recess.[53] The hostile tradition continues that, at the end of March,
Nero, 'beset by message after message', 'returned to Rome in a panic'.[54]
Once arrived, he still made no direct appeal to Senate or People. Instead,
he held a meeting of his 'chief advisers' but, 'after a hasty consultation',
spent the rest of the day exhibiting a new form of water-organ and
promising a public performance.[55] A positive interpretation is that, with
preparations for the expeditionary force now well in hand, the Establishment brought Nero back to Rome ready to take nominal command. Since
there was no dire emergency, there was no need to make any appeal to
Senate and People; and it mattered little that Nero failed to concentrate on
important business at meetings of his *Consilium*. The *Consilium* could not
meet without the *princeps*,[56] but if his attendance and co-operation could
be ensured by the prospect of interesting business to follow, his counsellors
could resolve serious matters quickly at the start by rubber-stamping
decisions reached elsewhere. Discussion could then move to the technology of water-organs or the exotic side of preparations for the campaign.[57]
The *Consilium's* priority was the creation of the force destined alone to

[48] Tac. *Ann.* 15.72.2; Cass. Dio 63. 27.1a. Birley 2005, 51–2.
[49] Tac. *Hist.* 2.99; Cass. Dio 63.27.1. Bradley 1978a, 264.
[50] Suet. *Ner.* 40.4; Plut. *Galb.* 4.2. Brunt 1959, 532; Bradley 1972, 452; 1978a, 203, 249–50.
[51] Suet. *Ner.* 41.1; Cass. Dio 63.26.1.   [52] E.g. Malitz 1999, 99 (quotation).
[53] Talbert 1984, 200, 211; Barratt *et al.* 2016, 268 n. 6.
[54] Suet. *Ner.* 41.2: *sed urgentibus aliis super alios nuntiis Romam praetrepidus rediit.* Bradley 1978a, 253.
[55] Suet. *Ner.* 41.2: *quosdam e primoribus viris domum evocavit transactaque raptim consultatione*; cf.
Cass. Dio 63.26.4.
[56] Above 81.   [57] Cf. Bradley 1978a, 253–4.

defeat Vindex under Nero. The commanders of the German armies Fonteius Capito in Lower Germany and Verginius Rufus in Upper Germany will have been forbidden to move into Gaul. This will have confirmed Vindex's hopes of their eventual co-operation and explains why it took Rufus so long to destroy Vindex: it was not that his loyalty to Nero wore thin and led to a 'temporising attitude' and 'incipient disloyalty' which caused such concern at Rome that it was the prime reason for the creation of the Italian army.[58] Though, in the event, Rufus' troops forced battle on him while he was negotiating with Vindex and offered him the principate, he should not be seen as a closet traitor.[59]

15.4   Galba

Nearly all the western governors and generals had dutifully reported Vindex's seditious approaches. The exception was Galba and, interpreting his silence as treachery, the government promptly ordered his assassination: further proof that, contrary to the impression given by the sources, it was not paralysed by events.[60] This, however, drove Galba into the arms of Vindex, and at the very beginning of April he rebelled in Cartagena (Figure 1). Like Vindex, he trod a careful constitutional path, styling himself not *princeps* and *imperator* but legate of the Roman people.[61] His coinage, referencing that of Vindex, bears such legends as *OB CIVIS SERVATOS* and *MARS VLTOR* and advertises *CONCORDIA HISPANIARVM ET GALLIARVM* ('the alliance of Spain and Gaul').[62] Galba also established a body comprising probably himself, his senatorial followers and distinguished non-senatorial provincial luminaries. This, Senate-like, might appear to contradict his claim to be no more than a representative of the Senate and People of Rome, content to wait upon the passing of a senatorial *lex de imperio* that would ratify his position as the new *princeps*.[63] However, as Suetonius emphasises, it was only 'like a Senate', so no-one should have taken it as an attempt at a Senate-in-exile.[64] As with his 'praetorian guard' of young equestrians,[65] Galba convened it for

---

[58] Bradley 1978a, 256–7 (quotation), 259 (quotation), 271.
[59] Tac. *Hist.* 1.8; Plut. *Galb.* 6.2–3; Cass. Dio 63.24.2–3, 63.25. Bradley 1978a, 257; Holland 2000, 224. Below 403.
[60] Plut. *Galb.* 9.2. Bradley 1978a, 255; cf. Bradley 1978a, 256.
[61] Suet. *Galb.* 10.2–3; Plut. *Galb.* 5.2; Cass. Dio 64.6.5². Brunt 1959, 536; Shotter 1975, 65; Rudich 1993, 224; Kienast 2004, 102.
[62] *RIC* I² pp. 197–8, e.g. Civil Wars, Group I nos. 3, 15, 16.   [63] Talbert 1984, 355; above 83.
[64] Suet. *Galb.*10.2: *vel instar senatus*. Syme 1982, 470–1; cf. below 397.   [65] Suet. *Galb.* 10.3.

practical reasons, as an extended *consilium*, made up of men 'to whom he might refer matters of special importance whenever it was necessary'.[66] In addition, by consulting senior provincials, he both underlined that he was more than the head of a narrow clique and forced local leaders to commit to his cause.[67]

Galba, born on 24 December 3 BC, had just turned sixty-nine. He was a living fossil, someone who had actually met Augustus. He was, indeed, an intimate of the Julio-Claudians. Livia had adopted him and named him a major beneficiary in her will; and Agrippina II is said to have set her cap at him on her return from exile.[68] He projected himself as a moral Roman of old, but he never travelled without a cart carrying HS 1 million in gold, and his reputation for frugality as a private citizen became one for meanness as *princeps*.[69] Physically tough, he was a capable soldier and administrator, though something of a martinet.[70] True to his high breeding, he craved honour in the service of the state. This helps explain why, after completing one successful career under Claudius,[71] Galba began another under Nero when, around the year 60, he accepted the governorship of Tarraconensis.[72] This was a large and important province, with its own garrison, the core of which was legion VI *Victrix*, based at León. Galba was therefore given an important position for an extended period of time. He must have been trusted so cannot have been, like Rubellius Plautus, sent into the provinces because politically suspect.[73] A more likely explanation for his appointment is that he was to keep watch on Otho, recently ordered to Lusitania as governor.[74] Although Otho long remained loyal (he must have been one of those governors who reported Vindex), there could be no harm in having him supervised. Suetonius claims that Galba eventually neglected his duties in order to avoid arousing the suspicions of Nero,[75] but this sounds like more prejudice. It is more likely that as he got older he was simply less active. There is no indication that he had become actively disaffected. His failure to report Vindex's initial approach may be explained as resulting from weary carelessness, not nascent rebellion.[76] Galba probably had no further contact with Vindex, learning of his actual

[66] Suet. *Galb.* 10.2: *ad quos de maiore re quotiens opus esset referretur*; cf. Tac. *Hist.* 2.52–3 (on the Othonians at Mutina).

[67] Cf. Syme 1937, 10.

[68] Suet. *Galb.* 2–4,5.2; cf. Plut. *Galb.* 3.1–2. Syme 1982; Kienast 2004, 102.

[69] Suet. *Galb.* 4.4, 8.1; Plut. *Galb.* 3.1   [70] Suet. *Galb.* 6.2–3, 7.2.   [71] Suet. *Galb.* 7–8.1.

[72] Suet. *Galb.* 8.1–2, 9.1; Plut. *Galb.* 4.2.   [73] *Contra* Wiedemann 1996a, 248; above 190.

[74] Suet. *Otho* 3.2. Cf. above 97.   [75] Suet. *Galb.* 9.1.   [76] Cf. Waldherr 2005, 254.

revolt from an urgent appeal for help from the governor of Aquitania.[77] Then came more communications from Vindex offering him leadership and, decisively, his interception of instructions for his assassination. These are plausible. Galba himself was soon to order the murder of Vespasian.[78] His response is equally plausible. The death threat was unexpected, unfair and a gross impugnment of his honour. As the leader of one great *domus* it was his duty to defend it against the attack of another. But also important was the influence of ambitious third parties, a political characteristic of the period. The ambition of Vitellius was later to be encouraged by Alienus Caecina and Fabius Valens, and that of Vespasian by Licinius Mucianus.[79] In 68, the most important third parties were Vindex, Vinius and Icelus. In the last resort, it was Vinius, probably acting commander of VI *Victrix* and Galba's chief-of-staff, who prevailed on him to take the final step to rebellion.[80] In his late forties, T. Vinius Rufinus was an ambitious and well-connected but somewhat erratic senator. After a colourful military career, he had fallen into disgrace under Gaius. He recovered under Claudius, becoming an *amicus*, but again fell into disfavour. Under Nero he had done well as proconsul of Narbonensis.[81] Icelus was a senior freedman of Galba. The activities of both will be examined further below.[82] Since Galba and his advisers were no fools, they too, perhaps misinformed by Vindex, must have seen no threat in the Rhine legions.[83]

Nero will have learned of Galba's proclamation around 7 April. According to Suetonius, he fainted in despair but then recovered and continued in his luxurious lifestyle, ridiculing the revolt's leaders in 'verses set to wanton music';[84] but this is again too negative. Galba's rebellion must have caused the Establishment consternation because it complicated the political situation. However, since clearly there had been no report of Galba's assassination, revolt cannot have come as a great surprise and, like Vindex's, it posed no existential threat. Though, unlike Vindex, Galba commanded one legion, VI *Victrix,* and raised another, VII *Galbiana,*[85] even he was relatively isolated and weak. He could be contained and, after Vindex had been disposed of, crushed by the expeditionary force and the

---

[77] Suet. *Galb.* 9.2.   [78] Suet. *Galb.* 23.   [79] Tac. *Hist.* 1.52, 2.76.

[80] Plut. *Galb.* 4.4. Syme 1982, 462. Plutarch describes Vinius as 'officer commanding the military unit' (*ho tou stratēgikou tagmatos hēgemōn*), usually taken to be legion VI *Victrix.* The Loeb translation of this as 'captain of the praetorian guard' cannot be correct. In a one-legion province it was usual for the imperial legate to be both governor and commander. Galba's delegation of this to Vinius hints at how age was affecting him.

[81] Tac. *Hist.* 1.48.2–4; Plut. *Galb.* 12. Crook 1955, 48, no. 346.   [82] Below 405–6, 408, 414.

[83] Above 392.   [84] Suet. *Ner.* 42.1–2: *carmina lasciveque modulata.* Bradley 1978a, 254–6.

[85] Tac. *Hist.* 1.16, 2.11 Cf. above 395.

German armies. There was no need for panic. Suetonius' accusation that at this time Nero contemplated the assassination of all army commanders and governors, the killing of all exiles and of all people of Gallic descent in Rome, the poisoning of the Senate and the firing of Rome may be ignored. His list is just a mixture of overexcited extrapolation from Nero's other alleged depravities': an 'interruption', comprising unhistorical calumnies based on what 'Nero was thought to be capable of doing, not what he actually did'.[86] It is, again, disproved by the very small number of provincial governors and senior generals who went against the *princeps*.[87] Equally unconvincing are Suetonius' dramatic statements that by the end Nero was boasting of his limitless power and threatening total destruction of the Senate. There is no sign of a senatorial surge against Nero or in favour of Galba in Rome.[88] Galba, indeed, threatened political stability. The extent to which his 'constitutional' claims were known, understood or believed is debatable. For some, indeed, his Spanish 'senate' may have revived memories of Sertorius' Spanish 'counter-senate' of the early first century BC, the mark of the renegade.[89] Galba's insurrection and Nero's reaction to it should not be seen as any turning-point.[90] The revolt does, however, appear to have resulted in Nero's one substantial personal intervention. This was the address – read, or made in person – to the Senate, requesting it to proclaim Galba a public enemy and so enabling the regime to confiscate his property.[91] Next, according to Suetonius, Nero regained his equilibrium and, 'feeling obliged to take the field', became extraordinary sole consul, 'alleging that it was a fated thing that the Gallic provinces could not be subdued except by a consul'.[92] I propose that this was the Establishment's initiating the final stage of its plan for a Gallic campaign. The consulship had nothing to do with ancient prophecy, but it made clear that conflict was now imminent and would be fought solely under Nero's leadership. Suetonius proceeds to further substantive preparations for war in the recruitment of slaves and the levying of extraordinary taxes. He diminishes their importance 'tendentiously, in order to reflect discredit on Nero', by associating them with descriptions of Nero's drunken and

---

[86] Suet. *Ner.* 43.1. Bradley 1978a, 258 (quotations); above 99.

[87] Bradley 1978a, 258, with 260–2; Cizek 1982. 386.

[88] Suet. *Ner.* 37.3: *negavit quemquam principum scisse quid sibi liceret*; cf. Cass. Dio 63.27.2. Above 118.

[89] *OCD*⁴, 1354 (quotation).   [90] *Contra* Bradley 1978a, 255–6.

[91] Suet. *Ner.* 46.3, with Bradley 1978a, 270; Plut. *Galb.* 5.4. Above 367.

[92] Suet. *Ner.* 43.2: *credensque expeditionem necessariam ... quasi fatale esset non posse Gallias debellari nisi a consule.*

sentimental campaign plans ('he would go before the soldiers unarmed and do nothing but weep') and ridiculously theatrical preparations (including the transport of his organs and concubines, dressed as Amazons).[93] Here, however, Nero's impracticality has a ring of truth:[94] the final step was to prove much more difficult than his advisers had hoped for. Galba's rebellion was of itself not catastrophic for the Neronian regime. Far more dangerous was that by the start of May Nero had still not stirred himself to lead an army against Vindex. He dallied in Rome; his army dallied in Italy;[95] and revolt spread.

15.5   Macer

Suetonius next notes unrest in Rome, resulting from a severe wheat shortage. Dismay at the arrival of a ship from Alexandria carrying sand for the court wrestlers, not much-needed grain, deepened suspicions that the *princeps* was in some way profiting from the situation. We can immediately dismiss profiteering. The Neronian administration will have been too concerned with destroying Vindex to engage in such complex skulduggery, and the more so when it will have needed calm in the capital. Suspicion of Nero probably arose, as with the Fire, out of popular inclination to blame government for calamity.[96] More plausibly, the shortage has been linked to a third rebellion, in the military region of Numidia, led by the officer commanding legion III *Augusta* and effective governor, Clodius Macer.[97] Our principal source of information for his revolt are his coins. On these, like Vindex and Galba, Macer professed allegiance to the Republic and advertised his movement as the bringer of liberty. They differed by bearing his name, but this should not be seen as a claim to the principate. Rather, on the model of the moneyers of the Republic, it indicated his responsibility for their minting.[98] Macer seized Carthage and appears to have had designs on Sicily. This put him in the position to halt grain shipments to Rome in early spring when, following the winter closure of the Mediterranean sea-lanes, stocks were low. With African supplies interrupted, the City would need to look to Egypt, hence popular dismay over the disappointing cargo from Alexandria.[99] Bradley

---

[93] Suet. *Ner.* 43.2: *inermem se in conspectu exercituum proditurum nec quicquam aliud quam fleturum*; 44.1. Charlesworth 1950, 70–1; Bradley 1972, 452 (quotation).
[94] Above 367, below 401.   [95] Cf. Tac. *Hist.* 1.9.   [96] Above 241.
[97] Suet. *Ner.* 45.1; Bradley 1972; Morgan 2000.   [98] Cf. Morgan 2000, 478; above 390.
[99] Plut. *Galb.* 13.3; *RIC* I² pp. 188–92. Bradley 1972, 454; 1978a, 266; Hewitt 1983; Rudich 1993, 220; Morgan 2000, 481–2; Waldherr 2005, 209.

dates Macer's rebellion to 'the very end of March' because this was when, knowing of the revolt of Vindex and that food was short in Rome, he might calculate that he could starve the capital into overthrowing Nero. This puts Macer's revolt before Galba's and envisages that he acted for himself.[100] Unilateral action by Macer appears to be supported by a statement in Plutarch:[101]

> Many were now falling away from Nero, and almost all of them attached themselves to Galba; only Clodius Macer in Africa, and Verginius Rufus in Gaul . . . acted on their own account (*autoi kath' heautous epratton*), though each took a different course.

Here, however, inaccurate about the loyalty of other generals, unclear about the chronology of the revolts and questionable over the stance of Verginius Rufus, Plutarch is writing for effect, not chronological accuracy. Others are more non-committal about the date of Macer's revolt;[102] and against a rebellion in late March is the fact that this would have Macer, far distant from Vindex, acting in dangerous isolation. Though he raised more troops, including a full legion, I *Macriana*, his military strength was slight;[103] and he had neither the dynastic nor the political clout to be a plausible replacement for Nero. It is more likely that he came out after Galba,[104] and in support of him.[105] As noted, independent action by self-declared allies of political leaders is a feature of the period.[106] Although Macer was eventually destroyed by Galba,[107] this is no proof of his being Galba's opponent. He could have been removed as an embarrassing ally. As Plutarch puts it, Macer 'could neither retain nor give up his command',[108] i.e. once Nero was gone, Macer could not be left in control of Africa or found a place in the jealous circle of Galba's counsellors.[109]

---

[100] Bradley 1972, 454, 456–7 (quotation); cf. Rudich 1993, 218.

[101] Plut. *Galb.* 6. Rudich 1993, 218.   [102] E. g. *RIC* 1^2 p. 188: 'about April'.

[103] Tac. *Hist.* 1.11; 2.97; *RIC* 1^2 p. 188; Bradley 1972, 454; 1978a, 260.

[104] Brunt 1959, 537; Shotter 1975, 67.

[105] *Contra* Brunt 1959, 537. For an alternative reconstruction based on the premise that Macer did not revolt in his own name see Morgan 2000, 467–76. I reject this because: the African legion was not need for the northern army; there was anyway no possibility of its being transferred in good order in time; and Calvia Crispinilla was not qualified to make a movement order in the name of Nero.

[106] Above 396; cf. below 400: Calvia Crispinilla.   [107] Tac. *Hist.* 1.7; Plut. *Galb.* 15.2.

[108] Plut. *Galb.* 6.2: *mēte katechein mēte aphienai tēn archēn dunasthai.*

[109] Cf. Plut. *Galb.* 10.4 (jealousy between Galba and Verginius Rufus); Tac. *Hist.* 1.13, Plut. *Galb.* 7 (between Icelus and Vinius). The precise sequencing of minting at Carthage is unknown, but the presence of issues of Galba hints at the possibility that at the very end of his uprising Macer openly acknowledged the new *princeps*: cf. *RIC* 1^2 pp. 202, 215; Butcher and Ponting 2014, 269–70.

We are told that he went because he abused his powers.[110] Such abuse may have been discerned in the fact that towards the end he put his own image on his coins.[111] However, even then he adopted no imperial title and, if his image did cause offence, it was probably just one in a list of misdeeds created from distortion of his actions. Chief among these must have been his 'starving' of Rome. Though he had the power to do so, it is most unlikely that he deployed it since he would thereby have hurt the Senate and People in whose name he professed to act. If there was a *fames* at this time, it was probably caused by a normal seasonal shortage exacerbated by private hoarding and profiteering on the scare of an African embargo. Plutarch in fact says that after the fall of Nero, the famine caused by Macer figured among other gross untruths told by Nymphidius Sabinus to Galba to dissuade him from hastening to Rome.[112] It is significant that all our literary sources associate Macer's killing with that of Fonteius Capito, commanding the military district of Lower Germany, never involved in revolt. Tacitus says that both executions were unfavourably received in Rome.[113] The new regime was ridding itself of embarrassing friends and potential enemies. Vindex would probably have suffered the same fate had he survived.

Acceptance of Macer as Galba's long-distance ally makes more understandable the activities of Calvia Crispinilla. According to Tacitus, it was she who crossed to Africa to instigate Macer to revolt and to threaten Rome with starvation.[114] Crispinilla, wardrobe mistress of Sporus/ 'Poppaea', was much more influential and politically astute than Macer.[115] She will have had knowledge of the secrets of Nero's bedchamber and of how the *princeps* was regarded at court. She was therefore well placed to realise before most that Nero would never produce a blood heir and that he would never lead his troops to victory over Vindex. Thus, probably immediately after she had heard the news of Galba's rebellion, she decided to support him by prevailing upon Macer to bring Africa out against Nero. She survived Macer's fall because, as a female, she posed no direct political threat to Galba who, followed by Otho and Vitellius,

---

[110] Tac. *Hist.* 1.11; Plut. *Galb.* 6.2.   [111] *RIC* 1² pp. 189, 191 nos. 32–42; Hewitt 1983, 66.
[112] Plut. *Galb.* 13.3. Cf. below 408; Morgan 2000, 485.
[113] Tac. *Hist.* 1.7; Suet. *Galb.* 11; Plut. *Galb.* 15.2.
[114] Tac. *Hist.* 1.73: *transgressa in Africam ad instigandum in arma Clodium Macrum, famem populo Romano haud obscure molita.*
[115] Above 164, 231.

actually made a point of protecting her.[116] Her desertion of Nero is of significance as the first crack in the edifice of loyalty of the court Establishment.

According to Suetonius, resentment at the corn shortage led to a collapse in Nero's popularity in Rome and cruel lampooning of the *princeps*. Suetonius further implies that it was now that Nero, terrified by nightmares and omens, finally appealed directly to the Senate, castigating Vindex.[117] The suggestion is that Macer's revolt was another turning-point, as Nero finally lost his nerve. All this is more distortion.[118] The food shortage was awkward, but no disaster. Nero had suffered occasional losses of public goodwill – for example, as a result of his treatment of Octavia and of rumours concerning his involvement in the Fire – but had always recovered it, and to the end and beyond he was generally well regarded by the Roman people. He could take the lampoons,[119] and his senatorial address was probably that made earlier, to get Galba declared a public enemy.[120] While Macer's revolt will have been worrying, it was again, like those of Vindex and Galba, no killer blow. There was still the prospect of an easy but memorable victory over Vindex in Gaul, after which Galba and Macer could be mopped up at will. Nero failed just by staying the same. The torpor that had gripped him following his triumph continued. His one remaining major enthusiasm, his fixation on Poppaea,[121] caused him to neglect Statilia Messalina and so fail to produce an heir. As for the Gallic expedition that could save his reputation, Nero did not want to go to war and was more concerned with the musical performances at the victory games to follow than with the practicalities of fighting.[122] This was his last, fatal, 'break-out'.[123] It convinced the Establishment that he was no longer up to the job of being *princeps* and would have to be removed.

15.6 Verginius Rufus

Nero's removal was accelerated by an event that, at first appearance, should have saved him. In Gaul, Verginius Rufus destroyed Vindex and his army of irregulars at the battle of Vesontio (Besançon: Figure 1).[124] By mid-68, both Roman commanders on the Rhine will have been under an enormous pressure of expectation from their men. They were in charge of troops who

---

[116] Tac. *Hist.* 1.73. Bradley 1972, 455–6; cf. above 399 n. 107 and Morgan 2000, 469, 478, 483, 486–7.
[117] Suet. *Ner.* 45.2–46.3.   [118] Cf. above 397–8.   [119] Above 106.   [120] Above 397.
[121] E.g. Cass. Dio 63.26.4. Champlin 2003, 2.   [122] Above 397–8.   [123] Above 168.
[124] Plut. *Galb.* 6.3; Cass. Dio 63.24; Drinkwater 1983, 42–3.

had seen others gain glory and booty on the Danube, in Britain and in the East, under generals who had been allowed free rein. They, in contrast, had been allowed to accomplish nothing of note.[125] In the spring of 68 the Rhenish troops saw a Gallic rebel on their doorstep: a male Boudica and a clear embodiment of the *terror Gallicus*.[126] They were mistaken, but such was their prejudice that, even if they had been aware of his constitutional aims, it is likely that they would have ignored them. As Tacitus was to put into the mouths of other Roman soldiers about a later provincial rebel, 'It was not for a turncoat to sit in judgement on matters Roman'.[127] Indeed, while providing sufficient information in the 'Histories' to support the idea of Vindex as a senatorial opponent of Nero, Tacitus himself projects him as a Gallic rebel who, with chiefs as his henchmen, waged outright war on Rome.[128] The troops on the Rhine must have expected to be ordered immediately into battle; but this did not happen. Key to my interpretation of Neronian strategy in respect of Vindex – that his suppression was to be reserved for an imperial expedition – is that initially both Verginius and Fonteius stayed away from the conflict. From the troops' viewpoint, Fonteius' behaviour will have seemed strange; but they must have been baffled by that of Verginius Rufus. His area of command had close links to important Gallic communities which had refused to follow Vindex and which must have looked to him for aid.[129] Even more, he had a duty to go to the aid of those besieged by Vindex in Lyon (Figure 1), a Roman colony and the capital of both Lugdunensis and the Three Gauls,[130] But Rufus did nothing, encouraging Vindex to see him as a secret sympathiser.[131] The extent of his inaction is indicated by the fact that he did not secure the town of Vesontio, which controlled access from the Rhine to central Gaul.[132] Rufus' failure even to gather necessary intelligence is reflected in his surprise when, after eventually calling up reinforcements from Lower Germany and moving on Vesontio, he found it closed against him.[133] Though this advance, probably at the behest of his men and the besieged of Lyon, will have been against orders, he might legitimately claim that it was a limited manoeuvre taken to keep Gaul open and maintain the spirits

[125] Tac. *Hist.* 1.51. Drinkwater 2007a, 22.   [126] Above 391.

[127] Tac. *Hist.* 4.21: *proinde perfuga ... abitrium rerum Romanarum ne ageret.*

[128] Tac. *Hist.* 1. 70: *bellum Vindicis,* 2.94: *duces Galliarum;* 4.57. Drinkwater 1983, 49; cf. Brunt 1959, 544–5.

[129] In particular, the Treveri and Lingones: Tac. *Hist.* 1.53.   [130] Tac. *Hist.* 1.65.

[131] Above 392.   [132] Syme 1953, 28; Drinkwater 1983, 43, 126; cf. 87.

[133] Cass. Dio 63.24.1. Brunt 1959, 537.

of Vindex's opponents. Then, however, he lost control and found himself fighting and defeating Vindex.

The story is told briefly by Cassius Dio and Plutarch.[134] Dio says that, under siege by Rufus, Vesontio called on Vindex for aid. Vindex arrived, camped near Rufus, made contact with him and then met him to strike a secret deal against Nero. As part of this deal, Vindex began to move his troops through Roman lines into the town. However, the Roman forces, interpreting this as an attack, spontaneously fought and defeated them. Vindex committed suicide. Rufus mourned his death but rejected the demands of his troops that he should become *princeps*. According to Plutarch, his troops offered Rufus the principate before the battle, and they and those of Vindex forced their leaders into a fight they did not want. After the battle, Rufus' men again unsuccessfully tried to get him to become *princeps*. Much has been made of the communication between Vindex and Verginius on the grounds that this signifies that Rufus had in principle turned against Nero.[135] However, Dio is careful to distinguish between initial communications, which must have occurred as Vindex sought to determine Rufus' intentions, and concrete negotiation and agreement, which he describes 'as conjecture'.[136] Since, following Syme, I believe that Rufus stayed loyal to Nero,[137] I propose a different reconstruction of events.

Rufus, rejected by Vesontio, found himself in an awkward position. He could not withdraw, since his men would have objected and withdrawal would have sent the wrong signal to Lyon. On the other hand, he could not ignore orders and attack the place even though it was a very easy target.[138] His only option was to stay where he was and await the outcome of events. Vindex, perhaps with his headquarters in Vienne (Figure 1), and perhaps participating in the blockade of Lyon, interpreted Rufus' inaction as a sign that he was about to declare for the rebels. Vindex therefore took his own army to join up with Rufus'. Vindex's arrival put Rufus in an even more awkward position, since he was under instruction not to engage him. He held back; and Vindex did not attack his prospective ally. The proximity of the two leaders, their common inactivity and awareness of communication between them produced rumours of negotiation. This became intolerable for the Roman soldiers, restrained for too long and

---

[134] Cass. Dio 63.24.1–25.1; Plut. *Galb.* 6.2–3.
[135] E.g. Kraay 1949, 18; Brunt 1959, 538; Rudich 1993, 214.
[136] Cass. Dio 63.24.2: *hōs eikazeto.* Townend 1961, 337.   [137] Syme 1953, 27; 1958, i.179.
[138] Cf. Drinkwater 1983, 151.

with the enemy in full view; they attacked without orders. The 'prevailing tradition' that the battle of Vesontio was an accident is correct.[139]

Rufus survived the fall of Nero and the civil war of 69–70, died in 97 aged eighty-three and was one of the last private individuals to be decreed a state funeral.[140] Yet his victory at Vesontio blighted his subsequent career, and to the end he was defensive of his achievement. His sensitivity was observed in a famous altercation with the historian, Cluvius Rufus. When Cluvius apologised to him for preferring truth to friendship in his account of the events of the period, Verginius replied:[141]

> *Tunc ignoras, Cluvi, ideo me fecisse quod feci, ut esset liberum vobis scribere quae libuisset?* (Don't you realise, Cluvius, that I did what I did so that the rest of you should be at liberty to write as you please?)

It was seen as even more powerfully expressed in the verses he composed as his epitaph:

> *Hic situs est Rufus, pulso qui Vindice quondam Imperium adseruit, non sibi sed patriae.* (Rufus is buried here, who, Vindex having been defeated, [did something to do with] the Empire to/for the fatherland, not himself.)[142]

Pliny II admires these lines so much that he cites them twice, verbatim; and Dio gives a close indirect quotation.[143] As befits a leading Neronian, they were clearly considered elegant and clever.[144] They are, however, as the problems in their translation show, like Verginius Rufus' retort to Cluvius, hugely enigmatic; and both retort and epitaph have provoked much discussion. I propose that Rufus' words reveal that in the post-Neronian world he found himself under two major charges. The first, immediate and simple, was that by defeating Vindex he had come close to keeping Nero in power.[145] The second, later and complex, was that his contention that this victory put the fate of the Empire into his hands was mistaken. It arose because Rufus, by maintaining that in 68 he had resisted the demands of his troops to take the purple and had instead deferred to the decision of the Senate, might appear morally superior to Vespasian, who in 69 did quite the opposite: 'Verginius' *gran rifiuto* ... was a permanent reproach to the man who had yielded to ambition and

---

[139] So Bradley 1978a, 257 (quotation); *contra* Rudich 1993, 216.
[140] Plin. *Ep.* 2.1–4. Talbert 1984, 370–1.   [141] Plin. *Ep.* 9.19.5.
[142] Trans. after Rudich 1993, 216.   [143] Plin. *Ep.* 6.10.4; 9.19.1; Cass. Dio 68.24.
[144] Above 373.   [145] Cf. Syme 1958, i.179; Shotter 2008, 163–4.

presented the senate with an accomplished fact'.[146] Rufus' uncompromising response was that he did right in destroying a Gallic rebel, and that after Vesontio he had, indeed, 'acquired' (*adseruit*) the Empire, but had not held on to it. Whom should we believe? Though Cluvius Rufus has attracted criticism as an historian,[147] he may well be correct in his negative judgement of Verginius Rufus if, before Vesontio, Verginius Rufus simply lost control of his men and, after it, he was a crypto-Neronian, concealing but never renouncing his loyalty to the Julio-Claudian line and ready to declare it again if permitted.[148] He will again have been under tremendous pressure. As his entourage must have included some urging him to take the purple, it contained others badgering him to give it to Galba.[149] His solution was to prevaricate by, like Vindex, Galba and Macer, leaving the decision to the Senate.[150] If Galba fell – which, after Vesontio, was highly likely – the only person that the Senate (in effect, the praetorians) could 'choose' was Nero, already in post. He further lengthened the odds on Nero's overthrow by rejecting Galba's desperate pleas for an alliance.[151] It is in this context of studied inaction that we may place Rufus' rejection of overtures from part, though by no means all, of the north Italy army,[152] whether these came before or, more likely, after news of Nero's death.[153] In terms of making the right things happen, Verginius Rufus was, indeed, no equal of Vespasian.

15.7 Desertion

After hearing of the disaster at Vesontio and being spurned by Verginius Rufus, Galba and his closest associates retreated to Clunia, deep in the mountainous hinterland of Tarraconensis, 488 km (*c.* 290 statute miles) from the provincial capital of Tarragona (Figure 1). Though loyal, the place was unsuitable as the headquarters of insurrection.[154] Galba could not anyway have expected to linger there for long.[155] His lieutenants would have demanded action one way or the other – recovery or death – and Galba was on the brink of suicide.[156] Awareness of this, together with personal ambition, explains the hasty return of Icelus and Vinius to Spain

---

[146] Joseph. *BJ* 4, 601–4; Tac. *Hist.* 2.80. Townend 1961, 339 (quotation); Talbert 1984, 354; Levick 1999a, 43, 47, 67; Kienast 2004, 106, 108.
[147] Townend 1961, 338–9.   [148] Townend 1961, 330; cf. Syme 1953, 27.
[149] Tac. *Hist.* 2.71.2. Syme 1982, 468, 477.   [150] Plut. *Galb.* 6.2, 10.2. Above 398.
[151] Plut. *Galb.* 6.4.   [152] Tac. *Hist.* 1.9: *Verginium legationibus adissent.*
[153] Before: Brunt 1959, 540; after: Syme 1982, 467; cf. below 410.
[154] Suet. *Galb.* 9.2. Kolb 2000, 322.   [155] Cf. Kraay 1949, 129, n. 5.   [156] Suet. *Galb.* 11.1.

with the news of Nero's fall and of Galba's acceptance by praetorians and Senate.[157] Delay could have destroyed them all. Such considerations are important in establishing the date of the battle of Vesontio. This is much disputed,[158] but the likeliest approximation is early/mid-May, allowing Galba around a month to declare himself and face mutiny and a second assassination attempt before hearing of Vindex's destruction.[159] More specifically, a date in early/mid-May suits a relatively short stay in Clunia. We may suppose that Galba contemplated remaining there for no more than a few weeks, and that by the time Icelus reached him these were almost at an end. We know that Galba first heard of events in Rome seven days after Nero's death, so around 16 June.[160] If he had arrived in Clunia about, say, four weeks earlier, around 20 May, he would have left the coast about 14 May.[161] Allowing about four days for the news of Vesontio to reach him on the coast, we can date the battle to around 10 May. This chronology requires that Verginius Rufus took over two months to crush Vindex, which is crucial to the understanding of the last weeks of Nero.

The battle of Vesontio was a disaster for Galba, but was an even greater disaster for Nero. According to Suetonius, Nero was immensely cheered by 'good news from the provinces', which must have reported the annihilation of Vindex.[162] He will have been delighted not only because Verginius' victory removed one rebel and seriously compromised the position of the remaining two, but also because it relieved him of the burden of a Gallic campaign. He could now resume his sporting and artistic round. The Neronian Establishment, on the other hand, will have taken a very different view. Rufus' victory had destroyed Nero's last chance of political redemption. The *princeps* and the northern army could have defeated Vindex perhaps as early as early April. This might have prevented the revolts of Galba and Macer but, even if it did not, Nero, having shown himself a true heir of Caesar and Germanicus, could have left both to others. But Nero never entered Gaul. The significance of Rufus' long delay is that it is a damning measure of the length of time Nero wasted in Rome

---

[157] Plut. *Galb.* 7.1. Cf. above 399 n. 109.

[158] E.g. Cf. Kraay 1949, 129, n. 5; Brunt 1959, 541; Shotter 1975, 69; Bradley 1978a, 257–8; Cizek 1982, 398; Griffin 1984, 181; Waldherr 2005, 258.

[159] Suet. *Galb.* 10.2–5.   [160] Plut. *Galb.* 7. Below 413.

[161] Cf. Kolb 2000, 322 for express times. I assume that Galba's train would have taken longer.

[162] Suet. *Ner.* 42.2: *prosperi quiddam ex provinciis nuntiatum.* Bradley 1978a, 257; *contra* Malitz 1999, 105.

because he did not want to play the general. This was his last, fatal, break-out.[163] As a result, the political situation became very complex. Verginius Rufus remained secretly loyal but, unable out of fear of those around him publicly to endorse Nero, was bound very quickly to be regarded with deep suspicion. Furthermore, even though Rufus had turned down the offer of the principate from his troops, the fact that this had been made will have raised doubts about the allegiance of all the main frontier armies.[164] Tacitus' 'secret of empire', or rather 'the dangerous truth' that everyone knew but 'anxiously covered up', was now revealed: a *princeps* did not have to be made in Rome.[165] Rufus posed no immediate threat; and if he was troublesome, Fonteius Capito could be ordered against him from Lower Germany. On the other hand, there was now the possibility of the emergence of a fresh contender, backed by another frontier army. The position was not immediately critical: in 68 the Empire was not a powder keg ready to explode in hostility to Nero.[166] There was, however, a new political situation which, if left uncontrolled, might threaten continuity, careers, fortunes and lives. A moment of decision had been reached. With Nero's irresponsibility making him a lost cause, and with no direct heir to bring on to replace him, the Establishment had just one course of action: to abandon the last Julio-Claudian *princeps* and to agree terms with a newcomer.[167] In 41, the Julio-Claudian dynasty had survived the fall of Gaius because there was a blood heir and 'hostility towards the imperial house was dwarfed by the inability of individual senators to stomach the prospect of a colleague taking over'.[168] In mid-68 there was no heir but, in Galba, an external candidate with whom those in charge felt they must do business.

Regime change, the formal renunciation by the political community of its acceptance of Nero's principate,[169] was a massive gamble but offered the Establishment the best chance of managing events. It came about astonishingly quickly. On my chronology, Nero died around only three weeks after the news of Vesontio reached Rome.[170] Furthermore, he was destroyed 'more by messages and rumours than by arms', before any enemy had crossed the Alps.[171] Equally remarkable is that both his fall and Galba's succession were engineered by interested third parties[172]

---

[163] Above 168; cf. Malitz 1999, 102.   [164] Cf. Waldherr 2005, 259.
[165] Tac. *Hist.* 1.4. Above 66; Syme 1953, 26 (quotations).
[166] *Contra* Cizek 1982, 381–9; Shotter 2008, 110.   [167] Cf. Grant 1970, 245.
[168] Barrett 1996, 71.   [169] Flaig 2011, 278, 280–1.   [170] Cf. above 406.
[171] Tac. *Hist.* 1.89: *nuntiis magis et rumoribus quam armis.* Henderson 1905, 405.
[172] Cf. above 396.

working in the capital but without the knowledge of the people of Rome (who played a remarkably passive role in events[173]) or ordinary praetorian soldiers, and without the direct participation of senior military commanders; the role of the army, for the most part still loyal to Nero, was minimal.[174] Those responsible comprised intimates, guard commanders, senior *liberti* and senior senators,[175] but the most important were the praetorian prefects, since without their approval nothing could have happened. It is significant, however, that Tigellinus, perhaps pleading illness, real or diplomatic,[176] was overtaken in importance by Nymphidius Sabinus, plainly determined not to be brought down in any political crash.[177] On the other hand, as is shown by his subsequent protection by Galba, Tigellinus did not oppose change, and so betrayed Nero as much as Sabinus.[178] The matching principal on the other side was Galba's freedman, Icelus, detained in Rome at the start of the Spanish insurrection. His presence allowed both parties speedily to agree terms. These are striking for the high number of leading Neronians they allowed to survive the fall of their patron, another example of important figures being 'too big to fail'.[179] Particular elements of agreement may be reconstructed from subsequent events:

(a)   Galba was accepted as Nero's successor.
(b)   He was to take over the Empire as quickly as possible.
(c)   To this end, the two generals commanding the north Italian army were to be invited (since none of the conspirators was in a position to give them direct orders) to take their forces off a war footing and not to impede Galba's progress to Rome from Spain. (There was in principle no reason why Rubrius Gallus and Petronius Turpilianus should be unwilling to accept an armistice, since the purpose of their expedition was gone and Rufus was no threat. Though Gallus proved happy to oblige, Turpilianus was more hesitant. His eventual compliance, in the face of some opposition from his troops, was the final piece of bad news for Nero, but he paid a high price for his hesitation, being executed by Galba as a 'Neronian general'.[180])

---

[173]   *Contra* Flaig 2011, 288.   [174]   Cf. Grant 1970, 246; Shotter 2008, 164; *contra* Cizek 1982, 290.
[175]   Cf. above 58.   [176]   Plut. *Otho* 2.1. Cizek 1982, 197.
[177]   Brunt 1959, 541–2; Cizek 1982, 399; Rudich 1993, 234; Waldherr 2005, 259–60.
[178]   Tac. *Hist.* 1.72; Waldherr 2005, 260.
[179]   Rudich 1993, 231–2; cf. Henderson 1905, 418; above 367.
[180]   Tac. *Hist.* 1.6: *dux Neronis*, 2.11; Cass. Dio 63.27.1a. Rudich 1993, 232.

(d)   Nymphidius Sabinus was to promise the main body of praetorians a large donative in return for their abandonment of Nero and acceptance of Galba. The high cost of this, at HS 30,000 per man, was to be met by Galba.[181] Their acceptance of the bribe made this 'the first time that the rank and file of the unit as a whole had forsworn their oath and deserted an emperor'.[182]

(e)   No-one knew how to end a dynasty and put an entirely new *princeps* in charge.[183] The 'wrong' end for Nero might produce a martyr and, knowing their half-baked Principate (especially, the fate of Cassius Chaerea, executed for the assassination of Gaius), those involved will have been aware that, even in what was still constitutionally a republic, regicide was perilous. The Neronian Establishment was therefore charged with destroying Nero in a way that would cause minimum embarrassment for themselves and the incoming regime, beginning with his peaceful removal from the City at the earliest possible opportunity.

(f)   Immediately after the abandonment of Nero by the praetorians and his removal from Rome, the Senate was to condemn him and acclaim Galba.[184] Galba was to become one of the *consules ordinarii* of 69.[185]

(g)   Tigellinus was to be pensioned off, but Nymphidius Sabinus was to be retained as Galba's senior praetorian prefect.

(h)   There was to be no general witch-hunt of Neronians among his family or intimates (so, no action against the 'wily' Statilia[186] – apparently now having prudently removed herself from Rome – or Sporus), or among senators and equestrians who had served the regime. This condition, generally respected, explains subsequent dismay over Galba's summary execution of Turpilianus.

(i)   There was, however, to be sacrifice of some leading *liberti*. Those involved in the negotiations and in managing the death of Nero, such as Ephaproditus and Phaon,[187] were to be spared and protected. Others, less complicit but influential and useful, such as Claudius of Smyrna, also survived.[188] On the other hand, many of those who had recently incurred aristocratic hatred were to be killed, in particular Helius and his associates, Patrobius, Petinus and Polyclitus.[189] A further victim was possibly another Narcissus. Such unlucky *liberti*

---

[181] Plut. *Galb.* 2.2.   [182] Below 412; Bingham 2013, 32 (quotation).
[183] Cf. Grant 1970, 249 and n. 19.   [184] Suet *Ner.* 48.2, 49.2.   [185] Kienast 2004, 102.
[186] Cizek 1982, 181: 'Elle savait ruser'.
[187] Below 413; cf. Henderson 1905, 496; Bradley 1978a, 275, 278–9.
[188] Crook 1955, 52; cf. above 363.   [189] Plut. *Galb.* 17.2; above 229.

are likely to have been those sent on a wild goose chase to Ostia.[190] However, for reasons unknown, unpopular Neronian *liberti* such as Halotus and Coenus were protected by Galba,[191] perhaps as clients of Icelus.

(j)   Until Galba's arrival, Rome was to be run by an interim adminis-
       tration under Nymphidius Sabinus.

One major issue which must certainly have surfaced at this time, but which was ominously left unresolved, was, given Galba's age and childless-ness, that of who was to succeed him.

15.8   Death

Probably the first inkling that Nero had of the movement against him was on the day before his death, when he learned of the defection of 'other armies', i.e. the units assembled to face Vindex: the northern army.[192] The sources then tell a very dramatic tale of Nero's panic-stricken reaction: his uncharacteristic destruction of rare *objets d'art*; his procuring poison for possible suicide; his moving his residence to the Servilian Gardens; his preparations for flight overseas; his consideration of going as a suppliant to Galba, of addressing the People to ask them for forgiveness or of appoint-ment to the prefecture of Egypt; and his ever more rapid desertion by his supporters.[193] Some of this rings true; Nero's sudden discovery that his own supporters had begun to turn against him must have been devastating, especially so soon after the good news of Vesontio, and he would reason-ably have sought to evade the consequences.[194] Much, however, smacks of prejudice and exaggeration, and we should not too readily follow its suggestion that Nero and his remaining supporters immediately accepted impending defeat. We can reconstruct his entourage during his move to the Servilian Gardens. These were: Sporus/'Poppaea'; most of his senior *liberti*; a number of *amici*; the duty praetorian cohort of the watch; and all or part of the German guards, under Spiculus.[195] Though the sources do not mention the *Augustiani*, we may assume that elements of these were also in attendance. In short, Nero was still accompanied by his court and,

---

[190] Cass. Dio 64.3.4. Below 411; Bradley 1978a, 272.   [191] Suet. *Galb.* 15.2; Tac. *Hist.* 2.54.
[192] Suet. *Ner.* 47.1: *ceteri exercitus*; cf. Cass. Dio 63.27.2. Brunt 1959, 541; Grant 1970, 246; Bradley 1978a, 271. (*Contra* Brunt 1959, 540: that some units had moved into Gaul; cf. Chilver 1979, 11; Syme 1982, 467.)
[193] Suet. *Ner.* 47.1–2; Plin. *HN* 37.29. Bradley 1978a, 271–2.   [194] Cf. Holland 2000, 225.
[195] *Contra* Bellen 1981, 92: that Spiculus, together with half the Batavian guard, remained in their camp.

the sign and instrument of power, by numerous men-at-arms who obeyed his commands and compelled others to do likewise. With the metropolitan plotters still to show themselves and so, as far as Nero was concerned, with the nearest threat in northern Italy, he might legitimately consider himself, and be considered by others, as the incumbent *princeps*. His transfer from the Palatine to the Servilian Gardens indicates how he still had freedom of movement and so access to a range of options. His loyal followers might have reasonable hopes of enabling him to survive the immediate crisis. Their solution was to leave Italy and the West and sail to Alexandria, already prepared as an imperial residence.[196]

The move to the Servilian Gardens, probably near the main road to Ostia,[197] appears to have been in anticipation of this. Though Suetonius indirectly ridicules the idea of an eastern flight by associating it with other, clearly hare-brained schemes,[198] it was brilliant in its simplicity. It would have immediately put Nero beyond the reach of the rebels and placed him under the protection of the loyal Tiberius Julius Alexander and Vespasian.[199] It was probably devised by those trusted *liberti* who were not part of the metropolitan plot, a number of whom, perhaps encouraged by those who were, went ahead to Ostia to arrange passage.[200] Likewise, Nero's failed effort to persuade the praetorians to join the enterprise should not be regarded as an act of foolish desperation. The meeting was not of itself a sign of weakness. It was fitting that praetorians should be asked to continue to protect the *princeps* during an unprecedented evacuation and proper that they should be assured about the withdrawal from Rome by the head of the *domus* which had created them and which they had served so loyally in the past. There was as yet no sign of mutiny in this quarter. The fact that Nero (probably, as ever, on the advice of his loyal counsellors) approached centurions and tribunes rather than prefects is no proof that he was aware of the duplicity of Tigellinus and Nymphidius Sabinus.[201] He might well have interpreted their absence as the result of, respectively, illness and attention to duty in difficult times. That other senior praetorian officers were willing to talk to him without obvious hostility (they did not kill him or arrest him) would further have confirmed his belief in the continuation of the status quo. Finally, we do not know

---

[196] Above 221; cf. Cass. Dio 63.27.2.

[197] Grant 1970, 246; Bradley 1978a, 272; cf. Winterling 2009, 83–4. *Contra* Cizek 1982, 399: from the Golden House.

[198] Suet. *Ner.* 47.2.   [199] Cf. above 391; cf. Holland 2000, 226; *contra* Bradley 1978a, 271.

[200] Suet. *Ner.* 47.2. Cf. above 410, below 413; Holland 2000, 226.

[201] *Contra* Bradley 1978a, 272–3; Cizek 1982, 399.

how these officers rejected the eastern scheme. Again, it is unlikely that they were obviously mutinous. Suetonius reports that only one of them urged Nero to give up and accept death, and even this is likely to be a literary flourish.[202] They may simply have pointed out the practical difficulties and urged Nero to take more time.

This is what the plotters needed. If Nero got away, all their plans would be ruined. They had to act quickly, and they were lucky that Nero, typically, prevaricated when it came to foreign travel and retired early to bed, probably still at the Servilian Gardens.[203] Over an evening of frenetic activity, the plotters worked to suborn his household. It was then that Sabinus showed his hand and, no doubt through their officers, bought the loyalty of Praetorians and Germans with tales of Nero's abandonment of them and the promise of generous donatives in the name of Galba.[204] It seems that Spiculus remained faithful to Nero and was deposed by his own men.[205] It is likely that the *Augustiani* were intimidated into desertion by the actions of the Praetorians and Germans: they would have had no stomach for standing alone. So Nero awoke around midnight to find all his guards – praetorians, *Germani* and *Augustiniani* – his *amici* and most of his attendants gone, the last having stripped his quarters of valuables. The sources stress the absence of an armed escort, the most telling sign of Nero's collapse in status.[206] With his loyal *liberti* presumably detained in Ostia, he was now wholly in the plotters' grasp. Now, probably for the first time, he became aware of the desperation of his position and may, again for the first time, have contemplated suicide. Finding his poison stolen by the defectors, and with no-one available to give him the coup de grâce, he considered death by drowning, but this was not in his nature. He lived on, and something else had to be done with him. He had to be destroyed but his destruction could not be perpetrated in Rome, which was needed for the Senate to declare against Nero and for Galba.[207] Nero's continued presence in the City, whether living or dead, might cause difficulties with the troops or the people. Phaon, who owned a villa four miles out of the city, persuaded Nero that he could safely hide and review his situation there. Suetonius gives a short but memorable account of

---

[202] Suet. *Ner.* 47.2.   [203] Bradley 1978a, 274; Champlin 2003, 4.
[204] Plut. *Galb.* 2.1–2; Bellen 1981, 92; Rudich 1993, 235.
[205] Suet. *Ner.* 43.3; Joh. Ant. Fr. 91, 23–35 (though, like Cass. Dio 63.27.2b, followed by Talbert 1984, 383, making the Senate the main agent in all this).
[206] Suet. *Ner.* 47.3; Cass. Dio 63.27.3; cf. Joseph. *BJ* 4.493. Bradley 1978a, 274–5; Bellen 1981, 93.
[207] Cf. Plut. *Galb.* 7.1.

Nero's terrifying night-flight northeastwards by the praetorian camp.
Nero was accompanied by Phaon himself, his *a rationibus*, Epaphroditus, his *a libellis*, Sporus/'Poppaea' and one Neophytus (named only in
a later source).[208] He was lured out of the capital by people he wrongly
considered still loyal, in a direction 'diametrically opposed to the Ostian
route'.[209] In the meantime, praetorians and Senate were declaring him a
hostis publicus, and formally accepting Galba as their new *princeps*.[210]
The one major figure whom we certainly know was never allowed a fair
trial under Nero was Nero himself.[211] Arrived at Phaon's villa, Nero's
party initially had difficulties in entering and Phaon suggested that
Nero hide 'in a pit'.[212] Having gained entry, they found themselves
poorly accommodated in the basement of the property.[213] 'Here was an
emperor who no longer commanded obedience, an emperor at last
bereft of his power ... Yet only a few hours, a few days, earlier,
thousands upon thousands of people had stood prepared to do [his]
bidding ...'[214] Wiedemann believes that by now Nero had 'lost his
nerve and effectively abandoned the administration of affairs',[215] but
this is too negative. Nero might think that his party, made up of two
key imperial secretaries and his 'empress', still constituted the core of a
functioning administration.[216] Used to being guided by others, he may
have believed that he was being helped to escape to a place from which
he might challenge Galba.[217]

It was now 9 June, the commonly accepted date of Nero's death.[218]
Nero, finally grasping that he must soon perish and at the urging of
companions whom he still believed were protecting him, contemplated
suicide for a second time and prepared for his subsequent cremation
and burial. He instructed his party to prepare a makeshift pyre and grave
and while he watched them he uttered his famous lament, 'What an
artist perishes in me!'[219] The force of 'artist' – in Latin, as in English, a
very loose term – has been hotly debated. As Reitz says, the essence of

---

[208] Suet. *Ner.* 48.1, 49.3–4; *Epit.* 5.7.
[209] Bradley 1978a, 276 (quotation); Holland 2000, 227–8; Reitz 2006, 138; Ranieri Pannetta 2011,
   29 figure 2.
[210] Suet. *Ner.* 48.2.   [211] Cf. above 325.   [212] Suet. *Ner.* 48.3: *in specum*.
[213] Suet. *Ner.* 48.4.   [214] Lendon 1997, 1.   [215] Wiedemann 1996b, 261.
[216] *Contra* Mordine 2013, 116: he was left only with 'the least distinguished and inconsequential'.
[217] Cf. Bradley 1978a, 273.
[218] A case may be made for 11 June: Bradley 1972, 452; Cizek 1982, 400; Champlin 2003, 5 n. 9, 49.
   See further Bradley 1978a, 274, 292–3; Kienast 2004, 97.
[219] Suet. *Ner.* 49.1: *qualis artifex pereo*; cf. Cass. Dio 63.29.2: *hoios technitēs parapollumai*.

discussion is whether he was commenting on his whole life or on his specific circumstances on 9 June. Cizek has him recalling his lifetime project to create a spectacular new world order. Bradley, more tightly focused, considers a possible reference to 'performer' or 'showman' but prefers an 'aesthetic context'. In this vein, Malitz very specifically proposes an allusion to his career as a citharode. Champlin, on the other hand, proposes that 'craftsman' best suits the immediate context, as Nero lamented that he, a great artist, had become a mere artisan.[220] This takes us in the right direction, but 'artisan' is not grand enough for Nero, even at the end. *Artifex* was probably a wry comment on his current situation: directing the fashioning of his own a grave from whatever materials lay to hand. 'Designer' seems its most apt translation. Striking here is the absence of any reference to divine status.[221] Nero, always the procrastinator, did not, however, proceed to kill himself. Though terrified to read in a letter then delivered to Phaon that he had been declared a public enemy and had been condemned to a horrifying death, he still hesitated, reproaching himself for cowardice. It was only when he heard the approach of horsemen come purportedly to take him alive that, helped by Epaphroditus, he stabbed himself in the throat.[222] Behind all this was more plotting, as the conspirators cold-bloodedly pushed Nero in the direction they wanted him to take. The 'secret' of his place of refuge was clearly known to everyone who mattered. This explains how Phaon's messenger and the pursuing cavalry knew where to come: 'The whole course of events smells of treachery'.[223] Nero could have been arrested at any time during his flight, but he had to be given the opportunity to take his own life. Even after having been declared a public enemy, he could not just be killed out of hand or put on trial and executed. Nero was terrorised into killing himself, unaccompanied by any of his self-professed intimates. At the end, Nero had begged that his corpse should not be decapitated. This, and the privilege of an unmutilated burial, was conceded by Icelus, who came to view the corpse before returning hotfoot to Galba.[224] Nero was given a funeral befitting a Roman magistrate, his body cremated and the ashes buried at great expense (HS 200,000). They were placed in the family

---

[220] Bradley 1978a, 277; Cizek 1982, 48; Malitz 1999, 36; Champlin 2003, 51; Reitz 2006, 12.
[221] Above 272.   [222] Suet. *Ner.* 49.3.
[223] Townend 1967, 75, 94 (quotation). Cf. Grant 1970, 246; Bradley 1978a, 274; Cizek 1982, 400; Holland 2000, 228; Waldherr 2005, 262.
[224] Suet. *Ner.* 49. 4; Plut. *Galb.* 7.2.

tomb by his nurses Egloge and Alexandria, accompanied by Acte.[225] In Rome there was great but short-term popular rejoicing at his disappearance. In Clunia, Galba first heard of Nero's deposition and death and of his own formal acceptance as *princeps* on 16 June, information which was confirmed two days later.[226]

---

[225] Suet. *Ner.* 50.1. Bradley 1978a, 279.   [226] Plut. *Galb.* 7.1.

CHAPTER 16

Conclusion

'My Nero' is neither the Nero of the main source tradition nor that of most modern reconstructions. Most characteristically, he is never in charge of the Empire. A team comprising Agrippina, Pallas, Seneca and Burrus put him into power. Agrippina then attempted to establish a regency based on her position as 'Queen Mother'. When this failed and when Nero, after initial engagement, showed diminishing interest in his routine responsibilities, a further series of teams took over allowing the *princeps* to take a back seat in government. Their chief members were Seneca, Burrus, Poppaea, Faenius Rufus, Tigellinus, Statilia Messalina and Nymphidius Sabinus. However, they were never rigorously exclusive and drew on the skills of a range of experts comprising *amici*, members of the *consilium*, senatorial commissioners, financiers and others. The Neronian administration always appreciated competence as well as loyalty. Its policies were pragmatic, not ideological. The principal aim of those involved was simply to survive and prosper.

They had to confront serious problems: for example, in Rome, the Fire and the chronic problem of succession; and in the provinces, dangerous revolt in Britain and Judaea and severe external pressure on Armenia. In addition, their lives were threatened directly by the Pisonian conspirators who, though divided and not part of any general movement against Nero, maintained remarkable secrecy and, by exploiting the lack of security around his person, came close to annihilating him and his regime. Most of the administration's major challenges were, however, not of its making. The Fire was almost certainly accidental; the succession issue derived from long-standing Roman social practice and Nero's failure to provide a viable heir; and, though the government should have been aware of impending trouble in Britain and Judaea, the causes of tension there, as over Armenia, antedated Nero. Indeed the regime's basic difficulties – arising out of the need to nest a developing autocracy run by a *princeps* within a supposedly 'restored' Republic run by the Senate and to meet the costs of the imperial administration and army from a fiscal structure that was systemically flawed – went back to Augustus.

The Neronian teams worked well. They faced these problems and generally overcame them. Teams ensured the smooth succession from Claudius to Nero; survived the collapse of Agrippina's regency; showed themselves capable of suppressing revolt and conspiracy; overcame and drew valuable practical lessons from the Fire; won spectacular military and diplomatic success in dealing with Parthia; and expanded the boundaries of the Empire. War was hugely expensive and, given the weak fiscal structure, might have brought about financial ruin. A crucial accomplishment of the Neronian administration was that, through careful management, it not only avoided bankruptcy but also implemented important reforms in the collection of indirect taxes and in the coinage system. Financial incompetence was not a cause of Nero's fall. A second crucial achievement was that there was no major break with the Senate. After early difficulties, the political community had grown used to the 'principate'/'Republic' paradox and wanted it to succeed. To maintain senatorial backing, all that was required was for an administration to demonstrate respect for senators' ancient Republican rights and privileges, and in this the Neronian teams were generally happy to oblige. Here it must be emphasised that those who composed them were no more cruel or heartless than was normal for their time. The administration subjected the Pisonian conspirators to heavy punishment and, in its determination to survive, showed itself generally pitiless in its treatment of enemies, real and perceived, including Agrippina, Octavia and a range of high aristocrats. In addition, history has some justification in condemning it in particular for its cold-blooded scapegoating of metropolitan Christians as arsonists. However, all this is typical of advanced pre-industrial court politics. Most political deaths and exiles were, though regrettable, carried out in the interests of stability. They were not huge in number, and conviction and sentencing usually took place within an established legal framework. A final key success was that there was no discord between the administration and the army, officers and men, praetorians and frontier troops. Indeed, as part of its appreciation of talent and its good relations with the Senate, the regime treated its senatorial generals exceptionally well by promoting men outside the Julio-Claudian family to important commands and, helped by the absence of any 'grand strategy', by trusting to their individual initiative. For this it was rewarded with victory, which culminated in Tiridates' grand entry into Rome in 66 to be formally crowned king of Armenia by Nero. It was success like this that, down to 68, secured the *princeps* the loyalty of his frontier troops, even though he himself never went to war. Likewise, though the Pisonian conspiracy could not have occurred without the grievances of a large proportion of senior officers, the praetorian rank and file remained faithful almost to the last. The people of Rome were rather more volatile. They had welcomed Nero in 54 but objected to his treatment of Octavia in 62 and found cause to doubt him after the Fire. However, they forgave him and by 68 had again taken him to their heart. Overall, the 'team experiment' worked well, and all those involved deserve credit.

Nero, in the background, was far from the deranged, murderous tyrant of the Flavian/Jewish/Christian tradition and *Quo Vadis?* He never harboured any crazed belief about his own omnipotence or divinity. Indeed, always in touch with reality, he, like his advisers, had no great ideological goals, religious or political. Devoted to sport and art, not administration and war, Nero wanted to be a different sort of *princeps*, not to establish a different sort of Principate or Empire. Until the very end, he worked tirelessly, if misguidedly, to achieve this goal. He was certainly not habitually lazy, but he was no saint. His self-indulgence, increasing absorption by his own interests and, at times, peculiar, especially populist, behaviour, provoked legitimate uncertainty about his character and suspicion of his motives. But this made him no 'monster'. He was neither vindictive nor indeed, with his great dislike of bloodshed, cruel. He was not morally depraved, not unusually anti-social in his behaviour, gluttonous, avaricious or lustful. He did not attempt to deprave others. In particular, he was neither a mad arsonist nor a vicious committed persecutor of Christianity. He was however, capable of occasionally breaking away from the direction of his advisers to assert his will in ways which could lead to odd, unsettling, expensive and short-lived projects, both civil and military. Behind such insistence lay self-doubt. Nero possessed the strength, skill and courage to drive a ten-horse chariot team, but always questioned his ability, and suffered occasional deep remorse for what he had done or for what others had done in his name. This explains his adoption of the mask of Apollo, his need for the catharsis of the Greek trip and his final 'burn-out'.

This imperfect but human Nero was genuinely curious about the world away from administration and politics. This caused him to ride an established cultural wave. Literature, art, architecture, science and geography were already attracting growing attention in an age of experts and handbooks. Nero's patronage gave this wave greater strength and, directly and indirectly, inspired a 'Neronian' age. Although the constitutional paradox complicated public discourse, it never stifled it, and Nero's relaxed attitude to personal criticism encouraged a relatively frank society which, from high to low, was permitted some degree of candid speaking and writing. As a result, there were notable 'spikes' of achievement in literature and various other fields. Neronian society's greatest legacy was, however, probably the part it played in encouraging eastern Greeks to participate in the full life of the Empire, which gives it a claim to be a progenitor of the Second Sophistic, the Constantinian Empire and Byzantium. It is little wonder that, apart from tendentious Jewish and early Christian loathing, the East remembered Nero favourably after his death.

Nero's principate demonstrated the strength of the Principate as an institution. With the accession of Tiberius, Gaius and Claudius, it had survived three changes of *princeps*, and it passed smoothly to Nero. By now somewhat less 'half-baked' than it had been at its beginning, Augustus' expedient was able to persist until the 'Crisis' of the third century. It may indeed be said that the Early Roman Empire ended with Nero and the High Roman Empire began with the Flavians. Since the Principate derived from Augustus' position as a legitimised warlord, it was always a covert military autocracy, a veiled monarchy. On the other hand, it was no arbitrary despotism, based on fear and repression. If it had been, it could not have survived for as long as it did. Though inherent constitutional paradox inhibited proper discussion of its nature – candour had its limits – the political community could see it for what it was; appreciate that for all its faults it guaranteed stability, peace and prosperity; and, for the most part, they showed themselves ready to work with it as long as the incumbent *princeps* did not declare himself king or work directly against their status and interests. Nero and the Neronian teams did neither, and most aristocrats recognised this and co-operated with the regime. Even the Pisonian conspirators aimed at the appointment of a new *princeps*, not the restoration of the old Republic.

The Julio-Claudian principate had matured, but it was not fixed in shape. We should not assume that its Antonine or Severan forms were inevitable. This is vividly reflected in the ambitions of Agrippina, who must have reckoned that she stood a good chance of succeeding in establishing female rule. The elasticity of the Principate, a major contributor to its strength, is also visible in the way in which during the summer of 68, in a wholly unprecedented situation, its supporters were able to withdraw consent from one *princeps* and his line and to give it to another without destructive empire-wide civil war. It was such resilience and plasticity that allowed the system to carry a passenger like Nero. This could not have happened without a central pool of informed and efficient executives and their advisers; and another Neronian lesson is that all *principes*, even those who were not carried as passengers, depended closely on a wide range of lieutenants. None could have governed successfully alone, and historians should always give close consideration to those working alongside and behind the current ruler. Two significant aspects of this essential delegation of power in Nero's final days are the part played by third parties, some independent and self-declared, in planning and implementing a change of *princeps*; and the clemency shown to the relatives and counsellors of the outgoing ruler, a vital guarantor of political continuity and stability.

Yet the Neronian period also revealed some of the weaknesses of the Augustan Principate. How the Neronian principate ended demonstrated that, because no *princeps* had sovereign power, the institution remained technically illegitimate and so, for all its developing strength, innately unstable. The events of 68 confirmed three generations of fear that the Empire could never again escape the danger of bloody civil war by establishing the precedent that a *princeps* might be challenged by military commanders on the periphery. Peripheral challenge and civil war were, in fact, the price to be paid for territorial hegemony and for the Principate: in the last resort a *princeps'* power was founded on the frontier armies, whose men had an historical claim to articulate the views of the People of Rome. The threat and reality of civil war were to haunt the Empire for the rest of its days. Major civil war was actually avoided under Nero, manifesting itself first under Galba. However, the process of his being replaced by Galba, in which all interested parties agreed to leave the formal repudiation of Nero and the acceptance of his successor to the Senate, was also to lead to centuries of centripetalism. For approximately the next 250 years, almost every usurper would feel obliged to march on Rome to be sure of recognition by the Senate. This held the Empire together, even during the third-century 'Crisis'. On the other hand, by confirming the nominal primacy of the Senate, and so blocking the development of autocracy into monarchy, it doomed the Principate to remaining half-baked. Furthermore, since civil war, and so the involvement of frontier troops in central affairs, was only intermittent, centripetalism left huge power in the hands of the real masters of the City, the praetorians. Finally, almost immediately and for centuries to come, it made Italy the cockpit of civil war and later, by requiring the removal of military strength from the frontiers, it encouraged foreign incursion.

The Neronian experiment worked well and achieved some remarkable successes. The regime presided over no age of 'dissolution', in either sense of the word. Yet in the end it failed because Nero fell and with him the Julio-Claudian dynasty. This came with little warning. By the end of 67 and the first half of 68 there was no gathering movement against the *princeps* caused, say, by acute provincial unrest arising out of a fiscal crisis and the consequent levying of unfair or irregular taxes. Nero had regained his popularity with the people of Rome, and the provinces and the troops remained loyal. The administration's trust in its most senior military commanders had paid off handsomely. Even in summer 68, none rebelled directly against Nero. Vindex's rebellion should not have happened, and once it had it should not have had such a devastating outcome. It was relatively minor and, with entirely adequate measures taken quickly to deal with it, there could have been no sense that the *princeps* was doomed. The revolt should, rather, have allowed the Neronian Establishment to confirm his position by handing him his own military victory on a plate. Nero fell because of his failure to take to the field. In the short term, this was caused by the 'burn-out' following his loss of Poppaea and the exhausting success of the Greek trip. In the longer term, it was due to his lack of interest in the responsibilities of his position. Behind this, however, was the fact that the successful experiment of a 'team' worked only because of Nero's own personality, which made him the wrong man for the job. A *princeps* was, again, a legitimised warlord. As such, he should ideally be a mature male, preferably one with real military experience and skills but, failing this, one (like Gaius and Claudius) prepared to make a nominal appearance on the battlefield when necessary. Nero failed to come up to this mark. He had reached office through dynastic succession, in itself no bad thing. As Roman imperial history shows, there was no alternative to it in creating long-term stability. There were bound to be unworthy heirs but, as in Nero's case, these could be supported by the innate strength of Principate. Such people had, however, to produce their own successors in order to give their supporters something to hope in and fight for, and in this Nero, obsessed with Sporus/'Poppaea' and ignoring his new wife, had already failed. The system could not indefinitely carry a passenger both disengaged and heirless. Without Vindex, Nero would either have been forced to name an heir or have been directly challenged by a strong man, probably Nymphidius Sabinus. Both would have resulted in further challenges by others thought capable of rule, certainly Vespasian but perhaps also Suetonius Paullinus. Civil war was unavoidable.

References

Alcock, S. E. (1994), 'Nero at play? The emperor's Grecian odyssey', in Elsner and Masters (eds), 98–111.

Alpers, M. (1995), *Das nachrepublikanische Finanzsystem. Fiscus und Fisci in der frühen Kaiserzeit* (Untersuchungen zur antiken Literatur und Geschichte Bd. 45), Berlin.

Asmis, E. (2015), 'Seneca's originality', in Bartsch and Schiesaro (eds), 224–38.

Ball, L. F. (2003), *The Domus Aurea and the Roman Architectural Revolution*, Cambridge: Cambridge University Press.

Bang, P. F. (2008), *The Roman Bazaar. A Comparative Study of Trade and Markets in a Tributary Empire*, Cambridge: Cambridge University Press.

Barrett, A. A. (1989), *Caligula: The Corruption of Power*, London: B. T. Batsford.
   (1996), *Agrippina: Sex, Power and Politics in the Early Empire*, London: B. T. Batsford.

Barrett, A. A., Fantham, E. and Yardley, J. C. (eds) (2016), *The Emperor Nero: A Guide to the Ancient Sources*, Princeton, NJ: Princeton University Press.

Barton, T. (1994), 'The *inventio* of Nero: Suetonius', in Elsner and Masters (eds), 48–63.

Bartsch, S. (1994), *Actors and Audiences: Theatricality and Doublespeak from Nero to Hadrian*, Cambridge, MA: Harvard University Press.

Bartsch, S. and Schiesaro, A. (eds) (2015), *The Cambridge Companion to Seneca*, Cambridge: Cambridge University Press.

Beard, M. (1980), 'The sexual status of Vestal Virgins', *JRS* 70, 12–27.
   (2007), *The Roman Triumph*, Cambridge, MA: Harvard University Press.

Bell, H. I. (1938), 'The economic crisis in Egypt under Nero', *JRS* 28, 1–8.

Bellemore, J. (2013), 'The identity of Drusus: the making of a *princeps*', in Gibson (ed.), 79–94.

Bellen, H. (1981), *Die germanische Leibwache der römischen Kaiser des julisch-claudischen Hauses*, Wiesbaden: Akademie der Wissenschaften und der Literatur.

Bergmann, M. (2013), 'Portraits of an emperor: Nero, the Sun and Roman *otium*', in Buckley and Dinter (eds), 332–62.

Berno, F. R. (2015), 'Exploring appearances: Seneca's scientific works', in Bartsch and Schiesaro (eds), 82–92.

Berti, E. (2011), 'La letteratura al tempo di Nerone', in Tomei and Rea (eds), 218–29.

Beste, H.-J. (2011a), 'La Domus Transitoria: un' ipotesi di collacazione', in Tomei and Rea (eds), 152–5.

(2011b), 'Domus Aurea, il padiglione dell'Oppio', in Tomei and Rea (eds), 170–5.

Beste, H.-J. and Hesberg, H. von (2013), 'Buildings of an emperor: how Nero transformed Rome', in Buckley and Dinter (eds), 314–31.

Bingham, S. (2013), *The Praetorian Guard: A History of Rome's Elite Special Forces*, London & New York, NY: I. B. Tauris.

Birley, A. R. (2005), *The Roman Government of Britain*, Oxford: Oxford University Press.

Bol, R. (2013), 'Nero in Olympia: Statuenehrungen für den neuen Hoffnungsträger', in Walde (ed.), 157–95.

Bowman, A. K. (1996a), 'Provincial administration and taxation', *CAH* 10², 344–70.

(1996b) 'Egypt', *CAH* 10², 676–702.

Bradley, K. R. (1972), 'A *publica fames* in AD 68', *AJPh* 93, 451–63.

(1973), '*Tunc primum revocata ea lex*', *AJPh* 94.2, 172–81.

(1977), 'Nero and Claudia Antonia', *Symbolae Osloenses* 52, 79–82.

(1978a), *Suetonius' Life of Nero: An Historical Commentary* (Collection Latomus vol. 157), Brussels: Société d'études latines.

(1978b), 'The chronology of Nero's visit to Greece AD 66/67', *Latomus* 37, 61–72.

(1991), *Discovering the Roman Family: Studies in Roman Social History*, Oxford: Oxford University Press.

(1992), 'Wet-nursing at Rome: a study in social relations', in Rawson (ed.), 201–29.

Bragantini, I. (2011), 'La pitturaa di èta neroniana', in Tomei and Rea (eds), 190–201.

Bransbourg, G. (2015), 'The later Roman Empire', in Monson and Scheidel (eds), 258–81.

Braund, D. (1985), *Augustus to Nero: A Source-Book of Roman History 31 BC–AD 68*, London: Croon Helm.

(2013), 'Apollo in arms: Nero at the frontier', in Buckley and Dinter (eds), 83–101.

Brunt, P. A. (1959), 'The revolt of Vindex and the fall of Nero', *Latomus* 18, 531–9.

(1977), '*Lex imperio Vespasiani*', *JRS* 67, 95–116.

Bryan, J. (2013), 'Neronian philosophy', in Buckley and Dinter (eds), 134–48.

Bryen, A. Z. (2012), 'Judging empire: courts and culture in Rome's eastern provinces', *Law and History Review* 30, 771–811.

Buckley, E. (2013a), 'Senecan tragedy', in Buckley and Dinter (eds), 204–24.

(2013b), '*Nero insitiuus*: constructing Neronian identity in the pseudo-Senecan *Octavia*', in Gibson (ed.), 133–54.

Buckley, E. and Dinter, M. T. (eds) (2013), *A Companion to the Neronian Age*, Malden, MA: Blackwell.

Butcher, K. and Ponting, M. (2014), *The Metallurgy of Roman Silver Coinage: From the Reform of Nero to the Reform of Trajan*, Cambridge: Cambridge University Press.

Cadario, M. (2011), 'Nerone e il "Potere delle Imagine"', in Tomei and Rea (eds), 176–89.

Campbell, J. B. (1984), *The Emperor and the Army 31 BC–AD 235*, Oxford: Oxford University Press.

Canter, H. V. (1932), 'Conflagrations in ancient Rome', *CJ* 27, 270–88.

Carandini, A. (with Bruno, D. and Fraioli, F.) (2011), 'Gli atri odiosi di un re crudele', in Tomei and Rea (eds), 136–51.

Carroll, K. K. (1979), 'The date of Boudicca's revolt', *Britannia* 10, 197–202.

Carson, R. A. G. (1990), *Coins of the Roman Empire*, London: Routledge.

Chaisemartin, N. de (2003), *Rome: Paysage urbain et idéologie des Scipions à Hadrien (IIe s. av. J.C.–IIe s. ap. J.C.)*, Paris: Armand Colin.

Champlin, E. (1978), 'The life and times of Calpurnius Siculus', *JRS* 68, 95–110.

(2003), *Nero*, Cambridge, MA: Harvard University Press.

Charlesworth, M. P. (1950), 'Nero: some aspects', *JRS* 40, 69–76.

Chilver, G. E. F. (1979), *A Historical Commentary on Tacitus' Histories I and II*, Oxford: Oxford University Press.

Cizek, E. (1982), *Néron*, Paris: Fayard.

Claridge, A. (1998), *Oxford Archaeological Guides: Rome*, Oxford: Oxford University Press.

Clarke, G. W. (1996), 'The origins and spread of Christianity', *CAH* 10², 848–72.

Closs, V. (2016), '*Neronianis temporibus*, the so-called *Arae Incendii Neronis* and the fire of AD 64 in Rome's monumental landscape', *JRS* 106, 102–23.

Coleman, K. M. (1990), 'Fatal charades: Roman executions staged as mythical reenactments', *JRS* 80, 44–73.

Coleman, K. M. (ed. and comm.) (2006), *Martial. Liber Spectaculorum*, Oxford.

Connors, C. (1994), 'Famous last words: authorship and death in the *Satyricon* and Neronian Rome', in Elsner and Masters (eds), 225–39.

Cottier, M., Crawford, M. H.,Crowther, C. V., Ferrary, J.-L., Levick, B. M., Salomies, O. and Wörrle, M. (eds) (2008), *The Customs Law of Asia*, Oxford: Oxford University Press.

Crook, J. A. (1955), Consilium Principis. *Imperial Councils and Counsellors from Augustus to Diocletian*, Cambridge: Cambridge University Press.

(1992), 'The development of Roman private law', *CAH* 9², 531–63.

(1996a), 'Political history, 30 BC to AD 14', *CAH* 10², 70–112.

(1996b), 'Augustus: power, authority, achievement', *CAH* 10², 113–46.

Dawson, A. (1964), 'Whatever happened to Lady Agrippina?', *CJ* 64, 253–67.

Dinter, M. T. (2013), 'Introduction: the Neronian (literary) "renaissance"', in Buckley and Dinter (eds), 1–14.

Doody, A. (2013), 'Literature of the world: Seneca's *Natural Questions and Pliny's Natural History*', in Buckley and Dinter (eds), 288–301.

Drinkwater, J. F. (1979), 'Gallic personal wealth', *Chiron* 9, 237–42.

(1983), *Roman Gaul: The Three Provinces 58 BC–AD 260*, Ithaca, NY: Cornell University Press.

(1997), Review of L. Wierschowski, *Die regionale Mobilität in Gallien nach den Inschriften des 1.bis 3. Jahrhunderts* (Historia Einzelschriften 91), Stuttgart, 1995, *Britannia* 28, 511–12.

(2001), 'Women and Horses and Power and War', in T. S. Burns and J. Eadie (eds), *Urban Centers and Rural Contexts in Late Antiquity*, East Lansing, MI: Michigan State University Press, 135–46.

(2005), 'Maximinus to Diocletian and the "Anarchy"', *CAH* 12², 28–66.

(2007a), *The Alamanni and Rome: Caracalla to Clovis 213–496*, Oxford: Oxford University Press.

(2007b), 'The principate: lifebelt or millstone around the neck of Empire?', in O. Hekster, G. de Kleijn and D. Slootjes (eds), *Crises and the Roman Empire*, Leiden: Brill, 67–74.

(2013), 'Nero Caesar and the half-baked Principate', in Gibson (ed.), 155–73.

(2014), Review of Walde (2013), *BMCR* 2014.09.37.

Drinkwater, J. F. and Lee, A. D. (2015), 'Civil wars: Late Empire', in Y. Le Bohec (ed.) *Encyclopedia of the Roman Army*, Chichester: Wiley-Blackwell, 211–18.

Droß-Krüpe, K. (ed.) (2014), *Textile Trade and Distribution in Antiquity/ Textilhandel und -distribution in der Antike* (Philippika 73), Wiesbaden: Otto Harrassowitz.

Eck, W. (1985), *Die Statthalter der germanischen Provinzen vom 1.–3. Jahrhundert* (Epigraphische Studien Bd. 14), Cologne: Steiner.

Editorial comment (2011), 'A theoretical framework for the neurobiology of chronic traumatization', *Acta Psychiatrica Scandinavica* 124, 329–30.

Edwards, C. (1994), 'Beware of imitations: theatre and subversion in imperial identity', in Elsner and Masters (eds), 83–97.

(2007), *Death in Ancient Rome*, New Haven, CT: Yale University Press.

Elsner, J. (1994), 'Constructing decadence: the representation of Nero as an imperial builder', in Elsner and Masters (eds), 112–27.

Elsner, J. and Masters, J. (1994), *Reflections of Nero: Culture, History, Representation*, London: Duckworth.

Erker, D. S. (2013), 'Religion', in Buckley and Dinter (eds), 118–33.

Esposito, P. (2013), 'Nerone in Lucano e nell'esegica lucanea', in Walde (ed.), 197–216.

Fantham, E. (2013), 'The performing prince', in Buckley and Dinter (eds), 17–28.

Fini, M. (1994), *Nero: 2000 Jahre der Verleumdung*, Munich: Herbig.

Flaig, E. (2011), 'How the emperor Nero lost acceptance in Rome', in B. C. Ewald and C. F. Noreña (eds), *The Emperor and Rome: Space, Representation, and Ritual* (Yale Classical Studies 35), rev. edn, Cambridge: Cambridge University Press, 275–88.

Fonagy, P. and Luyten, P. (2009), 'A developmental, mentalization-based approach to the understanding and treatment of borderline personality disorder', *Development and Psychopathy* 21, 1355–81.

Frere, S. S. (1978), *Britannia: A History of Roman Britain*, rev. edn, London: Routledge & Kegan Paul.

Freudenburg, K. (2015), 'Seneca's *Apocolocyntosis*: censors in the Afterworld', in Bartsch and Schiesaro (eds), 93–105.

Furneaux, H. (1896), *The Annals of Tacitus (Vol 1, Books 1–6)*, 2nd edn, Oxford: Oxford University Press.

(1907), *The Annals of Tacitus (Vol 2, Books 11–16)*, 2nd edn, Oxford: Oxford University Press.

Galsterer, H. (1996), 'The administration of justice', *CAH* 10^2, 397–413.

Giardina, A. (2011), 'Nerone o dell'impossible', in Tomei and Rea (eds), 10–25.

Gibson, A. G. G. (ed.) (2013), *The Julio-Claudian Succession: Reality and Perception of the 'Augustan Model'* (Mnemosyne Supp. 349), Leiden: Brill.

(2013), '"All things to all men": Claudius and the politics of AD 41', in Gibson (ed.), 107–32.

Ginsburg, J. (2006), *Representing Agrippina: Constructions of Female Power in the Early Empire*, Oxford: Oxford University Press.

Ginsburg, L. (2014), Review of Buckley and Dinter, (eds), 2013, *BMCR* 2014.02.29.

Goddard, J. (1994), 'The tyrant at table', in Elsner and Masters (eds), 67–82.

Gowers, E. (1994), 'Persius and the decoction of Nero', in Elsner and Masters (eds), 131–50.

Grant, M. (1970), *Nero*, London: George Weidenfeld & Nicholson.

Graves, R. (1956), *Lucan: Pharsalia*, Harmondsworth: Penguin Classics.

Green, S. J. (2010), '"(No) arms and the man": the imperial pretender, the opportunistic poet and the *Laus Pisonis*', *Classical Quarterly* 60, 497–523.

Griffin, M. (1976), *Seneca: A Philosopher in Politics*, Oxford: Clarendon Press.

(1984), *Nero: The End of a Dynasty*, London: B. T. Batsford.

(2013), 'Nachwort: Nero from zero to hero', in Buckley and Dinter (eds), 467–80.

Grünewald, T. (2004), *Bandits in the Roman Empire: Myth and Reality*, London: Routledge.

Günther, S. (2013), '*Res publica* oder *res popularis*? Die steuerpolitischen Maßnahmen des 'schlechten' Kaisers Nero zwischen Haushaltraison und Volksfreundlichkeit', in Walde (ed.), 105–28.

Halfmann, H. (1986), *Itinera Principum: Geschichte und Typologie der Kaiserreisen im Römischen Reich* (Heidelberger Althistorische Beiträge und Epigraphische Studien Bd. 2), Stuttgart: F. Steiner Verlag.

Hansen, D. U. (2013), 'Greek literature under Nero', in Buckley and Dinter (eds), 302–13.

Hardie, P. (2013), 'Lucan's *Bellum Civile*', in Buckley and Dinter (eds), 225–40.

Harl, K. (1996), *Coinage in the Roman Economy, 300 BC to AD 700*, London & Baltimore, MD: Johns Hopkins University Press.

Haynes, I. (2013), *Blood of the Provinces: The Roman Auxilia and the Making of Provincial Society from Augustus to the Severans*, Oxford: Oxford University Press.

Heil, M. (1997), *Die orientalische Außenpolitik des Kaisers Nero*, Munich: Tuduv Verlag.

(2008), 'Der Ritterstand', in K.-P. Johne, U. Hartmann and T. Gerhardt (eds), *Die Zeit der Soldatenkaiser: Krise und Transformation des Römischen Reiches im 3. Jahrhundert n. Chr. Zweiter Band*, Berlin: Akademie Verlag, 736–61.

Hekster, O. (2002), *Commodus: An Emperor at the Crossroads*, Amsterdam: Gieben.

Henderson, B. W. (1905), *The Life and Principate of the Emperor Nero*, London: Methuen & Co.

Henderson, J. (2013), 'The *Carmina Einsiedlensia* and Calpurnius Siculus' *Eclogues*', in Buckley and Dinter (eds), 170–87.

Hesberg, H. von (2011), 'L'attività edilizia a Roma all'epoca di Nerone', in Tomei and Rea (eds), 108–17.

Hewitt, K. V. (1983), 'The coinage of L. Clodius Macer (AD 68)', *Numismatic Chronicle* 143, 64–80.

Hine, H. M. (2006), 'Rome, the cosmos, and the emperor in Seneca's *Natural Questions*', *JRS* 96, 42–92.

Hohl, E. (1918), 'Domitius 29', *Paulys Realencyclopädie der classischen Altertumswissenschaft Supplementband 3*, Berlin, 349–94.

Holland, R. (2000), *Nero: The Man behind the Myth*, Stroud: Sutton.

Hurley, D. W. (trans.) (2011), *Suetonius: The Caesars*, Indianapolis, IN: Hackett.

(2013), 'Biographies of Nero', in Buckley and Dinter (eds), 29–44.

James, O.(2007), *They **** You Up: How to Survive Family Life*, rev. edn, London: A & C Black.

Jones, A. H. M. (1956), 'Numismatics and history', in R. A. Carson and C. H. V. Sutherland (eds), *Essays in Roman Coinage Presented to Harold Mattingly*, Oxford: Oxford University Press, 13–33.

(1964), *The Later Roman Empire 284–602*, Oxford: Taylor & Francis.

(1966), *The Decline of the Ancient World*, London: Longman.

Jongman, W. M. (2007), 'The Early Roman Empire: consumption', in Scheidel *et al.* (eds), 592–618.

Keppie, L.(1996), 'The army and navy', *CAH* 10², 371–96.

(2011), '"Guess who's coming to dinner": the murder of Nero's mother Agrippina in its topographical setting', *Greece & Rome* 58, 33–47.

Ker, J. (2015), 'Seneca in Augustan culture', in Bartsch and Schiesaro (eds), 109–21.

Kienast, D. (2004), *Römische Kaisertabelle: Grundzüge einer römischen Kaiserchronologie*, 3rd edn, Darmstadt: Verlag C. H. Beck.

Kimmerle, N. (2015), *Lucan und der Prinzipat: Inkonsistenz und Unzuverlässiges Erzählen im Bellum Civile* (Millennium Studien Bd. 53), Berlin: Walter de Gruyter.

Kolb, A. (2000), *Transport und Nachrichtentransfer im Römischen Reich* (Klio Beiträge n. s. 2), Berlin: Akademie Verlag.

Konstan, D. (2015), 'Senecan emotions', in Bartsch and Schiesaro (eds), 174–84.

Kraay, C. M. (1949), 'The coinage of Vindex and Galba, AD 68, and the continuity of the Augustan principate', *Numismatic Chronicle* 6, 129–49.

Kraus, C. S. (1994), Review of Elsner and Masters (eds) (1994), *BMCR* 1994.09.09.

Kreikenbom, D. (2013), 'Nero-Bildnisse zwischen Winckelmann und Bernoulli', in Walde (ed.), 129–56.

Krüger, J. (2012), *Nero: Der römische Kaiser und seine Zeit*, Cologne: Böhlau Verlag.

Lanfranchi, T. (2015), Review of F. J. Vervaet, *The High Command in the Roman Republic* (Historia Einzelschriften, Bd 232) (2014), *BMCR* 2015.06.08.

Lanius, R., Bluhm, R. L., and Frewin, P. A. (2011), 'How understanding the neurobiology of complex post-traumatic stress disorder can inform clinical practice: a social, cognitive and affective neuroscience approach, *Acta Psychiatrica Scandinavica* 124, 331–48.

Lavan, M. (2013), 'The Empire in the age of Nero', in Buckley and Dinter (eds), 65–82.

Lee, A. D. (2007), *War in Late Antiquity: A Social History*, Malden, MA: Blackwell.

Lendon, J. E. (1997), *Empire of Honour: The Art of Government in the Roman World*, Oxford: Oxford University Press.

Lenz, A. (2013), 'Nero, das Monster auf der Bühne. Zu Martin Walsers Stück Nero läßt grussen', in Walde (ed.), 273–85.

Levi, M. A. (1949), *Nerone e i suoi tempi*, Milan: Varese.

(1958), *Political Power in the Ancient World*, New York, NY: New American Library.

Levick, B. (1983), 'The *Senatus Consultum* from Larinum', *JRS* 73, 97–115.

(1990), *Claudius*, London: B. T. Batsford.

(1999a), *Vespasian*, London: Routledge.

(1999b), 'Messages on Roman coins: types and inscriptions', in G. M. Paul and M. Ieradi (eds), *Roman Coins and Public Life under the Empire* (E. Togo Salmon Papers II), Ann Arbor, MI: University of Michigan Press, 41–60.

Liebenam, W.(1909), *Fasti consulares imperii Romani*, Bonn: A. Marcus & E. Weber's Verlag.

Lintott, A. (1992), 'Political history, 146–95 BC', *CAH* 9 ², 40–103.

Littlewood, C. A. J. (2015), 'Theatre and theatricality in Seneca's world', in Bartsch and Schiesaro (eds), 161–73.

Lo Cascio, E. (2007), 'The early Roman empire: the state and the economy', in Scheidel *et al.* (eds), 619–47.

Lorenz, K. (2013), 'Neronian wall-painting: a matter of perspective', in Buckley and Dinter (eds), 363–81.

Maes, Y. (2013), 'Nero, NERO, Neronian literature', in Walde (ed.), 287–338.

Maier, H. O. (2013), 'Nero in Jewish and Christian tradition from the first century to the Reformation', in Buckley and Dinter (eds), 385–404.

Makin, E. (1921), 'The triumphal route, with particular reference to the Flavian triumph', *JRS* 11, 25–36.

Malitz, J. (1999), *Nero*, Malden, MA: Blackwell.

Malloch, S. J. V. (ed. and comm.) (2013), *The Annals of Tacitus: Book 11* (Cambridge Classical Texts and Commentaries 51), Cambridge: Cambridge University Press.

(2015), 'Frontinus and Domitian: the politics of the *Strategemata Chiron* 45, 77–100.

Mannering, J. (2013), 'Seneca's philosophical writings: *Naturales Quaestiones, Dialogi, Epistulae Morales*', in Buckley and Dinter (eds), 188–203.

Mantel, H. (2017), *Reith Lectures 2017*, (BBC).

Masters, J. (1994), 'Deceiving the reader: the political mission of Lucan *Bellum Civile* 7', in Elsner and Masters (eds), 151–77.

Matthews, J. F. (1975), *Western Aristocracies and Imperial Court AD 364–425*, Oxford: Clarendon Press.

Mayer, R. (1980), 'Calpurnius Siculus: technique and date', *JRS* 70, 175–6.

McCrumm, H. and Woodhead, A. G. (1961), *Select Documents of the Principates of the Flavian Emperors AD 68–96*, Cambridge: Cambridge University Press.

Meier, M. (2008), '"*Qualis artifex pereo*" – Neros letzte Reise', *Historische Zeitschrift* 286, 561–603.

Meyboom, P. G. P. and Moormann, E. M. (2012), 'Decoration and ideology in Nero's *Domus Aurea* in Rome', *Analecta Praehistorica Leidensia* 43/44, 133–43.

(2013), *Le decorazioni dipinte e marmoree della Domus Aurea di Nerone a Roma*, Louvain: Peeters.

Michel, A.-C. (2015), *La cour sous l'empereur Claude: Les enjeux d'un lieu de pouvoir*, Rennes: Presses Universitaires de Rennes.

Millar, F. G. B. (1977), *The Emperor in the Roman World*, London: Duckworth.

Milnor, K. (2005), *Gender, Domesticity and the Age of Augustus: Inventing Private Life*, Oxford: Oxford University Press.

Miziolek, J. (2011), '"Lux in tenebris": Nerone e i primi Cristiani nelle opera di Enrico Siemiradzki e Jan Styka', in Tomei and Rea (eds), 44–61.

Monson, A. and Scheidel, W. (2015), *Fiscal Regimes and Political Economy of Premodern States*, Cambridge: Cambridge University Press.

Moormann, E. M. (2003), 'Some observations on Nero and the city of Rome', in L. de Blois, P. Erdkamp, O. Hekster, G. de Kleijn and S. Mols (eds), *The Representation and Perception of Roman Imperial Power: Proceedings of the Third Workshop of the International Network Impact of Empire*, Amsterdam: Gieben, 376–88.

Mordine, M. J. (2013), '*Domus Neroniana*: the imperial household in the age of Nero', in Buckley and Dinter (eds), 102–17.

Morgan, G. (2000), 'Clodius Macer and Calvia Crispinilla', *Historia* 49, 467–87.

Mratschek, S. (2013), 'Nero the imperial misfit: philhellenism in a rich man's world', in Buckley and Dinter (eds), 45–62.

Murgatroyd, T. (2013), 'Petronius' *Satyrica*', in Buckley and Dinter (eds), 241–57.

Neri, V. (1996), 'L'usurpatore come tiranno nel lessico politico della tarda antichità', in F. Paschoud and J. Szidat (eds), *Usurpation in der Spätantike* (Historia Einzelschriften 111), Stuttgart: Steiner Verlag, 71–86.

Nichols, M. F. (2013), 'Persius', in Buckley and Dinter (eds), 258–74.

Osgood, J. (2011), *Claudius Caesar: Image and Power in the Early Roman Empire*, Cambridge: Cambridge University Press.

(2013), 'Suetonius and the succession to Augustus', in Gibson (ed), 19–40.

Panella, C. (2011a), 'Nerone e il grande incendio del 64 d.c.', in Tomei and Rea (eds), 76–91.

(2011b), 'La *Domus Aurea* nella valle del Colosseo e sulle pendici della Velia e del Palatino', in Tomei and Rea (eds), 160–9.

Pausch, D. (2013), 'Kaiser, Künstler, Kitharode: Das Bild Neros bei Sueton', in Walde (ed.), 45–79.

Payne, R. (1962), *The Roman Triumph*, London: Pan.

Perassi, C. (2002), 'Edifici e monumenti sulla monetazione di Nerone', in J. M. Croisille and Y. Perrin (eds) *Neronia VI: Rome à l'époque néronienne* (Collection Latomus 268), Brussels: Tournai, 11–34.

Perrin, Y. (2016) 'Main base sur la Ville? Les expropriations et confiscations de Néron à Rome', in C. Chillet, M.-C. Ferriès and Y. Rivière (eds), *Les confiscations, le pouvoir et Rome de la fin de la République à la mort de Néron* (Scripta Antiqua 92), Bordeaux: Ausonius, 229–46.

Pucci, G. (2011), 'Nerone superstar', in Tomei and Rea (eds), 62–75.

Quenemoen, C. K. (2014), 'Columns and concrete: architecture from Nero to Hadrian', in R. B. Ulrich and C. K. Quenemoen (eds), *A Companion to Roman Architecture*, Malden, MA: Blackwell, 63–81.

Ranieri Pannetta, M. (2011), 'Fine di una dinastia: la morte di Nerone', in Tomei and Rea (eds), 26–35.

Rathbone, D. (1996), 'The imperial finances', *CAH* 10², 309–23.

(2008), 'Nero's reforms of *vectigalia* in the inscription of the *Lex Portorii Asiae*', in Cottier *et al.*, 251–78.

Rawson, B. ed. (1992), *The Family in Ancient Rome: New Perspectives*, 2nd edn, London: Routledge.

Rea, R. (2011), 'Nerone, le arti e le ludi', in Tomei and Rea (eds), 202–17.

Rees, R. (2013), 'The lousy reputation of Piso', in Gibson (ed.), 95–106.

Reitz, C. (2006), *Die Literatur im Zeitalter Neros*, Darmstadt: Wissenschaftliche Buchgesellschaft.

(2013), 'Columella, *De Re Rustica*', in Buckley and Dinter (eds), 275–87.

Richlin, A. (2014), *Arguments with Silence: Writing the History of Roman Women*, Ann Arbor, MI: University of Michigan Press.

Rimell, V. (2015), 'Seneca and Neronian Rome: in the mirror of time', in Bartsch and Schiesaro (eds), 122–34.

Romm, J. (2014), *Dying Every Day: Seneca at the Court of Nero*, New York, NY: A. A. Knopf.

Rubiés, J.-P. (1994), 'Nero in Tacitus and Nero in Tacitism', in Elsner and Masters (eds), 28–47.

Rudich, V. (1993), *Political Dissidence under Nero: The Price of Dissimulation*, Abingdon: Routledge.

Ruffing, K. (2014), 'Seidenhandel in der römischen Kaiserzeit', in Droß-Krüpe (ed.), 71–81.

Rutledge, S. H. (2001), *Imperial Inquisitions: Prosecutions and Informants from Tiberius to Domitian*, London: Routledge.

Šašel Kos, M. (1986), *A Historical Outline of the Region between Aquileia, the Adriatic, and Sirmium in Cassius Dio and Herodian*, Ljubljana: Kulturna skupnost Slovenije.

Scheidel, W., Morris, I. and Saller, R. (eds) (2007), *The Cambridge Economic History of the Greco-Roman World*, Cambridge: Cambridge University Press.

Scheidel, W. (2015), 'The early Roman monarchy', in Monson and Scheidel (eds), 229–57.

Schofield, M. (2015), 'Seneca on monarchy and the political life', in Bartsch and Schiesaro (eds), 68–81.

Seager, R. (2013), 'Perceptions of the *Domus Augusta*, AD 4–24', in Gibson (ed.), 41–57.

Setaioli, A. (2015), 'Seneca and the ancient world', in Bartsch and Schiesaro (eds), 255–65.

Shaw, B. D. (2015), 'The myth of the Neronian persecution', *JRS* 102, 73–110.

Shotter, D. (1975), 'A time-table for the "Bellum Neronis"', *Historia* 24, 59–74.

(2008), *Nero Caesar Augustus: Emperor of Rome*, Harlow: Pearson.

Shumate, N. (2013), 'Nero *redivivus*: Nero, George W. Bush and the 'society of spectacle'', in Walde (ed.), 339–50.

Smallwood, E. M. (ed.) (1967), *Documents Illustrating the Principates of Gaius, Claudius and Nero*, Cambridge: Cambridge University Press.

Speidel, M. A. (1994), 'Scribonius Proculus: *curator aedium sacrorum et operum publicorum* in Rom oder Luna?', *Zeitschrift für Papyrologie und Epigraphik* 103, 209–14.

Stevens, C. E. (1951), 'The will of Q. Veranius', *Classical Review* 1, 4–7.

Stevenson, J. (ed.) (1967), *A New Eusebius*, London: SPCK.

Stover, J. (2015), 'Olybrius and Einsiedeln Eclogues', *JRS* 105, 288–321.

Syme, R. (1937), 'The colony of Cornelius Fuscus: an episode in the *Bellum Neronis*', *AJPh* 58, 7–18.

(1953), 'Tacitus on Gaul', *Latomus* 12, 25–37.

(1958), *Tacitus*, Oxford: Oxford University Press.

(1970), 'Domitius Corbulo', *JRS* 60, 27–39.

(1982), 'Partisans of Galba', *Historia* 31, 460–83.

Talbert, R. J. A. (1984), *The Senate of Imperial Rome*, Princeton, NJ: Princeton University Press.

(1996), 'The Senate and senatorial and equestrian posts', *CAH* 10 ², 324–43.

Thompson, D. J. (1987), 'Imperial estates', in J. Wacher (ed.), *The Roman World*, London: Routledge, 555–67.

Tinniswood, A. (2003), *By Permission of Heaven: The Story of the Great Fire of London*, London: Jonathan Cape.

Tomei, A. and Rea, R. (eds) (2011), *Nerone*, Milan: Electa.

Tomei, M. A. (2011), 'Nerone sul Palatino', in Tomei and Rea (eds), 118–35.

Too, Y. L. (1994) 'Educating Nero: a reading of Seneca's moral epistles', in Elsner and Masters (eds), 211–24.

Townend, G. B. (1961), 'The reputation of Verginius Rufus', *Latomus* 20, 337–41.

(1967), 'Suetonius and his influence', in T. A. Dorey (ed.), *Latin Biography*, London: Routledge & Kegan Paul, 79–111.

(1980), 'Calpurnius Siculus and the *munus Neronis*', *JRS* 70, 166–74.

Traina, G. (2009), *428 AD: An Ordinary Year at the End of the Roman Empire*, Princeton, NJ: Princeton University Press.

Treggiari, S. (1996), 'Social status and social legislation', *CAH* 10², 873–904.

Turner, E. G. (1954), 'Tiberius Julius Alexander', *JRS* 44, 54–64.

Viscogliosi, A. (2011a), '"Qualis artifex pereo." L'architettura neroniana', in Tomei and Rea (eds), 92–107.

(2011b), 'La *Domus Aurea*', in Tomei and Rea (eds), 156–9.

Vout, C. (2013), 'Tiberius and the invention of succession', in Gibson (ed.), 59–77.

Walde, C. (ed.) (2013), *Neros Wirklichkeiten: zur Rezeption einer umstrittenen Gestalt* (Litora Classica 7), Rahden: Verlag Marie Leidorf.

(2013), 'Einleitung Spurensuche: Alma Johanna Koenigs Nero in ihren Roman *Der jugendliche Gott* (1942)', in Walde (ed.), 1–43.

Waldherr, G. H. (2005), *Nero*, Regensburg: Friedrich Pustet.

Wallace-Hadrill, A. (1982), '*Civilis princeps*: between citizen and king', *JRS* 72, 32–48.

(1996), 'The imperial court', *CAH* 10², 283–308.

Warmington, B. H. (1969), *Nero: Reality and Legend*, London: Chatto & Windus.

Weaver, P. R. C. (1972), *Familia Caesaris: A Social Study of the Emperor's Freedmen and Slaves*, Cambridge: Cambridge University Press.

Whitton, C. L. (2013), 'Seneca: *Apocolocyntosis*', in Buckley and Dinter (eds), 151–69.

Wiedemann, T. E. J. (1996a), 'Tiberius to Nero', *CAH* 10², 198–255.

(1996b), 'From Nero to Vespasian', *CAH* 10², 256–82.

Wild, J. P and Wild, F. C. (2014), 'Berenike and textile trade on the Indian Ocean', in Droß-Krüpe (ed.), 91–109.

Williams, G. (1994), 'Nero, Seneca and Stoicism in the *Octavia*', in Elsner and Masters (eds), 178–95.

(2015), 'Style and form in Seneca's writings', in Bartsch and Schiesaro (eds), 135–49.

Winterling, A. (2007), *Caligula: Eine Biographie*, 4th edn, Munich: Verlag C. H Beck.

(2009), *Politics and Society in Ancient Rome*, Malden, MA: Blackwell.

Wirszubski, C. (1950), *Libertas as a Political Idea at Rome during the Late Republic and Early Principate*, Cambridge: Cambridge University Press.

Wiseman, T. P. (1991), *Death of an Emperor: Flavius Josephus*, Exeter: University of Exeter Press.

Wyke, M. (1994), 'Make like Nero! The appeal of a cinematic emperor', in Elsner and Masters (eds), 11–28.

Yavetz, Z. (1988), *Plebs and Princeps*, Oxford: Oxford University Press.

Index

In this index as in my text I have not striven for consistency or absolute accuracy in the naming of people (e.g. in the use of *tria nomina*) and places but give these in the form most familiar to anglophones. For help in running down topics, I also refer the reader to the chapter subheadings listed in the Contents.

434

Printed in Great Britain
by Amazon

20525051R00271